Law and Investment in Japan

Law and Investment in Japan

Cases and Materials

Yukio Yanagida
Founding Partner
Yanagida Nomura & Akai, Tokyo

Daniel H. Foote
Professor of Law
University of Washington

Edward Stokes Johnson, Jr.
Attorney
Paul, Hastings, Janofsky & Walker, Atlanta

J. Mark Ramseyer
Professor of Law
University of Chicago

Hugh T. Scogin, Jr.
Visiting Professor, Fordham University School of Law
Senior Research Scholar, East Asian Institute,
Columbia University

Published by the East Asian Legal Studies Program, Harvard Law School

and distributed by

HARVARD UNIVERSITY PRESS

Cambridge, Massachusetts
London, England

Studies in East Asian Law, Harvard University
The Harvard Law School, in cooperation with the John King Fairbank Center for East Asian Research, the Harvard-Yenching Institute, and scholars from other institutions, conducts a program of training and research designed to further scholarly understanding of the legal systems of Japan, China, Korea, and other jurisdictions in East Asia. In conjunction with this program, a series of publications was established in 1967.

Printed in the United States of America
ISBN 0-674-51375-4

Second Printing, 1995

For Oliver Oldman,
not only a teacher and a colleague
but a friend

Foreword

The publication of *Law and Investment in Japan: Cases and Materials* by the Harvard Law School's East Asian Legal Studies Program is a source of great satisfaction. This book is both an outstanding achievement on its own terms and a strong testament to the Law School's success in generating innovative international and comparative law scholarship.

Law and Investment in Japan grows out of materials developed for a highly successful course on foreign investment and joint ventures that Yukio Yanagida taught at the Harvard Law School in the academic years 1990-91 and 1991-92. The book provides an introduction to Japanese business law by means of a comprehensive case study of a joint venture between American and Japanese manufacturers. It is unique in its organization of Japanese legal materials, for it employs American analytical frameworks to understand substantive Japanese law. The result is a truly pathbreaking work of scholarship.

National legal systems are becoming increasingly intertwined. In all developed countries, the international dimension of law practice is expanding dramatically. The Harvard Law School recognizes that to meet the needs of a growing international legal profession, it must move further in the direction of internationalizing its curriculum. Yukio Yanagida's association with us has helped tremendously in giving us new insights not only into Japanese-American business relations but also into transnational business arrangements generally. This volume provides invaluable guidance in how lawyers from different legal environments should think about cross-border transactions and alliances.

Henry Clay, the distinguished legislator, speaking before the House of Representatives in 1812, proclaimed, "If you want to avoid foreign collision, you had better abandon the ocean." The alternative to withdrawal is to understand the foreign seas on which one is sailing. Yukio Yanagida and his colleagues, with this volume, help set us on the right course.

As Dean of the Harvard Law School, I take great pride in the role the School has played in the birth of *Law and Investment in Japan*. I am delighted that the perspectives of Mr. Yanagida and his colleagues can now be shared with a broader audience through the publication of this book.

Robert C. Clark
Dean, Harvard Law School

November 1994

Foreword

On behalf of the East Asian Legal Studies Program of the Harvard Law School, which I serve as Director, it is both an honor and pleasure to have the opportunity briefly to introduce *Law and Investment in Japan: Cases and Materials.*

This pathbreaking book uses a joint venture as its central organizing focus and is itself a highly successful joint venture in two important regards. It both bridges the worlds of scholarship and practice and is the product of a sustained collaborative effort between citizens of Japan and the United States deeply knowledgeable about each other's society. As such, we at Harvard Law School view this volume, in the facilitation of which we are proud to have played a role, as setting a standard for future efforts in comparative legal studies.

Substantively, *Law and Investment in Japan* represents a breakthrough in English language legal materials concerning Japanese business law. Building on the pioneering work of such leading scholars as Dan Henderson and John Haley, this is the first casebook in English that endeavors to present a comprehensive overview of all major facets of contemporary Japanese business law and foreign interaction therewith. The book commences with a thorough and insightful examination of the Japanese legal system, in which it both considers how Japan's civil law system and postwar experience with American business law have shaped its regulatory climate and surveys the country's principal legal institutions and professional personnel. Care is then taken to provide the reader with an understanding of Japanese business and administrative relationships before examining how Japan has sought to regulate foreign investment over the past five decades. The remainder of the book uses a hypothetical joint venture to delve imaginatively into issues of contract, corporate law, tax, intellectual property, fair competition law, and dispute resolution of consequence not only for potential foreign investors, but for anyone wishing to understand Japanese approaches toward these areas of the law.

Pedagogically, this book also is highly innovative. The many students who took Yukio Yanagida's courses during his year as the 25th Mitsubishi Visiting Professor of Japanese Legal Studies at the Harvard Law School were uniform in expressing a remarkable and unstinting level of enthusiasm for the class. They pointed out, quite rightly I believe, that in their use of a joint venture as an organizing focus, the materials (which were an earlier version of those upon which this book is based) were able to bring alive complex issues of law that might otherwise have seemed dry and excessively abstract. Indeed, it was in large measure because of the reaction of so many students and because the materials do such a fine job of integrating the best of theory and practice, that we prevailed upon Professor Yanagida and his colleagues to turn these materials into a book so that others might have the benefit of their efforts.

That the book succeeds so well ought not to be surprising when one considers its provenance. By any standard, Yukio Yanagida is an extraordinary individual, combining the wisdom gleaned during thirty years of practice as one of Japan's great legal figures with enormous creativity and a true *joie de vivre*. He has been joined in this project by a formidable American team representing the best and brightest of their generation of young American scholars of Japanese law—Professors Daniel Foote, J. Mark Ramseyer, and Hugh Scogin and Mr. Edward Johnson (who also ably assisted Professor Yanagida in offering the aforementioned classes).

In this era of periodic tension between the United States and Japan, it is heartening to see that experts from the two nations cannot only write about joint ventures, but in fact have masterfully carried one out themselves. And it is particularly gratifying for me as Director of East Asian Legal Studies to observe that what unifies these five accomplished individuals and what brought them to each other's attention was the Harvard Law School—where each of them earned a degree and each began or heightened his interest in legal relations between the United States and the nations and peoples of East Asia. I am sure that each joins me in hoping that others will have the opportunity to follow in their footsteps and undertake similar endeavors regarding other dimensions of East Asian legal studies.

William P. Alford
Henry L. Stimson Professor of Law
Director, East Asian Legal Studies
Harvard Law School

November 1994

Preface

This book grew out of a course I taught at Harvard Law School in the spring and again in the fall of 1991. Its materials were developed on the basis of my thirty years of experience as a *bengoshi* (Japanese lawyer) handling international and domestic legal affairs. The course utilized a comprehensive case study to examine the wide range of issues that commonly arise in connection with foreign investment in Japan. The approach used in the course seemed to work quite well, and my four co-authors, who are among the leading experts in the U.S. on Japanese and other Asian law, agreed that it would be valuable to refine and further develop the course materials in order to make available to English-readers the first comprehensive casebook on Japanese business law.

This book, as did the course, tracks a hypothetical joint venture from the initial negotiations and formation through operation of the venture, subsequent disagreements among the participants, and the ultimate breakup and dissolution of the venture nearly a decade later. This hypothetical joint venture, which is referred to throughout the book as the Principal Case, is based on one I advised after a dispute developed between the U.S. and the Japanese venturer.

Use of the Principal Case does not limit this book to issues particular to joint ventures. Rather, the Principal Case affords the opportunity to analyze legal issues in a realistic context, and to take into account the business environment and needs of clients. Moreover, it facilitates introducing the Japanese legal system and business law in a manner most suitable to those trained in the U.S. legal system.

The book opens with four chapters that provide an introduction to Japan's legal system and business environment. Chapter 5 then offers a description of the background of the Principal Case, outlining the parties' positions in their respective markets, their initial objectives (both stated and real), and their views and understandings at the time.

The remainder of the book, Chapters 6-12, covers substantive areas of Japanese law, including regulation of foreign investment, administrative law, corporations, intellectual property, antitrust and dispute settlement. Throughout these chapters, we return from time to time to the Principal Case, describing subsequent business developments as a means of bringing specific legal and practical issues into sharper focus. The book closes with a chapter on some special issues posed by publicly traded corporations (including mergers and acquisitions) in Japan.

In the Appendices appear the so-called "Principal Case Agreements"—the Joint Venture Agreement itself, the articles of incorporation for the joint venture company, and several related agreements. These agreements provide a focus for the wide range of specific questions and issues found in the book. The Appendices also contain ample statutory material necessary for analyzing these issues.

In preparing this book we have paid particular attention to making the materials on each topic stand on their own, so that they can be understood without having to track the Principal Case throughout the book. In doing so, we have sought to ensure that this work will serve as a valuable resource for practicing attorneys and others who may wish to use the materials on their own, as well as for professors and students in the classroom. The book may be treated as an integrated package, either with or without utilizing the Principal Case and Principal Case Agreements. The individual units may also be used separately for either teaching or reference purposes.

In a similar vein, while these materials are based on a joint venture, the issues they raise can be applied broadly to many types of foreign investment in Japan. In some ways the joint venture form is the most complicated and delicate form of investment. Its creators must establish complex control mechanisms that will balance the interests of the partners throughout the life of the venture. Joint ventures raise virtually all of the issues posed by other sorts of investment, plus a range of additional concerns. We have by no means, however, limited the materials to the joint venture situation.

This book could not have been realized without the assistance and encouragement of many people, all of whom it would be impossible to name here but a few of whom I would especially like to recognize. I should first mention Professor Emeritus of the Law Faculty of Tokyo University Hiroshi Kaneko, who, shortly after I accepted the offer to teach at Harvard Law School, offered valuable guidance on teaching and the farsighted advice that I should approach developing the materials for my course as though writing a book for publication. Also from the Law Faculty of Tokyo University, I would like to express my deep gratitude to Professor Tsuneo Ohtori and colleagues of his including Professors Mitsuo Matsushita, Nobuhiro Nakayama, Hiroshi Takahashi and Hideki Kanda, whose valuable assistance made it possible to develop the original version of this book used for my course at Harvard Law School.

At Harvard Law School, I would like especially to recognize Professor Oliver Oldman, whose advice was instrumental in organizing the original book and class and whose enthusiasm helped motivate the decision to publish this book to serve the growing interest in the Japanese legal system, Professor William P. Alford, who was a gracious host as Director of East Asian Legal Studies and whose leadership helps make EALS the foremost research center of its kind, Dean Robert C. Clark, whose deep commitment to internationalizing legal education has been an inspiration to many, and Dr. Myung-Soo Lee, then-Director of Research at the East Asian Legal Studies Program, whose blend of scholarly and administrative skills facilitated prompt production of this book. I would also like to offer thanks to the students in my two classes at Harvard Law School, whose feedback helped guide our revisions of the original materials, Ms. Sue Davidson, who typed the manuscript at an extraordinary pace, and those many others who offered advice or administrative assistance.

Finally, I would like to express my gratitude to my co-authors, Daniel Foote, Ted Johnson, Mark Ramseyer, and Hugh Scogin, without whose work it would have been impossible to compile all the materials and to convert over 2000 pages of course materials into this 725-page book. I would like to add a special word of thanks to Daniel Foote, who has been involved in this project from its early days and who served as coordinator during the revision, editing, and publication process.

Yukio Yanagida
Founding Partner
Yanagida Nomura & Akai

November 1994
Tokyo

Introductory Notes

Note Concerning Case Translations

Unless otherwise indicated, case translations used in this book were newly prepared for it. To aid readers in understanding the cases, for our translations we have deviated somewhat from the standard Japanese manner of presentation. We have divided the cases into five sections: 1) a heading, 2) "References," 3) "Facts," 4) "Judgment," and 5) "Reasons." The headings have been adapted to the U.S. style and do not correspond to the manner in which cases are typically identified in Japanese sources. As used in this book, the heading contains the names of the parties, a journal citation identifying where the opinion is reported or discussed, the name of the court whose opinion is presented and the date the opinion was issued. Official Japanese case reporters issued by the courts themselves normally contain the names of the parties. In contrast, reporters published by private companies, which represent the only readily available source for many important opinions, typically do not list the parties' names. In this same vein, the standard citation form used in Japan provides the name of the court and date of the opinion, but does not include the parties' names.

It is important to realize that the "References" and "Facts" sections of the cases in these materials are not parts of the opinions of the courts; those sections have been developed for these materials in order to facilitate understanding of the cases. The "References" section lists the laws most relevant to the legal issues raised by the case. All laws referenced for a given case are either explained in full in the introduction or text of the case or appear in the Appendices. The "Facts" section of each case, which details the relevant factual background and explains any lower court decisions in the case, has been drafted for these materials based on a review of the lower court opinions, commentaries in the journals cited and/or commentaries in other sources. The "Facts" sections are necessary because the facts provided in Japanese district court opinions tend to be extremely detailed and technical and because higher courts, instead of drafting their own findings of facts, often simply incorporate all or part of the facts as set forth in the opinions of lower courts.

Following each "Facts" section is a "Judgment" section. This section offers a short summary of the court's ruling. The bulk of the case presentation is then usually taken up by the "Reasons" section. The "Reasons" section for each case is taken from the text of the actual court opinion. Where we have omitted portions, we have so designated by ellipses or explanations in brackets. Finally, for ease in reference, we have referred to parties by their names rather than by designations such as "claimant," "appellee," etc.

A final note is that in the cases you will often encounter the abbreviation "K.K." As discussed in Chapter 8 on Japanese corporate law, the abbreviation stands for "Kabushiki Kaisha," the Japanese company form most similar to the corporate form prevailing in the U.S. and typically designated by "Inc." Some Japanese companies place the "K.K." before their name and some after, so you may just as likely encounter "Yamada K.K." as "K.K. Yamada."

Note Concerning the Principal Case (P.C.) Agreements

While hypothetical in nature, the Principal Case (P.C.) Agreements referenced throughout the book and reproduced in the Appendices are based on an actual joint venture between an American and a Japanese company. They are representative of documents frequently found in actual practice and this can make these agreements a valuable tool for teaching and studying the relevant issues. The P.C. Agreements, however, are in no way intended to be models for future drafters. To the contrary, in many respects these agreements are useful as a teaching tool precisely because they contain internal inconsistencies, drafting errors and drafting oversights. In short, any attorney who used the P.C. Agreements in their existing form as models for agreements for a new joint venture would not be engaging in good lawyering.

Note Concerning Statutory References and Citation Styles

Consistency has not yet been achieved in the terminology used for translating certain Japanese statutory terms into English. As prominent examples, some translators translate the Japanese *hō*, as used in the official title of statutes, as "Act," others translate the same word as "Law"; some translate the term *jō* as "Section," others as "Article"; and some translate *kō* as "Subsection," others as "Paragraph" or "Clause." In each of these instances, we prefer the former term, because that represents the terminology most commonly used in referring to U.S. statutory material. Accordingly, in the case translations and other materials newly compiled for this book, we have used the terms Act, Section (except for references to the Constitution, where the word "Article" corresponds to usage for the U.S. Constitution), and Subsection. For materials excerpted from other sources, however, we have followed the original authors' terminology.

There is even less consistency with regard to the citation style used for Japanese legal materials. Numerous variations in citation style exist even in Japanese-language materials, not to mention English renderings. Here again, for case translations and other materials newly prepared for this book, we have used the citation style we prefer. For excerpted materials, however, we have generally followed the original authors' own citation styles.

Summary of Contents

Table of Contents

ONE

Foreign Investment in Japan: Concerns Past and Present

I. Investing in Japan

Is Japan closed to foreign investment? If not, what barriers remain to such investment?

The answers to these questions of course differ depending on whom you ask, and when. Naturally, though, one of the groups that have followed these issues most closely is American businesspeople who have lived and worked in Japan for many years. Accordingly, their views represent an appropriate starting point for our examination.

The responses that follow are taken from a survey compiled in 1991 on behalf of the American Chamber of Commerce in Japan (ACCJ). The survey was sent to 1200 U.S. companies, of which 340 responded. Of the companies responding, 88% had operations in Japan, and on average those companies had over 17 years of experience in the Japanese market.

In some respects, the answers reveal major changes from earlier periods. Thus, for example, the respondents did not rank formal legal restrictions on investment very high on the list of remaining barriers to foreign investment. This reflects in large part the major relaxation in such restrictions over the past two decades, discussed in more detail in Chapter 6.

The great majority of the barriers listed, however, seem nearly timeless. Many of the concerns identified have affected foreign investors in Japan in every era to date and seem certain to continue for the foreseeable future. Moreover, many of these concerns are not unique to Japan. To the contrary, the same sorts of issues arise in virtually every cross-border investment situation.

A. T. KEARNEY, INTERNATIONAL, INC., TRADE AND INVESTMENT IN JAPAN: THE CURRENT ENVIRONMENT*

13-23 (1991)

Competing in a foreign market is not always easy. This is especially true for Japan, often referred to as the most competitive market in the world. * * *

[One finds] varying perceptions of U.S.-Japan economic and trade relations on both sides of the Pacific. In a recent study released by the Chicago Council on

*From *Trade and Investment in Japan: The Current Environment*, prepared for the American Chamber of Commerce in Japan by A. T. Kearney, International, Inc. (June 1991), at 13-23. Reprinted by permission.

Foreign Relations, more than 60% of the respondents viewed the most critical threat to the vital interests of the United States as the economic power of Japan. When further asked if Japan currently practiced fair or unfair trade with the U.S., 71% of the public and 78% of the opinion leaders who were interviewed replied that current trade practices were unfair. On the other side of the Pacific, Masaya Miyoshi, president of the influential Japanese Federation of Economic Organizations, or *Keidanren*, recently stated that "the Japanese market which appears to be a closed one when seen from the outside is, in fact, an open and intensely competitive one when seen from the inside."

Closed or open? Fair or unfair? As a part of this study, both "insiders," or U.S. companies currently operating in Japan, and "outsiders," or U.S. companies without significant experience in the Japanese market, were asked to share their perceptions, opinions and operating realities concerning these subjects, especially as related to success in Japan. Differences in perceptions do exist, especially as reflected through the eyes of seasoned Japan veterans versus their stateside counterparts. Although many American companies have been unable to gain a competitive foothold in Japan, even more have managed to carve a competitive niche for themselves and find some measure of success.

An appraisal of government policies and practices alone is insufficient for determining the competitive realities for companies operating in or seeking to enter the Japanese market. Motivations and restrictions encountered in a host country environment, in this case Japan's, are only the first part of a three-part strategic equation for assessing market attractiveness and viability. The other two parts of the equation are internal U.S. company capabilities and overall Japanese industry competitiveness in a particular sector. * * * A strategy for success in Japan should involve the proper evaluation of all three factors.

An evaluation of the environment for trade with and investment in Japan should focus not only on government or regulatory barriers, but also on barriers created by local business customs. Furthermore, developing a thorough understanding of overall Japanese industry competitiveness is critical for assessing one's niche in the market. Finally, a company must decide whether it possesses the internal capabilities to compete in Japan. Only by assessing these capabilities will a company executive understand whether the company has the managerial and financial stamina to compete in world markets. * * *

[From the survey of American businesses,] several key themes emerged concerning the current climate for trade with and investment in Japan. These include:

A. High costs due to high land prices/rents and staffing concerns were most frequently cited as the key restrictions on a company's ability to compete in the market;

B. "Japan-side" structural and business barriers such as distribution systems, *keiretsu* [corporate groups, a term discussed in Chapter 3], non-market pricing mechanisms and the exclusionary business practices of Japanese companies were viewed as being greater inhibitors than formal Japanese government regulations;

C. "U.S.-side" issues such as short-term management perspectives and product modification and quality requirements, as well as a general lack of understanding of the Japanese market, were equally significant barriers for American firms; and

D. Overall, the environment for foreign companies was viewed as favorable, with many companies more than doubling trade with or investment in Japan in the last five years. * * *

[1.] High Fixed Costs and Staffing Problems Keep U.S. Companies from Better Penetrating the Japanese Market

High land costs: There are several components to the issue of high operating costs in Japan, the most important being the high cost of land, especially in Tokyo, and related government land use policies. * * *

Staffing problems: The goal of Japanese parents has traditionally been to gain the best education for their children (usually sons) so that they can enter a top-notch Japanese university and go on to become a member of a large, well-known Japanese corporation. Until very recently, working for a foreign firm was not considered a part of this picture, and only a handful of U.S. companies such as IBM or Coca-Cola appeared on lists of the most desirable places for Japanese university graduates to work.

However, over the last few years, this picture has gradually changed. The growing individualism of Japanese youth, fostered especially by overseas travel, has been breaking down the stigma of working for a non-Japanese company. The ability to gain greater responsibility at an earlier age, and the possibility for international work experience offered by foreign firms, are becoming more attractive to younger Japanese not content to wait for years to gain the same opportunities with Japanese companies. Still, 27 out of 34 U.S. companies interviewed in Japan indicated that they had little or no access to graduates of top Japanese universities, and perceptions concerning American companies' lack of long-term commitment to the Japanese market hampered recruiting efforts. Even today, U.S. companies often come to Japan unprepared, only to exit the market within a short time, further bolstering their image as unreliable employers. * * *

High costs and staffing problems are two key issues in that they are symbolic of the types of structural and cultural issues so firmly embedded in Japan's economy and Japanese society that they may require a generation to change. Both the U.S. and Japanese governments are attempting to tackle the issue of land use policy through the [Structural Impediments Initiative (SII)] framework. * * * Cultural attitudes toward employment in foreign companies are not something that can be legislated for or against, however. Change is only likely to come as a product of time and the concerted efforts of foreign firms able to demonstrate their commitment to the market.

* * * The question "Which factors inhibit greater trade with Japan by your parent company?" was one of only a few in the survey which drew answers indicating a major concern regarding remaining Japanese government restrictions and regulations (28%). Such government restrictions and regulations were viewed as only slightly less inhibiting than tightly controlled distribution channels (31%).

Non-market driven pricing mechanisms and price distortion were specified as factors inhibiting trade by 25% of the respondents, followed by another 22% who pointed to a lack of market opportunities (due in part to *keiretsu* relationships).

[2.] "Japan-side" "Structural" and "Business" Barriers Were Viewed as Being Greater Inhibitors than Formal Japanese Government Regulations

Following the theme outlined above, high land costs and staffing problems topped the list of restrictions on a company's ability to do business in Japan. * * * Still, there are other issues which have a substantial impact on a company's ability to compete in the market. These follow ranked in the order of [importance reflected by] the survey.

Strong, interlinked business group relationships: Strong, interlinked business groups, or *keiretsu,* refer to the six large horizontally-integrated and numerous other vertically-integrated corporate or distribution groups whose structures are fairly unique among other industrialized nations. Three of the horizontal groups—Mitsui, Mitsubishi and Sumitomo—sprang up as the postwar successors of the old Japanese *zaibatsu,* or large industrial conglomerate/financial organizations, while the other three formed around the extensive holdings of the Sanwa, Fuji and DKB banks. The vertically-integrated *keiretsu* are independent industrial monoliths generally operating in one or a few industries. These groups include corporations such as automakers Toyota and Nissan and computer manufacturers Toshiba and NEC. Many of the vertical groups also maintain ties with one of the six horizontal *keiretsu.* [The *keiretsu* and related issues are the subject of Chapter 3.]

The U.S. government and American businesses have complained that many aspects of these organizations' relationships pose barriers to the market, making it difficult for foreign firms to compete against them in Japan. Companies within the *keiretsu* are bound together in several ways, including: mutual board of director appointments and presidential councils, extensive stock cross-holdings, groupwide financing through one main affiliated bank, and other long-term relationships such as those among suppliers and purchasers in the automobile industry. *Keiretsu* companies often prefer to purchase components and finished products from other members of their own groups instead of from outside firms. By recent A.T. Kearney estimates, anywhere from 20% to 40% of purchases in certain industries may be accounted for by such intra-firm arrangements. One recent report indicates that "the higher the share of *keiretsu* firms in an industry, the lower the share of imports in domestic consumption."

U.S. representatives maintain that these *keiretsu* activities hinder not only their entry into the Japanese markets in which the groups compete and/or dominate, but also hinder further investment by American firms in certain industries and imports of foreign products. * * * However, 32% of the survey respondents also pointed to positive aspects of the industrial groups as secure, but limited, sources once an initial sale within the *keiretsu* had been made. * * *

Exclusionary business practices: This issue is tied closely to that of *keiretsu* relationships. Business transactions based on long-term relationships and mutual commitments permeate all levels and sectors of Japanese industry. In many cases, these long-term relationships exclude dealings with outsiders such as U.S. firms or even Japanese newcomers to the market. * * * These types of relationships vary substantially from the arms-length transactions commonly practiced in the U.S., and the switching of suppliers for the simple advantage of a one-time cost break of 5-10% is virtually unheard of in Japan. On the other hand, Japanese companies enjoy lower transaction costs as a result of these long-term relationships. * * *

Distribution: The complexity of the Japanese distribution system is often cited as a barrier to both foreign imports and the ability of foreign firms in Japan to better penetrate the Japanese market. * * *

Ministry guidelines/policies and legal and regulatory restrictions: From the early postwar years, Japan's Ministry of International Trade and Industry (MITI) issued periodic "vision" statements targeting certain products and industries for growth in the following decade. As a means of aiding these "infant industries" on their path to competitiveness, certain benefits such as favorable loans, tax benefits, import restrictions and market protection were granted to companies within those targeted industries. [Regulation of foreign trade and investment is the subject of Chapter 6.] Foreign companies and products were effectively shut out of the market until their Japanese competitors gained strength. Examples of such guidelines today include the MITI interpretation of the Large-Scale [Retail] Stores Law [discussed in Chapter 3], Ministry of Health and Welfare (MHW) enforcement of annual reductions in pharmaceutical prices for both domestic and foreign products, and MHW interpretations of acceptable food additives for domestic and imported products.

Nonmarket pricing: Nearly 30% of the [U.S.] company representatives viewed the sustained high price levels in Japan as a significant restriction on their ability to conduct business in the market. After the rapid depreciation of the dollar and yen appreciation in 1985, companies exporting products to Japan expected to enjoy a distinct price advantage in the country over their competitors. In many cases, however, this was not true.

Since operating in a completely open market would allow for a certain amount of price arbitrage, many came to view the prolonged price discrepancies as an indication of nonmarket mechanisms supporting prices at artificially high levels. * * *

Testing association guidelines and procedures: Domestic and imported products in industries such as consumer products, cosmetics, food/agriculture, industrial equipment and automobiles are often subject to extensive testing requirements prior to being approved for sale in Japan. Testing advisory bodies composed of members of competing domestic firms sometimes require unnecessarily stringent or meaningless tests to be administered prior to approving new foreign products for sale in Japan. Other products are subject to strict standards and certification measures which are unreasonable or lack transparency in comparison to internationally accepted standards and practices. [These include] matters such as lengthy approval periods and limitations on food additives, formula restrictions on cosmetic and hair-care products, uneven enforcement of regulations, time-consuming testing procedures for technical and design standards of industrial equipment and components, and lack of acceptance of U.S. automotive features and safety standards. * * *

[*Other factors:*] While not ranking on the majority of companies' top ten factors inhibiting greater trade with or investment in Japan, two other issues deserve mention here as being major concerns for foreign companies attempting to do business in Japan. These issues are mergers and acquisitions (M&A) and patent/intellectual property protection.

M&A: Concern continues to mount regarding the difficulty for American companies to acquire Japanese firms. In comparison to the number of Japanese acquisitions made in foreign markets in the last few years, foreign M&A activity in Japan has been minimal and shrinking. For firms desiring to avoid the high cost of start-ups and the time required to build an organization, acquiring a local company generally provides the most expedient way for an "outsider" to gain ground in an "insiders" market. [M&A in Japan is discussed more extensively in Chapter 12.]

Several forces have contributed to this "M&A malaise" in the Japanese market. High land prices, high stock prices and the strength of the yen put the price of many Japanese companies out of the reach of U.S. buyers. Others find it difficult to obtain the proper information concerning potential acquisition targets given the lack of transparency in many Japanese business practices and customs. Another significant barrier is extensive cross-shareholdings among Japanese corporations. At any one time, it is estimated that only about 30% of all shares of stock in Japanese corporations are traded on the open market. The vast majority of remaining shares are generally held by other affiliated companies or financial institutions—usually members of the same *keiretsu* group. This pattern of stock ownership makes it difficult for any outsider to gain a majority of shares in a public corporation. Private companies therefore may be more attractive targets. However, Japanese social and business norms have prevented takeovers from becoming prevalent in the country. There has not been a single successful hostile takeover attempt by a foreign firm in Japan, and only 1% of survey respondents indicated they had entered the Japanese market through an equity purchase in an existing Japanese firm.

Patent/Intellectual Property Protection: Considerable friction has emerged between the U.S. and Japan concerning intellectual property protection for foreign products in the Japanese market, especially in high technology industries. The first area of concern is patent protection. * * *

U.S. complaints about the Japanese patent system fall into two categories: time and quality. The time required for processing a patent application can be extremely long due to staffing shortages in the Japanese Patent Office (JPO). In the past, applications have taken anywhere from two to ten years to clear, as compared to the average period of 18-24 months in the U.S. The most extreme example of this is the recent granting of an integrated circuit patent to Texas Instruments in Japan—29 years after the application was first filed! According to the [Office of the U.S. Trade Representative (USTR)], Japan has stated in the SII talks that patent processing time will be reduced to 24 months within the next five years.

The second area of complaint for the U.S. is the quality of patent protection. The scope of a Japanese patent is relatively narrow, and as a result patent "surrounding" has been commonly practiced in Japan. In this process, rival firms file numerous slightly modified versions of the original patent application in an attempt to force the patent holder into a cross-licensing of the technology. If a firm refuses, it may face costly and lengthy court battles to avoid losing the benefits of the patent. Enforcement in general has proven to be difficult and time consuming, and the outcome is often irrelevant by the time the process is completed. [Japan's patent system is discussed in Chapter 9.]

Looking at the "Japan-side" issues, however, is only taking into account half of the picture, since companies ranked certain "U.S.-side" restrictions as being at least as significant in influencing their ability to compete in the Japanese market.

[3]. "U.S.-side" Issues Such as Short-term Management Outlook and Product Modification and Quality Requirements Were Equally Significant Barriers for American Firms

While U.S. and other foreign companies frequently pointed to restrictions on their Japanese business due to existing government regulations or industry practices, many also identified domestic U.S. problems hampering American firms' ability to compete in Japan. As a result, survey respondents were given 10 "U.S.-side" issues from which to choose and asked to indicate whether these were major, minor or not restrictions on their ability to do business in Japan. The following were the top four responses.

Short-term management outlook: Nearly 55% of the survey respondents indicated a belief that the short-term management outlook of their home office in the U.S. inhibited their ability to compete in Japan and 24% classified it as a major restriction on their Japanese business operations. When ranked against the major "Japan-side" restrictions it was the third most frequently mentioned concern—preceded only by high land costs and the inability to attract and hire quality employees in Japan.

Interviewees indicated that this management outlook was due in part to quarterly pressures on top management from Wall Street and a traditional focus on short-term financial results. As a consequence of policies emphasizing rapid industrial growth and building market share, and less pressure to boost short-term earnings, thanks to extensive corporate cross-shareholdings, Japanese corporations have traditionally taken a much longer-term approach to building a business. Shareholder pressure in the U.S. for quick financial returns and increasing stock value conflicts with the more traditional Japanese goals of company growth and company stability.

Product quality requirements: [S]urvey respondents and interviewees alike placed the need for quality products and/or services as the number one priority for success in the Japanese market. Many foreign manufacturers underestimate the Japanese penchant for quality—so much so that they have difficulties finding places for their products in Japan's market. * * *

Product modification requirements: In the early 1960s and 1970s, many companies shipped products to Japan directly from the U.S., paying little or no attention to Japanese market needs and requirements. As a result, they encountered difficulties in finding distribution channels and/or sales outlets for their products. Although a majority of companies today are more aware of Japanese consumer needs and tastes, 46% of the respondents perceived their inability to sufficiently modify products to suit the Japanese market as a restriction on their ability to compete in Japan. * * *

Lack of experience in/knowledge of Japan: In the late 1970s, there were relatively few Americans studying Japanese language and culture either in Japan or in the U.S. Although by the end of the 1980s there had been a marked increase in this number, U.S. companies in need of American managers with greater experience in and knowledge of the Japanese market have only recently begun to benefit. Both in the surveys and interviews, executives indicated that not only the lack of bilingual employees but also the general lack of a true understanding of international practices and markets detracted from their ability to compete in Japan. Others classified this as the U.S. corporate "domestic" or "parochial" mentality, and they perceived a definite need for improvement in order to enhance their competitive position in Japan.

When grouped together, four of the top ten issues perceived to affect a company's ability to do business in Japan were U.S.-side issues. As some of the more prevalent barriers in the Japanese market, they are outgrowths of practices, policies, structures and attitudes ingrained in the U.S. system since the immediate postwar period.

- - - - - - - - - -

The following charts and graphs, which are taken from Appendix D of the above report, concern trade and investment among the U.S., Japan and certain European countries. Note carefully the differences among the countries in trade and investment levels and the trends reflected.

Table 1-1
Annual Direct Foreign Investment in Japan

Year	No. of cases	Value in U.S. $ Million
1985	3,370	930
1986	3,079	940
1987	3,946	2,214
1988	4,268	3,243
1989	5,688	2,860

Notes: Source: MOF
1) Annual flow; Approval basis; Equity portion.

Table 1-2
Annual Direct Foreign Investment in Japan by Country
(Number of Cases)

	1985	1986	1987	1988	1989	Cumulative 1950–1989
U.S.	525	489	684	670	727	7,681
U.K.	381	310	368	447	495	3,226
W. Germany	130	179	237	239	365	2,028
Total	2,774	2,502	3,946	4,268	5,688	37,196

Notes: Source: MOF
1) Figures for 1950–1984 are those of equity portion.
2) Annual flow; Approval basis.

Table 1-3
Annual Direct Foreign Investment in Japan by Country
(Value in U.S. $ Million)

	1985	1986	1987	1988	1989	Cumulative 1950–1989
U.S.	413	488	938	1,774	1,642	7,910
U.K.	61	35	49	112	81	599
W. Germany	25	47	53	195	144	690
Total	929	938	2,214	3,243	2,860	15,654

Notes: Source: MOF
1) Figures for 1950–1984 are those of equity portion.
2) Annual flow; Approval basis.
3) Cumulative figures include only acquisition of stocks and equities, and do not include liquid borrowed capital.

Table 1-4
Annual Japanese Direct Investment Abroad by Country
(Equity portion; Value in U.S. $ Million)

	1985	1986	1987	1988	Cumulative 1950–1988
U.S.	2,986	5,837	9,165	13,746	43,977
U.K.	313	727	2,168	2,570	7,473
W. Germany	107	88	251	311	1,473
Total	5,963	12,546	19,941	28,638	99,694

Notes: Source: MOF
1) 1989 figures of equity portion are not available.

Table 1-5
U.S. Direct Investment Position Abroad by Country
(Value in U.S. $ Million)

	1985	1986	1987	1988	1989
Germany	16,746	20,932	24,388	21,742	23,059
U.K.	33,963	35,389	44,512	49,274	60,810
Japan	9,095	11,472	15,684	17,927	19,341
Total	232,667	259,800	314,907	333,501	373,436

Source: U.S. Department of Commerce

Table 1-6
Direct Foreign Investment Position in the U.S. by Country
(Value in U.S. $ Million)

	1985	1986	1987	1988	1989
Germany	14,417	17,250	20,315	23,845	28,223
U.K.	43,766	55,935	79,669	101,909	119,137
Japan	19,116	26,824	35,151	53,354	69,699
Netherlands	37,056	40,717	49,115	48,337	60,483
Total	182,951	220,414	271,788	328,850	400,817

Source: U.S. Department of Commerce

Figure 1-1
Japan's Merchandise Trade Balance
(1977–1990)
(U.S. $ Million, customs clearance basis)

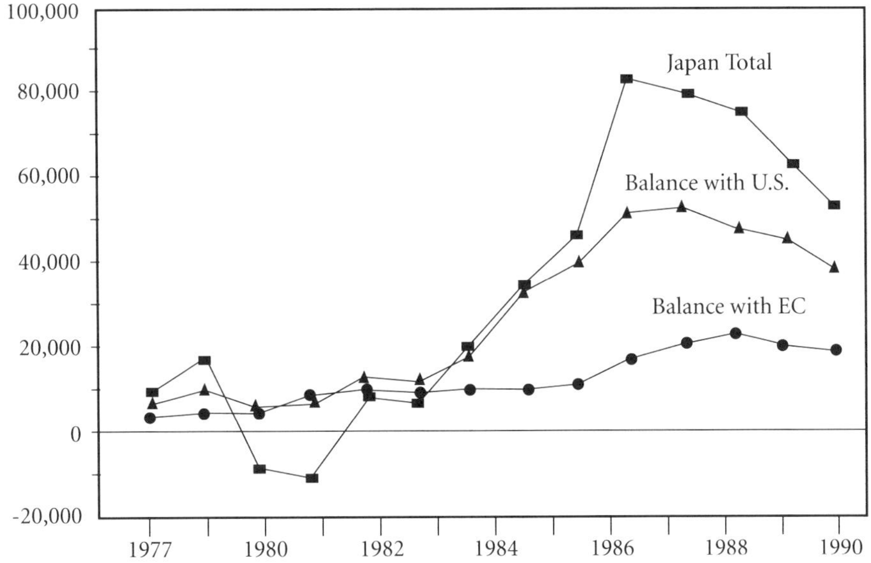

Sources: Japan Tariff Association, The Summary Report: Trade of Japan, *and U.S. Department of Commerce*

Figure 1-2
U.S. Merchandise Trade Balance
(1978–1990)
(U.S. $ Million, adjusted to balance-of-payments basis, excluding military)

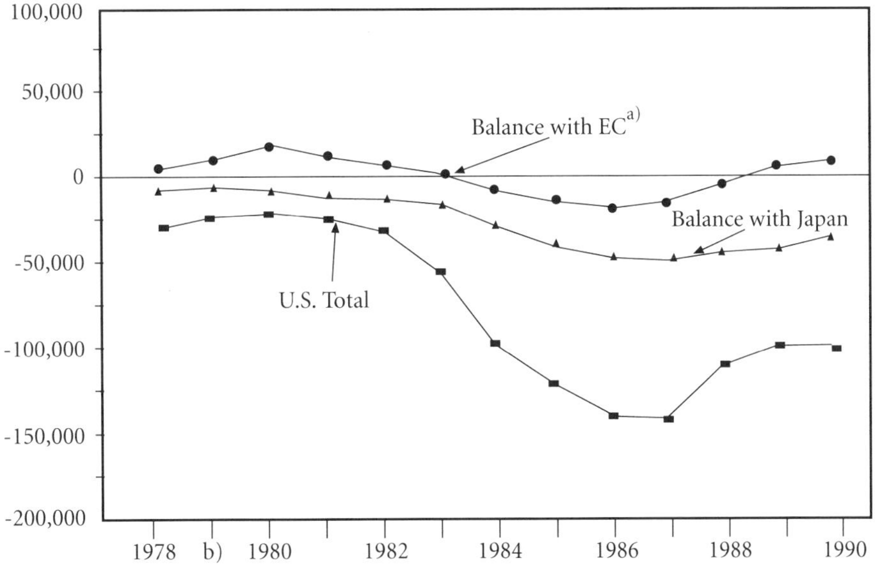

Sources: Japan Tariff Association, The Summary Report: Trade of Japan, *and U.S. Department of Commerce*
a) 1976–1980 nine countries, 1981–1985 ten countries, 1986–1990 twelve countries

Questions and Discussion Points

1. *Barriers to investment: Comparative evaluation:* Reexamine the barriers identified by the survey respondents. How different are they from barriers that foreign investors face in the United States?

2. *Relationship of the law to structural barriers:* To the extent that the remaining barriers in Japan consist of structural elements in Japan's market and business environment, what role does law play in maintaining those elements? Is any of those elements likely to be responsive to legal reforms?

3. *Role of lawyers in facilitating investment:* Given the extent of such structural elements, what role can lawyers play in facilitating foreign investment in Japan? Does the answer differ depending on whether the lawyer is a licensed Japanese lawyer (a *bengoshi*), a foreign lawyer residing in Japan and licensed to advise on designated foreign law, or a foreign lawyer outside Japan? As we will examine in Chapter 2, foreign lawyers in Japan are prohibited from advising on Japanese law and practicing before Japanese governmental agencies. To what extent are such functions essential to advising on foreign investment transactions? Can those functions be handled through cooperative relationships with licensed Japanese lawyers or other licensed legal professionals in Japan? Business consultants or other nonlicensed individuals?

4. *Role of lawyers with respect to U.S.-side factors:* The above survey identifies several important U.S.-side factors, including short-term management outlook, the frequent need for product modifications and greater emphasis on quality in entering the Japanese market, and a widespread lack of knowledge about Japan. What role, if any, should lawyers play with regard to factors such as these?

II. Concerns over Foreign Investment

A. Earlier attitudes in Japan

According to the above survey, formal legal restrictions on investment are no longer regarded as one of the top barriers to foreign investment in Japan. Moreover, that report describes recent efforts to reduce remaining barriers in several areas. This attitude of relative receptiveness (at least at the official level) to foreign investment has not always been the case, as revealed by the following account, published in 1967 in a major English-language newspaper in Japan, *The Daily Yomiuri*. In reading this selection, bear in mind that it appeared at just about the same time that the joint venture was being formed in the Principal Case, which appears frequently in later chapters.

JAPANESE-FOREIGN JOINT VENTURES PRODUCE MANY UNHAPPY MARRIAGES*

The Daily Yomiuri
5 (May 31, 1967)

It is being feared that liberalization of capital transactions will give foreign capital a chance to buy up Japanese enterprises. To prevent this from happening, the Japanese Government is taking a cautious approach [before] throwing the door wide open to foreign capital. But the current regulations on joint ventures with foreign capital, strict as they are for those who want to invest in Japan, nevertheless have loopholes that enable them to buy up their Japanese partners if they so wish.

One example where the loophole appears to have been taken advantage of is the case of Simmonds[1] Japan. The government intends to dispute the case in the Tokyo District Court. The government charges that violation of the Foreign Investment Law is suspected in the process of increasing the capitalization which, as a result, gave the right of management to the partner who had the minority share of the joint capital until then.

Simmonds Japan is a bed-manufacturing company originally called Simmonds-Tokyo Bed Manufacturing. Since the former [Simmonds] owned 55 percent of the joint capital and the latter [Tokyo Bed] the remaining 45 percent, the management right was in the hands of Tokyo Bed Manufacturing at the outset.[2] Production did not get under way even past the scheduled time for manufacture set for April 1965. Tokyo Bed contends that this was because Simmonds purposely delayed production with some ulterior objective. Simmonds, according to Tokyo Bed, kept on making market surveys on the pretext that the new company is to make beds most suited to the Japanese. When the machines for making beds arrived, they were from factories in the US that were closed down and were rusty. When Tokyo Bed wanted to repair them, the Simmonds' side prohibited the Japanese from touching them.

In the midst of this delay, talk of increasing the capital came up. The proposal by the American side was to increase the capital by ¥100 million to ¥310 million. This was quite a burden to Tokyo Bed which was capitalized only at ¥100 million itself. When Tokyo Bed was faced with the difficulty of raising the needed funds, Simmonds offered "to loan money without interest." But it later turned out that the interest was to be paid by the joint-venture company.

The joint venture became quite a burden to Tokyo Bed which had only a limited amount of funds on hand. It sucked up money and gave no returns. Unable to keep this up any longer, Tokyo Bed decided to give up its interests in the joint venture. In August 1965, it sold all its shares to the Japanese branch of an American company called Opemia, which is a subsidiary of Simmonds Company. Only two months after the Japanese partner withdrew, the company started manufacturing the beds. And in March this year, the company had its name changed to "Simmonds

---

*"Japanese-Foreign Joint Ventures Produce Many Unhappy Marriages," *The Daily Yomiuri*, May 31, 1967, at 5. Reprinted by permission.

Japan." Furthermore, it launched an all-out attack on the sales side too by making a sales agreement with Nishikawa Sangyo, one of the oldest and largest dealers in beds and beddings in Japan.

In the manner explained above, Simmonds Company captured the right of management of the joint-venture company. It is now virtually the Simmonds' company with all the shares owned by Simmonds and its subsidiary.

Earlier this month, the Ministry of International Trade and Industry (MITI) ordered the Development Bank to withhold a scheduled loan to Nishikawa Sangyo. Why did MITI come out with such a reaction when it had once recommended Nishikawa Sangyo as the desirable recipient of such a loan? This is because Nishikawa Sangyo made an exclusive sales agreement with Simmonds Company in February for the sale of beds manufactured by Simmonds Japan.

Simmonds Company is suspected of having deliberately captured the right of management of the joint-venture company. In other words, it is regarded as an "undesirable" foreign interest. And MITI cannot afford to see the low-interest long-term loan made to a company which specializes in the sale of products manufactured by such an "undesirable" foreign interest. * * *

[E]ven a foreign interest can buy the shares of a Japanese company freely if the purchase is made with yen by its branch in Japan. Simmonds Company took advantage of this "loophole." It first established a Japanese branch of its subsidiary, Opemia. This company borrowed yen from the Tokyo branch of Chase Manhattan Bank and bought the shares of Tokyo Bed. The government immediately summoned a representative of Simmonds Company and served notice to the effect that "this exception is applicable only when the branch of a foreign company in Japan buys shares in order to make use of the yen funds at its disposal" and that "this exception is not applicable when the shares are purchased with the object of seizing the right of management."

In refutation, Simmonds Company contends: "This exception is applicable to purchase of shares by yen by a branch of a foreign company in Japan irrespective of the intention with which the purchase is made." The case is scheduled to be disputed in the Tokyo District Court shortly. * * *

How can this kind of transfer of the right of management be prevented? One way is to establish a regulation whereby some restriction would be imposed on the Japanese branch of a foreign company in the purchase of shares in Japan. If there was such a regulation, the Simmonds case could have been prevented. But establishing such a regulation is a rather ticklish problem, because the mutual trade agreement between the US and Japan authorizes the foreign interests in Japan to enjoy freedom similar to that of the Japanese enterprises.

However, there is one clause in the mutual trade agreement which empowers the Japanese Government to exercise restrictions on the activities of foreign interests in Japan from the standpoint of protection of foreign exchange reserves. The government intends to take the Simmonds case to court and see if this clause could be applied. However, it must be noted here that the trend is moving toward easing capital transactions and that it runs counter to this world trend to enforce any further restrictions on capital transactions.

Since the Foreign Investment Law was put into effect in 1950, 380 joint-venture companies have been formed. (These exclude the joint-venture companies formed on a yen basis.) And the Japanese partner has the majority share in two-thirds of these companies. The government believed this would prevent foreign capital from taking over the reins of joint-venture companies, but it has now become clear that there are loopholes in the Foreign Investment Law which would allow the take-over by foreign interests if they so desired, as explained above.

* * *

Why do these takeovers occur? The root cause of it all lies in the "incompatibility of marriage" arising from the big difference in the capitalization of the partners. Furthermore, some Japanese companies seek tie-ups with large foreign interests with little or no preparation and with a vague idea that this will give them a chance to grow large quickly.

Unbalanced Marriage

One such typical example is that of wax maker Kentoku. During his world cruise in 1961, the president of Kentoku visited American wax maker Johnson Company and was deeply impressed by its immense facilities. Without hesitation, he accepted a proposal for a joint venture made by Johnson. But this proved fatal to Kentoku later. At first, Kentoku owned 60 percent of the joint capital, but when the capital was increased fourfold later, Kentoku had no money to pay for the increase and released a part of its stock to Johnson. Kentoku now owns only 24 percent of the capital.

Many of these joint ventures are like a "marriage of a Lilliputian and a Brobdingnagian," and it is only to be expected that "incompatibility" arises in the long run.

* * *

The difference in outlook is also one of the major causes for an unhappy ending of the marriage for the Japanese partner. One example is the joint-venture company formed by Nichiro Fisheries and Heinz (H.J.) Co. They had not been in full agreement as to the outlook of their business in Japan. Recently, Nichiro gave up its interests in the joint venture on the following grounds: "Five years have passed since the company was formed and we're still running in the red. The deficit has finally amounted to ¥700 million. There is no future in this business."

Heinz entertains a diametrically opposite view. "It is only natural that a new company will run in the red for four or five years in the beginning. It is strange to become so excited about this initial loss. We see a bright future in our business in Japan."

Unable to reach an agreement on the future outlook of this business, Nichiro handed over to Heinz the right of management of the new company.

* * *

In a word, it can be said that it is more desirable that the companies that go into a joint venture are of similar size in capital and business volume and that they have a similar outlook in their new project in Japan. If this condition can be met, many of the unhappy endings of the international marriages of enterprises can be prevented.

Divorce Case

In contrast to many cases of takeover of joint-venture companies by foreign interests, which are rather rampant these days, there are cases where the Japanese partner asks for a divorce.

Shinko-Smith was dissolved on May 22 and Shinko-Harnischfegur was divorced on May 25. In [each] case, the Japanese partner was Kobe Steel Works. What was the cause of divorce? * * * Shinko-Smith was formed in April 1961, as a joint-venture company. * * * The purpose of this company was to manufacture multi-stratum high pressure containers for chemical industry use with the technical know-how provided by Smith. * * *

The rationalistic-minded American partner unilaterally believed the product would sell if its price was low and its quality was good. But the Japanese market is quite different from the way the Americans see it. When it comes to the sale of large items like the high pressure container in question, personal ties of the buyer and the seller speak more eloquently than the quality or the price of the product. The market for this product was not as big as Smith International had envisioned.

The American partner agreed to withdraw and consented to provide the technical know-how hereafter too in exchange for royalty, realizing that it is wiser to do so than to continue to worry about the sale of the product by remaining a partner of the joint-venture company that does not pay.

The case of Shinko-Harnischfegur is not much different from that of Shinko-Smith. Shinko-Harnischfegur was formed in September 1960 by Kobe Steel and Harnischfegur as a company to build large shovels, with a joint capital of ¥150 million. Kobe Steel invested 60 percent of the capital.

The market for construction machinery becomes small when it comes to large items like the big shovel. Hence, the American partner recently proposed to manufacture small and medium shovels too. But Kobe Steel was already making medium shovels, one of its major items, and was thus reluctant to make another investment for manufacturing the same kind of product. Hence, it asked for a divorce.

The American partner understood the circumstances and agreed to dissolve the joint-venture company. Kobe Steel will continue to make big shovels by paying royalty to the American company. * * *

The above examples might give the impression that joint ventures are prone to fail. This is far from the truth. The successful ones far exceed the failures in number.

One example of a most successful joint venture is National Cash Register (Japan) Limited. Chairman W.S. Anderson of this company spoke of the secret of success and summed it up by saying, "When in Rome, do as the Romans do."

B. An alternative perspective on the "threat" of foreign investment

The preceding selection treats foreign investment in rather black and white terms, as have some contemporary American views on Japanese investment in the U.S. The issue is obviously not so simple, however. As elaborated in the following selection, in today's global economy it is not always an easy matter to define "foreign investment" or to determine the relative value of the investment to the host country.

ROBERT B. REICH, WHO IS US?*

Harvard Business Review 53
53-60 (Jan.-Feb. 1990)

[W]ho is "us"? * * * Consider two successful corporations:

Corporation A is headquartered north of New York City. Most of its top managers are citizens of the United States. All of its directors are American citizens, and a majority of its shares are held by American investors. But most of Corporation A's employees are non-Americans. Indeed, the company undertakes much of its R&D and product design, and most of its complex manufacturing, outside the borders of the United States in Asia, Latin America, and Europe. Within the American market, an increasing amount of the company's product comes from its laboratories and factories abroad.

Corporation B is headquartered abroad, in another industrialized nation. Most of its top managers and directors are citizens of that nation, and a majority of its shares are held by citizens of that nation. But most of Corporation B's employees are Americans. Indeed, Corporation B undertakes much of its R&D and new product design in the United States. And it does most of its manufacturing in the U.S. The company exports an increasing proportion of its American-based production, some of it even back to the nation where Corporation B is headquartered.

Now, who is "us"? Between these two corporations, which is the American corporation, which the foreign corporation? Which is more important to the economic future of the United States? * * * Typically, the assumed vehicle for improving the competitive performance of the United States is the American corporation—by which most people would mean Corporation A. But today, the competitiveness of American-owned corporations is no longer the same as American competitiveness. Indeed, American ownership of the corporation is profoundly less relevant to America's economic future than the skills, training, and knowledge commanded by American workers—workers who are increasingly employed within the United States by foreign-owned corporations.

So who is us? The answer is, the American work force, the American people, but not particularly the American corporation. The implications of this new an-

*Reprinted by permission of *Harvard Business Review.* "Who Is Us?" by Robert B. Reich (January–February 1990).

swer are clear: if we hope to revitalize the competitive performance of the United States economy, we must invest in people, not in nationally defined corporations. We must open our borders to investors from around the world rather than favoring companies that may simply fly the U.S. flag. And government policies should promote human capital in this country rather than assuming that American corporations will invest on "our" behalf. The American corporation is simply no longer "us."

Global Companies

American corporations have been abroad for years, even decades. So in one sense, the multinational identity of American companies is nothing new. What is new is that American-owned multinationals are beginning to employ large numbers of foreigners relative to their American work force, are beginning to rely on foreign facilities to do many of their most technologically complex activities, and are beginning to export from their foreign facilities—including bringing products back to the United States. * * *

Overall, the evidence suggests that U.S. companies have not lost their competitive edge over the last 20 years—they've just moved their base of operations. In 1966, American-based multinationals accounted for about 17% of world exports; since then their share has remained almost unchanged. But over the same period, the share of exports from the United States in the world's total trade in manufactures fell from 16% to 14%. In other words, while Americans exported less, the overseas affiliates of U.S.-owned corporations exported more than enough to offset the drop.

The old trend of overseas capital investment is accelerating: U.S. companies increased foreign capital spending by 24% in 1988, 13% in 1989. But even more important, U.S. businesses are now putting substantial sums of money into foreign countries to do R&D work. According to National Science Foundation figures, American corporations increased their overseas R&D spending by 33% between 1986 and 1988, compared with a 6% increase in R&D spending in the United States. Since 1987, Eastman Kodak, W.R. Grace, Du Pont, Merck, and Upjohn have all opened new R&D facilities in Japan. At Du Pont's Yokohama laboratory, more than 180 Japanese scientists and technicians are working at developing new materials technologies. IBM's Tokyo Research Lab, tucked away behind the far side of the Imperial Palace in downtown Tokyo, houses a small army of Japanese engineers who are perfecting image-processing technology. Another IBM laboratory, the Kanagawa arm of its Yamato Development Laboratory, houses 1,500 researchers who are developing hardware and software. Nor does IBM confine its pioneering work to Japan: recently, two European researchers at IBM's Zurich laboratory announced major breakthroughs into superconductivity and microscopy—earning them both Nobel Prizes.

An even more dramatic development is the arrival of foreign corporations in the United States at a rapidly increasing pace. As recently as 1977, only about 3.5% of the value added and the employment of American manufacturing originated in companies controlled by foreign parents. By 1987, the number had grown to almost 8%. In just the last two years, with the faster pace of foreign acquisitions and investments, the figure is now almost 11%. Foreign-owned companies now employ 3 million Americans, roughly 10% of our manufacturing workers. In fact, in 1989, affiliates of foreign manufacturers created more jobs in the United States than American-owned manufacturing companies. * * *

The New American Corporation

In an economy of increasing global investment, foreign-owned Corporation B, with its R&D and manufacturing presence in the United States and its reliance on American workers, is far more important to America's economic future than American-owned Corporation A, with its platoons of foreign workers. * * *

Ownership is less important. Those who favor American-owned Corporation A * * * over foreign-owned Corporation B * * * might argue that American ownership generates a stream of earnings for the nation's citizens. This argument is correct, as far as it goes. American shareholders do, of course, benefit from the global successes of American corporations to the extent that such successes are reflected in higher share prices. And the entire U.S. economy benefits to the extent that the overseas profits of American companies are remitted to the United States.

But American investors also benefit from the successes of non-American companies in which Americans own a minority interest—just as foreign citizens benefit from the successes of American companies in which they own a minority interest, and such cross-ownership is on the increase as national restrictions on foreign ownership fall by the wayside. * * *

Already Americans invest 10% of their portfolios in foreign securities; a recent study by Salomon Brothers predicts that it will be 15% in a few years. U.S. pension managers surveyed said that they predict 25% of their portfolios will be in foreign-owned companies within 10 years.

Control is less important. Another argument marshaled in favor of Corporation A might be that because Corporation A is controlled by Americans, it will act in the best interests of the United States. Corporation B, a foreign national, might not do so—indeed, it might act in the best interests of its nation of origin. * * *

But this argument makes a false assumption about American companies—namely, that they are in a position to put national interests ahead of company or shareholder interests. To the contrary: managers of American-owned companies who sacrificed profits for the sake of national goals would make themselves vulnerable to a takeover or liable for a breach of fiduciary responsibility to their shareholders. American managers are among the loudest in the world to declare that their job is to maximize shareholder returns—not to advance national goals. * * *

Obviously, this does not preclude American-owned companies from displaying their good corporate citizenship or having a sense of social responsibility. * * * But in this regard, American companies have no particular edge. * * * In fact, there is every reason to believe that a foreign-owned company would be even more eager to demonstrate to the American public its good citizenship in America than would the average American company. * * *

Just as empty is the concern that a foreign-owned company might leave the United States stranded by suddenly abandoning its U.S. operation. The typical argument suggests that a foreign-owned company might withdraw for either profit or foreign policy motives. But either way, the bricks and mortar would still be here. So would the equipment. So too would be the accumulated learning among American workers. Under such circumstances, capital from another source would fill the void; an American (or other foreign) company would simply purchase the empty facilities. And most important, the American work force would remain, with the critical skills and capabilities, ready to go back to work.

After all, the American government and the American people maintain jurisdiction—political control—over assets within the United States. Unlike foreign assets held by American-owned companies that are subject to foreign political control and, occasionally, foreign expropriation, foreign-owned assets in the United States are secure against sudden changes in foreign governments' policies. This not only serves as an attraction for foreign capital looking for a secure haven; it also benefits the American work force.

Work force skills are critical. As every advanced economy becomes global, a nation's most important competitive asset becomes the skills and cumulative learning of its work force. Consequently, the most important issue with regard to global corporations is whether and to what extent they provide Americans with the training and experience that enable them to add greater value to the world economy. Whether the company happens to be headquartered in the United States or the United Kingdom is fundamentally unimportant. The company is a good "American" corporation if it equips its American work force to compete in the global economy. * * *

In fact, because all of the other factors can move so easily any place on earth, a work force that is knowledgeable and skilled at doing complex things attracts foreign investment. The relationship forms a virtuous circle: well-trained workers attract global corporations, which invest and give the workers good jobs; the good jobs, in turn, generate additional training and experience. * * *

Foreign-owned corporations help American workers add value. When foreign-owned companies come to the United States, they frequently bring with them approaches to doing business that improve American productivity and allow American workers to add more value to the world economy. In fact, they come here primarily because they can be more productive in the United States than can other American rivals. * * *

In case after case, foreign companies set up or buy up operations in the United States to utilize their corporate assets with the American work force. Foreign-owned businesses with better design capabilities, production techniques, or managerial skills are able to displace American companies on American soil precisely because those businesses are more productive. And in the process of supplanting the American company, the foreign-owned operation can transfer the superior know-how to its American work force—giving American workers the tools they need to be more productive, more skilled, and more competitive. Thus foreign companies create good jobs in the United States. In 1986 (the last date for which such data are available), the average American employee of a foreign-owned manufacturing company earned $32,887, while the average American employee of an American-owned manufacturer earned $28,954. * * *

Now Who Is Us?

American competitiveness can best be defined as the capacity of Americans to add value to the world economy and thereby gain a higher standard of living in the future without going into ever deeper debt. American competitiveness is not the profitability or market share of American-owned corporations. In fact, because the American-owned corporation is coming to have no special relationship with Americans, it makes no sense for Americans to entrust our national competitiveness to it. * * *

The only practical answer lies in developing national policies that reward any global corporation that invests in the American work force. In a whole set of public policy areas, involving trade, publicly supported R&D, antitrust, foreign direct investment, and public and private investment, the overriding goal should be to induce global corporations to build human capital in America.

Questions and Discussion Points

1. *Desirable foreign investment:* The article about "unhappy marriages" in Japan reports that the government thought of Simmons, which bought out its Japanese co-venturer, as an "undesirable" foreign interest. What type of foreign investor would likely be regarded as a "desirable" foreign investor?

Would being a "desirable" foreign investor be desirable to most foreign investors?

2. *Relevant considerations:* Under the view expressed by Reich, is there such a thing as "undesirable" investment? What concerns are implicated by foreign investment in industry? Reich, citing average salary levels, assumes that the jobs created by foreign investment are raising the skills of American workers. If, instead, foreign investment is primarily utilizing nonskilled or semiskilled labor, should it be discouraged? By the same token, if, by investing abroad, American companies are simply exporting nonskilled or semiskilled jobs, should that be a major cause for concern in the United States?

Reich also largely dismisses concerns over foreign control, arguing that American executives are not in a position to put national interests ahead of company or shareholder interests and that, if the necessity arises, the U.S. government can impose direct restrictions on foreign-owned companies. Are you convinced? Does it matter what industry one is considering? How about agriculture? Aerospace? Computers?

3. *Level of economic development and regulation of foreign investment:* In considering whether a particular form of foreign investment is desirable or not, does the level of economic development of the host nation make a difference? Many developing nations have established strict limits on the percentage of foreign own-

ership of local industry or other restrictions on foreign investment, out of concerns over foreign oppression of local interests. Are Reich's arguments applicable, if at all, only to developed countries like the United States and Japan today? If so, might the attitudes contained in the 1967 *Daily Yomiuri* article simply reflect the level of economic development in Japan at that time?

4. *Joint ventures and foreign investment:* As we shall examine in detail later in these materials, for much of the postwar era Japan actively discouraged direct independent investment by foreign investors and instead promoted their entry into joint ventures with Japanese partners. For what reasons might the Japanese government have preferred foreign investors to use joint ventures?

If foreign investment in Japan had not been subject to government regulation, would most of the foreign investors described in the 1967 newspaper article have set up wholly-owned enterprises in Japan, or are there other reasons those foreign investors might have preferred investment through joint ventures?

FURTHER READING

Investment Issues

David E. Birenbaum and Sharon K. Zackula, "Foreign Investment in Japan: Current Limits and Restrictions," 10 *East Asian Executive Reports* 7 (1988).

Michael McAbee, "The Changing Face of Foreign Direct Investment in Japan," 9 *East Asian Executive Reports* 4 (1987).

Structural Barriers

Peter B. Edelman, "Japanese Product Standards as Non-Tariff Trade Barriers: When Regulatory Policy Becomes a Trade Issue," 24 *Stanford Journal of International Law* 389 (1988).

John O. Haley, "Weak Law, Strong Competition, and Trade Barriers: Competitiveness as a Disincentive to Foreign Entry into Japanese Markets," in Kozo Yamamura, ed., *Japan's Economic Structure: Should It Change?*, pp. 203-236. Seattle: Society for Japanese Studies, 1990.

Gary Saxonhouse, "Japan, SII and the International Harmonization of Domestic Economic Practices," 12 *Michigan Journal of International Law* 455 (1991).

NOTES TO CHAPTER ONE

1. Editor's note: This apparent misspelling of Simmons continues throughout the article.

2. Editor's note: This sentence apparently contains a misprint. From the remainder of the article, it appears that Tokyo Bed originally held 55 percent of the capital and Simmons 45 percent.

Two

Overview of the Japanese Legal System

Introduction

This chapter provides an overview of Japan's legal system. As the initial historical summary describes, Japan's current legal system is the product of a series of influences. Beginning in the eighth century, numerous legal reforms were adopted that were rooted in Chinese traditions, with a heavy Confucian orientation. Over the succeeding centuries, a series of legal institutions and traditions developed within Japan. These reached their highest level of refinement during the Tokugawa era, a period of nearly three centuries in which Japan maintained almost complete isolation from the Western world, limiting trade and other contacts to two ports.

This period of isolation was brought to a close by the arrival in 1853 of the so-called "black ships" of Commodore Matthew Perry of the United States, which helped precipitate the collapse of the Tokugawa regime and the advent of the so-called Meiji Restoration. In the drive to modernize and westernize that followed, Japan adopted a wide range of legal codes based primarily on French and German models. The resultant civil law system was then substantially modified during the U.S.-led Occupation that followed World War II. Throughout this process, societal and cultural forces within Japan influenced—though how strongly is a matter of debate—the manner in which each wave of legal reforms was implemented and interpreted. Accordingly, Japan's current legal system, though drawing substantially from both Continental and Anglo-American models, is distinct from both.

Despite the postwar reforms, Japan's current legal system, including the legal education process and attitudes toward law, reflects its civil law heritage. For this reason, in dealing with legal issues arising in Japan and with Japanese practitioners, one should understand some of the more basic differences between common law and civil law systems. Following an examination of that topic, these introductory materials turn to an overview of the structure of the current legal system and the existing institutional setting, as well as certain key constitutional issues. This chapter concludes by examining the legal profession in Japan, including the current status of foreign lawyers.

I. The Historical Development of Japan's Legal System

DAN FENNO HENDERSON, FOREIGN ENTERPRISE IN JAPAN: LAWS AND POLICIES*

164-172 (1973)

There are three major phases of Japanese legal development that need to be sketched in order to fathom the principal components of modern Japanese law: the Tokugawa phase (1603-1868), for the Japanese traditional institutions; the period before World War II (1868-1945), for the reception of civilian codes; and the postwar period (1945-), for the Anglo-American influences.

[1.] Tokugawa

Many Tokugawa values have been adapted to modern uses and exercise to some degree a continuing influence in Japanese life today. Some of them have found their way into the law itself, others remain vigorous in spite of the law, and still others operate in the interstices, neither heeding nor hindering the formal rules. But, in general, the traditional elements are receding in importance year by year as Japan industrializes, urbanizes, standardizes, and democratizes the fabric of its society. * * * [Yet] an understanding of the overall skeleton of the Tokugawa legal system [is] important, not only to indicate the starting point of modern legal development and consequently to show the vast distance traveled since 1868, but also to suggest some of the older ideas lingering at the very foundations of Japanese legal thinking.

In trying to achieve an overview of Tokugawa law, we find a new legal order emerging in Edo [currently Tokyo], which had developed the following relevant characteristics toward the end of the Tokugawa period.

1. There was an emergent state centering around the Edo shogunate, and its control system, decrees, and precedents were the beginnings of a positive law system that was rationalized by an orthodox Confucian natural law. At the same time, private relations in large part continued to be governed by a residual customary law.

2. The administration of justice was highly decentralized in that each of literally hundreds of fiefholders had the right to govern and administer justice to the people within their fiefs. Even the shogunate, in a sense, was but one of these fiefs, occupying, however, about one-fourth of Japan and strategic posts throughout the other three-fourths.

3. But judicial and administrative functions were not yet organized separately either in the shogunate offices or in the fiefs. The shogunate "judges" (*bugyō*, *daikan*, etc.) were primarily warrior-bureaucrats. Although some recording clerks * * * became officials specialized in lawsuits, they were mere clerks

*Reprinted from *Foreign Enterprise in Japan: Laws and Policies*, by Dan Fenno Henderson, at pp. 164-172. Copyright © 1973 by The University of North Carolina Press. Used by permission of the author and publisher.

and subject to the directives of their superiors.

4. Criminal and civil procedures were not entirely distinct, although generally the inquisitorial procedure (*gimmi-suji*) was used in criminal trials and a petition procedure (*deiri-suji*) was generally used in civil trials. * * *

7. In theory all civil litigation was a matter of grace, not of right.

8. The legal system had few professional jurists. * * *

9. Conciliation was the usual civil procedure, with veiled village coercion in the background to induce agreement.

10. No appeals were allowed.

11. The individual was legally only a member of a group; groups or their chiefs were the main objects of law and were vicariously liable for the conduct of members of their group (village, family, etc.).

12. Hence, suits brought to shogunate courts without approval of the village authorities and overlords were illegal and the petitioner without approval would be punished severely.

13. In no significant degree were schools and scholars factors in molding the positive law on a professional level, except perhaps as teachers of the bureaucracy.

14. Most personal and social relationships were governed by Confucianistic concepts of status, hierarchy, and authority, which left the individual wholly without legal recourse for abuse by his Confucianistic superior.

These features of the Tokugawa legal tradition added up to make authority, status, hierarchy, and official discretion the outstanding legal characteristics of a society of 30 million people, which found itself after 1853 for the first time in the full current of world affairs. If any single feature of the legal system stands out more than others, besides its fixed, static, and durable qualities, it is probably the unfettered authority of the warrior turned bureaucrat. His shadow has fallen noticeably over several decades of postrestoration legal development.

The present-day bureaucrat * * * is not, of course, identical with the warrior bureaucrat of the Tokugawa regime or even the new university-trained Imperial bureaucrat of prewar Japan. But these have all, until recently, been largely above the law in the sense of independent judicial review. It needs to be said, however, that, since the Meiji restoration, the civil branch of the bureaucracy has been generally motivated by a rather effective spirit of noblesse oblige, and judging from their overall performance in modernizing and, since World War II, rehabilitating Japan, they have shown a relatively high degree of competence and integrity.

[2.] Reception of Western Law

The forces behind the reception of western law in Japan in the 1880s and 1890s sprang from both internal and external sources. Within the ruling clique, at least after the first inept attempts to revert to the Chinese-style Imperial institutions of eighth-century Japan, there was no doubt a strong desire to centralize administrative power and to modernize Japanese legal institutions. By 1873 and onward, foreign legal advisers were employed to translate western legal materials and assist with the framing of new laws.

However, external pressures pushed the Japanese toward westernization of their law even more urgently. The chief reason was the unequal treaties that had established extraterritorial rights for foreigners in Japan. * * * [W]hatever the desire to reform for reform's sake may have been, the necessity to westernize Japanese law, before the treaties could be revised to abolish extraterritorial rights, was made clear enough. Treaty revision thus became a part of the program of successive Japanese governments after 1875. * * * By 1900, a complete system of European-style codes had been adopted, and simultaneously extraterritoriality was expunged from all of the treaties, except that full tariff autonomy was not realized until a decade later.

We have spoken of the reason for the western codification, but how did it come about and what were the major influences that made up the final product? Two distinct stages were followed: the first was a period of preparation and education (1870-85); the second was a period of debate, revision, and final adoption (1886-99). The preparatory phase began in earnest with the employment of a French jurist, Emile Boissonade, in 1873. After Boissonade, several English, American, and German jurists also served in Japan as advisers and lecturers.

In addition, several Japanese jurists (*e.g.*, Kentarō Kaneko, Harvard, 1871-78; Nobushige Hozumi, English barrister; Kazuo Hatoyama; Okamura; and others) had studied in the U.S. or Europe. Until about 1890, it seems that the English jurists were personally the more influential, followed by the French-trained group. The German-trained lawyers became especially influential after Hirobumi Ito's European trip during 1882-83. * * *

By the end of the preparatory stage (1885), * * * [a] new constitution was under active consideration. * * * A new civil code was being drafted along French lines by Boissonade, and a new commercial code was in progress under [Herman] Roesler, incorporating German, French, and English ideas. Also, work on the Code of Civil Procedure had been started. * * *

The reverse side of Japan's eager study of foreign law during this period was the noticeable neglect of the traditional customary law by the Meiji legal scholars, especially after the compilations of customary law were made in the early period. * * *

The second stage of Japanese codifications after 1889 centered around one of the most significant episodes of modern Japanese legal history. The "postponement campaign," as Hozumi called it, began as a dispute between the English-trained Japanese jurists and the French-trained Japanese jurists to postpone the effectiveness of the new civil and commercial codes promulgated in 1890 and to become effective in 1893. * * * The English-trained Japanese jurists * * * won a temporary victory when a bill was passed to postpone effectiveness for four years, after acrimonious debate in the newly established Diet of 1892. A drafting committee * * * substantially revised and improved the Civil Code, and another committee * * * redrafted the Commercial Code. Then the Civil Code became effective in 1898 and the Commercial Code followed in 1899. Curiously enough, though French influences remained strong, the new German codes, then in draft form in Germany, were finally relied upon most heavily in the new Japanese codes. So, while the English and French lawyers were at battle, the Germans, relative latecomers in Japanese legal circles, made the greatest contribution to the new codes, though actually much of the French doctrine remained.

[A]fter 1900, the Japanese codes, even the provisions clearly drawn from the Code Napoleon, were taught and interpreted by civil-law standards learned from the works of German professors. As Hozumi put it in 1912: "Within the past thirty years, Japanese law has passed from the Chinese family of law to the European family." Although this is in a sense so, it is important to be aware, as Hozumi was, that the new Japanese codes were but an imported skeleton. Only when the Japanese university, bar, and bench could give it flesh and the observance of the people give it life would it become Japanese. This has happened to a remarkable degree since 1945.

In its constitutional and administrative aspects, the new system was essentially authoritarian and remained so with only one significant glimmering of nascent liberality in the 1920s[, which] was ultimately snuffed out. * * *

[3.] The Anglo-American Infusion

Disillusioned and industrially demolished, Japan signed its surrender to the Allied powers on September 2, 1945, and in accordance with the Potsdam Declaration, the Supreme Command of the Allied Powers (SCAP) set about democratizing Japan. The legal formulation of this novel project—an unprecedented democratic revolution initiated paradoxically by aliens from the top down—was of profound significance to the formal legal order and potentially for the society. The constitution was fundamentally rebuilt; all of the five major codes underwent revisions, presumably to render them consistent with the constitutional changes; and a number of special implementing and regulatory laws (*e.g.*, antitrust, collective bargaining, securities exchange) previously unknown to Japan were enacted, with far-reaching implications for both the legal system and the society.

Clearly the new constitution was the center from which most of the other reforms emanated. * * * The Commercial Code was not changed until near the end of the Occupation (effective July 1, 1951), and the most important changes were confined to Book II on company law, which were very substantial changes, however, covering 203 of some 450 articles in Book II. Generally speaking, the major changes were related to shareholders' rights and management's responsibilities.

The Code of Civil Procedure was left largely intact, but two changes were made in 1948 which tended to give Japanese civil trials a more Anglo-American, adversary character. First, the power of the judge to take evidence *ex officio* was eliminated except for certain special situations, and secondly, the burden of presenting and cross-examining witnesses was placed upon the litigants and their counsel. These changes, supported by later Supreme Court Civil Procedure Regulations, were interpreted to relieve the judges of first instance of their prewar duty of clarification, and hence they have caused a shift somewhat away from the German-style, inquisitorial trial methods that lean heavily on the judge. This new tendency has increased the adversary character of Japanese civil trials, relying more on lawyers to present their cases.

In addition to the changes in the constitution and codes, profound changes were also effected * * * in the field of labor by setting up minimum standards of hours and wages and collective bargaining rights; in the field of business regulation by enacting antitrust laws and establishing a new Fair Trade Commission (*Kōsei torihiki iinkai*); in the field of securities by passing a Securities Exchange Act; and in maritime transportation by passing a Marine Transportation Act—to mention some of the most important special postwar legislation.

In all of the latter acts, * * * the legislative pattern followed models from the U.S. The most pronounced American influences found in the five codes themselves are in the Code of Criminal Procedure, the Commercial Code, and the Code of Civil Procedure. * * *

Cumulatively, these changes after World War II amount to a considerable infusion of Anglo-American influence into the Japanese legal system. Furthermore, the cumulative effect of the experience has greatly influenced the Japanese juristic method by producing an increased interest on the part of Japanese jurists in case studies and in the study of the social effects of law in Japan. * * * Nevertheless, it is probably fair to say that the Japanese lawyer still feels closer to the civil law world than the common law—in respect to private law problems at least.

II. The Civil Law System

A. Comparing the civil law and the common law

In the above selection, Professor Henderson notes the impact of French and, especially, German law on legal doctrines and legal thought in Japan. Despite the great infusion of Anglo-American legal concepts after World War II, Henderson concludes that Japanese legal practitioners today probably still feel closer to the civil law world than that of the common law. A thorough comparison of the civil law and common law systems, not to mention the differences between French and German approaches, lies beyond the scope of this book. By tradition, however, most comparatists have concluded that there are fundamental differences between the two systems. Accordingly, we begin with the following excerpt from Professor John Henry Merryman's *The Civil Law Tradition*, which highlights two of those allegedly key differences between the civil law and common law: attitudes toward the role and significance of codes and toward the role of the judiciary. The excerpt also describes the historical difference in basic orientation of the French and German approaches.

In at least one respect, the attitudes described by Merryman do seem to influence Japanese lawyers: when confronted with a legal problem, they will first look to the relevant Code (along with associated statutes and ordinances). In reading cases and other materials in the remainder of this book, consider whether the attitudes toward the role of the judiciary in civil law systems that Merryman describes also apply in Japan and whether basic attitudes in Japan more closely resemble the French or German approach. In addition, consider the following two questions: Are the distinctions between civil and common law systems of any substance? Is a continental jurist, who turns first to the relevant Code, undertaking a different exercise from an American tax lawyer, who turns first to the Internal Revenue Code? What do the alleged distinctions between civil and common law systems mean from a practical lawyering perspective?

JOHN HENRY MERRYMAN, THE CIVIL LAW TRADITION*

26-32 (2d ed., 1985)

One often hears it said, sometimes by people who should know better, that civil law systems are codified statutory systems, whereas the common law is uncodified and is based in large part on judicial decisions. The purpose of this [section] is to indicate the extent to which this observation oversimplifies and misrepresents, and at the same time the extent to which it expresses, an important set of basic differences between the two legal traditions.

The distinction between legislative and judicial production of law can be misleading. There is probably at least as much legislation in force in a typical American state as there is in a typical European or Latin American nation. As in a civil law nation, legislation validly enacted in the United States is the law, which the judges are expected to interpret and apply in the spirit in which it was enacted. The authority of legislation is superior to that of judicial decisions; statutes supersede contrary judicial decisions (constitutional questions aside), but not vice versa. The amount of legislation and the degree of authority of legislation are not useful criteria for distinguishing civil law systems from common law systems.

Nor is the existence of something called a code a distinguishing criterion. California has more codes than any civil law nation, but California is not a civil law jurisdiction. Codes do exist in most civil law systems, but bodies of systematic legislation covering broad areas of the law and indistinguishable in appearance from European or Latin American codes also exist in a number of common law nations. Conversely, a civil law system need not have codes. Hungary and Greece were civil law countries even before they enacted their civil codes: Hungarian civil law was uncodified until Hungary became a socialist state, and Greece enacted its first civil code after World War II. South Africa, whose legal system is based on Roman-Dutch law, is still uncodified, and citations of Justinian's *Digest* in South African judicial opinions are still encountered. The code form is thus not a distinctive identifying mark of a civil law system.

If, however, one thinks of codification not as a form but as the expression of an ideology, and if one tries to understand that ideology and why it achieves expres-

*From John Henry Merryman, *The Civil Law Tradition*, Second Edition, at 26-32. Reprinted with the permission of the publishers, Stanford University Press. © 1969, 1985 by the Board of Trustees of the Leland Stanford Junior University.

sion in code form, then one can see how it makes sense to talk about codes in comparative law. It is true that California has a number of what are called codes, as do some other states in the United States, and that the Uniform Commercial Code has been adopted in most American jurisdictions. However, although these look like the codes in civil law countries, the underlying ideology—the conception of what a code is and of the functions it should perform in the legal process—is not the same. There is an entirely different ideology of codification at work in the civil law world. * * * Justinian, when he promulgated the *Corpus Juris Civilis*, sought to abolish all prior law. Certain elements of the prior legal order were, however, included in the *Corpus Juris Civilis* itself, and were consequently preserved when he promulgated it. Similarly, the French, when they codified their law, repealed all prior law in the areas covered by the codes. Any principles of prior law that were incorporated in the codes received their validity not from their previous existence, but from their incorporation and reenactment in codified form. Justinian and the French codifiers sought to destroy prior law for different but analogous reasons: Justinian sought to reestablish the purer law of an earlier time, the French to establish an entirely new legal order. In both cases, the aims were essentially utopian. * * *

As in many utopias, one of the objectives of the [French] Revolution was to make lawyers unnecessary. There was a desire for a legal system that was simple, nontechnical, and straightforward—one in which the professionalism and the tendency toward technicality and complication commonly blamed on lawyers could be avoided. One way to do this was to state the law clearly and in a straightforward fashion, so that the ordinary citizen could read the law and understand what his rights and obligations were, without having to consult lawyers and go to court. Thus the French Civil Code of 1804 was envisioned as a kind of popular book that could be put on the shelf next to the family Bible. It would be a handbook for the citizen, clearly organized and stated in straightforward language, that would allow citizens to determine their legal rights and obligations by themselves.

Fear of a "gouvernement des juges" hovered over French post-revolutionary reforms and colored the codification process. The emphasis on complete separation of powers, with all lawmaking power lodged in a representative legislature, was a way of insuring that the judiciary would be denied lawmaking power. * * * At the same time, however, the judge had to decide every case that came before him. * * *

But if the legislature alone could make laws and the judiciary could only apply them (or, at a later time, interpret and apply them), such legislation had to be complete, coherent, and clear. If a judge were required to decide a case for which there was no legislative provision, he would in effect make law and thus violate the principle of separation of powers. Hence, it was necessary that the legislature draft a code without gaps. Similarly, if there were conflicting provisions in the code, the judge would make law by choosing one rather than another as more applicable to the situation. Hence there could be no conflicting provisions. Finally, if a judge were allowed to decide what meaning to give to an ambiguous provision or an obscure statement, he would again be making law. Hence the code had to be clear.

If insistence on a total separation of legislative from judicial power dictated that the codes be complete, coherent, and clear, the prevailing spirit of optimistic rationalism persuaded those in its spell that it was possible to draft systematic legislation that would have those characteristics to such a degree that the function of the judge would be limited to selecting the applicable provision of the code and giving it its obvious significance in the context of the case. * * *

In contrast to the essentially revolutionary, rationalistic, and nontechnical character of the Code Napoléon, the German Civil Code of 1896 (effective in 1900) was historically oriented, scientific, and professional. A large share of the credit (or blame) for the differences between the German and the French civil codes is owed to Friedrich Karl von Savigny, one of the most famous names in the history of the civil law tradition. * * *

Savigny's idea was that by thoroughly studying the German legal system in its historical context legal scholars would be able to draw from it a set of historically verified and essential principles. These features of the law could then be individually studied, studied in relation to other such principles, and eventually systematically restated. The result would be a reconstruction of the German legal system according to its inherent principles and features. This, in turn, would provide the necessary basis for the codification of German law. * * * [T]he proposed reconstruction of the German legal system was to be a *scientific* reconstruction. * * * Finally, the Germans were convinced that it was neither desirable nor possible to rid the world of lawyers. The idea that the law should be clearly and simply stated so that it could be correctly understood and applied by the popular reader was expressly rejected. The German view was that lawyers would be needed, that they would engage in interpreting and applying the law, and that the code they prepared should be responsive to the needs of those trained in the law.

Consequently, the German Civil Code of 1896 is the opposite of revolutionary. It was not intended to abolish prior law and substitute a new legal system; on the contrary, the idea was to codify those principles of German law that would emerge from careful historical study of the German legal system. Instead of trying to discover true principles of law from assumptions about man's nature, as the French did under the influence of secular natural law, the Germans sought to find fundamental principles of German law by scientific study of the data of German law: the existing German legal system in historical context. Rather than a textbook for the layman, the German civil code was thought of as a tool to be used primarily by professionals of the law.

Does this mean that the German civil code and the French civil code are totally dissimilar? It does not. There are differences, and they are important, but some overriding similarities remain. The Germans, like the French, have incorporated a sharp separation of powers into their system of law and government. It is the function of the legislator to make law, and the judge must be prevented from doing so. While displaying a more sophisticated awareness of the difficulty of making a code complete, coherent, and clear, the Germans nevertheless sought to do exactly that, and for the same basic reasons that motivated the French. The German code also served a unifying function, providing a single body of law for the recently unified nation. And like the French code, it thus supported the emergence of the monolithic nation-state.

An entirely different set of ideals and assumptions is associated with the California Civil Code, or with the Uniform Commercial Code as adopted in any American jurisdiction. Even though such codes may look very much like a French or a German code, they are not based on the same ideology, and they do not express anything like the same cultural reality. Where such codes exist, they make no pretence of completeness. The judge is not compelled to find a basis for deciding a given case within the code. Usually, moreover, such codes are not rejections of the past; they do not purport to abolish all prior law in their field, but rather to perfect it and, except where it conflicts with their specific present purposes, to supplement it. Where some provision of a code or other statute appears to be in possible conflict with a deeply rooted rule of the common law, the tendency will be to interpret the code provision in such a way as to evade the conflict. "Statutes in derogation of the common law," according to a famous judicial quotation, "are strictly construed."

Thus the conservative tendencies of the common law tradition stand in marked contrast to the ideology of the revolution from which the spirit of civil law codification emerged. It is this ideology, rather than the form of codification, that helps to bind civil law nations together in a common legal tradition.

B. Structure of the Codes

1. The six Codes

Reflecting its Continental underpinnings, Japanese law is centered around five basic Codes: the Civil Code, the Commercial Code, the Criminal Code, and the Codes of Civil and Criminal Procedure. As the most fundamental and the controlling legal document, the Constitution is of course different in nature from these Codes; but the five Codes and the Constitution collectively are referred to in Japan as the "six Codes"—or, literally, the "six laws" (*roppō*). These six Codes are supplemented by a wide array of statutes, ordinances, regulations and other provisions.

2. Relationship among the Codes and with other laws

Among the Codes (excluding the Constitution), the Civil Code stands at the top as the most general pronouncement of law. Compared to the Civil Code, the other Codes are regarded as more specific law. For example, the Code likely to be of greatest concern for doing business in Japan, the Commercial Code, is considered specific law vis-à-vis the general law of the Civil Code; and particular commercial legislation can be regarded as specific law compared to the general law of the Commercial Code. Normally, the specific prevails over the general. In the field of law governed by a statute or any other Code, if no provision applies, one refers back to the Civil Code, and if the Civil Code contains no applicable provision, one refers to custom and then to equity. Note, though, that Section 1 of the Commercial Code (reprinted in Section II.B.3 below) states that for commercial matters, if the Commercial Code contains no applicable provision, commercial custom should be referred to before referring to the Civil Code.

Japanese legal scholars and practitioners must become adept at maneuvering through the Codes, as these are typically the beginning points of legal analysis. The first step in doing so involves the ability to cross-reference between the Codes. In some cases, cross-referencing is explicitly called for by provisions in the Codes and cross-referenced provisions are incorporated as a matter of law. Most of the time, however, cross-referencing is only conceptual and doing it well entails considerable training and research.

The following is an example of cross-referencing in which the Commercial Code explicitly refers to, and incorporates provisions of, the Civil Code:

From the Commercial Code

Book II (Companies)

Chapter IV (Stock Company)

Division III (Internal Organization of Stock Company)

Subdivision 2 (Directors and Board of Directors)

Section 254. (Appointment, competency and relationship with the company)

(1) - (2) * * *

(3) The relationship between the company and the directors shall be governed by the provisions relating to mandate.

From the Civil Code

Book III (Obligation-rights)

Chapter 2 (Contracts)

Division X (Mandate)

Section 643. (Mandate)

A mandate takes effect when one party commissions another party to perform a juristic act and the other party accepts the commission.

Section 644. (Duty of [mandatory]—care of good manager)

A mandatory is obligated to manage the affairs entrusted to him with the care of a good manager in accordance with the tenor of the mandate.

(Note: There follow 12 more provisions concerning mandates in the Civil Code, Book III, Chapter 2, Division X.)

More often than not, maneuvering among the Codes is a matter of making and arguing for conceptual linkages rather than of following explicit references which are incorporated as a matter of law, as in the example above. Privately published books typically called *Roppō Zensho* (Complete Compendium of the Six Codes) are designed to help the scholar or practitioner of Japanese law in this endeavor. These books contain the text of the Constitution, the five Codes, and other important statutes, and for many of the provisions suggest cross-references to other Code provisions.

The annotated *Roppō Zensho* also refers one to various Cabinet and Ministerial Orders and occasionally to court precedents. For any given provision in the

Codes, ascertaining what the law is with respect to the provision is often far from clear based merely on a reading of the provision or cross-referencing to other provisions. Much of the significance of the relevant law may be subsumed in court cases, various Cabinet and Ministerial Orders, and related statutes. For example, consider Commercial Code, Section 281, which concerns the documents that must be submitted to a firm's auditors in advance of its annual shareholders' meeting. Subsection 1 of Section 281 lists four documents that must be submitted; an annotation in one *Roppō Zensho* that sets forth materials relevant to understanding the submission requirement contains nearly one hundred entries.

3. The public good and custom under the Civil and Commercial Codes

Recall the discussion by Merryman in the excerpt in Section II.A. of this chapter about the contrast between France's effort to repeal all prior law and Germany's effort to codify prior law in their Civil Codes. The Japanese Codes contain several provisions which reference custom and standards not defined within the Codes. Accordingly, in addition to being adept at maneuvering among the Codes, statutes, and relevant Cabinet and Ministerial orders, the legal scholar or practitioner of Japanese law must also be able to identify the proper standards for such concepts as "maintaining the public welfare" and "abuse of rights" and such practices as "commercial customary law." The following are examples of references in the Civil and Commercial Codes to customs and principles not defined in the Codes:

From the Civil Code:

Section 1. (Exercise of private rights)

1. All private rights shall conform to the principle of maintaining the public welfare.
2. The exercise of rights and performance of duties shall be carried out in accordance with the principles of good faith and trust.
3. No abuse of rights shall be permitted.

Section 1-2. (Construction)

This Code shall be construed in a manner consistent with respect for the dignity of individuals and the essential equality of the sexes.

Section 90. (The public order and good morals)

A juristic act whose object is contrary to the public order or good morals is null and void.

Section 91. (Discretionary provisions and declaration of intention)

If the parties to a juristic act have declared an intention which deviates from any provision of a law or ordinance not concerned with the public order, such intention shall prevail.

Section 92. (Effect of customs)

If there is a custom deviating from any provisions of a law or ordinance not relating to the public order, such custom shall prevail if the parties to a juristic act are deemed to have intended to be bound by such custom.

Section 236. (Ibid.—different custom)

If there is any custom different from what is provided for in the preceding two articles [both of which concern restrictions on the construction of buildings next to property lines], such custom shall prevail.

From the Commercial Code

Section 1. (Laws applicable to commercial matters)

As to commercial matters, in a case where there are no applicable provisions in this Code, commercial customary law shall apply; and where there is no applicable commercial customary law, the Civil Code shall apply.

A similar provision is contained in *Hōrei* (Act concerning the Application of Laws), which is Japan's choice of law statute. Section 2 of *Hōrei* provides:

Customs which are not contrary to public order or good morals shall have the same force as law insofar as they are recognized by the provisions of a law or ordinance or relate to matters which are not provided for by laws or ordinances.

4. Application of the Codes to a case

The case below reads almost as if drafted for the purpose of teaching about Japan's civil law. As with all cases translated for this book, in order to understand the case it is important to read carefully the Code provisions cited in the "References" section of the case (those provisions can be found in the Appendices) and to bear in mind the "Note Concerning Cases" contained in the Introductory Notes to this book.

Translation by Yanagida Nomura & Akai

Onoe v. Yasuda Marine & Fire Insurance K.K.
327 Hanrei Taimuzu 313
(Yokohama Dist. Ct., May 28, 1975)

REFERENCES:

Civil Code, §§ 90, 91, 651, and 709

Commercial Code, § 50(1)

Constitution, Art. 25

FACTS:

In 1966, plaintiff Onoe became an agent of defendant Yasuda Marine & Fire Insurance K.K. (Yasuda), a casualty insurance company, under an agency contract (the Contract) between them. Onoe operated his agency business in his own office, staffed by his own employees. For a period after he became an agent of Yasuda, Onoe was simultaneously engaged as an agent for two other insurance companies. Onoe was not paid a salary by Yasuda; his compensation came in the form of commissions paid by Yasuda in accordance with the volume of insurance sold by Onoe on behalf of Yasuda.

In 1970, Yasuda terminated the Contract pursuant to a termination clause which stated that Yasuda could terminate the Contract by giving Onoe thirty days' notice.

Onoe brought this suit against Yasuda for damages of ¥5,840,000, alleging that, since Yasuda's termination of the Contract was not justified, its interference with Onoe's right to engage in the agency business under the Contract constituted an intentional or negligent tort, and that Onoe suffered lost profits and mental distress as a result of Yasuda's tortious act. Onoe argued that Yasuda's termination was not justified for at least one of the following reasons:

(1) The termination clause of the Contract is an illustrative clause by which the parties did not intend themselves to be bound;

(2) Since the purposes of the Contract are not only for Yasuda's benefit, but also for Onoe's, Yasuda is required to have good cause, and to disclose the same, in order to terminate the Contract;

(3) Since the relationship between Onoe and Yasuda under the Contract is in substance like that of an employer and employee under a labor contract, Yasuda is required to have good cause to the same degree as required under the law governing labor contracts, and to disclose the same, in order to terminate the Contract; and/or

(4) The Contract has been in substance like a slave labor relationship in that Yasuda is a giant company with great resources, while Onoe is a small individual entrepreneur, who makes his entire living from commission fees by devoting himself to the agency business. Under these circumstances, the termination clause threatened Onoe's right to a livelihood, and thus the termination clause should be found void as jeopardizing the public order and good morals.

JUDGMENT:

Plaintiff Onoe's demands are denied.

REASONS:

I. [Omitted.]

II. Validity of Yasuda's Termination of the Contract

1. * * * Of the statutes governing the termination of an agency contract, the Civil Code provides that parties to an agency contract may terminate the same at any time (Civ. Code, § 651). By contrast, in light of the continuous and profit-making character of a commercial agency, the Commercial Code provides for two months' notice prior to termination of a commercial agency contract (Com. Code, § 50(1)). Section 50(1) of the Commercial Code should, however, be considered a discretionary provision. Accordingly, an agreement between parties to a commercial agency contract to extend or shorten the notice period for termination of the contract is valid.

* * * Onoe alleges that since the termination clause is an illustrative provision, the parties are not bound by it. Based on the following evidence [omitted], it could be found that Onoe signed the Contract without paying particular attention to the termination clause. Even if this were found, however, it does not follow that Onoe and Yasuda did not intend to be bound by the clause. There is insufficient evidence for us to reach such a conclusion.

2. Onoe alleges that since both parties to the Contract become bound thereunder for the purpose of profit-making, Yasuda is required to have good cause, and to disclose the same, in order to terminate the Contract.

For termination of an agency contract, neither the Civil Code nor the Commercial Code requires the existence or disclosure of good cause (*see* Civ. Code, § 651 and Com. Code, § 50). Given the nature of an agency contract, it is reasonable not to require a special cause to terminate it. This is true even if an agency contract creates mutual obligations.

Onoe entered into the Contract to make a profit and was paid certain fees by Yasuda for his services under the Contract. This, however, means simply that the Contract creates mutual obligations. The purpose of the Contract is not a reason to limit the right to terminate it.

Furthermore, there is no other law requiring Yasuda to give a reason for terminating the Contract.

3. Onoe argues that the relationship between Yasuda and Onoe under the Contract is that of employer and employee under a labor contract, and that Yasuda must thus give good cause to terminate the Contract.

(1) Needless to say, an agency contract is a contract the purpose of which is to supply labor services. If, as Onoe alleges, the relationship between Yasuda and Onoe under the Contract had been in substance an employer-employee relationship under a labor contract, the relationship between Yasuda and Onoe would have been subject to the relevant labor laws and regulations, such as the Labor Standards Act. In the case before the court, however, we find, upon all of the evidence, that no such labor laws or regulations have been applied to either Yasuda or Onoe.

(2) Instead, upon our review of the following evidence [omitted], we find that Onoe was paid commissions by Yasuda in accordance with the volume of insurance policies sold by Onoe on behalf of Yasuda.

He was not paid any salary or compensation as an employee, and when he became an agent of Yasuda, he was at the same time an agent of two other insurance companies, Capital K.K. and Dai Tokyo Marine and Fire K.K. Moreover, Onoe owned his own office for his agency business, hired employees himself, bore his own business expenses, and operated his business free of any time constraints imposed by Yasuda. Upon these findings, we find that Onoe, as a commercial agent under the Commercial Code, operated his agency business independent of Yasuda. Therefore, there was no employer-employee relationship between Onoe and Yasuda.

(3) We find, however, the following facts:

(i) Yasuda established a monthly sales target for each agent and made harsh demands that each agent achieve its target. As an incentive for each agent to do so, Yasuda honored the agent who achieved the greatest sales, had each agent post a list of the business results of all agents, and educated its agents by regularly issuing a newsletter, *Tobiguchi*.

(ii) In one case (for which Onoe experienced no similar occurrence) in which an employee of an agent embezzled an insurance premium, Yasuda demanded that the agent fire the employee or compensate Yasuda for the amount embezzled, and Yasuda expressed its intention to terminate the agency contract with the agent if the agent did not meet Yasuda's demand.

Fact (i) above does not, however, demonstrate that Yasuda had the right to order or direct its agents. Furthermore, Yasuda's requirements under fact (ii) above were reasonable since such requirements are necessary for Yasuda to prevent the recurrence of similar events, to maintain its reputation, and to make up for its losses. Therefore, the above-mentioned facts do not prove the existence between Yasuda and Onoe of an employer-employee relationship under a labor contract.

(4) There is no other evidence which would prove that Onoe had an employer-employee relationship with Yasuda.

4. [Omitted.]

5. Onoe argues that Yasuda's termination of the Contract pursuant to the termination clause is void since the clause jeopardizes the public order and good morals.

The termination clause, however, does no more than shorten the notice period for termination provided in Section 50(1) of the Commercial Code [from sixty] to thirty days. Since Section 50(1) is a discretionary provision, as mentioned above, the termination clause does not jeopardize the public order or violate good morals, and thus is not null and void. * * *

Questions and Discussion Points

1. *Cross-referencing between the Civil and Commercial Codes:* In the first paragraph excerpted from the "Reasons" section, the court refers to Civil Code § 651 and Commercial Code § 50(1). What is the relationship between these two sections? Which takes precedence and why?

2. *Compulsory and discretionary provisions:* Again in the first paragraph of the "Reasons" section, and also in the last paragraph, the court says that § 50(1) of the Commercial Code is a discretionary provision. What does this mean? Consider this with reference to Section 91 of the Civil Code. How can one determine if any given provision is compulsory or discretionary? Consider the following definition of "*kyōkō hōki*" (compulsory laws and regulations) from one of Japan's leading legal dictionaries:

> *Kyōkō hōki* are provisions that apply irrespective of whether a party(ies) so desires. In contrast, *nin'i hōki* (discretionary laws and regulations) are provisions that apply only absent a contrary expression by a party(ies). In the abstract, *kyōkō hōki* relate to the public order and *nin'i hōki* do not, but for a given provision there is no way of determining its classification except by evaluating its purpose. (From Takeuchi, et al., eds., *Shin-Hōritsugaku Jiten* (*New Legal Dictionary*) (3d ed., Yūhikaku 1989).)

3. *Public order or good morals, torts and the "right to life":* What is the relationship of Sections 90 and 709 of the Civil Code and Article 25 of the Constitution to the case? From what source(s) should one draw to learn what these provisions mean?

4. *The court's reasoning:* What is the court's holding and the basis for it? Is the court's reasoning convincing?

III. The Institutional Setting

A. The legislative and executive branches

JOHN OWEN HALEY, DANIEL H. FOOTE AND DAN FENNO HENDERSON, LAW AND THE LEGAL PROCESS IN JAPAN*

Part II, 4-6 (1994)

Japan's national government under the postwar constitution remained parliamentary in form with a bicameral legislature to which, unlike [under] the prewar system, the cabinet is accountable. Whether Japan should be classified as a constitutional monarchy or a republic continues to be debated. The emperor, whose formal status is described as a "symbol" of the state (Constitution art. 1), continues to perform such functions of a head of state as formal promulgation of treaties, statutes and cabinet orders, convocation of the Diet and dissolution of the lower house, attestation of the appointment and dismissal of ministers of state and certain other officials, reception of foreign ambassadors and award of honors (Constitution art. 7).

The principal lawmaking organ of government is the bicameral Diet, comprising a House of Representatives (*shūgi'in*) and a House of Councillors (*sangi'in*). The House of Representatives is politically the more significant of the two, despite its conventional description as the "lower house." For example, bills rejected by the House of Councillors still become law if subsequently passed by the House of Representatives by a two-thirds vote (Constitution art. 59[1]). Similarly, the House of Representatives controls the budget (Constitution art. 60). The House of Councillors in fact represents a rather awkward compromise between the advocates (mostly within SCAP) of a universal system and those (generally on the Japanese side) who preferred an appointive or corporative upper house.

The two houses are also differentiated by size and separate electoral systems. As of 1992 the House of Representatives had 512 members elected for four year terms from 130 local multi-member electoral districts. The upper house comprised 252 members, of whom 152 were elected from 47 "local constituencies" corresponding to Japan's 47 prefectures and 100 elected in a nationwide contest from the "national constituency." Because the lower house is subject to dissolution, the members rarely serve their full four year terms. In contrast, members of the upper house all serve their full terms of six years. Both houses suffer the problem of malapportionment. * * *

The constitution lodges executive power in the cabinet (Constitution art. 65), which is made collectively responsible to the Diet (Constitution art. 66[3]). Heading the cabinet is the prime minister (Constitution art. 66[1]), who has the author-

*From John Owen Haley, Daniel H. Foote and Dan Fenno Henderson, *Law and the Legal Process in Japan: Materials for an Introductory Course on Japanese Law,* Part II (Seattle: University of Washington School of Law, 1994 ed.), at 4-6. Reprinted by permission.

ity to appoint and dismiss all ministers of state (Constitution art. 68), at least half of whom must be selected from members of the Diet (Constitution art. 68). Under the cabinet are the Prime Minister's Office, twelve statutory ministries, eight commissions, and twenty-four agencies (see [Figure 2-1]). Within each ministry immediately below the minister are at least two vice-ministers, one of whom is also a political appointee. The other is the highest career official in the ministry. * * * Under the present system the emperor's position is purely symbolic and ceremonial. The cabinet and hence all organs of government, with the notable exception of the judiciary, are ultimately accountable to the Diet, and it to the people.

The influence of the bureaucracy is significant. It should be emphasized that Japan is not exceptional in this regard. Bureaucratic involvement in establishing policy and drafting legislation prevails in all industrial states. In parliamentary systems like Japan, bureaucratic participation and influence over policy is especially strong. * * * Japan also shares with European systems the presence of many former bureaucrats in the legislature. Between 1955 and 1965, for instance, nearly 30 percent of the members of the Diet affiliated with the ruling Liberal Democratic Party (LDP) were ex-bureaucrats and from a third to a half of the members of the cabinets of the various LDP governments during this period were former higher ranking bureaucrats.[1] * * *

[D]uring four decades of rule by the LDP and its predecessors[2] (aside from the brief interval from June 1947 to the beginning of 1948 during which a Socialist Party cabinet headed by Tetsu Katayama held power), it has often been difficult to distinguish between party, cabinet and bureaucracy.

The LDP lost its majority in the general election of July 1993 held in the wake of political scandal and the defection of nearly 20 percent of its lower house members, including its largest faction. The subsequent resignation of Kiichi Miyazawa as Prime Minister on July 22, 1993, ended 38 years of continuous LDP rule. * * * Morihiro Hosokawa * * * was elected prime minister to lead a coalition government. * * * The one issue uniting the new government [was] reform of the electoral system. * * *

[In January 1994, the Diet passed a compromise political reform proposal that replaced the existing multiseat electoral districts for the Lower House with a combination of single-seat constituencies and a proportional representation system. Under the new system, 300 Lower House members are to be elected from single-seat districts and 200 members based on proportional voting in eleven broad regions. (As of the publication of this book, the difficult task of drawing the boundary lines for the 300 single-seat districts had yet to be completed.) The reform legislation also placed certain limits on political fundraising. By mid-1994, Hosokawa had resigned and had been replaced by two successive coalition governments—the second of which consisted of a previously almost unthinkable alliance between the LDP and the Socialists. Despite some speculation that this coalition might try to roll back the electoral reforms, as of the completion of this book there had been no signs of such a move.]

Completing the institutional structure at the national level is the judiciary.

* * *

It should also be noted that although Japan is a unitary system, below the national level are two tiers of local government with some measure of autonomy. The first are the 47 prefectural governments (including Okinawa), which have a "presidential" system with independent executive-governors (*chiji*)—and legislative assemblies. Prefectures are ordinarily described in Japanese by the term *ken*. The capital Tokyo is the one *to* and, for historical reasons, the cities of Kyoto and Osaka are separately termed *fu* and Hokkaido *dō*. The second tier are the municipalities: cities (*shi*), towns (*machi*) and villages (*mura*). Counties (*gun*) no longer have formal existence, but the term continues to be used. Also, major cities are subdivided into wards (*ku*), which, with the exception of Tokyo's 23 *ku*, have only administrative significance.

B. The judicial branch

1. Overview

Japan's judicial system is a unitary nationwide system administered by the Supreme Court and its General Secretariat. There are five types of courts: the Supreme Court, High Courts, District Courts, Family Courts and Summary Courts.

As summarized in Figure 2-2, in civil cases, Summary Courts, of which there are some 575 throughout Japan, have jurisdiction over claims not exceeding ¥900,000. Proceedings in Summary Courts are handled by a single judge. (For a summary of the jurisdiction of Japanese courts in criminal cases, see Figure 2-3.)

There are 50 District Courts in Japan, plus nearly 250 separate branches of those courts. These courts have general jurisdiction over all civil cases not specifically assigned to other courts. Most civil cases are handled by a single judge, although three-judge panels hear certain types of cases. In addition, District Courts have jurisdiction over most appeals from Summary Courts, with three-judge panels hearing such appeals.

Family Courts, which have jurisdiction over domestic matters and most juvenile delinquency cases, are located wherever there are District Courts or branches. In addition, there are nearly 100 sub-branches of Family Courts in other locations.

There are eight High Courts and six High Court branches. In civil cases, these courts have appellate jurisdiction over appeals from District Courts (including second-level appeals from cases that originated in Summary Court and were first appealed to a District Court). In addition, if both parties agree, civil decisions of a Summary Court may be appealed directly to the High Court. The High Courts also have exclusive jurisdiction over certain types of civil cases, including election disputes and mandamus proceedings, and the Tokyo High Court has exclusive jurisdiction to review decisions of the Fair Trade Commission, Patent Office and other quasi-judicial bodies. Nearly all High Court cases are heard by three-judge panels.

The Supreme Court is an appellate court composed of fifteen Justices (assisted

Figure 2-1
Government Organization Chart

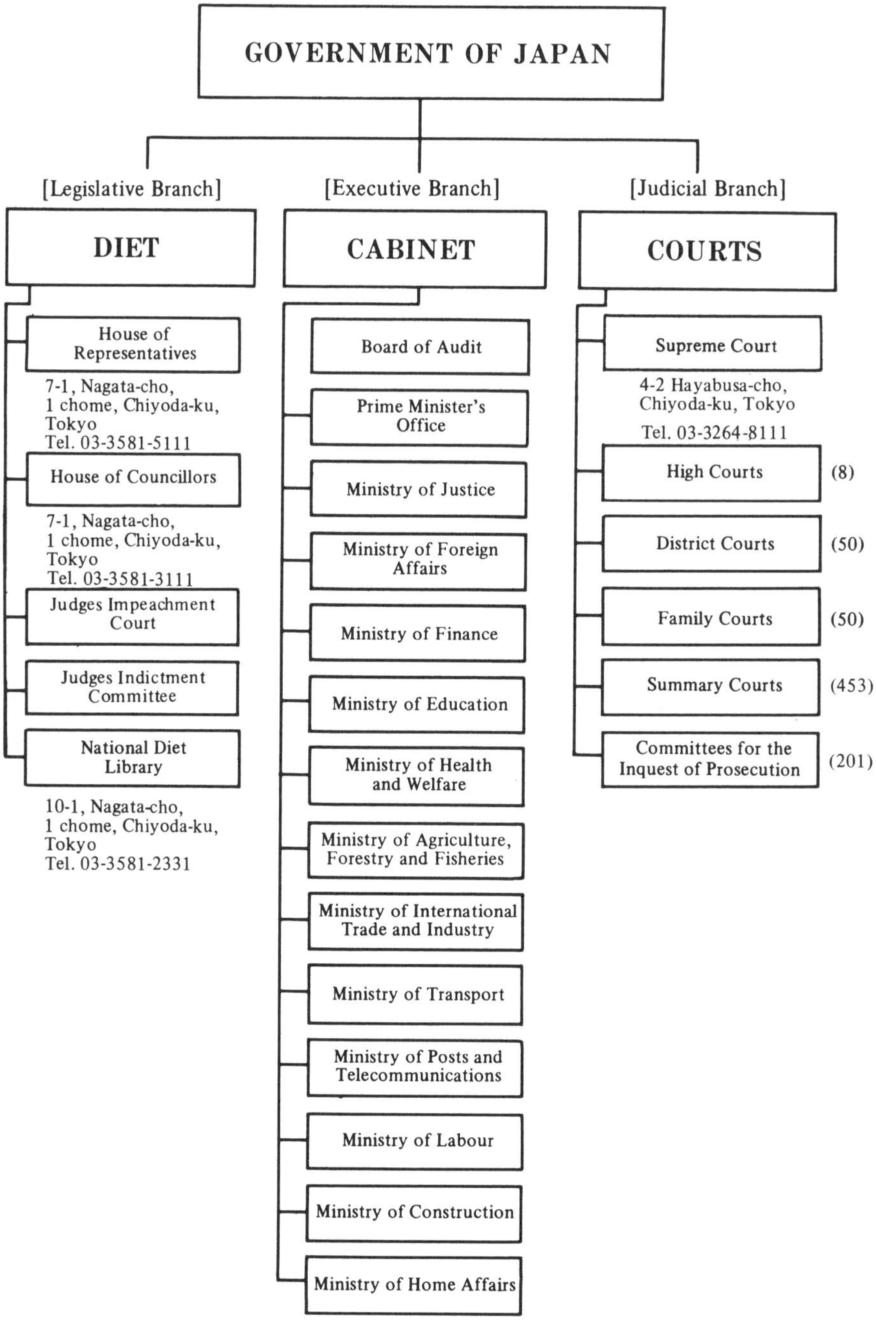

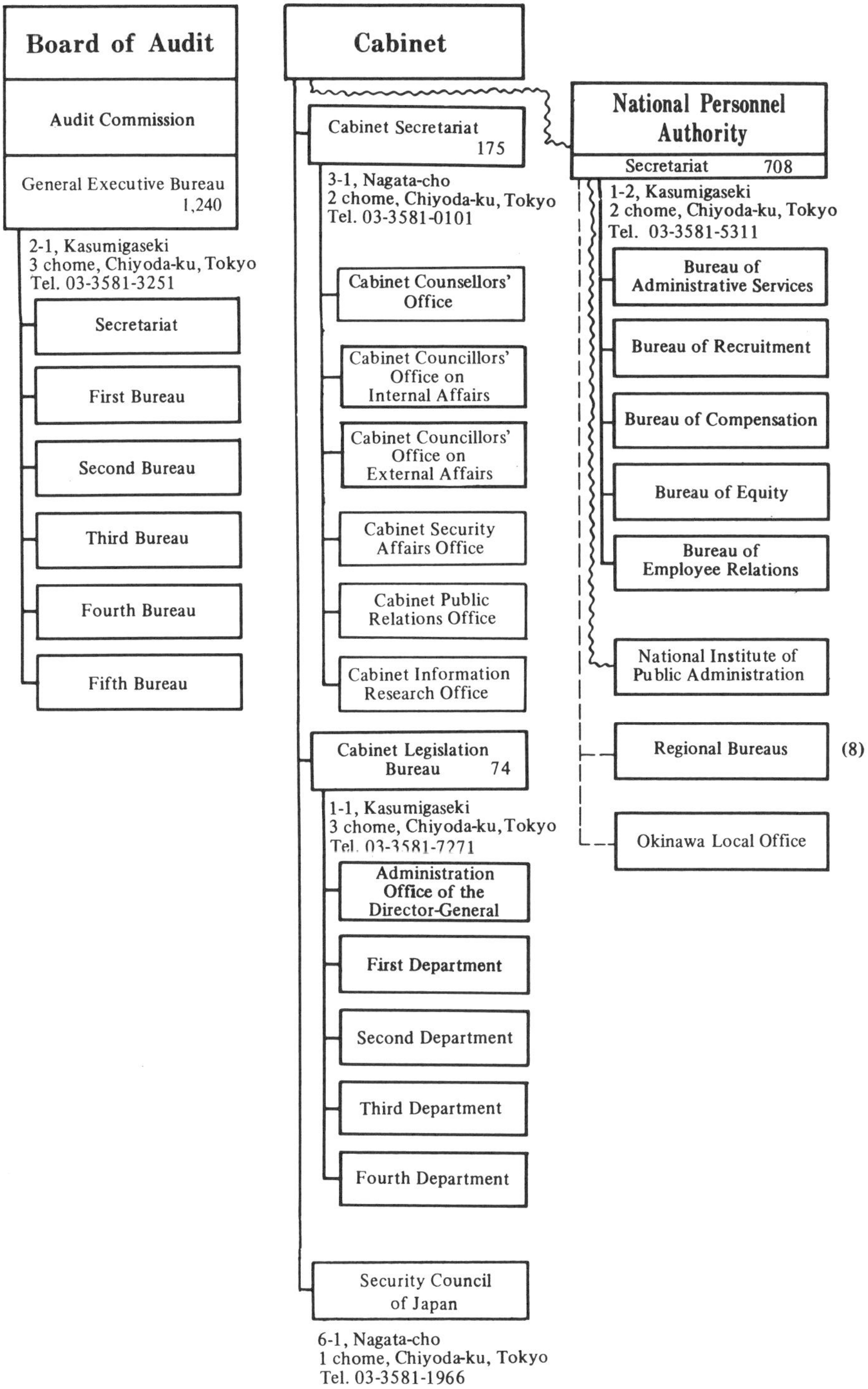
Board of Audit
Audit Commission
General Executive Bureau 1,240
2-1, Kasumigaseki
3 chome, Chiyoda-ku, Tokyo
Tel. 03-3581-3251
Secretariat
First Bureau
Second Bureau
Third Bureau
Fourth Bureau
Fifth Bureau
Cabinet
Cabinet Secretariat 175
3-1, Nagata-cho
2 chome, Chiyoda-ku, Tokyo
Tel. 03-3581-0101
Cabinet Counsellors' Office
Cabinet Councillors' Office on Internal Affairs
Cabinet Councillors' Office on External Affairs
Cabinet Security Affairs Office
Cabinet Public Relations Office
Cabinet Information Research Office
Cabinet Legislation Bureau 74
1-1, Kasumigaseki
3 chome, Chiyoda-ku, Tokyo
Tel. 03-3581-7271
Administration Office of the Director-General
First Department
Second Department
Third Department
Fourth Department
Security Council of Japan
6-1, Nagata-cho
1 chome, Chiyoda-ku, Tokyo
Tel. 03-3581-1966
National Personnel Authority
Secretariat 708
1-2, Kasumigaseki
2 chome, Chiyoda-ku, Tokyo
Tel. 03-3581-5311
Bureau of Administrative Services
Bureau of Recruitment
Bureau of Compensation
Bureau of Equity
Bureau of Employee Relations
National Institute of Public Administration
Regional Bureaus (8)
Okinawa Local Office

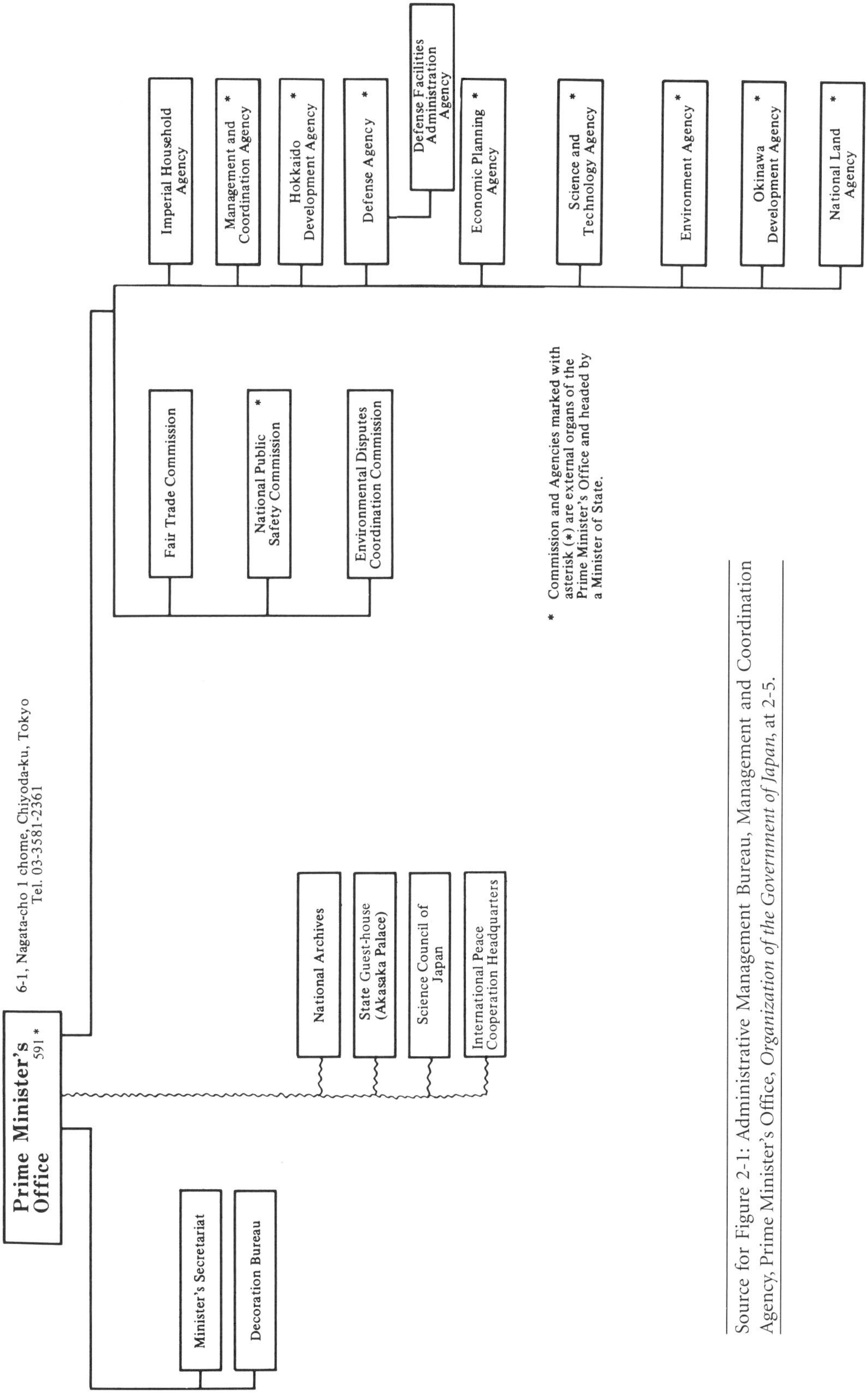

Source for Figure 2-1: Administrative Management Bureau, Management and Coordination Agency, Prime Minister's Office, *Organization of the Government of Japan*, at 2-5.

by a staff of research judges). Grounds for appeal to the Supreme Court are limited. In civil cases, available grounds include constitutional questions and material questions of law affecting the judgment in question.

The Justices are divided into three panels (often translated, somewhat misleadingly, as "Petty Benches") of five Justices each. These panels are not divided into specialties; rather, cases of all types are assigned to each of the panels. These panels dispose of the vast majority of all cases. Cases raising unresolved constitutional questions or involving changes in established precedent of the Court must be referred for an *en banc* decision (often called a Grand Bench decision). In addition, the panel may refer other cases for decision by the *en banc* Court if the panel concludes that the issue raised is important enough to warrant a decision by the entire Court. In recent years typically at most two or three cases per year have been referred to the *en banc* Court.

As described in more detail in the next section, Japan's is a career judiciary. Virtually all judges at the District, Family and High Courts are career judges who rotate among assignments at various courts. In addition, approximately one-third of the Supreme Court Justices are selected from among career judges, with most of the remainder coming from other branches of the profession.

Figure 2-2
Jurisdiction and Procedure of Japanese Courts I

CIVIL CASES

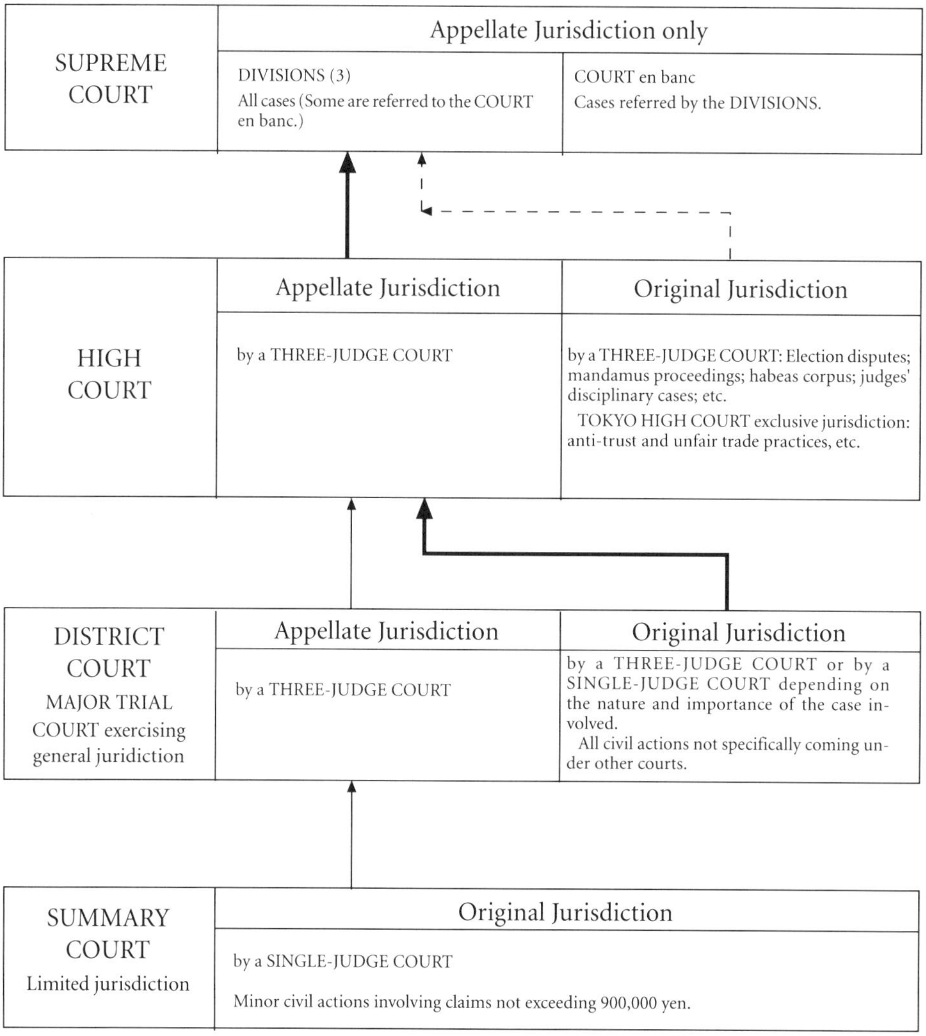

Note:

1) Where both parties agree, a jumping appeal may be made from a judgment of the SUMMARY COURT to the HIGH COURT or from a judgment of the DISTRICT COURT to the SUPREME COURT.
2) Where a SUMMARY COURT case involves constitutional questions, a special appeal may be made from a judgment of the HIGH COURT to the SUPREME COURT.

Figure 2-3
Jurisdiction and Procedure of Japanese Courts II

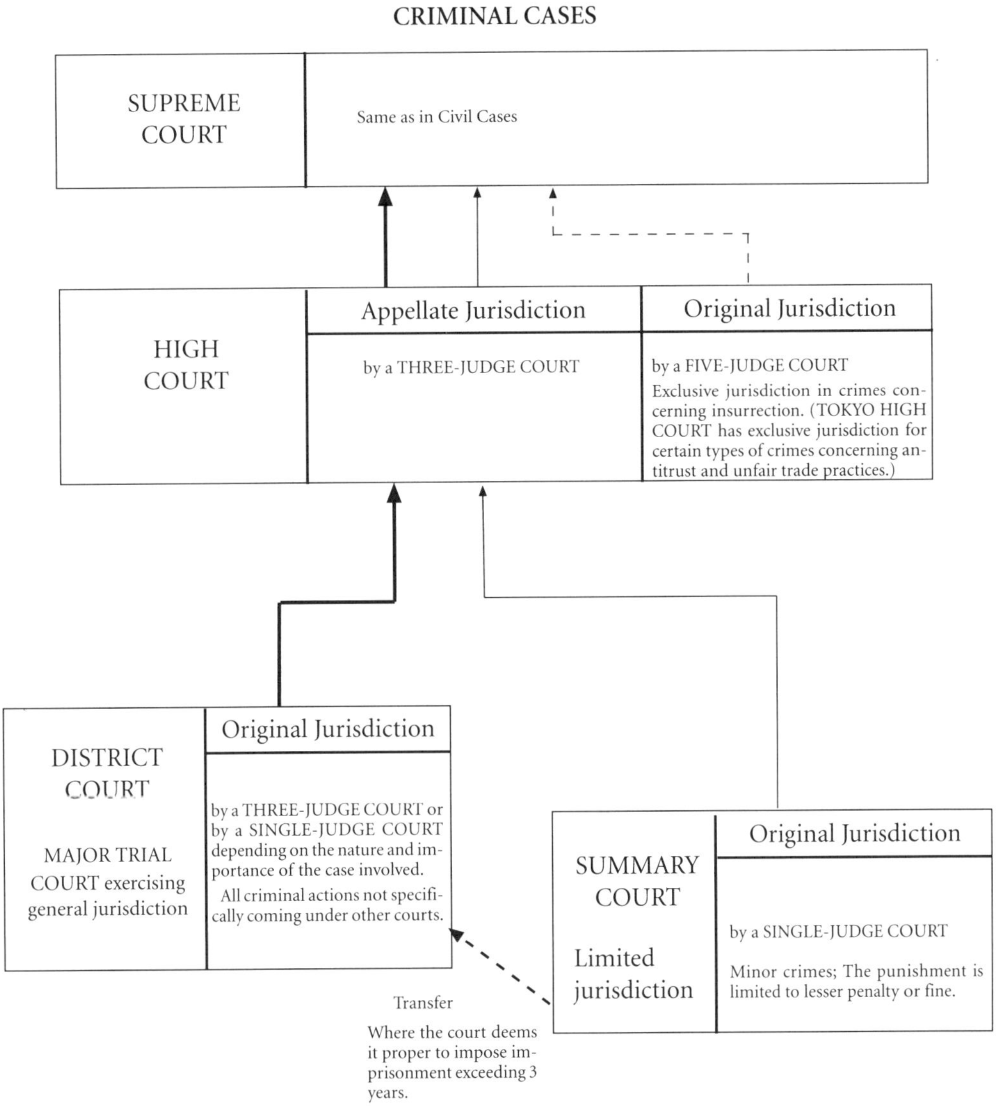

Note: A direct appeal may be made to the SUPREME COURT from a judgment of the DISTRICT COURT or the SUMMARY COURT in which the court determined a law, ordinance, etc., to be unconstitutional.

Source for Figures 2-2 and 2-3: The General Secretariat of the Supreme Court of Japan, *Justice in Japan* (Tokyo: The Supreme Court of Japan, 1990), pp. 14-15. Reprinted, with revisions supplied by the Supreme Court, by permission.

2. Enforcement of the rule of law

As the following excerpt highlights, one of the key postwar reforms relates to enforcement of the rule of law by Japanese courts.

DAN FENNO HENDERSON, FOREIGN ENTERPRISE IN JAPAN: LAWS AND POLICIES*

173-174 (1973)

Japanese governmental organization embodies a "double supremacy": legislative and judicial. The American type of separation of powers—legislative, executive, and judicial—is only partially observed in the new Constitution since Japan now has a parliamentary type of government with a prime minister. * * * This fusion of executive and legislative power resulting in the legislative supremacy of the Diet is, however, accompanied by a sort of Japanese judicial supremacy much like that of the U.S., which is, of course, not found in parliamentary English practice. [This] Japanese judicial supremacy is codified in the written Constitution. * * * Against the background of Japanese tradition, judicial supremacy as a formalism to support nascent political interest in a rule of law and right consciousness is * * * a structural change of revolutionary importance. * * *

In the new Japanese Constitution there were three major constitutional changes designed to implement the rule of law through judicial supremacy. First, the Supreme Court has been given the ultimate power to review all legislative, executive, and administrative acts for constitutionality. Secondly, the prewar separate administrative court for suits against officials, which was really a token device, was abolished, and the regular courts were given jurisdiction over all complaints alleging that officials had transgressed their authority or otherwise acted illegally. * * * Thirdly, the regular court system was taken out from under the administrative supervision of the executive branch (Ministry of Justice), and now the Supreme Court not only administers the entire court system but also has rule-making power.

3. The role of precedent

As discussed earlier, the Japanese legal practitioner would normally approach an issue by seeking first to identify the relevant Code provision and to determine the proper interpretation thereof. What, then, is the role of precedent in this civil law-based system? Does judicial precedent constitute "law" in the same sense that it would in a common law regime? If not, but if courts in Japan in fact act as though bound by precedent, is there any functional difference from a common law system? And what role do academic opinion and scholarly commentary play in Japan? The following selection examines these and related issues.

JOHN OWEN HALEY, DANIEL H. FOOTE AND DAN FENNO HENDERSON, LAW AND THE LEGAL PROCESS IN JAPAN*

Part II, 75-78 (1994)

Although the quasi-judiciary of the Tokugawa period relied consistently and expertly on its own case precedents over a span of two centuries, in 1875 the early Meiji government provided abruptly and explicitly in the Rules for Conduct of Judicial Affairs art. 4 that case precedents would not constitute law for future cases. One cannot but wonder whether the arrival of Boissonade in 1873, with his background in the French Civil Code (containing a similar provision [art. 5] to the effect that court decisions would not constitute law) did not have some influence on this marked departure from the past, which has vexed Japanese legal theorists ever since. The provision and legal theory underlying it are obviously inconsistent with the way in which the Japanese legal system operates.

In deference to this venerable provision of 1875 the well-informed Japanese lawyer, if asked whether case precedents are law in Japan, will say, "Substantially, yes; but formally, no." Also consistent with this old provision, the Court Organization Law (*Saibansho hō*) (Law No. 59, April 16, 1947), amending the 1890 law to conform with the 1947 constitution, simply provides:

> Article 4: A conclusion in a decision of a superior court shall bind courts below in respect of the case concerned.

The negative implication of this provision is that a superior court decision does not bind the lower courts except in the same case, and therefore not in similar future cases. However, upper court case decisions are in practice "substantially" binding on lower courts in similar cases. Also, courts on all levels follow their own decisions in Japan and overrule their own prior precedents only for strong reasons and with reluctance. Not only is this a matter of actual practice relied upon by both the bar and the bench in Japan, but there is also strong inference in the procedural provisions of Japanese law to support the idea that case precedence is in fact regarded as binding by lower courts, as well as by parties in planning their activities. * * *

One consequence of this schizophrenia (that case law is substantially but not formally law) has been that scholarly opinion and treatises too often tended to ignore what the courts were doing, yet at the same time the courts maintained a considerable degree of consistency in their code interpretations, despite the diversity and fluctuation of scholarly opinion. The result inevitably meant a great deal of professional pontification, often seeming to be an exposition of *the law*, when in fact it was instead a systematic analytical treatment of what the author thought the law should be. * * * Obviously from the standpoint of lawyers and their clients who are interested in knowing what law will be enforced, the case jurisprudence and its consistency are quite important. Of course, the courts have known

*From John Owen Haley, Daniel H. Foote and Dan Fenno Henderson, *Law and the Legal Process in Japan: Materials for an Introductory Course on Japanese Law*, Part II (Seattle: University of Washington School of Law, 1994 ed.), at 75-78. Reprinted by permission.

this and have, in very large extent, ignored recent scholarly opinion when it deviates from the courts' own precedents. Many scholars are well aware of this and those who wish to influence practice will accurately delineate between expositions of the law as shown in the cases and their own evaluations. * * *

[T]oday's legal scholar influences judicial practice and the growth of the law by persuasion rather than authoritative pronouncements.

The early tendency to deny decisions the force of law has also left some important marks in Japanese methodology related to case study. First, the case opinions, tied as they are to a positive law statute, are regarded as quite irrelevant once a statute has been repealed or amended. * * * Second, even the cases that were relevant (because interpretative of currently effective statutory provisions) were used differently than we would use them. It was not the factual similarity between one case and the next, to both of which the same law applied, that was significant, but rather what was important was the language employed by the judge in the prior case as a persuasive gloss on the statutory language.

Third, this also meant that case reports rarely included a precise and complete explanation of the facts, which a common law lawyer would regard as essential to any real understanding of the opinion. Finally, only a fraction of the total cases of the Supreme Court are reported. The decisions reported are doubtless the most important. They are usually selected * * * because the issues are considered important, the legal point novel or because the case is thought to be a contribution to the field of law covered. Still, it can hardly be denied that the editorial effect of this limited reporting has had an effect on the direction as well as the growth of case "law." Another point which has similarly constricted the flow of judicial opinion is the concept of collegiality, employed in all but the postwar Supreme Court, whereby the court always speaks unanimously without concurring (or "supplementary") or dissenting opinions * * * .

- - - - - - - - - -

According to one common characterization, in civil law systems, because the key inquiry relates to the proper interpretation of the relevant Code provision, commentary by noted scholars takes on greater weight than prior judicial precedent. As the above excerpt observes, that is not entirely the case in Japan. Though not technically bound (except in later proceedings involving the same case), Japanese courts place great weight on precedent, and scholarly commentary that ignores case law is unlikely to sway many judges.

As the excerpt notes, however, in Japan the prior opinion is looked to primarily for its "gloss on the statutory language"; the manner in which it has interpreted the relevant statutory language is normally of greater importance than distinctions between the basic facts of cases. This does not mean the factual distinctions are irrelevant, of course. Rather, the statutory reasoning constitutes the centerpiece of the opinion, with factual distinctions being relatively less important than in the typical common law case. In that sense, scholarly commentary that convincingly addresses the same statutory issue—especially if authored by a well-known expert—may prove influential. Accordingly, in addition to examining the relevant language of the Codes and related statutes, Japanese legal practitioners typically consider both prior precedent and scholarly commentary, but frame their arguments primarily in statutory construction terms.

IV. The Constitution and Regulation of Economic Activity

The Constitution of Japan was completely redrafted during the postwar Occupation, based on democratic principles. As noted earlier, the Constitution establishes the Diet as the exclusive law-making body in Japan and provides the judiciary with powers of constitutional review and review of administrative acts. The single provision of the Constitution that has generated the most controversy and commentary over the years is Article 9, pursuant to which Japan renounces war and the threat or use of force and pledges never to maintain land, sea and air forces and other war potential. In addition, in Articles 10 through 40 the Constitution proclaims a wide range of basic human rights, including equality under the law; freedom of thought, religion, association, speech and the press; and the rights to receive education, to organize and to bargain and act collectively, to own or hold property, and "to maintain the minimum standards of wholesome and cultured living" (Article 25). These rights and freedoms are not absolute, however. Article 12 sets forth the general principle that, in exercising the rights and freedoms guaranteed by the Constitution, the people "shall refrain from any abuse [thereof] and shall always be responsible for utilizing them for the public welfare." In a similar vein, Article 13 provides that "the right to life, liberty, and the pursuit of happiness shall, *to the extent that it does not interfere with the public welfare*, be the supreme consideration in legislation and in other governmental affairs" (emphasis added). (The full text of the Constitution appears in the Appendices.)

A detailed consideration of these and other constitutional issues lies beyond the scope of this book. One recurrent theme with considerable significance in the business context, however, concerns governmental regulation of business activities. Such regulation presents a possible tension with Article 22 of the Constitution, which proclaims the freedom of every person "to choose his occupation to the extent that it does not interfere with the public welfare," and with Article 27, which provides, "All people shall have the right and the obligation to work." That tension lies at the heart of the following two cases. These are leading decisions of the Supreme Court sitting *en banc* (commonly referred to as decisions "of the Grand Bench"), issued twenty years apart, in 1955 and 1975. The two decisions offer considerable insight into attitudes in Japan about the proper role of the government in regulatory matters and into views on free economic competition. They also provide a glimpse into the manner in which the Supreme Court treats its powers of constitutional review and an interesting example of the treatment of precedent.

The first of these cases is known as *The Bathhouse Case* (*Shimizu v. Japan*, 9 *Keishū* 89 (Sup. Ct., G.B., Jan. 26, 1955)). As its popular name implies, this case involved the establishment of public bathhouses, which at the time were a key facility for local residents, many of whom did not have showers or bathtubs in their homes. (Although the number of public bathhouses has declined considerably since that time, many bathhouses remain. Some apartments and homes still do not have showers or bathtubs, and a fair number of people who do have their own private baths nonetheless sometimes prefer the public bathhouses, which have large soaking tubs.)

The defendant-appellant in *The Bathhouse Case* had been found guilty of operating a public bathhouse without having obtained the license required by the Public Bathhouse Act. This law required anyone who intended to operate a public bathhouse to secure a license from the prefectural governor and stated that the governor should not grant a license if the governor regarded the site or proposed structure "improper from the standpoint of public sanitation" or "deem[ed] that the site for the establishment [of the bathhouse was] not properly located."

The Public Bathhouse Act further provided that each prefectural government could establish standards for distribution of bathhouse sites. Pursuant to this provision, Fukuoka Prefecture issued an ordinance establishing numerous further standards, including regulations on the minimum distances between bathhouses.

After being convicted for operating his bathhouse without a license, the defendant-appellant argued on appeal that the prefectural ordinance and the Public Bathhouse Act were unconstitutional because they restricted his freedom of choice of occupation. The defendant-appellant was unsuccessful on first appeal and so appealed to the Supreme Court.

The Supreme Court, in an *en banc* opinion, ruled against the defendant-appellant, holding as follows on his Article 22 claim:

> Public baths * * * are welfare facilities of a highly public nature, indispensable to the daily life of the majority of the people. If their establishment is left to the will of the entrepreneur himself and necessary measures are not taken to preserve their proper distribution or to prevent maldistribution and excessive numbers, such maldistribution may cause inconvenience to many people who wish easy access to public baths daily. In addition, the excessive numbers of bathhouses may lead to futile competition and have an unfavorable economic effect on the enterprises, thereby giving rise to undesirable consequences such as a deterioration in the sanitary facilities of the bathhouses. It is, therefore, desirable in view of the nature of the public bathhouses as stated above and from the standpoint of both natural hygiene and environmental sanitation, to prevent the above situation to the greatest extent possible. Accordingly, cases in which the sites for the establishment of public bathhouses are improperly located, thus leading to maldistribution or excessive numbers, run counter to the public welfare. The establishment of provisions to the effect that licenses for the operation of public bathhouses may not be granted on the grounds set forth above is, therefore, not in conflict with Article 22 of the Constitution.

A generation later, the Supreme Court faced similar issues in what is popularly referred to as *The Pharmacy Case* (*K.K. Sumiyoshi v. Governor, Hiroshima Prefecture*, 29 *Minshū* 572 (Sup. Ct., G.B., April 30, 1975). The relevant national legislation, the Pharmaceutical Affairs Act, stated that licenses for pharmacies "may be denied in a case where the proposed site is not a suitable location" (§ 6(2)) and directed prefectures "to prescribe by ordinance standards for the location of pharmacies * * * so as to ensure a proper distribution and supply of medicine for residents" and, in doing so, to "take into consideration distribution, population, traffic considerations, and other relevant circumstances" (§ 6(4)).

*K.K. Sumiyoshi v. Governor, Hiroshima Prefecture**
29 Minshū 572
(Sup. Ct., G.B., April 30, 1975)

REFERENCES:

Constitution, Arts. 13 and 22(1).

Pharmaceutical Affairs Act, § 6(2) and (4).

FACTS:

K.K. Sumiyoshi operated drug stores in several communities. Pursuant to the licensing requirement of the Pharmaceutical Affairs Act (the Act), it applied to the Governor of Hiroshima Prefecture on July 11, 1963, for a license to open a new pharmacy in the prefecture. On January 24, 1967, the Governor denied the application on the ground that it did not meet the standards applied to the location of new pharmacies under an amended prefectural ordinance (the Ordinance) authorized by amendments to the Act in effect only since July 12, 1963.

Sumiyoshi brought suit challenging the Governor's decision not to grant the license. The Hiroshima District Court ruled in favor of the plaintiff, holding that the Governor had retroactively applied both the Act and the Ordinance. In 1968, the Hiroshima High Court reversed, holding that the retroactive application of the laws was valid and that the revised Act and the Ordinance did not violate the freedom of occupation guaranteed in the Constitution. Sumiyoshi appealed to the Supreme Court.

JUDGMENT:

The judgment below is reversed.

REASONS:

Concerning the [claim of invalid retroactive application of the Act and Ordinance], in principle, administrative dispositions should be made in accordance with laws and orders at the time of the disposition. This is similarly true for licensing dispositions, unless otherwise provided by law at the time of applying for a license. This is because the license applicant does not acquire concrete rights under the law by virtue of his application for a license at the time he files. Such an interpretation is not contrary to the rule against retroactive application of law[, even

*Adapted from translation by Lawrence W. Beer and Hiroshi Itoh (publication forthcoming in Lawrence W. Beer and Hiroshi Itoh, eds., *The Constitutional Case Law of Japan, 1970-1990*). Used by permission.

though in this case the Governor] waited until the enforcement of the prefectural ordinance based on the amended law before disposing of the said petition. * * * [Concerning Sumiyoshi's claim of invalid retroactive application of the law,] the judgment below is in the end correct, and the assertion of unconstitutionality premised on alleged illegality is unjustified. * * *

Concerning [Sumiyoshi's claim that] the judgment below erred in applying and interpreting Articles 13 and 22 of the Constitution[, we hold the following:]

I. Freedom of Choice of Occupation

1. Article 22, paragraph 1 of the Constitution provides that every person is free to choose his or her occupation to the extent that it does not interfere with the public welfare. An occupation is a continuous activity in which an individual engages in order to maintain his or her own livelihood. In society, with its division of labor, an occupation is by nature an activity with a social function through which one contributes to the continuity and development of society; and as the locus where a person achieves his or her personal individuality, an occupation is inseparably related to the individual's [sense of] personal worth. The reason why the above provision guarantees one's freedom to choose an occupation as a fundamental human right may lie in this characteristic [relationship to personal worth] and the significance of one's occupation in modern society. When we consider the character and meaning of an occupation in these terms, an occupation must be free not only with respect to its independent choice, that is to say, in taking up, continuing and abandoning an occupation, but also must be free in principle with respect to one's performance itself within the chosen occupation, that is, with respect to the form and content of occupational activities. Therefore, the said provision should be interpreted to include not only freedom to choose an occupation in the narrow sense, but also a guarantee of freedom in one's occupational activities.

2. Because an occupation, as stated above, is in essence a social and * * * economic activity, and is by its nature something much involved with social relations, the demand for regulation by public authority is stronger than for other constitutionally guaranteed freedoms, especially the freedoms of the spirit, [which may well be why] the freedom of occupational choice in Article 22, paragraph 1 contains the reservation, "to the extent that it does not interfere with the public welfare."

Consequently, an occupation is a social activity within which a need for some sort of restriction is inherent. However, its type, nature, content, social significance, and effects are extremely varied, and * * * [t]he importance of restrictions varies. * * * Therefore, discrimination is necessary when discussing whether these regulatory measures can be approved as something demanded for the public welfare, under Article 22, paragraph 1 of the Constitution. * * *

In this case, it is primarily the right and duty of the legislative branch to undertake such study and deliberation. So long as the purpose of regulation is found to be in accord with the public welfare, and the judgment of the legislative branch remains within the bounds of reasonable discretion in terms of the necessity, reasonableness, and concrete content of the regulatory measures to achieve this purpose, that judgment of legislative policy should be respected by the Court. However, from the nature of the matter, the bounds of reasonable discretion differ with circumstances; and the Court should decide these [bounds] in light of the purpose, object, nature, and content of the concrete regulation.

3. Occupational licensing systems permit the carrying on of an occupation only by persons who fulfill conditions set by law and to whom licenses have been given, [and thus], in general, go beyond a simple regulation of the content and form of occupational activities and impose restrictions upon the freedom to choose a particular occupation in the narrow sense. For the constitutionality of such powerful restraints on the freedom of occupation to be affirmed requires in principle that they be necessary and reasonable measures for an important public interest. Also, where measures are not for a positive social or economic policy purpose, but rather are negative police measures to prevent harm to the public brought on by free occupational activities, it is necessary to find that the purpose could not be fully achieved simply by regulation of the form and content of occupational activities, a lighter restraint on freedom of occupation than a licensing system. This is required not only with respect to licensing itself, but also with respect to its content. Even where adoption of a licensing system is approved, a separate determination must be made on the suitability of individual conditions for granting a license in light of the above requirements.

II. *The Licensing System under the Pharmaceutical Affairs Act*

1. * * *

Drugs and other medical supplies are necessary to maintain the life and health of the people and have an enormous influence thereon. To guard the health and safety of the people from distribution of substandard drugs and medical supplies (including substandard preparation, hereinafter all referred to as "substandard drugs"), not only regulation of the content of the business, but also adoption of a licensing system limiting dealers to persons having set qualifications and forbidding the establishment of businesses by persons other than these, may be affirmed as necessary and reasonable measures for a purpose that accords with the public welfare. * * *

2. [Omitted.]

III. *The Legislative Purpose* * * *

1. * * * Those proposing [the 1963 amendments to the Act that concerned the suitable location of pharmacies] offered two supporting reasons: to prevent economic instability among some businessmen because of excessive competition resulting from the uncontrolled establishment of pharmacies in some areas, with the consequent danger of dispensing substandard drugs due to defective facilities; and, indirectly, to promote establishment of pharmacies in regions with too few or no pharmacies by restricting the tendency to establish more pharmacies in certain other areas. * * *

Accordingly, the regulations on the suitable location of pharmacies are regulatory measures for the negative police purpose of preventing hazards to the life and health of the people. The prevention of excessive competition among pharmacies and of instability of business operations contemplated therein are not themselves the aims, but are recognized clearly to be nothing more than means for preventing substandard drugs from being dispensed. The social and economic policy objective of protecting the business operations of pharmacies, among which small and medium enterprises are numerous, is not the intent of the regulations on the suitable location of pharmacies * * *. Furthermore, there are situations in which a type of monopoly status is accorded to those who furnish certain services indispensable to the life of the people, and measures are taken to stabilize their business operations in view of the highly public character of the services in question, in order to insure that they are offered in a suitable fashion. This is the reverse side of and balances the strict regulation * * * [of] persons who provide such services * * *. However, the Act and related laws and orders do not involve such far-reaching regulations as measures to insure the proper dispensing of drugs and other medical supplies. Nor is there a necessity or reason to grant monopoly status to existing pharmacies. We may, therefore, assume that the regulations on the suitable location of pharmacies in this case in no way include such intent and purpose. * * *

2. [Omitted.]

IV. *The Constitutionality of Regulations on the Proper Location of Pharmacies*

1. and 2.a. [Omitted.]

2.b. The defendant asserts that in the event there were no geographical restrictions * * * , pharmacies would be unevenly distributed, in some areas sales competition would be excessive, and the result of this * * * would be various abuses related to the proper dispensing of drugs. On this matter:

(1) First, * * * the Act establishes various strict regulations to maintain and guarantee quality throughout the entire process of manufacturing, storing and selling drugs. The Pharmacists Act (Law No. 146 of 1960) likewise establishes strict provisions to be observed during preparation of drugs, and the penalty of license or permit revocation has been provided for violations of these regulations. In addition, administrative correction measures, such as orders to repair the structure of faulty facilities, to increase the number of pharmacists, to discontinue substandard drugs, to make a change in management, and so forth, are all provided. Furthermore, compulsory investigation based on the authority of administrative organs to conduct spot inspections is also authorized. * * * In each case, these measures have been enacted to control the business activities of persons engaged in some aspect of the pharmaceuticals business; insofar as these are strictly observed and enforced by means of administrative supervision and criminal penalties, it should be possible fully to achieve the police purpose of preventing the dangers inherent in dispensing substandard drugs. To be sure, no matter how complete the [system of] regulation * * * , it remains difficult to eradicate all violations. Thus, as an ultimate measure for the complete prevention of dangers to the health of the people resulting from dispensing substandard drugs, it is not without merit to proceed further. * * * However, to uphold the constitu-

tionality of geographical restraints on the establishment of pharmacies, which substantially limit the freedom of occupation, * * * [w]e must also find it reasonable to say that if such restrictions were not enforced, there would be danger of hazards arising to the health of the people that outweigh [in importance] the restriction on the freedom of occupation imposed. * * *

(2) It is easy to imagine that if geographical restrictions on the establishment of pharmacies did not exist * * *, pharmacies could be distributed unevenly and * * * excessive competition could occur. Thus arises the fear that the business operations of some dealers might become unstable. The defendant argues that such instability would in turn lead to defects in facilities and equipment, and to inadequate storage and care of drugs, and that this would give rise to the danger of obstructing the supply of drugs of good quality. In theory, such a possibility certainly cannot be denied. However, as a matter of fact, the degree to which the danger exists has not been proved.

Also, regarding defendant's point that at the time of uncontrolled sale of drugs there was a threat that many substandard drugs would be sold, the extent of this is not clear. When we take into consideration the acknowledgment that the uncontrolled sale of drugs in some areas of major cities cited by the defendant was occasioned principally by the discount sales of cash wholesalers and supermarkets, and the fact that in general we may readily hypothesize that the uncontrolled sale of drugs was due substantially to surplus production at the manufacturing stage, heated price wars, and * * * management policies concerning the distribution process, then it is not reasonable [hastily to] conclude that the instability of business operations of some pharmacies was tied directly to * * * the sale of substandard drugs, or even less, to say that this resulted in inadequacies in storage and care of drugs. In particular, it would be unusual in the extreme for proprietors of pharmacies in general, especially pharmacists, who are restrained by penalties for violation of laws and regulations and are under constant administrative supervision, to dare to resort to violations of laws and regulations merely for economic reasons. * * * [I]f measures are deemed necessary to cure economic evils brought on by shortcomings in the structure and process of drug distribution, the questions of how to locate pharmacies, which are the final points in the distribution network, in order to rationalize distribution, or of how abuses resulting from unfair trade practices should be prevented, are questions of economic policy that should be investigated separately with no direct relation to the regulations in this case, which were established with the health of the people in mind.

(3) and (4) [Omitted.]

(5) The defendant also points out that unnecessary use of drugs by consumers is promoted by the uncontrolled sale of drugs. * * * However, the principal causes of uncontrolled sales of drugs and their abuse are the surplus production of drugs, sales wars, and the attendant exaggerated advertising. * * * Moreover, in addition to the regulation of exaggerated advertising under Section 66 of the Act, reinforcing consumer education also remains as a countermeasure against the above sort of abuse. It is hard to find geographical restrictions

on the location of pharmacies a reasonable way of dealing with this problem.
(6) [Omitted.]
2.c. The defendant asserts that a proper geographical distribution of pharmacies is necessary to regularize the supply of drugs, in that preventing someone from locating pharmacies in certain areas will indirectly promote entry into areas with too few or no pharmacies * * *. Correction of the geographical distribution of pharmacies does accord with the public welfare * * *. However, the extent to which such an effect can be anticipated is quite questionable. Rather, we believe that * * * the means to secure a supply of drugs in areas with too few or no pharmacies lie elsewhere. * * *
V. *Conclusion*

[S]ections 6(2) and (4) of the Act * * *, which provide geographical restrictions as a condition for granting a license to new pharmacies, are neither necessary nor reasonable for the purpose of preventing the distribution of substandard drugs and, therefore, are in violation of Article 22, paragraph 1 of the Constitution and are null and void. * * *

Questions and Discussion Points

1. *Reconciling the holdings:* How did the Supreme Court reconcile the holding in *The Pharmacy Case* with the holding in *The Bathhouse Case*? Did it even try? In Japan's civil law system, is it necessary for the Court to reconcile the holdings?

Can the holdings be reconciled? Consider the following arguments, which have been suggested by various Japanese scholars:

(a) *A change in the times:* Over the twenty years between the two cases, views may have changed on both the legitimacy of government regulation of economic activity and the virtues and vices of competition. If this is the case, however, how does one account for the fact that the Supreme Court reaffirmed *The Bathhouse Case* holding in 1989 (*see* Judgment of January 20, 1989, 2d P. B., 1302 *Hanrei Jihō* 159)?

(b) *Differences in the level of welfare concerns:* Unlike earlier periods, when pharmacists frequently mixed medications themselves, pharmacies today act as small retailers who simply sell preformulated products distributed by drug manufacturers. Accordingly, pharmacies have no direct control over the quality of the drugs they sell and regulating them will do little to serve the public welfare. In contrast, the bathhouse operator has direct control over the quality of the bathhouse, so regulating bathhouses in order to ensure quality serves an important public welfare purpose.

(c) *Excessive competition concerns:* Excessive competition in either the bathhouse or pharmacy industry could lead to a wave of bankruptcies. In the pharmacy situation this is not a major concern because it requires little capital to open a pharmacy, but in the bathhouse industry this would cause great problems since opening a bathhouse is very expensive.

On which of these arguments, if any, was the Supreme Court relying in

The Pharmacy Case?

2. *Excessive competition:* Even in *The Pharmacy Case*, the Court recognized the concept of "excessive competition." This concern over "excessive competition" is a recurrent theme in Japanese discussions about government regulation. When is competition "excessive"?

V. The Legal Profession

A foreign company doing business in Japan typically requires advice on Japanese law and must coordinate this with advice obtained on the law of other jurisdictions. If you are an attorney representing a company seeking to do business in Japan, to whom can you turn or refer your client for advice on Japanese law? If you think you know the relevant law to answer your client's questions, what constraints may affect your ability to give your client advice based on this knowledge? Answering these and related questions requires knowing how the legal profession is structured in Japan, the topic of this section.

A. Legal education

In Japan, as in most countries (with the notable exceptions of the United States and Canada), pursuing training in law is most commonly done by undergraduates rather than graduate students. Law is one of the more popular social science majors at Japanese universities, with some 35,000-40,000 students graduating each year with law degrees (considerably more per capita than the annual total of law school graduates in the United States). Law faculty graduates go on to a wide array of careers. For top graduates, these include careers in the bureaucracy, on the management track at medium-sized and large companies, and in the finance and service sectors.

The first one and one-half to two years of undergraduate education at a Japanese university are typically taken up by general liberal arts courses. Concentration on legal study thus occupies only the third and fourth years. Law faculties offer lecture courses that roughly parallel the subject matter of first-year courses in a U.S. law school, though tracking Japan's civil law system rather than the U.S.'s common law system and generally being more abstract and theoretical in orientation than U.S. courses. In addition, more specialized courses in legal history, comparative law and various business law subjects are offered. Such courses also tend to be rather abstract and rarely involve intensive application of law to specific cases. These courses, too, are generally taught in a lecture format with little class participation. (Considerably greater participation is the norm, however, in seminars, which are offered on a wide range of topics at most law faculties.)

Law faculties also have graduate departments offering master's and doctorate degrees in law. These degrees are not pursued by a great number of students and principally attract those who are interested in becoming professors of law.

In addition, in recent years a number of Japanese law faculties have begun offering separate master's programs, patterned after U.S. LL.M. programs. These new programs are aimed at candidates taking leaves from posts in law firms, corporations or government to return to school for up to two years of graduate-level study.

With certain exceptions mentioned below, becoming a lawyer, public prosecutor or judge entails entering Japan's one official law school, the Legal Training and Research Institute ("Institute"), which is affiliated with the Supreme Court. To enter the Institute one must pass the extraordinarily difficult National Legal Examination (*shihō shiken*) (NLE), which is offered once a year and is taken each year by about 25,000 people.

Taking the NLE and entering the Institute is a four-step process. The first step is a qualifying test, which is waived for those who have completed the first two years of general education at a Japanese university. The next step is a multiple choice examination on various fields of law that only about 3,000-4,000 of the test-takers pass. Next is an essay portion, which spans three days and includes six essays. The fourth and final step, an oral examination, eliminates another 50-75 candidates and leaves an entering class that from the mid-1960s until 1991 was usually somewhat under 500. (As described below, that number has since been increased.)

Most who pass the NLE do not do so on their first attempt. From the 1960s to the mid-1970s, those who passed on average did so on their fourth try. By the 1980s, the average passer required six attempts. From 1981-88, the highest percentage of passers who managed to do so on their first attempt was 2.5 percent (in 1982). Passers are overwhelmingly male but the gender imbalance is steadily, if slowly, decreasing: of graduates of the Institute (almost all who enter graduate), 26 of 484 were women in 1965 and 63 of 489 were women in 1988.

Passing the NLE entitles one to enter the two-year program at the Institute.[3] Trainees at the Institute are deemed to be public employees and receive pay from the government (as of 1990, ¥165,500 per month, which is a bit over $1,500/mo. at $1=¥110, plus semiannual bonuses equivalent in total to about six months' worth of the base pay). Trainees first spend four months at the Institute studying a variety of subjects under the instruction of judges, public prosecutors and practicing attorneys (*bengoshi*). The instructors are selected from among career judges, prosecutors and practicing lawyers and usually serve three-year terms. The emphasis at the Institute is on practical application of the law, and the instruction includes numerous drafting exercises and participation in, and observation of, mock trials. Though there is also opportunity to take more theoretical elective courses in subjects such as international business transactions, the bulk of the training one receives at the Institute is in skills needed for handling lawsuits and appearing in court.

Following the initial four-month period at the Institute, the trainees spend sixteen months in a series of four-month clerkships with courts, public prosecutors and *bengoshi*. For the last four months of the two-year program, the legal apprentices return to the Institute for classroom instruction. A final examination is required prior to graduation, but it is very rare for a trainee not to pass that exam.

Graduates of the Institute have three basic career paths available to them, and while it is possible to move from one path to another, far less of this is done than in the U.S. On graduating, legal apprentices can become career judges (in recent years chosen by about 60 out of each graduating class), government lawyers (primarily prosecutors, chosen by about 40), or *bengoshi* (practicing lawyers, chosen by the remaining approximately 400).

Traditionally, positions as judges and government lawyers were regarded as more prestigious and desirable than private practice. Given the limited number of openings for these positions, this meant that many graduates became *bengoshi* as their second or third choice. In recent years, though, the pattern has changed. An increasing percentage of the legal apprentices, including more of the top graduates of the Institute, have been opting for careers as *bengoshi* as their first choice. In part this reflects the higher pay typically enjoyed by *bengoshi*. Another important reason relates to the rotation system utilized by both the judiciary and the procuracy. Typically, judges and prosecutors must transfer to a new posting on a regular basis (generally every three to five years), and thus may have to move to many different regions of Japan over their careers. While this rotation system is regarded as an important means of protecting against local bias and corruption, it has come to make the judicial and, especially, the prosecutorial careers relatively less attractive to new graduates. *Bengoshi*, in contrast, can be virtually assured of the chance to stay in a single city throughout their careers (with the Tokyo area being the location of choice for many graduates).

The concern over the difficulty in attracting Institute graduates into public service constituted one of the most important factors influencing the recent decision to increase the annual number of trainees from about 500 to about 700. Hopes have been expressed that an increase in the number of trainees will lead to a greater proportion of younger admittees, who are thought to be more likely to want to become government lawyers. Even before the public sector experienced difficulties in attracting recruits, though, in some quarters there had been repeated calls for increases in the number of trainees for other reasons, including the view that the difficulty of the exam and consequent high passing age (the average age at the time of passing the NLE was about 28 during the 1980s) resulted in a waste of human resources and the view that legal consumers and the public would benefit from an increase in the number of legal practitioners.

In the late 1980s, meetings were held among the Japan Federation of Bar Associations (JFBA, the rough equivalent of the American Bar Association, though membership in the JFBA is mandatory for *bengoshi*), the Ministry of Justice, and the Supreme Court to discuss increasing the number of admittees to the Institute. None of the three groups released an official position, but most in JFBA sought to restrain increases, the Ministry of Justice appeared to desire an increase to an annual admission of about 2,000 trainees, and the Supreme Court also sought significant increases.

The three sides eventually reached an agreement to remain in effect through the 1995 offering of the NLE. The agreement calls for steadily increasing the number of passers of the NLE to 700 for the 1995 test. The three sides agreed that, if by that time the percentage of younger passers has not increased appreciably, they would consider the possibility of reserving a portion of the openings at the Institute for those who have made no more than three attempts at the NLE. The agreement is silent on the issue of whether to increase annual enrollment at the Institute further.

B. Types of legal professionals

1. *Bengoshi* and *shōgai bengoshi*

The great majority of graduates of the Institute become *bengoshi* and go into private legal practice. Most *bengoshi* are sole practitioners, although they often begin their careers under the tutelage of more experienced *bengoshi*; and most *bengoshi* devote the vast majority of their time to a traditional litigation-related practice. According to a 1981 survey, *bengoshi* working in the Tokyo area spend some 75% of their time on litigation matters and only about 10% on general business consulting and other non-dispute-related matters, and *bengoshi* outside the Tokyo area concentrate even more exclusively on litigation and dispute resolution.[4] One observer has characterized the work of traditional Japanese *bengoshi* in the following manner:

> [T]he practice of Japanese *bengoshi* is relatively pure, technically narrow legal work involving court-related disputes with a fair amount of money at stake. Medium-sized industrialists and those involved in a limited range of real estate transactions are the overwhelming beneficiaries of the services of *bengoshi*. Matters that are more central to the economic development of Japan, such as corporate organizations or even basic transactions, are not the object of their attention. Nor do *bengoshi* spend virtually any of their time on matters relating to personal injury, divorce, inheritance, estate planning, labor disputes, or the like. Such affairs that principally occasion individuals in Western societies to use the services of an attorney have little to do with the practice of the average *bengoshi*.[5]

Although the percentage of time devoted to non-dispute-related matters probably has increased somewhat over the past decade, especially for *bengoshi* practicing in the Tokyo area, the overall pattern described above is still the rule for most *bengoshi* practicing in Japan. The work of most *bengoshi* is centered entirely around trial practice. The vast majority of *bengoshi* spend very little time giving business or tax advice, reviewing mortgages and loan agreements, drafting contracts, or assisting on other such non-dispute matters.

The pattern is somewhat different for one group of *bengoshi*, though: the so-called *shōgai bengoshi*, or international practitioners. The *shōgai bengoshi* have joined together in firms of from 5-10 to as many as some 50 lawyers and provide many of the types of business-related advice and transactions-related services typical of large

U.S. law firms. They do so primarily in connection with international transactions. To date, general business consulting on purely domestic transactions continues to represent a minor aspect of the work of *bengoshi*. Many *shōgai bengoshi* also handle disputes, although for most *shōgai bengoshi* firms the dispute resolution work tracks the remainder of their practice and centers on transnational disputes. There are currently about 500 *shōgai bengoshi* in Japan, nearly all of whom are located in Tokyo, although the overall number is increasing rapidly and a few such firms have developed in the Osaka area. Given the nature of their practice, *shōgai bengoshi* naturally represent the most important segment of the Japanese bar for foreign companies doing business in Japan.

Many of the *shōgai bengoshi* have earned LL.M. degrees in the U.S. or received some legal education elsewhere in the West. It is estimated that roughly 600 *bengoshi* have LL.M. degrees from U.S. law schools and that recently about 50 have been receiving such degrees each year. In addition, in recent years it has become fairly common for *shōgai bengoshi* who have earned LL.M. degrees to take the New York or some other state bar examination before returning to Japan, so a small but steadily increasing number of *shōgai bengoshi* are now also members of a U.S. bar.

In response to the increasing demand in Tokyo for international legal services, the community of *shōgai bengoshi* is now growing rapidly, though not rapidly enough in the view of some. The *shōgai bengoshi* have begun to recruit graduates of the Institute vigorously. A few have publicly stated that the size of the entering class of the Institute should be at least doubled in order to meet the demand for more *bengoshi*. These calls are another reason for the recent increase in enrollment at the Institute; and they reflect a serious division within the Japanese bar between those, including some *shōgai bengoshi*, who are happy with the status quo and other *shōgai bengoshi*, who perceive a need to expand in order to meet the competition from large and highly specialized U.S. and other foreign law firms.

2. Judges and public prosecutors

MICHAEL K. YOUNG AND CONSTANCE C. HAMILTON, INTRODUCTION TO JAPANESE LAW*

1 Japan Business Law Guide
¶¶ 7-530 to 7-550 (1988)

[1.] Judges (saibankan)

With the exception of a few justices on the Supreme Court, Japanese jurists are career judges, choosing (and being chosen for) this option upon graduation from the Institute and remaining in this career path until retirement. Immediately upon graduation, aspiring judges are appointed assistant judges. While in this position,

*From Michael K. Young and Constance C. Hamilton, "Introduction to Japanese Law," in Mitsuo Matsushita, ed., 1 *Japan Business Law Guide* (CCH International, 1988, © CCH Australia Limited), at ¶¶ 7-530 to 7-550. Reprinted with the permission of CCH Australia Limited.

they can serve on district court panels and exercise limited judicial powers, but cannot try cases alone. They must serve at least ten years as an assistant judge before elevation to a full judgeship. Full judges are appointed by the Cabinet from a list drawn up by the Supreme Court. Full judges must graduate from the Institute and have at least ten years' experience as an assistant judge, public prosecutor, barrister [*i.e., bengoshi*] or law professor. They are appointed for a term of ten years which can be, and almost invariably is, renewed until age 65, when they must retire.

The career path of a judge is determined largely by the Secretariat of the Supreme Court, which assigns judges among the various family courts, district courts and high courts. It also assigns judges to serve in various administrative positions in the lower courts and the Supreme Court and its Secretariat. Approximately 30 to 35 judges also serve as research associates, or *chōsakan,* to the Supreme Court justices themselves. These judges, usually with considerable experience and a distinguished record, are assigned to various divisions to deal with cases that fall under particular substantive headings, such as civil, criminal and administrative, and to assist the justices in their research and drafting of Supreme Court opinions.

The selection process for the 15 Supreme Court justices differs from that of lower court judges. The Chief Justice is technically appointed by the Emperor, but in fact appointed by him only on the recommendation of the Cabinet. The remaining justices are appointed by the Cabinet alone. The law also requires that at least two-thirds, or 10 of the 15, justices must have been judges, public prosecutors, barristers or law professors for at least 20 years. The remaining five must be learned and have some knowledge of the law, but need not be qualified or experienced members of any of the three branches of the profession. Only a small handful of justices have been appointed from outside the three branches of the profession (and the university), and none in recent years. * * * Over time, a practice has evolved whereby the Cabinet selects approximately equal numbers from each of the three main branches of the profession, though law professors often fill one or two of the five seats generally allotted to the public prosecutors.

Article 79 of the Constitution requires that all justices elevated to the Supreme Court be submitted to the general electorate for approval in the first general election after their nomination and be again submitted every ten years thereafter. A justice rejected by a majority of the voters is immediately dismissed. No justice has ever been so removed. Since justices must retire at age 70 and are generally appointed while in their sixties, moreover, few justices are ever subject to a second round of voter approval.

[2.] Public prosecutors (kensatsukan)

Junior public prosecutors or public prosecutors of the second rank are selected from among the graduates of the Legal Training and Research Institute. The vast majority of senior public prosecutors or public prosecutors of the first rank are then chosen from among the ranks of the juniors who have served at least eight years. Assistant or full judges, judges of summary courts and barristers are also eligible for appointment after having served in their respective professions for an equal amount of time.

All prosecutorial activities come under the direction and control of the Public Prosecutor-General (*Kenji Sōchō*). Prosecutors must obey his and their superiors' orders in matters of general policy and even in particular cases. They must also, unlike judges, accept new postings when assigned. Prosecutors are immune from salary reductions or removal from office, however, except upon a hearing and suitable findings of the Public Prosecutor's Suitability Inquiry Board.

In order to enhance the independence of the prosecutors' offices, the Ministry of Justice cannot, at least since the end of the War, issue direct orders regarding specific cases except through the office of the Public Prosecutor-General. The Ministry retains the authority, however, to supervise prosecutorial activities in a general way. This is designed to insulate those offices from undue political influence, while allowing general control and oversight of prosecutorial activities to remain in those duly appointed administrative agencies that are at least indirectly responsible to the political process and democratic control. Despite these protections, during recent years, certain prosecutors' offices have come under fire, fairly or unfairly, it is hard to say, for their handling of prosecutions of major political figures.

The end of the War also saw the enactment of reforms designed to make prosecutors' offices a more integral part of an equally balanced adversarial system. As mentioned above, the most important of these reforms separated administrative control of the prosecutors' offices from that of the judiciary. Thus, prosecutors were no longer controlled by, responsible to, or, in too frequent practice, in charge of the same administrative organs that controlled the courts and the judges. Prosecutors' and judges' offices were moved to separate buildings and the prosecutor is now required to sit not on the dais with the judge, but on an equal level with the defense attorney near the front of the courtroom.

3. Other licensed providers of legal services in Japan

TAKAAKI HATTORI AND DAN FENNO HENDERSON, CIVIL PROCEDURE IN JAPAN*

Sec. 2.09 (1985)

In Japan, there are several kinds of licensed nonlawyer specialists who may act for and give advice to clients regarding specific fields of law. Patent agents (*benrishi*)[6] properly registered on the List of Patent Agents may file patent applications in the Patent Office (*Tokkyochō*), represent parties in hearings in the Patent Office concerning patents, utility models, designs and trademarks, and make oral statements in court in cases relating to these rights. Tax agents (*zeirishi*) registered on the List

*From Takaaki Hattori and Dan Fenno Henderson, *Civil Procedure in Japan* (Transnational Juris Publications 1985), at Sec. 2.09. Reprinted with the permission of Transnational Juris Publications, Inc., Irvington, New York.

of Tax Agents[7] may draft tax returns, represent clients seeking review of tax assessments, and give counsel on tax questions. Judicial scriveners (*shihō shoshi*) licensed to do business by the regional offices of the Ministry of Justice[8] may, upon the request of private persons, draft legal documents to be filed with the court, the public procurator's office, or the regional office of the Ministry of Justice. Administrative scriveners (*gyōsei shoshi*) registered on the List of Administrative Scriveners[9] may draft documents to be submitted to administrative agencies.

These licensed nonlawyer specialists greatly increase the number of those performing legal work in Japan.[10] The proportion of practicing lawyers is quite small compared with other developed countries. While in West Germany, for example, there is one lawyer for every [1,500] people, in Japan the ratio is one to [9,400]. This disparity is less striking when the nonlawyers are added; the ratio then becomes one to [1,070].[11]

4. Corporate in-house legal staff

A further class of legal advisors that should be considered in evaluating the Japanese legal profession is the personnel in legal and other departments of large corporations. Estimates of their numbers vary widely, ranging from one thousand to several thousand. Large corporations may have thirty or more members in their legal departments or doing legal work in other departments such as the patent, planning, general affairs, or debt collection department. These in-house legal staff members give legal advice to their companies, draft contracts and other documents, and communicate between management and outside lawyers retained by companies.

Most of the in-house legal staff members have undergraduate degrees in law, but others may be placed in the legal department simply because they have good reasoning skills. A very few companies include a *bengoshi* among their in-house legal staff and one firm, IBM Japan, has several. Traditionally, many of those in a corporation's legal department at any given time have been there only as part of a steady rotation through several departments. The recent trend in many companies, though, is for many staff members to spend virtually their entire careers in the legal or closely related departments or divisions. As with *shōgai bengoshi*, a sizeable (and rapidly increasing) number of corporate legal staff members have completed LL.M. or similar programs at law schools in the U.S. or United Kingdom, and some have become licensed in New York or some other state. Others are developing their legal expertise through postgraduate legal study in Japan in the recently instituted practice-oriented master's programs developed at a few universities.

Questions and Discussion Points

1. *Finding representation:* If you are a lawyer in the U.S. representing a U.S. client seeking to do business in Japan, and you have no connections in Japan, how do you go about obtaining advice on Japanese law?

If your client wants advice on registering and protecting patents, filing routine corporate documents to establish a subsidiary, negotiating a complete joint venture agreement, and determining all relevant Japanese tax considerations, will it be necessary or advisable to hire separately a patent attorney, administrative scrivener, *shōgai bengoshi*, and tax attorney?

2. *Size of the legal profession:* Even if all the various classes of legal professionals in Japan are added to the number of *bengoshi*, there are still far fewer "lawyers" per capita in Japan than in the U.S. (From the standpoint of true comparison, moreover, one should note that the U.S. also has many nonlawyer specialists performing law-related functions, including tax accountants and a wide range of consultants.) What reasons may there be for the differences in the size of the legal professions in the U.S. and Japan? Are there too many lawyers in the U.S., too few in Japan, or both?

C. Foreign legal professionals in Japan

1. The previous system for foreign lawyers and "trainees"

GLEN FUKUSHIMA, BACKGROUND*

Practice by Foreign Lawyers in Japan
10-11 (1989)

Between the enactment of the first Bengoshi Law in 1893 and 1933, foreign attorneys were freely allowed to establish offices in Japan. The scope of their practice, however, was limited to handling legal affairs in Japan involving aliens and international transactions. A new Bengoshi Law was enacted in 1933 which included a provision on foreign attorneys, but this provision appears to have had no impact on the then-existing *de facto* status of foreign attorneys in Japan.

Under the Allied Occupation, a third Bengoshi Law was enacted in 1949. This law contained a special provision allowing foreign attorneys to practice in Japan without passing the national bar examination if they could demonstrate that they possessed "an adequate knowledge of the laws of Japan." This provision was repealed in 1955, but a handful of American attorneys who had already obtained licenses were "grandfathered," making it possible for them to continue to practice in Japan despite the fact that no other foreign attorneys could be licensed. In addition, foreign attorneys were admitted to practice in Okinawa during the period the territory remained under U.S. occupation and control. This avenue was closed in 1972 when Okinawa reverted to Japanese jurisdiction, although a similar "grandfather" provision allowed existing foreign licensees to remain. Other than the few licensees admitted through one of these two avenues, any foreign attorneys who wanted to practice in Japan openly without fear of penalty could do so only as "trainees" affiliated with Japanese law firms or companies.

*From Glen Fukushima, "Background," in Richard Wohl, Stuart Chemtob and Glen Fukushima, eds., *Practice by Foreign Lawyers in Japan* (© American Bar Association 1989), at 10-11. Reprinted by permission.

Trainees have constituted the vast majority of younger American attorneys who gained work experience in Japan after 1955. Under the [Japan Federation of Bar Association's (JFBA's)] broad interpretation of Articles 3 and 72 of the Bengoshi Law, trainees are technically considered to be apprentices who serve as assistants to *bengoshi* and thus may not practice law, even of their home jurisdiction, in their own right. These attorneys, who typically assist Japanese "international" *bengoshi* prepare English-language documentation for international transactions, are usually granted one-year visas which, in the past, generally have been renewable only twice. Although the employment of trainees by *bengoshi* has been expressly sanctioned by the JFBA, in March 1972 it issued a document entitled *Standards Concerning the Prevention of Non-Attorney Activities by Foreigners*[12] aimed at severely restricting the legitimate activities of trainees in Japan. According to this document, "all aliens not permitted to engage in attorney affairs in Japan (regardless of whether or not they are qualified as attorneys abroad)" are deemed "unqualified aliens."[13] The following principles were set forth governing activities by trainees that are held to be prohibited or restricted:

(1) Activities such as the drafting and rewording of the text of technical assistance and joint venture contracts must be performed under the direction and supervision of a *bengoshi* or a foreign attorney recognized under former Article 7 of the Bengoshi Law.

(2) An unqualified alien may not independently express a legal opinion regarding such matters as the drafting or revision of a contract because to do so constitutes an act resembling the rendering of legal advice.

(3) An unqualified alien may not meet independently with a client for purposes of legal consultation and express a legal opinion or give independent legal advice.

Although this document had no legal binding force, it was prepared by an eight-man JFBA Committee on the Control of Unauthorized Practice by Foreign Lawyers and approved by the Board of Governors of the JFBA.

2. The current system for registered foreign lawyers

In 1974 the American Bar Association (ABA) initiated discussions with the JFBA over opening the legal market in Japan to foreign lawyers. As mentioned in the above selection, the only foreign attorneys then recognized in Japan were the dwindling population of "grandfathered" foreign attorneys who had qualified prior to revision of the Lawyers Law in 1955 and the growing community of "trainees"—foreign law clerks who were for the most part recent law school graduates and were supposed to work only under the direct supervision of a *bengoshi*. In addition, some foreigners who were qualified as lawyers in their home countries worked at foreign companies in Japan. For the most part, they worked as businesspeople, rather than as legal specialists. A handful, though, worked primarily on legal matters, in a manner similar to that of the (unlicensed) members of Japanese corporate legal departments. By the late 1970s and early 1980s, some Japanese corporations had also begun to hire foreign lawyers for positions in their legal departments. As with the trainees at law firms, these lawyers tended to be recent law school graduates, typically hired for periods of one to two years.

The ABA argued that these groups of foreign lawyers and the relatively small population of *shōgai bengoshi* were not adequate to meet the increasing demand for international legal services in Japan. The ABA also claimed that because growing numbers of *bengoshi* were passing bar exams and becoming fully qualified attorneys in the U.S., and because it is practically impossible for foreigners to pass Japan's National Legal Examination, Japan should provide some means for allowing foreign attorneys to practice.

In the meantime, some foreign attorneys, attracted by the rapidly growing Japanese economy, tried to practice in Japan in capacities other than that of trainee at a Japanese firm. In the 1970s, a few large U.S.-based law firms set up small offices or other presences in Japan.

This led to considerable controversy, with some *bengoshi* protesting the presence of foreign attorneys practicing in Japan without being licensed. Being lawyers, both the foreign attorneys arguing for the legitimacy of their presence and the *bengoshi* arguing against it came up with complex arguments supporting their positions.

In the short run, the *bengoshi* prevailed by convincing the Ministry of Justice to stop issuing visas to foreign attorneys setting up practice in Japan. For those who had already entered, there was tacit agreement that they could remain (and some additional foreign attorneys entered to join the existing offices).

Debate on the issue continued through the late 1970s and into the early 1980s, growing along with Japan's economy and Tokyo's emergence as a major financial center. The negotiations between the ABA and JFBA accomplished little, but several large American law firms eventually prevailed upon the U.S. government to make the so-called "lawyers issue" a trade issue and include it in its negotiations with Japan. Through the early 1980s there were extensive negotiations between the governments of Japan and the U.S. and between the ABA and the JFBA. These negotiations eventually resulted in the Foreign Lawyers Act, passed by the Diet in 1986. Over the following year ministerial ordinances were promulgated, providing further details on implementation of the law.

The Foreign Lawyers Act created a classification for foreign attorneys known as *gaikokuhō jimu bengoshi* (GJB). The following selections provide an overview of the requirements for becoming a GJB and the scope of practice permitted for GJB. They also provide an example of intergovernmental negotiations over the opening of a market and of the types of restrictions that may be imposed as conditions for market opening.

RICHARD WOHL, THE FOREIGN LAWYERS SYSTEM–AN OVERVIEW*

Practice by Foreign Lawyers in Japan
17-23 (1989)

Even a casual reading of the [Foreign Lawyers] Law, MOJ [Ministry of Justice] Ordinances and JFBA Regulations reveals a number of striking differences between the Japanese approach to licensure and the rules on foreign legal consultants adopted in various U.S. states. Three general points emerge from any comparison. First, the GOJ [Government of Japan] chose to create an independent, detailed system of regulation for a new profession as opposed to the option followed by U.S. jurisdictions of simply supplementing the existing set of rules that applies to lawyers admitted to the bar. This more specific pattern of oversight stems in part from the fact that Japan is a civil rather than common law country, but, more directly, from the GOJ's efforts to ensure that the opening of the Japanese market to foreign lawyers would not undermine the stability of the legal system or the economic position of the current body of legal practitioners in Japan.

Second, the substance of the Japanese system reflects a conservative view of the role played by lawyers in society. From beginning to end, the GOJ has perceived the foreign lawyers issue, despite its inclusion in the 1985 Action Program, as a problem of legal culture rather than trade. Foreign law offices would be significant economic agents in their own right and, more critically, the harbingers of a more assertive posture toward established institutions. Strict professional and financial controls were considered necessary in order to protect Japanese clients from "unscrupulous profiteers" and society at large from a surge in foreign-inspired litigation. In addition, the GOJ's positions were driven to a considerable extent by opposition from *bengoshi* to any accommodation that would dilute their professional or economic status. While the USG [U.S. Government] was willing to accept neutral standards, the GOJ's outlook gave rise to major disputes over whether foreign lawyers would have their qualifications judged according to Japanese or home country criteria, and whether, once licensed, they would be subject to restrictions not imposed on *bengoshi*.

Third, although the USG had significant substantive input into the form and structure of the foreign lawyers system in Japan, the actual provisions of the rules were drafted almost exclusively by the GOJ. * * * The GOJ's proposals were derived from the elements of existing laws regulating *bengoshi*, as well as from the then-current state of consensus within the JFBA on the admission of foreign lawyers. * * *

In addition to these three general points, there are a number of specific areas in which GOJ treatment of foreign lawyers differs from that accorded by U.S. jurisdictions. The first issue over which the USG and GOJ grappled was regulatory

*From Richard Wohl, "The Foreign Lawyers System—An Overview," in Richard Wohl, Stuart Chemtob and Glen Fukushima, eds., *Practice by Foreign Lawyers in Japan* (© American Bar Association 1989), at 17-23. Reprinted by permission.

authority—*i.e.*, what Japanese entity would license and supervise foreign lawyers. * * * [T]he JFBA asked to receive plenary responsibility over foreign lawyers by virtue of its preexisting role, codified in the *Bengoshi* Law, of regulating the practice of law in Japan. The USG opposed the JFBA's request, [taking] the position that the JFBA was an unsuitable regulatory authority because of its well-documented history of hostility toward foreign attorneys.

The key to resolving this issue proved to be the fact that the new regime would regulate foreigners as well as persons who practice law. In Japan, the legal status of foreigners is generally the province of the central government, while jurisdiction over lawyers is vested with the JFBA. The Law reflects this dichotomy by dividing administrative responsibility over foreign lawyers between the GOJ and JFBA. The MOJ decides whether applicants are qualified, although the JFBA retains initial power over registration and discipline. If the JFBA wishes to exercise its authority either to refuse to register or to impose disciplinary sanctions on a foreign lawyer, however, such action must be reviewed by hybrid entities composed of representatives of the JFBA, the GOJ and other groups, with a final right of appeal to the courts.

Related to the question of jurisdiction was the issue of the title that foreign lawyers would be able to use in Japan. The JFBA sought to have the appellation "*bengoshi*" included in the title in order to bolster its claim that the new entrants should come within its regulatory power. For this very reason, the USG pressed for a term without any statutory connotations. * * * In the end, the term "*gaikokuhō jimu bengoshi*," or "foreign law solicitor," was chosen. This term appears designed to emphasize both the foreign and lawyerly nature of the new breed of legal practitioner, while avoiding any confusion with *bengoshi*, who can appear in Japanese courts. However, a foreign lawyer also is permitted to use, in conjunction with this official title, his title as a member of the legal profession in his home country.

There are two major prerequisites for an applicant to qualify with the MOJ: reciprocity and experience. * * * [Under the reciprocity approach adopted by Japan,] the applicant must be licensed in a jurisdiction that has already adopted a rule permitting *bengoshi* to work as foreign legal consultants, regardless of whether any *bengoshi* actually wishes to take advantage of the rule.

A further difficulty arose out of the GOJ's early attempt to define the relevant jurisdiction for reciprocity purposes as the entire U.S. This proposal would have operated to bar any U.S. lawyer from practicing in Japan until all U.S. states became open to the licensing of foreign attorneys without examination. Since positive action by every U.S. state was unlikely for the foreseeable future, the GOJ's adoption of such a rule would have effectively blocked resolution of the underlying trade dispute. Subsequently, the GOJ agreed that applicants from a given state in federal countries such as the U.S. where regulation of the bar is a matter of local authority could qualify separately.

The Law requires an applicant to have engaged in legal practice in the jurisdiction where he is admitted for at least five years. U.S. states that license foreign legal consultants also impose minimum experience requirements. The principal subject of negotiation, therefore, was the definition of what would constitute qualifying experience. First, the GOJ sought to exclude from the five-year requirement any experience accumulated outside an applicant's home jurisdiction (*i.e.*, experience obtained in a state or country other than that of licensure). * * * In the end, the USG and GOJ did not succeed in completely reconciling their differences in this area, and the applicable standards are quite complex. The basic rule is that the GOJ will count experience accumulated in any state that has adopted a reciprocal system for admitting *bengoshi* as foreign legal consultants, even if such state is not the applicant's home jurisdiction. * * *

Second, the GOJ attempted to impose on foreign lawyers the Japanese view that only practice with a private law firm or office should count as actual legal experience. This standard would have prevented an applicant from relying on experience as a government or corporate attorney in order to qualify for licensing, thereby excluding a large number of potential applicants from the U.S. The manner in which this issue was resolved, however, ensures that government or corporate positions will constitute qualifying experiences so long as the applicant worked functionally as a lawyer during the period in question. * * *

Once the hurdles of reciprocity and experience are surmounted, the MOJ requires an applicant to fulfill a number of other criteria before it will approve his qualification. Foremost among these are proof of professional standing, the ability to compensate clients in cases of malpractice, a residence in Japan, a business plan and the financial wherewithal to set up an office according to that plan. * * *

Once a foreign lawyer is licensed, he becomes subject to a full panoply of rules governing his activities in Japan. The most important set of restrictions pertains to the permissible scope of practice. * * * The Japanese rules essentially provide that a foreign licensee may practice the laws of only those countries in which he is formally admitted. In order to render advice on the laws of another jurisdiction, he must demonstrate that he possesses knowledge and experience equivalent to a lawyer qualified in such jurisdiction. The initial Japanese position—as in the case of the experience requirement—was to define the "country" of admission for scope of practice purposes as the same jurisdiction used to satisfy the reciprocity test[, in the typical case meaning only the applicant's own home state]. After receiving objections from the USG and ABA, the GOJ adopted a more flexible interpretation that permits a U.S. lawyer to apply for and receive automatic designation to practice the laws of essentially all U.S. jurisdictions. The rules governing the practice of the laws of a third country, however, continue to require that the applicant either be formally qualified in that country or that he possess the same level of learning and experience as a qualified lawyer from that country. With respect to international law, a U.S. lawyer should be able to deal with any issue that relates to or involves the U.S. Finally, the foreign lawyer will be under severe restrictions regarding the practice of Japanese law and will be subject to criminal penalties in the event that he violates them.

Another issue that arose during the negotiations was the prohibition on certain forms of association between foreign lawyers and *bengoshi*. The Law forbids a foreign lawyer from employing a *bengoshi* and also prohibits the two from entering into a relationship that involves the division of revenues – *i.e.*, partnership arrangements. The GOJ justified these restrictions as essential to prevent foreign lawyers from engaging in the practice of Japanese law through the person of a Japanese partner or employee, and to ensure that *bengoshi* maintain their independent function. The USG argued that the transnational legal problems likely to be handled by foreign lawyers would require collaborative efforts, and that full service firms would be more efficient for the client. The GOJ agreed to define its restrictions narrowly so that joint activities between foreign lawyers and *bengoshi*, such as the sharing of offices and expenses, will be permitted so long as there is no sharing of profits. This concession is important because it allows the splitting of major cost items such as office rent, staff salaries, etc. The rules that apply to relationships between foreign lawyers and *bengoshi* also extend to interactions between foreign lawyers and the quasi-legal professionals in Japan, such as tax specialists (*zeirishi*), patent specialists (*benrishi*), administrative scriveners (*gyōsei shoshi*) and judicial scriveners (*shihō shoshi*).

There will be no limit on the number of junior attorneys (*i.e.*, persons not licensed in Japan) from abroad who may be employed in a foreign law office as "trainees." Initially, the GOJ proposed a ratio of one unlicensed lawyer per licensed foreign attorney, but dropped this idea in the face of opposition from the USG and ABA. * * * In addition, foreign lawyers may employ Japanese personnel who are not licensed to practice law in Japan but have some law-related background, a group that includes the many Japanese who studied law in college but have not passed the rigorous national bar examination.

There are specific rules in the Law and JFBA Regulations on a foreign lawyer's ability to use the name of his home country law firm, required disclosure of the limited license to practice, and advertising. * * *

The requirements for a foreign lawyer to maintain his license to practice in Japan are relatively straightforward. The major substantive condition is residency in Japan for at least 180 days per year. * * *

The substantive grounds for discipline of a foreign lawyer in Japan are similar to those in effect in U.S. jurisdictions, with several important additions. Any violation of the Law, MOJ Ordinances or JFBA Regulations may become a matter for discipline, so the unique Japanese rules on subjects such as residency, scope of practice and use of firm name will also be relevant in this context. Moreover, as in the case of registration, acts or omissions that endanger the order or reputation of the Japanese bar can be a basis for disciplinary sanction. The most significant parallel to the registration procedure, however, is the role provided for hybrid entities (consisting of representatives of the JFBA, GOJ and other institutions) in reviewing any disciplinary action.

Questions and Discussion Points

1. *Later developments:* At the time of publication of this book, amendments

to become effective in January 1995 had just been made to the Foreign Lawyers Act. Under the amended Act, up to two years of practice in Japan at a Japanese firm can often be counted toward the five years' experience requirement, reciprocity is in essence no longer required for GATT signatory countries (or for other countries where international treaty obligations restrict reciprocity requirements), and, to a limited extent, partnerships between *bengoshi* and GJB in their individual capacities (but not with any foreign firm with which the GJB is affiliated) are permissible.

2. *The number of GJB:* While applications to become GJB have increased steadily, between 1991 and 1993 the number actually practicing as GJB fell from 78 to 75 (presumably as a primary result of departures from Japan). The following shows the number of GJB in Japan as of September 16, 1993:

Law of Primary Qualification	Applicants	Currently Approved	Registered
U.S.A.	114	102	53
New York	61	56	28
California	30	26	14
D.C.	13	12	5
Hawaii	3	3	2
Illinois	2	1	1
Texas	2	1	0
New Jersey	1	1	1
Ohio	1	1	1
Louisiana	1	1	1
U.K.	38	37	18
France	1	1	1
Germany	2	1	1
Australia	3	2	1
Holland	1	1	1
Total	159	144	75

3. *Comparison of systems for registration of foreign lawyers:* In part to enable their lawyers to register as GJB in Japan, a gradually increasing number of U.S. jurisdictions have adopted systems for registration of foreign lawyers. The first such system, and the one that has attracted the most interest among *bengoshi*, is that of New York State. A brief comparison of relevant standards of the Japanese and New York regimes follows:

i) *Qualifications:* Both systems require that applicants be qualified lawyers in good standing in their home jurisdictions. As described in the preceding selection, under Japan's system applicants must have five years of practice experience. This may include service in government or corporate positions if the work is functionally equivalent to that of a practicing lawyer. Time spent in practice outside one's home jurisdiction may qualify under certain circumstances. In addition, as a special measure for trainees who were in Japan when the new system was adopted, a supplementary provision to the Foreign Lawyers Act grants them credit for up to two years of experience working in Japan under a *bengoshi.*

In New York, in accordance with the "Rules of the Court of Ap peals for the Licensing of Legal Consultants," applicants must have for at least five of the seven years immediately preceding application "been admitted to practice and [have been] in good standing as an attorney * * * in a foreign country and while so admitted ha[ve] actually practiced the law of such country."

Both systems also require foreign lawyers to be residents. Unlike Japan, however, New York's system does not require that the applicant's home jurisdiction maintain a reciprocal system for recognition of foreign lawyers.

ii) *Scope of Practice:* In Japan, at the time of registration, foreign lawyers must apply for designation of the laws they are licensed to practice. For U.S. lawyers, designation typically will also be granted for federal law and the laws of nearly all other U.S. states (with the possible exception of Louisiana). Practice of Japanese law is not permitted, and the Foreign Lawyers Act contains explicit prohibitions on such activities as appearing in court or before the Patent Agency, practicing before other governmental agencies, and preparing documents affecting real property, estates, or marital or family relations.

New York's rules provide similar prohibitions with respect to real property rights, trusts and estates, and family law matters. As to giving advice on New York or federal law, the New York rules prohibit doing so "except on the basis of advice from a person duly qualified and entitled (other than by virtue of having been licensed under this Part) to render professional legal advice on such law."

iii) *Association:* The Foreign Lawyers Act prohibits partnership between *bengoshi* and GJB and the hiring of *bengoshi* by GJB (but not the hiring of GJB by *bengoshi*). New York law contains no such prohibitions. Although a number of observers on the U.S. side expressed the hope during negotiations over the Foreign Lawyers Act that this restriction would not cause undue difficulties, particularly since GJB can share office space and expenses (but not profits) with *bengoshi,* a number of the U.S. firms that have established offices in Tokyo claim that these limitations on association in fact have impeded their practice. U.S. trade negotiators have also raised the issue of the association limitations, arguing that they hinder U.S. companies in obtaining advice necessary to do business in Japan. Accordingly, the association issue has become one of the most contentious remaining issues relating to the Foreign Lawyers Act.

4. *The experience requirement:* Consider the following situations. Would the applicant be qualified for registration in Japan? (Assume in each case that the applicant is a licensed lawyer in good standing in her home jurisdiction.)

i) A graduated from law school six years ago. After working as a law clerk for a federal judge in Vermont for one year, she became an associate at a major New York law firm. She did not take the New York bar exam until the following February. She passed and, after completing the necessary paperwork, was registered as a member of the New York bar in May of that year. She has continued to work as an associate at the firm's main office in New York for the four years since.

ii) Same situation as in (i), but B did not complete the necessary paperwork for a year and was not registered as a member of the New York bar until three years ago.

iii) Same situation as in (i), but C failed the bar exam on her first two tries and was not registered as a member of the New York bar until three years ago.

iv) Same situation as in (i), but D has spent the past two years working in the firm's Los Angeles office. (California has a system for registration of foreign lawyers that qualifies for reciprocity with Japan.)

v) Same situation as in (i), but E has spent the past two years working in the firm's Beijing office. (China does not have a reciprocal system.)

vi) Same situation as in (i), but F has spent the past two years working in the firm's Tokyo office.

vii) Same situation as in (i), but G quit the New York firm three years ago. After spending two years working as a trainee in the law firm of a *bengoshi* in Tokyo, she joined another large New York firm a year ago.

5. *Scope of permissible activity of GJB:* Consider the following issues. May a GJB give advice on the requested issue? (Assume in each case that the GJB is a member of the New York bar and has been designated as qualified to practice federal law and the laws of all U.S. states other than Louisiana.)

i) The client, a Japanese company, has asked advice regarding the acquisition of a chemical company in Ohio.

ii) The client, a U.S. company, has asked advice regarding the acquisition of a textile company in Osaka.

iii) The client, a Japanese company, has asked advice regarding the acquisition of a lumber company in Malaysia.

iv) The client, a U.S. company, has entered negotiations with a Japanese company on a contract to ship lumber from Oregon to Tokyo. The parties have not yet considered whether the transaction will be governed by Japanese law, Oregon law, or some other body of law.

v) The client, a Michigan company, has entered negotiations with a Japanese company on establishment of a joint venture to manufacture front-end loaders in Japan. The transaction will involve the negotiation of several contracts. These may all be governed by the same law, but it is also possible that one or more may be governed by Michigan law and one or more by Japanese law. The parties have not yet addressed the choice of law question.

6. *Actual activities of GJB:* If GJB cannot give advice on Japanese law, what kinds of advice are they giving, and to whom? What role, if any, can the GJB play in assisting a foreign company seeking to enter Japan? If a GJB is not in Japan, may he or she give a client advice on Japanese law? May any other foreign lawyer outside Japan give a client advice on Japanese law? Apart from the requirements under Japanese law, what other legal or practical factors should be taken into account in considering these questions?

7. *Japanese licensed in the U.S. and practicing in Japan:* Several Japanese who have graduated from undergraduate law faculties but who have not taken or have not passed the National Legal Examination have subsequently completed J.D. or LL.M. programs in the United States and then passed a state bar examination. Some of these lawyers have been hired by U.S. law firms with Tokyo offices. May such lawyers be transferred to the firms' Tokyo offices? If so, what is the permissible scope of their practice?

Several *bengoshi* who have obtained licenses in the U.S. have gone to work for U.S. law firms in the U.S. At least one of these *bengoshi* was transferred to his firm's Tokyo office, whereupon he was required to relinquish his license as a *bengoshi.*

8. *Views on Practice by Foreign Lawyers:* The U.S. Government and the ABA have treated restrictions on practice in Japan as a trade liberalization issue, while most *bengoshi* have viewed the issue in terms of protecting the style of practice and the conception in Japan of legal practice as a profession rather than a business. What are the merits of each side's position?

FURTHER READING

History

"Constitutional History Since 1867," in Hideo Tanaka, ed., *The Japanese Legal System*, Chpt. 7, pp. 621-685. Tokyo: University of Tokyo Press, 1988.

Dan Fenno Henderson, *Conciliation and Japanese Law, Tokugawa and Modern.* 2 vols. Seattle: Published for the Association for Asian Studies by University of Washington Press, 1965.

Ryosuke Ishii, *A History of Political Institutions in Japan.* Tokyo: University of Tokyo Press, 1980.

Masami Ito, "The Modern Development of Law and Constitution in Japan," in Lawrence W. Beer, ed., *Constitutional Systems in Late Twentieth Century Asia*, pp. 129-174. Seattle: University of Washington Press, 1992.

Charles L. Kades, "The American Role in Revising Japan's Imperial Constitution," 104 *Political Science Quarterly* 215 (1989).

Carl Steenstrup, *A History of Law in Japan until 1868.* Leiden: E.J. Brill, 1991.

Constitutional Rights

Nobuyoshi Ashibe, "Human Rights and Judicial Power," in Lawrence W. Beer, ed., *Constitutional Systems in Late Twentieth Century Asia*, pp. 224-269. Seattle: University of Washington Press, 1992.

Lawrence W. Beer, *Freedom of Expression in Japan: A Study in Comparative Law, Politics and Society.* Tokyo: Kodansha International, 1984.

Lawrence W. Beer, "Japan's Constitutional System and Its Judicial Interpretation," 17 *Law in Japan: An Annual* 7 (1984).

"Constitutional Guarantee of Human Rights," in Hideo Tanaka, ed., *The Japanese Legal System*, Chpt. 10, pp. 721-832. Tokyo: University of Tokyo Press, 1988.

Hiroshi Itoh and Lawrence Ward Beer, *The Constitutional Case Law of Japan: Selected Supreme Court Decisions, 1961-1970.* Seattle: University of Washington Press, 1978.

Percy R. Luney, Jr., and Kazuyuki Takahashi, eds., *Japanese Constitutional Law.* Tokyo: University of Tokyo Press, 1993.

John M. Maki, *Court and Constitution in Japan.* Seattle: University of Washington Press, 1964.

The Japanese Legal System and the Japanese Judiciary

Edward I. Chen, "The Legal Training and Research Institute of Japan," 22 *University of Toledo Law Review* 975 (1991).

Edward I. Chen, "The National Law Examination of Japan," 39 *Journal of Legal Education* 1 (1989).

John Owen Haley, *Authority without Power: Law and the Japanese Paradox.* New York: Oxford University Press, 1991.

Hiroshi Itoh, *The Japanese Supreme Court: Constitutional Policies.* New York: Markus Wiener, 1989.

Hiroshi Oda, *Japanese Law.* London: Butterworths, 1992.

J. Mark Ramseyer and Frances McCall Rosenbluth, *Japan's Political Marketplace.* Cambridge, MA: Harvard University Press, 1993.

Frank K. Upham, *Law and Social Change in Postwar Japan.* Cambridge, MA: Harvard University Press, 1987.

Statutory Interpretation and the Role of Custom and Precedent in Japan

"'Legal Process' in Japan," in Hideo Tanaka, ed., *The Japanese Legal System*, Chpt. 2, pp. 61-162. Tokyo: University of Tokyo Press, 1988.

J. Mark Ramseyer, "Water Law in Imperial Japan: Public Goods, Private Claims, and Legal Convergence," 18 *Journal of Legal Studies* 51 (1989).

Masataka Taniguchi, "Judicial Binding Force and Law-Making by Judges," 4 *Ritsumeikan Law Review, International Edition* (1989).

The Domestic Legal Profession in Japan

Takaaki Hattori, "The Legal Profession in Japan: Its Historical Development and Present State," in Arthur T. von Mehren, ed., *Law in Japan: The Legal Order in a Changing Society*, pp. 238-273. Cambridge, MA: Harvard University Press, 1963.

Richard Rabinowitz, "The Historical Development of the Japanese Bar," 70 *Harvard Law Review* 61 (1956).

J. Mark Ramseyer, "Lawyers, Foreign Lawyers and Lawyer-Substitutes: The Market for Regulation in Japan," 27 *Harvard International Law Journal* 499 (1986).

Takao Tanase, "Urbanization of Lawyers and Its Functional Significance: Expansion in the Range of Work Activities and Change in Social Role," 13 *Law in Japan: An Annual* 20 (1980).

Michael K. Young, "The Legal Profession in Japan: Misleading Comparisons and Unasked Questions," in Institute of Comparative Law in Japan, ed., *Conflict and Integration: Comparative Law in the World Today*, pp. 131-160. Tokyo: Chuo University Press, 1989.

Negotiation and Content of the GJB Law

Glen Fukushima, "The Liberalization of Legal Services in Japan: A U.S. Government Negotiator's Perspective," 21 *Law in Japan: An Annual* 5 (1988).

John O. Haley, "The New Regulatory Regime for Foreign Lawyers in Japan: An Escape from Freedom," 5 *UCLA Pacific Basin Law Journal* 1 (1986).

Susan Sayuri Kigawa, "Gaikoku bengoshi ho, Foreign Lawyers in Japan: The Dynamics Behind Law No. 66," 62 *Southern California Law Review* 1489 (1989).

Reaction of Japanese Bar to GJB

Kunio Hamada, "The Reaction of Japanese Lawyers to the New Law," 21 *Law in Japan: An Annual* 43 (1988).

Tasuku Matsuo, "Recent Developments in and Japanese Attorneys' Perceptions of *Gaikokuhō Jimu Bengoshi* Status," 21 *Law in Japan: An Annual* 27 (1988).

NOTES TO CHAPTER TWO

1. H. Fukui, *Party in Power* (1970), p. 66.

2. The two conservative parties of the immediate postwar period—the Liberal Party and the Democratic Party—merged to create the LDP in November 1955.

3. Aside from those who pass the NLE and complete the two-year program at the Institute, four additional groups of people can become *bengoshi*: 1) those who have served as a Justice on the Supreme Court (under the Court Organization Act up to five of the fifteen Justices may come from backgrounds outside the legal profession); 2) those who have passed the NLE but instead of enrolling in the Institute have entered certain other government jobs and have been employed in those jobs

for at least five years; 3) those who have for at least five years been professors of law at a Japanese university with a graduate department in law; and 4) those with a total of at least five years combined in positions in the second and third categories above (Practicing Attorneys Act, § 5). In 1988, about 15% of those who became attorneys did so through one of these alternative paths.

4. *See* Kahei Rokumoto, "Bengoshi gyōmu no keizaiteki kihan ni kansuru jittai chōsa kihon hōkoku" ("Basic Report on the Survey of Actual Circumstances concerning the Economics of Bengoshi Business"), *Jiyū to Seigi,*Vol. 32, No. 10, 1, at 72-80 (1981).

5. Michael K. Young, "Foreign Lawyers in Japan: A Case Study in Transnational Dispute Resolution and Marginal Reform," 21 *Law in Japan* 84, 102 (1988).

6. Patent agents are registered after passing the patent agent examination. However, qualified lawyers or persons who have served as an examiner or commissioner of the Patent Office for more than seven years are also eligible for registration as patent agents. Patent agents are under the supervision of the Ministry of International Trade and Industry.

7. Tax agents are registered after passing the tax agent examination; practicing lawyers or certified public accountants are also eligible to register as tax agents. They are subject to discipline by the Japan Federation of Tax Agents Association.

8. Anyone who has served for more than five years as a secretary of a court (*jimukan*), a court clerk (*shokikan*), or a secretary of the Ministry of Justice or the public procurator's office may function as a legal scrivener with the permission of a chief of the appropriate regional office of the Justice Ministry, subject to supervision by the chief of such offices.

9. Those who have passed the administrative scrivener examination or are qualified lawyers, patent agents, tax agents, or certified public accountants, and those who have served as an official of the national or a municipal government for more than twelve years may be registered as administrative scriveners. They are subject to the supervision of the governors of their respective prefectures.

10. In 1983, the number of licensed non-lawyer specialists was as follows:

Tax Agents	40,985
Patent Agents	2,660
CPA (including assistant CPA)	8,684
Notaries	446
Administrative scriveners	30,908
Judicial scriveners	14,862
TOTAL	98,545

See Shimin no tame no hōritsuka (Law Specialists for the Citizenry) 213, 219, 222, 227, 231, 235 (Tokyo: Nihon Hyōron-sha, 1983).

In addition to the people mentioned above, there are other kinds of licensed specialists who handle transactions involving legal matters. They are Immovable Property Appraisers (*Fudōsan kantei-shi*) (app. 4,000), Land and House Investigators (*Tochi kaoku chōsa-shi*) (app. 18,000), and Specialists in Charge of Building, Land and House Transactions (*Takuchi tatemono torihiki shunin-sha*) (app. 299,000). *See Shimin no tame no hōritsuka*, at 236-247.

11. In recent years, the population per practicing lawyer in major developed countries is reported to be approximately as follows:

Country	Lawyers	Per capita
Japan (lawyers only)	12,700	9,400
France	15,700	3,400
Federal Republic of Germany	41,500	1,500
United Kingdom (including barristers and solicitors)	38,500	1,400
United States	612,000	370
Japan (including non-lawyer specialists)	111,245	1,070

Source: Materials prepared by the Supreme Court of Japan in 1984.

12. "Gaikokujin hiben katsudō bōshi ni kansuru kijun" (1972), reprinted in 23-8 *Jiyū to Seigi* 39 (1972).

13. Tadao Fukuhara, "The Status of Foreign Lawyers in Japan," 17 *The Japanese Annual of Int'l Law* 21, 36 (1973).

Three

The Business Environment

Introduction

For foreign companies doing business in Japan or considering entering the Japanese market, and for business lawyers counseling them, understanding the overall business environment in Japan is vital. One aspect of the business environment that has attracted much attention in recent years is the so-called *keiretsu,* or business grouping. As noted in Chapter 1, many executives at American companies doing business in Japan regard the business group relationship as one of the strongest barriers to increased trade. As a reflection of that view, in the Structural Impediments Initiative (SII) talks, the U.S. Government argued that reform of the *keiretsu* system was essential in order to allow foreign companies to compete on a fair and equal footing in Japan.

The materials in the first part of this chapter explore the *keiretsu* and related issues in more detail. As the initial section explains, the term *keiretsu* is often used in a loose fashion and in fact covers a wide range of different types of business groupings. Subsequent readings consider whether these different types all raise the same sorts of concerns and advance arguments in favor of retaining the *keiretsu* system—arguments that have led some to argue for greater utilization of the *keiretsu* approach in the United States, as well.

The next section of this chapter considers two other aspects of the long-term orientation of Japanese companies: typical financing patterns and the so-called lifetime employment system.

Japan's distribution system has been identified by foreign businesses as another major barrier to the Japanese market. The final section of this chapter explores the distribution system in more detail, concluding with an examination of an issue that has garnered great attention in the SII talks, the so-called Large-Scale Retail Stores Act.

I. *Keiretsu* and Ongoing Business Relationships

A. Overview

Journalists and commentators, both in foreign countries and in Japan itself, frequently use the term *keiretsu* as though its meaning is fixed and clearly understood. In fact, however, that term may be used in several different senses. At its narrowest, the term refers to six horizontal industrial groupings centered around major banks. For many commentators, the term also embraces vertically integrated business groups operating within a single industry (such as automobiles or computers) or at most a few industries. Sometimes the word is even used to refer to close ongoing business relationships between companies where no shareholding or other formal control mechanism exists.

By the end of World War II, a number of large commercial and industrial combines, called *zaibatsu*, had developed in Japan. Each *zaibatsu*, which typically included a bank, a trading company and strength in several industries, was joined through a central holding company (normally controlled by members of a single family). Following the War, the Occupation prohibited holding companies and ordered the dissolution of these *zaibatsu* and the public distribution of the shares in the former *zaibatsu* companies.

In many cases, however, former *zaibatsu* companies continued to work rather closely with one another. Although the resultant relationships have never approached the degree of centralized control through a single family or holding company of the old *zaibatsu*, in some cases they have led to business groups sharing a significant degree of coordination and cooperation. Thus, the Mitsubishi, Mitsui and Sumitomo *keiretsu*—three of the six major horizontal *keiretsu* today—all have roots in prewar *zaibatsu*. Three other major horizontal business groupings developed around Fuji, Daiichi-Kangyo and Sanwa Banks, large banks that were able to supply needed funding in the years after the War.

Strictly defining membership in these groups in legal terms would be difficult. For purposes of financial disclosure, the Ministry of Finance treats a company as a "subsidiary" if the filing company (the registrant) owns 50 percent or more of its shares and treats a company as a "related company" if the registrant owns 20 percent or more of its shares and exercises control over a major part of its business activities through an "uninterrupted and close relationship."[1] Yet, as the term *keiretsu* is commonly used, even in its narrow sense, the group may include companies in which the cross-shareholding level is less than 20 percent. In fact, in its figures on horizontal group companies, the Fair Trade Commission, while using the same 50 percent figure to define subsidiaries, classifies affiliates into two subsets: those for which the cross-shareholding level is between 25 percent and 50 percent and those for which it is between 10 percent and 25 percent. According to those figures, as of 1983 the six major horizontal *keiretsu* and their related companies accounted for 34 percent of all corporate assets in Japan.[2]

Despite the difficulties in attaining precise definitions, the horizontal *keiretsu* groups share certain characteristics. As set forth by Professor Dan Fenno Henderson, these characteristics include the following:

1. The members are all "independent" major firms in their own oligopolistic industries.

2. The *keiretsu* is a confederation pursuing the "one-set" formula (*i.e.*, aiming at representing all lines within the confederation).

3. Service firms (for example: banking, trading, insurance and shipping companies) from within the *keiretsu* perform special functions for industrial member firms in varying degrees (not usually to the complete exclusion of outsiders).

4. Between the firms there are several cross-ties: *e.g.*, borrowing from the same banks, mutual shareholding, interlocking directorates, using the same trademark and the same trading company, and liaison planning by presidents' clubs.

5. Much interfirm business, horizontal and vertical, is done within the group.

6. Holding companies at the top have been eliminated so that the relationship is now more cooperative than controlled.[3]

In addition to the horizontal *keiretsu*, a large number of vertical *keiretsu* have developed in various industries. These include automobile makers such as Nissan and Toyota and electronics makers such as Hitachi and Toshiba. In most of these vertical *keiretsu*, group companies are concentrated into one or at most a few industries (although many are increasingly branching out into a fairly wide range of fields related to the core industry). Accordingly, these vertical *keiretsu* do not attempt to cover all fields, nor do they include the full range of central banks and other service firms typical of the horizontal *keiretsu*. Otherwise, however, they share most of the characteristics listed above, several of which are described in more detail in the following selection.

ROBERT BALLON AND IWAO TOMITA, THE FINANCIAL BEHAVIOR OF JAPANESE CORPORATIONS*

67-69 (1988)

Basically, the *keiretsu* is a loosely knit organization of independent companies with a balanced combination of growth industries. At the same time, it is well organized in the sense of its competitive position vis-à-vis other groups. Interdependence within the group, with the main bank at its center, is cultivated by business and human ties.

In the early postwar years, mutual shareholding was a powerful instrument in the formation of the major [horizontal] *keiretsu* attempting to reestablish their prewar importance. Later, much mutual shareholding took place under the label of stable shareholding. City banks, within the constraints of the Antimonopoly Law, are among the largest shareholders of their major corporate clients, followed closely by the other financial institutions in the group (trust banks and insurance companies). * * *

*From Robert Ballon and Iwao Tomita, *The Financial Behavior of Japanese Corporations* (Kodansha International, 1988), at 67-69. Reprinted by permission.

Business transactions within the group manifest a similar trend; currently they average about 10% among nonfinancial members [of horizontal *keiretsu*] (see Table [3-1]). [Such intragroup transactions have been estimated to be as high as 20% to 40% in vertical *keiretsu* in some industries.]

Human ties play an important role in group cohesiveness as well. They take the form of presidents' meetings, interlocking directorates, and transfer of personnel. Meetings of presidents of the *keiretsu*'s major member companies are held regularly, often backed up by meetings of directors and of upper-level managers. These meetings are not organs of decision making in the sense that a majority vote would carry the day, but they are manifestations of the very dynamic process of consensus. Views are exchanged, opinions heard, and actions reciprocally adjusted, more on an ad hoc basis than in terms of binding policy, a process that characterizes Japanese management.

The dispatch, permanent or temporary, of executives among group members is standard practice in ordinary times. In troubled periods a former bank official may be installed as president or board member of the company concerned. It is also fairly common that when the president or a director of a bank retires, he becomes president or director of a related company (although the reverse is never seen!). * * *

> The top six trading companies, as of March 1982, had dispatched executives to 57.5% of the companies in which they held 10% or more of the shares (an average of 1.4 directors per company or 14.2 % of the board), to 89.6% of their affiliates (2.7 directors per company or 30.1% of the board), and to 97.6% of their subsidiaries (5.0 directors per company or 66.2% of the board) [citation to FTC materials omitted].

Interlocking directorates are a feature of the *keiretsu* found in 70% of the member companies, and in about half of the member companies at least the main bank (or the trading company) has dispatched an executive to them. * * *

* * * * *

Table [3-1]

Six Major Industrial Groups: Intragroup Transactions (1981)

(percentage)

	Nonfinancial Members		Member-Manufacturers	
	Purchases	Sales	Purchases	Sales
Total of six groups	11.7	10.8	12.4	20.4
Former *zaibatsu* groups	14.8	13.4	18.6	29.0
Other three groups	9.1	8.6	8.2	14.9

Source: [Citation to FTC materials is omitted.]

* * * * *

In addition, human ties within the group are accumulated by transfers of personnel (*shukkō*). This practice is identical to the one found among related companies. It takes one of the following two forms: either the transferee, initially sent on a temporary basis, later becomes a permanent member of the company, or the transfer is only temporary, usually for a term of two or three years. The transfer may supply the following benefits to the two corporations: manpower supply and technical assistance; training (the parent's) personnel, especially young promising managers, through broader experience and business contacts; strengthening the subsidiary's managerial and financial operations, if not also directly controlling it; and promoting (the parent's) managerial staff by transferring them to the subsidiary after the mandatory [retirement] age limit. When reduction of personnel must take place, it is a major responsibility of management to first seek the transfer of surplus personnel to other companies. This practice has been nicknamed the "Japanese-like lay-off," as when the shipbuilding industry, hit by the oil shock, transferred some of its workforce to the automobile industry.

Interdependence is thus the key to a thriving group life. * * * It flourishes in times of prosperity but works best in times of need. During tight-money periods (a recurring phenomenon in postwar Japan) as well as in the face of oil shocks or yen appreciation, cooperation among member companies remains the first privileged recourse.

B. Refining the definition of *keiretsu*

The first of the two selections below offers a response to the asserted tendency of government negotiators from the U.S. to identify all types of persistent business ties as *keiretsu*. After arguing that the term *keiretsu* carries so many ambiguities that it should not be used, the author refers to relational contract theory and Japan's postwar economic history to explain the prevalence of long-term relationships in Japan. The second selection below provides further commentary on the logic of ongoing trading relationships and on the factors which appear to make them more common in Japan than in the U.S.

Although the two selections are phrased in terms of business practice and economic theory, they are of great value in understanding not only the business environment, but certain legal principles, as well. Given the important role played in Japan by long-term trading relationships, views shaped by such relationships have influenced attitudes toward contract, good faith, custom, and other principles.

In approaching these two selections, consider what difference it makes to foreign companies seeking to do business in Japan where the parameters of the definition of *keiretsu* are drawn. If business relationships are exclusionary, does it matter how they are labeled? Alternatively, does the tendency to label all persistent business ties as *keiretsu* blind one to significant distinctions that need to be recognized to do business in Japan effectively?

Consider also whether Japanese companies and/or the government should be required to alter their practices, if their practices are sound and rational but happen incidentally to operate to exclude foreign competitors. Finally, if you think certain practices in Japan should be altered, could this be accomplished through legal reform?

1. Distinguishing *keiretsu* from ongoing business relationships

BANRI ASANUMA, LONG-TERM RELATIONSHIPS, NOT *KEIRETSU*

Japan Views, Vol. II, No. 3
12-16 (March 1992)

Japanese industrial groupings, called *keiretsu*, emerged as a major bone of contention during the Structural Impediments Initiative trade talks of 1989-90. Since then, the debate over them has raged unabated.

Many U.S. lawmakers and business leaders denounce these groups as collusive, exclusionary, and a cause of America's trade deficit. On the other hand, a number of Japanese government officials and industrialists insist that to some extent they possess economic rationality and can enhance productivity.

The controversy has become complicated. Several Japanese commentators have joined in the attack on *keiretsu*, while some U.S. opinion leaders propose that America form its own industrial groups to bolster the country's manufacturing sector. Academic opinion also is split on the issue, not necessarily along national lines.

But are *keiretsu* really the proper focus for study and discussion? My answer is no. The debate is bound to be unproductive because the term is too loose to be of much help in analyzing Japanese industrial organization. Worse, it can actually mislead us when we attempt international comparisons.

The Old Dichotomy: Market vs. Keiretsu

The concept of "relational contracting," which originated in the legal literature and recently has been adopted by prominent American economists, gives a far clearer picture of an industry. Furthermore, it helps us see that both the United States and Japan can contribute to the development of a new kind of business tie—long-term relationships based on international cooperation.

Keiretsu include two different types of corporate groupings: "horizontal" and "vertical." Failure to differentiate between them has led to confusion. The former applies to a number of big firms, including manufacturers and trading companies, that cluster around a large bank and other financial institutions. Some, such as the Mitsubishi and Sumitomo groups, are the successors to pre-World War II *zaibatsu*

*From Banri Asanuma, "Long-Term Relationships, Not *Keiretsu*," *Japan Views*, Vol. II, No. 3, pp. 12-16 (March 1992), at 12-16. Reprinted by permission.

combines, which the American Occupation dismantled after 1945. Unlike their predecessors, though, these contemporary versions lack the holding companies that directed group members from the top, hence their designation "horizontal."

Vertical groups are collections of companies consisting of a single large manufacturer and an extensive network of suppliers, dealers, and other service firms. These firms are positioned upstream or downstream of the manufacturer in the production and distribution process. In economists' jargon, they engage in vertically related activities. The traditional notion is that a particularly close relationship exists between the manufacturer and each member of the group.

It is not clear whether the name "*keiretsu*" should apply to both types of corporate groupings. But even in the case of vertical groups, which I examine below, the exact meaning is still unclear. The existence of a "particularly close" relationship is usually considered the criterion for distinguishing group members from outsiders.

The meaning of "particularly close" is ambiguous, however. In some cases, it refers to such ties as shareholding by, and the dispatch of directors and other personnel from, the core manufacturer. In others, the presence of a longstanding transactional relationship itself is taken as the decisive mark in classifying a specific firm as a member of some group. Obviously, the size and content of a corporate grouping change depending on the criterion used.

Another problem with the term "*keiretsu*" stems from some of the basic assumptions people make about the market. Many critics of these groups, for example, believe that relations between firms should normally take the form found in the competitive spot market, where each participant continually changes its partner * * * as fluctuation in demand and supply dictates. Such critics also believe that this is how most Western economies actually work.

This set of assumptions creates a very clear-cut dichotomy. On the one hand, the U.S. and European economies, where the market prevails, are taken as the norm. The Japanese economy, on the other hand, where *keiretsu* ties dominate, is seen as idiosyncratic and a serious deviation from the norm.

But in reality, given certain conditions, long-term relationships emerge as a normal response of the parties concerned. This is true of any industrial economy, Asian or non-Asian. * * *

A New Concept: Relational Contracting

Textbook economics supposes that, for any kind of goods, a competitive spot market is the ideal exchange mechanism. In this type of institutional arrangement, discrete, one-time transactions are the normal form of economic exchange. According to this model, continuous dealings between a given pair of parties are an aberration. This has led to the widespread misconception that long-term business relationships are illegitimate.

Since the 1970s, however, a new economics of organization has evolved. Economist Oliver E. Williamson * * * has pioneered this endeavor. He advises us to make transactions rather than "the market" the basic unit of analysis, classify them systematically, and try to find the optimal governance structure, *i.e.*, the mode of transacting that minimizes the costs associated with organizing and executing each kind of transaction.

Concerning institutional arrangements for procuring parts or materials, Williamson has divided transactions into three cases: 1) where the supplier provides standard items that call for minimal investment in specialized machinery or processes; 2) where the manufacturer on the buyer's side orders customized goods necessitating a fair investment by the supplier; and 3) where the buyer's needs are paramount and idiosyncratic, as in the case where the supplier is required to locate adjacent to the assembly plant.

In the first case, Williamson agrees with textbook economics: the competitive spot market is most efficient. In the second, however, he submits that the optimal arrangement is a "relational contract" with a fixed supplier as the source of the customized item over a period of time. In the third case, he says, vertical integration is the way to go.

Relational contracts were first analyzed by the American legal scholar Ian R. MacNeil. They specify only the general terms and objectives of a relationship and allow for adjustments of specific terms as circumstances dictate. They also provide the decision-making and dispute-resolving mechanisms for such adjustments. * * *

Suppliers' Involvement

Following Williamson's model, let's look at manufacturer-supplier relationships focusing on the nature of the transaction and the corresponding governance structure and compare the empirical results internationally. This method illuminates many interesting points that the "market vs. *keiretsu*" dichotomy obscures.

* * * [A] 1991 book on the product-development performance of the world auto industry by Kim B. Clark * * * and Takahiro Fujimoto [found] that the purchasing practices of auto makers in the United States, Japan, and Europe have something in common: a surprisingly small percentage of the money these makers spend on parts from outside suppliers goes for standardized, off-the-shelf parts. The bulk are customized products.

According to Williamson's theoretical findings, this suggests that relational contracting is the most appropriate governance structure for auto-part transactions not only in Japan, but also in the United States and Europe, where holders of the conventional dichotomy view assume that the market prevails.

Regional differences exist between the United States, Japan, and Europe in the composition of customized parts purchased from outside suppliers. * * * [I]n the United States most outlays for parts are for those where the automaker not only sets specifications but also provides the supplier with drawings made by its own engineering staff. (Let's call these "Drawings-Supplied parts," or DS parts for short.)

In Japan, however, a major portion of parts expenditures are items for which the automaker issues only specifications and approves the final drawings, most development work and drawings being done by the supplier's engineering staff. (Let's call these "Drawings-Approved parts," or DA parts for short.) The European situation falls in between.

The contractual practice developed in the United States to regulate parts transactions has features of relational contracting * * * . But it is also relatively close to the competitive spot market in that automakers solicit new bids, after one year, from a large number of suppliers, switching from a given [supplier] to a new one if the latter proposes a lower price. This practice has been possible because the drawings belong to the buyer. Automakers can reclaim them from the current supplier and lend them to another one quite easily.

Since such transactions are terminated within a relatively short interval, there is somewhat less incentive for the supplier to invest in developing skills that would enable him to meet the manufacturer's specific needs. Furthermore, U.S. suppliers have had relatively less opportunity to cultivate skills required to develop customized parts in response to an automaker's requirements, since the makers historically have completed development work themselves in-house.

U.S. automakers have recently begun to cultivate longer relationships with a select number of suppliers who take a more active role in product development. Nevertheless, the above features still remain.

In contrast, Japanese automakers have relied to a much greater extent on the capabilities of suppliers, both in cost reduction and product development. Since this has required suppliers to invest considerably in developing skills of the kind that help them meet exact customer specifications, transactions are of longer duration than in the United States.

In addition, in the case of DA parts, the drawings belong to the suppliers. This has also compelled the buyer to lengthen the duration of the transaction. Consequently, the relational contract as developed in Japan has evolved a more complex structure than in other countries and includes incentives to enhance suppliers' skill formation.

* * *

A New Business Relationship

This explanation applies to non-Japanese and Japanese firms alike. Some may ask at this point whether some features are specific to Japanese manufacturer-supplier relationships. As I noted earlier, a larger proportion of suppliers in Japan provide DA parts and are used to participating in product development from a very early stage.

Furthermore, even suppliers of DS parts are regularly asked by the buyer, before and after commercial production begins, to present ideas for improvement. The buyer also suggests possible improvement to suppliers.

In other words, communication and productive interaction between the buyer firm and its suppliers have been closer and more effective in the Japanese system. This does not stem from Japanese "cultural uniqueness," contrary to popular arguments, but is explained by historical conditions.

Japanese automakers in the 1950s and 1960s were so short of capital that they had to rely more heavily than their counterparts in other countries on the capabilities of their suppliers. This produced the know-how for initiating and sustaining productive interaction between firms throughout the development and manufacturing stages.

This know-how is worth sharing worldwide. Japanese manufacturers should try their best to use suppliers based in other countries in order to facilitate this transfer, which, in the long term, is the surest way to reduce trade friction. * * *

2. The logic of ongoing business relationships

MOTOSHIGE ITOH, INTER-ENTERPRISE RELATIONS AND ONGOING BUSINESS RELATIONSHIPS*

Nihon no Kigyō

109, 112-118, 124-126 (1989)

The essence of market transactions lies in the extreme standardization of the goods being traded and the absence of any major information gap between the buyer and seller of those goods. As a result, once a price is established, the exchange takes place in a very simple manner.

In actual transactions, however, these premises of standardization and perfect information do not pertain and simple transactions do not function well. As one example, let us consider the case of the transactions between an automotive parts maker and an automobile maker.

The parts supplied by the parts maker to the automobile maker are often highly specialized products. Even when the products themselves are not so highly specialized, when one takes into account services for research and development, shipping, and other matters, special investments relating specifically to the automobile maker are often essential. And these investments often cannot easily be utilized for other purposes. Moreover, from the automobile maker's viewpoint, once that maker has decided to purchase parts from a given parts maker, it would not be easy to shift to another parts maker if the supply of parts is cut off. In these respects, the parts maker and the automobile maker are entering into a long-term relationship.

Even in a relationship such as this, if the two companies were able to conclude and implement a perfect contract, a situation fundamentally identical to the simple market transaction could be attained. Before the contract is entered, there are a number of automobile companies that the parts maker could do business with, and there are also a number of companies that could supply parts to the automobile maker. In short, at the stage before the contract is entered, the necessary conditions for competition exist (although once the parties commence their dealings, each party will have committed to the other).

---

*From Motoshige Itoh, "Kigyōkan Kankei to Keizokuteki Torihiki" ("Inter-Enterprise Relations and Ongoing Business Relationships"), in Ken'ichi Imai and Ryūtarō Komiya, eds., *Nihon no Kigyō (The Japanese Enterprise)*, pp. 109-130 (Tokyo: University of Tokyo Press, 1989), at 112-118, 124-126 (translation by Daniel H. Foote). Reprinted by permission.

In such a case, fierce bargaining would occur at the contractual level. Once the parties have entered into the business relationship and concluded the contract, however, all that would be left would be to conduct business in accordance with the contract. Of course, various imperfections may enter into play. To the extent that the contract has covered all the possible contingencies that might arise in the future, *and* to the extent that the parties strictly observe the contract, there will be no problem whatsoever. * * *

In the real world, however, it is difficult to establish a perfect contract and even more difficult to implement one. When two companies seek to conclude a relatively long-term business relationship and conduct transactions, it is almost impossible for them to cover all the possible contingencies that may arise after the contract is entered. * * *

Even if the contract is concluded, more difficulties await in implementing it. Let us assume that a contract has been concluded and the business relationship entered. If the market for the automobile maker's cars takes a downturn, do you suppose the automobile maker will continue to observe the contract?

So long as the penalties under the contract are not too severe, the automobile maker presumably would not observe the contract. In order to force the automobile maker to obey the contract, some third party such as a court would have to enter the picture and decide whether or not the automobile maker breached the contract. * * *

Even if a court or other third party does enter the picture, though, it still is not easy to force implementation of a contract. * * * When one is dealing with a contract between enterprises that by its nature must be very detailed and technical, it is very difficult for a third party to determine whether a party is obeying the contract. At a macroeconomic level, moreover, if every such dispute between companies were taken to court, the litigation costs and the losses in production that would be sacrificed to the dispute resolution process would be great indeed.

* * * Where two or more companies undertake economic activities on the basis of a relatively long-term economic relationship, a variety of unanticipated events are bound to occur. When they do, there is no guarantee that the companies will approach them harmoniously. To the contrary, they will pursue their own respective interests. In most cases, that will result in a situation far removed from the maximization of their collective interests. * * *

Another problem resulting from the inability to maintain a business relationship very well by means of contract is that, because of attempts to foresee all such potential future troubles, the initial investment itself may be shaped in undesirable ways. * * *

For the above reasons, when two or more companies enter into a long-term relationship under circumstances of uncertainty, it is not easy for them to conduct simple transactions pursuant to contract. * * *

In the real world, how are these sorts of problems resolved? One method of resolution is to integrate the entire set of transactions into the same enterprise, as in the case of a vertical consolidation. * * *

* * * Another possible method of resolution is for completely independent enterprises to enter into transactions, but to devote great efforts to devising transactional methods and business relationships that will resolve the various types of business problems described above. It is possible to understand such approaches as cross-shareholding, exchange of personnel, establishment of complex pricing formulae, and the like from this viewpoint. The concept of the ongoing transaction is the mechanism lying behind this sort of business relationship.

The Theory of Ongoing Business Relationships

As game theory has made clear, when a business relationship is turned into an ongoing relationship, a cooperative relationship can result. Without going into great detail here, that mechanism works in essentially the following manner. If a transaction is an isolated one time transaction, each enterprise will likely act with regard only to its own temporary interest. This maximization of the individual interest of each participant will not necessarily result in the maximization of the collective interest of the enterprises engaged in the transaction. If, however, the business relationship is to continue permanently in the future, the enterprises will not necessarily act simply to maximize their respective temporary interests. * * *

* * * Using the automobile parts example, let us assume that the transaction between the parts maker and the automobile maker is not a one time deal, but rather is a relationship that will continue into the future. In that case, the parts maker and the automobile maker will not have in mind simply the current transaction; in deciding upon their behavior they both will take into consideration future transactions.

From the standpoint of the parts maker, it will compare whether to engage in conduct that will disappoint the automobile maker, thereby losing the future transactions, with whether to maintain cooperative relations and continue to do business with the automobile maker. The greater the benefit from continuing the transactions and the smaller the gain from betraying the automobile maker at the current time, the more likely the parts maker is to engage in cooperative conduct with the automobile maker.

The same circumstances exist for the automobile maker. If the automobile maker is dependent on the parts maker in a variety of ways, the automobile maker will likely maintain cooperative relations rather than betray the parts maker for a temporary gain. The automobile maker will also have business relations with numerous other parts makers. If the automobile maker betrays a number of those parts makers, it may also lose the trust of the other parts makers. This is undesirable from the standpoint of maintaining good relations over the long term. In this respect, a reputation mechanism is also at work.

If the sort of self-generating cooperation explained above is possible, it should not be necessary, even when one is entering into a long-term transaction, to prepare a detailed contract and conduct transactions in simple obedience to that document. Rather, it should be sufficient to exchange a relatively brief contract agreeing on matters up to a point, enter into a business relationship, and thereafter engage in cooperative conduct in accordance with the circumstances and in consultation with the other party. When the two sides have this sort of cooperative relationship, it is just as though they are acting in accordance with an implicit contract. * * *

* * * The ongoing business relationship has significance in various other respects, such as the accumulation and joint possession of information, diversity in methods of payment, changes in incentives for competition, and the like.

[Among other things, the] existence of an ongoing business relationship means that information concerning technology, the business environment, and other matters will be accumulated by both sides and possessed jointly by both sides. * * *

Mutually understanding information and utilizing that information in a cooperative relationship are not something that can be accomplished merely through manuals and short-term exchange of information. There is no way to accomplish this other than by spending a long period of time and accumulating information in the course of business experience. * * *

Mechanisms that Support Implied Contracts

* * * [B]enefits that cannot be obtained in the case of a simple one time transaction thus can be obtained through the use of ongoing business relationships. Ongoing business relationships do not by any means, however, just arise and continue spontaneously. To the contrary, the incentive always exists for the principals in the transaction to deviate from the ongoing business relationship. * * *

In a society with many economic entities linked only through economic relationships, there is great incentive to secede from an ongoing business relationship. If seceding from a business relationship is not subject to any penalty and a better economic opportunity arises for one of the parties, that party will presumably pursue the better opportunity. * * *

[Conversely,] one factor supporting ongoing business relationships in Japan is the existence of deep regional or societal ties underlying economic transactions. When an enterprise thinks of seceding from an ongoing business relationship, its managers and workers will presumably consider what sorts of societal penalties would be imposed after the enterprise secedes. Even if the sanctions do not go all the way to the glorified level of a "societal penalty," the people working at an enterprise have a broad variety of relationships with business partners and may be subject to a variety of penalty-like influences in those relationships. * * *

Regional and societal relationships constitute what we may refer to as noneconomic factors supporting ongoing business relationships. At the same time, economic factors supporting ongoing business relationships also exist. The first such factor is the steady economic and industrial growth Japan has experienced. [When sales and production levels are rising, opportunities for future gain take on added importance. In such a situation, there may be less incentive to engage in an act of betrayal for the purpose of temporary gain, thereby sacrificing future gains.] This factor may have had a strong influence on the strengthening of various so-called "Japanese style" business relationships during the high-growth period.

A second factor supporting the ongoing business relationship is a lack of developed external markets. Ongoing transactions are transactions among a small number of specified economic entities. When this sort of transaction occupies a substantial portion of the economy, the development of external markets is stifled. * * *

The third economic reason supporting ongoing transactions is the so-called "hostage" mechanism. In the transactional process, maintenance of ongoing transactions may be rendered easier when one side provides the other with some sort of hostage. Furthermore, there are cases where one side deliberately introduces such a hostage into the relationship precisely to achieve that sort of effect.

Let us return to the business relationship between the automobile maker and the parts maker. Assume that the parts maker undertakes an investment that is of use only for that particular automobile maker. If the parts maker were to terminate the transactions with the automobile maker, it would not achieve a sufficient return on that investment. The investment in this case is precisely a form of hostage.

* * *

Of course, it is by no means clear that a transactional relationship will function well simply because one side has handed over a hostage. In the above case, for example, the automobile maker might take advantage of the weakness afforded by the parts maker's delivery of this hostage and demand a revision of the business terms. * * *

Accordingly, for the hostage mechanism to work well in the real world it may be essential that, for example, both sides have delivered hostages to each other. Or else, as in the automobile industry, where a large number of parts suppliers are engaged in transactions with one large automobile maker, it may be necessary for there to be a reputation mechanism so that if the automobile maker breaks its promises to one parts maker, the reputation for failure will impair its relations with others. In the real world, it is common to find both of the above sorts of relationships that prevent one side from oppressing the other by taking advantage of a hostage.

Questions and Discussion Points

1. *The role of independent firms:* One thing that is crucial to understand when studying the *keiretsu* in Japan is that many firms operate independently from the *keiretsu, i.e.*, their business activities are not characterized by an unusually high level of transactions with a single grouping of firms, they do not hold shares in many firms within any given group, and their shares, if available at all, are not held in large portion by any given group. Many smaller companies are partnerships or closely held corporations owned by management and operate wholly independently of the *keiretsu*. Many large firms are also independent. Honda and Sony, for example, though both certainly have strong ongoing relationships with suppliers and subcontractors, are generally not regarded as being part of any of the *keiretsu*.

2. *Genesis of long-term relationships:* What accounts for the greater degree of ongoing business relationships in Japan than in the United States? Economic hardship in the 1950s and early 1960s, as Asanuma explains? The rapid economic growth Itoh points to?

3. *Economic efficiency and the* keiretsu: Are the *keiretsu* and ongoing business relationships inefficient anachronisms likely to end in the face of increased competition or freer trade? Some commentators suggest instead that the *keiretsu* are an advanced form of economic organization that American firms should copy. For example, a former IBM analyst has argued in the *Harvard Business Review* that U.S. and European electronics firms should form *keiretsu*, and he maps out a proposed structure of tie-ups between prominent large firms and emerging specialized companies.[4] Is he right? Should the U.S. government encourage such tie-ups?

4. *Subcontractor oppression:* The Asanuma and Itoh readings both emphasize the benefits to the manufacturer of having suppliers who are willing to make specialized investments that would be of little value to other manufacturers. Given the vast difference in size between the manufacturers and the suppliers, what protects the subcontractors against opportunistic strategies by the manufacturers?

5. Keiretsu *and foreign companies:* What difficulties do the *keiretsu* and ongoing relationships present for foreign companies seeking to do business in Japan? Might the *keiretsu* and ongoing relationships in fact offer opportunities to foreign companies? Can foreign companies become "members" of *keiretsu*?

II. Long-Term Elements in the Practices of Firms

In recent years Japanese firms have often been lauded for their management styles and in particular for having long-term orientations, while U.S. firms have been criticized for giving too much attention to quarterly profits. The practice of lifetime employment at Japanese firms has also received considerable attention. This section considers these supposed attributes of Japanese firms and how the attributes may relate to the *keiretsu*.

A. The corporate finance practice of Japanese firms

In the first selection below, a well-known Japanese economist offers a comparison between the corporate finance strategies and profitability of Japanese companies that are *keiretsu* members and those of companies that are not and argues that membership contributes to financial stability and a long-term strategic orientation. In the brief second selection, a Japanese professor argues for a distinct Japanese style of capitalism, based on control by managerial workers.

IWAO NAKATANI, THE JAPANESE FIRM IN TRANSITION*

45-53 (1988)

Japanese companies have been managed to maximize profits for their company groups. This was made possible by the decrees to democratize the economy

*From Iwao Nakatani, *The Japanese Firm in Transition* (© 1988, Asian Productivity Organization), at 45-53. Reprinted by permission of the Asian Productivity Organization. Distributed in the U.S., Canada, and Western Europe by Quality Resources, White Plains, New York 10601.

after the Second World War abolishing the capitalist class and producing a situation in which managers and employees could work together as allies. Share-issuing corporations without capitalists (investors) at the helm may be the exception worldwide, but Japanese companies maintain this situation with seemingly effortless ease—in part by maintaining large groups of companies.

Postwar Japanese company groups represent an ingenious system to provide a safety net to insure the survival of companies operated as alliances of managers and employees. This mechanism is also one of the prerequisites for Japanese-style management.

A company requires a stable supply of capital to execute its investment plans. * * * [B]ank borrowing * * * was the mainstay providing capital to Japanese companies during the rapid-growth era. Group financing, with city banks selectively financing companies in the same group, often played a central role.

Knowing this, the reader may be surprised to hear that group financing is not that big a proportion of the total supply of funds. * * * Despite its small proportion of the total, group financing is still important. First, for other suppliers of capital, membership in a group with a large city bank is the equivalent of loans being guaranteed. * * * Default is unlikely, as the group bank will provide the necessary funds to bail the company out.

Second, the group bank acts as a lender of last resort for the company. Even if the company does not borrow much from its group bank, the fact that it has a ready source of funds in an emergency is an indispensable support for the company. As such, the main bank in a group often takes on the functions of a safety net.

But why would the main bank want to act as a safety net? Why discard simple business considerations to save a company about to go belly-up? The response to these questions is found in the balancing "insurance premiums" that companies in the group pay to the main bank. * * *

[H]ow do the other companies pay the main bank for this service? * * * [First, g]roup companies rely on bank borrowings for a greater proportion of their investment funds. * * * Group companies also tend to maintain a large and stable debt with their main banks. When, for example, the enterprise has surplus funds and money is not tight, it does not repay its loan from the main bank but keeps the outstanding debt at a stable level. * * * Maintaining a higher debt level than justified to maximize profits may be seen as the premium the group companies pay their main bank. Likewise, the failure to repay the main bank in periods of easy money is confirmation of this debt's function as an insurance premium.

[Secondly, i]nterest rates fluctuate less for group companies than for non-group companies. * * * The main bank and group companies maintain a long-term client relationship. More concretely, the interest rates paid to the main bank by the company in periods of easy money, when interest rates generally fall, were somewhat higher than the market rates. Even when it would be possible to borrow cheaper in the market, the company dutifully maintained "obligatory borrowings" at the main bank. Conversely, interest rates generally rise when money becomes tight, but here the main bank maintains lower interest rates for group companies. * * *

What is the significance of the close relationship between the major city banks and group companies? The most significant feature is the Balkanized capital market. The main bank has easy access to information on the group companies and supplies capital preferentially to these companies. This is the main reason for the higher debt ratios of the group companies and their lower ratio of net worth to total capital. When this is the situation, it becomes obvious that the stock market is not the main provider of funds for these companies. * * *

Under these conditions, companies in groups (each group centered on a major bank) rely on capital supplied by the group, and there is a relatively low dependence on outside capital (particularly the stock market). Recently, major companies have been relying less on the main bank as Japanese capital markets have internationalized, but the pattern still holds. As a result of increasing cross-holdings and group financing, the regular capital markets have been Balkanized and mini-markets centered on enterprise groups have been created to serve the group members. * * *

Japanese companies are managed somewhat like communities, without influence from the investors. This has become possible only because of the peculiar company group with its cross-holdings and group finance. If managers did not support each other through cross-holdings and there was no way to provide operating capital without going hat-in-hand to investors, Japanese corporate management would have become very straightforwardly capitalist. The company would then have had to rely on the regular capital markets to supply capital, and management would have had to follow the dictates of the market. * * *

[Instead, Japanese] companies in a company group can be supplied with capital from the group's own mini-market and have their operational plans approved within the group. This leaves the company with a high degree of independence and frees it from the need to maximize profits. Compared with a non-group company that is subject to direct supervision by the capital markets, the group company has a greater degree of operational freedom and can pursue profits for its community-like organization. * * * At the group company, where investor influence is weak, it is enough to pay the going rate of return on the capital, or as much as is generally acceptable, and the remaining profit can then be distributed among the parties that are involved with the enterprise. * * *

[Finally, stable growth is very important for group companies.] Lifetime employment is an imperative at the group company, and as the transfer of workers between enterprises is a limited option, it becomes obvious that employees have a strong interest in stabilizing and improving their own company's performance. Nobody wants upsets that may result in unnecessary fluctuations in salaries and employment. It is the same for managers. Their status improves if there is a solid record of strong performance. * * *

[Thus,] the very strong company-community-oriented Japanese management environment may be explained by the presence of company groups centered on the major city banks. Japanese management would probably be untenable otherwise.

TADANORI NISHIYAMA, THE STRUCTURE OF ENTERPRISE CONTROL IN MODERN JAPAN*

63-65 (1980)

In capitalistic society the enterprise belongs to the shareholders, and since one can freely buy and sell the shares of a company, the "takeover artist" represents the essence of capitalism. Judging from the logic of capital, Japanese managers, who hate takeover artists and are prejudiced against takeover bids, seem like parasites who view the company as their own private property. If one assumes, however, that Japan is not a capitalistic society, so there is no need to adhere to the logic of capital, things look much different and can be explained clearly. In Japan, enterprises do not belong to the shareholders, but rather belong to the employees and workers, including management. Accordingly, for someone in the mere status of shareholder to seek to usurp the managerial authority of existing managers represents a preposterous antisocial act. This fact proves that Japanese society has no connection at all to capitalistic society of the sort found in the United States. * * *

The control by managers as the managerial structure of present-day Japanese enterprises is, put more bluntly, "control by managerial workers" and represents the establishment of one form of bureaucracy. Expressed in a somewhat different fashion, this signifies the collapse of capitalistic society and the establishment of managerial society. * * * Since this "control by workers" depends largely upon the capital of others—especially lendings from banks, the enterprises will shift to control by creditors if results deteriorate. In that case, the "control by creditors" will mean control by banks. We find, however, that those banks in turn are under "control by workers" who are also dependent upon the capital of others, namely, the deposits of depositors. This thus constitutes complete control by managerial workers in which one cannot find a single sign of capitalists.

If we go further and examine the share capital of banks and of those enterprises with relatively high equity levels, we find that those entities are dependent on life insurance companies. And almost all of those life insurance companies are mutual companies rather than stock companies. Accordingly, they have neither capital raised from capitalists nor capital under the control of capitalists; rather, the capital for these life insurance companies comes from the premiums of contract holders. Here again we find complete control by managerial workers.

B. Lifetime employment and seniority-based advancement

The following selection describes the systems of lifetime employment and seniority-based advancement, which, along with company unions, are frequently referred to as the "three pillars" of Japanese labor practices. Lifetime employment

*From Tadanori Nishiyama, *Shihai Kōzō Ron* (*The Structure of Enterprise Control in Modern Japan*), at 63-65 (Tokyo: Bunshindō, 1980) (translation by Daniel H. Foote). Reprinted by permission.

and seniority-based advancement do not apply to all workers in Japan. As the selection notes, these features are the norm for regular employees (as opposed to part-time and temporary employees) at large Japanese companies, but it has been estimated that those covered by these systems account for no more than 25-30 percent of the total workforce in Japan.

Nonetheless, many observers argue that the systems of lifetime employment and seniority-based advancement exert strong influence over a much broader range of Japanese companies, for they are widely regarded as the ideals for which small and medium-sized companies should also strive, although economic realities may prevent their full realization. Thus, these systems affect the attitudes many Japanese have toward employment.

The notion of long-term relationships embodied in lifetime employment may constitute an important barrier for foreign companies seeking to recruit skilled Japanese employees. In many industries, these skilled employees are precisely the sorts of workers most likely to be sought by large Japanese companies offering long-term job security and stable prospects for advancement.

KEN'ICHI IMAI AND RYŪTARŌ KOMIYA, CHARACTERISTICS OF THE JAPANESE ENTERPRISE*

Nihon no Kigyō

3, 4-7 (1989)

In their employment practices, large Japanese enterprises are characterized by the systems of lifetime employment and seniority-based advancement. * * * We believe that these features are tied to the strong growth orientation of Japanese firms. * * * Under the systems of lifetime employment and seniority-based advancement, rapid growth is advantageous for people working at the firm, since it provides them with opportunities for promotions and pay increases, as well as prospects for obtaining new jobs at related companies after retirement. Accordingly, strong pressure for growth arises from within the enterprise. On the other hand, in order to engage in continuous technological innovation and maintain growth, it is essential, for reasons we will turn to next, to develop human resources within the enterprise through the systems of lifetime employment and seniority-based advancement and to build up learning and problem-solving abilities. These two aspects are interrelated synergistically and together have produced the dynamic quality of the Japanese firm.

Large firms in present-day Japan are somewhat different from the classical image of a firm in which the capitalist or the person who has provided the capital employs workers and seeks to maximize the return on capital. It is more appropriate to understand the large Japanese firm as "an organized body in one specific field of

*From Ken'ichi Imai and Ryūtarō Komiya, "Nihonkigyō no Tokuchō" ("Characteristics of the Japanese Enterprise"), in Ken'ichi Imai and Ryūtarō Komiya, eds., *Nihon no Kigyō* (*The Japanese Enterprise*), pp. 3-26 (Tokyo: University of Tokyo Press, 1989), at 4-7 (translation by Daniel H. Foote). Reprinted by permission.

business that is composed of managers who have accumulated management ability, technicians, skilled workers, and persons in charge of clerical and business matters." It is not simply a collection of labor inputs hired with capital, but is instead an accumulation of "human capital" possessing the above-described abilities. Furthermore, the separation of ownership from control is probably more advanced in Japan's big business sector than in any other developed nation in the world. Shareholders have little voice or influence, and Japanese managers hold a strong role as representatives of these "human organizations."

Lifetime employment * * *

The system of lifetime employment consists of the customary practice by which an enterprise will not, at the enterprise's convenience, terminate or lay off an employee who has been hired as a "regular" employee unless the enterprise has experienced extraordinary business difficulties. The employment of "regular" employees means the process of widely advertising for new graduates from high school, college, etc., and hiring them as permanent employees. Temporary workers, part-time workers, and other such workers hired on a temporary basis are not included in the term "regular" employees, nor are workers who have been dispatched from other companies. (In some cases, though, temporary workers may be elevated to "regular" status if they satisfy certain conditions.)

Although referred to as "lifetime employment," this system does not really mean that an employee will be employed at one enterprise right up until his or her death. For general employees, enterprises have adopted a retirement age of between 55 and 60. Among relatively young workers, especially those in their twenties, there are also quite a few cases in which workers voluntarily quit one company and switch to another.

It is difficult to explain the legal nature of lifetime employment in any simple fashion, and we suspect that this system is rather difficult for foreigners to understand. It is not as though a clear written contract exists guaranteeing employment through retirement age. If an enterprise terminates a "regular" employee without an "appropriate" reason, however, the terminated employee may sue for relief in the local Labor Relations Commission or in court, and enterprises have been ordered to withdraw the termination and provide employees with continued employment.

Recently it has been said that white collar employees at certain leading companies in the United States and Europe are in effect close to being employed for life; and in its broad sense the lifetime employment system may not be unique to Japan. Comparative international research on this point remains a task for the future. Moreover, the extent to which this lifetime employment system has eroded in recent years and the question of how that system will change in the future are both open to great debate.

The traditional lifetime employment system, however, represents the employment pattern at the great majority of large Japanese enterprises. It is an uncontroversial fact, moreover, that the concept of lifetime employment remains widely held as the commonly accepted view among those seeking work at firms and those currently working at firms, and among the employers, as well.

In short, this means that the firms will seek to avoid firing regular employees except in extreme circumstances. Even when reductions in personnel prove unavoidable because of technological innovation, changes in industrial structure, or the like, the normal practice is for a firm first to seek to transfer regular employees to subsidiaries or related companies and thereafter to seek voluntary resignations by offering special retirement bonuses; only if over-employment still exists at that point will the firm normally undertake so-called "designated termination."

* * *

[Seniority-based advancement]

Under the system of seniority-based advancement, "regular" employees receive raises and promotions at fixed intervals. It is wrong, however, to assume that the seniority-based advancement system means that salaries and positions are determined mechanically in accordance with age. For a time after they enter the company, employees with the same academic background and years of experience will receive nearly identical raises in their base pay and bonuses and nearly identical job promotions. After a time, however, differences will arise in their base pay, bonuses and job rankings based on evaluations of their job performance and ability. In the case of white collar workers, after about the age of forty tough choices are made in determining who will be appointed to positions such as department head and section head. Moreover, even though there are many different posts labeled "section head," for example, there are great differences among those posts; some are very good positions, some not so good, some are cushy, others very demanding, and so on. From immediately after people enter the company, fierce competition begins among employees of the same age cohort with an eye toward future advancement. Nevertheless, while such tough choices and fierce competition may exist, the enterprise itself seeks to improve the abilities of every employee equally and to decide on promotions in accordance with evaluations that most people will recognize as fair. These decisions on promotions are made on the basis of evaluations resulting from competition over the long term; many people will have participated in those evaluations, and care is taken so that the evaluations are made as fairly as possible on the basis of each employee's ability over the broad range of work and so that the persons affected will accept the results of the evaluations.

The seniority-based advancement system at Japanese enterprises is very closely linked with internal policies for improvement of ability and employee development. In the typical pattern of personnel policies at firms in the United States and Europe, periodic pay raises, promotions, and reassignments are almost never carried out. Rather, personnel are hired as necessary from the external labor market, or else appropriate persons are identified from within the company and promoted without regard to seniority. Thus, the pattern in the United States and Europe is fundamentally different from the personnel policies at Japanese firms.

The manner of appointment of managers at Japanese enterprises constitutes an extension of this seniority-based advancement system. Most of the managers of large Japanese enterprises—by this, we refer to the directors, managing directors, senior managing directors, vice presidents, and presidents (as well as chairmen)—are chosen from among employees who entered the company directly after graduation from school and progressed steadily up the ladder of seniority-based advancement. And at most large enterprises the custom is for the president, who is ordinarily the highest-ranking officer, to designate a successor. At certain major American enterprises, including GE, Exxon, IBM, and Texas Instruments, it is the custom for the president to be chosen from among long-term employees; but it is probably safe to say that the pattern in which nearly all the managers, including the president, are promoted from among long-term employees and each president chooses the successor represents a custom that is unique to Japan. As a result of these above-described customs of lifetime employment, seniority-based advancement, and the appointment of executives and presidents, the managerial ranks at large Japanese enterprises bear the deep hue of representatives of the employees.

Note

Responsiveness to shareholders in Japan and the U.S.: Nakatani and Nishiyama assume that dependence of U.S. corporations on financing through the stock market has ensured that those corporations are sensitive to the wishes of stockholders and gear their activities toward maximization of the interests of stockholders. In contrast, they seem to assume that there are few such capital market-based checks on the activities of Japanese corporations, which depend more heavily on debt financing and which, in their view, are more responsive to the interests of employees.

In an article in the *Harvard Business Review* (Sept.-Oct. 1989) entitled "Eclipse of the Public Corporation," Professor Michael C. Jensen has taken issue with both of these assumptions. He argues that, with the wide dispersal of shares, most large U.S. publicly traded corporations need not be particularly responsive to the views of stockholders and that, while Japanese corporations may not be tightly constrained by shareholders, they traditionally have been subject to rather close oversight by the main bank and other large lenders. From this perspective, he concludes that leveraged buyouts (LBOs) in the United States may place the bought-out company in a position similar to that of the traditional Japanese corporation—subject to close ongoing oversight by a small and clearly defined group of individuals at the LBO fund. In contrast, he argues, Japan is going in the opposite direction:

> Ironically, even as more U.S. companies come to resemble Japanese companies, Japan's public companies are becoming more like U.S. companies of 15 years ago. Japanese shareholders have seldom had any power. The banks' chief disciplinary tool, their power to withhold capital from high-growth, cash starved companies, has been vastly reduced as a result of several factors. Japan's victories in world product markets have left its companies awash in profits. The development of domestic and international capital markets has created ready alternatives to bank loans, while deregulation has liberalized corporate access to these funds. Finally, new legal constraints prevent banks from holding more than

> 5% of the equity of any company, which reduces their incentive to engage in active monitoring. * * *
>
> In short, Japanese managers are increasingly unconstrained and unmonitored. They face no effective internal controls, little control from the product markets their companies already dominate, and fewer controls from the banking system because of self-financing, direct access to capital markets, and lower debt ratios. Unless shareholders and creditors discover ways to prohibit their managers from behaving like U.S. managers, Japanese companies will make uneconomic acquisitions and diversification moves, generate internal waste, and engage in other value-destroying activities. The long-term result will be the growth of bureaucracy and inefficiency and the demise of product quality and organizational responsiveness—until the waste becomes so severe that it triggers a market for corporate control to remedy the excesses.[5]

Given the bursting of Japan's so-called "bubble economy" in the early 1990s and the subsequent recession, was Professor Jensen prescient?

III. The Distribution System

In recent years Japan's distribution system has been the focus of much commentary in the foreign media. The system is often criticized not only for being inefficient, but also for being inefficient in ways that make it harder for foreign companies to do business in Japan. In the survey of foreign executives excerpted in Chapter 1, the complexity of the distribution system was one of the items mentioned most often as a barrier to the Japanese market. The following selections examine the organization of the distribution system and then explore a particular law that has helped shape its characteristics.

A. Overview

The first selection provides a description of some basic features of the distribution system from the perspective of an American businessman with several years of experience doing business in Japan.

MARK A. ZIMMERMAN, HOW TO DO BUSINESS WITH THE JAPANESE: A STRATEGY FOR SUCCESS*

134-140 (1985)

The Japanese distribution system is one of the most complicated jigsaw puzzles ever contrived by human beings, and is the most dramatic difference between our

*From Mark A. Zimmerman, *How to Do Business with the Japanese: A Strategy for Success* (Tokyo: Charles E. Tuttle, 1985), at 134-140. Reprinted by permission.

way and their way of doing business. The system is tightly controlled. A product ends up in the consumer's hands only after it has passed through a distribution chain consisting of at least two and sometimes as many as five layers of wholesalers before landing on the retailer's shelf. Each layer (primary, secondary, tertiary wholesalers, etc.) adds a margin. A typical flowchart of a distribution channel for a product from a Japanese consumer-products company would look like [Figure 3-1]. The product moves from the factory to the sales company, which is a wholly owned subsidiary of the company that manufactures the product, but has usually been kept separate. * * *

The next layer (Layer One) is the large wholesaler or institutional customer and the small wholesaler who will take the product out to the secondary wholesalers and the hundreds of thousands of mom-and-pop shops throughout Japan. The large general wholesalers will be the most efficient channel, as they usually sell directly to large retailers, such as the Daiei and Seiyu Supermarket chains, who in turn sell to the consumer at a much lower price than can be found in the corner stores that have to buy their products from a secondary wholesaler. By the time the product passes through Layer Two (the secondary wholesalers) and into Layer Three (the retailers) it has acquired an additional cost of 50 to 60 percent. With a factory price of $1.00, a product will cost about $1.50 to $1.60 at the retail (small shop) level. This compares with $1.30 in the United States for a non-food product and as low as $1.10 for a food product. Finally the product reaches the retail shelf. Occasionally it doesn't sell and the retailer decides he wants to return it. Unless the Japanese company is very strong and has a definite policy against it, the shopkeeper can usually return the item to the sales company and get full credit. It will then pass back up through the system, and eventually returns to the factory for repackaging and resale or destruction.

In the field of nondurable consumer products (over-the-counter drugs, toiletries and the like), the Japanese strive to maintain retail prices at the same level in all classes of trade. The concept of *wa* (harmony) prevails even in the arena of marketing policy. In the United States the Robinson-Patman Act would prevent this covert price fixing, but in Japan retailers who break the price line are often boycotted by manufacturers. They are regarded as untrustworthy, and wholesalers and manufacturers alike treat them as pariahs for violating the sacred code of retail-price maintenance. There may be minor differences between the prices of toiletries in pharmacies as compared with those in supermarkets, but this is the exception rather than the rule. * * * To be sure, price control for cameras and electronic consumer goods has broken down, but this has occurred only recently, since the pressure of the discounters in Tokyo's low-price shopping areas (Akihabara and Shinjuku) has forced the issue. * * *

Another key aspect of the Japanese distribution system is the use of exclusive distributors and the way credit is used (the infamous "P note," or promissory note) to make it even easier for each level to buy, and even more expensive for the consumer in the long run. Essentially, the system cannot adjust to serving two masters. A large general wholesaler of consumer goods usually has a showroom on the ground floor decked out like a model store, and there one can see the merchandise beautifully displayed. There may be more than one brand on display, and the casual observer may assume that the situation is the same as in the West, where multibrand distributors are the norm. In fact, each distributor is a dedicated and exclusive wholesaler for one manufacturer in each product category, and he will not push (even though he may carry) any brand other than the exclusive one that he is contractually committed to sell aggressively. Japanese businessmen are amazed by the American or British system of grocery wholesalers who carry all the brands of each product that is selling well. In Japan such a practice would be a violation of the loyalty (*giri*) that the wholesaler has to the manufacturer.

This [exclusive distribution system] is also true of the appliance shop. The customer who walks into a Curry's in England, for example, or a J.C. Penney's in the United States, will find every major brand of appliance displayed, and there will usually be salespeople to explain and demonstrate any brand of merchandise. Not so in Japan, where the consumer must visit ten shops to see ten brands. It is possible to see different brands displayed in department stores, but they can't compete with the one-brand shops in certain product categories (for example, electronic goods), where the manufacturers have built up chains of exclusive distributors. The department stores will not even have people trained to demonstrate such merchandise, since the manufacturers refuse to cooperate with non-exclusive distributors. The Japanese think the Western way of selling very strange. They find it difficult to accept the fact that a Toyota dealer can give equal emphasis to Volkswagen or Chevrolet. To them a distributor is worth working with only if he is totally committed to their company's line of products.

In addition to being exclusive, the Japanese wholesaler acts as a sort of finance company for the retailers that buy from him. Similarly, the manufacturer is expected to finance the wholesaler. Normal terms between a Japanese manufacturer and his key wholesalers are six months, with a promissory note exchanged at an interval of forty-five to ninety days after the sale has taken place. This "P note" can be discounted at the bank and the manufacturer will have the cash flow after ninety days, but discounting is usually an additional five to six percent off the invoice (factory price) value.

The key lesson about how the distribution system operates is that the Japanese manufacturer is conditioned to a market situation where he has a network of some fifty to five hundred primary wholesalers who are exclusively his. Their livelihood depends on his ability to continue to provide products that will compete successfully against rival chains of distributors. The distribution network is therefore an extension of the company itself, and is of primary concern to the Japanese manufacturing company. * * *

It would be difficult for any company, domestic or foreign, to ignore or bypass any layer in the Japanese distribution system. Procter & Gamble made a major commitment to the Japanese market in the mid-seventies, and it took them years to build a solid and cooperative network of primary wholesalers and distributors. They were not used to paying so much attention to the distribution network because in the United States and most other markets it is expected that the multiproduct distributor will go where the action is. In short, the marketplace will dictate the behavior of a distributor in other countries. In Japan the marketplace is important and decisive in the long run, but in the short run—and this can be five to ten years—the importance of the exclusive network is even greater. * * *

Although it looks as though exclusivity is here to stay, some aspects of the traditional distribution system in Japan are under attack. For example, the traditional corner grocery stores are threatened by the rapid growth of supermarkets. To meet the new demands created by the steep rise in quantity and variety of consumer products being sold, many innovative ideas have found a place in the system. It is important to remember, therefore, that the distribution system is, in the words of a study put out by McKinsey & Co. for the United States-Japan Trade Study Group, "undergoing a major evolution. Opportunities to participate and accelerate are available to both entrepreneurial Japanese and American corporations."

- - - - - - - - - -

Figure 3-1

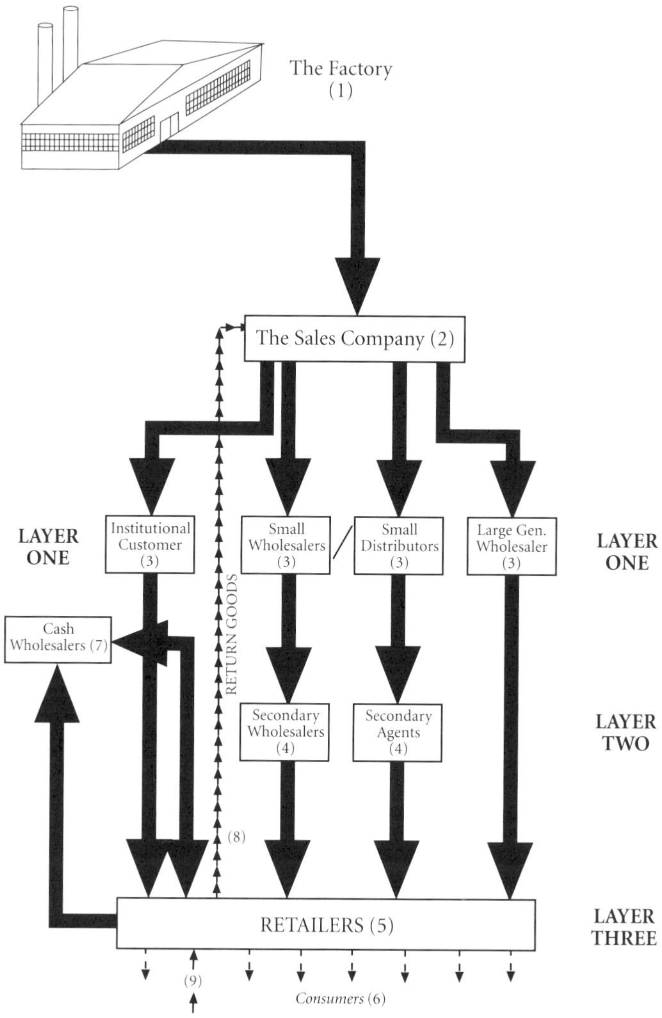
The Factory
(1)
The Sales Company (2)
RETURN GOODS
LAYER
ONE
Institutional
Customer
(3)
Small
Wholesalers
(3)
Small
Distributors
(3)
Large Gen.
Wholesaler
(3)
LAYER
ONE
Cash
Wholesalers (7)
Secondary
Wholesalers
(4)
Secondary
Agents
(4)
LAYER
TWO
(8)
RETAILERS (5)
LAYER
THREE
(9)
Consumers (6)

The next selection and the table that follows it provide further details concerning Japan's distribution system and the extraordinary number of very small retailers in Japan.

FRANK UPHAM, PRIVATIZING REGULATION: THE IMPLEMENTATION OF THE LARGE-SCALE RETAIL STORES LAW*

Political Dynamics in Contemporary Japan
264, 265-267 (1993)

Whatever its long term social and economic contribution to Japanese social welfare, Japan's distribution system in the 1980s was woefully inefficient by conventional economic measures * * *. In its "Cost of Living '88" report, [Japan's] Economic Planning Agency (EPA) estimated that the cost of living in Tokyo was 97 percent higher than in New York and traced part of the cause to the distribution system * * *. The EPA also estimated that 40 percent of the retail price of domestic goods and 59 percent of [that of] imported goods were attributable to distribution costs and that 30 percent of the savings theoretically achievable by the rise of the value of the yen in the two years between October 1985 and December 1987 was absorbed by the distribution sector rather than passed on to the consumer.

Part of this inefficiency was produced by a complex wholesale network. In the early 1980s, for example, the number of employees per wholesale store was the lowest in surveyed countries, and in one EPA survey the ratio of the value of wholesale to retail sales was more than double that of any other country. These figures portray a wholesale industry dominated by large numbers of small firms, each of which added to the product's price while adding little to its value.

But high distribution costs were also attributable to the inefficiency of Japanese retailing. In 1982, for example, the number of retail stores per capita was 75 percent higher in Japan than in the United States, the next highest country, and the value added per employee was 28 percent less. Stores with only one or two employees accounted for 60 percent of all stores and yet generated less than 14 percent of all sales. * * *

Many factors contributed to the structure of Japanese distribution networks. Historically, Japanese manufacturers had been heavily involved in all levels of the distribution chain and had been able to dominate a system that has often been described according to production estimates more than consumer desires. Manufacturers guaranteed their distributors' margins and, in turn, received price stability. The result was a system largely organized along *keiretsu* (affiliated enterprise) lines in which long-term relationships and uniform and inflexible pricing reduced

*From Frank Upham, "Privatizing Regulation: The Implementation of the Large-Scale Retail Stores Law," in *Political Dynamics in Contemporary Japan*, pp. 264-294 (Gary D. Allinson and Yasunori Sone, eds., Ithaca: Cornell University Press, 1993), at 265-267.

bargaining and other transaction costs and provided an effective barrier to both non-*keiretsu* consumer goods and new entrants into the industry, including foreign entrants. One reason this system worked, one is told, is that Japanese consumers emphasized quality and service more than price in consumption decisions. Uniform prices, therefore, were not a major source of concern. Another reason, however, was the effectiveness of government intervention to favor both manufacturers and merchants more than consumers, as represented by the Large-Scale Retail Stores Law and its predecessors dating back to the 1930s.

\- - - - - - - - - -

Table 3-2: Number of Retailers by Number of Employees (1988)*
(Excluding restaurants)

No. of employees	No. of retailers	Composition ratio (%)	Increase ratio 1988/1985(%)
1-2	874,377	54.0	–7.0
3-4	422,067	26.1	3.4
5-9	214,046	13.2	12.4
10-19	70,394	4.3	21.6
20-29	19,186	1.2	25.1
30-49	12,250	0.8	22.1
50-99	5,362	0.3	12.6
Over 100	2,070	0.1	5.7
Total	1,619,752	100.0	–0.5

Source: Census of Commerce, MITI.

B. Manufacturers' distribution networks

The discussion of vertical *keiretsu* in Section I of this chapter focused on the production side of the manufacturing sector. As the preceding selections reflect, however, *keiretsu* structures also exist on the distribution side, in the form of exclusive networks of small retailers controlled by major manufacturers. The two newspaper articles that follow give some further flavor to the operation of such distribution *keiretsu* and help in understanding the concerns of foreign businesses.

ELECTRONIC FIRMS AIM TO KEEP KEIRETSU**

The Japan Economic Journal
3 (June 2, 1990)

Japanese home appliance manufacturers did not come to worldwide domi-

*From Japanese External Trade Organization, *The Japanese Market: A Compendium of Information for the Prospective Exporter* (Tokyo: JETRO, 1990), at 73. Reprinted by permission.
**From "Electronic Firms Aim to Keep *Keiretsu*," *The Japan Economic Journal* (now *The Nikkei Weekly*), June 2, 1990, at 3. Reprinted by permission.

nance by dint of innovative technology and high quality alone. They also got a big boost from a nurturing domestic market. For industry leader Matsushita Electric Industrial Co., for example, its 25% share of the domestic refrigerator market is supported by 24,000 "National" shops that sell nothing but its National and Panasonic products.

In exchange for special rebates and other remuneration, these *keiretsu* shop proprietors also promise to sell Matsushita goods at the manufacturer's suggested prices. Other leading manufacturers, such as Hitachi Ltd. and Toshiba Corp., maintain similar *keiretsu* distribution networks in the ¥6.25 trillion domestic home appliance market.

Useful as the outlets have proven to ensuring domestic profit margins and market shares, they are now facing affronts from several quarters. To outsiders, namely the U.S., the *keiretsu* have come under fire for allegedly exclusive cross-shareholding, but there is now concern the barbs will be directed at their *keiretsu* retail networks of 63,000 exclusive shops.

Such worries were exacerbated in April [1990] when Matsushita called a press conference to deny reported plans to alter its *keiretsu* retail system for fear of a U.S. backlash. In defending the *keiretsu* shops, Matsushita Vice President Shoji Sakuma said the home appliance industry's retail practices are not exclusive because they are an inherited sales method established by the Japanese industry.

Market forces

Whether or not the U.S. buys that logic or presses the issue further, liberalization of Japan's distribution is putting *keiretsu* retailers under increasing pressure and conjuring up strong ambivalence among manufacturers about how much support to provide them. "If you have *keiretsu* shops, you can take leadership in pricing the market against discounters and you can make a solid production projection," says Matsushita spokesman Akinori Kimura.

On the other hand, huge networks of mom-and-pop shops are inherently inefficient and increasingly burdensome to manufacturers. That cost has been especially troubling since the sharp appreciation of the yen from 1985 re-focused attention on the home market.

In addition to an average 25% sales margin, Matsushita *keiretsu* shops enjoy higher rebates than independent retailers. Moreover, Matsushita maintains unique financial reserves for dealer business development and dividend payments. "I guess the company is obliged to pay several billion yen to dealers every year," calculates Tatsuo Taki, a National shop-owner in Gifu Prefecture.

Another problem for the manufacturers is that the sophistication of products is beginning to outgrow that of *keiretsu* proprietors. Most shopowners are now over 60 years old and have a tough time keeping up with new technology. In addition, consumers are demanding greater diversification than even the largest manufacturers can offer alone. "Even home appliance stores cannot appeal to consumers with just one company's brand," says Hitachi's spokesman Takeshi Okamoto. In response, Hitachi now allows its 9,000 *keiretsu* shops to chalk up about 20% of their sales from other manufacturers' products.

Changing market

Even with such changes, the market appears to be moving inevitably away from *keiretsu* shops toward more efficient, price-competitive large-scale retailing. Over the past decade that trend became apparent in the decline of *keiretsu* home appliance sales to 40% from 60% of the domestic market. For Matsushita, more than 50% of home appliance products are still sold through its National shops, and the company sees its large retail network as a key to holding market share.

At the same time, large independent retailers have gained considerable clout over the past five years, while buying in bulk and requiring much less hand-holding from manufacturers. As such outlets gained market share, manufacturers have vied for room on their shelves by upping rebates even higher than accorded *keiretsu* shops, says Akira Takemura, chairman of the Electrical Products Retailers Association.

Recently, however, manufacturers have begun to have second thoughts. Most of all, they fear the independents will gain too much leverage and erode their price-setting power. "If such retailers become very powerful, manufacturers will be impoverished by harsh price competition as in the U.S.," says Tomoo Shimizu, executive director of the Nippon Electric Big-Stores Association. Even some *keiretsu* shops have defected from the manufacturers to join retail franchisers, claiming they offer better sales support.

The dependence of manufacturers on *keiretsu* shops and reluctance to hand over too much power to large retailers are likely to keep the smaller outlets up and running for some time to come. Toshiba and Hitachi, for example, recently reduced rebates to large retailers. Although Toshiba suffered a decrease in sales last spring as a result when retailers turned to hawking other companies' items, the company claims the trade-off was worthwhile. "We decided to implement the new rebate plan even if we would lose our market share because we believed it would help us in the long run," says Toshiba's senior manager of consumer products marketing, Kazuhiro Ohe.

For its part, Matsushita is trying to breathe new life into its *keiretsu* retailers by upgrading their operations with new appliances. It has a pilot project of 100 "Human Shop" outlets up and running with entirely revamped layouts.

2 FIRMS STILL A-FEUDIN' AFTER ALL THESE YEARS*

The Daily Yomiuri

8 (July 24, 1990)

It has been 26 years since Matsushita Electric Industrial Co. stopped supplying its products to Daiei, Inc., the largest supermarket chain in Japan.

In 1964, Daiei sold Matsushita products at a 20 percent discount, ignoring Matsushita's request not to cut more than 15 percent off the suggested retail price.

*From "2 Firms Still A-feudin' After All These Years," *The Daily Yomiuri*, July 24, 1990, at 8. Reprinted by permission.

Konosuke Matsushita, the founder of Matsushita Electric, believed that retailers should sell at a certain price level in order to secure an appropriate profit, even when the products were mass-produced and supplied at low prices. This philosophy clashed with that of Isao Nakauchi, president of Daiei, who wanted to sell as cheaply as possible and destroy the conventional pricing system.

Daiei began trying to mend fences immediately after Konosuke Matsushita's death last year. At Matsushita's funeral in Osaka on April 30, 1989, Nakauchi told Matsushita officials that he wanted to resume business with the company by year's end. His proposal was flatly rejected.

Daiei's next approach took place in June after the U.S.-Japan Structural Impediments Initiative talks in Tokyo, when the Fair Trade Commission compiled guidelines for the Antimonopoly Law, saying that suspension of business because of underselling is illegal. Nakauchi again told reporters that he hoped to resume negotiations with Matsushita.

Matsushita again refused, saying the lack of relationship between the two companies would not violate the Antimonopoly Law because Matsushita had not done business with Daiei for many years.

An International Trade and Industry Ministry official said the ministry has no intention of offering to mediate because it could be interpreted as administrative intervention.

Since Matsushita is the only maker not supplying Daiei, consumers' rights are not infringed upon. In fact, Daiei now sells Matsushita products without dealing directly with Matsushita. Industry sources say that Daiei sales of Matsushita products are estimated at ¥30 billion annually, but that profits are slim because of margins paid to middlemen.

In the past 20 years the environment surrounding the two companies has greatly changed. Daiei, whose organization has grown to gigantic proportions, is said to have reached the limits of the cut-price strategy. Matsushita also faces an urgent need to restructure its nationwide network of outlets.

It is doubtful how long Matsushita can close its doors to Daiei while the United States demands that Japan change every part of its distribution system and big U.S. shops are eager to join the competition.

[**Note:** In March 1992 Matsushita Electric announced plans to reorganize its distribution system and disband the National shop network, replacing it with a new network, called the Mast network, consisting of far fewer shops and concentrated on medium-sized and larger outlets. A simplified rebate system is also being adopted. These moves are in part a response to Fair Trade Commission guidelines and foreign pressures, but some observers see them as a response to market pressures cloaked under the guise of a response to international pressures.]

Questions and Discussion Points

1. *Economic rationale for the distribution system:* What holds the distribution system together? What is in it for manufacturers, wholesalers, and retailers? Consumers?

2. *Role of law:* What, if anything, is the role of law in maintaining this system? Is this the sort of issue that can be easily influenced through legal reform, or is the distribution system so rooted in established practices and societal attitudes as to resist change? Consider the role of law as you read the following selections concerning the Retail Stores Act.

C. Law and the distribution system: The Retail Stores Act

In Japan numerous laws and government policies protect small and medium enterprises. Examples are the Liquor Tax Act, which imposes a licensing system for liquor retailers that has been used to limit strictly their supply (in the interest of protecting existing small retailers rather than in promoting temperance), and the provision of low-interest loans through the Small Business Finance Corporation. Another law protecting small and medium enterprises that has attracted great attention is the Large-Scale Retail Stores Act (the Retail Stores Act). The following section examines the Retail Stores Act and U.S. Government objections to it in more depth. This examination also introduces the concept of administrative guidance, the primary topic of Chapter 4.

1. Outline and operation of the law

SURVEY: OVER 1,190 LARGE STORE APPLICATIONS AWAITING APPROVAL*

The Daily Yomiuri

3 (April 6, 1990)

A total of 1,195 large store applications are currently being processed under the Large-Scale Retail Stores Law in Japan * * *, of which the longest running application has been in train for 10 years and four months. * * *

The law, which has become the chief focus of the Japan-U.S. Structural Impediments Initiative talks, requires retailers who wish to open large stores to seek approval for the move from local shopowners. Adamant opposition from these merchants appears to prolong the application process indefinitely, analysts said. The main reasons given by local shopowners for opposing the opening of large retail stores were "loss of customers" and "fear of being forced to close down." A number of local community assemblies dominated by local shopowners have already passed resolutions opposing revision or abolition of the Large-Scale Retail Stores Law. * * *

One supermarket industry executive has said that it usually takes three to five years from the announcement of intention to build a new store to the actual open-

*From "Survey: Over 1,190 Large Store Applications Awaiting Approval," *The Daily Yomiuri*, April 6, 1990, at 3. Reprinted by permission.

ing date. The survey revealed, however, that store applications take more than five years to complete in 32 of Japan's 48 prefectures. The longest application process ever, by Nichii Co. in Isawa, Yamanashi-ken, took 12 years and eight months. * * *

The longest running application at present is one by Jusco Co. in Takamatsu. The company presented its application in December 1979. Local storeowners finally granted permission to open on March 6 of this year, a waiting period of 10 years and three months from the original application date, but only on condition that the proposed store's floor space be reduced by half. Jusco has yet to respond to this demand, and the store's opening appears likely to be delayed still further.

In Shizuoka, four members of the local shopowners' association were arrested after invading a meeting of the Shizuoka Chamber of Commerce and Industry, which was considering an application for a new Ito Yokado store. Since that incident, the city has revised its large store ordinances to make it virtually impossible for a new large store to open.

In addition, the Osaka city assembly and the Kanagawa prefectural assembly have recently passed resolutions opposing abolition or relaxation of the Large-Scale Retail Stores Law because of the damage it would do to small shopowners.

- - - - - - - - - -

In the explanation of the Retail Stores Act that follows, the author refers to its procedures in the past tense because, as discussed in the next section, the Act has been and likely will continue to be modified.

FRANK UPHAM, PRIVATIZING REGULATION: THE IMPLEMENTATION OF THE LARGE-SCALE RETAIL STORES LAW*

Political Dynamics in Contemporary Japan
264, 270-279 (1993)

Although its passage might be adequately explained as the result of a political struggle among department stores, small and medium retailers, and superstores, official MITI commentaries on the LSRSL [Large-Scale Retail Stores Law] invariably cited a desire for strengthened consumer protection and industry rationalization as statutory goals. Besides guaranteeing small merchants an enterprise opportunity, Articles 1 and 11 of the law specifically required due consideration to the interests of consumers and to the well-being of the retail industry as a whole, which contributed to a generally positive initial appraisal of the law by economists and large retailers.

The procedural requirements of the LSRSL were simple and straightforward. Persons wishing to construct a building (Article 3) with more than fifteen hundred

*From Frank Upham, "Privatizing Regulation: The Implementation of the Large-Scale Retail Stores Law," in *Political Dynamics in Contemporary Japan*, pp. 264-294 (Gary D. Allinson and Yasunori Sone, eds., Ithaca: Cornell University Press, 1993), at 270-279.

square meters of retail space and prospective retailers (Article 5) within the building had to notify MITI of their plans. If MITI determined (Article 7) that the operation of the new store would have a significant impact on local small and medium retailers, it had four months to issue a recommendation (*kankoku*) that the prospective retailer delay the proposed opening date, decrease the floor space, or otherwise modify its plans.

During these four months, MITI had to solicit the opinion of two tripartite deliberative bodies made up of merchants, consumers, and representatives of the public interest: the Large-Scale Retail Stores Deliberative Council at the regional level and the Commercial Activities Adjustment Board established within the local chamber of commerce. The latter was to investigate local conditions, negotiate with the prospective large retailer regarding possible changes in its plans, and report to the regional council, which, in turn, gave its opinion to MITI. Acceptance of a recommendation was voluntary, but Article 8 of the law gave MITI the power to order compliance if necessary to prevent severe injury to the interests of local merchants. The statute contemplated that the entire process would normally take no more than eight months.

Commercial Adjustment under the Large Stores Law

From the first, however, implementation under the LSRSL was only loosely related to its formal structure. The shift from the permit system of the [prior] Department Store Law [DSL] to the notification system of the [new] LSRSL ostensibly meant that government intervention would be the exception rather than the rule, and an emphasis on free market principles played a role in convincing large retailers and others to support the law. * * * At the same time that it was extolling free market competition to the large retailers, [however,] MITI and the Liberal Democratic Party were promising small and medium retailers that the notification system would operate "just like a permit system." In the subsequent fifteen years MITI more than fulfilled this promise and oversaw the creation of a system that erected barriers to entry into the retail industry far surpassing those of the Department Store Law in everything but formal legal authority.

* * * In the first five years of operation, almost fifteen hundred new large stores were opened under the law, approximately doubling the number existing before 1974, and many chain retailers began avoiding the law altogether by shifting to stores of just under fifteen hundred square meters. In response, local governments passed ordinances and [undertook] administrative guidance restricting stores of less than fifteen hundred square meters, and independent retailers began pushing hard for extended coverage and tighter restrictions on new entrants into the industry. By 1977 the Diet had passed a resolution urging action to protect small retailers, and MITI had established a series of study commissions on the "retail problem." In 1978 the Diet extended the LSRSL's coverage from stores of more than fifteen hundred square meters to all stores of more than five hundred square meters. The former became "class one" stores under the direct jurisdiction of MITI; the latter became "class two" stores under local government jurisdiction. In addition, in 1979, MITI issued administrative guidance that required Article 3 notifica-

tion [to MITI] thirteen months prior to the proposed opening date rather than the statutory seven months.

When 1979 and 1980 saw both an increasing number of store openings and sluggish consumer expenditures, however, small retailers began to call for the return to the permit approach of the DSL and a reorientation to regulate stores on the basis of type of retail activity as well as floor space. The latter was necessary to protect independent stores from yet another new competitive threat, the convenience store chains, which competed not on the basis of size but on price and hours.

Any attempt to pass legislation that favored small retailers would have elicited substantial opposition, but, as it turned out, recourse to the Diet was unnecessary. In January 1982, MITI issued guidance entitled "Interim Measures Concerning the Notification of Large-Scale Retail Stores" that accomplished the small retailers' goals without legislative action. One set of measures modified the statutory adjustment process by requiring builders of class one outlets and their primary tenants to "explain" their plans to local merchants *before* [initial] notification [to MITI] under Article 3 of the law. Previously, [such] notification had been the initial step in the adjustment process. Similarly, it moved the formal adjustment process, which statutorily was to commence after each retailer had completed notification under Article 5, to commence before that notification. These new requirements became known as "prenotification explanation" and "prenotification adjustment," respectively.

This guidance frontloaded the adjustment process so that contact between prospective retailers and local merchants was to begin before any steps were taken under the statute and be completed before the individual retailers had even filed their formal plans. As a result, official adjustment after Article 5 notification was to be a mere formal endorsement of the prenotification adjustment results. These changes did not necessarily mean a complete transformation of the system, however. The thirteen-month time limit of the 1979 administrative guidance remained, and the prenotification adjustment was still to be carried out by the Commercial Activities Adjustment Board, which had to include consumer and public interest representatives as well as local merchants.

These administrative measures took the implementation of the LSRSL some distance from its statutory framework. Actual practice under the law, however, was removed even farther from the original intent; so far removed, in fact, that in many instances it was inconsistent with both the statutory requirements and even the administrative guidance itself. Local variations make generalizations dangerous, but one consistent feature was the removal of real power under the LSRSL from the regional MITI bureaus and their statutory advisory councils to local merchants operating under the umbrella of local chambers of commerce. Beginning in 1979 and accelerating in the 1980s, MITI refused to accept Article 3 notification unless the builder appended a document setting forth the terms under which local merchants unanimously agreed to the new store's opening. As a result, even the prenotification adjustment process envisioned by the 1982 administrative guidance before Article 5 notification became a meaningless formality, replaced by an even more informal process known as "pre-prenotification adjustment."

At this stage, before any formal steps had been taken under the law at all, the large-store and local merchants entered negotiations on the four items generally covered by adjustment: opening date, floor space, daily hours, and annual days of operation. Sometimes these negotiations were carried out by the members of the formal Adjustment Board but more frequently by local merchants themselves in a Large-Store Countermeasures Task Force or Large-Scale Retail Stores Policy Subcommittee loosely affiliated with the local chamber of commerce.

This distortion of the statutory procedure and the general withdrawal of MITI from its statutory role of final decisionmaker corrupted the implementation of the Large-Scale Retail Stores Law. Instead of the contemplated seven to eight months between initial notification and opening, it became common for negotiations to take seven to eight years, and delays of ten years were not unheard of. The resulting agreements clearly reflected the veto power given to local merchants. They covered not only the four statutory items but also frequently extended to matters wholly unrelated to the legitimate concerns of the LSRSL itself. They included, for example, requirements that the new store include specified local merchants as subtenants on favorable terms, make large "donations" to local merchant groups, and maintain prices or services at the same level as surrounding merchants.

Questions and Discussion Points

1. *Purpose of the Retail Stores Act:* What was the purpose of the law? Small retailers can naturally be expected to have a favorable attitude toward the Retail Stores Act. Are there reasons that large department stores or large discount retailers might support the law? Are there any reasons consumers might support the law?

2. *Effects of the law:* One obvious effect of the law is to preserve a greater number of small retailers than would presumably continue to exist in the absence of any such legislation. What other effects might operation of the Retail Stores Act have? To what extent might the Retail Stores Act account for the continued existence of distribution *keiretsu*?

3. *"Adjustment" boards and commissions:* As the above selection describes, responsibility for negotiations in the "adjustment" process was delegated to a Commercial Activities Adjustment Board composed of representatives of local merchants, consumers, and representatives of the public interest. Such tripartite boards and commissions are common in Japan. Does their continued existence and utilization discriminate against foreign firms? Are they objectionable on other grounds? Or are they a desirable means of involving those affected by certain activities in the decisionmaking process?

2. U.S.-Japan trade friction and the Retail Stores Act

During 1990, the governments of Japan and the U.S. began the extensive SII discussions ostensibly aimed at ameliorating the long and persistent trade imbalance between the two countries. In those discussions, the U.S. government complained about the Retail Stores Act. In the end, the Japanese government agreed to amend the act.

The American government argued that the Retail Stores Act disadvantaged foreign companies because small retailers are less likely to carry foreign products than are large retailers. In addition, of course, it may also have been concerned about the prospects for U.S. and other foreign companies opening their own retail operations in Japan. At the time of the SII talks, the U.S.-based company Toys 'R Us was engaged in negotiations to open its first retail store in Japan.

MITI regulations implementing the law have recently been amended and the law itself may be amended or even repealed in the next few years. The excerpt below explains how MITI has changed its implementation of the law. At least to outward appearances, the U.S. interest in reform of the Retail Stores Act was the paramount factor leading to changes. Nonetheless, many consumers, some retailers (particularly the larger discount stores), and a few segments of the bureaucracy (such as the Fair Trade Commission) also pushed for change.

FRANK UPHAM, PRIVATIZING REGULATION: THE IMPLEMENTATION OF THE LARGE-SCALE RETAIL STORES LAW*

Political Dynamics in Contemporary Japan
264, 285-287 (1993)

On May 24, 1990, * * * MITI announced a package of short- and long-term reforms pursuant to the Structural Impediments Initiative talks with the United States. First, immediate steps would be taken under current law to make opening a large store quicker and easier. Second, MITI would submit to the 1991 regular session of the Diet amendments to the LSRSL that would further streamline the process. Third, MITI pledged to reevaluate fundamentally its policy toward the retail industry within three years, including consideration of total liberalization.

The immediate measures meant substantial changes in the operation of the law. MITI announced that it would accept all notifications regardless of the area, an implicit acknowledgment of the illegality of its former system of "restricted zones," where authorities had refused even to accept any notifications whatsoever. The fundamental nature of the process of commercial adjustment was changed. The first step was still to be the explanation by the prospective retailer before Article 3 notification of its plans to local merchants, but the new rules limited this stage to four months and eliminated the requirement of the local merchants' consent. If they remained dissatisfied, the formal process moved to the next stage regardless. The entire process from initial announcement of intention by the large

*From Frank Upham, "Privatizing Regulation: The Implementation of the Large-Scale Retail Stores Law," in *Political Dynamics in Contemporary Japan*, pp. 264-294 (Gary D. Allinson and Yasunori Sone, eds., Ithaca: Cornell University Press, 1993), at 285-287. Copyright © 1993 by Cornell University. Used by permission of the publisher.

retailer to the final decision was to take no more than eighteen months.

In addition to the measures relating directly to the process of commercial adjustment, MITI also increased immediately the permissible hours and days of operation for large stores and exempted retail space devoted to imports from the law in certain circumstances. It also initiated measures to increase the "transparency" of the process by requiring quarterly reports on the status of pending notifications, establishing a bureau within MITI to answer inquiries regarding notifications, and providing for limited disclosure of the results of meetings of the various entities involved in the adjustment process.

MITI explained these measures to the Americans as the maximum changes possible under the LSRSL. They were not. Not only was the eighteen-month deadline almost double the maximum time anticipated by the statute itself, but the liberalized hours and days of operation were well short of what MITI could have established by simply revising its ministerial order. Furthermore, true transparency remained impossible as long as the informal and nonstatutory prenotification explanation meetings were a significant part of the process. If MITI had simply decided to follow the formal process delineated by the law, the degree of liberalization would have been much greater, but to do so would have meant an immediate and substantial loss of control of the speed of reform.

Despite the lack of change in the nature of LSRSL implementation, the results changed dramatically. In the first six months following the measures, more than nine hundred prospective new large stores were announced, more than double that of the previous year and more than nine times the rate during 1982-1985. The American toy retailer, Toys 'R Us, became the first foreign store to be allowed to open under the LSRSL and announced that it planned one hundred stores by the end of the decade. Large Japanese retailers also reported that the adjustment process had become easier. Small merchants and local governments accelerated the trend toward using large stores as the nucleus for the revitalization of established areas, and trade associations for small and medium retailers began to lobby on the national level for various forms of subsidies to replace the declining protection of the law.

In December 1990, MITI, through a joint report by subcommittees of the Industrial Structure Council and the Small and Medium Enterprise Policy Council, announced the shape of the proposed amendment of the LSRSL to be submitted to the Diet in 1991. The eighteen-month period for store opening established in May was to be further shortened to one year and increases in floor space devoted to import goods further liberalized. To streamline the process, prenotification explanation, which had taken up to ten years in the mid-1980s, was to be eliminated entirely * * *.

Crucial to the shortening of the period in the proposed amendment was the elimination of the Commercial Activities Adjustment Boards. Instead, initial deliberation on the impact on local retailers and consideration of reductions in size or operating conditions were to be performed by the Large Stores Council. It was hoped that the regional rather than local nature of the council and the status of its members as quasi-public servants, which made them subject to criminal liability for bribery or self-dealing, would eliminate the corruption and deliberate delay that had marked the history of the boards.

In May 1991, the Diet passed a series of bills effective in 1992 that largely carried out MITI's proposals. If implemented in accord with their spirit, these amendments meant a fundamental change in the nature of retail regulation in Japan. The replacement of the boards and elimination of the prenotification stage would require MITI and the Large Stores Council to make the substantive decisions required by the statute. Instead of forcing large retailers to negotiate with their competitors, both sides would present their cases to a supposedly neutral decisionmaking body in a process that would be considerably more open and accountable than its predecessor. In themselves, these changes would not necessarily mean a greater number of large store openings or any substantive change in the results of the process. In practice, however, the procedural regularity and the clear deadlines for action would likely mean that the retailing industry would develop in closer conformity with the natural demands of the market than under the LSRSL as it operated until 1990. Supporting this interpretation was MITI's concurrent reiteration of the strong possibility that the LSRSL would be repealed in 1994.

Reform and even repeal of the law did not mean abandonment of small retailers, however. Simultaneous with its announcement regarding the future of the law, MITI stated its intention to introduce further legislation that would provide a wide range of subsidies to small merchants and would integrate protection of small merchants' interests into the city planning process. Consistent with the strategy already adopted by many small retailers and local entities, the proposed law would aim at the "coexistence and coprosperity" of individually owned stores and large-scale retail stores within the framework of large integrated shopping centers complete with parking lots and other facilities necessary to revitalize the surrounding commercial area. The law would require each local municipality to draft a shopping zone plan under the City Planning Law, which, when approved by the governor and the Ministries of International Trade and Industry, Construction, and Local Autonomy, would entitle participating merchants to a wide range of financial subsidies and tax relief. The goal for the first decade of the law was to be one hundred such shopping zones throughout Japan.

FURTHER READING

Keiretsu, Etc.

Ronald Dore, *Flexible Rigidities: Industrial policy and structural adjustment in the Japanese economy 1970-80.* Stanford: Stanford University Press, 1986.

Michael Gerlach, *Alliance Capitalism: The Social Organization of Japanese Business.* Berkeley: University of California Press, 1992.

Ronald J. Gilson and Mark J. Roe, "Understanding the Japanese *Keiretsu*: Overlaps Between Corporate Governance and Industrial Organization," 102 *Yale Law Journal* 871 (1992).

Takeo Hoshi, Anil Kashyap and David Scharfstein, "The Role of Main Banks in Reducing the Costs of Financial Distress in Japan," 26 *Journal of Financial Economics* 67 (1990).

J. Mark Ramseyer, "Columbian Cartel Launches Bid for Japanese Firms," 102 *Yale Law Journal* 2005 (1993).

J. Mark Ramseyer, "Legal Rules in Repeated Deals: Banking in the Shadow of Defection in Japan," 20 *Journal of Legal Studies* 91 (1991).

Mark J. Roe, "Some Differences in Corporate Structure in Germany, Japan, and the United States," 102 *Yale Law Journal* 1927 (1993).

Paul Sheard, "The Main Bank System and Corporate Monitoring and Control in Japan," 11 *Journal of Economic Behavior & Organization* 399 (1989).

Jiro Tamura, "U.S. Extraterritorial Application of Antitrust Law to Japanese Keiretsu," 25 *N.Y.U. Journal of International Law and Politics* 385 (1993).

Aron Viner, *Inside Japanese Financial Markets*. Homewood, IL: Dow Jones-Irwin, 1988.

Ulrike Wassman and Kozo Yamamura, "Do Japanese Firms Behave Differently? The Effects of *Keiretsu* in the United States," in Kozo Yamamura, ed., *Japanese Investment in the United States: Should We Be Concerned?*, pp. 119-149. Seattle: Society for Japanese Studies, 1989.

Organization of Japanese Firms

James Abegglen and George Stalk, Jr., *Kaisha, The Japanese Corporation*. New York: Basic Books, 1985.

Masahiko Aoki, ed., *Economic Analysis of the Japanese Firm*. Amsterdam: North-Holland, 1984.

Rodney Clark, *The Japanese Company*. New Haven: Yale University Press, 1979.

Jackson N. Huddleston, Jr., *Gaijin Kaisha: Running a Foreign Business in Japan*. Armonk, NY: M. E. Sharpe, 1990.

Employment Practices

James C. Abegglen, *Management and Worker: The Japanese Solution*. Tokyo: Sophia University Press, 1973.

R. E. Cole, *Work, Mobility and Participation*. Berkeley: University of California Press, 1979.

T. A. Hanami, *Labour Law and Industrial Relations in Japan*. Deventer, The Netherlands: Kluwer, 1985.

Taishiro Shirai, ed., *Contemporary Industrial Relations in Japan*. Madison, WI: University of Wisconsin Press, 1983.

Kazuo Sugeno, *Japanese Labor Law*. Seattle: University of Washington Press, 1992.

Distribution System

David Flath, "The Economic Rationality of the Japanese Distribution System," Working Paper No. 29, Center on Japanese Economy and Business, Columbia University, 1989.

David Flath and Tatsuhiko Nariu, "Returns Policy in the Japanese Marketing System," 3 *Journal of Japanese and International Economies* 49 (1989).

Takatoshi Itoh and Masayoshi Maruyama, "Is the Japanese Distribution System Really Inefficient?," Working Paper No. 3306, National Bureau of Economic Research, March 1990.

U.S.-Japan Trade and Investment Relations

Clyde Prestowitz, *Trading Places: How We Allowed Japan to Take the Lead.* New York: Basic Books, 1988.

Gary Saxonhouse and Kozo Yamamura, eds., *Law and Trade Issues of the Japanese Economy: American and Japanese Perspectives.* Seattle: University of Washington Press, 1986.

Lester Thurow, *Head to Head: The Coming Economic Battle Among Japan, Europe and America.* New York: Morrow, 1992.

Kozo Yamamura, ed., *Policy and Trade Issues of the Japanese Economy: American and Japanese Perspectives.* Seattle: University of Washington Press, 1982.

Impact of Keiretsu on Foreign Trade and Investment

Joel Davidow, "Keiretsu and U.S. Antitrust," 24 *Law and Policy in International Business* 1035 (1993).

Ken'ichi Imai, "Japanese Business Groups and the Structural Impediments Initiative," in Kozo Yamamura, ed., *Japan's Economic Structure: Should it Change?*, pp. 167-202. Seattle: Society for Japanese Studies, 1990.

Daniel Okimoto, "Outsider Trading: Coping with Japanese Industrial Organization," in Kenneth Pyle, ed., *The Trade Crisis: How Will Japan Respond?*, pp. 85-116. Seattle: Society for Japanese Studies, 1987.

Gary Saxonhouse, "Differentiated Products, Economies of Scale and Access to the Japanese Market" (with Comments by Laura D'Andrea Tyson and Harry P. Bowen), in Robert C. Feenstra, ed., *Trade Policies for International Competitiveness*, pp. 145-183. Chicago: University of Chicago Press, 1989.

Small Enterprise Policy

David Flath, "Why Are There So Many Retail Stores in Japan?," Working Paper No. 17, Center on Japanese Economy and Business, Columbia University, 1988.

Hugh T. Patrick and Thomas P. Rohlen, "Small-Scale Family Enterprises," in Kozo Yamamura and Yasukichi Yasuba, eds., *The Political Economy of Japan, Volume 1: The Domestic Transformation*, pp. 331-384. Stanford: Stanford University Press, 1987.

NOTES TO CHAPTER THREE

1. *See* Robert Ballon and Iwao Tomita, *The Financial Behavior of Japanese Corporations* 39 (Kodansha International, 1988).

2. *See id.* at 42.

3. *See* Dan Fenno Henderson, *Foreign Enterprise in Japan* 131-132 (Univ. of No. Carolina Press, 1973).

4. Charles Ferguson, "Computers and the Coming of the U.S. *Keiretsu*," *Harvard Business Review*, July-Aug. 1990, at 55-90. For reactions to Ferguson's article by several prominent business and policy leaders and academicians, *see* "Can a *Keiretsu* Work in America?," *Harvard Business Review*, Sept.-Oct. 1990, at 180-197.

5. Michael C. Jensen, "Eclipse of the Public Corporation," *Harvard Business Review*, Sept.-Oct. 1989, at 61.

Four

Administrative Guidance

Introduction

Both in Japan and abroad, many commentators have characterized the Japanese administrative process as unique. By consensus, they have come to call the allegedly peculiar aspects of this process "administrative guidance." To most observers, Japanese administrative guidance is bureaucratically driven, informal, and part of a carefully orchestrated industrial policy. In turn, the Japanese bureaucracy is powerful and adept, and much of Japan's economic success derives from that administrative guidance.

Several recent critics have challenged this orthodox view. Some have pointed to prominent firms that have bucked the bureaucracy's leadership. Others have argued that the use of informal regulatory techniques shows that the bureaucracy is weak. Still others have shown the political—not economic—logic to the bureaucracy's actions. In this chapter, we explore how administrative guidance operates in individual cases, and what chance private parties have to challenge it. Primarily, we focus on the retailing, construction, and petroleum industries.

I. Administrative Guidance in Operation

MICHAEL K. YOUNG, JUDICIAL REVIEW OF ADMINISTRATIVE GUIDANCE: GOVERNMENTALLY ENCOURAGED CONSENSUAL DISPUTE RESOLUTION IN JAPAN*

84 Columbia Law Review
923, 926-932 (1984)

Administrative guidance (*gyōsei shidō*) is a common Japanese regulatory technique that, although generally nonbinding, seeks to conform the behavior of regulated parties to broad administrative goals. Two examples of administrative guidance clarify its scope. The first of these developed during late 1980 and early 1981,

*From Michael K. Young, Fuyo Professor of Japanese Law and Director, Center for Japanese Legal Studies, Columbia University School of Law, "Judicial Review of Administrative Guidance: Governmentally Encouraged Consensual Dispute Resolution in Japan," 84 *Columbia Law Review* 923 (1984), at 926-932. Reprinted by permission.

when the dispute between Japan and the United States over the import of Japanese automobiles reached crisis proportions. Threatened with the possibility of executive and legislative action restricting Japanese auto imports into the United States, the Japanese government agreed, in what is euphemistically known as an "Orderly Marketing Agreement," to restrict automobile imports "voluntarily" for a three-year period. To implement this agreement, the principal ministry dealing with trade matters, the Ministry of International Trade and Industry (MITI), informed auto manufacturers that during each of the next three years they were to limit exports of passenger cars to the United States. In its notification letter, the MITI found authority for this action in its enabling legislation and in article 48 of the Foreign Exchange and Foreign Trade Control [Act (FECA)]. To assure compliance, the MITI required each manufacturer to submit periodic reports on car exports. Falsification of such reports would be considered a violation of the reporting requirements under article 67 of the [FECA] and would subject firms to liability for punishment under articles 72 and 73 of that same law. The MITI also indicated that if any company threatened to exceed its export allotment, the Government would amend the Export Trade Control Order [Cabinet Order No. 379 of 1949] to subject car exports to the United States to export licensing, in accordance with article 48 of the [FECA]. The MITI would then be able to seek sanctions against any noncomplying company under article 70 of the [FECA].

Another interesting, important and, at least within Japan, well-known example of administrative guidance involves local governments' attempts at land use planning. During the postwar period, Japan experienced tremendous urban growth, much of it concentrated in the Tokyo metropolitan area, where almost one-quarter of Japan's population resides. This rapid urban development seriously undermined the general living environment and placed tremendous strains on the ability of the government to provide adequate services.

While the national government undertook reasonably successful efforts to solve serious air pollution problems in Tokyo, additional concerns surfaced in the late sixties that were not directly addressed at the national level. Two areas became the particular focus of residents' energies. First, concerned parents began to focus on the dislocations this rapid urban development caused in the schools. To a large degree, education is the key to an individual's future in Japan. Even the slightest diminution in educational opportunity evokes great concern. The strain placed on the school systems during this period threatened the quality of educational opportunities and parents were quick to demand solutions.

Second, residents became increasingly concerned about the effect of high rise buildings on ventilation and sunlight. This concern might strike Americans as odd, but Japan's climate, especially the high humidity of the Tokyo area, and the relatively late advent of air-conditioning and central heating, elevated sunlight and air above mere aesthetic interest. To enhance ventilation, walls are thin, windows and doors large, and many rooms are cross-ventilated. Few dwelling places are without a small patio used for ventilation, drying laundry, and growing plants. To the growing alarm of residents, the construction of apartment buildings, even if only three stories high, undermined ventilation and its significant benefits. Moreover, while Japanese courts have created a right to sunlight (*nisshōken*), thereby affording some minimal protection against undue interference, effective injunctive relief is rarely available and damages are usually low.

The national government addressed national standards for housing construction by adopting the Construction Standards Law. The Law establishes a basic construction permit process, requiring builders to submit a complex set of plans and blueprints to the construction supervisor, an employee of the local municipal government. The supervisor determines whether those plans conform to the requirements of the orders (*meirei*) and local ordinances (*jōrei*) based upon it. Construction cannot lawfully proceed without a permit. Despite this regulatory mechanism, the law attempts only to guarantee health and safety and not to assure the availability of adequate educational facilities or of sunlight and ventilation. Nothing expressly authorizes the construction supervisor to deny a permit because a building might block sunlight from surrounding buildings or because the increase in population resulting from the occupancy of the new building would put a strain on schools. Moreover, while the law allowed municipalities to establish additional building standards through local ordinances (*jōrei*), no municipality enacted ordinances dealing with ventilation and local schools. Some commentators even doubted the legality of such ordinances, as they would arguably exceed the scope of the law. Indeed, given the specificity of the law's provisions, these regulations might directly conflict with it, a preemption problem. Moreover, while municipalities have a general mandate to enact local ordinances on matters within their jurisdictional ambit, direct, legally binding solutions such as the requirement that developers donate land and money for the construction of educational facilities would probably conflict with the takings clause of the Japanese Constitution. [Article 29, paragraph 3, provides: "Private property may be taken for public use upon just compensation therefor."]

Despite these disabilities, local constituencies placed considerable pressure on local governments to safeguard education and ventilation. Local interest groups focused their energies on local solutions in part because they felt their needs and circumstances varied tremendously from area to area. The residential groups' resources would clearly be most effectively marshalled against the local—not national—government. Moreover, these groups refused to accept as an excuse for local-level nonaction the national government's failure to address their concerns adequately.

Municipalities initially responded to constituency pressure by urging national authorities either to undertake regulation of the incursions on sunlight and ventilation occasioned by housing construction, or to permit local regulation. The national authorities, however, were unresponsive and six concerned municipalities issued so-called "guidelines," known more formally as Outline Guidance (*Yōkō Shidō*).

The Outline Guidance of the city of Musashino, a suburb in the Tokyo metropolitan area, typifies the response of the six original municipalities as well as that of the almost 800 municipalities that shortly followed suit. Musashino issued "Outline Guidance Concerning Housing Development in the City of Musashino," which became effective on October 1, 1971. This Outline Guidance encouraged developers or builders of medium and large scale housing developments or apartment buildings to take two steps of particular significance. First, in projects over a certain size, the developer was encouraged to provide free land for the construction of one elementary school for every 1,000 units or fraction thereof and one junior high school for every 2,000 units. Developers were also encouraged to bear the expense of constructing educational facilities on the land. Second, developers were to reach an agreement with the surrounding residents regarding the degree to which the planned building might permissibly interfere with the residents' sunlight and ventilation.

Although such Outline Guidance was not legally binding, the municipalities did not leave compliance entirely to the developers' good will. Musashino's Outline Guidance, for example, indicated that the city would not provide water or sewage services to uncooperative developers. Moreover, the city would not issue the construction permits required under the Construction Standards Law. Other municipalities outlined additional ways in which they would refuse to aid uncooperative developers. Some localities, for example, threatened to refuse uncooperative developers a waiver that would allow them to bring construction equipment to the construction site under legislation entrusting to local officials' discretion the permissible size of vehicles allowed to pass over the roads. These informal sanctions encouraged developers to heed residents' concerns over sunlight and ventilation.

Questions and Discussion Points

1. *Administrative guidance in the two different contexts:* What differences exist between the guidance given in the export control example and that in land use planning? What legal authority did the bureaucrats in the two contexts have?

2. *Difference from U.S. administrative practice:* Is administrative guidance different from informal administrative practice in the U.S.?

II. Challenging Administrative Guidance

Prior to the enactment of the Administrative Procedure Act (the APA, Law No. 88 of 1993) in November 1993 (to become effective within one year thereafter), the primary general avenues for challenging administrative actions in Japan lay in two statutes, the Administrative Case Litigation Act (Law No. 139 of 1962) and the Administrative Complaint Inquiries Act (Law No. 160 of 1962). In some cases, these general standards have been supplemented by specific procedural standards contained in specialized regulatory statutes. Even with the enactment of the APA, these avenues remain important. Yet under the above statutes, parties may contest only those actions that constitute administrative dispositions (*gyōsei shobun*). The problem for parties that want to challenge administrative guidance is that much guidance does not involve any administrative disposition at all.

At least two questions present themselves. First, what prevents a party facing administrative guidance from ignoring it? For instance, when a party wants permission to construct a new retail store, why does it not simply submit its notification pursuant to the Retail Stores Act? In doing so, it would initiate the statutory process that would mandate a formal response by the local MITI office. Presumably, it could then contest that response in court.

Second, if informal bureaucratic action is essentially dispositive (as it almost certainly sometimes is), does or should a party have the same recourse under the law that would be available after a formal administrative disposition? The materials directly below address—even if they do not answer—these issues. We then turn to the treatment of administrative guidance under the new APA.

A. Challenges under the Administrative Case Litigation Act and specific regulatory statutes

FRANK UPHAM, PRIVATIZING REGULATION: THE IMPLEMENTATION OF THE LARGE-SCALE RETAIL STORES LAW*

Political Dynamics in Contemporary Japan
264, 274-279 (1993)

Given the gap between the goals of the Large-Scale Retail Stores Law [LSRSL] and the actuality of its operation, one might expect that one or more of the many individuals and groups injured by the process would have convinced the courts to force MITI to implement the statute in accord with its content and intent. As in the United States, if a Japanese plaintiff can show that a government act violates the statute on which it is based, a court will nullify it, and a common way to demonstrate illegality is to show that the government agency has used the wrong criteria or followed incorrect procedures in making a decision. Why no one successfully brought such an action against the implementation of the LSRSL can be explained by the litigation that grew out of the opening of a store in Iwate Prefecture.

On March 20, 1979, the Etsurigo Shopping Center Cooperative notified MITI of its plan to build a three-story, 23,904 square meter shopping complex in Etsurigo Village. The superstore, Jusco, was to occupy 14,000 square meters and local merchants 6,000 square meters. The Etsurigo Commercial Activities Adjustment Board met six times between May 18 and July 23 and recommended that Jusco's space be reduced to 7,500 square meters and the local tenants remain at 6,000 square meters. Jusco accepted this recommendation, and on September 12, 1979, Jusco and the

*From Frank Upham, "Privatizing Regulation: The Implementation of the Large-Scale Retail Stores Law," in *Political Dynamics in Contemporary Japan*, pp. 264-294 (Gary D. Allinson and Yasunori Sone, eds., Ithaca: Cornell University Press, 1993), at 274-279. Copyright © 1993 by Cornell University. Reprinted by permission.

prospective local tenants filed their Article 5 notification.

The Regional Board reconvened on October 19. Ten days later, at its eighth meeting, the board adopted, over two dissents, a resolution accepting the stores' Article 5 notification and forwarded it to the Tohoku Large Stores Council. The council, in turn, submitted its opinion to MITI on November 27, recommending a further 15-percent reduction of total space. MITI then issued a recommendation to Jusco calling for the reduction suggested by the council and for certain reductions in operating hours, which Jusco accepted. The whole process took less than nine months.

In January 1981, 117 local merchants sued for the nullification of MITI's recommendation. The plaintiffs claimed that the recommendation was too lenient to Jusco because it did not give local small merchants the enterprise opportunity provided by Article 1 of the LSRSL and that the process by which the recommendation was formed violated both the statute and the detailed administrative guidance issued by MITI stipulating how the adjustment process was to be conducted. Specifically, they alleged that President Takahashi of the Etsurigo Chamber of Commerce, whose son was the president of the Etsurigo Shopping Center Cooperative, had had a direct conflict of interest and had selected members of the regional board solely on their pro-shopping center views as demonstrated by the fact that the spouses of three of the members were scheduled to become tenants in the complex. They argued that the participation of these persons in the board's deliberations violated both Article 1 of the LSRSL and MITI's own administrative guidance requiring the president of the local chamber of commerce to appoint members who will "represent the views of all local small-scale retailers."

Even if the blatant conflict of interest of the board members did not in itself invalidate its action, the plaintiffs further alleged that the board's investigation and deliberations were insufficient. They argued that the board had failed to consider the current condition of small-scale retail operations in the area, local retailers' prospects for modernization, consumer convenience, and the extent of the detrimental impact on existing retailers and that it had not followed the detailed computation formulas provided in MITI's guidance and handbooks. Nor had the regional MITI bureau supervised the board's deliberations as required by ministry rules. The MITI representative failed to attend a single meeting despite repeated requests by local merchants to investigate improprieties in the composition and activities of the board. Plaintiffs pointed to parts of the Diet debates on the LSRSL for proof of the importance of adequate governmental supervision to proper implementation of the law and argued that the failure of the local MITI office to exercise such supervision rendered the board's process unfair and illegal. Because MITI did not conduct its own investigation and based its eventual action solely on the board's findings, the plaintiffs argued that it, too, was illegal.

Journalistic reports and practices elsewhere under the LSRSL leave little doubt that the plaintiffs' factual claims were largely accurate and that the facts amounted to a blatant conflict of interest on the part of Takahashi and the board members and a clear abdication of its statutory duties by MITI. Such procedural irregularities would probably have been enough to convince the courts to declare the whole process illegal. Because the doctrines of Japanese administrative law so restrict judicial review of government action, however, it made little difference what improprieties the plaintiffs might have been able to prove. And in the end, the district and high courts had little trouble either rejecting the local merchants as proper plaintiffs or finding that the MITI recommendation to Jusco was not the type of administrative act that could be challenged in court.

Under Article 3 of the Administrative Case Litigation Law (ACLL), which governs judicial review of bureaucratic action in Japan, a plaintiff must show that the allegedly illegal act is an "administrative disposition or other exercise of public power," which the Supreme Court has interpreted narrowly to include only "official conduct which forms rights and duties in citizens or confirms their scope." To be actionable, in other words, bureaucratic action must either deny citizens a previously existing legal right or compel them to perform a new legal duty, and the effect must be immediate and directed at the plaintiff specifically. Actions that affect one's economic interests, as opposed to legal rights, are considered too informal to be judicially cognizable. In the *Etsurigo* case the challenged act was the MITI recommendation based on Article 7 of the LSRSL. The plaintiffs argued that such a recommendation was, in practice, the equivalent of a permit to operate and as such gave the shopping center a right that it did not previously have. It followed that the opening of the shopping center would infringe the rights of local merchants to be protected from such competition unless proper procedures were followed and a legally valid recommendation issued.

Japanese courts interpreting the ACLL, however, are generally uninterested in the substance of government actions or their practical effect on citizens. They are centrally concerned with the legal nature of the action, and the recommendation in *Etsurigo* changed no one's legally enforceable rights or duties. Unlike in an Article 8 order, Jusco had no legal duty to abide by the recommendation; technically, it was completely free to ignore it. Similarly, it gave Jusco no right it did not have before because it was legally free to open its store without any action by MITI whatsoever. Because the recommendation gave Jusco no new right, indeed had no legal effect at all beyond providing the basis for a possible order to follow, it could not possibly have legally affected the plaintiffs.

Furthermore, even if the recommendation had created a right or duty in Jusco, it would have made no difference in the ultimate result, because the courts also found that the merchants did not have the standing to bring the action. ACLL Article 9 limits standing in administrative actions to persons with a "legal interest" in the administrative disposition: "Legal interests are created by provisions vesting an administrative agency with the duty of protecting some personal interest. But where an agency is to act for the general public interest, personal interests affected by the action are only reflex interests. A plaintiff with only a reflex interest does not have standing to sue." A legal interest, therefore, requires injury to an individualized interest that the agency is specifically charged to protect under the relevant statute.

In the *Etsurigo* opinions, the courts concluded that the goal of "enterprise opportunities" for local merchants set forth in Article 1 of the LSRSL was not enough to give any individual merchant more than a reflex interest in the adjustment process. Nor did the whole of the 117 plaintiffs' interests amount to more than the sum of their individual interests. Had the situation been reversed and consumers been suing MITI on the grounds that the 6,390 square meters allotted to Jusco in the recommendation was too small to serve their interests, the result would have been the same. Neither regional consumers nor merchants have the individuated interest under the LSRSL to grant them standing to challenge MITI action.

The only potential plaintiffs under the LSRSL would have been prospective large retailers dissatisfied with the amount of space given them through the adjustment process. Even then, the retailers could not have sued on the basis of a MITI recommendation because they would not have had any legal obligation to follow it. They would have had to defy the recommendation and wait until MITI issued a legally binding order under Article 8. At that point the retailer would have lost the right to open a store under any terms other than those of the order and would have had the right to challenge the order for illegality, including grounds such as those alleged by the *Etsurigo* plaintiffs.

The problem is that MITI rarely, if ever, resorted to a formal order in the implementation of the LSRSL. The large retailer invariably either reached a compromise with local merchants, waited it out, or gave up. According to the pre-prenotification procedures in effect during most of the 1980s, MITI did not even accept Article 3 notifications from retailers without an appended agreement with local merchants. Under these circumstances, MITI was not formally involved until the deal had been cut and there was no reason for it even to issue a recommendation, much less an order.

Theoretically, a large retailer could have attempted to notify MITI without appending the required agreement with local merchants and, when MITI refused to accept the notification, sued to force MITI action. Its argument would have been that requiring such an agreement with local merchants was an illegal delegation of MITI's public duty to implement the statute to private parties. Precedent exists for such a suit, and MITI subsequently admitted that its blanket refusal to accept notifications during the 1980s had been illegal, but victory at this stage would only have gotten the plaintiff the right to proceed with the formal adjustment process as provided for in the statute. Although the formal process might have been more sympathetic to the interests of the retailer and consumers, it would have been time consuming and, given MITI's great discretion under the statute, might easily have resulted in an eventual order no better than what the retailer could get from the merchants directly. If MITI eventually did issue an order, the retailer would finally be able to challenge it directly, but by that point any victory would have been pyrrhic indeed.

Note on the Nakaya case

The plaintiff in the case below is "Nakaya G.G." The "G.G." refers to *gōmei gaisha*, a type of business form used in Japan that is much like a partnership. We study *gōmei gaisha* in Chapter 8.

The following is from the Construction Standards Act discussed in the case:

Section 6 (Application and Permit with Respect to Building Construction, etc.)

1. [This paragraph contains a list of 4 items, each of which describes buildings in terms of size, materials, use, and placement. For buildings falling within one of these four categories, this paragraph requires an application to the local Construction Director.]

2. * * *

3. In the event that the Construction Director receives the application provided in Paragraph (1) of this Section, he shall investigate whether the submitted plan for such building complies with laws concerning the land, the structure and the construction equipment used in the construction of such building, and the orders and ordinances based thereupon, and he shall give the applicant a construction permit in writing within twenty-one (21) days from the receipt of the application in the case of the buildings listed in Items (i) through (iii) of Paragraph (1) of this Section and within seven (7) days in the case of a building listed in Item (iv) of the same Paragraph, upon confirmation of the compatibility with such laws, orders and ordinances.

4. In the event the Construction Director does not confirm the compatibility with laws, orders or ordinances or he with good reason is unable to determine the compatibility of laws, orders and ordinances owing to the description included in the application, he shall give the applicant written notice thereof setting forth such reasons within the period provided in the immediately preceding paragraph.

Translation by Yanagida Nomura & Akai

Nakaya G.G. v. City of Tokyo
1168 Hanrei Jihō 45
(Sup. Ct., P.B., July 16, 1985)

FACTS:

Nakaya G.G., a construction company, planned to construct a condominium and office building. Since a permit was necessary before it could proceed with the construction, on October 28, 1972, it applied to the Construction Director of the City of Tokyo for the required permit.

Some neighboring lot owners opposed construction of the building. They protested, and a city officer in charge of dispute settlement, by administrative guidance, ordered Nakaya to resolve the dispute amicably. During the negotiations between Nakaya and the neighbors, the Construction Director withheld his response to Nakaya's application. He did so despite the fact that the Construction Standards Act (the Act) required him to respond to construction applications within 21 days.

While Nakaya was trying to settle the dispute with the neighbors, the City of Tokyo on February 15, 1973, announced a new height-regulated district plan. The plan applied to all applications filed after April 19 of that year as well as to all applications pending on that day. This new plan would have required Nakaya to modify its proposed design. Because Nakaya thought it would be hard to settle its dispute before the April 19 deadline, it wanted the Construction Director to respond to its application immediately. Hence, on March 1, 1973, it petitioned the Tokyo Construction Review Board for a response to its application. On April 2, 1973, the Construction Director issued Nakaya its permit.

Though having finally obtained the permit, Nakaya sued the City of Tokyo in the Tokyo District Court for damages it suffered as a result of the Construction Director's allegedly illegal delay. The Tokyo District Court ruled against Nakaya. It held that since the delay was reasonable given the purpose of the Act and general social mores, the Construction Director's delay in responding to the application was not illegal.

Nakaya appealed to the Tokyo High Court. The High Court reversed. It reasoned that the Construction Director could justifiably delay only so long as Nakaya voluntarily followed or cooperated with the administrative guidance. Accordingly, once Nakaya showed that it intended not to follow the administrative guidance by petitioning the Tokyo Construction Review Board, any further delay was illegal.

The City of Tokyo has appealed to this Court.

JUDGMENT:

The decision of the Tokyo High Court is affirmed in all respects.

REASONS:

* * * Paragraphs (3) and (4) of Section 6 of the Act provide that when a Construction Director receives a construction permit application under Section 6(1) of the Act, he shall review that application. In that review, he shall determine whether the plan for the proposed building conforms to laws and regulations concerning land, structure, and construction requirements. He shall then notify the applicant accordingly (a confirmation disposition). This investigation and confirmation disposition must occur within 21 days * * * of the receipt of the application. The Act sets forth the period within which the Director must issue his confirmation disposition and does so in order not to inconvenience the lot owner. After all, the owner will need to procure financing, secure a substitute residence or place of business during construction, and make other preparations before he can commence construction. To aid him in these matters, the Act requires a prompt response to his permit application.

Through this approach, the Act balances the general freedom of construction against the need for a system that will prevent illegal buildings. The lot owner must have his construction plan reviewed by the Construction Director for conformity with applicable laws and regulations, and he must obtain a construction permit from the Construction Director before constructing a building or undertaking major repairs. Should he fail to comply with these requirements, he incurs certain penalties (*see* Act §§6(1) and (5) * * *).

In making his confirmation disposition, the Construction Director has little discretion. If an applicant has filed an application whose construction plan conforms to the applicable laws and regulations and which includes the consents from such people as the competent local fire chief required by Section 93 of the Act, the Construction Director must promptly issue a confirmation disposition. Nonetheless, this obligation of the Construction Director is not absolute. Consider the cases where either (i) a building owner has consented to the withholding by the Construction Director of the confirmation disposition, or (ii) the owner has not clearly consented but the withholding was reasonable under the circumstances in the light of the purpose of the Act. In such cases, the Director does not break the law when he withholds his response to an application for a construction permit.

[Neither does the Construction Director necessarily break the law when he withholds his response after an applicant has been told—through administrative guidance—to negotiate with the neighbors.] Suppose a dispute arises between a lot owner and the owners of neighboring lots over a building construction permit. Suppose further that the lot owner has received administrative guidance from the relevant local government agency to settle the dispute amicably. If the lot owner complies with this guidance and conducts those talks, it does not follow that he necessarily has consented to having his application deferred. Local government agencies have a responsibility to maintain local public order, to secure the security, health and welfare of the residents, to maintain the environment, and to prevent public nuisances * * *. Accordingly, the Act establishes minimum standards for structures, facilities, and building uses on lots of land. These standards exist to enhance the public welfare by protecting the lives, health, and property of citizens (Act §1).

Suppose that a relevant local agency, in light of the purpose of these laws, were to conclude that the construction of a building according to the proposed plan would cause damage (significantly obstruct sunlight, for example, or cause wind damage or otherwise harm the local environment). If it issued administrative guidance to the lot owner to cooperate and concede certain points in his construction plan, and if the lot owner appears voluntarily to be cooperating in this process, the Construction Director might decide to defer the confirmation disposition temporarily. If he withheld it for a period of time reasonable under the circumstances, and if he did it in expectation of the response to the administrative guidance, he would not thereby have acted illegally.

In these cases, the withholding of the confirmation disposition is merely the natural consequence of the administrative guidance to which the owner has voluntarily complied. If the owner clearly declares his intent not to comply with that administrative guidance, the Construction Director may not force him to endure delays in the issuance of his confirmation disposition. If the owner declares that he will not cooperate with the guidance, the public welfare that the administrative guidance supposedly advances must be weighed against the disadvantages the owner suffers. Unless there exist special circumstances that make the lot owner's lack of cooperation unreasonable, the administrative guidance does not justify delays in the confirmation disposition. Such delays are, accordingly, illegal. * * *

Given the above facts, when Nakaya filed its March 1, 1973, petition, it indicated a clear and sincere intent to seek an immediate confirmation disposition, and a refusal to cooperate further with the administrative guidance. Until that point, Nakaya had cooperated with the administrative guidance of the City of Tokyo. Nakaya is not alone responsible for the fact that the dispute with its neighbors had not been resolved in accordance with the administrative guidance. And Nakaya's own reasonableness is especially apparent given the way that the City of Tokyo had issued new administrative guidance to Nakaya in late February of 1973, ordering Nakaya to modify its design to comply with its new height-regulated district plan promulgated more than three months after Nakaya had applied for its construction permit. At this point, Tokyo planned to enforce the new height-regulated district plan within about a month. Under these circumstances, Nakaya did not act improperly in declaring its intent, through its March 1, 1973, petition, not to cooperate further with any administrative guidance during the pendency of its disposition.

Accordingly, no special circumstances justify forcing Nakaya to endure delays in its confirmation. Had the Construction Director objectively reviewed the process of the administrative guidance, the contents of Nakaya's petition, the timing of its measures, and so forth, he would (or should) have understood that Nakaya did not file the petition in ill temper or as a tactic in its negotiations with its neighbors. Instead, he would (or should) have observed a sincere desire to obtain a response to its permit application. Therefore, the Director's actions in withholding the confirmation disposition after the March 1, 1973, petition in order to further administrative guidance were illegal. With respect to those delays, the Construction Director was clearly negligent.

The judgment of the Tokyo High Court holding the City of Tokyo liable for damages under the National Compensation Act is hereby upheld as just. There is no error in the judgment from which this appeal was taken. * * *

Questions and Discussion Points

1. *Judicial review of administrative guidance:* Is there a clear holding by the Supreme Court in the *Nakaya* case? If so, what is it? At what point does an administrative body's insistence that an applicant negotiate with other interested parties or comply with "recommendations" of the agency constitute a refusal or other disposition the applicant may challenge in court? Is the issue clear after the *Nakaya* case?

2. *Retroactive application:* Will standards contained in a new ordinance adopted while an application is pending apply to that application? (*Cf. The Pharmacy Case*, Chapter 2, Section IV.)

3. *The strength of the bureaucracy:* Given both the lack of a clear legal basis for much of the guidance and the reluctance to use available mechanisms for enforcing guidance, is the guidance really coercive? Or is it instead benefiting the private parties being "guided"? Might there be contexts where such an argument is more persuasive than in relation to the Construction Standards Act?

B. Administrative guidance under the Administrative Procedure Act

LORENZ KÖDDERITZSCH, JAPAN'S NEW ADMINISTRATIVE PROCEDURE LAW: REASONS FOR ITS ENACTMENT AND LIKELY IMPLICATIONS*

24 Law in Japan 105
105-108, 110-111, 115-119, 125-128 (1991)

Following passage by the Diet, Japan's new Administrative Procedure Act (the APA, Law No. 88 of 1993) was officially promulgated on November 12, 1993. By its terms, the APA is to take effect on a date to be specified by Cabinet Order, within no more than one year from the date of promulgation. This will mark the end of a long history of endeavors to codify in a comprehensive manner rules of administrative procedure in Japan. * * *

Although Japan had never previously enacted a uniform and general administrative procedure law, this does not mean that no legislation has set forth procedural rules. Quite to the contrary, a great number of laws dealing with specialized regulatory policies contain procedural standards in varying degrees[, as with the Construction Standards Act discussed in the *Nakaya* case]. The problem with these rules, however, is that they lack any consistency and are often insufficient to properly defend citizens' rights. * * * Even where laws do provide for procedural rules, they often single out one or two aspects (such as prior notice or hearing), without establishing comprehensive standards.

* * *

[Moreover,] courts have been extremely reluctant to grant procedural rights if there is not at least some reference to procedural standards in the applicable law. * * *

A further weakness of existing Japanese law is the relative absence of a means for effective after-the-fact judicial review. * * *

A further problem of the use of administrative guidance is that the outcome of the decision-making process is very much dependent on the particular circumstances and the "negotiating power" between the administration and the addressee. Thus, not only the rationale but even the outcome of such compromise may not be clear to a third party, which may be either a competitor of the first addressee or later itself a recipient of guidance. Given that no standards of comparison are readily available, it is difficult to ensure equal and fair treatment. Some commentators have likened this nontransparent decision-making procedure to a "black box" which helps ensure a cooperative relationship between the administration and incumbent competitors but which may pose a serious obstacle for new entrants, be they Japanese or foreign. This perception [has] prompted the United States govern-

*From Lorenz Ködderitzsch, "Japan's New Administrative Procedure Law: Reasons for its Enactment and Likely Implications," 24 *Law in Japan: An Annual* 105 (1991), at 105-108, 110-111, 115-119, and 125-128. Reprinted by permission.

ment to demand, in the context of the Structural Impediments Initiative discussions, clearer procedures and greater transparency for administrative behavior in Japan. This lack of transparency also prompted the third commission on administrative reform * * * to set up a subcommittee in January 1991 entitled "fair and transparent administrative procedure" * * * with the task of drafting an administrative procedure act[, which ultimately resulted in the newly enacted law]. * * *

Overview of the APA

* * *

The main elements of the APA are the rules concerning licenses (arts. 5-11), disadvantageous dispositions (arts. 12-31) and administrative guidance (arts. 32-36). The structure and provisions of the act differ substantially from [an earlier] draft * * *, as well as the U.S. and German administrative procedure laws. Notably, the APA does not include any provisions concerning party capacity nor does it provide for rulemaking and planning procedures. * * *

The general provisions define the aim, scope and terminology of the law. Art. 1, subsection 1, states the law's aim as protecting citizens' rights by providing general and uniform rules for administrative actions such as dispositions, administrative guidance and notifications, and thereby contributing to a fair and transparent administrative procedure. It is noteworthy that * * * previous drafts [by] two study commissions had both emphasized the concept of participatory democracy. This concept has been deleted, concurrently with the decision not to formulate rules concerning planning and rulemaking procedures. * * *

Although the APA is intended to enact general rules for administrative procedure, art. 1, subsection 2, states that, when any law contains specific procedural standards, those standards shall apply, rather than the APA. * * *

Art. 2 defines basic terminology such as "laws and orders" (*hōrei*), "administrative disposition" (*shobun*), "application" (*shinsei*), "disadvantageous disposition" (*furieki shobun*), "administrative body" (*gyōsei kikan*), "administrative guidance" (*gyōsei shidō*) and "notification" (*todokede*).

The most noteworthy of these definitions is that of *gyōsei shidō*, which not only is defined but also is used as such for the first time in a statute. Until now that term has only been used by administrative practitioners and legal scholars exclusively as a hermeneutical—not a legal—concept. Such a legal definition is of great importance since *gyōsei shidō* has hitherto been an ambiguous and broad concept. It is defined in the APA as any "act, not being a disposition, such as a direction, recommendation or suggestion by an administrative body, in order to ask for the performance or nonperformance by a particular citizen with a view of achieving a policy aim within the sphere of competence of said administrative body." * * *

The scope of application is dealt with in art. 3. The law is generally applicable to all actions and administrative guidance by national administrative bodies, except those matters specifically exempted in the enumeration of art. 3, subsection 1, and all actions of local administrative bodies, provided that the actions are based on national statutes. Actions by local administrative bodies based upon ordinances or regulations (*jōrei mata wa kisoku*), together with all administrative guidance conducted by local administrative bodies, are exempted from coverage by art. 3, subsection 2. * * * (Art. 38, however, admonishes the local authorities to respect the spirit of this law when applying administrative guidance.) * * *

General rules pertaining to administrative guidance

The rules concerning administrative guidance reflect most strongly the impact of the administrative style in Japan and are probably the most interesting and innovative feature of the APA. This is the first attempt at dealing with the phenomenon of informal means of administrative actions through procedural rules. * * *

Similarly to scholars in Germany, Japanese legal scholars have come to recognize and analyze the phenomenon of informal means of administrative actions in a very reluctant way. Administrative guidance was first described by practitioners and only later with considerable delay treated from a legal perspective. The main reason for this may be that administrative law theory in Japan and in Germany sees its task in analyzing exclusively legal phenomena and not sociological occurrences. Thus for a very long time administrative guidance was viewed not as a legal phenomenon but as an anomaly or as a violation of the legal system. As such the initial reaction was one of skepticism: The usage of extralegal means runs contrary to the basic theory of the German and Japanese concept of 'rule of law.'

The obvious answer would be to devise mechanisms to oblige the administration to act exclusively according to the intent and means described in the substantive laws * * *. Yet occasionally these substantive laws do not provide sufficient rules for the agencies to cope with the demands of administration. Again, the standard academic answer would be to call for more detailed legislation. However, some legal scholars have come to accept the inevitability of extralegal actions by the administration, since no law can keep up with the changing needs in society. Furthermore, overregulating may put the administration in an impasse out of which it can only escape through either inaction or extralegal means. * * * Given this situation, some Japanese scholars have supported the necessity and even the positive role of administrative guidance. Yet, just as the concept of administrative guidance is very broad and diverse, so has the assessment of it been very diverse, from outright rejection to moderate support.

The new law does not in itself make any judgment on the phenomenon of administrative guidance but tries (i) to reiterate fundamental principles derived from the Japanese concept of 'rule of law' as an admonishment to the administrative bodies and (ii) to provide for some procedural mechanism in order to minimize the risk of abuse by administrative bodies.

Arts. 32-34 state the general principles regarding administrative guidance and the rules to be observed by the administration when issuing administrative guidance in connection with procedures for review of applications. Art. 32 stresses the fact that administrative guidance is based on voluntary compliance and that no administrative body may impose any unfavorable treatment on an addressee who refuses to comply with the administrative guidance. Furthermore, an administrative body may not exceed its statutory authority when issuing administrative guidance. These general principles are further clarified in arts. 33 and 34, which forbid the administrative agency to abuse its authority to issue licenses in order to secure an addressee's compliance. Thus, the administrative body is not allowed to insist on its administrative guidance, for instance when asking an applicant to modify the content of his application, when the applicant has made it clear that he is not willing to comply with the administration's wishes.

These rules as such do not add anything to the principles of 'rule of law' as understood by the courts and legal scholars in Japan. Also, in a narrow sense, they are not procedural rules. This led critics of the [draft on which the APA was based] to question the necessity of such rules, and in a counterproposal they exclusively focused on procedural mechanisms to contain the administration's excessive use of administrative guidance. However, clarifying the basic principles may be understood as a powerful signal to the administrative bodies to respect the boundaries of law and may be helpful to citizens when opposing a nonstatutory request by an administrative body.

Besides the danger of abuse of the administration's regulatory rights and the possible coercion of addressees into compliance with administrative guidance, criticism has mainly focused on the fact that in many cases the content and aim of the administrative guidance and the designation of the responsible civil servant or administrative body are kept unclear. In order to avoid such lack of transparency and lack of attributable responsibility, art. 35, subsection 1, requires the administrative body to clearly inform the addressee of the aim and content of the administrative guidance and the name of the responsible official. Subsection 2 entitles the addressee to request to have this information stated in writing unless there are special administrative impediments (*gyōseijō no tokubetsu shishō*). Having to put in writing the content of administrative guidance will undoubtedly force the administrative body to think through the rationale and legal implications of its request. However, part of the success of administrative guidance has been the process of give-and-take between the administration and an addressee and the blurring of legal boundaries. The impact of art. 35 on the administrative style in Japan will essentially depend on whether the addressee will have either the interest or the courage to request a written statement.

A second procedural rule addresses the problem involved in issuing administrative guidance with the same aim or content to different addressees. Art. 36 requires administrative bodies to set up rules for the common points of administrative guidance and, unless there are special administrative impediments, to make these rules publicly available. The publication of such rules will be of crucial importance in order to ensure fair and equal treatment by the administration, since the lack of means of comparison often has proved to be a major obstacle when considering filing a suit against an administrative body. On the other hand, this rule may be perceived as a way of legitimizing administrative bodies to set up rules quite independently of statutory bases, as is the case in building law through so-called "outline guidance." * * *

Questions and Discussion Points

1. *Impact of the APA:* Is the APA likely to have a significant impact on administrative guidance? Why or why not?

2. *The Nakaya Case under the APA:* Assuming the APA had been in effect at the time of the *Nakaya* case, what effect would it have had on that case?

3. *Influence of German administrative law principles:* Ködderitzch refers from time to time to principles of German administrative law. These references derive particular significance in that Japanese administrative law has been profoundly influenced by German law and Japanese scholars continue to pay close attention to developments in German administrative law doctrine. Consider whether the German and Japanese attitudes toward the 'rule of law' described by Ködderitzsch may have produced views on administrative guidance that differ from those in the United States.

III. Administrative Guidance and Criminal Liability

Consider the position of a firm asked by one branch of the government bureaucracy to do something which violates a law administered by another branch. Does complying with the first agency's administrative guidance immunize it from liability if sued by the second agency? Should it? The following case explores the problem in more detail.

*[Japan] v. Idemitsu Kōsan, et al.**
985 Hanrei Jihō 3
(Tokyo High Ct., Sept. 26, 1980)[1]

Defendants Jun'ichi Saitō and Ichiyuki Okada are sentenced to ten months in prison; defendants Yasuichi Tamura, Ryōichi Aichi, Takashige Hashida, Kenji Ishiwata, Junkichi Izumi, Kiyoshi Inoue, and Tatsuo Matsui are sentenced to four months in prison; and defendants Jirō Kawazoe, Taisuke Ōhashi, Akira Takenobu, Nagahiko Tokida, and Yoshitaka Enomoto are sentenced to six months in prison.

Defendant corporations Idemitsu Kōsan K.K. and Nihon Sekiyu K.K. are fined 2.5 million yen; defendant corporation Taiyō Sekiyu K.K. is fined 1.5 million yen; and defendant corporations Daikyō Sekiyu K.K., Maruzen Sekiyu K.K., Kyōdō Sekiyu K.K., Kigunasu Sekiyu K.K., Kyūshū Sekiyu K.K., Mitsubishi Sekiyu K.K., Shōwa Sekiyu K.K., Sheru [Shell] Sekiyu K.K., and Zeneraru [General] Sekiyu K.K. are fined 2 million yen.

The execution of the prison terms for the defendants is deferred for two years following the confirmation of this trial.[2]

[I.A. THE FACTUAL AND LEGAL CONTEXT]

[When the Arab nations reduced the quantity of oil they were willing to sell to

*Translation from J. Mark Ramseyer, "The Oil Cartel Criminal Cases: Translations and Postscript," 15 *Law in Japan: An Annual* 57 (1982). Reprinted by permission.

Japan in 1973, the Japanese economy faced one of the most serious challenges it had encountered since the Second World War. Numerous firms, including those in the petroleum industry, attempted to deal with the crisis by entering into cartel-like arrangements, and the Fair Trade Commission (FTC) responded by trying vigorously to enforce the Antimonopoly Act. The petroleum industry, however, had been heavily regulated by the Ministry of International Trade & Industry (MITI) for years, first through the Ministry's control over the allocation of foreign exchange, and later through the Petroleum Industry Act.[3] The Ministry had always been more skeptical than the FTC of the need for a strong antitrust policy, and had been directly involved in coordinating the cartelization of the petroleum industry. Thus, when the FTC attempted to curtail the concerted activity among the petroleum refiners, it directly interfered with MITI's policies and created one of the central issues in this case: should firms, trade associations, and personnel in heavily regulated industries be held criminally liable for violating the Antimonopoly Act when they do so pursuant to instructions and authorizations issued by a government ministry?]

[The case arose under Section 3 of the Antimonopoly Act, which provides: "No entrepreneur shall effect any private monopolization or unreasonable restraint of trade." Section 89(a)(i) makes the violation of Section 3 a criminal offense, and Section 2(f) defines an unreasonable restraint of trade as activity "by which an entrepreneur * * * engages in concerted activity with other entrepreneurs to fix prices * * * and bind their business activities mutually * * *, and thus substantially restrains competition in any particular line of commerce in a manner contrary to the public interest."]

[I.B. ARGUMENT OF THE DEFENDANTS]

The argument of the defense counsel, amplified, is as follows:

Petroleum products have been under governmental control and management since the pre-war years. After the enactment of the Petroleum Industry Act in 1962, MITI used that law and administrative guidance based on the law to regulate the business activities of firms in the industry and to determine the basic price structure of the market for petroleum products. To respond to the OPEC offensive begun in 1970, MITI in April of 1971 used a ten cent burden[4] to control the average increase in petroleum product prices. It then allocated that average increase to the various products by establishing guidelines for the maximum price increases of the different types of petroleum, and demanded that firms obey those guidelines. MITI thus determined prices through the guideline system of administrative guidance. It issued such guideline administrative guidance again in April 1972, and this time demanded that a firm report to the Ministry whenever it believed that an increase in crude oil prices necessitated an increase in the price of its petroleum products above the ceiling established by the guidelines. At this point, the guideline system of administrative guidance had become established, and firms could no longer raise the prices of petroleum products except by obtaining a revision of the guidelines.

From 1972 through 1973, the defendants did, as charged, discuss at the meetings of the Business Committee [of the Petroleum Federation] the five increases in the price of petroleum products that took place. They did so, however, because the price of crude oil had risen. As they wished to raise their prices in compliance with the guideline system, they hoped to obtain the requisite changes in the guidelines and met to construct a proposal for those changes. In order to construct the proposal, they calculated the average price increase necessary for the industry as a whole, allocated that amount to the different types of oil in order to determine the price increase needed for each of the various products, and determined the date on which they hoped to make the increases effective. The chairman of the Business Committee then sought an acknowledgment of the proposal from MITI officials. When he obtained the acknowledgment, the proposal became the industry's guidelines. All sellers, including the defendant companies, then raised (or sometimes lowered or maintained) their prices within the range of the guidelines according to the applicable pricing standards, and made those increases effective on the date the Ministry had acknowledged as the date to execute the changes.

Thus, the defendants claim that, contrary to the charge, they did not in their capacity as executives of the various firms meet and decide to raise prices together. Instead, they argue that they merely cooperated with MITI's administrative guidance.

[II. FINDINGS OF FACT]

Even before the OPEC offensive, * * * the national government partially controlled the price of petroleum products. It did so largely to further its industrial strategy. In order to try to correct market allocations, it intervened in the market through administrative guidance to the extent necessary, once the Petroleum Industry Act took effect. As part of that guidance, it issued the pricing standards authorized by the Petroleum Industry Act; for example, it issued guidance directly setting some prices, and attempted to eliminate excess competition. After the OPEC offensive, the government intervened in the market through a form of administrative guidance that strongly resembled price control, and did so to promote not only its industrial strategy but also its pricing policy and the public welfare. * * *

It was the industry, however, that initiated the price increases of April 1972 and determined their scope. Yet, in the course of doing so the industry found itself at odds with MITI officials—officials who generally favored price restraints. Because of this conflict, industry leaders conferred with officials of the Mining & Coal Bureau [of MITI], provided MITI officials with data and explanations, and collaborated with MITI officials in making calculations. Nevertheless, although MITI officials acknowledged the industry's agreement to raise prices, the industry initiated the increases. The increases were not, as defense counsel argue, the result of price guidance by MITI's guideline system. * * *

Considering these facts and the above testimony of MITI officials, we conclude that the April 1972 price increases involved positive guidance (like that described above) which MITI issued on its own initiative in response to the drastic changes that had taken place in the crude oil market. After that time, however, the Ministry issued price guidance only for certain oil products like kerosene, and then only out of consideration for the public welfare. Instead, it investigated price fluctuations in order to understand the actual situation; it adopted the stance of trying to restrain price increases in the industry and issued general warnings to the industry not to raise prices by taking advantage of the market or by any other undesirable means; and it tried to enforce its past measures and advice regarding the scope of the average price increases. It sought, however, to entrust the price of the various types of petroleum to the marketplace. It generally avoided intervening in the market on its own initiative so drastically as to specify the scope of the maximum price increases for the different types of petroleum and then to enforce those price directives.

The above discussion indicates that the defendants at bar customarily deferred to MITI's administrative guidance. No doubt they remembered the forceful administrative guidance the Ministry had issued at the time of the April 1971 price increases, and the fact that it had demanded at the time of the following April's price increases that the industry consult with it before raising prices. The defendants knew on the basis of their information about the opinions and attitudes of past MITI officials that the Ministry might, depending on the increases to which the industry members agreed, issue guidance restraining such increases unless it had already acknowledged the price hikes.

Nevertheless, we reject the defense counsel's claim that the price guideline system of guidance had become so established as to be a permit system whereby industry members could not raise prices unless they obtained MITI's acknowledgment. This "acknowledgment" was in fact merely negative—an indication from the MITI officials that they did not intend to issue guidance restraining the increases so long as the prices to which the industry leaders agreed did not exceed the proposed price limits. The defendants obtained the acknowledgment because they considered it to their advantage to raise prices only by obtaining MITI's acknowledgment and thereby to forestall any guidance restraining their price increases. MITI did, in other words, administratively intervene in the process by which the price increases at bar were set, and the defendants did in part cooperate with that administrative effort. Such a finding of cooperation does not, however, lessen the fact that the defendants engaged in the concerted activity described above.

[III. THE LEGALITY OF THE DEFENDANTS' BEHAVIOR]

[A. Was the Agreement Between the Firms Binding?]

The defendants believed that by engaging in the concerted activity at bar and conducting the business of their firms accordingly they would benefit their respective firms. They hoped to realize the aims of that concerted activity, and adhered to their agreement because they believed that the other defendant firms would do so as well. The concerted activity, therefore, mutually bound the business activities of the defendant companies and falls within the scope [of Section 2(f) of the Antimonopoly Act]. The legality of an agreement depends on its power to bind firms [within the group], not on whether firms may freely choose to join or to leave the group. Because an unreasonable restraint of trade is illegal under the Antimonopoly Act, a firm cannot realistically expect such a restraint to be fully effective. Accordingly, a court need not find that the defendant firms had a duty to abide by the terms of the agreement establishing the concerted activity in order to find a violation [of the Act]. In the case at bar, the defendant firms did not go to the lengths suggested by the defense counsel to ensure that they each engaged in the concerted activity, although as noted above they did consider some measures that would have prevented firms from acting contrary to the agreement. Therefore, even though the firms maintained the freedom to refuse to participate in the concerted activity and the activity was not fully effective, the defendants' behavior falls within the scope [of the Antimonopoly Act].

[B. Was the Activity Contrary to the Public Interest?]

The criminal sanctions against unreasonable restraints of trade apply only if the substantial restraint of competition is "contrary to the public interest." The significance of that requirement and the reasons for its adoption can be understood only in light of the purpose of the Antimonopoly Act and its structure as a whole.

According to Section 1 of the Antimonopoly Act, the Act was drafted to "promote fair and free competition"—to promote the antimonopolistic policy of maintaining a freely competitive economic order. The drafters sought the realization of this antitrust policy in order "to protect the interests of general consumers" and "to promote the healthy and democratic development of the national economy." To further these aims, the Act prohibits private monopolization, unreasonable restraints of trade, and unfair business practices, as defined in Section 2 of the Act, and prevents the excessive concentration of business power. This concern for a healthy and democratic national economy clearly reflects no concern for the protection of those business managerial interests at odds with the interests of general consumers.
* * *

If one considered the Antimonopoly Act as a whole in light of these revisions in the Act,[5] one might conclude that some concerted activity to restrict competition substantially in a given line of commerce, depending on its content, would not violate the purpose of the Act. The purpose of the Act as described above, however, indicates that activity "contrary to the public interest" is activity contrary to the purpose of the Act and contrary, therefore, to the freely competitive economic order whose maintenance is the direct aim of the Act. Nevertheless, even if the defendants' activity appeared to violate the letter of the Act, one might in some cases conclude, after comparing the interests protected by the statute with the interests protected by the defendants' activity, that the activity was not substantially contrary to the purpose of the Act as a whole. One might, therefore, reasonably decide that the "contrary to the public interest" provision was included in the Antimonopoly Act to exclude from the scope of the Act such exceptional cases.

In light of that analysis, we conclude that the defendants' activities were contrary to the public interest. Through their concerted activity to raise the price of petroleum products—which are some of the commodities most important to our nation—the defendants restricted competition in those products and had a major impact on the national economy. As noted above, they acted pursuant neither to administrative guidance nor to an effort to assist MITI in its administrative duties. Cost factors like the rise of crude oil prices did necessitate an increase in the price of the defendants' products. Yet, the evidence does not indicate that the defendants would have found it extremely difficult or impossible to remain in business or that the nation's maintenance of a stable supply of inexpensive petroleum products[6] would have been jeopardized, had the defendants not engaged in the concerted activity. While the defendants did not attempt to garner especially large profits for their firms, they did engage in the activity at bar in order to make their price increases profitable.

[C. Did the Agreements Substantially Restrain Competition?]

Section 2(f) of the Antimonopoly Act defines binding concerted activity as that activity which has the natural effect of restraining competition. It limits the coverage of the prohibition of concerted activity unreasonably restricting trade to that activity which "substantially restrains competition in any particular line of commerce." An unreasonable restraint exists, in other words, when parties engage in concerted activity sufficiently binding to restrain substantially, contrary to the public interest, competition within a given line of commerce. The illegal restraint exists even when the substance of the concerted activity has not been realized—a realization that represents the external manifestation of the substantial restraint of competition brought about by the concerted activity.

[IV. THE PRESENCE OF CRIMINAL INTENT]

[A. The Assertions of the Defense Attorneys]

Defense counsel assert that even if the defendants' activities met the criminal statutory requirements for a finding of illegality, the defendants lacked the requisite intent. The Antimonopoly Act prohibits only behavior contrary to the public interest and the defendants, they claim, were not conscious of the fact of violating that interest. The Act prohibits only activity that mutually binds the business activities of the firms and substantially restrains competition in a given line of commerce, they continue, and the state has failed to prove that the defendants were conscious of the fact of engaging in such activity. Thus, counsel argue that the defendants believed that they were acting legitimately and legally when they engaged in the activity which they considered to be pursuant to MITI's legal administrative guidance and to be the execution of the Ministry's administrative responsibilities. These mistakes by the defendants, they claim, constitute mistakes of fact sufficient to preclude a court from finding the defendants' conduct illegal. Furthermore, they argue, because of these mistakes the defendants lacked any consciousness of the illegality of their actions, and the circumstances of the case justified their ignorance.

[B. The Decision of the Court]

In light of the substance and purpose of the statutory provisions to which the defendants' attorneys have referred, we believe that the defendants' behavior itself indicates that the defendants were conscious of all facts necessary for conviction. Judging the behavior of the defendants in the context of the administrative intervention that took place, we reject the claim of the defense counsel that there were mistakes of fact sufficient to preclude a finding of illegality. Various factors point to the conclusion that the defendants were conscious of the illegality of their actions: the content of their concerted activity; * * * the fact that the defendants feared that their pending administrative litigation[7] with the FTC—although initiated under somewhat different circumstances when the Commission attacked, as an Antimonopoly Act violation, the content of the defendants' April 1971 price increases—might lead the Commission to expose their present activities as well; and [citation to various testimony omitted]. The evidence to the contrary is not credible. The fact that the defendants may have believed that MITI and the FTC disagreed on several points concerning the proper interpretation of the Antimonopoly Act and about the legality of administrative intervention restricting competition does not affect our conclusion.

Questions and Discussion Points

1. *Purpose of the guidance:* What was the purpose of the administrative guidance? Who gained from it? Who lost?
2. *Purpose of the suit:* Why did the FTC bring suit?

FURTHER READING

John O. Haley, "Administrative Guidance versus Formal Regulation: Resolving the Paradox of Industrial Policy," in Gary Saxonhouse and Kozo Yamamura, eds., *Law and Trade Issues of the Japanese Economy: American and Japanese Perspectives*, pp. 107-128. Seattle: University of Washington Press, 1986.

John O. Haley, *Authority without Power: Law and the Japanese Paradox*. New York: Oxford University Press, 1991.

Kiminobu Hashimoto, "The Rule of Law: Some Aspects of Judicial Review of Administrative Actions," in Arthur T. von Mehren, ed., *Law in Japan: The Legal Order in a Changing Society*, pp. 238-273. Cambridge, MA: Harvard University Press, 1963.

Wolfgang Pape, "*Gyōsei Shidō* and the Antimonopoly Law," 15 *Law in Japan: An Annual* 12 (1982).

J. Mark Ramseyer, "Japanese Antitrust Enforcement After the Oil Embargo," 31 *American Journal of Comparative Law* 395 (1983).

J. Mark Ramseyer and Frances McCall Rosenbluth, *Japan's Political Marketplace*. Cambridge, MA: Harvard University Press, 1993.

Lawrence Repeta, "The Limits of Administrative Authority in Japan: The Oil Cartel Criminal Cases and the Reaction of MITI and the FTC," 15 *Law in Japan: An Annual* 24 (1982).

Allan D. Smith, "The Japanese Foreign Exchange and Foreign Trade Control Law and Administrative Guidance: The Labyrinth and the Castle," 16 *Law and Policy in International Business* 417 (1984).

Frank Upham, "The Legal Framework of Japan's Declining Industries Policy: The

Problem of Transparency in Administrative Process," 27 *Harvard International Law Journal* 425 (1986).

Jonathan Weinberg, "Broadcasting and the Administrative Process in Japan and the United States," 39 *Buffalo Law Review* 623 (1991).

Russell Allen Yeomans, "Administrative Guidance," 19 *Law in Japan: An Annual* 125 (1986).

NOTES TO CHAPTER FOUR

1. All footnotes have been supplied by the translator.

2. 985 Hanrei Jihō at 8. The execution of the sentences was deferred and made contingent on the behavior of the defendants during those two years.

3. *Sekiyugyō hō* (Petroleum Industry Act), Law No. 128 of 1962 [hereinafter cited as the Petroleum Industry Act].

4. MITI ordered the firms to absorb ten cents per barrel of the increased costs. *See* 985 Hanrei Jihō at 12.

5. Enacted in 1947 by American occupational authorities eager to refashion Japanese society, the Antimonopoly Act soon encountered strong Japanese opposition. Within a year after the end of the Occupation, the Japanese Diet substantially revised the Act to weaken many of its prohibitions. Law No. 259 of 1953. * * *

6. Quoting the Petroleum Industry Act, art. 1.

7. The FTC staff brought an administrative action before the Commission, as provided in the Antimonopoly Act, Section 48.

FIVE

Doing Business in Japan and the Principal Case

Introduction

With this chapter we begin our consideration of the Principal Case (P.C.). The P.C. involves a business relationship between two construction equipment manufacturers, American Heavy Equipment, Inc. (A.Co) and Japan Construction Machinery K.K. (J.Co). Their twelve-year relationship provides the opportunity to survey much of the law relevant to doing business in Japan from the perspective of the practical business objectives of the two companies. Accordingly, materials in later chapters will refer frequently to the relationship between A.Co and J.Co.

The P.C., although framed in hypothetical terms, is based on an actual case. Names and certain details have been changed, various revisions and some simplifications have been made for pedagogical purposes, and some aspects of the timing have been adjusted. With few exceptions, however, the letters exchanged by the parties, the agreements they entered, and the other documents concerning the relationship are derived from actual documents, either in that case or in other U.S./Japan ventures.

The P.C. spanned a twelve-year period from 1969 to 1981. This was an important period both for law and for business in Japan. It was a key transitional period with respect to the attitudes toward and the legal regulation of foreign investment in Japan. Not entirely coincidentally, it was also a time during which Japanese industry greatly increased its ability to compete effectively in worldwide markets. Because the primary purpose of this book is to examine the relevant law as it exists today, these materials focus primarily on current legal standards. At times, however, we have also given attention to the law prevailing at the time of the P.C., both to enable readers to understand the P.C. and to explain the historical antecedents to the current legal standards.

After describing the factual background of the P.C., this chapter turns to a consideration of factors influencing the choice of investment vehicle, followed by an examination of key issues relating to joint ventures. The next section of this chapter is designed to introduce the P.C. Agreements, primarily through a series of questions focusing on specific key provisions of each agreement. To simplify consideration, the initial discussion in this chapter does not include tax aspects of the structuring decision. The final section of this chapter, however, provides an overview of basic principles of Japanese tax law that may affect the choice of investment vehicle.

PART A: Introduction to the Principal Case

I.Business Setting

In order to provide good legal advice regarding a business transaction, it is usually vital to understand the business setting and objectives of the parties. The following provides background for the negotiations between A.Co and J.Co, which began in 1969.

1. *Description of the parties, as of 1969*—Both A.Co and J.Co are in the business of manufacturing heavy machinery, such as bulldozers, graders, cranes, excavators, and backhoes, for use in construction and mining projects. A.Co is focused primarily on the production of excavators and excavator/cranes (cranes built onto excavator frames). It holds a substantial market share in the U.S. for these products, but is one of a few second-tier companies which are considerably smaller than, and do not have the broad product lines of, the three giant construction equipment manufacturers in the U.S.

J.Co has focused primarily on the production of bulldozers. It has had great success with its bulldozers, holding a 60% share of the bulldozer market in Japan and making substantial exports to other Asian countries. Based on its dominance in the bulldozer market, J.Co has one of the largest shares of the total construction machinery market in Japan. J.Co, however, has not had great success with other products.

2. *Hydraulic technology and excavators*—In the 1960s, European and U.S. manufacturers have commercialized hydraulic technology for use in certain construction equipment, especially excavators, which are machines used for digging and moving earth. Hydraulic excavators, as compared with traditional mechanical excavators, offer substantially greater strength, precision of movement, control, and reliability.

Western companies are far ahead of Japanese companies in the use of hydraulics and have an overall lead in almost all construction machinery technology. A.Co and other Western companies have obtained patents in Japan relating to hydraulics and in particular to application of hydraulic technology to excavators. J.Co has undertaken some limited R&D in hydraulics, but it is not yet close to commercializing the technology.

The excavator market in Japan is substantially smaller per capita than in the U.S., but J.Co expects the demand for excavators to rise sharply. The excavator market in Japan is dominated by one company which has only a 7% share of the total construction equipment market in Japan but a 61% share of the excavator market. The excavators it has been selling are the old mechanical type. J.Co produces no excavators.

A.Co's sales of excavators in the U.S. have been strong. It has a broad line of highly regarded excavators of varying sizes, several models of which can, by attaching different front ends, also operate as cranes, machines that lift materials and equipment.

3. *Worldwide construction industry*—The industry is fiercely competitive in each of the U.S., Europe, and Japan, but the three markets have been fairly isolated from one another. There has, however, been some cross-Atlantic trade and joint venturing, and though the Japanese government has restricted imports of construction machinery into Japan, it has throughout the 1950s and 1960s allowed limited importing when necessary for major public works projects. A.Co exported some machinery for these projects and on this basis has a good reputation within the Japanese industry.

4. *Trend toward tie-ups between Japanese and Western construction equipment makers*—J.Co's main competitors in Japan have concluded or are in the process of negotiating licensing agreements and other tie-ups with Western manufacturers through which they can obtain access to hydraulic and other technologies and through which the Western companies can participate in the fast growing Japanese market. No Western company on its own has manufacturing facilities in Japan or extensive exports to Japan.

If J.Co does not quickly develop or obtain access to similar technology, it will likely be at a severe competitive disadvantage. A.Co has not yet entered into any relationship with a Japanese company but is aware that several of its U.S. competitors have.

J.Co, in addition to proposing that A.Co license its hydraulic and other technologies for excavators, has begun talks with International Reaper, one of A.Co's principal competitors in the U.S., to obtain technology related to backhoes and loaders. J.Co is also considering approaching one of the major U.S. construction equipment engine manufacturers to gain access to its technology and know-how.

II. Business Objectives

From the foregoing factual background, you should be able to make some predictions about the business objectives of the two companies. The first letter below was sent from J.Co to A.Co after the parties attended introductory meetings initiated by J.Co. At these meetings, J.Co made a general proposal that A.Co license its hydraulic and other excavator technologies. The second document is an internal memorandum of A.Co summarizing some preliminary discussions with J.Co representatives.

- - - - - - - - - - -

[J.Co letterhead]
August 20, 1969

A.J. Rose
Sales Manager, Commercial Cranes and Excavators
A.Co
[address omitted]

Dear Mr. Rose:

Thank you for your letter dated August 11, 1969. We are pleased that you are seriously considering this matter.

We enclose our report on "The Excavator Business in Japan." As you will see, the demand for bulldozers has grown rapidly, and we expect to see a similar increase in the demand for excavators. Construction companies are now experiencing a boom and are rapidly buying the necessary machinery. Also, the remarkable economic growth in Japan has raised the price of labor and forced construction companies to adopt mechanized methods.

The current supply of excavators will not meet the expected demand. Therefore, we believe this is the ideal time to enter the excavator market. We are the largest bulldozer manufacturer in Japan with a 61% market share. It is common for bulldozer purchasers later to become purchasers of excavators. As a result, we believe we have a natural access to potential excavator buyers.

We would be pleased to discuss with your staff the following, even on an informal basis, as soon as is convenient:

i) Details of a manufacturing collaboration,
ii) Export of the manufactured machines,
iii) Stocking parts,
iv) Service facilities, and
v) Major construction projects planned in Japan and elsewhere.

We appreciate your attention to these matters.

Very truly yours,

[signed]

____

A. Kurasaka, Chief
First Machinery and
Engineering
J.Co

- - - - - - - - - -

To: Mr. P.E. Berger
Copies to: Messrs. Alson, Charles, and Rose
From: T.R. Griggs
Re: Discussions with J.Co
Date: 10/15/69

As expected, we were visited today by two Japanese gentlemen from

J.Co, Mr. Kurasaka and Mr. Matsumoto.

Mr. Kurasaka opened by saying that the price for machinery imported into Japan can be as much as double that for the locally manufactured product. We can appreciate that from our own experience several years back when Kobe Steel quoted for copies of our heavy mining shovels for delivery to Manchuria a price about half of the F.O.B. price if built by us.

This supports our thoughts about the possibility of using low-cost manufacturing in Japan to supply markets all over Asia and perhaps the world. This could also position us well if the government ever opens up China. Of course I agree that we can hold off on these issues for now and focus on capitalizing on the economic boom in Japan.

Having regard for the cost advantages, the Japanese Government encourages local manufacture and provides exchange and import facilities for firms to be able to arrange technical assistance contracts. On the other hand, because of its dependence on outside sources for raw materials, Japan is very anxious to export, and we shall, undoubtedly, hear more about this as we go along.

I am not sure what the situation is if we decide we want to try and get into our own manufacture there, but I think there are all sorts of regulations in Japan to discourage this. Basically, they probably want their own companies involved in manufacture. We could look into this more and of course would have to give serious consideration to the huge capital outlay, greatly increased risk, delays in earnings, and other issues related to going it alone.

The Japanese side seemed to receive our preliminary thoughts about possibly providing them technical information on our hydraulic excavators with a considerable degree of hopefulness. They said and I agree that we'll have to move fast on this or get shut out of the market now that Excavators 'R Us and International Reaper have apparently already negotiated tie-ups with J.Co's main competitors. Basically they seem very concerned, so our bargaining position should be strong.

We questioned our visitors as closely as we could about the size of excavators which are most popular in Japan and were informed that these range in size from 3/4 cubic yard to 1-1/2 cubic yards. The market for machines of larger size is said to be very limited. They said they plan to send us a detailed report on their market forecasts for various size excavators.

The metric system prevails by law in Japan, but Japanese manufacturers are prepared to make their own conversions and drawings and to translate other forms of know-how.

If we want to license the know-how to J.Co, we'll have to negotiate a technical assistance contract through the Ministry of International Trade and Investment. I've heard this can take as long as six months but I also think there may have been some recent changes in the regulations to loosen things up a bit. We were given to understand that the Japanese are accustomed to paying substantial fees for the disclosure of know-how as well as royalties of up to say 5%, depending on the size of the machine concerned.

I emphasized that we wouldn't be interested in short-term licensing as we are looking to a long-term future in Japan. I said that we would want some sort of permanent arrangement and a means of ensuring that our technology is put to the best use.

When I get back from the New York trip we can discuss how to proceed.

Questions and Discussion Points

1. *Business objectives of each side:* Generate a list of the business objectives of J.Co and A.Co. Are these objectives compatible?

2. *J.Co's letter:* Why is J.Co's letter so vague? Might J.Co be afraid to mention licensing, out of fear that A.Co will lose interest? Or has J.Co simply not resolved its own desires?

J.Co might also have mentioned other factors, such as the availability of an established sales network, funding, or possibly even an idle plant. Why didn't it?

3. *Form of relationship:* What type of business relationship would each side likely prefer?

III. Legal Advice

Once A.Co and J.Co begin to assess how they might structure any business relationship between them, they will have embarked upon some basic legal analysis. Doing so will not require A.Co and J.Co to consult lawyers, but either might at this point decide to do so. Should they?

On what subjects might A.Co need advice? Recall the discussion of the legal profession in Japan in Chapter 2. If A.Co were today seeking to do business in Japan, from whom could it get what types of advice on Japanese law?

Assume that representatives of A.Co showed J.Co's letter to you, as their attorney, and asked your advice on how to respond. If you are a U.S. lawyer, what limitations are there on the advice you can give to A.Co?

Available options for A.Co range all the way from flatly rejecting the feeler or sending an equally vague response to formulating a firm proposal and attaching detailed drafts of agreements. If A.Co is a typical client, it will want your best estimate of the future based on the various options available now. Making such predictions requires two levels of analysis. The first level is *static analysis.* This involves analyzing the current state of affairs, both from your client's point of view and from the other side's likely point of view. You should consider the law, the economics of the transaction, and the psychology of the two parties. The second level is that of *process analysis,* in which you put the static analysis into an analysis of developing trends and foreseeable future events, in order to predict future results as well as possible.

With these thoughts in mind, what additional information do you need to answer A.Co? To what sources can you turn for assistance in advising A.Co?

Consider also the perspective of J.Co. If J.Co's letter to A.Co represents the sum of the collective thinking of J.Co management, should J.Co now begin seeking legal advice, and if so, what type of advice might J.Co need? To what types of lawyers should J.Co turn?

Finally, are there professionals other than lawyers to whom either of A.Co and J.Co might want to turn for advice? Should nonprofessionals also be consulted?

PART B: Vehicles for Foreign Investment

I. Legal Forms for Doing Business in Japan

Even before having been approached by J.Co, A.Co was interested in developing a presence in Japan. This presence might take any of a number of forms. A.Co might want to minimize its commitment in Japan and simply export its construction machinery to be distributed in Japan by some Japanese company. Alternatively, A.Co might prefer to establish its own company in Japan to distribute its U.S.-made excavators. A.Co would also need to consider whether manufacturing in the U.S. for shipment to Japan would be most cost effective. For supplying the distant Japanese market, manufacture in Japan might be the best choice, and if so, A.Co will have to decide whether the manufacture in Japan should be done by an A.Co subsidiary, by a Japanese subcontractor, or by licensing the technology to a Japanese company. Furthermore, before A.Co chooses any one approach to selling its excavators in Japan, it might simply want to station one or two employees in Japan to do some preliminary research.

J.Co, too, having concluded that there is a market for excavators in Japan but that it does not yet have the technological ability to make marketable excavators itself, would need to consider its options. For example, J.Co might simply try to become the sales agent in Japan for A.Co's or another company's excavators. Another option would be to convince A.Co to sell the rights and training necessary for J.Co to use A.Co's technology to manufacture excavators in Japan.

In this section, we will survey the principal legal forms by which A.Co and J.Co might do business and consider the relationship between business objectives and legal forms. Naturally, much of what we discuss will apply to any foreign manufacturer seeking to do business in Japan and to any Japanese manufacturer seeking a business tie-up. Some of the discussion will also apply to companies in services or finance. Note, however, that one means of doing business in Japan, by acquiring an existing Japanese company, will be reserved for Chapter 12 on mergers and acquisitions.

DAVID A. AAKER, STRATEGIC MARKET MANAGEMENT*

284-294 (1984)

During the past few decades an increasing number of firms have seen their strategies affected by multinational competitors and the opportunities of foreign markets. The world is indeed getting smaller and more interdependent technologically, politically, socially, and economically. * * *

The development of multinational strategies * * * involves consideration of threats, opportunities, key success factors, and strategy options and issues which do not appear when the analysis is restricted to operations within a single country. In particular, the evaluation of a market must take into account the political and economic risks associated with individual countries. Thus, the external analysis becomes much more demanding.

Among the alternative strategies that are possible for a firm in a multinational environment are exporting, licensing, joint venture, foreign subsidiary, and engagement in a global strategy. Of course, many multinationals engage in more than one of these strategies in different countries. Further, the strategies are not necessarily mutually exclusive. A firm could engage in exporting or a global strategy using joint ventures, for example. However, a discussion of each of them will provide a good overview of the involved issues.

[1.] Exporting

The simplest way to enter a foreign market is to export. Manufacturing remains in the home country. The product may be identical or it might be modified somewhat if the foreign market warrants. The exporting can be done through an export organization in either the home country or in the foreign market. Such an exporting organization can provide expertise with respect to distribution, marketing, and negotiations as well as administrative skills at handling any export approvals and credit arrangements. Alternatively, the exporting firm can sell directly to its foreign customers. Direct selling could also be done by correspondence or with traveling representatives. It can also include sales offices in the foreign market, perhaps under the control of a sales subsidiary. Further on the continuum would be the inclusion of a sales/service dealer network. * * *

There is, in many strategic choices, a tradeoff between commitment and flexibility. Exporting minimizes the commitment and accompanying risks. The other extreme is to establish manufacturing operations in the foreign market. Compared to the commitment of manufacturing, exporting would be a logical choice when:

- The firm is small and does not have the resources to make the commitment of manufacturing.
- Heavy commitment is inadvisable because of political risk or because the market is either not sufficiently attractive or its prospects are too uncertain.

*From David A. Aaker, *Strategic Market Management* (© 1984, John Wiley & Sons), at 284-294. Reprinted by permission of John Wiley & Sons, Inc.

• There is no political or economic pressure to manufacture in the foreign market. Several Japanese automobile manufacturers have considered or have begun manufacturing in the United States because of political factors. The American Congress has warned of political risks in expanding imports indefinitely.

[2.] Licensing

In a licensing arrangement, a firm will provide, for a fee or royalty, some technology needed to operate its business in the foreign market. This technology could involve a brand name, operations expertise, manufacturing-process technology, or access to patents or other trade secrets. The licensee gains a competitive advantage and access to information that would perhaps be prohibitively expensive. The licensor gains access to a foreign market with very low investment and, in some instances, obtains the investment and market knowledge of an able organization.

Exporting allows the flexibility of later expanding the scope of commitment from a sales office to a marketing operation and even to manufacturing. However, by inhibiting or prohibiting such options, the licensing arrangement provides less flexibility. More generally, a licensing arrangement contains upscale risk—if the business turns out to be extremely successful, the profit potential will be limited by the licensing arrangement. Further, a commitment may be made to a firm which could turn out to be either less competent than expected or unwilling or unable to put the expected resources into the project. Of course, termination clauses can be included in any agreement, but they rarely can prevent the loss of a considerable amount of time. * * *

[3.] Joint Ventures

A joint venture is an alternative approach to entering a market. It involves a joint-ownership arrangement which can vary on the extent of ownership and the involvement of both parties, from a 50/50 proposition to a combination in which one partner is virtually a silent participant. Joint ventures involve more commitment than either exporting or licensing and have more risk and less flexibility associated with them.

One motivation for joint ventures is to accommodate existing or potential political problems associated with exporting into the foreign market. * * * [Local content requirements, for example, may make] an exporting strategy * * * unrealistic. Potential restrictions can also loom. Thus Toyota and GM agreed to make a subcompact car to be sold through GM dealers using an idle California GM plant. A prime Toyota motivation is to sidestep U.S. import quotas and to avoid the import taxes that have been proposed for cars without any U.S.-made parts. Further, some countries such as India and Mexico have been insisting that joint ventures replace corporate subsidiaries.

The importance of the motivation of political factors in foreign investment was shown by a survey of 108 large U.S.-based multinational firms. As Figure [5-1] shows, two of the primary reasons offered for foreign investment [were] to overcome tariff barriers and to respond to government pressures to produce locally. Another involved the enticement of government incentives.

* * * * *

FIGURE [5-1] Reasons for Foreign Investment—108 U.S. Multinational Firms

Reasons	*Percent*
Overcome tariff barriers	27.6
Gain economies of scale	26.7
Take advantage of government incentives	21.0
Follow customers	20.0
Respond to government pressures to produce locally	19.0
Lower wage rates	13.3

Source: [omitted].

* * * * *

A second motivation is to obtain the use of assets that would be very expensive to establish. Thus, Renault's motivation for its joint venture with American Motors is to gain access to existing production facilities and to a network of over 2,000 dealers. American Motors, of course, obtains critically needed investment and a new car (the Renault Advantage) for its dealers that will meet emission standards and that will be competitive with respect to gas mileage.

Another motivation for joint ventures is to obtain local expertise in terms of marketing or operating a production or service operation. Given the differences in culture and language, it can be risky for the most assured firm to attempt to manage production employees or a marketing effort in a foreign culture. * * *

Sometimes an undertaking is so big that a joint venture is needed to spread the economic and political risk. In aviation, joint ventures are often needed because of the huge investment. Also, governments are likely to inhibit purchases of equipment by firms in their countries when it does not include substantial portions manufactured in their countries. * * *

Difficulties with Joint Ventures

Some obvious difficulties and disadvantages are associated with joint ventures. A commitment made to a partner may become inappropriate or undesirable when conditions change. One study found that 30 percent of a sample of 1,000 pre-1967 ventures between American companies and partners in other developed countries proved unstable because of organizational or strategic changes made by one of the partners. A change in a product-market mission for one partner can make a once-attractive and synergetic joint venture become a nuisance or even a liability. The loss of flexibility associated with a joint venture may be particularly costly if the industry evolves to the point that a global strategy, a strategy option which will be discussed shortly, seems more appropriate.

The joint-venture commitment may also become undesirable if the results are disappointing to one partner. Mitsubishi became frustrated with the sales performance of its cars sold through Chrysler. The result was a decision to establish a set of Mitsubishi dealers to handle models not being sold through the Chrysler dealership. Another Mitsubishi motive was pride. It looked with envy on the other Japanese manufacturers which had all established their names in the American market while Mitsubishi remained in the Chrysler shadow. * * *

Another potentially serious problem for a joint venture is that one of the partners may be very uncomfortable with sharing market data and technology. Security of trade secrets, proprietary methods, and market intelligence can be difficult enough without being concerned with possible leaks by a partner. A further possibility is that the partner might at some time in the future be competing or desire to join in partnership with a competitor firm. In [one] jet-engine joint venture, the partners were very sensitive about transferring technology. The solution was for each partner to contribute its own technology and handle the associated production so in fact very little technology transfer was needed.

Joint ventures can create severe tensions when a multinational partner cannot delegate decision making to the joint venture because of dependencies between the local operation and other activities of the multinational.[1] * * *

[4.] Direct Investment—A Foreign Subsidiary

The ultimate commitment is developing a foreign manufacturing subsidiary to service the host-country markets. It would normally involve at least a final assembly operation and perhaps component production as well. The major characteristic is that it would have as its primary focus the host country and its market. Thus, the operation would have considerable leeway to determine product lines and to make operating decisions. The parent company may provide financing, R&D effort, production technologies, marketing methods, and coordination of exporting but mainly as a support service. * * *

Direct investment, unlike a joint venture, allows control over the operation. There need be no concern that the lack of experience, judgment, or competence of a partner will cause it to fail. Further, the shared management problems and the loss of flexibility associated with joint ventures [are] avoided.

Some of the same motivations for joint ventures apply to direct investment. It can be an approach to overcome political resentment of exporters exploiting a foreign market and the associated import restrictions that either exist or may be threatened. It can also be a way to exploit local assets in terms of labor, raw materials, or facilities. * * *

Types of Risks

The major disadvantage of direct investment is that the risks are usually high. Figure [5-2] provides an overview of the two major types of risks involved. The first are the macro risks, those affecting the country as a whole and thus all firms operating there. The second are the micro risks, those affecting only some industries and thus some foreign firms.

The macro risk is the least common but the most visible. It involves political and economic uncertainties that can be a threat to the recovery of the investment. The political events of countries like Cuba, Chile, Iran, and Afghanistan have illustrated that extreme scenarios can occur. Less extreme but very relevant is the expropriation of foreign business that has occurred in a host of countries including Mexico and France in the early 1980s. Also included here are financial instability, a potential in countries with large debts such as Mexico and Brazil, and the economic difficulties associated with high inflation.

* * * * *

FIGURE [5-2] The Nature and Causes of International Business Risk

Macro Causes	**Investment Recovery Risks**
• Competing political systems	• Expropriation with compensation
• Armed conflicts and revolutions	• Expropriation without compensation
• Social unrest and disorders	• Property/personal damage
• New international alliances	• Loss of transfer freedoms (money, ownership, goods)
• Hyperinflation	• Asset deterioration
Micro Causes	**Profitability/Cash-flow Risks**
• Changing market conditions	• Competitive advantage damaged
• Unstable/depressed economy	• Market deterioration
• Vested political interests	• Discriminatory taxes or regulation
• Vested local business interests	• Operating restrictions

Source: [omitted].

* * * * *

The micro risk impacts more on profitability and cash flow than on asset recovery. Government actions well short of expropriation can make the host country less hospitable and therefore less profitable. Included would be discriminatory taxes or regulations, operating restrictions, or unilateral revisions of contracts. They can also be caused by changes in the local environment that affect the market and the firm's ability to compete in that market. * * *

[5.] Global Strategies

A global strategy, in contrast to running autonomous strategies in several countries, considers competition in a worldwide setting. A firm's worldwide system of product positions, manufacturing and logistical operations faces other globally oriented firms as well as local competitors. The various country subsidiaries are highly interdependent in terms of manufacturing and perhaps marketing. Strategy is usually centralized although aspects of operations may be decentralized.

A global strategy will usually involve the achievement of economies of scale by using plants to make components or final products for many or perhaps all markets. A key ingredient is usually a common product such as the "world car" concept of Ford, GM and others. The plants will be located to help provide entry into markets as well as to exploit low-cost sources of labor or raw materials. * * *

Factors Inhibiting the Use of Global Strategies

Global strategies are not always appropriate or even possible. The factors that can inhibit the use of global strategies include:[2]

- *Heavy transportation or storage costs such as those found in concrete or hazardous chemicals.*
- *When localized markets demand very different products.* For example, appliances needed in underdeveloped countries are smaller and less complex than those needed in more established markets.
- *Strong established local distribution channels and sales organizations.* Japan has effectively excluded outside firms from entering because of these factors. That is one reason joint ventures like Caterpillar's are more attractive in Japan than elsewhere.
- *A lack of world demand.* * * *
- *A difficulty in providing intensive local customer systems, service, or other needed customer interaction.* A local firm that can be more responsive and is more skilled at local management of such services may have a decisive advantage over a global competitor.
- *A complex, segmented local market which might be more suitable for a local firm more intimately embedded in it.*
- *Government barriers.* Trade barriers protecting local firms or government subsidies of local industries can be a significant impediment to a global strategy.

Note on legal forms and legal restrictions

The decisions to do business in a foreign country and on what form to use are not purely a product of marrying a company's business objectives to one of the legal forms available. Other laws may directly or indirectly affect the desirability of utilizing any given investment form. Tax issues, for example, may dramatically affect the evaluation of what form to use to do business in a foreign country (see Part D of this chapter). Other laws and regulations should also be taken into account. For example, at the time A.Co and J.Co were negotiating their tie-up, there were severe restrictions on foreign manufacturers establishing wholly owned manufacturing subsidiaries in Japan. It is entirely possible that based purely on business considerations A.Co would have decided against establishing a wholly owned subsidiary, but even if it had preferred such an approach at first glance, further analysis of the legal restrictions would likely have dissuaded it.

Another example of how legal considerations may affect the choice of legal form involves the Japanese automakers and their operations in the U.S. Initially, these companies manufactured their cars in Japan and exported the cars to U.S. distributors. In recent years, however, Honda, Nissan, Toyota and Mazda have established manufacturing plants in the U.S.; and Toyota (again) and Mitsubishi Motors have undertaken manufacturing in the U.S. through joint ventures with General Motors and Chrysler, respectively. While there may be good business reasons for these changes in the manner of doing business in the U.S., "voluntary" export limits, along with the threats of formal import limits and of high tariffs, undoubtedly influenced the decisions to establish local manufacturing operations.

II. Joint Venture Issues

Given the focus of this book on joint ventures in Japan, it should come as no surprise that A.Co and J.Co eventually settled upon the joint venture form of doing business. But what is the joint venture form? What precisely does it mean to say that two firms have entered into a joint venture together?

A. The form of the joint venture company

"Joint venture" is a very general term. There is no particular joint venture form in the sense that there is a corporate or partnership form. Furthermore, there is not even agreement on the point at which a relationship between two companies moves from being a simple cooperative arrangement (as with any two companies doing business with one another) to being a joint venture. A joint venture does become identifiable, however, when two (or sometimes more) venturers, through an agreement typically called a Joint Venture Agreement, together form a third company which they will jointly own and to which they will commit various resources.

Once two or more parties have determined to enter into a joint venture that entails establishing a separate entity, they must choose the form the joint venture company will take. Should it be a corporation, a partnership, or something else? Answering this question first involves study of the corporate and partnership law of the jurisdiction in which the entity is to be established. A given jurisdiction might not have a form that corresponds to the partnership form typically found in the U.S., or it might have a variety of corporate forms, such as a specialized form for closely held corporations. And the partnership or corporate form of a given jurisdiction may create rights and obligations between the venturers that differ from those found under U.S. law.

In addition, considerations such as tax liability must be taken into account. For instance, when establishing a joint venture company in the U.S., a desire for limited liability and clearly established legal standards may argue for utilization of the corporate form, but tax considerations often argue for a partnership form. For joint venturing in Japan, then, it is essential to study Japan's corporate law, which we will take up in detail in Chapter 8, and to consider other areas of law such as tax, which we will address in Part D of this chapter.

B. Joint venturing between manufacturers

The following selection discusses motivations of manufacturers in forming joint ventures and some of the problems that may be created by joint ventures. Consider which of the points discussed in the article may be applicable to the joint venture formed between A.Co and J.Co and how they may be able to structure their joint venture to take advantage of the opportunities created by their union and to minimize the difficulties.

THOMAS NOWINSKI AND D. KERRY CRENSHAW, JOINT VENTURING IN THE MANUFACTURING INDUSTRY*

The Handbook of Joint Venturing

144, 144-149 (1988)

[1.] What Motivates the Formation of Joint Ventures in the Manufacturing Industry?

Technology

More than any other factor, the exploitation of technology in one form or another drives the formation of joint ventures for manufacturing. Typically, one party to the venture will have conceived and developed (or partially developed) a particular manufactured product or manufacturing process having a potentially significant market. If that party lacks the production and/or marketing resources to realize the full potential of the product or process, and also lacks the financial ability to create such resources on its own, it may seek out a joint-venture partner who has the requisite characteristics.

This is the traditional "Mr. Idea/Mr. Money" theme, and there are numerous variations on the theme. * * *

Marketing Expertise

Not every manufacturer has a marketing research arm. A company may have the manufacturing capability to produce huge quantities of a technically superior product, but may have no idea what type of product is needed or how that product should be marketed. Thus, the impetus for forming a joint venture may come from a nonmanufacturer that has discerned a market for a particular product, has developed a performance specification for it, and perhaps has even begun to test the market for the product with potential customers. Having discovered or created a market for the product, that company may then seek out a joint venture partner with the technical capability to design, develop, and manufacture the product in profitable numbers.

Furthermore, there are industry segments in which market entry would be difficult for a newcomer because of high entry costs or because the market is insu-

*From Thomas Nowinski and D. Kerry Crenshaw, "Joint Venturing in the Manufacturing Industry," in John Carter, Robert Cushman and C. Scott Hartz, eds., *The Handbook of Joint Venturing*, pp. 144-159 (Dow Jones-Irwin, © 1988), at 144-149. Reprinted by permission.

lar in other ways. * * * This easy market entree may be contrasted with the enormous logistical and financial difficulty involved in setting up a distributor network for a completely new entry. * * *

Risk-spreading

Sharing the risk of developing a particular product is a traditional motivation for forming a joint venture, but it has particular applicability in the manufacturing industry. The cost of research and development, tooling, and manufacturing machinery to produce a new manufactured product may run into millions of dollars. The balancing of risks against potential rewards may make such a development financially infeasible unless there are two or more solvent participants willing to accept a share of the cost.

Production of Raw Materials

A manufacturer may not need any help in developing, producing, or marketing products, but may find it crucial to have a guaranteed source of the raw materials or components from which its products are manufactured. Many years ago, for example, Henry Ford decided that the best way to insure a steady supply of quality steel to manufacture his automobiles was to build his own steel mill.

Few manufacturers are willing to undertake this type of capital commitment today, but the concept survives in joint ventures between manufacturers and suppliers for the production of certain specialized materials and components. What this represents is a version of vertical integration that can be significantly less costly to the manufacturer than building its own facility, while offering the supplier an assured market for its output. * * *

Other Factors

The list of factors which may [counsel] the formation of manufacturing joint ventures is as varied as the participants themselves. The GM-Toyota venture offers one additional illustration of this point. At the time the venture was formed, "voluntary" trade restraints prohibited Japanese manufacturers from exporting to this country more than a slated number of automobiles. These restraints did not apply to vehicles assembled in the United States. Several Japanese manufacturers had taken advantage of this exception by constructing and staffing manufacturing facilities here, an extremely costly and time-consuming enterprise. Toyota was able to avail itself of the same exception at a much smaller cost by entering into a venture to utilize GM's existing facility.

[2.] Advantages and Disadvantages

The advantages and disadvantages of joint ventures in the manufacturing industry are likely to be typical of those of joint ventures generally. The advantages tend to track the motivations discussed in the previous section for forming the venture in the first place. The disadvantages are not unlike those that plague such ventures in other segments of the industry. * * *

A universal disadvantage of joint ventures is the potential for "culture clash" in the management of the venture, and manufacturing joint ventures are no exception. This is especially true where a design-oriented, "creative" firm enters into a venture with a no-nonsense manufacturing company to exploit the intellectual property of the former. By contrast, the likelihood of a clash is probably less severe where the venturers are of approximately equal sizes and are drawn from the same industry segment.

Different factors may account for differences in "culture." The GM-Toyota venture is again a prime example. The differences between U.S. and Japanese approaches to management and manufacturing are well known and have been extensively debated. The operating agreement between the two companies permits Toyota to appoint the chief executive officer and the chief operating officer, and one might assume that this arrangement comprises a tacit agreement that the Japanese management philosophy will be permitted to predominate. Nevertheless, the venture must operate in this country, and GM will remain a highly visible presence in its operation. GM may have made a corporate decision to permit its management style to be submerged, but it remains to be seen how well individual managers will adapt to that decision.

Another potential difficulty with a manufacturing joint venture is product-oriented. When a product designer enters into a venture with a manufacturer, the two may have different goals. The designer may be interested primarily in the further development of the product, and may view the joint venture as a means to that end. The manufacturer, by contrast, may be motivated principally by a desire to establish a high volume of production and sales of the existing product as quickly as possible, in order to derive the maximum potential profit in the shortest practicable time frame. This is the type of issue that requires careful consideration in planning stages, leading to detailed agreement on goals and objectives.

C. Finding a corporate partner in Japan

The selection below includes a brief discussion about the importance of assessing the competitive relationship between any joint venture partners. What is the competitive relationship between A.Co and J.Co? What opportunities and what problems does this create between A.Co and J.Co? How might these opportunities and potential problems affect their structuring of the joint venture relationship?

RICHARD COOPER, JOINT VENTURING IN JAPAN*

The Handbook of Joint Venturing
360, 369-373 (1988)

Choosing a joint-venture partner in Japan is both easier and more difficult than choosing one in most other countries of the Far East. It is easier in Japan with regard to such factors as reputation and ability to deliver what is promised, since sources of information in a developed economy such as Japan are generally quite

*From Richard Cooper, "Joint Venturing in Japan," in John Carter, Robert Cushman and C. Scott Hartz, eds., *The Handbook of Joint Venturing*, pp. 360-382 (Dow Jones-Irwin, © 1988), at 369-373. Reprinted by permission.

good. This is particularly true when the Japanese company is large and maintains a high profile. For smaller Japanese companies—as with smaller companies anywhere—one needs to be a bit more careful. But even in this instance, information sources are still usually available.

Where Japan is more difficult is from the strategic viewpoint. Western companies should take greater care than they often do to answer such questions as "Is there a strategic fit?" and "Are there strategic pitfalls or dangers?" These same two questions are equally appropriate, whether it is the Western company that is seeking a Japanese partner or whether a prospective Japanese partner has approached the Western company.

Beginning with the question of fit, it is useful to think of the joint venture and the potential joint-venture partners in two different respects. First is whether the underlying motivation for the joint venture is strategic, tactical, or portfolio (*i.e.*, investment). Second is the type of competitive relationship between the companies:

- Direct competitors. Examples would be GM and Toyota or Kodak and Fuji Film.
- Producers in the same industry, but not typically competing in the same markets. An example would be Young & Rubicam and Dentsu.
- Producers of similar or related products, but not usually direct competitors. Examples would be Olin and Asahi Chemical or Fujitsu and Microsoft.
- Vertically related companies—that is, in an industry somewhere up or down the production or distribution chain. An example would be Sara Lee and Seiyu supermarkets.

With this framework in mind, Table [5-1] illustrates how a company may use its underlying motivation to assess the type of Japanese company it should consider as a joint-venture partner. For example, if a company is looking to link its product with those of another company, then it would most likely look to a vertically related company.

More broadly, it is clear from Table [5-1] that the strategic opportunities lie mainly with producers of similar or related products that are not typically direct competitors. To a lesser extent, strategic opportunities may also lie with vertically related producers of the same products that sell in different markets. Direct competitors, on the other hand, are generally much less viable as partners for strategic ventures, except when the two want to develop a new product together. The reason for this, of course, is that the success of one partner is more likely to come at the expense of the other when the two are direct competitors. Direct competitors thus find it more difficult to use the joint venture as a tool for meeting their strategic objectives. For producers of different but related products or services, the joint venture can help to satisfy a common strategic need without generating the kind of conflict that direct competitors face.

By way of contrast, direct competitors will often be the most attractive choice for tactical joint ventures, although other kinds of companies can be worthwhile partners as well. To understand why, consider first that tactical joint ventures are typically intended to realize nearer-term, less-strategic opportunities or to solve nearer-term, less-critical problems. In this instance, the direct competitor typically brings more to the joint venture than a company not in the same industry or market. The key, however, lies in structuring the joint venture such that the joint-venture partner cannot use it to gain a larger strategic advantage.

This brings us to the second issue raised earlier—namely, the pitfalls and dangers of joint ventures with Japanese companies. Unlike the past and unlike the joint-venture situation in many other Asian countries, where the concern may have been or may be about piracy of technology, the principal danger today in Japan is much more likely to center on whether the Japanese partner will be able to use the joint venture to seize a strategic advantage of its own. Japanese companies have shown themselves to be particularly adept at taking and combining various ideas, recognizing the market opportunities, and focusing on quality and manufacturing cost to achieve strategic advantage. To avoid this danger, the Western company needs to keep two things in mind, particularly when joint venturing with a direct competitor. It must be sure to structure the joint venture in a way to minimize the chances of its partner using the joint venture to successfully gain strategic advantage. It must also not be content with its existing product and manufacturing technology, as too many Western companies have been in the past. It must instead continually work toward improved quality and reduced cost, for it is clear that its Japanese partner will be doing so.

* * * * *

Table 5-1

A Guide to Choosing a Joint-Venture Partner in Japan*

If your specific objectives are listed in the table, then look for a joint-venture partner that is a:

If your broad objectives are:	*Direct Competitor*	*Producer of Same Products Selling to Different Market*	*Producer of Similar Products*	*Vertically Related Producer*
Strategic	Develop new product Divestiture	Develop new product Strategic marketing Access to mfg. technology	Develop new product Strategic marketing Access to product technology Access to mfg. technology Management know-how Diversification Acquisition	Access to product technology Divestiture Acquisition
Tactical	Consolidate markets Protect markets Access to mfg. technology Reduce technology risk Management know-how Obtain capacity Low-cost production Reduce costs Buy time	Sell more into Japan Access to product technology Reduce technology risk Obtain capacity Utilize excess capacity Low-cost production Reduce costs Buy time	Sell more into Japan Access to products Reduce technology risk Utilize excess capacity Reduce cost	Access to related products Ensure suppliers
Portfolio	Reduce management burden Clean up balance sheet		Reduce management burden Clean up balance sheet	

*To use this table, begin with the broad objective on the left. Then look for the specific objective(s) in the main body of the table. Then look up to the top of the table to see the type of joint-venture partner to choose.

* * * * *

Beyond these broader issues of strategic fit and the pitfalls and dangers, the Western company needs to be aware of two additional aspects of Japan's industrial structure in order to identify specific partner candidates. The first, which is particularly important if the joint venture intends to sell in Japan, is that distribution channels in Japan are very specific and often narrower than in the West. It is therefore important to be sure that the prospective joint-venture partner has access to the necessary distribution channels. Second, just as Japanese society is structured much more according to rank and status than is the case in the West, especially in the United States, so Japanese industry is much more structured along these lines. Thus, if it is the Western company that is seeking the joint venture, it should begin by approaching companies of its approximate status. Fortune 100 companies can feel comfortable approaching Japan's industrial giants. Smaller- and medium-sized Western companies will usually have greater success in approaching second- or third-tier Japanese companies, or second- or third-tier subsidiaries of larger Japanese companies.

Once the type of potential joint-venture partner has been selected, then the company should identify the specific candidates. In general, the Japanese company should be approached at a high level by a high-ranking member of the Western company, lest the joint venture get lost in the bureaucracies of the two companies.

One final consideration bears mentioning. * * * Japanese companies often operate as part of a group of companies, the so-called *Keiretsu* or *Shūdan*. The issue then becomes the extent to which joint venturing with a member of one of these groups can be used to gain better access to other members of the group. The Western company should thus first compile a list of the group's member companies, examine the extent to which other members of the group might have something to contribute, and then explore the extent to which they are willing to do so.

Questions and Discussion Points

Business objectives of A.Co and J.Co: With these additional readings in mind, reconsider the positions and objectives of A.Co and J.Co. If no legal requirement limits the legal vehicles available to either party, is the joint venture form desirable? What special concerns does it raise?

PART C: The P.C. Agreements

I. Analyzing the Basic Structure of the P.C. Agreements

The principal materials for this and the following sections are the agreements entered into among J.Co, A.Co and the joint venture company formed between them known as Newco. These agreements, referred to collectively as the P.C. Agreements, consist of six agreements and the Articles of Incorporation of Newco, and appear in the Appendices. Reading and understanding the P.C. Agreements is not as daunting a task as it may at first appear. Explanations of the agreements are provided in this section, and you will see in going through the agreements that the heart of each agreement comprises only a few clauses and that many other clauses are repeated through the agreements (you should observe which clauses get repeated and try to ascertain why).

This section contains directions and questions to guide you through your initial reading of the P.C. Agreements. Answering the questions should lead you to an understanding of the basic structure of the P.C. Agreements and of the roles of A.Co, J.Co and Newco under the agreements. Section II then offers questions that will be of most value after you have worked your way through the P.C. Agreements once. Answering those questions will provide you with further insight into the rights and obligations the P.C. Agreements create in the various parties. These questions will also introduce you to several complex issues we will investigate in greater detail later in the materials.

The P.C. Agreements appear in full in the Appendices. Note that in this chapter we will not study the Trademark Agreement. Note also that the last agreement in the Appendices, Amending Agreement No. 15, is not discussed in this chapter as it is an amendment to the P.C. Agreements that we will not encounter until Chapter 9.

Follow the directions and questions below to guide your way through the P.C. Agreements for the first time.

1. *The JVA:* The Joint Venture Agreement between A.Co and J.Co (the JVA) is the centerpiece of the P.C. Agreements. Read the clauses of the JVA referenced below.

Section A (DEFINITIONS): This section defines the terms that will be used throughout the JVA. Refer back to it if you encounter capitalized terms in the JVA that you do not understand.

Section B (FORMATION OF NEWCO KABUSHIKI KAISHA): This section concerns formation of the joint venture company, Newco.

When is Newco incorporated?

For what purpose have A.Co and J.Co formed Newco?

What control does each of A.Co and J.Co have over Newco?

Is it possible for either A.Co or J.Co to exercise unilateral control over Newco?

Section C (AGREEMENTS BETWEEN THE PARTIES AND NEWCO): This section lists and briefly describes the rest of the P.C. Agreements, excluding the Articles of Incorporation of Newco.

What seems to be the purpose of the Technical Agreement (the TechA)?

What do the descriptions of the Manufacturing Agreement (the MA) and Distribution Agreement (the DA) indicate about Newco and its relationship to J.Co?

Section D (OWNERSHIP AND PROTECTION OF DATA): This section references matters that will be covered in greater detail in other P.C. agreements.

Section E (OFFERS, SALES, AND SERVICE): Read carefully the first two paragraphs in this section. For the rest of the section, simply note the subject areas covered.

Section F (DISCOUNTS AND MARKUPS): This section contains the complex formula for determining the compensation to be provided to J.Co for manufacturing excavators for Newco. It is not necessary at this point to analyze the formula in detail.

Section H (GENERAL PROVISIONS): Skim through all the paragraphs in this section to see the subject areas covered, but note carefully paragraphs 3, 4, and 10.

What law governs the JVA?

Section I (TERMINATION): This section concerns the length of time the JVA is to remain in effect, the conditions under which it can be terminated, and the consequences of termination.

How long is the term of the JVA?

What provisions of the JVA remain in force even if the JVA is terminated, and why have these provisions been chosen?

Section J (EFFECTIVE DATE): Simply note the purpose of this section.

2. *The Articles of Incorporation of Newco K.K.:* The Articles of Incorporation of Newco K.K. (the Articles) are rules concerning the governance of Newco. Note especially Articles 1, 2, 5, 7, 14, 16, 19, 22, 27, 28, and 32.

How do the provisions concerning governance of Newco in the Articles coordinate with the JVA provisions concerning governance of Newco?

3. *The remaining P.C. Agreements*: You should next try to develop a basic understanding of the function of each of the P.C. Agreements within the entire structure of the joint venture.

What is the basic function of each of the P.C. Agreements?

4. *Manufacture under the P.C. Agreements*: Under the P.C. Agreements, the excavators to be manufactured are referred to as Licensed Products. How is the manufacture of Licensed Products to be accomplished under the P.C. Agreements? To answer, analyze:

JVA §§B and C; TechA §§B, E and F; MA §§B, C and E.

5. *Distribution under the P.C. Agreements*: How is the distribution of Licensed Products to be accomplished under the P.C. Agreements? To answer, analyze:

JVA §§A, B, C and E; TechA §B; DA §§A and C.

6. *Role of each party*: Having analyzed how both the manufacture and the distribution of Licensed Products are to be accomplished, the basic role of each party under the P.C. Agreements should be becoming clear. What specifically is each party committed to doing in effecting the manufacture and distribution of Licensed Products? To answer, analyze:

A.Co's role:
JVA §§B and C; TechA §§B, E and F; MA §E.
Newco's role:
JVA §§B, C and E; TechA §§B, E and F; MA §§B and C; DA §C.
J.Co's role:
JVA §§B, C and E; MA §§B, C and E; DA §C.

How well do the roles of A.Co and J.Co correspond to their respective business objectives, as reflected by the materials in Part A of this chapter?

7. *The function of Newco:* Understanding the function of Newco is the key to understanding the basic structure created by the P.C. Agreements. Many manufacturing joint venture companies have their own manufacturing facilities, workers, and management, and some even conduct their own research and development. In contrast, Newco, as should now be clear, hires J.Co to accomplish both the manufacture and the distribution in Japan of Licensed Products.

Given that Newco simply contracts all of its work out to J.Co, why does Newco even exist? For what reason is the relationship not simply structured as one between A.Co and J.Co?

In answering these questions, we will learn how the joint venture between A.Co and J.Co is unusual and examine virtually all of the areas of law presented by the typical joint venture, along with additional issues particular to this venture's unique structure.

II. Further Analysis of Rights and Responsibilities under the P.C. Agreements

The discussions and questions in Section I above were designed to guide you in developing an appreciation for the basic structure created by the P.C. Agreements. The questions in this section delve more deeply into the rights and obligations created by the P.C. Agreements and introduce issues we will return to throughout these materials. Answering these questions will be of most value after you have read through all of the P.C. Agreements one time.

1. *Licensing/sublicensing vs. contracting/subcontracting:* Under the TechA, A.Co licenses its excavator technology to Newco for the purpose of manufacturing and selling Licensed Products. Newco is thus the licensee of A.Co. As we have learned, however, Newco does not conduct the manufacturing or selling of Licensed Products by itself; it instead arranges for J.Co to undertake these activities.

For J.Co. to manufacture Licensed Products, it must obtain the right to use the technology licensed by A.Co to Newco. For this to be accomplished, there are two basic options: 1) Newco could sublicense to J.Co the right to use the technology, or 2) Newco could hire J.Co as a contractor. In the MA, Newco utilizes the second option; it hires J.Co as a contractor to perform the specified work of manufacturing Licensed Products. (Note that if one thinks of A.Co and J.Co as having hired Newco as a contractor, then Newco hires J.Co as a *sub*contractor, and this term is, in fact, used in some places in the P.C. Agreements, *e.g.*, in JVA §F-1 (a).) Consider how the situation would be different if Newco were instead to utilize the first option and sublicense A.Co's technology to J.Co.

To understand why the contracting option was chosen over the sublicensing option, it is necessary to analyze the substantive difference between the two options. Compare carefully the terms of A.Co making Newco its licensee in the TechA with the terms of Newco making J.Co its contractor in the MA. What rights and obligations are created in each case and how do these differ? To answer, analyze: TechA §B-1; MA §§B-1 to 3.

2. *Non-compete obligation*: Consider the non-compete clauses in MA §B-3 and in DA §F. How is the non-compete obligation structured and on what parties is it imposed?

Which parties does the non-compete obligation benefit?

Why do the non-compete clauses appear in the MA and DA, both of which are between Newco and J.Co, and not in the JVA or TechA, to both of which A.Co is a party?

3. *Compensation to A.Co for its technology*: What compensation is A.Co to receive for providing Newco with its excavator technology? To answer, analyze TechA §G.

TechA §§G-4(a) and (b) create an obligation on Newco's part to pay minimum fees to A.Co. Do these clauses create any obligation on the part of A.Co?

For how long is Newco required to continue paying A.Co royalties? To answer, analyze the TechA carefully. In your analysis, consider also the relevance of the JVA and the Articles.

4. *Compensation to J.Co for its manufacturing work*: What compensation is J.Co to receive for its manufacturing work for Newco? To answer, analyze: MA §F-1(a); JVA §F.

Why is JVA §F so complicated? What problems might be presented by the way the compensation to J.Co is to be determined? Why was this means of calculating the compensation for J.Co's manufacturing work chosen? Is there some other manner in which the payment of J.Co's manufacturing work might be structured?

Note that §F-5(b) of the JVA states that the key elements of the formula—C_1, J.Co's costs associated with manufacture of Licensed Products, and C_2, Newco's similar costs—are to be finally determined in accordance with Schedules III and IV of the JVA. Turn to these at the end of the JVA. Careful analysis of Paragraph 5 of each of Schedules III and IV reveals that, as an alternative to the method in §F, C_1 and C_2 can simply be determined by agreement of the board of directors of Newco. In the actual case on which the P.C. is based, the two joint venturers always negotiated C_1 and C_2 in this fashion. Given this, what is the purpose of the complex formula in §F of the JVA?

5. *Compensation to J.Co for its selling work*: What compensation is J.Co to receive for selling Licensed Products for Newco? To answer, analyze DA §§H and A.

6. *Territorial division of distribution responsibilities*: Distribution of Licensed

Products is handled in the Selling Agreement (the SA), which outlines basic rules on distribution, and the DA, which concerns J.Co's distribution activities in Japan for Newco. Under the JVA and SA, for what territories do A.Co and Newco have responsibility for distributing Licensed Products? To answer, analyze JVA §E; SA §§A-13 and B-1.

Why is J.Co not assigned any territory in the JVA or SA?

What responsibility does J.Co have for distribution? To answer, analyze SA §B-2(b) and the appropriate provisions of the DA.

Can Newco or J.Co make sales in A.Co Territory? To answer, analyze JVA §E-2; SA.

Why are the U.S. and Panama Canal Zone excluded from A.Co Territory? Does their exclusion mean that Newco and/or J.Co is free to sell Licensed Products in the U.S. and Panama Canal Zone, and, if not, what prohibits either Newco or J.Co from doing so? To answer requires analysis of many of the P.C. Agreements.

7. *Relationship among the agreements:* Consider Paragraphs 1-5 of §C of the JVA and §H-10 of the JVA. What is the purpose of these clauses?

What does it mean for the referenced agreements to be "made a part hereof to the same effect as if set forth herein in full"?

If this is the case, why is each agreement separately executed between the parties to each agreement?

8. *Terminability of the agreements:* Before entering into a contract, it is crucial to analyze under what terms one can terminate the contract. Consider carefully §I of the JVA. For how long is the JVA to remain in effect?

Under what terms can A.Co or J.Co terminate the JVA?

Note the distinction between §I-2(a) and §I-2(b) of the JVA. Why does breach by Newco allow A.Co but not J.Co to terminate the JVA?

What are the consequences of termination?

Consider TechA §§I-1 and J-2. What is the relationship between these clauses, and what is the term of the TechA?

Consider TechA §I-2. If either A.Co or Newco can terminate the TechA, and if, as noted above, JVA §H-10 makes the TechA a part of the JVA, what effect would termination of the TechA have on the JVA?

What is the term of the MA and under what conditions can either Newco or J.Co terminate the MA?

What are the consequences of termination of the MA?

If J.Co terminated the MA, could Newco hire another party to manufacture Licensed Products?

Consider the term and termination clauses of the DA. What is the term of the DA?

Why does the DA allow either party to terminate the agreement without cause?

If the DA is terminated, can Newco hire another party to distribute Licensed Products in Japan?

PART D: Tax Considerations

Tax considerations can have a tremendous impact on foreign investment in Japan. Japanese tax law and the interplay of that law with the tax law of a firm's home jurisdiction will affect both how the firm initially structures its business in Japan (to this point we have simplified matters by omitting tax considerations) and how it resolves operational issues once it has begun that business.

Japanese law firms rarely offer tax advice. Clients who need tax advice instead generally obtain that advice from a Japanese C.P.A. Nonetheless, international lawyers cannot remain aloof from tax issues. The materials below outline some of the basic tax issues in international transactions.

I. Tax Law and Foreign Investors

MICHAEL WHITENER, TAXING FOREIGN INVESTMENTS*

International Financial Law Review

41-46 (Special Supplement, September 1990)

Although Japan's tax treatment of foreign investment has roots that go back to the Meiji era (1868-1912), following World War II the tax system was radically revised to conform to the pattern of the U.S. system. Further revisions have been made over the years to allow the tax rules to keep pace with Japan's spectacular economic growth. The result is a generally equitable, nondiscriminatory tax system that, despite some quirks, holds few surprises for the Western tax practitioner.
* * *

This article will focus on the taxation of the two most common forms of foreign corporate direct investment in Japan: (i) the establishment of a branch or other fixed place of business in Japan, including an office, factory or warehouse; and (ii) the establishment of a Japanese subsidiary, either wholly owned or pursuant to a joint venture.

[1.] Taxation of Japanese Branches

The "Permanent Establishment" of a Foreign Corporation

Under Japan's Corporation Tax Law (*Hōjin Zeihō*), a foreign corporation doing business in Japan is liable only for taxes on income derived from sources within Japan. A "foreign corporation" is defined as any corporation that does not have its head office or principal office in Japan.

If a foreign corporation has a "permanent establishment" in Japan, it is taxed on its entire income from Japanese sources. Article 141 of the Corporation Tax

*From Michael Whitener, "Taxing Foreign Investments," *International Financial Law Review* (Spec. Supp., Sept. 1990), at 41-46. Reprinted by permission.

Law defines a permanent establishment to include a branch, factory or other fixed place of business, including an office, warehouse, or "any other fixed place of business which is similar in nature"; a construction, installation or assembly project which a foreign corporation has supervised for more than one year; and a person who has authority to conclude contracts in Japan on behalf of a foreign corporation (except contracts exclusively for the purchase of goods or merchandise).

The Corporation Tax Law Enforcement Order, however, exempts certain types of enterprises from treatment as a permanent establishment. These include fixed places of business engaged solely in purchasing or storing goods or merchandise, or activities such as advertising, promotion, supply of information, market survey, basic research or other activities having an auxiliary function in carrying on the business of the enterprise. As a result, a foreign representative or liaison office generally is not subject to Japanese corporate income tax.

Determining Foreign Corporate Income

A foreign corporation with a branch or other fixed place of business in Japan is presumably receiving income from sources both within and outside Japan. Japanese corporate tax law lays down the following rules regarding what constitutes Japan-source income:

[i] Income from doing business in Japan. If goods or merchandise are sold in Japan without manufacturing, the total income from such sales is considered to be derived from Japan. A sale is deemed to have been made in Japan if (a) the goods or merchandise are actually in Japan or under the control of the permanent establishment of the seller situated in Japan immediately before delivery, or (b) the contract for the sale is concluded in Japan, or (c) an important part of the negotiations for the sale or disposal is performed in Japan.

If the goods or merchandise to be sold are manufactured abroad in whole or in part, income from the sale is allocated among the countries involved on the basis of normal transactions "at arm's length."

In the case of construction, installation or assembly projects undertaken in Japan, the total income derived from such activities is treated as having arisen in Japan, even though the contract is concluded or necessary labor or materials are furnished from outside Japan. * * *

[ii] Income from assets held in Japan. This category includes income derived from the following sources:

[a] The sale or disposal of assets (other than inventories) located in Japan.

[b] The sale or disposal of goodwill from a business carried on in Japan.

[c] The sale of national or local government bonds, domestic corporation debentures, and shares of domestic corporations.

[d] The sale of securities on a Japanese securities exchange or through a place of business of a dealer or broker located in Japan, or when the securities are located in Japan.

[e] Income from the sale or disposal of a right or license granted under Japanese law.

[iii] Other types of income. The following sources of income are also subject to Japanese corporate tax:

[a] Income from a business providing personal services (such as professional services) performed in Japan.

[b] Rent from immovable property located in Japan.

[c] Interest on national or local government bonds, debentures issued by a Japanese corporation, and deposits made with entities that have a place of business in Japan.

[d] Dividends or distributions of surplus, and distributions of profits on securities investment trusts, received from domestic corporations.

[e] Interest on loans relating to the debtor's business.

[f] Royalties for the right to use industrial property (including know-how), copyrights and equipment, as well as proceeds from the sale of industrial property or copyrights, when such properties are used with respect to business carried on in Japan.

Effect of Tax Treaties with Japan

The taxation of foreign companies and foreign nationals under Japanese law may be modified by the bilateral income tax treaties that Japan has entered into with 36 countries. These treaties generally follow the OECD model treaty in avoiding double taxation and reducing the withholding tax rate on dividends, interest and royalties payable to a nonresident.

Taking the Japan-U.S. Income Tax Treaty as an example, the most significant tax-reducing features are as follows:

i) Business profits. Under Japan's Corporation Tax Law, if a foreign corporation has a permanent establishment in Japan (as defined above), all income from Japanese sources is taxed to that permanent establishment even if the income is not connected with that establishment. Under the Japan-U.S. Tax Treaty, however, Japan may tax only that portion of business profits that are directly attributable to the permanent establishment.

In addition, the general administrative expenses of a head office of a foreign corporation that are allocated to a Japan branch may be deducted from the foreign corporation's taxable Japan-source profits. This allocation must be done on some reasonable basis. * * *

ii) Withholding of dividends, interest and royalties. Under Articles 212-215 of Japan's Income Tax Law, the withholding income tax rate on dividends, interest, royalties, rents, salaries, and personal service income payable to a nonresident is 20 percent. Japan's tax treaties reduce this withholding rate as applied to dividends, interest and royalties to between 10 and 15 percent.

In the case of the Japan-U.S. Tax Treaty, the withholding rate on interest and royalty income received by a U.S. permanent establishment in Japan is reduced to 10 percent. With respect to dividend income, the withholding rate is reduced to 10 percent if the dividend is paid to a U.S. corporation owning at least 10 percent of the Japanese corporation making the distribution, and in other cases is reduced to 15 percent.

iii) Capital gains. In Japan's tax treaties with some countries, including the United States, capital gains on the sale of shares in domestic corporations are exempt from corporate tax.

iv) Salaries. Salaries paid to U.S. residents present in Japan for less than 183 days are exempt from withholding unless such salaries are counted as expenses of the permanent establishment in Japan.

Taxation Distinctions

The tax treatment of a Japanese subsidiary of a foreign corporation * * * and of a Japanese branch or other permanent establishment of a foreign corporation are identical in most respects. But the methods of calculating taxable income differ in the following ways.

A Japanese branch may make an allocation of sales and general administrative expenses between itself and its head office abroad. No such allocation is permitted between a Japanese subsidiary and its parent company abroad.

The distribution of profits from a Japanese branch of a foreign corporation to its head office abroad is not viewed as a dividend payment and therefore is a tax-free transaction. Dividends paid by a Japanese subsidiary to its parent company abroad, however, are fully taxable and subject to withholding.

Interest paid by a Japanese branch to its head office abroad is not recognized as an expense under Japanese accounting principles and so may not be deducted from taxable income, while interest paid by a Japanese subsidiary to its parent corporation abroad is deductible. However, a foreign corporation may reasonably allocate to its Japanese branch interest payments made to other parties by the head office abroad.

[2.] Taxation of Japanese Subsidiaries

The Japanese subsidiaries of foreign corporations are given the same tax treatment as wholly domestic corporations, except as modified by tax treaties. The most important features of such tax treatment are described below.

Income Subject to Taxation

A subsidiary incorporated in Japan is subject to Japanese corporation tax on its entire worldwide income, not only on Japan-source income. Net profit or loss for each accounting period must be calculated on an accrual basis. * * *

Exclusions from Taxable Income

The following are among the income items that the Corporation Tax Law excludes from the calculation of income:

[i] Dividends received from domestic corporations. However, the interest expense on money borrowed to purchase stock on which dividends are received must be deducted from the amount of dividends received.

[ii] Appraisal gain on assets.

[iii] Refunds of corporation and other taxes.

Deductible Expenses and Losses

The following items are deductible for corporate tax purposes:

[i] Certain taxes. The enterprise tax, excise taxes (national and local), interest

tax on various national and local taxes, and foreign taxes not eligible for a foreign tax credit are deductible. However, most taxes, including the corporation tax, the inhabitants tax, and withholding income tax on non-assessable foreign corporation income, are nondeductible.

[ii] Salaries, wages and pensions. Salaries and wages paid to employees, as well as pensions paid to former employees, are deductible. Compensation paid to directors is deductible only to the extent that it is not unreasonably high. * * *

[iii] Entertainment expenses. The deductibility of entertainment expenses is restricted based upon the capitalization of the corporation. Corporations with capital of ¥10 m[illion] or less may deduct up to ¥4 m[illion] in entertainment expenses per year; corporations with capital of more than ¥10 m[illion] but no more than ¥50 m[illion] may deduct up to ¥3 m[illion] in entertainment expenses per year; and corporations with capital in excess of ¥50 m[illion] may not deduct any entertainment expenses.

[iv] Donations or contributions. Contributions to the Japanese national or local governments or to certain public interest organizations designated by the Ministry of Finance are fully deductible. Other contributions, however, are deductible only up to half the amount of the sum of 2.5 percent of profits plus 0.25 percent of capital. * * *

[v] Interest expenses. Interest is a deductible expense except that, if a corporation owns land which it acquired on or after December 31, 1988, and does not fully use, interest which amounts to six percent of the acquisition cost of that land is not deductible in business years which commence within four years from the date of the acquisition of that land. * * *

Foreign Tax Credits

Although Japanese branches of foreign corporations are not eligible for foreign tax credits—because they are taxed only on Japan-source income—the Japanese subsidiaries of foreign corporations may receive credit for foreign taxes paid. Creditable items include direct foreign taxes such as foreign corporation tax, local tax and withholding tax, and indirect foreign taxes such as tax assessments on dividends received from foreign subsidiary shares (if the Japanese subsidiary owns at least 25 percent of the voting shares or capital of such foreign subsidiary).

Capital Gains and Liquidation Income

Corporate capital gains are not granted special treatment under the Corporation Tax Law, and therefore are subject to the normal corporation tax of 37.5 percent. With regard to the sale or transfer of land or land rights held for 10 years or less as of January 1 of the sale or transfer year, a 20 percent capital gains surtax is assessed.

Under Japan's tax treaties with certain countries, including the United States, capital gains from the sale of shares are exempt from taxation.

The Japanese subsidiary of a foreign corporation, like a domestic Japanese corporation, is subject to a corporate tax of 33 percent on the excess of its residual assets over its capital and accumulated earnings at the time of liquidation or absorption by merger. * * *

[3.] An Overview of Japanese Corporate Taxes and Rates

Foreign businesses operating in Japan (both branches and subsidiaries) may be subject not only to taxes imposed by the Corporation Tax Law, but * * * local and consumption taxes as well. The following provides a quick overview of all of these taxes.

Corporation (National) Tax (*Hōjin Zei*). Imposed on either Japan-source income (in the case of the "permanent establishment" of a foreign corporation) or worldwide income (in the case of the Japanese subsidiary of a foreign corporation). The corporation tax rate is currently 37.5 percent, reduced from 40 percent as of April 1, 1990 (until April 1, 1989, the rate was 42 percent). This rate applies to both retained earnings and earnings distributed as dividends; a reduced rate on distributed income that previously was in effect for Japanese domestic corporations was repealed for tax years beginning after March 31, 1990.

Business Tax (*Jigyō Zei*). Imposed by prefectural governments, rates are graduated based upon income by prefecture and range from six percent for a corporation with a taxable income of up to ¥3.5 m[illion] per year up to 12 percent for a corporation with a taxable income of over ¥7 m[illion] per year. Business taxes are deductible from income in the accounting period in which they become due.

Prefectural and Municipal Inhabitants Tax. Both the prefecture and the municipality in which a corporation has a permanent establishment impose an Inhabitants Tax on the corporation. This tax has two components: (1) A per capita tax based on the amount of the corporation's capital and capital surplus and the number of corporate employees. The amount of the tax ranges from ¥50,000 per year for corporations with less than ¥10 m[illion] in capital to ¥750,000 per year for corporations with greater than ¥5 b[illion] in capital. For foreign corporations, capital is based on the amount of the corporation's worldwide capital, but employees include only those working in the prefecture. (2) A tax calculated as a percentage of the corporation tax, ranging from 17.3 to 20.7 percent of the corporation tax. The Inhabitants Tax is not deductible from taxable income.

Consumption Tax (*Shōhi Zei*). Since April 1, 1989, Japan has assessed a flat-rate three percent tax on sales, transfers or leases of assets, provision of services and receipts of imported products. For automobile sales, the tax rate [was] six percent until March 31, 1992 [and is now three percent]. Exports and international transactions involving the provision of services outside Japan are exempt from the tax.

II. Taxes on Enterprises in Japan

Earlier in this chapter we considered possible forms for doing business in Japan and began by focusing on the joint venture. In the P.C., A.Co acquired its 50% interest in the joint venture company, Newco, by buying half of the shares initially issued by Newco. There are other ways A.Co might have acquired half of Newco. The selection below discusses the tax implications of this choice.

RICHARD COOPER, JOINT VENTURING IN JAPAN*

The Handbook of Joint Venturing
360, 379-381 (1988)

[1.] Investment Through a Japanese Subsidiary

The foreign corporation can establish a subsidiary in Japan, usually in the form of a K.K., which is a domestic corporation. The foreign company's subsidiary K.K. then makes the investment in the joint-venture K.K. Under this format, a 20 percent withholding tax is imposed on the payment of dividends from the joint-venture K.K. to the subsidiary K.K., as well as to the Japanese investor. When the subsidiary K.K. pays a dividend to the foreign parent, another 20 percent withholding tax is imposed for companies from non-tax-treaty countries. Companies from tax-treaty countries pay a smaller withholding tax on the repatriation of dividends from the subsidiary in Japan to the foreign parent (for the United States, the withholding tax rates are 10 percent if the U.S. investor holds more than 10 percent of the joint-venture K.K. and 15 percent if the U.S. investor holds less than 10 percent—*i.e.*, so-called portfolio investors).

[2.] Investment Through a Japanese Branch

Alternatively, the foreign company can establish a branch in Japan, which in turn invests in the joint-venture K.K. The tax treatment for the joint-venture K.K. is the same as described above. Regarding the tax treatment for the branch, the branch is still liable for the 20 percent withholding tax on dividends paid from the joint-venture K.K. to the branch, as is the case for the subsidiary. But, there is no withholding tax on moneys paid from the Japanese branch to its foreign parent since, technically, this is not viewed as a dividend payment. Note, however, that if the branch has other income-producing activities beyond its investment in the joint-venture K.K., this income is not eligible for the reduced tax rate on amounts earmarked for repatriation since, again, these are not technically viewed as dividend payments. The reduction of national tax rates from 42 percent to 32 percent for income earmarked for dividends only applies to domestic corporations, which include subsidiaries incorporated in Japan and owned by foreign companies, but not Japanese branches of foreign corporations.

[3.] Direct Investment from Abroad

As a third alternative, the foreign company can invest in the joint-venture K.K. directly from abroad, thus bypassing any local presence. Again, the tax treatment of the joint-venture K.K. has already been discussed. However, the withholding tax is imposed directly on the payment of dividends from the joint-venture K.K. to the

*From Richard Cooper, "Joint Venturing in Japan," in John Carter, Robert Cushman, and C. Scott Hartz, eds., *The Handbook of Joint Venturing*, pp. 360-382 (Dow Jones-Irwin, © 1988), at 379-381. Reprinted by permission.

foreign investor, since there is no intermediate entity such as a branch or subsidiary. The amount of this withholding tax is again governed by the relevant tax treaty. For foreign investors from countries without a tax treaty, the rate is 20 percent. In the case of a U.S. investor, for example, the rate will be 10 percent or 15 percent, depending on whether the U.S. investor holds more than 10 percent of the joint-venture K.K. or less, respectively.

Thus, the overall tax burden for the foreign investor, including both the taxes paid directly by the K.K. and the withholding taxes paid on dividends, is greatest if the foreign company invests in the joint-venture K.K. through its own wholly owned Japanese subsidiary. But its freedom of permissible activities in Japan is also the greatest. By way of contrast, the total tax burden is the least if the foreign company invests directly from abroad, but its range of activities in Japan is also the most circumscribed. Investing in the joint-venture K.K. through a Japanese branch represents a middle ground in terms of both taxes and range of business activities that can be conducted in Japan. Alternatively, some companies follow the two-pronged approach of investing in the joint-venture K.K. from the foreign parent while operating an unrelated subsidiary for their other operations in Japan. * * *

Questions and Discussion Points

1. *Impact of tax considerations*: Given the tax considerations, would you advise A.Co to reconsider its choice of investment vehicle? Why or why not? To what extent should tax considerations drive the decision?

2. *Obtaining tax advice*: While some Japanese *bengoshi* are true tax specialists, most *bengoshi* do not practice in the tax field. In fact, relatively few have even taken courses in taxation. If such *bengoshi* nonetheless choose to give advice on tax issues, are they permitted to do so? (Consider section 3 of the Lawyers Act, which appears in the Appendices. Might ethical obligations nonetheless bar *bengoshi* from practicing in a field in which they lack expertise or experience?)

Where else should the foreign company turn for tax advice? To C.P.A.'s? *Zeirishi* (tax attorneys)? Foreign law firms? Are *gaikokuhō jimu bengoshi* permitted to advise on Japanese tax issues?

FURTHER READING

Forms for Doing Business in Japan

Japan External Trade Organization, *Setting Up a Business in Japan.* Tokyo: Japan External Trade Organization, 1989.

Joint Ventures Generally

Michael Geringer, *Joint Venture Partner Selection: Strategies for Developed Countries.* New York: Quorum Books, 1988.

David N. Goldsweig, ed., *Joint Venturing Abroad: A Case Study*, Washington, D.C.: American Bar Association, Section of International Law and Practice, 1985.

David N. Goldsweig and Roger H. Cummings, eds., *International Joint Ventures: A Practical Approach to Working with Foreign Investors in the U.S. and Abroad.* Washington, D.C.: American Bar Association, Section of International Law and Practice, 1990.

Kathryn Harrigan, *Managing for Joint Venture Success.* Lexington, MA: Lexington Books, 1986.

J. Peter Killing, "How to make a global joint venture work," *Harvard Business Review*, pp. 120-127, May-June 1982.

Joint Ventures in Japan and with Japanese Firms

The American Chamber of Commerce in Japan, *High Adventures in Joint Ventures.* Tokyo: The American Chamber of Commerce in Japan, 1972.

Robert Ballon, ed., *Joint Ventures in Japan.* Tokyo: Charles E. Tuttle, 1967.

Michael Gerlach, "Business Alliances and the Strategy of the Japanese Firm," 30 *California Management Review* 126 (1987).

R. Geoffrey Grice, "Government Reporting and Review Requirements Concerning the Establishment of Joint Venture Companies in Japan," 3 *Butterworths Journal of International Banking and Financial Law* 306 (1988).

Jackson N. Huddleston, Jr., *Gaijin Kaisha: Running a Foreign Business in Japan.* Armonk, NY: M. E. Sharpe, 1990.

Zenichi Shishido, "Problems of International Joint Ventures in Japan," 26 *International Lawyer* 65 (1992).

Jeremiah Sullivan and Richard Peterson, "Factors Associated with Trust in Japanese-American Joint Ventures," 22 *Management International Review* 30 (1982).

Tax System

Yuji Gomi, *Guide to Japanese Taxes.* Tokyo: Zaikei Shoho Sha, 1990.

John Huston, Toshio Miyatake, Griffith Way and Vicki L. Beyer, *Japanese International Taxation.* Irvington, N.Y.: Transnational Juris Publications, 1994.

Hiromitsu Ishi, *The Japanese Tax System.* Oxford: Clarendon Press, 1989.

Takashi Kuboi, *Business Practices and Taxation in Japan.* Tokyo: The Japan Times, 1989.

Griffith Way, Rosser H. Brockman and Masatami Otsuka, *Business Operations in Japan: Tax Management, Foreign Income.* Washington, D.C.: Tax Management Inc., 1990.

Tax Policy

Vicki L. Beyer, "The Legacy of the Shoup Mission: Taxation Inequities and Tax Reform in Japan," 10 *UCLA Pacific Basin Law Journal* 388 (1992).

Seiritsu Ogura and Naoyuki Yoshino, "The Tax System and the Fiscal Investment and Loan Program," in Ryutaro Komiya, Masahiro Okuno and Kotaro Suzumura, eds., *Industrial Policy of Japan*, pp. 121-153. Tokyo: Academic Press, 1988.

John Shoven and Toshiaki Tachibanaki, "The Taxation of Income and Capital in Japan," in John Shoven, ed., *Government Policy Toward Industry in the United States and Japan*, pp. 51-96. Cambridge: Cambridge University Press, 1988.

NOTES TO CHAPTER FIVE

1. Richard H. Holton, "Making International Joint Ventures Work," in Lars Otterbeck (ed.), *The Management of Headquarters-Subsidiary Relationships in Multinational Corporations*, Gower Pub. Co., Aldershot, Hampshire, England, 1981, pp. 255-267.

2. *See* Michael E. Porter, *Competitive Strategy* (New York: The Free Press, 1980), pp. 282-286.

Six

Regulation of Foreign Investment

Introduction

One threshold legal issue that a firm confronts when seeking to do business in any foreign country is how the country regulates foreign trade, foreign investment, and the flow of currency. A firm that prefers to export to the country, for example, might find that preference subverted by high tariffs or stringent quotas. Or a firm that prefers to establish a wholly owned manufacturing subsidiary might find that preference subverted by limits on the activities in which foreign-controlled firms can engage. In this chapter, we consider Japan's regulation of foreign investment, foreign trade, and currency flows. Given the P.C.'s activities, we primarily focus on the regulation of foreign investment.

I. History and Policy

A. Postwar control of direct investment

To appreciate the developments in the P.C., one must first have some sense of the regulation of foreign investment in Japan during the 1970s, a topic discussed in the following selection.

BOOZ, ALLEN & HAMILTON, INC., HISTORY OF LEGAL RESTRICTIONS ON DIRECT INVESTMENT IN JAPAN*

Direct Foreign Investment in Japan: The Challenge for Foreign Firms
A-7 to A-12 (1987)

Broadly speaking, from the Meiji Restoration until World War II foreign direct investment in Japan was limited by the government to the minimum necessary for establishing trade and finance links with the international community, and later for obtaining technology or establishing industries important to national development. In all there were probably less than 100 foreign affiliated enterprises in exist-

*From "History of Legal Restrictions on Direct Investment in Japan," Appendix III in *Direct Foreign Investment in Japan: The Challenge for Foreign Firms*, prepared for The American Chamber of Commerce in Japan and The Council of the European Business Community by Booz, Allen & Hamilton, Inc. (1987), at A-7 to A-12. Reprinted by permission.

ence at any one time and most of these were under Japanese control. Approximately 30 foreign affiliated enterprises survived through to the postwar period.

After World War II the underlying thrust of this negative regulatory environment continued, but was tempered by the practical realities of the intensified national effort for economic development.

From 1949 there were two methods of direct investment:

[1] Make a "validated" direct investment under the Foreign Investment Law, [or]

[2] Establish a yen based company.

A "validated" investment was one which was officially approved and carried a guarantee of access to foreign exchange for repatriation of dividends and capital. "Validated" investments were usually restricted to cases where a valuable foreign technology was unavailable through licensing or where licensing was impractical. The foreign ownership ratio was invariably limited to a maximum of 50% and control was always maintained by the Japanese side. In addition, there were various limitations placed on the right of the foreign investor to charge for its technology, to limit the joint venture's export markets, and to require the joint venture to give it access to further technological developments based on the original technology.

A yen based company could be established without government approval under a special provision in the Foreign Investment Law, * * * and as such involved no guarantee of access to foreign exchange. In fact, the foreign investor was considered to have waived any claim to foreign exchange for repatriation of returns and/or capital. Yen based companies could be up to 100% foreign owned subject to approval. They were typically established by foreign companies which possessed an important product or technology, but would neither license it nor agree to enter a 50:50 joint venture. A number of important foreign manufacturers began operations in Japan in this way.

In the period up to about 1955 the weakness of the economy discouraged most foreign companies from investing in Japan unless there was strong official encouragement for the project. Most of the investments in this period were "validated" investments in very basic industries such as oil, chemicals and metals. Many of these projects had the encouragement of the U.S. Government in accordance with its policy of promoting the economic rebuilding of Japan.

In the second half of the 1950s the growing attractiveness of the market prompted the establishment of a stream of yen based companies and new "validated" companies. "Validated" companies were increasing in the machinery industry and subsequently in consumer product industries.

In the early 1960s Japan began to gear up for greater participation in the international community, an effort that was spearheaded by entry to the OECD [the Organization for Economic Cooperation and Development, a group largely consisting of economically advanced Western nations], hosting of the Tokyo Olympics and introduction of permission for Japanese to travel overseas as tourists. Part of the requirements for entry to the OECD was fundamental agreement to the principle of capital liberalization, and as a first step towards this the government decided to guarantee foreign exchange privileges for all foreign affiliated enterprises. In doing so it simultaneously prohibited the establishment of any new yen based companies after July 1963.

At the same time it committed the country to a programme of liberalization of foreign direct investment which was carried out over the following 17 years, culminating in the reform of the Foreign Exchange Law in 1980. Real liberalization in most industries took place between 1970 and 1976. * * *

The perception among many foreign observers is that the government began by liberalizing industries in which domestic Japanese competitors were already in an unassailable position or industries which were unattractive to foreigners.

In July 1967 the "First Liberalization" introduced a system of automatic approval which initially permitted up to 50% foreign ownership in industries such as the manufacturing of household appliances, cameras and watches, and up to 100% foreign ownership in the manufacture of certain types of steel, and of motorcycles, cement and spinning.

The "Second Liberalization," in March 1969, allowed 50% foreign ownership in insurance, various types of food production, and the manufacture of industrial machinery, materials and instruments. Up to 100% foreign ownership was allowed in more areas of the steel industry, electric lamp manufacture and other industries. This was a much more substantial liberalization than the first, at least in the 50% category.

The "Third Liberalization," which became effective from September 1970, liberalized a wide range of manufacturing industries in the areas of food, textiles, pulp & paper, chemicals, metals and machinery, as well as banking, securities, transport and other services. All these were only liberalized, however, for up to 50% foreign ownership, and the list of industries liberalized for 100% foreign ownership was somewhat less impressive. Nevertheless, this was a very significant expansion of the boundaries for foreign involvement.

In April 1971 the automotive industry was substantially liberalized and in August of the same year the "Fourth Liberalization" opened up all except seven industries to 50% foreign ownership, and made a very significant expansion in the range of industries in which 100% foreign ownership was approved.

The most substantial liberalization was in May 1973. Automatic approval for up to 100% foreign ownership of newly established corporations was effected for all except 22 (albeit important) industries. Acquisition of stock in existing enterprises was liberalized for up to 100% foreign ownership where the target company's agreement was obtained. Where the target company's agreement was not obtained, a single investor's share was approved up to 10%, and the total foreign ownership ratio was approved up to a maximum of 25% (or 15% in the case of utilities, broadcasting, transportation, fisheries, mining and the financial services industries).

Over the next five years 18 of the 22 excepted industries were liberalized through individual liberalization schedules designed to allow domestic competitors time to consolidate their positions. At the same time the automatic approval process was simplified and speeded up.

Finally, in 1980 the Foreign Exchange Law was reformed, elevating the previous 17 years' changes to full legal status. The basis of the system was changed from one of prior * * * approval to one of prior notification. In addition, foreigners were permitted in principle to make equity investments (*i.e.*, acquire stock) in existing enterprises up to the 100% level with or without the target company's agreement.

The remaining exceptions and caveats, which are still applicable today, are as follows:

[1] Four industries are excepted under the OECD Code of Liberalization of Capital Movements:
[i] Agriculture, fishery and forestry;
[ii] Mining (up to 50% foreign ownership permitted);
[iii] Petroleum refining; [and]
[iv] Leather manufacturing.
Foreign investments in these industries are subject to stricter individual screening.

[2] The major financial services industries and the telecommunications industry have special provisions dealing with foreign participation contained in industry specific legislation separate from the Foreign Exchange [and Foreign Trade Control] Act.

[3] The government may prohibit investments in any industry where it:
[i] Considers the investment will adversely affect the interests of national security, public order or public safety;
[ii] Believes the investment will have adverse implications for Japanese competitors or the general performance of the national economy;
[iii] Wishes to maintain reciprocity with a particular country's restrictions on Japanese investment; [or]
[iv] Judges the investment to be an attempt to evade controls in a national emergency.

The procedure for notifying the authorities (and obtaining approval where necessary) for a direct investment has now been greatly simplified. Notification is made by submitting the appropriate forms to the Bank of Japan, and, where there is no objection by the Ministry of Finance or the Ministries responsible for the industries concerned, the investor may proceed with the investment the following day. [As explained later in this chapter, 1991 amendments to the relevant law allow for after-the-fact notice for most types of investment.] Where the relevant authorities wish to investigate the investment and its possible effects more closely, the investor can be made to wait for up to five months.

In industries affected by industry-specific legislation, direct investment may be subject to a completely separate system of restrictions and/or approvals. Industry legislation for financial services and telecommunications has specific provisions governing establishment of operations by foreigners, whereas for other industries the legislation applies to all companies whether domestic or foreign.

Note on the liberalization process and the P.C.

As we saw in Chapter 5, the negotiations between A.Co and J.Co began in the summer of 1969, and the firms signed the P.C. Agreements in the spring of 1970. They thus negotiated and began the agreements during the "Second Liberalization" described in the preceding selection. At that time, the construction machinery industry had been liberalized enough to allow foreign firms 50% equity positions.

B. Coordinating trade and investment controls

The effectiveness of investment controls in protecting domestic industries could be severely constrained if such controls did not go hand-in-hand with import restrictions. The selection below explains postwar Japanese policy on industrial imports and offers further detail on investment restrictions.

MOTOSHIGE ITOH AND KAZUHARA KIYONO, FOREIGN TRADE AND DIRECT INVESTMENT*

Industrial Policy of Japan

155, 158-160, 166-167 (1988)

[1.] Import Restrictions and Trade Liberalization

The initial import control measures in Japan consisted of a series of foreign exchange allocations and other quantitative restrictions. Faced with severe foreign exchange shortages, the Japanese government placed restrictions on the type and amount of imports as well as the number of importers over a wide range of commodities from raw materials to finished products. Imports of raw materials, capital goods, and advanced technology required for expanding production in the existing foreign-exchange-earning export industries and for the growth and development of the strategic industries targeted for development as future export industries were given preferential treatment in terms of allocation of the meager foreign exchange resources. Allocation of foreign exchange for imports competing with the products of the infant industries in their development throes as well as for luxury goods was severely restricted. This system of foreign exchange allocations proved to be an effective tool in the policy kit aimed at protection and promotion of indigenous industry.

Import quotas formed the core of the protection policy until the early 1960s. The quantitative barriers came down sharply beginning in 1960, on the heels of Japan's entry into the IMF (1952) and GATT (1955), raising the relative importance of tariffs, the pecuniary import control measures. This is also revealed in the heavier tariff burdens in Japan as compared to the United States and EEC countries in the 1960s and the first half of the 1970s in contrast to those in the 1950s. There was a built-in tariff escalation system imposing higher tariffs on imports of more

*From Motoshige Itoh and Kazuhara Kiyono, "Foreign Trade and Direct Investment," in Ryutaro Komiya, Masahiro Okuno and Kotaro Suzumura, eds., *Industrial Policy of Japan*, pp. 155-181 (Tokyo: Academic Press, 1988), at 158-160 and 166-167. Reprinted by permission.

processed goods. Further, the effective rates of protection (ERP) were above the nominal tariff rates. In other words, the actual protection enjoyed by the industries at higher levels of processing was thus much higher than nominal figures. * * * [T]his trend continued, though in a weaker form, into 1968, the first year after the Kennedy Round (1967). * * *

Trade liberalization in terms of the removal of quantitative restrictions proceeded at a fast pace for a short period during the early 1960s, just before Japan's entry into the ranks of Article 8 countries of the IMF (1964), followed by a period of sluggishness, whereafter the program began dragging its feet. The international criticism of Japan arising out of its rising trade surplus and the development of trade friction with the United States over textiles, color televisions, and iron and steel forced Japan to proceed with trade liberalization at a faster pace during the late 1960s and early 1970s. The items affected by the trade liberalization were buses and trucks (1961), color televisions (1964), and passenger cars (1965) during the 1960s and color film (1971), high quality electronic calculators and cash registers (1973), integrated circuits (with over 200 elements) (1974), and electronic computers and related equipment (1975) during the 1970s. It, however, took considerable time for trade in these items to be liberalized after the initiation of promotory measures for these industries taken by the Japanese government, especially MITI. For example, the government's intent to promote the automobile industry was translated into protection policy in 1952 and MITI came up with "People's Car Promotion Guidelines" in 1955. As for the machinery and electronics industries, the protection policy was formalized in the Laws on Temporary Measures for the Promotion of the Machinery Industry (1956) and the Electronics Industry (1957), respectively. The indigenous industries on the way to growth were thus protected for quite a long period of time. * * *

[2.] Regulating Inflow of Direct Foreign Investment and Capital Liberalization

* * *

[C]lassified by industry, the capital liberalization lagged behind the trade liberalization, all coming in the 1970s: automobiles (1971), integrated circuits (1974), electronic computers (1975), and information processing (1976). In the presence of the fears mentioned above, the policy authorities opposed the adoption of the alternative development strategy inviting foreign firms through liberal inflows of foreign investment.

Table [6-1] reveals the consequences of adopting such controls. The ratio of foreign direct investment and hence the proportion of manufacturing production held by foreign firms in Japan was far lower than in other developed countries throughout the 1960s and the 1970s. The high returns on foreign investment relative to its share in investment and production reflected the strict control exercised by the policy authorities.

* * * * *

Table 6-1
International Comparison of Trends in Foreign Direct Investment

	Direct Investment Outflow (%)[a]			Direct Investment Inflow (%)[a]			Return on Investments[b,c] 1970 - 78		Proportion of Mfg. Prodn. Held by Foreign Affiliate Firms	
	1961-67	1968-73	1974-79	1961-67	1968-73	1974-78	Receipts (%)	Payments (%)	Participation Ratio (%)	Proportion (%, Year)
Canada	2.3	4.5	6.2	16.2	12.1	3.2	2.8	12.3	≥50	56.6 (1977)
United States	61.1	45.8	29.3	2.6	11.1	26.7	50.6	34.6	n.a.	n.a.
Japan	2.4	6.7	13.0	2.0	1.7	1.2	5.9	8.5	≥25	4.2 (1978)[5]
Australia	0.7	1.4	1.6[1]	15.6	12.9	9.5[1]	n.a.	n.a.	≥25	36.2 (1972/73)
Belgium	0.3[2]	1.4	2.5	4.5[2]	6.1	9.4	n.a.	n.a.	n.a.	n.a.
France	6.9	5.2	7.8	8.2	8.2	15.2	8.2	10.0	≥20	27.8 (1975)
West Germany	7.2	12.5	17.0	21.3	16.4	14.7	9.7	12.7	≥25	21.7 (1976)[6]
Italy	3.6	3.3	2.0	11.5	8.3	5.0	n.a.	n.a.	>50	23.8 (1977)[6]
Netherlands	4.4	6.8	9.6[3]	4.7	8.5	6.0[3]	5.6	7.6	n.a.	n.a.
Sweden	2.0	2.4	3.7[4]	2.4	1.7	0.5[4]	n.a.	n.a.	≥20	10.8 (1976)
United Kingdom	8.7	9.1	9.2	9.7	7.4	6.1	13.0	13.6	≥50	21.2 (1977)
Spain	0.0	0.3	0.6	2.7	3.7	3.7	n.a.	n.a.	>50	11.2 (1971)
Norway	0.0	0.3	0.9	0.8	1.4	4.1	n.a.	n.a.	≥20	18.7 (1977)

Source: Miyazaki et al. [1981]; OECD, [1981].
[a]Proportion among 13 countries.
[b]Returns on direct investment, equity, and other investments abroad (including reinvestment). (Service incomes such as royalties, management fees, etc. are not included.)
[c]Proportion among seven countries.
[1]1974-76
[2]1965-67
[3]1974-78
[4]1974-77
[5]Sales
[6]Transactions

Questions and Discussion Points

1. *Policy of encouraging joint ventures and blocking imports and foreign majority-owned investment:* Note that the construction machinery industry was not fully liberalized at the time A.Co and J.Co entered into the P.C. Agreements. As a result, A.Co may have agreed to the joint venture form because of pressure from the Japanese government. If A.Co would have preferred to use a wholly owned subsidiary, what implications might this have had for A.Co's approach to the joint venture? Do the P.C. Agreements suggest whether A.Co would, in fact, have preferred a wholly owned subsidiary?

2. *Protective efforts not desired by a presumed beneficiary:* Suppose that both A.Co and J.Co, absent regulation, would have preferred to have A.Co establish in Japan a wholly owned manufacturing subsidiary that would sell excavators to J.Co for distribution through J.Co's network. If J.Co believed that such an arrangement was in its own interests, why might the Japanese government still have prohibited it?

II. The New FECA and the Change in Approach Toward Foreign Investment

A. From "prohibited in principle" to "free in principle"

Above we considered several aspects of the two laws that until 1980 governed foreign trade, investment, and currency flows in Japan: the old versions of the Foreign Exchange and Foreign Trade Control Act (old FECA) and the Foreign Investment Act (FIA). Under these laws, foreign investment was prohibited unless shown to be beneficial to the Japanese economy. The laws themselves, however, were both nominally established as "temporary" laws to be relaxed in due course.

By the mid-1960s, the Japanese restrictions on foreign investment had attracted considerable criticism. In response, the government announced a policy of granting "automatic" validations under the old FECA and FIA for various categories of transactions. Foreigners continued to complain, however, that no industries susceptible to foreign competition were covered by the newly liberalized regime, and that even the "automatic" validations were far from automatic. Further liberalization followed in 1973. Criticism continued, but at a reduced level.

Finally, in 1979, with the enactment of the new FECA, the government radically changed its regulatory scheme for foreign investment. The new FECA took effect on December 1, 1980, and replaced the old "prohibited in principle" approach with a new "free in principle" regime. Under the old scheme, all transactions within the scope of the FECA or FIA had been banned unless specifically approved by the "competent Minister." Under the new regime, all "foreign exchange, foreign trade, and other foreign transactions" were permitted unless shown to be detrimental to the Japanese economy. Only notice—not validation—was required.

B. Overview of the FECA

The new FECA regulates the same types of transactions regulated by the old FECA and FIA: foreign exchange transactions by banks and other money exchangers (§§10-15); payments into and out of Japan (§§16-19); capital flows for inbound and outbound investment (§§20 to 25-2); direct investment in Japan (including technology induction contracts) (§§26-46); and foreign trade transactions (§§47-55). The selection below outlines the structure and operation of this revised Act.

ALLAN SMITH, THE JAPANESE FOREIGN EXCHANGE AND FOREIGN TRADE CONTROL LAW AND ADMINISTRATIVE GUIDANCE: THE LABYRINTH AND THE CASTLE*

16 Law & Policy in International Business 417
450-453, 456-464, 468-471 (1984)

[1.] Capital Transactions

* * * A capital transaction involves the transfer of funds which are to be repatriated at some later date. Capital transactions are distinguished from current transactions, which presume the simultaneous or near simultaneous transfer of goods or services in return for the transfer of funds. Current transactions are regulated primarily by the provisions on payments and export-import trade.

Capital transactions, as defined in the new [FECA], include some transactions that affect the current account rather than the capital account of the balance of trade. Those transactions affecting the current account are "service transactions," which are sales abroad by Japanese residents of industrial property rights and similar transactions. Some investment transactions are singled out for separate treatment under the heading of direct domestic investments because they are large transactions undertaken in Japan by foreigners. All capital transactions are subject either to a license requirement or a prior notification requirement by MOF or MITI.

Capital Transactions Subject to MOF Regulation

Four categories of transactions require a license from MOF [the Minister of Finance]. Three of these categories include payment and banking transactions which make up the AFEBs' [Authorized Foreign Exchange Banks'] business activities in foreign exchange. In these three categories, MOF coordinates the flow of foreign exchange through the new [FECA] provisions on AFEBs and payments. The fourth category of capital transactions subject to an MOF license includes the issuing or offering abroad of yen-denominated securities by a nonresident. This area of regulation is an attempt to impose some control in the Euro-yen market.

The capital transactions subject to an MOF notice requirement include lending, securities, real estate, and other investment and investment-like transactions

*From Allan Smith, "The Japanese Foreign Exchange and Foreign Trade Control Law and Administrative Guidance: The Labyrinth and the Castle," 16 *Law & Policy in International Business* 417 (1984), at 450-453, 456-464 and 468-471. Reprinted by permission.

involving Japan but not performed by a foreign investor. While nonresidents report few problems, Japanese parties acquiring the shares of a foreign corporation, engaging in loan and loan guarantee contracts, and making direct foreign investments conduct discussions with the ministries before submitting notice and receive administrative guidance concerning the prospects of a transaction in the same way they did under the old [FECA]. * * *

Capital Transactions Subject to MITI Regulation

MITI has authority primarily over capital transactions denominated as service transactions. Service transactions are sales or grants of rights to industrial property from a resident to a nonresident. MITI subjects service transactions to a license requirement. The 1980 revision reduced the number of service transactions as they existed under the old [FECA], mainly by redefining them as special methods of payment transactions and as transactions relating to technology induction contracts. Significantly, MITI still lists 150 items as strategic under the license criteria, and includes technology related to weapons and nuclear energy production as well as technology designated by the Consultative Group Coordinating Committee (COCOM) as strategic items restricted from sale to Soviet bloc countries. MITI applies a license requirement to sales of COCOM designated technology to the advanced capitalist countries as well as Soviet bloc countries, but not developing countries. MITI officials attribute the COCOM restriction to the ease with which technology transfers can be rerouted and the resultant need to inquire into their ultimate destination. Computer and optic technology is prominent on the list and the license requirement stands as a potential barrier to foreign access to technology developed in Japan in those areas.

This practice typifies a MITI pattern of broadly interpreting recognized categories of exceptions to free trade principles in order to expand its control. Often the extension of these controls bears a strong relationship to regulatory objectives other than the objective used to justify the existence of the authority. For example, MITI regulation of foreign computer and optic technology is done in the context of MITI plans to develop domestic industries in those areas. Restriction of transfers of these technologies to advanced industrialized countries and not to developing countries, however, is justified solely on the basis of the potential for rerouting of the technology to Soviet bloc countries. This practice allows MITI to monitor flows of certain technology out of Japan to its Western trading partners and potentially halt such flows by refusing to take action on license applications.

Licensing High Technology

Many license agreements from a nonresident to a resident in high-technology areas contain provisions for a grant-back or a cross-license from a resident to a nonresident. A grant-back or a cross-license from a resident to a nonresident is a service transaction which may itself be subject to a license requirement, even though the principal license from the nonresident is subject only to a notice requirement as a direct domestic investment. The license requirements on a grant-back or cross-license agreement give MITI more leverage with the foreign investor. Unlike a notification requirement, a license requirement allows the ministry to delay a transaction until the party convinces the ministry of the positive attributes of the transaction. In this way, the provisions on service transactions potentially provide MITI with some residual power to separate foreign ownership from foreign control in technology developed in Japan. MITI could, for example, attach conditions to granting MITI licenses or stipulate that technology developed in Japan, even if owned indirectly by a nonresident through a branch or subsidiary, remain in Japan. MITI, however, has not exercised its licensing authority to negotiate terms in a manner similar to that exercised in order to grant validation under the old [FECA].

Parties report that problems over technology licensing occur with the Fair Trade Commission under the antimonopoly laws but not under the new [FECA]. This is consistent with the nature of trade friction between Japan and its trading partners. The European Community and the United States show a commitment to their antimonopoly laws. Shifting the regulation of the degree of competitiveness of foreign entrants from the foreign exchange and investment laws to the jurisdiction of antimonopoly laws makes it more difficult for Japan's trading partners to complain of closed markets because these countries have similar legal regimes.

Requirements for Divulging Information

Although MITI has not used the license requirement as an impediment to foreign entry, MITI regulation thereunder is not entirely benign. A license application requires that the applicant divulge extensive information on its intended transaction and activities. Filing a license application also entails discussions with MITI in the period prior to the formal reception of the application form concerning the details of the transaction. MITI is involved in the development and maintenance of Japanese industries, and utilizes these ties with domestic enterprises to achieve its goals for the development of a strong international position for Japan in the industries. The information required in the pre-acceptance period is related to MITI's plans for the industry involved, and allows MITI to monitor the activities of foreign enterprises to make sure that their activities are consistent with MITI's plans. * * *

[2.] Direct Domestic Investment

Provisions in the new [FECA] on direct domestic investment primarily monitor the flow of investment and technology into Japan, including transactions between related entities in and out of Japan as well as between foreign controlled and Japanese controlled residents. Transactions within the definition of direct domestic investment, unlike other transactions, involve a "foreign investor." A foreign investor is defined as a natural person who is a nonresident, an organization established under foreign legislation or having its main office in a foreign country, or a company whose stock is held by nonresident entities above a certain percentage. Generally, resident legal entities are deemed to be foreign investors under the new [FECA] if they are under the control of a foreign person. The application of different terminology is an indication of the importance of protecting domestic industries from disruptive foreign competition already in Japan as well as coming into Japan.

Direct domestic investment is subject to the joint jurisdiction of MOF and the ministries charged with oversight of the particular industry into which the direct domestic investment is made. This dual oversight is reproduced in the provisions regarding the acquisition of shares in a designated corporation. Once again, this emphasis reflects ministerial concern of foreign control over the industries subject to their jurisdiction.

Notice Requirement and Waiting Period

All direct domestic investment, unless specifically exempted, is subject to a notice requirement and a thirty-day waiting period. During the waiting period the proposed transaction is screened to determine whether its implementation will bring about any of the adverse consequences set forth in the new [FECA]. The Supplemental Provision covering the acquisition of the shares of designated publicly traded corporations provides for similar treatment.

The requirements of prior notice and a thirty-day waiting period are reduced in many categories of direct domestic investment. Standard transactions are treated routinely, and notice accepted with only minor discussion. Several categories of direct domestic investments are singled out for particular scrutiny by a decision to retain the full notice and waiting requirements. This treatment indicates that the government and ministries view these transactions as more likely to bring about adverse consequences. Strictly scrutinized transactions include those falling within Japan's OECD reservations, "designated" technology and "designated" companies. These are substantially the same as transactions under the [FIA] and in each of these areas, the 1980 revision has not created any real difference in the way the transactions are treated. * * *

Direct Domestic Investments Not Reserved Under the OECD Agreements

Recommendations or orders to change or suspend a transaction involving direct domestic investments, including areas not reserved under the OECD agreements, have never been invoked under the new [FECA]. Although the BOJ [Bank of Japan] and the ministries may conduct discussions with parties before accepting notice, there does not appear to be extensive administrative guidance to alter the terms of these proposed transactions in areas not subject to an OECD reservation. Unusual transactions in these categories may require detailed discussions to gather information in the prereception period even though they are ultimately accepted.

An example of the routine handling of foreign investment in areas not reserved under OECD agreements is the formation of two Japanese subsidiaries to handle imports and sales for their foreign parent, a manufacturer of high-technology medical equipment. In one instance, the parent established a subsidiary under the [FIA] in 1974. The second subsidiary, which was essentially the reorganization of the earlier subsidiary on a larger scale, did not encounter the difficulties under the new [FECA] which its predecessor did in the 1974 incorporation. In the 1974 incorporation, representatives of the subsidiary were required to visit MITI on several occasions to discuss problems related to the terms of the transaction before submitting the application for validation. MITI was particularly concerned with the level of capitalization, large by Japanese standards, and the royalty rate.

MITI's demand to reduce the royalty rate was a typical MITI practice under the [FIA]. MITI justified the use of administrative guidance to reduce royalty rates through the negative principle which required that the terms of a transaction be "fair" to the Japanese party, as defined by MITI, before it allowed the transaction to go forward. MITI's ability to engage in this type of administrative guidance, however, was greatly reduced by the shift to a positive principle. The criterion for a recommendation or order under the new [FECA] is whether a transaction threatens the Japanese economy as a whole, or a particular industry group in Japan. Thus, to restrict a royalty rate, MITI must sustain this burden to make the threat of an order or recommendation an effective foundation upon which to base administrative guidance.

The 1983 incorporation of the new subsidiary was more easily accepted by MITI because of the greater sophistication of the foreign investor. All business purposes not vital to the intended line of business were omitted from the articles of incorporation to simplify notification and avoid problem areas. In addition, the familiarity of MITI with the prior subsidiary also eased the acceptance of the procedure in 1983.

In contrast, the establishment of a trading company subsidiary by a resident petroleum company in 1982 presented more difficulty for the parties due to more stringent controls on the transaction. The petroleum company was required to submit notice because its level of foreign ownership qualified it as a foreign investor even though it was a Japanese corporation. Petroleum manufacturing is an OECD reservation, sea floor petroleum production is a designated technology, and the petroleum company is a designated company. Thus, to preclude additional requirements, the mention of petroleum in the articles of incorporation and notification under the new [FECA] of the subsidiary was avoided to ease acceptance.

The trading company subsidiary was organized to supply goods other than petroleum products to service stations. The articles of incorporation and notification under the new [FECA] were drawn broadly to allow the subsidiary to expand its line of business into any other area. Nevertheless, the activities of the parent company in the petroleum industry made its subsidiary a subject for particular scrutiny. Also, the number of product lines into which the subsidiary could expand required that the parent submit notice to several ministries. The parent petroleum company, therefore, followed the advice of the BOJ and visited several ministries in the prereception period. The parent followed the advice of the ministries in drawing its notification because it found that doing so eased acceptance and, although time consuming, did not affect its ability to engage in its intended lines of business. * * *

Technology Induction Contracts

Technology induction contracts are a separate category of transactions within direct domestic investment that involve the transfer of industrial property rights. A technology induction contract is an agreement for the transfer of a nonresident's industrial property rights or know-how, or for the rendering of technical guidance related to management, to a resident. In technology induction contracts, parties are differentiated as residents and nonresidents, rather than foreign investors and domestic investors. The use of this distinction allows the ministries to monitor flows of technology between related companies into Japan when the company in Japan is a foreign investor by definition. If only transactions between domestic parties and foreign investors were monitored, some transfers into Japan would be missed because the new [FECA] defines foreign-controlled Japanese companies as foreign investors. Such agreements, with the possible exception of know-how related to commercial sales, are subject to a notice requirement. Notice reports are submitted to the MOF and the "competent ministers," which invariably include MITI because of MITI's role in the oversight of technology transfers.

Treatment of Designated Technologies

The thirty-day waiting period requirement applicable to technology induction contracts is waived in all industry categories except twelve denominated as "designated technologies." At present, these designated technologies are: 1) aircraft, 2) weapons, 3) gunpowder, 4) nuclear power, 5) space exploration, 6) electronic computers, 7) electronic components for the "next generation" of computers, 8) laser-processing and optical communication, 9) innovative materials (amorphous or super-conductive materials), 10) nonmercurial electrolysis of salt, 11) seabed petroleum recovery, and 12) leather and leather goods. The list reproduces the [FIA] Class A technological assistance contracts subject to validation, with the exception of technology related to the production of heat-resistant ceramic metal amalgams, which was dropped. * * *

MITI Oversight of Designated Technologies

These categories of information suggest a MITI concern that excess foreign control may undercut the domestic market. The provisions concerning designated technology primarily serve as a means to gather information and monitor development in these areas. The designation of technology indicates that MITI views the induction of these types of technology as likely to bring about the consequences justifying a recommendation or order to either change or suspend the transaction. It is notable in that regard that computer and optical technology are included in the designated technologies list and in the list of service contracts requiring a license. MITI has a policy of fostering the growth of domestic industry in these fields through cooperative efforts between MITI and private enterprises.

The provisions for a recommendation or an order have never been invoked. If a problem were to arise, MITI officials would attempt to handle it through prior discussions. MITI officials state that they would not accept a notice that did not give them sufficient information to make a determination. This would include a failure to conduct prior discussions or a failure to provide extra information when requested to do so. MITI officials recognize that they are required to accept notice without that discussion or further information if the parties insist that they do so. However, they state that the result would be a formal recommendation or order either to change or halt the transaction. At present, the provisions on designated technology serve only this information-gathering function. A diligent inquiry does not indicate that nonresidents are having difficulties in notifying agreements under the new [FECA], as they did under the [FIA] validation requirement.

C. From prior notice to notice after the fact

Notwithstanding the previous selection's optimistic account as of 1984, not all foreign investors were satisfied with the liberality of investment rules or the benign nature of the prenotification process. As a response to continued complaints from some American companies, the U.S. government placed the FECA on the agenda for the Structural Impediments Initiative talks. These negotiations led to the Japanese government's announcement of changes concerning the prior notice requirement. The following document summarizes these changes.

OUTLINE OF LAW AMENDING THE FOREIGN EXCHANGE AND FOREIGN TRADE CONTROL LAW*

Official Gazette, Extra Edition No. 58, April 26, 1991

Taking into consideration the recent circumstances of the international economy and with a view toward enhancing the international flow of capital and for the purpose of clarifying and making more open the procedures for direct domestic investment, etc., and the conclusion, etc., of technology induction agreements under the Foreign Exchange and Foreign Trade Control Act ("FECA"), the Japanese government has amended the FECA as follows:

1. Direct Domestic Investment, etc.

1. The prior notice requirement under the old FECA is amended. The amended FECA provides that in the event a foreign investor makes a direct domestic investment, etc., he or she shall report such investment to the Minister of Finance (MOF) and the Minister(s) in charge. The amended FECA still provides, however, that in cases where it is necessary to examine whether a direct domestic investment, etc., affects national security, etc., the old prior notice requirement shall apply [§§26(3) and 27(1)] .

2. The prior notice requirement of the old FECA that could broadly restrict direct domestic investments, etc., is amended. The amended FECA states that only direct domestic investment, etc., not subject to liberalization requirements of multilateral conventions and other such international agreements may be restricted [§27(3)].

3. The amended FECA states that in the event the MOF or any Minister(s) in charge has extended the period during which a direct domestic investment, etc., is prohibited, the Minister may nonetheless shorten such period prior to the expiration thereof if he or she judges that such direct domestic investment, etc., will not affect national security, etc. [§27(4)].

*From "Outline of Law Amending the Foreign Exchange and Foreign Trade Control Law (Law No. 40, 1991)," *Official Gazette*, Extra Edition No. 58, April 26, 1991.

2. Conclusion, etc., of Technology Induction Agreements

1. The prior notice requirement under the old FECA is amended. The amended FECA provides that in the event a resident concludes, etc., a technology induction agreement with a non-resident, he or she shall report such agreement to the MOF and the Minister(s) in charge. The amended FECA provides, however, that in cases where it is necessary to examine whether the conclusion, etc., of a technology induction agreement affects national security, etc., the prior notice requirement shall still apply [§§29 and 30(1)].

2. Although the old FECA required both residents and non-residents to give prior notice, the amended FECA requires only residents to make the *ex post* reports or to give prior notice [§§29 and 30(1)].

3. The prior notice requirement of the old FECA that could broadly restrict the conclusion, etc., of technology induction agreements is amended. The amended FECA states that only conclusion, etc., of technology induction agreements not subject to liberalization requirements of multilateral conventions and other such international agreements may be restricted [§30(3)].

4. The new FECA states that in the event the MOF or any Minister(s) in charge has extended the period during which the conclusion, etc., of a technology induction agreement is prohibited, the Minister may nonetheless shorten such period prior to expiration thereof if he or she judges that such technology induction agreement will not affect national security, etc. [§30(4)].

Questions and Discussion Points

1. *Effect of the new notice requirement*: The explanation above states that notices no longer need be made in advance, except where the government needs the prior notice to determine issues of national security. How does this operate in practice? For example, how can the government determine whether prior notice is required unless it receives prior notice?

2. *Impetus for the change in the notice requirement*: Why might the U.S. government have been concerned about the prior notice requirement, and what does it hope to accomplish through a change to an *ex post* notice regime?

III. The Principal Case Under the FECA

Consider how the current FECA would regulate the transactions contemplated by the P.C. Agreements and other transactions that companies like A.Co and J.Co might undertake.

1. Acquisition by A.Co of shares in Newco—Direct domestic investment

The P.C. Agreements call for A.Co and J.Co to create Newco, a Japanese corporation, and for each to buy half of the Newco shares. A.Co's purchase of Newco's shares would be a "direct domestic investment"(§26)[1] by a foreign investor (§26(1)(ii)). As such, the foreign investor, A.Co, would have to make an ex post report to the Minister of Finance (MOF) and to the "Minister(s) in charge of the industry involved" (§26(3)), unless the investment constitutes a direct domestic investment for which prior notice is required under §27(1).

An investigation of whether the prior notice requirement would apply to A.Co's purchase of shares in Newco leads first to §27(3), then to the Cabinet Order concerning Direct Domestic Investments, Etc. (CODDI), then to the Ordinance concerning Direct Domestic Investments, Etc. (ODDI), and finally to a Designation (issued in the form of a ministerial notification in 1991 and slightly revised in 1994) specifying a very broad range of businesses that are *not* subject to the prior notice requirement. That Designation, it turns out, includes the manufacture and sale of construction machinery, Newco's main business. Accordingly, A.Co would not have to give prior notice, but would have to make an ex post report, within fifteen days from the date when the direct domestic investment is made.[2]

Suppose, however, that Newco's business was not of a type listed in the Designation and A.Co faced the prior notice requirement under §27. This might be the case, for example, for (a) investments exempted from liberalization requirements under multilateral conventions, such as the Code of Liberalization of Capital Movements under the OECD Treaty [to which Japan is a party], and which (i) imperil the national security, disturb the maintenance of public order, or hamper the protection of the safety of the general public, or (ii) adversely and seriously affect the smooth performance of Japan's national economy (§27(3)(i)); (b) investments to be undertaken by an investor from a country which is not a member of multilateral conventions and has not entered into a treaty with Japan, where reciprocity reasons exist for altering or suspending the investment (§27(3)(ii)); and (c) investments which might constitute a capital transaction requiring permission under §21(2) (§27(3)(iii)). In such a case, A.Co could not make its investment in Newco for thirty days from the day when the MOF and the Minister(s) in charge have received such prior notice (the Prohibition Period) (§27(2)). The MOF and the Minister(s) in charge may shorten such thirty-day period when they deem that there is no need for review under §27(3) in terms of the business purpose and other particulars of the investment (proviso to §27(2)). If a direct domestic investment falls within a category that is still subject to review, that review is likely to be more than just cursory. However, to expedite the review process, under a 1991 amendment to ODDI, the Prohibition Period is, in practice, shortened, as a rule, to two weeks.

The MOF and the Minister(s) in charge can extend the Prohibition Period for any transaction to a maximum of five months if they perceive certain risks (§§27(3) and (6)). These include the chance that the direct domestic investment will "imperil the national security * * * or hinder the protection of the safety of the general public," or "have a seriously adverse effect on the smooth operation of Japan's economy" (§27(3)(i)).

If they conduct such an inquiry, the MOF and the Minister(s) in charge would first request the opinion of the Committee on Foreign Exchange and Other Transactions (the CFE). They could then recommend either that the firm alter the particulars of its transaction or that it suspend its execution (§27(5)). If the firm does not respond favorably to the recommendation within ten days, the MOF and Minister(s) in charge could then order it to make the changes or prohibit the transaction entirely (§27(10)). Note that there is no record of the government ever having given such an order, either under the old FIA and FECA or under the current FECA. Finally, continuing to assume that the investment is one for which prior notice is required, after buying the Newco shares, A.Co within thirty days would have to notify the Bank of Japan (BOJ), and through it the MOF and the Minister(s) in charge.[3]

2. Acquisition by A.Co of shares in J. Co—Capital transactions

Suppose that instead of forming a joint venture with J.Co, A.Co acquired shares in J.Co. Its strategy would be to license its technology to J.Co and earn royalties on the license and equity returns. If A.Co acquired shares listed on the Tokyo Stock Exchange, its FECA requirements would depend on the percentage of shares in J.Co that it bought. If it bought less than 10% of J.Co's listed shares, it would be undertaking a "capital transaction."[4] Accordingly, if it bought such listed shares directly from a shareholder, it would have to file a report with the MOF within 10 days before the acquisition;[5] if it bought the shares through a designated securities company such as Nomura Securities, it would not need to file prior notice (§22(1)). If A.Co instead bought more than 10% of J.Co's listed shares (or if A.Co's purchase brought its total J.Co holdings above 10%), it would be undertaking a "direct domestic investment"[6] rather than a capital transaction. The discussion above would then apply.

3. Loan by A.Co to Newco—Loans

Suppose that Newco needed a loan from A.Co to start operations. A.Co's loan would constitute either a "capital transaction" or a "direct domestic investment," depending on the amount and term of the loan. If (i) the loan was for ¥100-¥200 million and for a term of more than five years or (ii) it was for more than ¥200 million and for a term of more than one year, it would qualify as a "direct domestic investment."[7] All loans not qualifying as direct domestic investments would constitute capital transactions.[8]

4. Licensing technology to Newco—Technology induction contracts

Under the P.C. Agreements, A.Co licenses to Newco its patents and know-how relating to excavators. This transaction would constitute "an agreement * * * for the transfer of * * * technology." As such, the resident, Newco, would have to make an ex post report to the MOF and to the Minister(s) in charge (§29), unless the conclusion of the technology induction contract is of a type for which prior notice is required under §30.

An investigation of whether the prior notice requirement would apply in this case leads first to §30(3), then to CODDI, then to ODDI, and finallly to Schedule II to ODDI. As technologies for which prior notice is required (the Designated Technologies), Schedule II specifies the following: (i) technology concerning aircraft;

(ii) technology concerning firearms; (iii) technology concerning the manufacture of gunpowder; (iv) technology concerning nuclear energy; and (v) technology concerning space development.

Since the technolgy to be provided by A.Co to Newco concerns the manufacture of construction machinery and does not fall within the Designated Technologies, Newco is not required to give prior notice but must make an ex post report to the MOF and the Minister(s) in charge. That report must be made within fifteen days from the date when the technology induction contract is concluded.[9]

Suppose, however, that the technology was among the Designated Technologies and Newco had to file prior notice under §30(1). In that case, Newco could not conclude the TechA for thirty days from the day when the MOF and the Minister(s) in charge have received such prior notice (the Waiting Period) (§30(2)). The MOF and the Minister(s) in charge may shorten such thirty-day period when they deem that there is no need for review under §30(3) in terms of the kind and other particulars of the subject technology (§30(2)). To expedite the review process, under a 1991 amendment to ODDI, the Waiting Period is, in practice, shortened, as a rule, to two weeks.

For technology induction contracts that concern a Designated Technology, the Waiting Period can last as long as five months (§§30(3) and (6)). During that time, the MOF and the Minister(s) in charge would determine whether the technology might "imperil the national security * * * or hinder the protection of the safety of the general public" (§30(3)(i)) or "have a seriously adverse effect on the smooth operation of Japan's economy" (§30(3)(ii)). Again, should the ministers, after consulting the CFE, advise the firms to modify the terms of their agreement or to suspend its execution (§30(5)), and should the firms not respond favorably within ten days, the ministers could order the firms to make the recommended changes or cancel the transaction (§§30(5) and (7)).

Today, recommendations to modify the terms of direct domestic investment and technology induction contracts are uncommon. In the days of the P.C., however, the ministries often intervened under the FIA to recommend changes such as lower foreign equity holdings, lower royalty rates, lower licensing fees, or more generous rights to the Japanese party regarding technology improvements.

5. Newco's royalty payments to A.Co—Payment transactions

Royalty payments from Newco to A.Co for the license and dividend payments from Newco to A.Co would both constitute payment transactions. However, whether A.Co or Newco is required to file prior notice or to make an ex post report in connection with the direct domestic investment or the technology induction contract, under the current FECA and relevant regulations, neither A.Co nor Newco would have to obtain any permission with respect to the relevant payment transactions involved.[10]

6. Newco's import of parts from A.Co—Trade transactions

Suppose that Newco needed to import excavator parts from A.Co. This would constitute a trade transaction. As discussed earlier, we have avoided a discussion of trade matters in this chapter. For our purposes, therefore, merely note that the FECA's scope extends to trade. In order to import the parts, Newco would need to consult various Cabinet Orders to determine the relevant restrictions, applicable import duties, and so forth (§§52 and 54).

IV. Private Law Obligations and the FECA

The following case arose under the old FECA, but addresses issues still relevant under the current statute.

Translation by Yanagida Nomura & Akai

Tōkai Denki Kōji K.K. v. K.K. Ryūkyū Bank
29 Minshū 1029
(Sup. Ct., P.B., July 15, 1975)

REFERENCES:

[Old] Foreign Exchange and Foreign Trade Control Act, §§ 13 and 30.

FACTS:

In August 1967 when Okinawa was not yet under Japanese sovereignty, Tōkai Denki Kōji K.K., a Japanese resident and defendant and appellant at both the Nagoya High Court and the Supreme Court, executed a guaranty contract with K.K. Ryūkyū Bank, an Okinawa resident and plaintiff and appellee at both the High Court and the Supreme Court. Under this contract, Tōkai guaranteed the payment of certain debts to Ryūkyū Bank jointly and severally with the debtor. Tōkai's maximum liability under the guaranty was US $250,000.

The debtor having defaulted, Ryūkyū Bank instituted this suit in Japan, where Tōkai was resident, demanding payment of ¥90,000,000 under the guaranty agreement. At the then-effective exchange rate, this amount was equivalent to US $250,000.

In the District Court, Tōkai asserted that the guaranty contract was invalid. Its argument was that, because no one had obtained the approval of the Ministry of Finance or other competent minister as required under the Foreign Exchange and Foreign Trade Control Act (FECA), the contract violated the FECA and was thus unenforceable. The District Court held for Ryūkyū Bank, however, and ordered Tōkai to pay to Ryūkyū Bank ¥90,000,000 plus interest. Tōkai appealed that judgment unsuccessfully to the Nagoya High Court, and then appealed to the Supreme Court.

JUDGMENT:

The appeal by Tōkai is dismissed.

REASONS:

According to the High Court's statement of facts, the guaranty contract was between Ryūkyū Bank and Tōkai. Through the contract, Tōkai guaranteed payment of certain debts up to the amount of US $250,000. The execution of this guaranty contract required government approval under Section 13(2) of the [old] Foreign Exchange Control Order (the FEC Order), in conformance with Sections 30(3) and 13(1)(i) of the [old] FECA.

The provisions of the FECA and the FEC Order, however, are regulatory provisions (*torishimari hōki*) that are temporarily to regulate transactions with foreign entities. In principle, these transactions should be unregulated. As such, the violation of such provisions does not affect the validity of a transaction under private law. * * * Therefore, the guaranty contract is valid under private law even without the required regulatory approval . * * *

Questions and Discussion Points

1. *Regulatory provisions*: The court holds that the violation of the regulatory provision requiring the obtaining of an approval under the old FECA has no impact on the private obligations created by the guaranty agreement. What are the limits of this segregation of public and private obligations? Recall from Chapter 2, Section II.B.4, the discussion of compulsory versus discretionary provisions. Regulatory provisions (*torishimari hōki*) are defined in a leading Japanese legal dictionary as follows: "provisions that, for administrative purposes, prohibit or impose conditions upon certain activities under the law or in fact. For violations of regulatory provisions, penalties are commonly provided. The validity of the activity constituting the violation depends upon the particular provision and circumstances." (From Takeuchi, et al., eds., *Shin-Hōritsugaku Jiten* (*New Legal Dictionary*) (3d ed., Yūhikaku, 1989).)

2. *The problem of side letter agreements*: What about transactions that have been validated pursuant to the FECA, but for which the parties have secretly negotiated other terms? In countries that strictly regulate foreign investment, the domestic and foreign parties sometimes submit to the government for approval a version of their agreement to which the foreign party has not actually agreed. The parties then simultaneously execute a "side letter agreement" that gives the real terms of their agreement. These side agreements present considerable enforcement problems if the promisor later reneges on the secret terms. In Japan, should the *Tōkai* holding apply to such side letters?

FURTHER READING

Robert C. Christopher, *Second to None: American Companies in Japan*. New York: Crown, 1986.

R. Geoffrey Grice, "Government Reporting and Review Requirements Concerning the Establishment of Joint Venture Companies in Japan," 3 *Butterworths Journal of International Banking and Financial Law* 306 (1988).

Dan F. Henderson, "Access to the Japanese Market: Some Aspects of Foreign Exchange Controls and Banking Law," in Gary Saxonhouse and Kozo Yamamura, eds., *Law and Trade Issues of the Japanese Economy*, pp. 131-156. Seattle: University of Washington Press, 1986.

Dan Fenno Henderson, *Foreign Enterprise in Japan: Laws and Policies.* Chapel Hill: University of North Carolina Press, 1973.

Mitsuo Matsushita and Thomas J. Schoenbaum, *Japanese International Trade and Investment Law.* Tokyo: University of Tokyo Press, 1989.

NOTES TO CHAPTER SIX

1. Citations are to the FECA unless otherwise indicated.

2. That time limit is specified in Cabinet Order concerning Direct Domestic Investments, Etc. (amended in 1991) (CODDI), §2(10).

3. Ordinance concerning Direct Domestic Investments, Etc. (amended in 1991) (ODDI), §7(i).

4. §§20(v) and 26(2)(iii) and CODDI, §2(5).

5. §§22(1)(iii); Foreign Exchange Control Order (FECO), §12(1); and Ministerial Ordinance concerning Foreign Exchange Control (MOFEC), §9(1).

6. §26(2)(iii) and CODDI, §2(5).

7. §26(2)(vi); CODDI, §2(7); and ODDI, §2(1).

8. §20(ii). For exemptions, see §22(1); FECO, §12(4); and MOFEC, §16 and Schedule II.

9. That time limit is specified in CODDI, §4.

10. *See* §16(1); Notification of Minister of Finance, No. 117, Nov. 28, 1980. Note, however, that if the methods of payment fall within those provided under §17, peremission of the MOF will be required.

Seven

Negotiating and Drafting Agreements

Introduction

This chapter considers issues related to negotiating and drafting international agreements, with a focus on negotiations between U.S. and Japanese parties. Over the years, many writers in both the West and Japan have attempted to elucidate key differences in the negotiating style of Westerners and Japanese. We begin by considering a few of those accounts. We then turn to an issue of potentially great importance in any negotiation: at what stage in negotiations may the parties become bound? As with the other legal issues covered in these materials, we look at this issue under Japanese law. Section II then considers a variety of substantive issues relating to many of the standard provisions that appear in agreements for international business transactions. To close out this chapter, we return to another issue concerning basic attitudes of Japanese and Westerners: the attitudes toward contract and the impact that differences in such attitudes may have on the negotiating and drafting process.

I. Negotiations between Japanese and Westerners

Much has been written for Western businesspeople, lawyers, and other professionals about how negotiations with Japanese parties can be quite a different affair from negotiations with Western parties, and about the difficulties encountered by those who have not realized this. While some of these "how to" books on negotiating with the Japanese may be helpful, one should be wary of the stereotypes and generalizations that typify works of this sort.

The first selection below is by an Australian who has considerable experience with business negotiations between Japanese and Western parties. Following it is a brief excerpt concerning the *ringi* process of decision making within Japanese firms and the impact it may have on negotiations. The next selection, by an American attorney experienced in U.S./Japan negotiations, offers a rather different perspective on several aspects of the debate. Finally, the last selection, which was written by a Japanese for a Japanese audience, offers one example of Japanese views on negotiating with Americans.

A. Western views on negotiating with the Japanese

ROBERT MARCH, THE JAPANESE NEGOTIATOR: SUBTLETY AND STRATEGY BEYOND WESTERN LOGIC*

8-9, 162-168 (1988)

[1.] Introduction

* * * I have used this technique for many years in business negotiation courses in Japan that are attended by both American and Japanese graduate students. At our first class meeting, without any introduction to the subject, I often split the class into an American negotiating team, a Japanese negotiating team, and a mixed group of observers and monitors. I then give each team very different instructions for negotiating, for instance, how class grades will be calculated. The Japanese must argue for grades based 100 percent on work assignments, while the Americans must insist on 50 percent grades for participation in class discussions.

Each team, along with observers, retires to a separate room to prepare for the negotiating session. Thirty minutes later, the session begins and runs for about an hour and a half. Observers, by means of a standard form, record details of the teams' behavior and their interpersonal dynamics throughout the negotiation. Then we analyze what has happened. Invariably, the experiences and lessons drawn from the exercise are similar every year. In addition, they are strikingly like real-life Japanese-American business negotiations.

A summary of the reports of observers for a typical year notes that, in preparing for negotiations, the Japanese will develop defensive arguments with no consideration of persuading, selling, or converting the other side. They do not consider what the other side might be thinking or offering, or try to foresee its strategies. Nor do they consider concession options. A strong consensus is reached based on the arguments supporting their position after the leader has reviewed the arguments and everyone has jotted them down. There is strong group cohesion.

In the actual negotiations, the Japanese side gives the "appearance of being somewhat overwhelmed by the Americans, although it did not in fact make as many concessions." The tone of the negotiation "seemed to indicate that the Americans were dominating, when in fact the Japanese were only being out-talked, not out-negotiated."

The Japanese typically show little physical or verbal activity, but they nod frequently, suggesting to Western observers, and to the American team, that their minds are being changed. An aggressive approach easily pushes them into a defensive position, and they become less willing to yield.

The observers also point out the following Japanese characteristics in negotiation: the Japanese are frustrated by the difficulties of negotiating in English, where

*From Robert March, *The Japanese Negotiator: Subtlety and Strategy Beyond Western Logic* (Kodansha International, 1988), at 8-9 and 162-168. Reprinted by permission.

their skills are imperfect; they have problems in conveying what they mean in English; they are unwilling either to form a consensus or to express disagreement in front of their opponents; they give strong nonverbal support to their leaders; and their final counteroffers are often innovative, offering benefits to both sides.

As for the American team's preparation for negotiations, observers stated that they (unlike the Japanese) will take time to try and predict how the other side will conduct the negotiations. In the actual negotiations, they decide to explore the other side's approach and then go on the offensive. They agree to ask initially for more than they want and to take a low-keyed approach. In reality, however, they are not low-keyed but are concerned with proving that their position is right in order to convert the Japanese to their viewpoint. Americans show a stronger and more explicit desire to win, emphasize the benefits to the other party, and make passionate presentations with the goal of winning, in contrast to the Japanese goal of defending their position. Observers repeatedly describe the American negotiating style as highly aggressive. But Americans only appear to dominate as they keep agreeing with each other and disagreeing with the other side. * * *

Culturally, there are sharp differences in the way Japanese and Westerners prepare for negotiation. The Japanese priorities are, first, to develop a working organization around a discussion leader, who will usually become the spokesman; second, to ensure that everyone has a thorough understanding of the issues; and, third, to develop a position on which everyone can agree. This position is usually arrived at in what we might call an intuitive way, for there is rarely any discussion of position options. The essence of the Japanese approach is organization, and they can be expected to come into a negotiation with a cohesive team, a single spokesman, a shared understanding of the issues, and consensus on one position even if they are ill-prepared in other respects.

In contrast, Americans and Europeans make the following their priorities: first, to understand the issues; second, to debate possible strategies and positions they could adopt and reach some majority agreement on initial and second-line positions; and, third, to try to assess the likely approach of the other side. So the Western approach is predominantly strategic, with little or no attention paid to team leadership, cohesion, or achieving a genuine consensus on position.

The serious consequences of such lopsided preparation in face-to-face negotiation cannot be stressed too strongly, for Westerners discover that they are less committed to their position than the Japanese, and are readier to make concessions in order to reach agreement. Westerners, irritated by the rock-solid commitment of the Japanese, may attempt to persuade them by vigorous argumentation, directed not only at their spokesman but at other team members, although I have to say that I have never seen this approach succeed. It has only resulted, ironically, in worsening the internal cohesion and commitment to its position of the Western team, for failure to influence the Japanese leads to internal dissent over new strategies.

Another aspect of preparation that needs thought by Westerners is in their selection of a suitable team leader as spokesman and negotiator. Westerners have a curious ambivalence here. A great deal has been written in the West about the ideal qualities of a negotiator. * * * Kniveton and Towers are perhaps representative when they specify "unlimited patience," "persuasion," "knows himself as others know him," "knows and understands others," "good socializer," "strongly committed but can be flexible." This emphasis reflects interest in individual negotiators (not team performance), and it is true that Westerners can be capable individual negotiators. On the other hand, there is a good chance that a team of Westerners will be inferior to either one competent Westerner operating alone or a cohesive Japanese team.

In contrast, the Japanese behave as though they do not believe that the spokesman of a negotiation team has to be an outstanding or even especially competent negotiator. To them it is sufficient if he follows instructions, is supported by effective teamwork, and has in his team people who do possess good negotiation skills (though they may not be suitable as spokesmen). * * *

[2.] The Opening Stage

With their penchant for establishing sound human relations, the Japanese place greater emphasis upon trust-building social conversation at the beginning of a negotiation than do Westerners. This pre-business small talk, handled in a friendly and sympathetic way, typically covers travel, quality of accommodation, mutual friends, and sports (especially golf). Five or ten minutes spent in this way establishes an amicable relationship with most Japanese groups, [yet i]nternationally inexperienced Westerners dealing with the Japanese usually avoid personal conversation and dive head-first into business discussion. * * *

Another common problem in the opening stage is to assume (as Americans often do) that a negotiation is nothing but a set of specific items or issues, each to be settled independently. This is not the way the Japanese see matters. Whereas Americans are prone to proceed point by point, from the beginning of the first meeting, many Japanese (at home, if not abroad) will often begin with the general issue, talking unsystematically around it, meandering without agenda or structure, and thoroughly annoying their counterparts with a seeming lack of logic or of a plan. This conversational meander, in fact, is a part of the process of becoming comfortable with one another, of building bridges, and is common in many Asian countries. Those who would deal effectively with the Japanese should learn to go with the flow of conversation in this opening stage, confident that the time will soon come when you can both get down to business with an agenda mutually agreed on.

In many international negotiations, when the actors may have little or no prior experience, they will be unsure how to proceed. As a result, they may fail in the opening stage to check that both sides share the same understanding of what the negotiation is about, what special terms or expressions mean, what has been agreed up to that time, and, not least, they omit to communicate to each other their interpretation or slant on the subject (which will be the basis of their attempt to persuade the other side to their way of thinking). The failure to do such things creates a variety of problems later, from misunderstandings to distorted perceptions, which can eventually lead to hostility, postponement, or abandonment.

[3.] The Bargaining Stage

This stage begins when one side makes concrete proposals for acceptance by the other side. The broadest difference in this stage is the Japanese desire to achieve an overall agreement first (for example, in a joint venture negotiation, to agree only on capitalization, a broad mission statement, and a manning profile), versus the Western desire to negotiate point by point (for example, in a similar joint venture negotiation, Westerners typically want to hammer out policy for each area, especially marketing, personnel, R&D, and product development, whereas the Japanese would want to leave these to be settled after the agreement is concluded), with the final result being overall agreement. However, if the negotiation is for a simple deal, such as commodities purchase where only price, delivery, and quality have to be settled, the bargaining style of Japanese with substantial international experience (which you can check by discreet questioning) will usually be similar to that of Westerners.

This bargaining stage also sees Westerners much readier to make concessions than the Japanese. Westerners tend to use what they believe will be persuasive, "winning" arguments, but these rarely achieve their goal. The Japanese tend to be skeptical of such arguments, and may analyze them semantically, search for hidden meanings, insist on them being repeated, or apparently ignore or be unresponsive to them to such an extent that the Westerner may become impatient, lose the thread of his own rhetoric, and readily make concessions in order to speed up and complete the negotiation process.

In contrast, the Japanese bargaining style is slower, more deliberate, with much time given to re-stating and re-clarifying their position to the other side. It takes a comparatively long time for them to make concessions, and this only happens when they feel they are close to agreement in other respects.

[4.] The Complication Stage

The problems that emerge from these contrasting negotiation styles and stem, in turn, from the values of two very dissimilar cultures, can color the entire negotiation. As persuasive and strategically creative as Western teams can be, the Japanese can be psychologically better prepared for complex negotiations. Their patience, indifference to pressures of time, and cautious style repeatedly show up as more rooted and stable than the more volatile Western style. Their team structure, organized usually around one spokesman, is important, for he is the one who puts requests, makes demands, or offers concessions, and then only after he has checked with his team or his boss. Most likely, as the negotiation unfolds, most Western members will speak up spontaneously, even interrupting one another, on occasion making sudden new offers or changes in proposals without checking with the rest of the team or the spokesman.

[T]he list below presents some reactions that occur when complications emerge.

Japanese

1. Are less concerned with pressure of deadlines;
2. Retreat into vague statements or silence;
3. Require frequent referrals to superiors or head office;
4. Appear to slow down as complications develop;
5. Quickly feel threatened or victimized by aggressive tactics or a stressful situation.

Western

1. Are more conscious of time/feel pressure of deadlines;
2. Become aggressive and/or express frustration sooner;
3. Often have more authority for on-the-spot decisions;
4. Fail to understand, or else misinterpret, Japanese non-verbal behavior;
5. The breakdown of team organization, with members competing to outargue the Japanese and control their team.

Note on the *ringi* system of decision making

In discussions of negotiations with Japanese companies, one frequently finds references to the so-called *ringi* process of decision making within Japanese firms. The following brief excerpt describes the *ringi* system and the impact it may have on negotiations.

ELLIOTT J. HAHN, JAPANESE BUSINESS LAW AND THE LEGAL SYSTEM*

38-39 (1984)

Besides the length of the socializing process, there is another reason why an American usually should not expect to achieve a speedily negotiated contract with the Japanese. The typical method of contract approval in Japanese corporations (at least in the larger ones) is significantly different from that in the United States. It is very rare for the Japanese employees of a larger corporation to have authority themselves to agree to contract provisions, as is common in the United States. Instead, the larger Japanese companies usually use a system of group decision making called "*ringi-sho*."

* * * In this process a contract is written up by a low-level manager and circulated among all the concerned parties of the Japanese company for their approval. Under the system the draft contract winds its way up the corporate hierarchy, not down. Even though the draft contract goes up the corporate chain of com-

---

*From Elliott J. Hahn, *Japanese Business Law and the Legal System* (Quorum Books, 1984; Copyright © 1984 by Elliott J. Hahn), at 38-39, an imprint of Greenwood Publishing Group, Inc., Westport, CT. Reprinted with permission.

mand, it has been wryly written that if a superior does object, the most he can do is put his seal of approval on it upside down. As one can see from Figure [7-1] depicting the typical *ringi-sho* system in a Japanese corporation, ultimately a consensus on the appropriate course of action is hammered out, although the process does take a considerable amount of time by American standards. The rendering of the ultimate decision on any given significant contractual matter is thus, by American standards, time consuming. What is especially important to Americans involved in contract negotiations with the Japanese is that the inherent need in the *ringi-sho* process to confer with other individuals in the company and receive their approval invariably makes it exceedingly difficult for a Japanese negotiator to give a definite "yes" or "no" to the foreign businessman with whom he is negotiating. Thus, the American discussing contractual issues with employees of the larger Japanese companies should invariably not expect to receive quick answers to his proposed provisions. What the American should do at the start of the negotiations is to ascertain the authority of the Japanese on the other side of the bargaining table. Although it is not uncommon in the United States for a negotiator to have authority to bind his employer to a contract by his assent, the opposite is true in Japan. The *ringi-sho* system is used by the Japanese to reach the consensus which is usually so very important to the Japanese.

* * * * *

Figure 7-1
Japanese Decision-Making Process, "Ringi-sho"

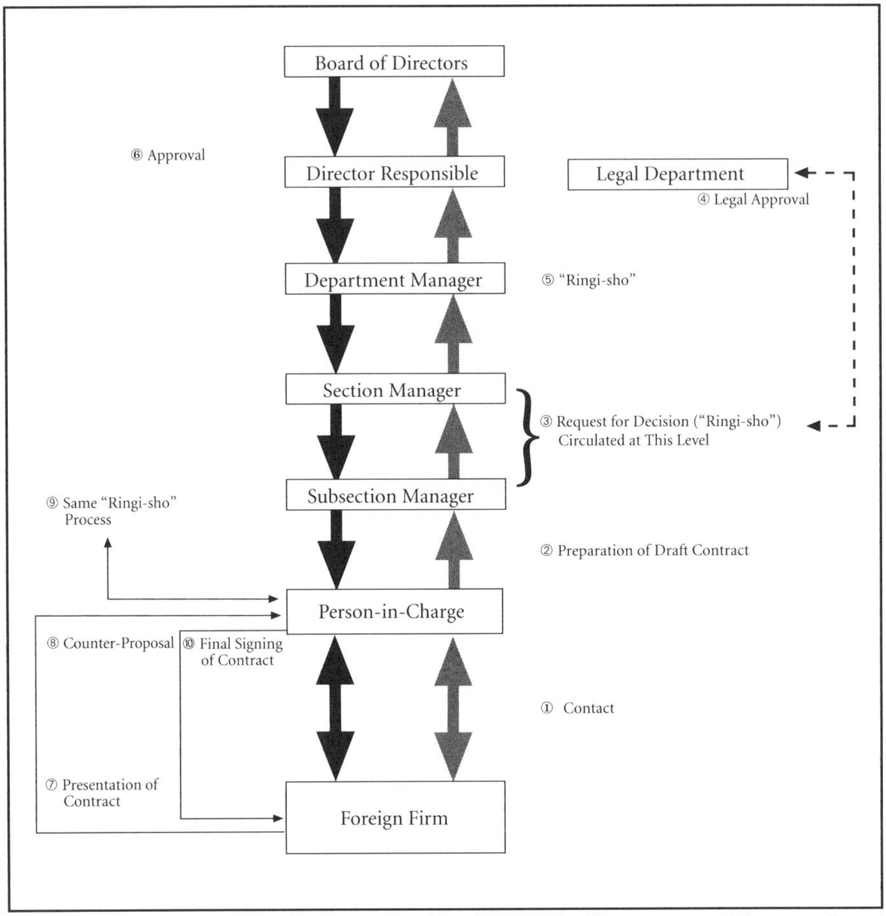

Source: Japan External Trade Organization (JETRO), *Contracts and International Trade* 13, "Business Information Service No. 6," reprinted in 1 *The International Contract* 572 (1980).

A less sanguine view of Japanese decision-making and negotiating: The following account, by an American lawyer with many years of experience handling U.S./Japan negotiations, offers a quite different view of both internal corporate dynamics in Japan and the nature of negotiations.

E. ANTHONY ZALOOM, OBSTACLES TO THE EFFECTIVE RENDERING OF PROFESSIONAL ADVICE TO JAPANESE COMPANIES*

It is interesting and ironic that what is perhaps the most serious of these obstacles [features of Japanese companies that make rendering professional advice for them difficult]—decision by consensus—is a feature of Japanese organization which it is currently quite fashionable to praise as a source of Japanese strength. * * * Equally misleading is another category of literature which tells the reader that he will do well in dealing with the Japanese so long as he is prepared to spend a lot of time in doing so, does not get angry, and remembers to bring a small present for his Japanese counterpart. * * *

Decision by Consensus

The diffuse nature of the decision-making process in Japanese corporate clients is the biggest obstacle to effectively giving them advice. When an American client visits his attorney's office for advice, he often makes his decisions with respect to the advice right there in the attorney's office or within a very short time after leaving it. Through further discussion, the lawyer can then give the client what further advice he needs to implement his decision or tell him what part of his decision might pose problems. * * * With respect to large Japanese corporate clients, no individual will ever walk into the lawyer's office who has any authority to make a decision on any important matter. * * * Japanese individuals and groups that visit the lawyer do ask for advice. But since they are not yet engaged in, or are only beginning, the decision-making process, the lawyer's advice tends to stay at a very general level and with respect to a larger number of competing solutions. Most of the decision-making process then takes place very far away from the lawyer, so there is no further opportunity to offer necessary further advice with respect to tentative decisions.

Therefore, when a decision is reached by the Japanese client it is more likely to be the wrong one from a legal point of view. Sooner or later this decision is usually communicated to the American lawyer, and he then has a chance through his advice to try to change it. Unfortunately, however, the diffuse nature of the decision-making process which contributed to the wrong decision having been made now operates to make it very difficult to change that decision. * * * By way of example, * * * a Japanese individual will tell the lawyer that the joint ven-

*From E. Anthony Zaloom, "Obstacles to the Effective Rendering of Professional Advice to Japanese Companies," Speech presented at Columbia University School of Law, 1982. Reprinted by permission.

ture that his company is planning to enter with an American company will be done through a new corporation established in the United States, the stock of which will be owned in equal shares by the Japanese and the American companies. The lawyer quickly points out to him that such a structure would be very disadvantageous from a tax point of view and that rather the joint venture should be conducted through a partnership agreement (an unfamiliar concept in Japan) between the American and Japanese venturers. [I]t appears that use of a corporate rather than a partnership structure would cost an additional $5 or $6 million in unnecessary taxes over the life of the venture.

The Japanese individual listener's reaction to this news is not positive; he is not happy to hear that there is a way of structuring this venture to save several million dollars in taxes. Rather, he is unhappy that the lawyer should suggest a different structure, one which would require him to send telexes and written reports and perhaps himself back to Tokyo to convince the very large number of people that are involved in this project. Within a few minutes he has made a decision: * * * the additional tax cost of several million dollars is nothing compared with the delay to the project which will ensue if he has to explain this to the people back in Japan. The lawyer's warning that the American side will not consent to such a needlessly tax-expensive structure is unavailing. * * * (Incredible as it may seem, the author has actually had this experience not once but twice, and in each case the outcome was the same: after the American venturer had overcome his initial amazement, it acquiesced in the Japanese side's request only on condition that the Japanese side pay the American side in cash for its additional tax burden. In both cases, this resulted in a reconsideration by the Japanese side and a switching to the more rational partnership form.)

Weakness of Internal Communication

A Japanese company suddenly finds itself in the midst of a crucial investigation in the United States and faces an imminent possibility of indictment for the activities of its employees. In a desperate attempt to prevent the indictment, the company's American lawyers arrange to travel to Japan, meet for four hours with the top management of the company, and return to the United States that same day, hopefully in time to make an effective presentation to the American authorities. The meeting is planned by the lawyers as a means of determining both the degree to which the employees' activities were approved by top management of the company and the most appropriate manner of presentation to the authorities.

After being ushered into the presence of several senior executives in Tokyo, the lawyers gradually realize to their amazement and chagrin that the precious four hours of meeting time are to be almost completely preempted by an emotional monologue by the president of the company on such subjects as how hard the company has worked to get where it is in the industry today, the enormous contribution it is making to Japanese-American economic harmony, and how unfair it is that the American authorities should be giving the company trouble about activity that everyone else engages in to some extent anyway. Attempts by the American lawyers to interrupt the monologue and discuss the immediate very serious problems of the company are unsuccessful. They are particularly disappointed that the younger company employees present, who are thoroughly briefed on the issues and who had seemed before the meeting to have intended that it be a fruitful one, do nothing to get things back in focus, but rather listen intently to the president for the entire four hours, continually nodding agreement and murmuring assent to his emotional appeals and anecdotes. * * *

At another Japanese company, a license agreement is about to be negotiated with a German company for advanced technology that is very critical to the Japanese company's success in its markets. The marketing department head who has been strongly pushing for a license from the German company visits the head of his company's R&D department with the intention of persuading him that a license from the German company is preferable to trying to develop substantially similar technology within the company and also to clear with him what he thinks the basic terms of the licensing agreement with the German company are likely to be.

The conversation lasts for about two hours, most of it taken up by reminiscing about the work that the two individuals have done together in the company and how far the company has come in the last ten years. The marketing head spends some time talking about the need to go outside the company for this critical technology and also the basic terms on which the technology may be so obtained. Although the R&D manager seems somewhat saddened by this last part of the conversation, he makes no objection. The marketing manager could go into more detail on the terms to be negotiated, but feels that he has already been successful enough, probably because of the emotional appeal he has been able to make to his old friend, and decides to quit while he is ahead.

The next day he begins negotiations with the German company's representatives, assuming that there will probably be no objection from the R&D department when the time comes to execute the final agreement. It occurs to him that he has not talked at all with the R&D department head about the terms of any grant back license provision that may be required by the German company, but he feels that to talk with the R&D department head, especially about something so concrete and so relevant to the R&D department's interests as this, would be so delicate and expend so much of his emotional energy that he decides to delay the conversation until later.

Both of these fact situations illustrate the very serious problems that the Japanese have in communicating with each other, let alone their foreign professionals.
* * *

This surprising phenomenon is generally explained by the fact that in any conversation in Japan the fact that one participant is inevitably senior to the other results in at least a partial inability to convey information that might be unpleasant to the more senior listener, or to respond critically to information from that senior. The result for the professional advising Japanese companies is that he can never be sure that his oral advice is being adequately disseminated within the company. A partial solution to this is to give advice as often as possible in writing, even where it would not be so given to an American client, thus decreasing the possibility that the advice will be watered down or even not conveyed at all. * * * When more than one Japanese company is involved in a matter, or even when more than one department in a single Japanese company is involved, the American professional should conservatively assume that there has been insufficient communication among them, and be prepared for last minute problems resulting from that. * * *

Fear of Fixing Responsibility

A Japanese company once extended too much credit to one of its American customers, who was unable to pay it back. * * * After the customer had finally taken his company into a rearrangement proceeding under Chapter 11 of the Bankruptcy Act, he gave his Japanese creditor a choice: he would either settle with a partial payment of 25 cents on the dollar or he would transfer his entire business, including some real estate, to the Japanese company.

The cash offer was clearly more beneficial to the creditor, since the amount offered, although much less than the outstanding amount of the debt, was considerably more than the value of the customer's business assets, whether computed on a liquidation or going-concern basis. * * * Although the American lawyers representing the Japanese company in the rearrangement proceedings immediately advised it to accept the cash offer, to their surprise, the Japanese company opted in favor of taking over the customer's business. Their "explanation" was that at least with the business, which included some real estate, there was some chance of appreciation and recoupment of more of the money that had been lent to the customer. When the American lawyers suggested the obvious, that the cash offer be accepted and the cash invested in real estate for what would seem to be an even greater possibility of recoupment, an officer of the Japanese company explained the real motivation of himself and others in the company. Acceptance of the cash offer would make taking a loss on the loan to the customer unavoidable. Taking over the business and carrying it on the books of the Japanese company at the full amount of the loan made to the customer—an arrangement that the Japanese accountants were willing to acquiesce in—would keep the matter from becoming a *hito no sekinin mondai*—a question of a person's responsibility. Apparently, most people in the company knew the individual who had been primarily responsible for the mistaken credit judgment about the customer. * * *

Preference For Simple Non-Innovative Solutions

Finally, an important obstacle to effectively rendering advice to Japanese companies is their very strong preference for simple non-innovative solutions to problems. It is certainly true that when advising any client, Japanese or not, everything else being equal, the simple non-innovative solution is to be preferred over that which is complicated and untested. In the case of the Japanese client, however, the simple non-innovative solution is many times more preferable. The large number of people involved in any decision, the poorness of internal communication, and the fears of being responsible for any kind of a mistake make complex innovative solutions to problems much less "digestible" in Japanese companies than American companies. Also, the only tentative acceptance by Japanese companies of outside professionals and their advice further decreases the possibility that the client will accept solutions of any complexity.

B. A Japanese view on negotiating with Americans

The following selection about negotiating with Americans, which is reportedly a translation of an article written by a Japanese, has appeared in at least three publications in the U.S., even though its origin is not entirely clear. The article's first publication in English apparently was in a 1985 book, *Getting Your Yen's Worth: How to Negotiate with Japan, Inc.*, by Professor Robert Moran of the American Graduate School of International Management. Moran reported that he received the article from someone at the U.S. Information Agency who was not sure of the article's origin.

The article also appeared in the April 18, 1988, issue of the *Northern California Real Estate Journal* ("NCREJ"), which reported that it was reprinting the article with the permission of a magazine entitled *Contract Management.* The editor of NCREJ wrote that the article had been contributed to *Contract Management* by James T. Fellita, a "former U.S. government contract negotiator," who reported that the article was an unpublished essay written by "a Japanese negotiator."

ANONYMOUS, A JAPANESE VIEW OF AMERICAN NEGOTIATORS

Negotiators from the United States are difficult to understand because they come from a background of different nationalities and experiences. Unlike Japanese, the Americans are not racially or culturally homogeneous. Even their way of speaking English varies. Gaining a good understanding of one U.S. representative is only a little help in understanding others. Americans from large cities are different from those coming from small towns. There are differences between East, West, North and South, as well as in religion and national origin.

Thus, much of what they do is truly unpredictable and erratic. At the same time, there is no reason to suspect that beneath the rather disorderly appearance of U.S. negotiating teams, whose members often seem to not be listening to each other and who may not even dress in the same style, there is a calculated set of tactics and objectives that guides them. Sometimes U.S. representatives seem to make mistakes or to be ignorant of commonly known facts, but their lack of humility in such cases may mean that they really know what they are doing.

The background of American history is an important influence on their attitudes. The American frontier was a major factor from the arrival of the first settlers from Europe and for about 250 years. American books describe how the West was conquered or won. In some strange way the empty spaces of America had to be captured from nature, which was like an enemy. This is a complete contrast to our idea that one must live with harmony and nature.

Adversarial Approach

Americans also highly value what they call adversary proceedings. This seems to come from their court system, where two sides argue their cases in a direct confrontation with no effort made to find any harmony at all. Then the judge issues a ruling one way or the other without private consultation with the two sides and with no value given to conciliating the feelings of those in the case. Americans believe this undemocratic system is the best way to learn the truth and impose justice.

Americans sometimes say "truth is relative," or that "there is no such thing as black and white, only shades of grey," but often they act differently. They are seekers of truth and morality, just as we are, but they think truth and morality exist apart from the practical world around them. So in a negotiation it is common for American negotiators to say what basic principles are important. Later they may reject a sound practical idea because it violates principle. Therefore, it is necessary to be cautious about agreeing to any statement of principles and always point out the need for workable understandings. One possibility is that their fixed ideas about truth come from the Christian religion, which promises perfection at some future time or after death, so many American negotiators try to negotiate perfect and final agreements, which they think will never need reinterpretation or adjustment. Indeed, once an agreement is signed they may be very rigid about it because they think it is perfect. * * *

They often talk about how hard we Japanese work, but many Americans work hard and they can be extremely clever sometimes. However, they seem to attribute their leadership status not to hard work but to the idea that they know the truth and are moral. Thus, they are convinced that their ideas are right and others must follow or reveal themselves as fools or knaves. This may seem a harsh judgment, and it is overstated, but Americans are often ethnocentric without knowing it. * * *

U.S. Negotiating Preparations

Without access to their secrets, I can only guess, from their behavior and what they tell me, how the Americans prepare for negotiations. * * * Often they argue among themselves in public, so it is safe to assume that they argue even more in private. This is part of their idea of adversary proceedings and they seem to feel no shame about such embarrassing behavior.

The procedures they use include careful study of the Japanese position, the reasons for it, and the negotiating pressure each side can apply. They spend the most time on their own position. Like the Japanese government, they have many different agencies with different interests that must be reconciled. This is done by circulating draft papers and holding meetings at which middle level officials discuss what to do. Each of these officials represents his own superiors and has limited power to express his own ideas, unlike Japanese officials at that level whose advice is usually accepted since they have more time to study and become experts on detailed matters.

U.S. negotiators often have fallback positions which they can use if they do not win agreement to first proposals. These fallbacks are worked out in advance almost as if they knew their first offers were unreasonable. They do not prepare one approach as the best under the circumstances, while giving their negotiators the authority to approach the matter flexibly. Therefore, it is necessary for us to learn what the final fallback is as early as possible. Once that information is obtained, it is often possible to get the U.S. side to offer its fallback proposal in return for a concession of no consequence.

The Americans also try to predict what our reactions will be. They prepare contingency plans, which they hope will counter our statements, again believing that confrontation and rebuttal are necessary. They seem to value highly winning such arguments. When arguments do develop, U.S. negotiators may become tense; after that they may try to distract attention from a difficult situation by resorting to humor. Their humor is hard to understand since it is based on their own rather strange cultural experience, but it is safe to laugh when they do.

In the Negotiating Room

U.S. negotiating teams are sometimes small and are sometimes large. Their delegations are often large when the internal disagreements between agencies have not been reconciled before the meeting, and therefore each department must send an agent, or, on the other hand, perhaps because of internal jealousy. They do not always admit observers from interested agencies and seldom have anyone present for training purposes or as an extra notetaker. Thus our delegation is usually larger.

* * *

Americans are quite conscious of protocol, so it is necessary to consider seating and the matters of introductions and entertainment. They often say that rank means nothing to them, but it really does. On the other hand, when mistakes are made they adapt easily and are not offended if the matter is quietly corrected. In short, they want the proper gestures made but are satisfied with that. They also like to be invited to social events where they say they dislike discussing business and then in fact they easily agree to do so. Such occasions are useful for testing compromises and obtaining information on their fallback positions.

The Progress of Talks

Americans are energetic and persistent. They are enthusiastic negotiators who seldom take naps during talks even if the topic at hand is of no real concern. They enjoy arguing the logic of their position, which they like to describe as good for all and not just for them. They have a disturbing habit, however, of passing over very quickly the areas of agreement and giving high emphasis to disagreements. In fact, they talk about little else, as if that were the most important subject.

Americans like to concentrate on one problem at a time. They seem not to understand that the whole picture is more important, and they spend little time on developing a general understanding of the views and interests of both sides. Since their habit of focusing on one issue often forces a direct disagreement, they often propose setting the issue aside, but they come back to it later with the same attitude and concentration. A negotiation with them may therefore become a series of small conflicts and we must always make a special effort to give proper attention to the large areas of agreement and common interest. * * *

C. The negotiations between A.Co and J.Co

Conditions in the era in which A.Co and J.Co negotiated the P.C. Agreements were quite different from those of today. There were not shelves of books in English offering advice to foreign businesspeople on how to negotiate with the Japanese; very few *shōgai bengoshi* were available to advise Japanese companies; Japanese companies' corporate legal departments were far smaller than they are today and had far less accumulated expertise; and foreign parties often had considerably more bargaining power than their Japanese counterparts. This state of affairs was reflected in the P.C., as A.Co entered the negotiations with J.Co with very little experience in dealing with Japanese parties, and J.Co undertook the negotiations without assistance from any *bengoshi* or U.S. lawyers.

Initial meetings between A.Co and J.Co led to agreement to form a joint venture company and on the basic structure of the relationship among A.Co., J.Co, and the joint venture company. A.Co's attorneys then produced drafts of the agreements and sent those to J.Co. After analysis of the drafts, J.Co dispatched personnel to the U.S. to negotiate with A.Co and its attorneys and to explain the substantive changes J.Co wanted to make in the drafts.

A.Co's response was essentially, "take it or leave it." Presented with this choice, J.Co agreed to sign the agreements as drafted by A.Co.

Consider how A.Co was able to achieve this negotiating triumph of having its first drafts become the final agreements. Why do you suppose J.Co was willing to accept A.Co's position? Eagerness to complete the deal at any cost? Lack of a full understanding of the potential ramifications of the agreements? A belief that, regardless of the legal niceties reflected in the agreements, future relations between the parties would, as a practical matter, be subject to renegotiation and modification as developments warranted? What might J.Co have done differently to have had the agreements reflect its viewpoints?

Also, consider just how much of a triumph the negotiations were for A.Co. In drafting agreements strongly advantageous to itself, what assumptions was A.Co making? What costs might there be to A.Co's approach?

II. Negotiations Becoming Agreements— The Issue of Contract Formation

Before negotiating and drafting agreements to be governed by Japanese law and/or performed in Japan, one should know some of the basics of Japanese contract law. On some of these basics, there are rather clear and substantial differences in U.S. and Japanese law. For example, in Japan consideration is not required to make contracts enforceable, oral contracts ordinarily are enforceable, and there is no parol evidence rule. Another basic issue of contract law is determining the point during negotiations when a contract is formed, or, more precisely, the point at which contract-like rights and duties arise.

In this section we consider this issue of contract formation. We begin by examining some of the provisions in the Civil Code and Commercial Code on point. We then turn to an important recent case dealing with this issue under both contract and tort theories.

A. Key provisions of the Codes

Review in the Appendices the following key Code provisions concerning contract formation: Civil Code, §§ 521, 523, 524 and 526; Commercial Code, §§ 507-09.

Questions and Discussion Points

1. *Open offers at a distance*: What is the relationship between Section 524 of the Civil Code and Section 508 of the Commercial Code? Assuming the offeror has second thoughts after making an open offer at a distance, can the offeror improve his or her position by promptly sending a notice of revocation, or would he or she end up in the same position through the operation of the lapsing provision in Section 508 of the Commercial Code?

2. *Code interpretation*: Do the above provisions answer all the questions about offer and acceptance that you can imagine? If not, and if ambiguities remain in Japan's civil law-based system, how should one go about resolving those ambiguities? Would the applicable approach be the same as that for a U.S. court in a sale of goods case faced with an offer and acceptance issue not squarely addressed by the Uniform Commercial Code?

B. Reliance on a promise to contract

Even before arriving at the point of formal contract formation as defined in the Civil and Commercial Code provisions, negotiations between parties may give rise to an expectation that a contract will be formed, and a party may take actions based on that expectation. If a contract is not then entered, does the party who has taken such actions have any recourse? The case below addresses this issue.

Translation by Yanagida Nomura & Akai

D. James Wan Kim Min v. Mitsui Bussan K.K.
1232 Hanrei Jihō 110
(Tokyo High Ct., March 17, 1987)

REFERENCES:

Civil Code, §§ 1(2) and 709

FACTS:

Beginning in August 1973, Plaintiff Min, a Malaysian politician and businessman, conducted negotiations with Mitsui Bussan K.K., a Japanese general trading company (Mitsui), concerning a joint venture project to log and develop a forested area in Indonesia (the Project). Min and the employees of the Lumber Division of Mitsui had several conferences in both Tokyo and Singapore in the course of the negotiations, more than half of the conferences being held in Tokyo. In January 1974, Min and the manager of the Lumber Division of Mitsui (the Manager) reached the following basic understanding at a conference held in Tokyo:

(1) For the price of US $4,000,000, Mitsui shall purchase from Min 50% of the shares of a certain Brunei corporation which holds a majority of the shares in a certain Indonesian corporation that has lumbering rights in Indonesia.

(2) Mitsui shall pay the share purchase price to Min on April 30, 1974.

(3) Payment by Mitsui of the share purchase price shall be subject to approval by the Board of Directors of Mitsui.

(4) By the end of February 1974, Mitsui and Min shall enter into a basic contract covering the matters necessary for the Project.

After this conference, the Manager sent Min a letter dated January 29, 1974, (the Letter) to confirm these understandings, and on February 6, 1974, Min responded with his own letter, which stated that he accepted the offer made in the Letter.

From February 21 to February 27, 1974, Min and the employees in charge at Mitsui held a conference in Singapore at which they completed a draft of a contract between Min and Mitsui for the sale and purchase of the shares in the Brunei corporation and a draft of a basic contract between Min and Mitsui concerning the Project. Min and employees of Mitsui also agreed that Min should rent an office in Singapore to proceed with the Project, and in April 1974 Min began to rent such an office.

By the April 30, 1974, deadline, however, Mitsui neither signed the draft contracts nor paid to Min the US $4,000,000 purchase price for the shares in the Brunei corporation. Instead, Mitsui continued negotiations with Min. In July 1974, Mitsui proposed to Min a loan of US $4,000,000, rather than proceeding with the purchase of the shares in the Brunei corporation. Mitsui then suspended the offer of the loan when Min was arrested and detained by Malaysian authorities in October 1974 under the Public Security Maintenance Regulations (an arrest that Min claims was politically motivated).

After Min's arrest, Mitsui maintained contact with representatives of Min, and in July 1975 Mitsui agreed with them that after Min's release it would make its best efforts to execute the loan it had suspended.

Min was released on January 31, 1976, and requested Mitsui to proceed with the suspended loan. Mitsui refused and in May 1976 told Min that it had no legal obligation to him.

Min then brought suit against Mitsui, raising both contract and tort claims and seeking (1) damages caused by depreciation in the market price of shares in the Brunei corporation, (2) interest on the purchase price of the shares in the Brunei corporation, (3) expenses for preparation for the Project, such as expenses for transportation and correspondence and the rental of the office, (4) damages for mental distress, (5) lost profits associated with the Project, and (6) attorney's fees associated with the tort claim.

With respect to the contract claims, Min alleged that the exchange of letters between himself and the Manager constituted the offer and acceptance of a sales contract for the shares in the Brunei corporation (the alleged Share Purchase Contract); that at the February 21-27, 1974, conference in Singapore, he and Mitsui entered into an oral contract concerning the Project (the alleged Joint Venture Contract); and, thus, that Mitsui breached both of the alleged contracts by its nonperformance.

Min's tort claim, offered as an alternative to the contract claims, was that even if the two alleged contracts were not formed, Mitsui was liable to Min for breach of a duty created by Mitsui's leading Min to rely on the expectation that the two contracts would be concluded.

The District Court rejected Min's contract claims, stating that for the following reasons the Letter should not be regarded as an offer to enter into the alleged Share Purchase Contract:

(1) Since, in general, only the representative director of a company has the authority to execute an agreement such as a joint venture agreement which requires the company to purchase shares in the joint venture company, the Manager should not be regarded as having had the authority to make an offer binding Mitsui.

(2) After the exchange of letters between Mitsui and Min, which Min argued constituted offer and acceptance, the two parties completed drafts of both the alleged contracts, neither of which was ever signed.

(3) Since the purpose of the alleged Share Purchase Contract was not to make profits with respect to the market value of the shares, but rather to make profits in proceeding with the Project, it would be reasonable to expect that both the alleged contracts should be concluded at the same time, or at the least, that the alleged Share Purchase Contract would not be concluded until the substance of both contracts had been determined.

Furthermore, with respect to the alleged Joint Venture Contract, the court found that the existence of the unsigned draft of the agreement indicated that no oral agreement had been concluded.

With respect to Min's tort claim, however, the court held in favor of Min, finding that Mitsui was liable to Min for approximately ¥6 million for Min's expenses in preparation for the Project and for his attorney's fees. The court gave the following reasons:

(1) Given that Min and Mitsui exchanged drafts of the two alleged contracts, both of which were expected to be executed soon, first, it was reasonable for Min to proceed with preparation for the Project in reliance on his expectation of the conclusion of the contracts, and secondly, Mitsui was obligated under the principles of trust and good faith to make good faith efforts to conclude the contracts in order not to injure Min's expecta-

tion. If Mitsui breached this duty, it should be regarded as having committed a tort against Min, unless special circumstances existed.

(2) It could be said, however, that Min's arrest by the Malaysian authorities would reasonably cause Mitsui to have concern for the prospects for the Project, and Mitsui should thus not be held liable for refusing to proceed with the Project following Min's arrest.

(3) Therefore, Mitsui is held liable to compensate Min only for the preparatory expenses he incurred prior to his arrest, plus attorney's fees. Mitsui's infringement of Min's expectation that the two alleged contracts would be concluded cannot be said to have caused the losses alleged by Min due to the drop in the market price of the shares of the Brunei corporation, his mental distress, or his lost profits.

Min appealed the adverse ruling on his contract claims and the damages awarded for his tort claim. Mitsui appealed the finding of its tort liability.

JUDGMENT:

1. The appeal by Mitsui of the judgment on Min's tort claim is dismissed.
2. Based on Min's appeal the original judgment is hereby modified as follows:
   (1) Mitsui is liable to Min in the amount of ¥55,892,947, plus interest thereon at the rate of 5% per annum from September 8, 1976, until the principal amount is paid in full.
   (2) All other claims by Min are denied.

REASONS:

1. [Omitted—In this part of the opinion, the court discusses whether Japanese, Malaysian, or Brunei law should apply to the contract and tort claims of Min. This portion of the opinion will be provided when we revisit this case later in Section III.D.1 below, when studying choice of law issues. For present purposes, it is enough to know that the court applied Japanese law to all Min's claims.]

2. [Omitted—In this section, the High Court, though making some corrections, essentially makes the same findings of facts relating to the negotiations between Min and Mitsui as those found by the District Court.]

3. With respect to Min's contract claims, we also hold against Min.

We adopt the District Court's reasoning on this issue, with the following exceptions:

(1) [The High Court's disagreement related to the first reason given by the District Court in its assessment of the contract formation issue, the question of whether the Manager could bind Mitsui. The District Court held that the Manager did not have authority to bind Mitsui, but the High Court noted that Min had asserted that even if the Manager had no such authority, the offer should bind Mitsui in accordance with the principle of apparent agency under Sections 38(3) and 43(2) of the Commercial Code, Section 42 of the Commercial Code, or Section 110 of the Civil Code. To respond to these assertions, the High Court replaced the first reason of the District Court on the substantive contract issues with the language that follows:]

Paragraph 3 of the Letter provides that payment of the purchase price of the shares shall be subject to approval by Mitsui's Board of Directors. Furthermore, Paragraph 4 of the Letter provides that a basic contract covering other matters necessary for the Project shall be concluded by the end of February 1974. According to the foregoing provisions, the Letter as a whole should be interpreted as a confirmation that Mitsui intended to purchase the shares after all necessary matters were agreed upon, rather than being interpreted as a final and definite offer by Mitsui to purchase the shares. Furthermore, although a sales contract is a consensual contract [which is not necessarily required to be made in writing], making a written contract is usual for an important agreement concerning a joint venture project of a large contract amount. In fact, in the case before the court, the parties had continued to draft written contracts concerning the Project and the sale of the shares. * * * Therefore, since the Letter should not be regarded as an offer by the Manager to purchase the shares, Min's assertion [of application of the principle of apparent agency], which is based upon the assumption that the Manager made an offer, is not reasonable.

(2) [Omitted.]

4. We next will discuss Min's alternative claims. The first of Min's alternative causes of action is to the following effect: In light of the negotiations toward the conclusion of an agreement, Min came to have a right of expectation of, or an interest in, the conclusion of the agreement. Mitsui was thus obligated under the principle of good faith to make efforts to enter into the agreement in order not to infringe upon Min's right or interest. Nonetheless, Mitsui failed to perform its duty and, despite its repeated assurances that it would enter into and perform the agreement, it later reversed its course and concluded that entering into the agreement would be impossible, thereby injuring the said interest of Min.

We shall review the foregoing allegation of Min: In the modern world, the principles of good faith and trust govern not only contractual relationships, but also all relationships under private law, and such principles thus apply not only after conclusion of an agreement but also at the stage of preparations toward conclusion of an agreement. In the event that preparation between two parties progresses toward conclusion of an agreement and the first party comes to expect that the agreement will surely be concluded, the second party becomes obligated under the principles of good faith and trust to try to conclude the agreement, in order not to injure the expectation of the first party. Therefore, if the second party, in violation of its obligation, concludes that the agreement is undesirable, [absent certain circumstances], it is liable for damages incurred by the first party as the result of its illegal acts. * * *

In this case, we find that the Letter sent by the Manager and Min's response, to which Mitsui offered no subsequent objection, caused Min to expect that the agreements would be concluded. Mitsui, therefore, should be considered to have become obligated from that time to make good faith efforts, under the principles of good faith and trust, to conclude the agreements. Absent special circumstances that justified suspension of efforts to conclude the agreements, Mitsui should not have been allowed unilaterally and unconditionally to suspend conclusion. Mitsui should thus be found liable to Min for any damages incurred by Min due to such suspension.

In response, Mitsui alleges that the reason the agreements were not concluded was that no agreement was reached between Min and Mitsui concerning the issue of the Indonesian minority shareholders.

We find, however, as follows: Consideration of Mitsui's figures for its lumber business in March and in September of 1974 reveals that Mitsui showed profits for March but losses for September. Accordingly, Mitsui's prospects for profits from the lumber business declined during the time of the negotiations with Min. Mitsui's interest in concluding any agreement with Min weakened owing to the change in circumstances in the lumber market. Furthermore, there was a provision in the alleged Share Purchase Contract to the effect that Min would not arrange a meeting between Mitsui and the Indonesian parties until after Mitsui completed the stock purchase. In light of the foregoing facts, the main reason the agreements were not entered cannot be the fact that no agreement was reached between Min and Mitsui on the issue of the Indonesian minority shareholders.

It is the case, however, that Min was arrested by the Malaysian authorities on October 30, 1974, under the Public Security Maintenance Regulations, and that he was detained in the Thaipin Detention House. Min was released on March 10, 1975, by virtue of a writ of habeas corpus, but then was rearrested on the same day under the Domestic Security Maintenance Act and once more was detained in the Thaipin Detention House. On January 31, 1976, Min was finally released, although with restrictions on his freedom of movement. Min claims that the foregoing arrests and detentions were politically motivated and illegal. Whatever the reasons for the arrests, the fact that Min, who not only would have been a party to the agreements but also was to be the main person in charge of the Project and who would have been critical to it in other respects, was arrested by local authorities and detained for a long time must have caused apprehensions about the venture's future. This may be one of the reasons Mitsui suspended efforts to conclude the agreement to enter into the joint venture. The main reason, however, was clearly the drop in prices in the lumber market. Mitsui had consistently behaved in a way that would cause Min to expect that the agreements would be concluded, Min's detentions notwithstanding. This remained the case until the end of May 1976, when Mitsui made it clear to Min that it had no intention of concluding the agreements. [The High Court determined later in the opinion that the date on which the Project was finally and definitely cancelled by Mitsui was September 8, 1976.]

Since there were no special circumstances that would justify Mitsui's suspension of efforts to conclude the agreements, we hold that Mitsui must compensate Min for damages he suffered from the time of the exchange of letters until the end of May 1976, the time Mitsui made it clear to Min that it had no intention of concluding the agreements [and thus not for the shorter period for which the District Court found Mitsui liable, from the exchange of letters until Min's arrest and incarceration].

[The High Court next discussed the damages due from Mitsui. With respect to Min's alleged damages resulting from depreciation in the market price of the shares, mental distress, and lost profits, the High Court held that such damages did not reasonably relate to Mitsui's breach. With respect to Min's expenses in preparing for the Project, the High Court found Mitsui liable for the amount claimed by Min, ¥55,892,947, for expenses relating to transportation, accommodations, and correspondence from February 1974 to May 1976, compensation paid to representatives of the Project, rent on the office paid from April 1974 to May 1976, expenditures on investigation into lumbering forests, and attorney's fees. The High Court dated Mitsui's liability from September 8, 1976, when it finally and unequivocally rejected the Project, and assessed the statutory 5% interest rate on such amount until paid to Min in full.]

Questions and Discussion Points

1. *Formation of contracts*: As both courts note, Japanese law does not require sales contracts to be in writing to be enforceable. In this case, the parties had not only reached a basic understanding orally. In addition, Mitsui had put that basic understanding into writing in a letter of confirmation to Min, and Min had responded in writing less than ten days later with a letter accepting that "offer." Given the provisions of the Civil Code and Commercial Code discussed previously, why didn't this result in a binding contract? What does the District Court say on this point? The High Court? On what Code provisions are they relying for their decisions? Do you agree with the courts' reasoning? Suppose this case had arisen between two Japanese entities for a logging project to be performed in Japan. Would the judgment have been the same?

2. *Potential tort remedies*: Where does the tort remedy in the Min case come from? On what Code provisions, if any, are the courts relying in finding tort liability? Do you agree with the finding of liability?

Both courts found liability based on a violation of the principles of good faith and trust. What factual circumstances were particularly relevant to the courts in finding such a violation? Did the courts look at the same factors as for the contract claims? Suppose the price of lumber had increased during the period in question, rather than dropping. Do you suppose the High Court would have reached the same decision? The District Court?

Did it matter to Min whether he won in tort or in contract? What damages are available under the respective theories? Why did the High Court disagree with the District Court's measure of damages? Which decision is correct, if either?

3. *Business customs*: With regard to both the contract and tort claims, the courts refer to business norms and reasonable expectations of the parties to business dealings. In fact, as discussed in Chapter 2, several provisions in *Hōrei*, the Civil Code, and the Commercial Code require courts to consider relevant customs. Given the career system for the judiciary, where do the judges obtain their knowledge of business customs?

4. *Other considerations*: As discussed in Section III.D.1 below, in this case the

Japanese courts elected to apply Japanese law. In transnational business transactions (especially where, as here, the negotiations have taken place in both nations or the bulk of the activities are to take place in the other nation), however, it is entirely possible that courts will reach different conclusions on which law applies. Accordingly, it is important to bear in mind the possible need to assess contract formation and related issues under both nations' laws.

III. Drafting Issues

In negotiating and drafting agreements, there is usually no clear demarcation between the act of negotiating and the act of drafting. Negotiations often take the form of the parties' sending back and forth successive revised drafts of an agreement. At the other extreme, though, face-to-face negotiations may resolve all substantive issues with the result that all that is left is pure draftsmanship, with the legal technician trying to express clearly the parties' intent and to take account of the myriad ways in which the background legal rules can affect the final agreement and might frustrate the parties' intentions.

In addition to being aware of substantive and technical legal issues, the drafter must be attuned to strategic issues related to the drafting process. Should the initial draft be made strongly advantageous to the drafter's client, thereby risking unnecessary friction with the other party, or should the initial draft be balanced, but at the risk of offering unnecessary or premature concessions? Which concessions should be offered for which counterconcessions? It goes without saying that both strategic and purely legal concerns are important in drafting. While we will focus in this section on some of the substantive legal issues that the drafter must consider in drafting international joint venture agreements, in approaching these materials you should also be thinking about strategic issues.

The topics in this section do not exhaust those which need to be considered—some drafting issues are particular only to a given joint venture, many others are considered in later chapters, such as corporate law issues in Chapter 8 and antitrust issues in Chapter 10, and still others lie beyond the scope of this book. In this section, though, we introduce several basic drafting issues that routinely arise in U.S.-Japan transactions (most of which come up in many settings, not just joint ventures).

A. Initial drafting concerns

1. Determining who makes the first draft

One of the first issues that often arises is determining which party will produce the initial draft of an agreement. Consider a complex series of agreements such as those making up the P.C. Agreements. What are the advantages in being the party to produce the initial drafts of the agreements? What are the disadvantages?

2. The legal effect of vague drafting

What is likely to be the legal result of drafting that is vague or that does not address substantive issues that later arise? The following is a case in which the clauses in the agreements between the parties concerning the terminability of the agreements were not clear. The claimant in the case was seeking a provisional disposition, a ruling similar to a declaratory judgment or an injunction under U.S. law, declaring that the supply agreements terminated by the respondents were not terminable and thus that the respondents had continuing obligations to supply the claimant pursuant to the agreements.

Translation by Yanagida Nomura & Akai

K.K. Miyagi Family Club v. Nihon Columbia K.K. et al.
1110 Hanrei Jihō 13
(Tokyo Dist. Ct., March 29, 1984)

REFERENCES:

Code of Civil Procedure, § 760
Civil Code, §§ 540 and 555

FACTS:

Since 1976, claimant K.K. Miyagi Family Club (Miyagi), a music record retailer, had been supplied records, tapes, etc. (records) by respondents pursuant to distributorship agreements (collectively the Agreements) entered into with a record wholesaler, respondent K.K. Seikōdō (Seikōdō), and two record manufacturers, respondents Nihon Columbia K.K. (Columbia) and K.K. Tōshiba E.M.I. (Tōshiba) (collectively Respondents).

In 1981, Miyagi began to sell records to record rental shops, which began to appear in Japan in about June 1980 and which expanded rapidly. [Under the so-called home use exception to Japan's Copyright Act, taping an album in one's home for private use is not regarded as copyright infringement. Record rental shops rented albums for a modest per day fee. Most shops also sold blank tapes, and some had high-speed dubbing machines available for use on the premises. Record rental shops have since been displaced by CD rental shops, which have been the object of protests by foreign recording artists and record companies. At the time of this case, Japanese record companies also strongly opposed the record rental shops, but a subsequent amendment to the Copyright Act, described below, quieted the domestic protests.] Respondents repeatedly requested Miyagi not to sell records to rental shops, but Miyagi continued to do so. In August 1981, Tōshiba stopped supplying Miyagi with the records it ordered; in September 1981, Columbia and Seikōdō did the same. Eventually Respondents all terminated their Agreements with Miyagi.

The Agreements provided that Respondents should supply Miyagi with records, but did not provide how individual sale and purchase contracts between Miyagi and Respondents were to be formed. In practice, however, Respondents supplied Miyagi with records ordered by Miyagi upon receiving orders from Miyagi. The Agreements with Tōshiba and Columbia did not contain language limiting Miyagi's sales to ordinary consumers. While the Agreement with Seikōdō did indicate that Miyagi's sales were to be for consumers, the language was not limiting language drafted with the knowledge that record rental shops would develop.

Miyagi has filed a petition with this court seeking a provisional disposition to confirm its continuing rights under the Agreements and to order Respondents to deliver the records it ordered.

Respondents assert that their ceasing to supply Miyagi is justified for the following reasons:

(1) Under the Agreements, Respondents were not obligated to accept purchase orders placed by Miyagi. Therefore, none of the Respondents was obligated to supply Miyagi with any records until an individual sales contract was formed by one of the Respondents accepting an offer made by Miyagi in the form of a purchase order;

(2) If individual sales contracts had been formed between Miyagi and Respondents by Respondents' having accepted Miyagi's purchase order offers, Respondents would thereby have become obligated to deliver records, and Miyagi could thus obtain a provisional disposition ordering the Respondents to deliver. In the case before the court, however, Respondents have not in fact accepted Miyagi's purchase orders. Since a court cannot order Respondents to accept Miyagi's offers and thereby assume an obligation for which provisional disposition could be ordered, Miyagi has no cause of action;

(3) Respondents could rightfully terminate the Agreements in accordance with the terms thereof on account of Miyagi's breach.[1] Since the purpose of the Agreements was to enable Miyagi to sell records to ordinary consumers, Miyagi was required to sell only to ordinary consumers, and, therefore, Miyagi's sales to record rental shops constituted breach of the Agreements; or

(4) [Omitted.]

JUDGMENT:

The Claimant's petition is denied on all counts.

REASONS:

I. - II. [Omitted.]

III. Miyagi alleges that under the Agreements Respondents do not have the right to reject its purchase orders and that Respondents are obligated to supply it with the records it orders.

We find as follows: It is true that there is a provision in each of the Agreements (Article 1) to the effect that Respondents shall supply Miyagi with records handled by Respondents. Further, it has been the practice under the Agreements that Respondents supplied Miyagi with records in accordance with Miyagi's orders, so long as the records ordered were in stock. We also find that, generally speaking, if Respondents did not deliver goods as ordered by their distributors, it was only due to special circumstances such as that Respondents did not have sufficient goods in stock or that a distributor had been in default of payment for previous purchases.

* * * In the event that a retailer becomes unable to obtain a supply of records from a particular manufacturer or wholesaler, it will be very difficult for

the retailer to find a source of supply elsewhere. Therefore, it is a basic condition for the business of a record retailer that its contractual relationships with record manufacturers or wholesalers are maintained and that it is supplied with records in accordance with its orders. * * * [T]aking into consideration the provisions in Article 1 of the Agreements, as well as the past conduct of the Respondents in delivering records, we determine that under the Agreements Respondents did not have unrestricted freedom to accept or reject Miyagi's orders, and that they were obligated to enter into individual sales contracts with Miyagi by accepting Miyagi's orders and supplying Miyagi with records in accordance therewith. * * *

IV. [Omitted.]

V. [In this section, the court discusses Respondents' assertion that Miyagi cannot, by means of a provisional disposition, be granted the type of relief it sought.]

* * * Under the Agreements, however, Respondents were obligated to accept Miyagi's orders unless special circumstances existed. * * * Taking these facts into consideration, we determine that there could be cases where Miyagi could obtain provisional relief requiring delivery of goods it orders, even if the orders were not accepted by Respondents, on the basis that unless special circumstances exist which justify Respondents' rejection of Miyagi's orders, Respondents must accept the orders. * * *

VI. - VII. [Omitted.]

VIII. [In this section, the court discusses whether Miyagi's sales of records to record rental shops constituted breach of the Agreements.]

1. - 4. [Omitted.]

5. * * * Upon review of all of the allegations and evidence provided by the parties, we find that the purpose of the Agreements was Miyagi's selling of records to ordinary final users who intended to buy them from retailers for the purpose of hearing the recordings recorded therein; that Miyagi and Respondents entered into the Agreements with the assumption that they would maintain a traditional market flow in which record manufacturers or wholesalers sell records to retailers, who then sell them to ordinary final users; that the nature of record rental shops, the purpose of which is to make profits by renting records to their customers, is different from that of sales to ordinary final users; and that record manufacturers were granted the right to reproduce recordings and to protect that right based on the assumption of the traditional market flow. Furthermore, the fact exists that the purpose of the Copyright Act, under which record manufacturers are granted a right to reproduce recordings, has been jeopardized by the development of the large number of record rental shops that have interfered with the traditional market flow and given their customers opportunities to reproduce recordings by renting records to them.[2] Taking into consideration the foregoing facts, as well as the fact that the Agreements are continuous agreements, Miyagi could be found liable for breach of the Agreements based on its breach of the principle of good faith and trust by selling records supplied by Respondents to record rental shops, when doing so was against the will of Respondents and jeopardized their profits.

6. - 8. [Omitted.]

IX. We next discuss whether Miyagi's sales of records to record rental shops constituted good cause for termination of the Agreements.

We find it reasonable to hold that the Agreements could be terminated only for such a serious breach on the part of Miyagi in the performance of its obligations as to render it unreasonable for Miyagi to expect the Agreements to continue, but not for a trivial default because the Agreements were continuous agreements and, as stated earlier, the continuation of the Agreements was crucial for the continuation of Miyagi's business. Considering, however, the adverse effects of the activities of record rental shops on the business of record manufacturers and retailers, sales of records to record rental shops might not constitute a trivial breach, depending on the extent and manner thereof.

[The court next discusses the great extent to which Miyagi's orders increased as it began selling to rental shops, how Respondents became aware of the source of Miyagi's new sales and protested, how Miyagi continued sales to rental shops, and how Respondents began to refuse to fill Miyagi's orders and terminated the Agreements.]

Based on the foregoing facts, we find that Miyagi's supply of records to record rental shops was against the will of Respondents and became detrimental to the interests of Respondents in its extent and manner. The actions of Miyagi, thus, did not constitute a mere trivial breach, but such a serious breach as to disrupt the trust underlying the Agreements and thereby to render the continuation of the Agreements not to be expected. It is, therefore, held that Miyagi's actions constituted a lawful cause for termination of the Agreements. * * *

X. - XIII. [Omitted.]

Questions and Discussion Points

1. *The court's reasoning*: What is the holding in the *Miyagi* case? Given the ambiguity of the termination clauses in the agreements between Miyagi and Respondents, to what sources or standards did the court turn to resolve the issue?

2. *Foreign opposition to the rental system*: Under the amended Copyright Act, Japanese record manufacturers have agreed to permit rental shops to rent CDs within one to three weeks after their release, subject to payment of royalties. Foreign record companies have demanded that their CDs not be made available for rental for one full year after their release, the maximum period stipulated under the revised Copyright Act. What do you suppose accounts for this difference in attitude? Does the record (and CD) rental system represent a hidden barrier to foreign trade and business in Japan?

B. Standard clauses

1. Governing language

It is quite likely, especially as of the late 1960s when the agreements in the P.C. were executed, that personnel of J.Co were relying on Japanese translations of the

P.C. Agreements. What legal status, if any, would such translations have? Note that no reference is made in the JVA or collateral agreements to any Japanese versions of the agreements. Consider what would or should happen if a future dispute between A.Co and J.Co is heard by a Japanese court. Are there reasons the Japanese court should or should not rely on the Japanese translations to interpret the agreements?

Though no such clauses appear in the P.C. Agreements, contracts governing international relationships now almost always contain clauses designating the governing language of the contract. The examples below are from actual contracts. Consider the reasons different approaches to wording governing language clauses have been chosen and try to evaluate the merits of each clause as drafted.

Standard wording is represented by the following example from an agreement between a U.S. and a Japanese company:

> This Agreement shall be executed in English and shall be governed by and interpreted in accordance with the laws of Japan.

In the example below, from another agreement between a U.S. and a Japanese company, consider the meaning of the phrase "official, original agreement":

> This Agreement shall be prepared in both the Japanese and English languages. The English version shall be deemed the official, original agreement.

The final example is from an agreement between a Korean and a Japanese party. Consider why it might be that the agreement is drafted in English:

> The official text of this Agreement is prepared in the English language, which shall be the controlling version. Any version prepared in Korean or Japanese is done merely for the convenience of the parties hereto and shall have no bearing on the interpretation of the English language version of this Agreement.
>
> The language to be used at the General Meetings of Shareholders, the meetings of the Board of Directors and the consultations between the Operating Directors of NewCo shall be English.
>
> The notices summoning such meetings, the agenda and minutes thereof, and the notice and communications between the parties hereto shall be made in the English language as official language and the Korean or Japanese languages as support languages.

In all three of the examples above, the contracts were drafted or reviewed by a native speaker of English. Consider what sorts of problems may be presented when a contract drafted in English is negotiated and executed without the involvement of a native English speaker.

2. Force majeure

Almost all contemporary international agreements contain a "force majeure" clause such as the one below. Note that no such clause appears in the JVA in the

P.C., but that very brief "suspension of performance" clauses appear in §H-5 of the TechA and in §G-4 of the MA. Consider whether the "suspension of performance" clauses in the TechA and MA accomplish the same thing as the typical "force majeure" clause below, which comes from an agreement between a Japanese and a U.S. company:

> (1) Neither Party shall be liable to the other or in breach of this Agreement for non-performance or delay in performance of the terms and conditions herein due to any cause force majeure such as acts of God, acts of governments, riots, wars, strikes or other labor disturbances, accidents in transportation or other causes beyond the control of said Party; provided, however, that the Party so prevented from complying herewith shall promptly give notice thereof to the other Party and shall continue to take all actions reasonably within its power to comply as fully as possible herewith.
>
> (2) The Party not directly affected by the cause force majeure may elect to terminate this Agreement if the non-performance as hereinabove by the affected Party continues for six (6) months or longer.

3. Government approvals

Review the "government approvals" clause of the JVA (§H-5). From our study of the FIA and old FECA in Chapter 6, you should be able to ascertain why such a clause was necessary at the time the P.C. Agreements were entered into by A.Co and J.Co. Given the reform in the FECA which included a shift from the "prohibited in principle" approach to the "free in principle" approach to foreign investment and the consequent shift from the requirement of obtaining the government's approval to the requirement of giving the government notice of foreign transactions, should such clauses still be necessary in agreements between Japanese and foreign parties?

The following is from a contemporary agreement between a U.S. and a Japanese company and is an example of the type of clause that in many contemporary agreements has replaced the type of "government approvals" clause typical in the era the P.C. Agreements were drafted:

> If any provision of this Agreement is held invalid by any competent authority, the remainder of this Agreement shall continue in effect. The parties shall replace any invalid provision with a valid provision which most nearly conforms to their original intent.

Might a foreign company still prefer a more restrictive provision? Suppose trade secrets and know-how are to be transferred. How does one restore the status quo if provisions deemed vital by the party providing the information are held invalid?

C. A fundamental issue in joint venture agreements—contributing and withdrawing funds

In this section we will focus on two issues which go to the heart of any joint venture and which can easily give rise to conflict between the venturers: 1) how to determine whether additional funds for the joint venture company are necessary and, if so, how these should be raised, and 2) how to determine when and how much of the earnings of the joint venture company should be distributed to the venturers.

Though there are exceptions, in the typical joint venture between two parties, each venturer provides half the initial capital and anticipates receiving half the profits. The joint venture agreement designates the initial capital contributions to be made by each venturer at the time of formation of the joint venture company. Decisions about the future capital needs of the joint venture company and whether to distribute profits are then left, in the case where the joint venture company is a corporation, to the Board of Directors of the corporation, and in the case where it is a partnership, to the partners. In either case, in practical terms this means that the venturers themselves must reach agreement on these issues.

For the venturers to reach agreement on the capital needs of the joint venture company and whether to extract profits can be difficult, especially if the capital resources available to each venturer differ significantly. As the 1967 *Daily Yomiuri* article in Chapter 1 describes, difficulties arose in several 1960s joint ventures in Japan in which the foreign venturers had considerably more available capital than did their Japanese counterparts. This led to situations where the Japanese venturer felt compelled to sell its interest in the joint venture company or to allow its interest to become diluted as the foreign venturer contributed all the additional capital needs of the joint venture company. Such disparity in the resources of two venturers can also lead to disagreement over whether to reinvest earnings of the joint venture company or to extract them as profits.

Even where partners have similar resources, they may have different business philosophies, management styles, or long-term visions of what role the joint venture company should play. This may lead to disagreement over the issues of funding and taking funds from the joint venture company. Often it may not be possible to detect these differences at the outset of the relationship; abstract discussion about how to run the new entity may not reveal the considerable differences that arise as the joint venture company and each venturer confront concrete and unpredictable problems and opportunities.

Some venturers do seek in advance greater clarity in the joint venture agreement than a simple recognition that in the future they will have to reach agreement on the issues of the capital needs of the joint venture company and whether to extract profits. Below are examples from actual joint venture agreements of such efforts at greater clarity. Consider whether these drafting efforts ultimately commit the parties to anything more than an agreement to agree and, if their wording accomplishes no more than this, what purpose the clauses may serve.

1. Raising new funds

Compare the two examples below with §B-4(c) of the JVA in the P.C.

The following is from an agreement between a Japanese and a British company:

5.3 Britain Co. and Japan Co. agree that after the establishment of an agreed capital base (initially anticipated to be £____), the requirements of JV.Co for funds which the Board of Directors of JV.Co recommends [each party controls half the Board] and which are approved by the shareholders [each party owns half the shares], for the development or the proper running of JV.Co's business (including the provision of working capital), shall be met first out of internally generated cash, and then by any or all of the following:
a) increasing the issued share capital of JV.Co;
b) borrowing from either Party hereto; or
c) borrowing from banks or similar institutions, in a manner agreed by the Parties hereto (having regard to the underlying reasons for such additional requirements for funds by JV.Co). It is intended that at no time shall borrowings from external sources other than the Parties hereto exceed forty per cent (40%) of the aggregate of total borrowings from external sources and/or Britain Co. and Japan Co., as determined in accordance with normally accepted UK accounting practice and principles.

5.4 Any necessary guarantees of the repayment or discharge by the Company of its borrowings and other obligations shall be discussed between Britain Co. and Japan Co., and if it is agreed that guarantees should be provided, such guarantees shall be provided by Britain Co. and Japan Co. so far as practicable equally but severally.

The following is from an agreement between a Japanese and a U.S. company which established a joint venture partnership in the U.S.:

(a) Upon execution of this Agreement, each Partner shall open an account at a bank agreed upon by the Partners (each such account hereinafter referred to as a "Capital Account") and shall deposit one million dollars ($1,000,000.00) in its respective Capital Account. Subsequent capital contributions shall be made in the ratio of fifty percent (50%) by Japan Co. and fifty percent (50%) by U.S.Co. up to the total joint capital contribution of five million dollars ($5,000,000.00). After a Partner has contributed two million five hundred thousand dollars ($2,500,000.00) to its Capital Account, no further capital contribution shall be required of that Partner without its consent.

In addition, each of the Partners shall deliver to the other a letter of credit or other evidence of financial capability satisfactory to the other

Partner in the amount of one million five hundred thousand dollars ($1,500,000.00), as evidence of its commitment to provide the remainder, after its initial contribution above, of its one-half share of JV.Co's total projected financial requirements of five million dollars ($5,000,000.00). The Partners shall, after making the above initial capital contributions and at all times thereafter, hold equal ownership interests in JV.Co, except as otherwise hereinafter provided.

(b) In the event either Partner fails to make any required capital contribution, it is agreed that JV.Co may charge the delinquent Partner interest on the outstanding amount of the capital contribution due until said contribution is paid, at the current prime rate charged by JV.Co's financial depository. Neither Partner shall make any withdrawal from its Capital Account without the written consent of the other Partner.

(c) The Net Income of JV.Co, as defined in Article 6(a), shall be calculated monthly and distributed to each Partner's Capital Account until each Partner has contributed two million five hundred thousand dollars ($2,500,000.00) to its Capital Account. After reaching two million five hundred thousand dollars ($2,500,000.00) in each Capital Account, the Net Income shall be distributed into each Partner's separate bank account provided for in Article 6(c), in proportion to the amount of the total capital contribution of each Partner.

(d) If JV.Co at any time needs funding in excess of the amount of capital contributed to it by the Partners at that time, each Partner shall deposit in its Capital Account that amount remaining due on its total obligation of two million five hundred thousand dollars ($2,500,000.00).

2. Withdrawing profits

Note that the JVA in the P.C. does not contain any provision stating a policy on Newco's payment of dividends to A.Co and J.Co.

The following is from an agreement between a U.S. and a Japanese company:

> Japan Co. and U.S.Co. recognize and agree that their own best interests and the best interests of JV.Co will be served by taking all reasonable steps to insure that the expansion and growth of JV.Co will occur as rapidly as market conditions permit. To this end, Japan Co. and U.S.Co. agree that, in lieu of making dividends and distributing profits to the shareholders of JV.Co, the Board of Directors may, until Japan Co. and U.S.Co. otherwise agree, provide for the retention by JV.Co of such amount of the net income as shall reasonably be required under the then existing circumstances to provide for such expansion and growth and to continue to conduct the business and affairs of JV.Co according to sound business practices.

D. Dispute resolution and governing law

In this subsection we will consider a set of negotiating and drafting issues that commonly arises with respect to the mode of dispute resolution: the choice of governing law for the agreement and the enforceability of that choice. Another set of common negotiating and drafting issues related to dispute resolution concerns whether to provide for arbitration and, if so, how to deal with the site for and rules governing the arbitration. Because those issues are so closely bound up with broader questions relating to arbitration generally, we defer consideration of them to Chapter 11, which concerns arbitration and other means of dispute resolution.

1. Choosing and failing to choose the governing law

Review §H-4 of the JVA in the P.C. This clause designates Japanese law as the law governing the JVA. The P.C. Agreements' reliance on Japanese law is a product not of the negotiations between A.Co and J.Co, but of the pedagogical requirements of a course on Japanese law—in the actual case on which the P.C. is based, the governing law was the law of the state in the U.S. in which A.Co was incorporated.

In international agreements, each party usually prefers the governing law to be that of its home jurisdiction. The ultimate choice is a product of their relative bargaining strength and any "horse-trading" that may go on with respect to other provisions. Why would A.Co prefer U.S. law to govern an agreement to be performed almost entirely in Japan? In answering the foregoing question, consider what it means to designate a governing law. What types of legal issues that might arise from the P.C. would be covered by the governing law clause? What legal issues would not be affected by the governing law clause?

Complex international agreements like the P.C. Agreements always should (and almost always do) contain a governing law clause, and, as shown by the two articles below from *Hōrei* (Act Concerning the Application of Laws), which is the basic Japanese law concerning choice of law rules, parties have broad freedom under Japanese law to choose the law governing their agreements.

Hōrei (Law No. 10 of 1898)

Section 7. (Formation and effect of juristic act)

1. With regard to the formation and effect of a juristic act, the question as to which country's law is to govern shall be determined by the intention of the parties.
2. In cases where the intention of the parties is unclear, the law of the place where the juristic act is done shall govern.

Section 9. (Juristic acts involving a person resident in a place governed by different law)

1. For a declaration of intention made to a person residing in a place governed by a different law, the place from which notice of the same is dispatched shall be regarded as the place of the act.
2. For the formation and effect of a contract, the place from which the offer

is dispatched shall be regarded as the place of the act. In cases where the offeree is unaware, at the time of his acceptance, of the place from which the offer has been dispatched, the place of the offeror's domicile shall be regarded as the place of the act.

What happens when the parties fail to designate a governing law and subsequent tort claims arise? Japanese law on choice of law for tort claims is governed by Section 11 of *Hōrei,* which is reprinted below.

Section 11. (Formation and effect of obligations arising by operation of law)

1. The formation and effect of obligations arising from the voluntary management of affairs, unjust enrichment or torts, shall be governed by the law of the place where the events giving rise to such obligations occurred.
2. The provisions of the preceding paragraph shall not apply to torts in cases where the events occurring in a foreign country are not unlawful according to Japanese law.
3. Even when events occurring in a foreign country are unlawful according to Japanese law, the injured person may claim compensation only for damages or other remedies recognized by Japanese law.

In *Min v. Mitsui Bussan K.K.*, other aspects of which we considered in Section II of this chapter with regard to contract formation, Japanese courts considered choice of law issues in both the contract and tort context. Relevant portions of the opinion follow.

Translation by Yanagida Nomura & Akai

D. *James Wan Kim Min v. Mitsui Bussan K.K.*
1232 Hanrei Jihō 110
(Tokyo High Ct., March 17, 1987)

REFERENCES:

Hōrei, §§ 7, 9 and 11.

FACTS:

[See Section II.B above for the basic facts of the negotiations, dispute, and rulings on the substantive claims.]

The first issue considered by the Tokyo District Court was the law applicable to Min's contract and tort claims. With respect to the alleged Share Purchase Contract, the District Court held that determination of whether a contract had been formed should be governed by Japanese law because:

(1) There was no explicit or implicit agreement between Min and Mitsui concerning the governing law of the alleged Share Purchase Contract.
(2) Therefore, the governing law should be the law of the site of the act.
(3) Taking into consideration that more than half of the negotiations between Min and Mitsui were conducted in Tokyo and that the Letter, which Min argued should be regarded as an offer to enter into the alleged Share Purchase Contract, was sent from Tokyo, the site of the relevant acts was Tokyo, and thus Japanese law should be applied.

With respect to the law governing the contract formation issue for the alleged Joint Venture Contract, the District Court held that Japanese law should apply for the reason that since the alleged Joint Venture Contract was closely related to and inseparable from the alleged Share Purchase Contract, it was reasonable to infer that the parties intended to apply the same law to the former as to the latter.

With respect to the law governing Min's tort claim, the court held that because more than half of the negotiations were conducted in Tokyo, Japan was the place where the principal cause of the tort took place and thus Japanese law should govern. Both sides appealed.

JUDGMENT:

[Omitted.]

REASONS:

1. With respect to the law governing the two alleged agreements and the tort claim, we hold that Japanese law is the governing law in all respects.

We quote the District Court's reasoning on this issue, with the following addition:

> Although review of the evidence demonstrates that there exists evidence [copies of two drafts of the alleged Share Purchase Contract] which may show that the parties considered adopting Brunei law as the governing law for the alleged Share Purchase Contract, such drafts were only drafts and were never signed.
>
> [The rest of the opinion is omitted.]

Questions and Discussion Points

1. *The application of Japanese law*: Why did the Japanese courts apply Japanese law on the contract issue? What are the relevant statutory provisions? Do they provide a clear answer? What was the relevance, if any, of the references to Brunei law in drafts of the Share Purchase Contract? If the key inquiry under *Hōrei* is the intent of the parties, should the references to Brunei law be accorded more weight than they were given?

Why did the courts apply Japanese law to the tort claim? What statutory provision applies? Where did the events giving rise to the claims occur? Is the decision correct? If you do not think Japanese law should apply, what law should govern the tort claim?

2. *Failing to designate the governing law*: In *Min*, no formal written agreement was ever executed. When written contracts are drafted for complex international transactions, though, they can almost always be expected to include a governing law clause. Yet in simple one-time transactions the parties sometimes neglect to designate the governing law. If a dispute over such an agreement between a Japanese and a foreign party comes to a Japanese court, what law should the court apply? Consider the following example.

> Professor Splurge, a wealthy sports car enthusiast and U.S. citizen living in Cambridge, Massachusetts, reads that Japan Motor Works (JMW) has developed a limited edition high performance car called the Double Turbo 300XX. While guest lecturing in Palo Alto, California, Professor Splurge faxes JMW's Customer Sales Office in Tokyo a letter offering to purchase a Double Turbo 300XX and stating the price and other terms. JMW sends a fax letter accepting Professor Splurge's offer to the return fax number indicated.

If JMW then fails to deliver and Professor Splurge sues JMW in a Japanese court, what law should the court apply? The first step in the court's analysis, which you could not ascertain from *Hōrei*, should be to determine whether there is any effective convention governing the sale of goods between the U.S. and Japan. The U.N. Convention on the International Sale of Goods specifies rules for the choice of law in sale of goods transactions when the parties have not specified the governing law. As it turns out, however, Japan has not yet ratified that Convention, nor is there any other applicable convention between the U.S. and Japan. Thus the court would move to consideration of *Hōrei*, from which it would determine the applicable law by reference to Sections 7 and 9, reprinted above. What should be the first step of the court in applying *Hōrei*? If the intention of the parties is unclear, what does *Hōrei* direct the court to do? Suppose that JMW, the offeree, was not aware, at the time of acceptance, of the place from which Professor Splurge sent the offer. What law should govern the agreement?

2. Applicability of public law obligations

Though private parties have strong freedom in Japan to designate the governing law, such a designation does not permit the parties to avoid all public obligations in Japan or relating to Japanese nationals. In drafting the governing law provision, it is critical to understand that even if a law other than Japanese law is chosen, various obligations under Japanese law will still exist and need to be taken into account in drafting agreements and conducting business pursuant to such an agreement. The following case concerns application of Japanese labor laws and provides an excellent example of some of the principles and policy concerns involved in this interface of public and private obligations. The following is the provision of the Labor Union Act at issue in the case:

Article 7. (Unfair Labor Practices)

Employers shall not engage in the following practices:

(i)(a) dismissing or subjecting to any other unfair treatment any employee because of such employee being a member of a labor union, joining a labor union, or engaging in protected activity of a labor union, or (b) making it a condition of employment that an employee not join a labor union or give up membership in a labor union.

*Frank S. George v. International Air Service Co., Ltd.**
408 Hanrei Jihō 14
(Tokyo Dist. Ct., April 26, 1965)

REFERENCES:

Code of Civil Procedure, § 4(3)

Hōrei, § 7

Labor Union Act, § 7(i)

FACTS:

International Air Service Company Limited (IAS) was a corporation organized under the laws of California with its head office in California. Its main business was supplying crew members to airlines and air transport companies in various countries. As of the mid-1960s, IAS was supplying 52 crew members to airlines in Japan for their domestic operations, including 45 assigned to Japan Air Lines (JAL). It conducted business relating to this supply from an office in JAL's Operations Center at Tokyo International Airport.

Frank S. George, a U.S. citizen, was employed by IAS as a planemaster on April 1, 1960. He was initially hired for a period of one year, but that period was extended through the time of this dispute. The Labor Agreement between IAS and George stated that he would be assigned to JAL. It also provided that any claims concerning death, disease or injury suffered in the course of his employment, even when he was on assignment to JAL, would be settled in accordance with the Worker's Compensation Law of California. George was sent to JAL at the start of 1961 and had worked as a planemaster for JAL's domestic lines since that time.

On April 1, 1964, IAS established a seniority system for crew members assigned to JAL. At the same time, it entered an agreement with JAL containing the following items (the Agreement): (1) JAL would have authority to supervise, instruct and control crew members supplied by IAS, but, subject to JAL's prior consent, IAS would have the right to substitute crew members assigned to JAL in accordance with the new seniority system; and (2) IAS would be responsible for settling any complaints from crew members relating to terms of employment or working conditions, and both companies would make their best efforts to settle any complaints regarding interpretation of the Agreement.

The Agreement was deemed to be part of George's Labor Agreement with IAS when that Labor Agreement was renewed on April 1, 1964. On September 11, 1964, George complained to James C. Jack, a manager in IAS's Tokyo office, that his seniority rights had been ignored when IAS recommended to JAL two crew members with less seniority for promotion to jet crews. Many other planemasters also voiced concerns about operation of the seniority system. Along with two other employees assigned by IAS to JAL, George formed a "Temporary Employees Committee" (the "Temporary Committee") to discuss such issues with IAS. On Sep-

---

*Translation adapted from Dan Fenno Henderson, *Justiciability in U.S./Japanese Disputes* (Seattle: University of Washington School of Law, 1988), at 83-92. Reprinted by permission.

tember 21, they notified H. Odagiri, who was in charge of the foreign operations center of JAL, of the complaint and proposed that the selection of jet crew members be postponed until the complaint was resolved in accordance with the Agreement. At the same time, George distributed circulars to the crew members of IAS assigned to JAL, informing them of his complaint to IAS, the notice he had sent to JAL, and the formation of the Temporary Committee.

On October 3, the three members of the Temporary Committee met with Jack to discuss their concerns. They reached agreement with him for regular meetings between IAS and a committee representing the employees. Two days later, George, as chair of the Temporary Committee, sent all crew members a report summarizing the above agreement and requesting an election to determine the representatives of the employees, as well as ballots for that election. The ballots also asked whether the employees favored establishing a labor union and included a statement that it was illegal in Japan as well as in the U.S. to prevent the employees from uniting for the purpose of collective bargaining.

Meanwhile, on September 28, R. Henderson, IAS's acting chief pilot, ordered George to provide a detailed explanation of the document he had sent to Odagiri of JAL. George provided that explanation on October 3. IAS then sent George a written notice dated October 7 announcing his dismissal as of October 30. As reasons, the notice stated that George had acted against the interests of IAS and its employees assigned to JAL by sending the document to Odagiri and by using IAS stationery without permission in preparing that document.

At the time of his dismissal, George's monthly salary was U.S. $1,710. No salary was paid to him after October 1, 1964.

George sued in Tokyo District Court, asserting that the reasons given for dismissal were a pretext and that the dismissal was in fact for the purpose of interfering with organization of a labor union, and therefore was null and void as a violation of Section 7, Item (i) of the Labor Union Act.

IAS raised the following defenses: (1) Japanese courts lack jurisdiction because IAS has no office, place of business, or person in charge of its business in Japan; (2) even if Japanese courts have jurisdiction, the dismissal should be considered under the laws of California, because the dismissal relates to the Labor Agreement; (3) even if Japanese law applies, the dismissal was valid because George, by arbitrarily engaging in direct negotiations with JAL over complaints, had committed a "breach of the Agreement, especially an act of grave misconduct" (a ground for dismissal specified in the Labor Agreement); and (4) even if the dismissal was invalid, George could only claim wages through November 30, 1964, since the number of planemasters assigned to JAL was cut by about 50% on that date and, given George's seniority level, his assignment would, in any event, have been terminated on that date.

On December 14, 1964, George also filed a complaint with the National Labor Relations Board in the United States, asserting that his dismissal constituted an unfair labor practice under U.S. law. This complaint was rejected by a local NLRB official on January 21, 1965.

JUDGMENT:

IAS shall provisionally pay George $10,260. Expenses for the petition shall be borne by IAS.

REASONS:

The court will consider IAS's defenses in order:

I. **Jurisdiction.**

It goes without saying that a corporation organized under the laws of a foreign country is subject to the jurisdiction of the Japanese courts if it has an office in Japan and is engaged in business in Japan. Section 4, paragraph 3 of the Code of Civil Procedure presupposes this conclusion. Accordingly, IAS's assertion that the Japanese courts have no jurisdiction over it cannot be supported, since IAS is doing business at an office in Japan by offering 52 crew members to Japanese airlines. * * * Incidentally, the fact that George filed a complaint before a local division of the National Labor Relations Board of the United States does not affect this judgment.

II. **Applicable Law.**

With respect to the Labor Agreement, this court concludes that both parties have selected, as the applicable law, either the federal laws of the United States or the laws of the State of California, since the Labor Agreement (1) was concluded in California, U.S.A., between IAS, a California corporation, and George, a U.S. citizen, and (2) was conditioned on George having his domicile in the United States or its territories during the term of the Agreement, "in order to avoid a jurisdiction of any government other than that of the United States concerning labor conditions."

However, the declaration of intent to dismiss George was made by James C. Jack, a manager at IAS's Tokyo office, to George, who resides in Tokyo, was assigned to JAL, and has been working as a planemaster for domestic airliners in accordance with JAL's instructions. Under such circumstances, although the dismissal relates to the Labor Agreement, the effect of the dismissal must be considered in accordance with the labor laws of Japan, where the labor is actually supplied, and the provisions of Section 7 of the *Hōrei* should not apply to this matter. Laws regulating labor relations in different nations do not share a common nature, unlike general private laws which regulate contractual relations between management and labor. Moreover, each nation intrudes on labor agreements by which labor is actually supplied in that nation, based on the interests that the nation views as essential, and in doing so nations restrict or regulate the freedom to conclude labor agreements in different ways. Based on these factors, this court finds it reasonable to conclude that, if the labor is actually supplied in Japan on a continuous basis as in this case, the principle of freedom to designate the governing law provided for in Section 7 of the *Hōrei* is restricted by the labor laws, which reflect a public policy with only a limited territorial effect.

III. This court will now consider the effect of dismissal in light of the public policy contained in Section 7, Item (i) of the Labor Union Act. The reason IAS has given for the dismissal is that George, by using IAS's stationery and by negotiating directly with JAL, gave JAL the impression that IAS itself was requesting changes in the promotion recommendations. However, although it may have been a bit imprudent of George to have used IAS's stationery, there was no fear whatsoever that the letter might cause the misunderstanding that the request came from IAS itself. * * * Moreover, it is not conceivable that George's acts * * * necessarily impaired the interests of IAS and its employees. * * * On the other hand, this court has found that: Although the dismissal was pretended to have been made after George submitted his explanation on October 3 * * *, the dismissal was in fact made in accordance with instructions given by [a director of IAS] on September 19. * * * Taking all the facts into consideration, this court finds it reasonable to conclude that those instructions and the dismissal based thereon were made for the purpose of interfering with preparations to establish a labor union. Therefore, the dismissal is null and void because it conflicts with the public policy contained in Section 7, Item (i) of the Labor Union Act.

IV. [The Labor Agreement between George and IAS was renewed on April 1, 1964, for a twelve-month period. The court found no evidence to support IAS's contention that the Labor Agreement would have been terminated in any event on November 30. Accordingly, the court held that George was entitled to wages for the six months remaining on the contract, from October 1, 1964, when IAS stopped paying George, through March 31, 1965.]

Incidentally, as mentioned above, the parties to the Labor Agreement selected as the applicable law either the federal laws of the United States or the laws of the State of California. However, it is not necessary to inquire into which of these laws the parties intended to select, since, in each case, a labor agreement gives an employee the right to receive wages from the employer. Moreover, although it is not entirely clear to this court whether George can sue directly for the payment of wages under either of the above sets of laws, in the event IAS defaults in performing its obligations, then the laws of Japan, where the litigation has been instituted, should govern with respect to (1) the possibility of suing for performance of a contractual obligation by an obligor who is in default in that performance and (2) the procedures to preserve the rights of the obligee. * * *

[George had sued for provisional disposition, which, similar to injunctive relief, is handled through an expedited proceeding and may result in an order for immediate relief, without the need to await the conclusion of the full trial on the merits and possible appeals. In granting provisional disposition, the court must find both a valid basis for the claim and an urgent necessity for the relief. The court concluded that the difficulties that nonpayment of wages would cause for George in his daily life constituted such a necessity. The court also rejected IAS's argument that the provisional disposition order would be meaningless, since IAS had no assets in Japan; the court noted that, even if IAS had no assets in Japan, "there is a possibility of voluntary performance of the order."]

Questions and Discussion Points

1. *Holding in the George case*: Why did the court reject the parties' choice of law? What public policy concern is implicated by the employment of a foreign

worker by a foreign company? In this case, the U.S. tribunal had rejected George's claim. What relevance, if any, should that ruling have? Suppose George had recovered on his claim in the U.S. Should he still be able to maintain the claim in Japan?

2. *Other public law obligations*: What further public law obligations might affect a joint venture like that between A.Co and J.Co? Other forms of doing business in Japan?

IV. Japanese Attitudes Toward Contract

It is often said that contracts are understood and utilized differently in Japan than in the U.S., or perhaps in Western countries generally. In this section we will explore the key distinctions (if any) between Japanese and U.S. approaches to contract and will consider the practical ramifications (if any) of any such distinctions for negotiating and drafting contracts.

A. Distinct attitudes toward contract?

1. Evidence of distinct attitudes in typical U.S. and Japanese contracts

The most salient evidence of different approaches to contract in Japan and the U.S. may be the greater reliance on oral agreements in Japan than in the U.S., even for rather major transactions that would almost never proceed without a written agreement in the U.S. Although little empirical research has been conducted to substantiate this difference, many practitioners feel that such a difference does exist: Japanese are much more likely than U.S. parties to rely on oral agreements. Assuming this popular view is correct, consider what the respective preferences may reflect about the basic attitudes toward contract. Is the fact that one is written and one oral the sole distinction between written and oral agreements?

Practitioners and other observers point to another characteristic (again, one on which there has been little empirical study, but that is widely agreed to exist) that may reflect similar differences in attitudes toward contract: when Japanese parties use written contracts in deals with other Japanese parties, those contracts tend to be less detailed than agreements between U.S. parties undertaking similar transactions.

Those who perceive a basic difference in attitudes toward contract may also point to two sharply contrasting provisions, one typical of U.S. contracts, the other typical of Japanese contracts. These are, respectively, the so-called "merger" or "entire agreement" clause and the "meet to discuss" clause.

"Entire agreement" and "meet to discuss" clauses are significant because both explicitly seek to define the function of the contract. The JVA in the P.C., which was drafted by A.Co., contains in §H-3 a typical "entire agreement" clause:

(a) This Agreement sets forth the entire agreement and understanding between the Parties as to the subject matter hereof.

(b) No modifications, amendments, or supplements to this Agreement shall be effective for any purpose unless in writing signed by each of the Parties. Approvals or consents required hereunder of a Party shall also be in writing.

Contrast this approach to the "meet to discuss" clause, a typical example of which appears below. This example is taken from a translation of a joint venture agreement between two Japanese parties. Consider what sort of attitude toward the role of contract this clause reflects.

1. Concerning the establishment and management of NewCo, X.Co and Y.Co promise to behave in a cooperative spirit, to maintain mutual confidence, and to make efforts to promote mutual development.
2. Should matters arise that are not provided for herein or should some doubt arise as to the matters provided herein, X.Co and Y.Co shall resolve the same upon consultation with each other, to be conducted in a cooperative manner and in good faith.

Questions and Discussion Points

1. *Harmonizing the two approaches*: Can the "entire agreement" approach be reconciled with the "meet to discuss" approach? What conditions are necessary for the "meet to discuss" approach to operate effectively?

2. *Oboegaki*: Japanese parties often seek to include a "meet to discuss" clause even in detailed written agreements. Yet in many instances, especially between two Japanese parties, the written agreement may consist solely of a few very general provisions and a clause promising to "meet to discuss" any other issues that may arise. Such documents are sometimes designated as "*oboegaki*," a term that is often translated as "Memorandum of Understanding," but at times is referred to as "Letter of Intent." Is it appropriate to call such a document a "contract," as that term is used in U.S. law? Is the document likely to be binding?

Assume that you are a lawyer and a Japanese client seeking to commence a business transaction with a U.S. company comes to you with a rough translation of such a document and asks you to "put it into proper English so it can be signed." What advice would you give? What additional questions would you ask?

3. *Choosing between the two approaches*: When Japanese and U.S. parties enter a contract, as in the P.C., how is it determined whether to utilize the U.S. or the Japanese approach? Might Japanese companies ever prefer the "entire agreement" approach in contracting with foreign parties? Might foreign parties prefer the "meet to discuss" approach when dealing with Japanese parties? Might U.S. parties ever prefer the "meet to discuss" approach when dealing with other U.S. parties?

2. Evidence of differences in A.Co's and J.Co's views

Several years after entering into the JVA, J.Co and A.Co exchanged the letters set forth below. These letters provide some insight into the views of contract held by the parties. To fully appreciate the letters, however, some background information is necessary.

J.Co previously had developed new models of small excavators. At that time, J.Co took the position that the new models did not utilize know-how supplied by A.Co and that J.Co thus could manufacture them independently, without infringing any of the P.C. Agreements. A.Co disagreed, arguing that the new models were based on A.Co know-how and were competitive with Licensed Products, and that their manufacture by J.Co thus was prohibited by the JVA and collateral agreements. As described in Chapter 9, where the small excavator dispute is examined in more detail, the parties eventually resolved that dispute in 1975 by amending the P.C. Agreements to classify the small excavators as "Related Licensed Products," which were treated somewhat differently from the standard Licensed Products.

The following letters were exchanged one year later, in the fall of 1976. They involve a similar controversy, relating to J.Co's proposal to manufacture two new models of mini-backhoe independently. A.Co took the position that the issue was identical to that of the small excavators. Rather than going through the process of amending the agreements every time J.Co suggested new product lines, A.Co proposed settling the competition issue on an overall basis by executing an amending agreement classifying all excavators and similar equipment by weight categories and declaring that all machines within the same weight category would be regarded as competitive with one another. Prior to the exchange of letters set forth below, A.Co had sent J.Co the draft of this proposed amending agreement.

As with the small excavators, J.Co took the position that the mini-backhoes did not utilize any A.Co know-how. In addition, J.Co objected to the proposed weight classification scheme.

In reading the following exchange, consider whether the letters reflect a different conception of the role of contract. Do the differences in approach stem simply from the self-interest of the respective parties? Or do the differing approaches reflect deeper differences in basic attitudes?

- - - - - - - - - -

[J.Co Letterhead]
September 20, 1976

Mr. J. A. Theory
V.P. Sec'y, Gen. Atty.
A.Co
[address omitted]

Subject: New Model Excavators

Dear Mr. Theory:

With respect to both your proposed Amending Agreement No. 25, as well as your letter of August 24, 1976, in support of such proposal, which concern the treatment to be accorded J.Co's new 2-Ton and 4-Ton Size Mini-Backhoes, we now wish to state our opinion, as follows:

The parties have already orally agreed that the 2-Ton and 4-Ton Size Mini-

Backhoes do not constitute any part of the subject matter of either the Joint Venture Agreement or its collateral agreements. It is, therefore, entirely illogical to confirm this oral accord concerning the status of the Mini-Backhoes in the form, as proposed by you, of an amendment to the Agreements—which in no way govern the treatment of such models.

According to your proposed Amending Agreement No. 25, however, any Mini-Backhoes in excess of 10,000 lbs. which are manufactured by J.Co would be deemed to come under the scope of the JVA and collateral agreements. We maintain that all distinctions between licensed and non-licensed products and the resultant model classifications must be based solely upon whether the manufacture of any given product has utilized or proceeded on the basis of patents and/or know-how supplied by the Licensor—the underlying principle of all licensing agreements in general, with which aforesaid proposed amendment No. 25 is inconsistent.

In order properly to position any given product in relation to the Joint Venture Agreement and collateral agreements, the parties must first undertake a careful technical review of the situation. They should first isolate and identify the licensed technology on the one hand, and the technology used in the manufacture of the product in question on the other. They should evaluate the relationship between the two. By following such procedures the rights and obligations of all parties would be clarified and firmly secured, and, thus, the status and treatment of any given product under the various agreements would be smoothly determined.

In conclusion, we have determined that no amendment to our present agreements is warranted and wish to propose that the following memorandum be exchanged between us, in settlement of this matter:

(a) J.Co's Mini-Backhoes shall be defined as excavators equipped with hoes, whether hydraulic or cable operated, whether full-turn or half-turn, or whether crawler or wheel mounted, and having a weight of less than that of the most current model of the Related Licensed Product 10-H.

(b) J.Co's Mini-Backhoes do not constitute products covered by the JVA or its collateral agreements.

We would appreciate your prompt attention to this proposal.

Very truly yours,

[signed]

____

I. Higashi
Coordinating Director
J.Co

- - - - - - - - - -

[A.Co Letterhead]
October 24, 1976

Mr. I. Higashi
Coordinating Director
J.Co
[address omitted]

Subject: Amending Agreement No. 25

Dear Mr. Higashi:

In response to your letter of September 20, 1976, on the above subject, A.Co has the following comments:

(1) JVA Exhibit D (the Manufacturing Agreement), Paragraph B-3(a) provides:

> J.Co shall not at any time during this Agreement manufacture, sell or handle, or directly or indirectly be concerned in the manufacture, sale or handling of any items competitive with Licensed Products.

(2) As to the Mini-Hoes specifically, A.Co feels that it is not correct to state that the JVA does not govern such models. In fact, the 4-Ton Mini-Hoe is a hydraulic backhoe similar in design and function to the 10-H small excavator, which is a Related Licensed Product. Accordingly, if the weight of the Mini-Hoe were to be increased to *more* than 10,000 lbs., A.Co feels that it could in many applications be an alternative for and therefore competitive with a 10-H. Therefore A.Co is not willing to agree to exempt *all* Mini-Hoes regardless of weight or size, and Amending Agreement No. 25 merely reflects this position. A.Co feels that it is essential that Amending Agreement No. 25 clearly define once and for all by appropriate criteria the line between a Related Licensed Product and a non-competitive Mini-Hoe.

(3) At no time in connection with any amendment of the JVA, by Amending Agreement, Letter Agreement, or otherwise, has any oral statement by an A.Co or J.Co representative been taken as the equivalent of or substitute for a formal Amending Agreement. Were such statements to modify the formal agreements, free exchange of thoughts between representatives would become impossible. A.Co wishes to be clearly understood that the only way the JVA can be modified is by a formal, properly-signed Amending Agreement. No officer or other representative of A.Co is authorized to make any *informal* arrangements or modifications to the JVA.

(4) A.Co feels that it is in the best interest of all parties to the JVA that clearly defined lines be established between Licensed Products, Related Licensed Products, products agreed to be competitive with such Products, and products agreed *not* to be competitive with such Products. If reasonable and clear definitions can be established, then much unnecessary discussion and many possible misunderstandings will be avoided, and the accounting status of any given model will be known regardless of minor changes in design. With this in mind, Amending Agreement No. 25 proposed to establish a gross weight criterion for fixing the line between a "non-competitive" Mini-Hoe and a Mini-Hoe that might

constitute a Related Licensed Product. Obviously, merely calling a machine a "Mini-Hoe" does not necessarily free it from constituting a Related Licensed Product. Merely specifying a model without specifying weight and/or size limiting characteristics is not a sufficient or practical definition of category under the JVA.

Future confusion and misunderstandings are likely to occur if weight, size and other characteristics of a model that is originally non-competitive are changed to render it competitive. A.Co desires to avoid such misunderstandings.

We look forward to further discussions leading to conclusion of a formal Amending Agreement No. 25 in the near future.

With kind personal regards,

Sincerely yours,

[signed]

J. A. Theory
Vice President & Secretary
A.Co

B. Scholarly views on the Japanese attitude toward contract

In this section we consider views held by three scholars on distinctions in the approaches to contract by Japanese and U.S. parties. The first and third commentators argue that there are significant differences in U.S. and Japanese attitudes, but offer quite different explanations for those differences. The second commentator suggests that the whole notion that there is a considerable distinction between U.S. and Japanese attitudes toward contract may be flawed.

1. Japanese legal consciousness

TAKEYOSHI KAWASHIMA, THE LEGAL CONSCIOUSNESS OF CONTRACT IN JAPAN*

7 Law in Japan 1
5-7, 15-21 (1974)

Among merchants (among businesses) there are many occasions where there is no way to clarify whether or when a contract for a business transaction has been formed. There is, as a result, the example of a lawsuit between two of the largest

*From Takeyoshi Kawashima, "The Legal Consciousness of Contract in Japan," 7 *Law in Japan: An Annual* 1 (1974), at 5-7 and 15-21. Reprinted by permission.

enterprises in Japan. During the Korean War Marubeni-Iida K.K. had sold soy beans to Aji-no-Moto K.K. pursuant to international business terms known as C.I.F. Aji-no-Moto K.K. rejected delivery when the international market price of soy beans dropped, and Marubeni-Iida K.K. brought suit against Aji-no-Moto K.K. claiming damages. In that suit the important point at issue was whether the effective formation of a contract should be recognized where there had only been mutual assent concerning a C.I.F. price or whether the effective formation of a contract to buy or sell should be initially recognized only upon the drafting of both English language and Japanese language contracts. In this case an English language contract had been drafted but a Japanese language contract had not been drafted. The Tokyo District Court entered its judgment in this case as follows:

> * * * When a sales contract is made within our country with regard to imported freight, the contract document is not necessarily drawn up in the English language, and there are also cases in which the contract is drawn up only in Japanese. * * * In any event, we recognize that normally a written agreement is drawn up expressing the contents of the agreement. * * * Drafting a contract document meets the need to preserve evidence of the existence of an agreement in order to be prepared for quarrels that arise later.
>
> Basing our thoughts on these facts in case there is a change in the market price of soy beans, for instance, and even in the case of so-called futures transactions (*sakimono torihiki*) there is no justification for upsetting the general rules for consensual contracts set forth in the Civil Code and adopting reasoning that depends on the formal act of drawing up a written document to determine the existence of an agreement. Moreover, generally the *existence is well-known of a custom in our country's society that the drawing up of a written document incorporating the agreement is disliked.* We acknowledge that Hōnen Oil Refining K.K., which is one of our country's foremost oil refiners, does not demand written contracts for precisely the reason set forth above. Taking all of these factors into account, we hold that in purchase and sale of imported freight, a contract has been formed when there has been a concurrence of the intentions of the parties; that the commercial custom asserted by the defendant does not exist; and that although, as is mentioned above, it is normal for a written contract to exist, such a written contract is considered only as an instrument for verifying the existence of an agreement. *Marubeni-Iida K.K. v. Aji-no-Moto K.K.*, 8 Kakyū minshū 1366 (Tokyo Dist. Ct., July 31, 1957).

Shiro Hattori, a professor of linguistics of The University of Tokyo, made the following observations concerning Japanese attitudes toward contracts, basing his conclusions on his experiences during a two-year stay in the United States. His comments are interesting in his comparison of American attitudes:

> Americans carefully observe the law, regulations and contractual agreements, and they make full use of these legal forms. Japanese do not have a sufficiently clear conception of such legal forms but honor and trust *jōjō* [the surrounding circumstances], *giri* [moral or social obligation to others], *ninjō* [human feeling], *yūjō* [friendship], *magokoro* [sincerity] and so forth. * * * It is perhaps well-known that Americans observe contractual obligations more closely than Japanese. Conversely, an American will say that he is not responsible for what he did not agree to. When a Japanese makes an agreement with another person, the *goodwill and friendship that gave rise to the agreement is more important to him than the agreement itself.* If there is sincerity, it does not matter if the contract itself is not executed exactly according to its terms. To Americans legal agreements and feelings of friendship are completely different things. In these circumstances Japanese tend to be preoccupied with a *friendly atmosphere and are not careful to see that the agreement itself is thorough.* This is a mistaken attitude to take toward a contract. When Japanese make a contract with Americans, they have to treat the contract very gingerly. I personally have suffered many unpleasant experiences in these situations.

* * * The contracts given above are typical examples that illustrate traditional legal consciousness in regard to contracts. However, this legal consciousness penetrates many kinds of contracts and those contracts are by no means exceptional. As an illustration I offer the following facts:

The following tendency can be seen in many contracts in our country—even in the contracts of businesses of the largest scale. In Japan, not only are there many instances where written agreements are not drafted, but even when written agreements are drafted their contents are generally very simple and in many cases include only the most important elements. When we compare this situation with the situation in European and American business transactions (and also in transactions between European or American businesses and Japanese businesses) where contractual rights and duties are set forth in detail "to the point of being permeated with minutiae" that provide for every possible contingency and where contracts are often printed in their full particulars in letters that are so small that one cannot read them without a magnifying glass, we can understand the very conspicuous Japanese peculiarity in this regard. Moreover, one can all the more appreciate the differences between Western and Japanese contract documents by comparing the detailed provisions of a lease contract providing for every contingency in regard to property being leased anywhere in America—such a lease is usual even when the landlord is not in the business of managing real property—with the typical lease contract in Japan.

An interesting point is the consciousness of the people toward these contractual methods. An American who views Japanese contract documents, which are simply written as if they contain only "three chapters," will often wonder if he would become embroiled more easily in disputes over these [Japanese] types of contracts that are "full of holes" * * * and would ask whether such contracts would not be insecure since it is unclear what rights and duties the parties have and do not have. However, the way of thinking of Japanese businessmen is diametrically opposed to this. On one occasion I suggested that the contents of the standard provisions of the construction work contract of the Ministry of Construction be made as concrete, inclusive and definite as possible. This was because I thought that it was, above all, necessary to narrow the margin for deciding disputes between the contracting agency and the contractor through negotiation in order to correct the fact that public works contracts are in reality quite one-sided (*henmuteki*). There was opposition to my proposal from the business world, which had always requested that such one-sidedness be corrected. If the obligations under the contract were made definite and fixed, it was said, an uneasiness was felt that such contracts would "lack flexibility" (*yūzūsei ga naku naru*). That is to say, indefinite contractual provisions that give a feeling of uneasiness to Westerners give a feeling of security to Japanese. However, even in Japan the contracts of businesses such as banks, trusts and insurance companies naturally are drafted with very great detail and attention to minutiae; and banks, trust companies and insurance companies are engaged in constant efforts to make the contents of their contracts more definite. This, however, represents an exception to the general rule[, to which I will return.] Before that, but in connection with it, I want to point out one other form of legal consciousness that can generally be seen in the contracts of our country. In many Japanese contracts there are clauses such as:

> If in the future a dispute arises between the parties with regard to the rights and duties provided in this contract the parties will confer in good faith (*sei-i o motte kyōgi suru*).[3]

or, in a similar situation,

> * * * will settle the dispute harmoniously by consultation (*kyōgi ni yori emman ni kaiketsu suru*).[4]

I have never seen such clauses in the contracts of Western countries; in their place there are arbitration clauses (*chūsai jōkō*). For example:

> If in the future a dispute arises between the parties in connection with this agreement, it shall be settled by arbitration [by the decision of an arbitrator who is a third party].

I think that these two different methods for dealing with disputes that can arise under a contract illustrate very clearly the legal consciousness of contracts in the West and in Japan.

One might think that Japanese clauses such as those quoted above came into existence because they are necessary since there are no detailed provisions in the written agreement concerning the rights and duties of the parties. It is, of course, undeniable that there is this aspect to the confer-in-good-faith clause.

However, * * * the insertion of a confer-in-good-faith clause cannot be explained on the basis of this reason * * * alone.

I believe that the more valid reason for inserting confer-in-good-faith clauses in many Japanese contracts is as follows: In Japanese contracts the parties not only do not stipulate in a detailed manner the rights and duties under the contract but also think that even the rights and duties provided for in the written agreement are tentative rather than definite. Accordingly, when a dispute arises, they think it desirable at that time to fix such rights and duties by means of ad hoc consultation. Therefore, even something such as the due date of a debt is not thought of as something strictly defined but as fixed "give or take a few days." The creditor who demands payment of the penalty for delay when payment is only a day or two overdue is thought of as a shylock or an inflexible person. Therefore, it is possible to state that a confer-in-good-faith clause, even if it is not written in a contract document, is, so to speak, tacitly implied in all contracts.

From the viewpoint of Westerners who see contractual rights and duties as something fixed and definite, a confer-in-good-faith clause seems to be nonsense. Even if the contract states that the parties "will confer in good faith," what will happen if they do not confer in good faith? Also, even though one "confers" in good faith, in what form will the dispute be resolved? Will it be possible for them to reach an agreement to resolve the dispute? All are unknown. Therefore, in the West one must provide clauses that can definitely settle disputes by means of arbitration methods. This is a Western way of thinking.

From the point of view of Japanese legal consciousness, such clauses are not unsettling. Rather, conversely, as was explained above, it is unsettling to determine rigidly and definitely rights and duties in advance and not to leave room for requests [for mitigation] between the parties, for the granting of mitigation (*onkei*), and for the exercise of flexibility (*yūzū*). Therefore, even if detailed provisions are inserted in contracts, they do not have very much significance; and, consequently, the parties do not read them carefully or regard them seriously. Rather, when problems arise, it is very important for them to "confer in good faith," to arrive at a harmonious settlement (*emman na kaiketsu*), and to let the dispute "wash away" (*arasoi o mizu ni nagasu*). In this sense the confer-in-good-faith clause is the core of our country's contracts. Accordingly, arbitration is not employed in Japan and *a fortiori* courts cannot be adapted to such purposes. There is a great fondness for conciliation (*chōtei*), and it has been affirmed as an institution of national law and is used extensively.

* * * Nevertheless, we must not forget that some of the contracts in our country are very dissimilar from the legal consciousness described above—namely, as we have previously noted, the contracts of institutions such as banks, trust companies, and insurance companies. * * * In insurance contracts in particular, such provisions are printed compactly on the reverse side of the policy in print that requires a magnifying glass to read. Indeed, these latter contracts are exceptional phenomena among our contract documents. Why do such phenomena occur in a society that is used to indefiniteness in the relations between contractual

parties and that feels comfortable with such indefiniteness? Also, in recent years there have arisen demands that contractual relations be made more clear and fixed in construction contracts where attitudes toward contracts have been more "Japanese," and there has been movement toward realizing this goal. Also, in many industries efforts to make contractual documents more thorough can be observed. Why is such so-called Western legal consciousness, which differs from traditional legal consciousness, appearing in the contract area? What is the social setting for this change?

These are extremely meaningful phenomena. From a macroscopic historical viewpoint, I presume that they are one manifestation or indication of Japan's "modernization." * * * Needless to say, the contents of contracts depend on what is desired by the parties—particularly by the party who possesses the power (social ascendance) to force the contractual terms that he desires upon the other party. Thus the problem is what kind of contractual contents do persons with different kinds of legal consciousness want: sketchy contractual contents in which the rights and obligations of the parties are indefinite or imprecise and which anticipate that disputes will be resolved by consultation; or detailed contractual provisions in which the rights and obligations of the parties are definite and precise and in which such rights and obligations are settled objectively without resort to consultation?

First, the differences in the terms of the contracts described above depend on whether the parties—particularly the party who possesses the power * * * to force the contractual terms that he desires upon the other party—are aware of (recognize or desire) their mutual contractual relationship as something "functionally specific" (a relationship concerning only one specific aspect of their lives) or as something "functionally diffuse" (a diffuse relationship not limited to any particular aspect of their lives). For instance, in a relationship that is conceived of by the parties as a purely economic transaction like the purchase and sale of goods, problems between the parties are settled only within the limits of the economic transaction. Accordingly, in this sense the contents of such problems are clear. However, when this is not the case and the parties conceive of their relationship as an economic transaction that is at the same time connected with another interest relation (for example, protection or dependence) or human feelings—especially, continuing human feelings (family or friendship)—it is difficult to solve problems connected with the economic transaction without the solution having an effect at the same time upon other problems. When such other interest relations are not clear and not specific or when such relationships are connected with human feelings that by nature can change with unlimited diversity, to the extent that the parties take such other problems into consideration, it probably follows that they will not desire beforehand to make the contents of their contracts definite or precise.

Second, the differences in the terms of the contractual contents described above probably depend on whether the parties are aware of (recognize or desire) their mutual contractual relationship as something "particularistic" or whether they conceive of it as something "universalistic." * * *

However, we should make it clear before we go on that there can be a gap between what is verbalized in an agreement (especially what is in the written contract) and the consciousness described above. * * * For instance, by importing the contractual terms of foreign countries, by using as a model and copying contractual terms used by other persons, or by buying form contracts such as those sold in stores, written contracts are spread throughout the society. As a result, it is not unusual for gaps to arise between written agreements and the consciousness of a specific individual party. * * *

Needless to say, the traditional contractual consciousness described above is changing. * * * However, in spite of this, it is still significant that attitudes such as those described above are emphasized even today. It is not rare for many Japanese businesses that are engaging in transactions with foreign businesses not to read or to ignore the clauses written in contracts, to invite economic disaster, and to damage their commercial reputations. * * *

The attitudes described above are contradictory to the requirement of foreseeability of contractual claims that is necessary for rational profits in capitalistic businesses. Because of such attitudes, judicial protection for contractual claims cannot be considered important, and the function of litigation in Japan has been distorted as a result. Thus this explanation, which emphasizes the [contractual] consciousness described above, is not by any means out of idle curiosity or nostalgia for antiquity.

2. The fallacy of comparing the attitudes of U.S. lawyers and Japanese businesspeople

WHITMORE GRAY, THE USE AND NON-USE OF CONTRACT LAW IN JAPAN: A PRELIMINARY STUDY*

17 Law in Japan 98
101-103 (1984)

[An] enquiry regarding the use of rules of contract law brings with it * * * broader questions about the use of contract as an institution—*i.e.*, the use of oral or written contracts, the elaborateness of the planning reflected in the terms, the extent to which the parties provide in the agreement for what the consequences of non-performance should be, etc. While these are not strictly questions concerning the use of rules of law, there is really no clear dividing line, for clauses exempting one party from liability in certain circumstances or providing for a particular pattern of remedy are usually drafted and agreed upon in the light of what result the rules of contract law and the available enforcement mechanism would have given in the absence of such clauses. Even though the choice to use these clauses is non-legal, presumably the choice of content and their drafting call for the use of legal knowledge and skills.

*From Whitmore Gray, "The Use and Non-Use of Contract Law in Japan: A Preliminary Study," 17 *Law in Japan: An Annual* 98 (1984), at 101-103. Reprinted by permission.

One thing that became increasingly clear to me [in the course of a survey of Japanese and non-Japanese lawyers and businessmen] was the need to attribute every conclusion concerning attitudes to a definite group of actors in contract transactions. A good deal of the misleading comparison of United States and Japanese "attitudes" may have been caused by a failure to do this. For example, when people compare the careful drafting of contracts and strict insistence on contract rights in the United States with informality and a tendency toward accommodation and compromise in Japan, they are usually talking about the attitudes of different groups in the two countries. They are often comparing the attitudes of Japanese businessmen with the attitudes of American lawyers. It seems clear from common experience, and is certainly suggested in a number of [Stewart] Macaulay['s] interviews,[5] that U.S. businessmen would also prefer to deal with people they know well, and when they do, do not feel the need for such elaborate contracts. Moreover, when problems arise in such a relationship, they feel they can be settled by mutual accommodation, without the need to resort to any insistence on legal rights.

By contrast, if the attitudes of American lawyers were compared with those of Japanese lawyers, there would also be a similarity of views. Many lawyers in Japan comment on the unfortunate tendency of businessmen to leave important questions unresolved. In fact, since Japanese lawyers are commonly consulted only for litigation, their principal exposure is to cases where there was no adequate provision in the contract for the difficulty which occurred. The lawyer in the United States may be considerably more knowledgeable about business practices, for he is more likely to be involved on a regular basis in the negotiation and drafting process. One American attorney commented that he found the Japanese lawyers too inflexible and legalistic when they were brought into business negotiations, due in part to their orientation toward litigation.[6]

As for contract practices, the interviews made me very cautious about attributing distinctive features in the two systems to cultural factors or general legal consciousness. In many cases there are other possible causes which should be identified and whose impact should be explored. For example, a fact which is often overlooked in comparing long contracts used in the United States with shorter Japanese agreements in similar situations is the inherent uncertainty of the rules of law in the United States. First there is the problem of choice of law in complex interstate transactions. In addition there is the general difficulty of spelling out precisely the rules of our case law. Since the courts do continue to refine and even change these rules, a prudent lawyer may feel it is desirable to make the contract as self-sufficient as possible. Long lists of definitions of words used are common, and so is the spelling out of legal results of default, etc., in order to minimize differences in results in the various jurisdictions which might be involved, or the inherent uncertainty involved in determining a precise rule of law in a particular jurisdiction according to the case law.

Another thing to consider in comparing both attitudes toward and the use of contract law in the two countries is the difference in the extent of general legal knowledge. While there are many more legal specialists in the United States, *i.e.*, persons whose professions are built on their specialized legal knowledge, in Japan the proportion of the general business population with a legal education is much higher than in the United States. Only an insignificant number of graduates of law faculties become legal specialists, and the vast majority go into general careers in business.

In 1980, for example, there were approximately 150,000 students in university law departments, almost all of whom were headed for careers in business rather than law in the American sense. Each year only about 500 [now about 700] are able to enter the training program required to become a *bengoshi*, though a sizable number who go to work for corporations will at some point in their careers spend some time doing work that in the U.S. is done by house-counsel "attorneys." A question to pursue, then, is the effect of widespread knowledge of legal rules in a business community regarded by American lawyers as extremely casual toward the technical legal questions that arise in the course of commercial transactions.

The legal background of Japanese businessmen may help explain why they often seem somewhat skeptical when lawyers talk about the uncertainty of law in the United States. They have learned academically a system of legal rules which appear to lead to relatively clear answers to many legal problems. While Japanese lawyers are a little more aware of the problem of uncertainty in determining precise rules of law because of their greater familiarity with actual practice in which Japanese courts have to give specific content to general rules case by case, differences in "legal method" continue to be at the root of many misunderstandings. In fact, one Japanese lawyer told of his surprise when he found that American law was still rather uncertain, for he had supposed that the large number of case decisions would have resolved most of the questions, unlike Japan, where many questions are as yet unresolved by the courts because of the small number of decisions. He was not sufficiently aware of the uncertainty caused by the wide range of often conflicting authorities from many jurisdictions, as well as our lack of rigid adherence to *stare decisis*—in particular, our acceptance of the idea that rules can be reexamined and changed in the light of new circumstances.

3. Relational contracting

DANIEL H. FOOTE, EVOLUTION IN THE CONCEPT OF CONTRACTS*

United States/Japan Commercial Law & Trade 689

689-694 (1990)

The standard characterization of contracts in Japan, as opposed to those in the United States, is that Japanese contracts tend to be short, composed primarily of

*From Daniel H. Foote, "Evolution in the Concept of Contracts," in *United States/Japan Commercial Law & Trade*, pp. 689-695 (Valerie Kusuda-Smick, ed., Transnational Juris Publications, 1990), at 689-694. Reprinted with the permission of Transnational Juris Publications, Inc., Irvington, New York.

general conditions, with at least one broad catch-all provision stating that the parties will consult in good faith to resolve any questions of interpretation or issues not covered by the contract. In contrast, according to the standard view, American contracts tend to be long, complex documents dealing in detail with all foreseeable contingencies. In a closely related point, the standard view is that Japanese take a very flexible attitude toward the written document, with both sides being willing to revisit (and revise) the terms of their agreement in the event of a change in circumstances, whereas Americans tend to insist upon the letter of the contract if it is in their favor, even if conditions have changed dramatically.

As with any generalization, one can inevitably point to numerous exceptions—on both sides of the Pacific. Nevertheless, traditionally the standard view has been surprisingly accurate.

A number of theories have been suggested for these rather striking differences. Some commentators have noted that Japan does not have a general statute of frauds. While a few special statutes effectively require written contracts in certain rather narrow circumstances, the key inquiry concerns the intent of the parties, and if that intent can be proven an oral agreement may be binding, regardless of the amount of money involved or the duration of services required by it. Others have pointed to the old standby, the number of lawyers in the respective countries.

I must confess that at times I am struck by the extent to which fertile lawyers' minds can conceive of risks that, while remote, in the heat of drafting and negotiating an agreement just beg for inclusion. To my mind, though, that's just a matter of degree; it may add a few pages to an agreement, but it by no means explains the fundamental difference in traditional approaches toward contract in the United States and Japan. The absence of a general statute of frauds and consequent enforceability of oral agreements in Japan, while significant for other reasons, do not explain why, in drafting agreements, Japanese are typically much more willing than Americans to leave terms vague and open for future discussions.

[A] much more promising approach to trying to understand this difference lies in what is known as a "relational contract"—this is to say, one involving an ongoing relationship of the parties. It would seem readily apparent that the nature of a contract, as well as the parties' attitudes toward and willingness to renegotiate that contract in the event of changes in circumstances, would vary depending on the nature and duration of the relationship of the parties. The longer and deeper the relationship of the parties * * *, the more likely those parties should be to enter simpler, more general agreements; and the greater the mutual benefits of an ongoing relationship, the more likely a party would be to renegotiate terms if circumstances change, in order to preserve the relationship.

In this regard, rather than thinking only of relationships between the parties (*i.e.*, the companies) themselves, it may be worthwhile to consider relationships at several levels: first, the personal—employee to employee—level; next, the company level; then the level of the corporate group or even entire business community; and finally the level of society as a whole. * * *

On first blush, personal relationships might appear likely to play a significant role in Japanese attitudes toward contracts. Given Japan's "lifetime employment system" (which, while by no means universal, does cover most white-collar workers in major companies who would be intimately involved in contract negotiations), one might perhaps assume that the same individuals negotiate with each other year after year, in the process developing such deep familiarity with prior agreements and such great trust that they would feel no need to draft detailed agreements and would be more understanding if conditions have changed. This is by no means true, though, since Japanese employees normally rotate regularly from one position to another. Nonetheless, while Japanese employees are of course evaluated on the basis of their personal performance, the fact that they are likely to remain in their companies for their entire careers may well make them more willing to take a long-term outlook; thus, they may be less likely, on average, than American businesspeople to insist upon a narrow adherence to existing contractual provisions resulting in short-term gains, if such insistence might ultimately affect the long-term prospects of the company.

This leads to the second level of relationships—company-to-company. I have frequently heard American businesspeople comment that the important thing is to establish the initial relationship with a Japanese company, but that once established it will take a major failure before the Japanese would terminate the relationship. If, by that, one were to suggest that once you get your foot in the door, you can take advantage of a Japanese trading partner, it would be a big mistake. But it does accurately reflect the importance most major Japanese companies place upon developing long-term, stable relationships, based upon trust and mutual benefit. And the prevalence of such long-term relationships within Japan may help explain the short agreements and relative willingness to renegotiate upon changes in circumstances.

An even more important factor, though, may be found at the next level up—the corporate groupings in Japan. Although the prewar *zaibatsu*—the so-called combines—were broken up after World War II, they have been replaced by numerous *keiretsu*—corporate groupings, such as the Mitsui, Mitsubishi and Sumitomo groups, often consisting of hundreds of subsidiaries and affiliated companies grouped around a central bank, trading company or major manufacturer. While levels of cross-shareholding vary, and are frequently well under 30 percent, as a practical matter these companies are often closely tied and highly interdependent. It is, for example, not uncommon for a central company in a group to send certain of its employees to serve as key executives in affiliated companies. Under these circumstances, it is hardly surprising that contracts between affiliated companies are frequently brief and interpreted quite flexibly.

For a somewhat different complex of factors, a similar situation arises when a contract is entered into between a company within a major corporate group and a company from outside that group. In such a case, if the outside company were to develop a reputation within the corporate group as untrustworthy or unreasonable, it might well find itself cut off from any future dealings with any company in that group. And at an even broader level in Japan, if a company develops a reputation as unreasonable or otherwise somehow "tainted" in the business community as a whole, other companies will be reluctant to deal with it again.

One could undoubtedly make that last statement in the United States, too, but the definition of what is "unreasonable" would be very different. In the United States, typical businesspeople would not consider it unreasonable if a major corporation were to institute litigation against even a large trading partner over interpretation of a disputed contract term. In contrast, in Japan, public controversy between two companies could well lead to rumors that both were difficult to deal with, and Japanese businessmen[—the vast majority still are men—]widely feel that any adverse publicity could lead to a significant drop in business. In part for this reason, Japanese companies tend to be very sensitive to adverse publicity of any type. And the combination of direct—albeit nonlitigious—sanctions through the withdrawal of business by both the other party to an agreement and members of that company's corporate group, together with the potential indirect impact resulting from moral opprobrium of the business community as a whole, would appear to be major reasons why Japanese companies are relatively willing to revise contract terms in the event of a change in circumstances and why they place such great importance on resolving disputes through mutual discussion.

The final level of relationships I will discuss is what I earlier called the societal level. * * * I scarcely accept the theory—voiced by some—that Japanese attitudes toward contract are somehow linked to the origins of Japanese society, reflecting the trust and harmony required in a farming culture, in contrast to the aggressive, pioneer spirit of a hunting culture supposedly reflected by the American model. Nor is it accurate to describe Japan as completely homogeneous. Nonetheless, * * * Japanese businessmen tend to be far more homogeneous, sharing far more views in common, than their American counterparts, and the perception of homogeneity within Japan undoubtedly also bears on the willingness to enter short, general agreements and rely upon mutual discussions to fill any gaps.

[In this context, an experience in representing a Japanese corporation purchasing a cattle ranch in Montana provided a striking example that the attitudes described here are by no means uniquely Japanese. Local Montana counsel for the transaction had represented buyers and sellers of ranchers for many years. He reported that a decade or so earlier, when one Montana rancher was selling to another, the negotiations had often been just about as hard, but the final agreement was typically embodied in a brief one- or two-page terms sheet. Given the shared context and common understandings, there was no need for more. Then, major out-of-state corporate investors began buying ranches. And suddenly the shared context no longer existed and contracts expanded to 30 or 40 pages. Finally, with the arrival of a foreign investor, the contract grew yet again. In the meantime, he reported, agreements between Montana ranchers had also become longer and more detailed than had previously been the case, albeit still far shorter than the contracts with out-of-state and foreign buyers.]

* * * One other—perhaps fairly obvious—point relating to the length of

contracts [bears note]. When a contract is short and general and leaves many matters for future discussions between the parties, the party with the greater bargaining power naturally tends to be favored. After working in-house at a major Japanese manufacturing corporation's legal department and being imbued with the notion that short contracts were somehow almost uniquely Japanese, I remember being struck after I returned to private practice in the United States that Americans, too, can write very short contracts, so long as they hold the balance of power.

Lest this be taken solely as a cynical indictment of motives, though, I might recount one episode from my in-house experiences. The Japanese manufacturer had been sued on a patent infringement claim, and the downstream supplier of the component in question had signed a very brief contract containing a one-line agreement to bear responsibility for any patent infringement claim. Despite the clarity of the language, it was also apparent that, if the claim was recognized, the liability could potentially bankrupt the supplier. During the initial negotiating session with the supplier over ultimate liability in the event of an adverse judgment, the manufacturer took a very hard line, pointing to the language in question and insisting that the supplier bear the entire amount, as the faces of the supplier's representatives turned white. After that meeting, I was wondering if what I'd heard about Japanese willingness to revisit contractual terms was grossly exaggerated, when one of the other members of the legal staff explained to me that their position had been largely a show, to impress upon the supplier the importance of care in the patent area, but that in the event of any significant judgment or settlement the manufacturer itself would undoubtedly bear the lion's share.

Are U.S. and Japanese attitudes concerning the length of contracts converging? [Despite some indications that Japanese companies increasingly insist upon relatively detailed contracts even when dealing with other Japanese companies, my sense is that, when Japanese companies deal with other Japanese companies, the practices described at the outset remain relatively well entrenched.] On the other side of the picture, for the most part I have not seen what I would consider a true indication that American companies, either when dealing with other American companies or when dealing with Japanese companies, have evinced a sudden willingness to sign brief, general agreements. In certain cases, such as where two companies have entered into a joint venture and have developed a close working relationship over a substantial period of time, the parties have rather naturally dispensed with many of the earlier procedural formalities. Yet in major transactions, even where the two parties have worked closely with each other on prior projects, the parties generally wish to enter comprehensive agreements.

Rather than a convergence as such, the key development in this area (although by now not so recent) is an increased willingness—and in many cases, desire—of Japanese companies to enter into comprehensive contracts when dealing with foreign companies. (In some cases, in fact, Japanese clients have suggested * * * provisions covering contingencies that even American lawyers have felt are too remote to warrant inclusion.) And given the fact that a number of the factors discussed earlier that underlie attitudes toward contract in Japan do not apply with respect to agreements between U.S. and Japanese companies, I would expect the American-style contract to continue to prevail in general. As commercial relations continue to expand, however, I would anticipate that relations between certain companies will become so deep-rooted that simpler contracts will suffice.

On the other hand, there may well be some movement by American companies toward a greater willingness to revise contractual terms in the event of a change in circumstances. To the extent such a change occurs, though, I would not expect it to come from a fundamental change in attitude as such. Rather, I would expect such a change, if it comes, to reflect an increased awareness by American companies of the financial and commercial strength of Japanese trading partners, and a recognition that the long-term benefits of the relationship might outweigh any short-term gains that could be derived by insisting on a narrow interpretation of the contract. In short, I would expect such a change only to the extent that the long-term balance of power, so to speak, in a particular relationship may have shifted.

Questions and Discussion Points

Detailed contracts as evidence of modernization: Kawashima points out that contracts in the finance industry in Japan tend to be detailed and that "Western legal consciousness" is also developing in other fields of economic activity. What explanation might be given for "Western legal consciousness" first appearing in the finance sector?

Kawashima suggests that the degree of use of detailed contracts may be a measure of the "modernization" of a society. Would Foote agree?

FURTHER READING

Negotiating With the Japanese

John L. Graham and Yoshihiro Sano, *Smart Bargaining: Doing Business with the Japanese*. Cambridge, MA: Ballinger, 1984.

Don R. McCreary, *Japanese-United States Business Negotiations: A Cross-Cultural Study*. New York: Praeger, 1986.

Stephen E. Weiss, "Creating the GM-Toyota Joint Venture: A Case in Complex Negotiation," *Columbia Journal of World Business*, Vol. 22, No. 2, pp. 23-37 (Summer 1987).

Drafting and Dispute Resolution

Jeremiah Sullivan, Richard Peterson, Naoki Kameda and Justin Shimada, "The Relationship Between Conflict Resolution Approaches and Trust—A Cross Cultural Study," *Academy of Management Journal* 803 (1981).

Japanese Contract Consciousness

Ronald Dore, *Flexible Rigidities: Industrial policy and structural adjustment in the Japanese economy 1970-80*. Stanford, CA: Stanford University Press, 1986.

Michael Gerlach, "Trust is Not Enough: Cooperation and Conflict in Kikkoman's American Development," *Journal of Japanese Studies,* Vol. 16, No. 2, pp. 389-425 (1990).

Shinichiro Michida, "Contract Societies: Japan and the United States Contrasted," 1 *Pacific Rim Law & Policy Journal* 199 (1992).

J. Mark Ramseyer, "Legal Rules in Repeated Deals: Banking in the Shadow of Defection in Japan," 20 *Journal of Legal Studies* 91 (1991).

Hiroshi Wagatsuma and Arthur Rosett, "Cultural Attitudes Towards Contract Law: Japan and the United States Compared," 2 *UCLA Pacific Basin Law Journal* 76 (1983).

NOTES TO CHAPTER SEVEN

1. The agreement between Miyagi and Seikōdō included the following termination clause:

> In the event one of the following occurs to Miyagi or its joint guarantor, Seikōdō may suspend the supply of Goods to Miyagi or terminate this Agreement, without giving prior notice thereof:
>
> (i) breach by Miyagi of this Agreement;
>
> (ii) - (iv) [Omitted.]

Although the court does not cite the language of the termination clauses in the agreements between Miyagi and Columbia and between Miyagi and Tōshiba, it states that Columbia and Tōshiba terminated the agreements with Miyagi based upon clauses providing for termination in the event of breach by Miyagi.

2. In a part of the opinion that is omitted, the court recognizes that the copyright issues implicated by the rental businesses do not directly affect wholesalers such as Seikōdō, since wholesalers are neither manufacturers nor performers, but that the rental businesses have still had a damaging effect on wholesalers.

By amendments made to the Copyright Act in 1985, after the decision in this case, record manufacturers and performers were granted the exclusive right to supply their records to the public by renting commercially reproduced records. Agreement was then reached on the payment of royalties by record rental shops. Thus, the effect of the amendments was to provide legal recognition of the rental business, while preserving manufacturers' and performers' rights to profit from the recording of records.

3. The "confer in good faith" clause.

4. The "harmonious settlement" clause.

5. Editors' Note: This is a reference to Stewart Macaulay, "The Use and Non-Use of Contracts in the Manufacturing Industry," 9 *The Practical Lawyer* 13 (1961), and Stewart Macaulay, "Non-Contractual Relations in Business: A Preliminary Study," 28 *American Sociological Review* 55 (1963).

6. An American attorney who has often used correspondent Japanese attorneys

complained that even with their extensive experience in litigation, Japanese lawyers tend to be much less flexible in their doctrinal thinking. American lawyers are used to being able to find respectable authority to support almost any position. The American attorney's explanation was that the *bengoshi*'s civilian doctrinal training and the limited amount of case authority in Japan tend to make him take the black letter statement of the legal rule too much at face value.

EIGHT

Corporate Law

Introduction

In this chapter we will seek a broad understanding of Japanese corporate law, but we will probe most deeply into issues relevant to the Principal Case, *i.e.*, issues most relevant to joint ventures and closely held corporations. In Chapter 12, we will investigate publicly traded corporations and mergers and acquisitions.

To begin our inquiry, Part A surveys the principal "corporate" forms available under Japanese law. We will then investigate the structure of Japanese corporate management and consider who has authority to oversee management. In Part B we will focus on the duties directors owe to their companies and the particular problems these duties can present in the context of joint venture corporations. Following this, Part C examines three particular issues where Japanese corporate law diverges significantly from U.S. law and considers how these issues might affect Newco in the Principal Case. In Part D we will consider the degree to which shareholders may alter the applicability of certain Commercial Code provisions by agreement, and, finally, in Part E we will study the resolution of deadlock in close corporations and the dissolution of corporations when deadlock is irresolvable.

PART A: Company Forms and Management Structure of Corporations

I. Available Business Forms

There is no particular legal status associated with the term "joint venture corporation"; it is used in these materials simply to refer to corporations whose shares are owned by joint venturers. In the U.S., denominating a business arrangement as a "joint venture" charges the joint venturers with broad-ranging fiduciary duties to each other apart from the obligations that arise from the underlying business organization itself. In Japan, it is important to focus on the underlying business form and the statutory obligations that are functionally analogous to the U.S. notion of fiduciary duty.

There are several different forms in which a business enterprise might be organized in Japan. The four "corporate" forms are outlined below. Each of the forms described below is treated from the time of formation as a merchant (*shōnin*), *i.e.*, a legal entity to which many of the Commercial Code's general provisions apply (Commercial Code (Com. Code), §§ 4 and 52). The overarching obligations of merchants under the Commercial Code fill gaps in the more specific provisions dealing with each of the business forms under discussion. Note also that all merchants are required to register certain matters in the Commercial Registry, as discussed further in Part C.

A. Partnership (*Gōmei Gaisha*)

Partnerships are similar in many ways to general partnerships organized under the Uniform Partnership Act in the U.S. In Japan, each partner is personally liable to creditors of the company (Com. Code, § 80(1)); each has an equal right to manage and the ability to bind the company, unless otherwise agreed in the company charter (the partnership agreement) or by later unanimous agreement of the partners (Com. Code, §§ 70 and 76); and partners share gains and losses in accordance with their respective contributions (Com. Code, § 68). Contributions may be in cash or in kind (Com. Code, § 89) and must be listed in the company charter (Com. Code, § 63). Only natural persons may become partners (Com. Code, §§ 55 and 80).

No partner may transfer all or a part of his or her interest without the permission of all other partners (Com. Code, § 73). Partners may withdraw at the end of the company's fiscal year by giving six months' notice (Com. Code, § 84(1)). A partner may be expelled for personal bankruptcy, acts of dishonesty, failure to perform a duty, or similar reasons (Com. Code, §§ 85 and 86). Partners leaving the company must register their withdrawals in the Commercial Registry. After having done so, they remain liable for a certain period of time for company debts incurred while still a partner (Com. Code, § 93). New partners become liable for all previous company debts (Com. Code, § 82).

The non-competition obligation required of partners is a crucial point for prospective partners to remember. Unless all other partners consent, no partner may engage, on his or her own or another's behalf, in transactions of the same type of business as engaged in by the company. In addition, a partner may not become a partner with unlimited liability in or a director of another company engaging in the same type of business (Com. Code, § 74(1)).

In spite of the apparent similarities between Japanese and American general partnerships, partnerships play a much more limited role in Japan than in the U.S. The limitation to natural persons, for example, greatly restricts its usefulness in business. The non-competition provisions mentioned above also make the partnership most appropriate to those persons for whom it is their sole activity.

B. Limited partnership (*Gōshi Gaisha*)

The limited partnership company form has many similarities with the limited partnership in the U.S. Limited partnerships have general partners with unlimited liability as well as limited partners (Com. Code, § 146). General partners must be natural persons (Com. Code, § 55). Limited partners are liable only to the extent of their contributions (Com. Code, § 157), which must be disclosed in the company charter (Com. Code, §§ 148 and 63). Contributions from limited partners must be in the form of money or other property (Com. Code, § 150).

Limited partners have no right to participate in the management of the company or to represent the company (Com. Code, § 156). If they do participate in management, they may be treated as general partners and incur unlimited liability for company debts (Com. Code, § 159). To oversee their investment, limited partners do, however, have a right at the end of each fiscal year, or at any time with a court's permission, to inspect the company's records and property (Com. Code, § 153).

With the permission of all general partners, a limited partner may transfer his or her shares in the company (Com. Code, § 154), and even without the general partners' permission a limited partner may engage in competitive activities (Com. Code, § 155). A general partner must get the permission of both general and limited partners in order to transfer his or her shares (Com. Code, § 147).

Other than provisions concerning the status of the limited partners, the limited partnership company form is like the partnership company form, and the Commercial Code provisions applicable to the latter apply *mutatis mutandis* to the former (Com. Code, § 147).

C. Public corporation (*Kabushiki Kaisha*)

The public corporation form, the most popular form for large, and for many small, enterprises in Japan, is the principal form we will study in this chapter on corporate law. The fundamental features of the public corporation are similar to those of the corporation forms prevailing in the U.S., but there are important differences.

Shareholders of public corporations are liable only to the extent of their capital contributions (Com. Code, § 200(1)), and can recover their investment only by selling their shares (*i.e.*, redemptions are not allowed). Shares are freely transferable unless the articles of incorporation stipulate that transfer requires the approval of the board of directors (Com. Code, § 204(1)). Each shareholder is generally entitled to one vote per share held (Com. Code, § 241(1)).

In theory, this capital structure may be varied by provisions in the articles of incorporation establishing different categories of shares. These categories of shares may have preferences similar to those familiar to U.S. investors, and may be voting or nonvoting (Com. Code §§ 222, 290, 291, 293, 293-5, and 242).

Shareholders exercise their formal influence over the management of the company through shareholder meetings, which must be held at least annually (Com. Code, § 234(1)) and which may be held at any time as determined by the board of directors (Com. Code, § 231), or, with court permission, upon demand of shareholders holding at least three percent of the issued shares (Com. Code, § 237). Shareholder resolutions are by a majority vote of shares, unless otherwise specified in the Commercial Code or the company's articles of incorporation (Com. Code, § 239(1)).

The proper subject matter for shareholder meetings is established by statute. According to corporate law doctrine, the meetings, and presence at them, are of central importance to the governance of the corporation. As in most societies, however, shareholder meetings are seldom the real focus of decision making. Participation often requires a minimum holding of 1,000 shares. Proxies are often in the form of open-ended powers of attorney granted to management. Moreover, although somewhat less important than in the past, specialized gangsters called *sōkaiya* sometimes ensure that contrary opinions are not expressed at shareholder meetings. The meetings are therefore often perfunctory. (Shareholder meetings and *sōkaiya* are discussed in greater detail in Chapter 12.)

To manage the company, the shareholders elect directors. The directors must by resolution appoint one or more representative directors to represent the company (Com. Code, § 261(1)). Directors cannot be required by the articles of incorporation to be shareholders (Com. Code, § 254(2)). Each director's relationship to the company is governed by a duty of care (Com. Code, § 254(3)) and a duty of loyalty (Com. Code, § 254-3).

D. Close corporation (*Yūgen Gaisha*)

The statutory close corporation is designed to combine limited liability with a more flexible structure than that required of public corporations. Generally, a close corporation can have no more than 50 shareholders (Limited Liability Company Act (*Yūgen gaisha hō*), Law No. 74 of 1938 (LLCA), § 8(1)). While freely transferable among existing shareholders, shares cannot be transferred to nonshareholders unless approved by a general meeting of shareholders (LLCA, §§ 19(1) and (2)). If the other members do not approve the transfer desired by the requesting shareholder, they must designate another person to whom the shareholder may transfer the shares (LLCA, § 19(4)). All shareholders have preemptive rights in proportion to their shareholdings to new shares issued by the company and thus can maintain their relative shareholding ratios (LLCA, § 51).

- - - - - - - - - -

The chart on the following page lists the numbers of Japanese firms using each of the forms described above as of 1986 and their levels of capitalization.

* * * * *

Utilization of Company Forms

Amount of stated capital	less than ¥5 million	¥5 million to ¥10 million	¥10 million to ¥100 million	¥100 million to ¥1 billion	¥1 billion or more		
Types						Total	%
Public corporations	414,584	183,102	252,548	16,003	2,718	868,955	53.5
Close corporations	562,257	104,168	37,564	106	4	704,099	43.3
Partnerships	5,372	568	514	15	2	6,471	0.4
Limited partnerships	29,886	3,645	1,501	17	—	35,049	2.2
Miscellaneous	4,906	1,453	3,175	151	2	9,687	0.6
TOTAL	1,017,005	292,936	295,302	16,292	2,726	1,624,261	100

Source: 89 *Bessatsu Shōji Hōmu* 9 (Aug. 1986).
Note: Figures give stated capital as of March 1986.

Note on choosing between the public corporation and close corporation

The above chart shows that as of 1986 nearly half the firms in Japan choosing the public corporation form were businesses with stated capital of less than ¥5 million (at $1=¥110, about $45,000). Many such small businesses might seem more suited to be close corporations, as this form was essentially designed to accommodate closely held corporations. Consider also that Newco, which A.Co and J.Co organized as a public corporation, has limited assets and only two shareholders and thus seems to be a natural candidate for the close corporation form.

Early explanations for the Japanese reliance on the public corporation form for small companies pointed to the greater prestige attached to operation as a public corporation. Later commentators have argued that the ease of organization, low minimum capital requirements, and relatively low level of required disclosure for public corporations, as well as the ability of shareholders in public corporations to alter their management structure by agreement among themselves (this ability is discussed in detail in Part E), mean that the close corporation form offers no distinct advantage for smaller companies.

The lack of utilization of the close corporation form has prompted reform of the Commercial Code and Limited Liability Company Act. Amendments to these laws made in 1990 may affect decisions on whether to use the close or public corporation form. The 1990 amendments raised the minimum capitalization requirements for new close corporations from ¥100,000 to ¥3 million and the minimum capitalization requirements for new public corporations from ¥350,000 or ¥400,000 (the amount depending on the method of incorporation) to ¥10 million. (Existing companies have a schedule of several years over which they must increase their capitalization to the applicable minimum.)

II. Management of the Japanese Corporation

A. Overview of the role of directors and auditors

We will begin our study of the management of Japanese corporations by considering the roles of directors and auditors. The most fundamental provisions of the Commercial Code concerning these roles are Sections 260 and 274.

Note that the first paragraph of each of the two provisions goes to the issue of supervision. What is the significance of the board of directors' supervising the performance of the directors? What sorts of activities might directors be undertaking in performing their "duties"? Is the board's supervision of individual directors meaningful supervision? What role do corporate officers play, and who supervises them? And what about the supervisory role of auditors? What powers do auditors have to audit the performance of the directors and officers?

The following two selections address these questions. The first provides a quick outline of the management of Japanese corporations, and the second offers an interesting critique of the law on supervision of management of Japanese corporations as compared to the laws of the United States and some European countries.

SURVEY, CORPORATE GOVERNANCE IN JAPAN: THE POSITION OF SHAREHOLDERS IN PUBLICLY HELD CORPORATIONS*

5 University of Hawaii Law Review 135
153-161, 163-164 (1983)

Although the Commercial Code [was reformed in the postwar era] based on an American model, it is more detailed and less flexible than its statutory counterparts in the United States, "where procedures and formalities have been eliminated to the extent possible." The Code originally applied uniformly to all stock companies, but various amendments passed over the years interjected distinctions among companies based on size and whether or not their stock was listed. The major amendments to the Commercial Code and related laws passed in 1981 expanded these distinctions. Thus, while most of the description below applies to all stock companies, distinctions * * * are noted that in particular affect Japan's approximately 1850 publicly listed stock companies.

1. Directors

Every stock company must have at least three directors. Directors are elected at shareholder meetings and serve terms of office of two years or less. The board of directors is granted broad statutory powers to "manage" the corporation. Japanese boards do not delegate their management powers to corporate "officers" as they commonly do in the U.S. The American concept of corporate "officers" does not

---

*From Survey [Christopher Lee Heftel], "Corporate Governance in Japan: The Position of Shareholders in Publicly Held Corporations," 5 *University of Hawaii Law Review* 135 (1983), at 153-161 and 163-164. Reprinted by permission.

exist in Japan. Everyone who would be considered "senior management" by American standards occupies a place on the board of directors. Consequently, Japanese boards tend to be large, often numbering over thirty.

The directors are split into a hierarchy of several ranks. Seniority usually determines ranking. The lower ranking directors tend to be salaried employees, such as department chiefs. Higher up are "managing directors" (*Jōmu torishimariyaku*) who have in essence retired from employee status. Above the one or more ranks of managing directors are a variety of vice-presidents (*Fuku shachō*) and a president (*Shachō*). The most senior members of the typical board take on such titles as vice-chairman (*Fuku kaichō*), chairman (*Kaichō*), advisor (*Sōdan yaku*) and senior advisor.

The size of the typical Japanese board of directors necessitates division into more compact decisionmaking units. Directors often form working and executive committees that meet more frequently than the full board. These committees are not recognized by statute. However, the Code does recognize the position of "representative director" (*Daihyō torishimariyaku*). Representative directors are appointed by the board from its ranks to act on behalf of the corporation.[1] The boards of most large stock companies appoint several directors, including the president, to function as representative directors to deal with third parties on behalf of the company. Representative directors implement decisions made at shareholders' or board meetings and are empowered to make decisions on matters delegated by the board.

Beginning with incidents such as the Lockheed scandal, concern grew that individual directors needed to be more accountable to the board as a whole and that the board's supervising authority needed to be strengthened. Disagreement existed over what kinds of matters could be delegated by the board to a representative director. Thus, the 1981 Commercial Code amendments specifically enumerated four subjects[2] which the board may *not* have a director decide and further prohibited the board from delegating the "execution of any other important business affairs."

The new Code has other provisions designed to exact greater responsibility on the part of individual directors. For example, the amended Code provides that "[a] director shall report to the board of directors the status of execution of business affairs not less than once every three months."[3] These reports must include concrete descriptions of how corporate affairs are being handled, thus providing the entire board with all the information necessary to enable proper supervision. The new Code also imposes heavier duties and liabilities on directors,[4] increases an individual director's ability to carry out his duties[5] and specifies criteria for the disqualification of directors.[6]

The board has other enumerated obligations including: convocation of general meetings of shareholders; approval of transactions between a director and the company; and submission of certain financial reports to the auditors prior to each ordinary general meeting of shareholders and then again to the shareholders at the general meeting, [and prior to any] transfer from statutory reserve to stated capital, and [prior to any] declaration of stock-splits [or] interim dividends. Unless stricter requirements are provided in the articles of incorporation, a majority of the board constitutes a quorum, and all board resolutions must be passed by a majority of those present at a board meeting.

In practice many boards have been ineffective in overseeing the affairs of the company, often being considered just "hollow shells" controlled by powerful presidents. Regardless of how actively these directors in fact supervise the company, their loyalties are not generally to the shareholders but to the corporate insiders and to the employees. While the trend for publicly held firms in the U.S. has been toward greater numbers of "outside directors," Japanese boards continue to be comprised almost entirely of "inside directors." Most of these directors are the survivors of a seniority system in which they worked their way up to the position of director after many years with the same firm. Outsiders are few in number and are usually not independent from the company in the American sense of outside directors. Instead, they are transplanted or retired from major bank creditors, sister companies and government agencies that regulate the company.

2. Auditors

The shareholders must also appoint auditors,[7] who are in charge of supervising the management track records set by the directors. They are appointed for [three]-year terms and may not concurrently serve as directors or employees of the company. Most companies fill these positions with retiring employees who did not quite excel enough to become directors; in some cases middle level directors who are not going to be promoted to a more powerful position on the board are appointed as auditors.[8] Auditors may be employed on a full-time or part-time basis.

Amendments in 1974 strengthened auditors' powers and duties.[9] Auditors are empowered to: investigate corporate affairs and documents, make reports to the directors and at the shareholders' meetings, enjoin directors' illegal acts, and bring certain suits on behalf of the corporation. Auditors are jointly and severally liable to the company for damages due to nonperformance of their duties. In spite of the 1974 amendments, auditors often function as mere "rubber stamps" for the board of directors and often lack the professional expertise to carry out their duties.[10]

In an effort to strengthen the self-regulating functions of the company, the auditors' powers and duties were greatly enlarged by the 1981 Code revisions. Large companies must now have at least two auditors [raised to three by amendments in 1993, as explained below], of which at least one must be full-time. Auditors have the option of obtaining employee reports from the directors or can circumvent the directors and obtain the report directly from the employee.[11] Auditors may also demand the convocation of a meeting of the board of directors whenever necessary. Auditors' rights to remuneration and compensation for expenses have been increased. This further shields auditors from undue influence by directors and makes it easier for them to hire specialists to assist in their auditing and other technical duties. The duties which expose auditors to liability to the company have been expanded and clarified. The new Code imposes liability to third persons as well where false statements have been made in any audit report.

Unlike many statutory changes in the past, these amendments are expected to significantly increase the effectiveness of auditors in practice.[12] There are already concerns about the role of part-time auditors,[13] and speculation that the average salaries of auditors will increase substantially.

[Editors' Note: Because the 1981 amendments were seen by many (including U.S. government negotiators, who included the power of auditors as a topic in the Structural Impediments Initiative talks) as not having increased sufficiently the effectiveness of auditors, in 1993 further amendments were made to the Commercial Code and to the Act Regarding Exceptional Rules of the Commercial Code Concerning Auditing, etc., of Stock Corporations (the "Special Audit Act"). Under these amendments, the term of office for auditors was increased from two to three years. In addition, for large companies, as defined in the Special Audit Act, the minimum number of auditors was increased from two to three, at least one of whom must not have been a director, manager or employee of the company or any of its subsidiaries in the five years before assuming office.

The 1993 amendments to the Special Audit Act also require every large company to establish a board of auditors, consisting of all the auditors. In addition to the powers auditors already possess under the Commercial Code and the Special Audit Act, the board of auditors has been given the authority to determine the company's auditing policy and the methods used for investigating the company's financial affairs.]

3. Accounting Auditors

In large companies financial statements must not only be audited by company auditors but also by outside "accounting auditors" (*Kaikei kansanin*). An accounting auditor must be a certified public accountant or an audit corporation. Accounting auditors were previously appointed and removed by the board of directors but the new Code shifts these powers to the general meeting of shareholders. Other new provisions further insulate accounting auditors from undue influence by directors or inside auditors.[14] Accounting auditors are liable to the company and to third parties for damages caused by their negligence.[15]

4. Shareholders

a. Stock System

Although different classes of stock are allowed,[16] almost all stock issued in Japan is voting common stock. * * *

b. Voting

* * * The Commercial Code enumerates a limited number of matters upon which shareholders have the power to vote at a general meeting. These can be extended by the articles of incorporation. Cumulative voting is possible for the election of directors,[17] but in practice is rarely, if ever, used.

Most matters may be passed upon by a simple resolution of the shareholders. Some of the matters which may be passed by ordinary resolution include: declaration of cash dividends, declaration of stock dividends, approval of financial statements, and election of auditors and accounting auditors. This requires a quorum of a majority of the outstanding voting shares and affirmative votes of a majority of the shares represented at the meeting. These quorum and voting requirements for simple resolutions can be changed by the articles of incorporation, but elections for directors and auditors must in any event have a quorum of not less than one-third of the outstanding voting stock.

Certain matters can only be passed by special resolution requiring a quorum of a majority of the outstanding stock and the favorable vote of two-thirds of the shares represented at the meeting. These requirements cannot be relaxed by the articles of incorporation. Some of the matters requiring a special resolution include: amending the articles of incorporation, removing directors and auditors prior to the expiration of their terms, approving mergers and consolidations, reducing paid-in capital, and issuance of new shares at favorable prices to persons other than shareholders. There are certain matters which require even more stringent voting or quorum requirements: for example, releasing directors and auditors from liability for various acts usually requires unanimous consent.

B. The supervisory role of auditors

Translation by Yanagida Nomura & Akai

Hitsugi v. K.K. Hasegawa Kōmuten
1200 Hanrei Jihō 154
(Tokyo High Ct., June 26, 1986)

REFERENCES:

Commercial Code, §§ 247(1), 273, 274 and 276

FACTS:

Plaintiff-appellant Hitsugi, a shareholder of defendant-appellee K.K. Hasegawa Kōmuten (Hasegawa), brought an action seeking a declaration of the invalidity of a shareholder resolution approving a certain disposition of the profits of Hasegawa (the Resolution). Hitsugi objected to the Resolution since it was based in part on an audit prepared in part by Gorō Hasegawa (Gorō), a statutory auditor of Hasegawa, who had audited the Balance Sheet and Profit and Loss Statement for the sixty-eighth fiscal year of Hasegawa. During part of that year, from June 1 to August 29, 1984, Gorō had been a director of Hasegawa. Hitsugi asserted that Gorō should not have been eligible to become a statutory auditor of the company since doing so required him to audit his own prior activities as director. Hitsugi argued that the self-audit made the audit report illegal and, thus, that the Resolution, which was based on the audit report, should be nullified.

The court of first instance ruled against Hitsugi, holding that although such self-audits are not desirable, they are not *per se* illegal.

Hitsugi appealed the judgment to the Tokyo High Court.

JUDGMENT:

The appeal is dismissed.

REASONS:

I. * * * Section 276 of the Commercial Code provides that an auditor of a corporation may not concurrently be a director, manager or employee of the corporation or of any subsidiary of the corporation. Section 276, however, does not prohibit a corporation from electing a former director, manager or employee to the position of statutory auditor. Furthermore, Section 273 does not require that the term of office of a statutory auditor be the same as the term which the statutory auditor audits. The Commercial Code, therefore, should be construed to permit a self-audit, even if self-audits are not necessarily desirable.

If a director of a corporation resigns from office as director and is elected a statutory auditor of the corporation at a general meeting of shareholders held at the midpoint of the corporation's fiscal year, the statutory auditor then audits the activities of the directors, including himself, for the period during which he was a director. It is possible for a statutory auditor to audit his own prior activities as a director by exchanging his position of director for that of statutory auditor. (Furthermore, there may well be certain advantages to this situation, inasmuch as a statutory auditor, who has been a director of the corporation before taking office as a statutory auditor, may be able to audit more efficiently than a statutory auditor elected from outside the corporation, since the former is familiar with the recent circumstances and activities of the corporation.)

Accordingly, whether a corporation elects as a statutory auditor a person who was formerly a director is a matter to be decided by resolution of the general meeting of shareholders. Election by the general meeting of shareholders of a person to the position of statutory auditor who has been a director until immediately before such election does not constitute a violation of the law.

II. [Omitted.]

Questions and Discussion Points

1. *Function of auditors*: Does the reasoning of the court follow from the language of the Commercial Code sections concerning the role of auditors? Does the link between the Code provisions and the court's ruling come from a vision of the corporation that emphasizes the importance of protecting the interests of shareholders? If not, what are the interests that are served by the auditors and directors?

2. *Appeal of the case*: Hitsugi's appeal of the Tokyo High Court's ruling was dismissed by the Supreme Court, *see* 1110 *Shōji Hōmu* 79 (Sup. Ct., April 21, 1987).

3. *1993 auditor amendments*: Assuming K.K. Hasegawa Kōmuten was not a large company, as defined in the Special Audit Act, the 1993 amendment to that Act requiring large companies to have at least one auditor who was not a director, manager or employee of the company or a subsidiary during the previous five years would not directly apply in this case. Should that amendment affect the court's interpretation of the requirements of Section 274 or 276 of the Commercial Code? What supports the implicit view in the Special Audit Act that there is a greater need in large companies than in small ones for auditors with greater independence?

PART B: Directors' Duties to the Corporation

Introduction

Any attempt to consider the adequacy of supervision of Japanese corporate management must take into account two underlying issues. First, by what goals is adequacy to be measured? Are the key factors shareholders' interests, the long-term interests of the employees, the fate of related companies, or the good of the community? The second issue is that of available mechanisms for effectuating supervision. The previous section focused on the formal structures of corporations and on the roles assigned to directors and auditors. By itself, the existence of such formal structures does not ensure effective supervision. Other mechanisms supplementing these structures include market discipline and specific legal duties.

Many commentators discussing the adequacy of management supervision in U.S. corporations have pointed to the pressure exerted on the management of publicly traded companies by an active market in the companies' shares. Many observers argue that this market factor is less effective in Japan than it is thought to be in the U.S.

In Japan, directors are typically managers. In their capacities as directors, the law imposes various duties upon them. We will first consider these duties generally and then in the context of a joint venture corporation such as Newco. In approaching these materials, consider the efficacy under Japanese law of these duties in ensuring supervision over the management of Japanese companies.

I. The Duties of Care and Loyalty under the Codes

The most basic provisions of the Commercial Code concerning the duties of directors to their companies are Sections 254-3 and 254(3). To understand the latter provision, one must also consider Sections 643 and 644 of the Civil Code. Note further that under Section 267 of the Commercial Code, directors' duties can be enforced by the company or, in a derivative action, by the shareholders.

Consider the relationship between Section 254-3 and Section 254(3) of the Commercial Code. The former is usually described as imposing a duty of loyalty and the latter as imposing a duty of care. Are these duties distinct? Does one elaborate on the other or is one superfluous? There is considerable debate among Japanese corporate law scholars on these and similar questions. Plaintiffs bringing claims against directors for breach of their duties typically rely on both Sections 254-3 and 254(3).

While Sections 254-3 and 254(3) of the Commercial Code constitute the general law concerning the duties directors owe to their corporations, there are two more specific provisions of importance: Section 264, which is relevant to the case that follows, and Section 265, which concerns what is usually called self-dealing in the U.S. and is treated later in this chapter.

Translation by Yanagida Nomura & Akai

Yamazaki Bakery K.K. v. Iijima
1015 Hanrei Jihō 27
(Tokyo Dist. Ct., March 26, 1981)

REFERENCES:

Commercial Code, §§ 254(3), 254-3, 264, 266, 268(2), 275-4 and 284[18]

FACTS:

Plaintiff Yamazaki Bakery K.K. (Yamazaki) was established by defendant Iijima in 1948 and has been continuously engaged in the production and sale of bread and confectioneries since its incorporation. Iijima was representative director of Yamazaki from its founding until 1976. For the first twenty-one years of Yamazaki's existence, Iijima exercised absolute power in managing the company without ever convening a meeting of the board of directors. In 1969, the company elected several outside directors and began to hold meetings of the board of directors, but Iijima continued to wield absolute power in managing the company.

In 1963, Yamazaki, whose sales territory extended throughout the Kantō region, including Tokyo and Chiba, desired to acquire Kawaguchi Bakery K.K. (Kawaguchi), a wholly owned subsidiary of Chiba Mills K.K., as Kawaguchi was engaged in Chiba in the same business as Yamazaki. A director of Yamazaki, under Iijima's direction, reached agreement with Chiba Mills on behalf of Yamazaki for the purchase of 290,000 of the 320,000 issued shares of Kawaguchi. Iijima, however, without consulting Yamazaki's board of directors, modified the agreement at the time of the closing so that Iijima purchased 258,000 of the agreed 290,000 shares of Kawaguchi in his own name and Yamazaki purchased the balance of 32,000 shares. Iijima paid for his 258,000 shares with the proceeds of a loan made to him by Yamazaki. In 1965, the remaining 30,000 shares in Kawaguchi were transferred from Chiba Mills to Iijima's wife, Kazu Iijima.

Following the transfer of the 290,000 shares of Kawaguchi from Chiba Mills to Iijima and Yamazaki, the corporate name of Kawaguchi was changed to K.K. Yamazaki Bakery Chiba Factory (Chiba Factory), which later merged with Yamazaki in 1973. By the time of such merger, Iijima, his wife, other Iijima family members, and other persons close to Iijima had come to own 3,554,999 shares in Chiba Factory. Although Iijima was never made a director or representative director of Chiba Factory, he exercised absolute power in managing the company, acting alone in deciding all corporate matters of Chiba Factory until the merger with Yamazaki in 1973.

Chiba Factory was engaged in the same business in Chiba and Tokyo as was Yamazaki. When Chiba Factory encountered difficulty in expanding its business in Chiba, Iijima transferred 508 Yamazaki distributors operating in Chiba to Chiba Factory without consulting the board of directors of Yamazaki. Furthermore, Yamazaki, represented by Iijima, made major loans to Chiba Factory to support its operations and also guaranteed significant debts of Chiba Factory. All employees at Chiba Factory were dispatched from Yamazaki, and daily operations and sales of

Chiba Factory were carried out by Yamazaki's management. Chiba Factory used Yamazaki's brand name and production and packaging technology for its bread and confectioneries and paid Yamazaki royalties for such use.

Having rapidly developed its business and established its sales network in the Kantō region, in 1966 Yamazaki began to contemplate the expansion of its business to the Kansai region centered around Osaka. Following preliminary market research, a suitable factory site was found in Suita City.

Instead of having Yamazaki purchase the factory site and enter the Kansai market, Iijima decided to form and capitalize a separate company, which he named K.K. Yamazaki Bakery Osaka Factory (Osaka Factory). All shares in Osaka Factory were owned by Iijima, a corporation wholly owned by him known as "Iijima Kōsan," or by family members and others close to Iijima. Iijima was the representative director of Osaka Factory.

Since incorporating Osaka Factory involved some delay, Yamazaki, represented by Iijima, purchased the factory site on behalf of Osaka Factory and later transferred title to the property to Osaka Factory following its incorporation. The purchase price for the factory site was paid primarily from a large loan made by Yamazaki to Osaka Factory and in smaller part out of Iijima's own funds.

Osaka Factory was merged with K.K. Yamazaki Bakery Fukuoka Factory (Fukuoka Factory) in 1971 and its corporate name changed thereafter to K.K. Kansai Yamazaki. Iijima was made representative director of Kansai Yamazaki and remained as such until 1976.

The business initiated by Osaka Factory in the Kansai region in 1966 was the same as Yamazaki's business in Tokyo and Chiba. Almost all of Osaka Factory's operating funds came from loans made by Yamazaki or from loans made by banks or trading companies that were guaranteed by Yamazaki. All employees in Osaka Factory were dispatched from Yamazaki, and Osaka Factory used Yamazaki's brand name and production and packaging technology for its bread and confectioneries in exchange for the payment of royalties.

In 1976, an auditor of Yamazaki brought suit on behalf of Yamazaki under Commercial Code §275-4, demanding that Iijima pay damages equivalent to approximately ¥5,000,000,000. This amount was calculated as being equal to the sum of the value of the shares originating in Chiba Factory and Osaka Factory held by Iijima, his wife, Iijima Kōsan, Iijima's other family members and other persons close to Iijima, less the purchase price of such shares actually paid by the aforementioned shareholders, and ¥240,685,832, which had already been paid as dividends on such shares to the aforementioned shareholders. In the alternative, the auditor, on behalf of Yamazaki, demanded the transfer of all such shares originating in Chiba Factory and Osaka Factory to Yamazaki.

On behalf of Yamazaki, the auditor alleged that Iijima's conduct, as described above, violated his duty as a director under Commercial Code §264 to avoid competition, his duty under Commercial Code §254(3) and Civil Code §644 to use the diligence of a good manager, and his fiduciary duty under Commercial Code §254-3. A shareholder of Yamazaki intervened in this suit pursuant to Commercial Code §268(2).

Iijima denied the allegations. Concerning the operation of Chiba Factory, he argued that as a mere shareholder of Chiba Factory he did not act on that company's behalf and, therefore, did not violate any duty to Yamazaki to avoid competition. Concerning the operation of Osaka Factory, Iijima argued that since one of Yamazaki's major shareholders had opposed the expansion of Yamazaki's business to the Kansai region, Yamazaki itself did not intend to extend its operations to the Kansai region and, therefore, Osaka Factory's business was not competitive with Yamazaki's business.

As to the alleged violations of his duty to use the diligence of a good manager and his fiduciary duty as a director, Iijima argued that Yamazaki succeeded in promoting its brand name in Chiba and Osaka by allowing Chiba Factory and Osaka Factory to use its brand name and technology under Yamazaki's control, and that Yamazaki earned profits from the royalties paid by Chiba Factory and Osaka Factory for such use. Iijima also asserted that in order to limit Yamazaki's risks from expansion he formed Chiba Factory and Osaka Factory with little or no capital relationship with Yamazaki but, in substance, as subsidiaries or cooperative companies of Yamazaki so as to promote Yamazaki's profits, and thus that there could be no competition between Yamazaki and Chiba Factory or Osaka Factory. Finally, Iijima asserted that the shareholders' meetings of Yamazaki had accepted the financial reports of the company each year and had not considered any resolution to hold Iijima liable and, therefore, that Yamazaki should be deemed to have released Iijima from any liability pursuant to Commercial Code §284.

JUDGMENT:

1. [As to the shares originating in Chiba Factory,] Iijima shall transfer or cause to be transferred to Yamazaki a total of 3,554,999 shares in Yamazaki held by Iijima, his wife and others listed below in exchange for receipt of the sum equal to the purchase prices of all such shares ("Purchase Price"). For any shares Iijima is unable to cause to be transferred to Yamazaki, Iijima shall pay Yamazaki ¥500 per share in exchange for receipt of the respective Purchase Price.

[List of names omitted.]

2. [As to the shares originating in Osaka Factory,] Iijima shall transfer or cause to be transferred to Yamazaki a total of 751,546 shares held by Iijima, Iijima Kōsan and others listed below in exchange for receipt of the amount of ¥500 per share. For any shares Iijima is unable to cause to be transferred to Yamazaki, Iijima shall pay Yamazaki ¥2,507 per share in exchange for receipt of ¥500 for each such share.

[List of names omitted.]

3. Iijima shall pay Yamazaki ¥240,685,832 and interest accrued and accruing thereon at the rate of 5% per annum from the date the complaint was served on Iijima.

REASONS:

[I. - V.—Omitted. In these sections, the court found generally the same facts as described above.]

VI. **Liability of Iijima**

1. *Violation of the Duty to Avoid Competition*

(1) There is no dispute that Iijima was representative director of Yamazaki from the time of incorporation of Chiba Factory until its merger with Yamazaki; that Chiba Factory was engaged in the same business as Yamazaki; and that the Kanto region, including Tokyo and Chiba, was within the business territory of Yamazaki. As determined above [in an omitted section], Iijima operated Chiba Factory as its *de facto* president.

We conclude that Iijima's actions on behalf of Chiba Factory should be deemed competitive with Yamazaki's business. This conclusion is not affected by the fact that Chiba Factory paid Yamazaki royalties for use of Yamazaki's brand name and technology. Thus, Iijima's acts constitute a violation of his duty to avoid competition.

(2)(i) There is no dispute that Osaka Factory was engaged in the same business as Yamazaki; that Iijima was representative director of Osaka Factory from the time of its incorporation until its merger with Fukuoka Factory; that after such merger, Osaka Factory and Fukuoka Factory assumed the corporate name of Kansai Yamazaki; that Iijima was representative director of Kansai Yamazaki from the time of the merger until March 31, 1976; and that Iijima managed both Osaka Factory and Kansai Yamazaki as representative director of each at the same time as he managed Yamazaki as its representative director. As determined above [in an omitted section], Yamazaki had contemplated expanding its business to the Kansai region and in 1966 conducted market research related to such expansion.

(ii) As determined above [in an omitted section], with respect to the circumstances of the incorporation and operation of Osaka Factory, although Iijima supplied Osaka Factory with capital, he used Yamazaki's funds, goodwill, brand name, technology and employees in the operation of Osaka Factory. Osaka Factory's success owed mainly to Iijima's access to Yamazaki's tangible and intangible property, including the results of the aforementioned market research. Had Osaka Factory failed as a business, the effect upon Yamazaki would have been the same as if Osaka Factory had been operated as a division of Yamazaki. If, conversely, Osaka Factory succeeded as a business, Iijima, and Iijima Kōsan, Iijima's family members and other persons close to him would earn dividends on their capital investment owing largely to Yamazaki's contributions to Osaka Factory's business. Therefore, at the time Yamazaki purchased the factory site in Suita City, Yamazaki itself might have entered the Kansai market had Iijima decided to establish Osaka Factory as a division of Yamazaki.

In view of the foregoing, Yamazaki should have established Osaka Factory as a division of Yamazaki unless some special circumstance called for incorporating Osaka Factory as a separate entity with a close capital relationship with Yamazaki. Therefore, with respect to assessing the extent of Yamazaki's interest in entering the Kansai market, the extent of Yamazaki's market territory and the extent of damages to Yamazaki caused by Osaka Factory's infringement of its market, we should assume that Yamazaki had already decided to establish and operate Osaka Factory as one of its divisions.

(iii) Therefore, in acting as representative director of and actually controlling operations of each of Osaka Factory and Kansai Yamazaki, Ijima was doing nothing other than conducting business competitive with Yamazaki, for which he was also a representative director. It is clear that such conduct by Iijima constitutes a violation of the director's duty to avoid competition. This conclusion is not affected by either the fact that Iijima supplied Osaka Factory with capital or the fact that Osaka Factory paid Yamazaki royalties for its use of Yamazaki's brand name and technology.

2. *Violation of the Duty to Use the Diligence of a Good Manager and of the Fiduciary Duty*

Iijima was obliged, as representative director of Yamazaki, to oversee operations of the company with the diligence of a good manager and to heed his fiduciary duty to the company. As determined above [in an omitted section], however, Iijima acquired almost all the shares in Chiba Factory and brought it under his control; he deprived Yamazaki of opportunities to strengthen its business in Chiba by siphoning off its employees, property and funds for the benefit of Chiba Factory; and he injured Yamazaki's marketing capabilities by reappointing 508 distributors of Yamazaki as Chiba Factory distributors without consideration and without consulting the board of directors of Yamazaki. In such actions, Iijima acted competitively with Yamazaki as the *de facto* president of Chiba Factory. Furthermore, Iijima deprived Yamazaki of the opportunity to penetrate the Kansai market either by itself or through a subsidiary by establishing Osaka Factory as a company with no capital relationship with Yamazaki. In this manner, Iijima also acted competitively with Yamazaki.

It is clear that such competitive acts by Iijima constitute a violation of his fiduciary duty as a director of Yamazaki and, therefore, a violation of his duty to use the diligence of a good manager as a director of Yamazaki.

3. *Violation of the Duty of a Mandatary*

(1) As determined above [in an omitted section], Iijima acted as a one-man board of Yamazaki and solely decided all corporate matters, from business strategy and personnel affairs to daily operations, and he did not convene any meetings of the board of directors for a long period of time. All competitive actions by Chiba Factory and Osaka Factory were conducted during this period. Corporate matters are properly decided by a board of directors, and the representative director of a corporation acts merely to execute decisions reached by the board of directors. Therefore, it is very abnormal when the board of directors has lost such function and the representative director decides and executes all corporate matters, as was the case with Yamazaki. Under these circumstances, the board of directors of Yamazaki should be deemed to have mandated Iijima to decide and carry out all corporate matters acting alone.

In such an event, the board of directors would have naturally mandated Iijima to decide matters on behalf of the corporation in accordance with the law. It is clear, therefore, that decisions made in violation of his duties as a director under the Commercial Code are not within the scope of such a mandate. Such a representative director should decide matters within the scope considered proper under the circumstances from time to time, and any decision outside these bounds constitutes a breach of the board's mandate.

(2) We have already determined that Iijima's actions in establishing and operating Chiba Factory and Osaka Factory were competitive with Yamazaki and constituted violations of his duty to use the diligence of a good manager and his fiduciary duty as a director. Therefore, it is clear that these acts by Iijima constitute a breach of the aforementioned mandate by the board of directors of Yamazaki.

Accordingly, Iijima should have acquired the shares in Chiba Factory (*i.e.*, Kawaguchi) on behalf of Yamazaki. As to Osaka Factory, Iijima should have established it as a division of Yamazaki or, if special circumstances warranted, as Yamazaki's subsidiary, acquiring its shares on behalf of Yamazaki. Since no other way presented itself to Yamazaki to enter the Kansai market than by establishing Osaka Factory as one of its divisions or as a subsidiary, Iijima should have adopted one of these alternatives under the mandate of the board of directors of Yamazaki. Iijima, however, breached the mandate by having the shares in Chiba Factory and Osaka Factory vested in parties other than Yamazaki.

Assuming that the board of directors of Yamazaki had decided to purchase a targeted company or to incorporate a subsidiary, had mandated Iijima to execute such a decision, and had provided him with necessary funds therefor, and that Iijima had instead acquired the shares of the targeted company or established a new company for himself and others, Yamazaki could demand that Iijima transfer such shares of the targeted company or the newly established company to Yamazaki pursuant to the mandate of the board of directors of Yamazaki.

Accordingly, in the case at hand, which corresponds to our assumptions above, it is reasonable that Yamazaki demands that Iijima transfer to it the shares controlled by Iijima in Chiba Factory and Osaka Factory, unless such transfer is impossible; or that Iijima instead pay Yamazaki damages, if the transfer of such shares to Yamazaki is impossible. This approach affords Yamazaki a more direct and fitting remedy than would damages based on Iijima's violations of his duty to avoid competition, his duty to use the diligence of a good manager, and his fiduciary duty as a director.

VII. **Assertions by Iijima**

1. Iijima asserts that, in order to limit Yamazaki's risks from entering a new market, he arranged for Chiba Factory and Osaka Factory to have little or no capital relationship with Yamazaki while at the same time operating as *de facto* subsidiaries or cooperative companies whose objects were to promote Yamazaki's profits. Given the special circumstances that both Chiba Factory and Osaka Factory were operated pursuant to Yamazaki's direction and that the directors of those companies could be replaced at Yamazaki's behest, the activities of Chiba Factory and Osaka Factory could not be competitive with those of Yamazaki.

As determined above: in order to limit Yamazaki's risks in entering a new market, it would have been sufficient to establish a separate company with a strong capital relationship with Yamazaki, and it was not necessary to acquire or establish a company with little or no such capital relationship; both Chiba Factory and Osaka

Factory were entities only remotely related to Yamazaki; management of both companies was conducted entirely as a function of Iijima's personal will; Yamazaki was deprived of opportunities to strengthen its business in Chiba by Iijima's reappointment of 508 of Yamazaki's distributors as Chiba Factory distributors; Yamazaki was deprived of an opportunity to enter the Osaka market by Iijima's establishment of Osaka Factory; and, thus, Yamazaki suffered large damages. On the other hand, Iijima, Iijima Kōsan, Iijima's family members and other persons close to him increased their wealth at Yamazaki's expense. Therefore, Iijima's assertions are unfounded.

2. There is no dispute that, as asserted by Iijima, the annual financial reports of Yamazaki were accepted by each shareholders' meeting, and no shareholder resolutions seeking Iijima's liability were made within two years after any such acceptance.

However, * * * Iijima conducted the abovementioned acts for his own benefit with knowledge that his acts would deprive Yamazaki of opportunities to expand its business. Such acts by Iijima constitute separate instances of a "dishonest act," as set forth in the proviso of §284. Therefore, this assertion by Iijima is also unfounded.

[VIII. and IX.—Omitted. In these sections, after the court determines the value of the shares of Yamazaki originating in Chiba Factory and Osaka Factory and the dividends paid thereon, it reaches the conclusions described above in the Judgment section.]

Questions and Discussion Points

1. *Duties under Sections 254-3 and 254(3)*: Does the court distinguish between the duties owed under Commercial Code Sections 254-3 and 254(3)? Do the duties appear to be distinct? Is the court's reasoning in holding that Iijima breached these duties compelling?

2. *Duty under Section 264*: What is the relationship between the duty owed under Section 264 and those owed under Sections 254-3 and 254(3)? Is the court's reasoning in holding that Iijima breached the duty owed under Section 264 compelling?

3. *Management of close corporations*: The court states that it is very "abnormal" for a board of directors not to function and for the representative director to determine and execute all corporate matters. On what basis does the court declare this to be "abnormal"? How does the court resolve the problem of Iijima's unilateral actions and why does it choose such a resolution?

II. The Business Judgment Rule

What distinguishes, or should distinguish, breaches by directors of their duties to the company from mere poor business decisions that prove to have bad consequences for the company?

*Fukuokaken Uoichiba K.K. v. Kobayashi**
433 Hanrei Taimuzu 149
(Fukuoka High Ct., Oct. 8, 1980)

REFERENCES:

Commercial Code, §§ 254(3), 254-3 and 266(1)(v)

(Note: At the time of this decision, Section 254-3 was numbered 254-2. The change in numbering came through the 1981 amendments to the Commercial Code. For convenience, the subject provision is referred to in this translation in accordance with its current numbering.)

Civil Code, § 644

FACTS:

Kobayashi, defendant, was representative director of plaintiff Fukuokaken Uoichiba K.K. (F.U.), a wholesale trader of marine products. Kobayashi had delegated all managerial authority to a senior managing director, Yamauchi.

Daitoku Suisan K.K. (D.S.), a subsidiary of F.U. in which F.U. held more than 50% of the shares, had been established to promote F.U.'s business. In April 1962, F.U. received information that D.S. had become financially troubled. F.U. investigated the situation and discovered that D.S. had issued excessive amounts of promissory notes and was on the verge of bankruptcy.

Yamauchi instructed the Investigation Section of F.U. to develop proposals to submit to him for improving D.S. and F.U.'s control and supervision of it. In July 1962, the Investigation Section presented two alternative proposals. The "negative" proposal called for minimizing F.U.'s losses by immediately ceasing financial support for D.S. and, in the event D.S. became insolvent, attempting to sell it or liquidate its assets. The "positive" proposal called for extending further loans to D.S. to keep it afloat until the next fishing season. This proposal noted that one bumper catch would dramatically improve D.S.'s financial condition. The risk of the positive proposal, however, was that fishing prospects were generally considered to be poor and D.S.'s fishing methods were thought to be unreliable.

Yamauchi decided to adopt the positive proposal for two reasons. First, F.U. had already made substantial unsecured loans to D.S. for which there would be no recovery if F.U.'s suspension of financial support led, as expected, to D.S.'s bankruptcy. Second, a majority of F.U.'s Business Section supported the positive proposal.

F.U. thus continued financing D.S., by issuing D.S. negotiable promissory notes secured as much as possible by boats and personal property of D.S. that had not already been encumbered. From April through August 25, 1962, F.U. issued 60 notes totaling ¥66,300,000. F.U. also began to institute a new plan for exercising greater control over management of D.S.

Before the new management plan was fully implemented and before the next fishing season opened, D.S. went bankrupt. One of the principal reasons was that

---

*Translation adapted from Misao Tatsata & Richard O. Kummert, *Cases and Materials on Japanese and U.S. Business Corporation Law*, Vol. II (Temp. Ed. 1994), at 8-26 to 8-29. Reprinted by permission.

the president of D.S. had caused it secretly to borrow over ¥10 million at high interest rates, despite strict orders from F.U. that D.S. was not to issue additional debt. F.U. had to pay off all the promissory note financing and was able to recover only ¥2,399,500 from D.S.

Following D.S.'s bankruptcy, Kobayashi resigned from his position as representative director. F.U. then brought suit against Kobayashi to recover its loss on the promissory notes, alleging that Kobayashi had violated his fiduciary duty to F.U. by failing to supervise Yamauchi, who had in turn been negligent in managing F.U.

The District Court found that Yamauchi should have known that D.S.'s properties were far from sufficient for securing the new promissory notes and thus could not support the decision to continue financing D.S. Yamauchi's judgment concerning D.S.'s business performance was thus defective, held the court, and constituted a violation of his fiduciary duties, which by extension reached Kobayashi, who had failed to supervise Yamauchi.

JUDGMENT:

The judgment for the plaintiff is reversed.

I. & II. [Omitted.]

III.

1. [In this part, the court finds facts as described above.]

2. It is generally accepted that the fiduciary duty of directors set forth in Section 254-3 of the Commercial Code simply amplifies the duty of diligence of a good manager, which is derived from the mandate relationship between directors and the company (see Com. Code, §254(3) and Civ. Code, §644). Such duty does not impose on directors a duty greater than that required of a good manager, nor does it require directors to assume strict responsibility for the consequences of the business performance of their companies. The inherent risks and responsibilities in operating an enterprise must be accepted. Therefore, it is not proper to state that in the event a director of a parent company causes it to extend new loans to a subsidiary that would become insolvent without such loans, at the parent's own risk and with the expectation that the subsidiary's business performance will be improved, such director violates his fiduciary duty merely because the parent's efforts to rebuild the subsidiary fail and most of the parent's loans cannot be recovered. The director should not be held to have violated his fiduciary duty if his actions were done in the best interests of the parent company and if the decision to make the loans was not beyond the bounds of rational choices made by businessmen.

Applying this general rule to the instant case, * * * we find that even though Yamauchi could be accused of having been too optimistic in his business judgment, he exercised such judgment with the expectation that it would be to F.U.'s benefit. Further, we regard his decision as being within the range of reasonable options that might be considered by ordinary businessmen under such circumstances. Therefore, it would be improper to find that Yamauchi violated his fiduciary duty as a director simply because, contrary to his expectations, his decisions resulted in F.U.'s suffering a loss.

Kobayashi, as the representative director of F.U. with exclusive power to administer its business affairs, had responsibility for supervising the administration of F.U.'s business by Yamauchi, as the senior managing director. Since Yamauchi's actions did not violate his fiduciary duty as a director, however, there is no reason to charge Kobayashi, as representative director, with negligent supervision, nor is there reason for charging Kobayashi with having violated his fiduciary duty as a director. Therefore, F.U.'s claim against Kobayashi for compensation for damages suffered by it is improper.

IV. [Omitted.]

III. Fiduciary Problems of Directors in Joint Venture Companies

Consider directors' duties of loyalty and care in the context of the Principal Case. Pursuant to the JVA, A.Co and J.Co each nominate three of the six directors constituting the board of directors of Newco (§B-7(a)). One from each group of three then serves as a representative director of Newco (§B-8(a)). As directors of Newco, those nominated and elected to fill Newco's directorships will have duties of care and loyalty to Newco under Sections 254-3 and 254(3) of the Commercial Code. Consider, however, to whom each of these directors is likely to feel most duty-bound.

In addition to their duties of care and loyalty to their companies, directors have specific duties under Commercial Code Section 264 to avoid competition and under Section 265 to refrain from self-dealing. Recall the various transactions between Newco and each of A.Co and J.Co called for in the P.C. Agreements—might any director feel pressured to violate either the Section 264 prohibition against competition or the Section 265 requirement of obtaining board approval to "make any transaction with the stock company on his or her own behalf or on behalf of a third person"? How should the obligations imposed on directors by the Commercial Code affect their responses to such types of conflicts? Since Newco exists solely for the benefit of A.Co and J.Co, should the duties imposed under the three articles on corporate directors in general be made applicable to Newco's directors?

Several of these issues arise in the following case, concerning Section 265(1) self-dealing. Note that the second sentence of Section 265(1), which deals with indirect benefits, was added to the Code in the 1981 amendments (as a codification of the holding in this case) and was therefore not relevant to the court's analysis. Would that sentence have made any difference?

*Nippon Bikutā K.K. v. San'ei Denki K.K.**
22 Minshū 3511
(Sup. Ct., G.B., Dec. 25, 1968)

REFERENCES:

Commercial Code, §265

Civil Code, §108

FACTS:

Non-party Shirō Fukao had operated a retail electrical appliance store as a sole proprietorship in his wife's name. In 1959, he incorporated the enterprise as San'ei Denki K.K., the defendant. He was immediately appointed to the office of representative director.

Nippon Bikutā K.K. [Japan Victor Co., or JVC], plaintiff, had supplied electrical goods to the Fukao proprietorship prior to the establishment of San'ei Denki. At the time San'ei Denki had been formed, Fukao owed Nippon Bikutā ¥2,654,008 for credit purchases of merchandise. San'ei Denki listed this debt as a liability in its report for its first fiscal year. At no time, however, did its board of directors adopt a resolution approving the assumption of Fukao's liabilities to Nippon Bikutā.

Nippon Bikutā continued to supply electrical goods to San'ei Denki. In April 1961, Fukao, representing San'ei Denki, confirmed that the company owed to Nippon Bikutā the debt that San'ei Denki had assumed and more than ¥4,079,612, the sum of credit that had been extended to the Fukao proprietorship and to San'ei Denki since its incorporation. By March 20, 1965, as a result of further payment and credit transactions, this total figure had been reduced to ¥3,205,840. Nippon Bikutā requested full payment of this amount, San'ei Denki refused, and Nippon Bikutā brought suit.

The Nagoya District Court held in full for Nippon Bikutā.

San'ei Denki appealed, arguing that it had not assumed Fukao's liabilities. Further, it could not have assumed the debt because doing so would have required the approval of its board of directors, which had not occurred. Absent action by the board and absent consideration, asserted San'ei Denki, the assumption of Fukao's liabilities was invalid.

Nippon Bikutā argued that: (1) the approval of each of the directors had in fact been obtained; (2) even absent formal board approval of assumption of the debt of the Fukao proprietorship, San'ei Denki had continued transactions with Nippon Bikutā, had gradually paid a portion of Fukao's liabilities, and thus had implicitly approved the assumption of all of Fukao's liabilities; (3) San'ei Denki was in essence Fukao's personal corporation and thus there was no need for approval by the board of directors; and (4) Nippon Bikutā, believing that there had been a valid

*Translation adapted from Misao Tatsata & Richard O. Kummert, *Cases and Materials on Japanese and U.S. Business Corporation Law*, Vol. II (Temp. Ed. 1994), at 8-100 to 8-103. Reprinted by permission.

assumption of Fukao's liabilities, had continued transactions with San'ei Denki in good faith and had obtained the ratification of representative director Fukao, and San'ei Denki should not be permitted to escape responsibility for the proprietorship's debts because such a ruling would sacrifice transactional security and the interests of bona fide third parties.

The Nagoya High Court found that there had been no approval by San'ei Denki's board of directors and held that "transactions lacking the approval of the board of directors are invalid in proportion to their lack of authority." The court thus granted Nippon Bikutā's claim only to the extent that debts actually assumed by San'ei Denki itself (and not including amounts owed by Fukao individually) exceeded payments to Nippon Bikutā, a sum of ¥551,832.

JUDGMENT:

The decision below is vacated except for the payment order of ¥551,832. In addition, San'ei Denki shall pay ¥2,654,008 to Nippon Bikutā.

REASONS:

Commercial Code §265 attempts to take account of the interests of individual directors and to prevent the unauthorized execution of acts disadvantageous to the company in situations where the interests of a director and the company are in conflict. We hold that so-called Section 265 transactions include not only those which directly exhibit a conflict of interest between the director and the company, but also those that are done for the benefit of a director and that cause a disadvantage to the company. Included in the latter category are transactions whereby an individual director, while representing the company, effects a debt assumption with a creditor with regard to his personal debts. (We should add that our decision of March 24, 1964, Sup. Ct., P.B., 72 *Saibanshū* 619, has been altered by this interpretation and that our decision of October 21, 1958, P.B., 34 *Saibanshū* 303, is not relevant to the instant case.)

When a director effects such an action without approval of the board of directors, that action should be held invalid. Section 265 states that where the board of directors' approval is subsequently obtained, Civil Code §108 does not apply. This implies that actions that do not obtain the approval of the board, like acts in contravention of §108, are invalid.

With regard to a transaction between a director and the company that presents a direct conflict of interest, the fact that the company can insist on the invalidity of that action vis-à-vis the director, due to his not having received the approval of the board, is justifiable as stated above. However, with regard to other transactions (*i.e.*, those between a third party and a director representing the company that are for the benefit of the director himself), in the interest of transactional security it is necessary to protect bona fide third parties. It is, therefore, appropriate to hold that a company can insist on the invalidity of such a transaction against a third party only by pleading and proving that, in addition to lack of approval by its board of directors, the third party was acting in bad faith (*i.e.*, knew that board approval had not been obtained).

With regard to Fukao's liabilities to Nippon Bikutā, Fukao himself, as a director of San'ei Denki, represented San'ei Denki and arranged its assumption of his liabilities. This action falls within the type of transactions covered by §265 because it was made with a third party entirely external to the corporation and was made for the director's personal benefit, and the director effected the action while representing his company. Therefore, unless San'ei Denki were to plead and prove that Nippon Bikutā had been acting in bad faith (*i.e.*, knew that the approval of the board of directors had not been obtained), we would have to hold that San'ei Denki cannot assert the invalidity of that transaction against Nippon Bikutā.

The decision below, in applying §265 to the issue of whether San'ei Denki had assumed the liabilities of Fukao, held that no such assumption had taken place because the approval of the board of directors had not been obtained. This facile rejection by the court below of the corresponding portion of Nippon Bikutā's claim is contrary to law, and the argument for appeal on this point is meritorious. [W]e must quash the portion of the decision below holding against the claim of Nippon Bikutā.

As stated above, it is clear that the instant assumption of liabilities was between a third party outside the company and a director representing the company, and that the transaction was on his own behalf. With regard to the nonexistence of a resolution by the board of directors of San'ei Denki regarding the subject transaction, no claim was made nor evidence provided that Nippon Bikutā was acting in bad faith. Accordingly, San'ei Denki cannot assert against Nippon Bikutā the invalidity of the transaction. For that reason, the instant lawsuit by Nippon Bikutā seeking payment of the liabilities of Fukao assumed by San'ei Denki is proper based on the facts found in the decision below. * * * [Judgment was unanimous, but several Justices wrote supplementary opinions.]

PART C: Distinct Issues of Japanese Corporate Law

Introduction

This section examines three aspects of Japanese corporate law that differ significantly from corporate law in the United States. First is the Commercial Register, the public document in which companies must register information such as their business objectives, their capital contributions, and the identity of persons with authority to bind the company. The existence of the Commercial Register raises the important issue of who can be charged with knowledge of its contents.

We next consider the liability of directors to third parties with whom their corporations transact business. The Commercial Code provision imposing this liability has been an important weapon for creditors of shell corporations formed by individuals seeking to protect their personal assets.

The third and final issue is the doctrine of disregard of the corporate entity.

This doctrine is the Japanese analogue to the concept of "piercing the corporate veil" under U.S. corporate law, but differs in important respects.

All three provide possible avenues for creditors to reach the assets of corporations or, in some cases, the assets of directors or shareholders. Cases involving at least one of these issues make up the bulk of all reported corporate law cases in Japan. The prevalence of these cases can to some extent be attributed to the prevalence in Japan of small thinly capitalized corporations. Consider whether creditors might use these strategies with respect to the company established in the P.C., Newco, which is also a rather thinly capitalized company, and the implications of these doctrines for A.Co, J.Co, and the directors and officers of Newco.

I. Registry System

MICHIYO HAMADA, THE RELATIONSHIP BETWEEN THE COMMERCIAL REGISTRATION SYSTEM AND PROVISIONS THAT PROTECT RELIANCE ON EXTERNAL APPEARANCES IN JAPAN*

4 Journal of Comparative Corporate Law & Securities Regulation 143
143-145 (1982)

Japanese law requires that certain matters concerning corporations be entered in the Commercial Register. One of these items of information is the name of the company's representative director. Similarly, the resignation of this person, or the lapse of his authority to represent the company, must also be registered. At the same time, however, the law permits a third party who is unaware of the registered information to rely on the mere external appearance of representative authority. These two threads have given rise to numerous liability problems. In 1974, the Japanese Supreme Court addressed these, but, in turn, created new controversies. * * *

1. Decision of the Japanese Supreme Court

The liability issue arose out of the following fact situation.[19] A representative director A of defendant corporation Y was made to resign and the resignation was entered in the Commercial Register. At some time later, A drew a promissory note as representative director of Y on B. B in turn transferred the note to plaintiff X. X brought action against [Y] to demand payment on the note.

The Court of Appeals found for X. The Supreme Court, however, found differently:

---

*From Michiyo Hamada, "The Relationship Between the Commercial Registration System and Provisions That Protect Reliance on External Appearances in Japan," 4 *Journal of Comparative Corporate Law & Securities Regulation* 143 (© 1982, Elsevier Science Publishers B.V.), at 143-145. Reprinted by permission.

> [S]ince resignation of a representative director of a stock corporation and lapse of authority to represent the corporation are matters that must be registered pursuant to Articles 188 and 15 of the Commercial Code * * *, only Article 12 of the Code should be applied to resolve this case. Therefore, subsequent to registration, the facts of the resignation and the lapse of authority can be invoked against a third party who did not know of these facts, provided that there was not a reasonable cause for his ignorance of the registered facts. It should be understood that Civil Code Article 112 is not applicable to this case.

Reversing the Court of Appeals, the Supreme Court instructed the trial court to try the issue of reasonable cause.

2. Constructive notice theory

Commercial Code, Article 12, provides:

> Matters required to be registered cannot be set up against a bona fide third person until the registration and public notice thereof will have been duly effected; even after the registration and public notice of such matters will have been effected, they cannot be set up against a third person who for any reasonable cause has been unaware of them.

The prevailing scholarly interpretation of the article rests upon the so-called constructive notice theory, which presumes that a third person has notice of registered information. One of the most celebrated textbooks on the subject maintains that the "commercial registration system serves as a means to publicize certain important information and regulate conflicts between merchants and third persons by deeming a third person to have notice of publicly registered matters and by no longer allowing a third person to plead ignorance of such matters." Furthermore, the constructive notice theory construes the phrase "any reasonable cause" very narrowly to mean objective obstacles encountered by a third person when he investigates the Commercial Register, *e.g.*, interference with the mails or traffic, or loss of or stain on the Commercial Register entry itself.

The Supreme Court decision is perfectly consistent with this theoretical framework. Civil Code Article 112 maintains that "lapse of the power of representation cannot be set up against a bona fide third person, unless such third person was unaware of such fact through negligence," thus requiring proof of the third person's ignorance of the lapse of representative authority. If Commercial Code Article 12 presumes knowledge of the lapse of authority as the constructive notice theory understands, Civil Code Article 112 cannot be applicable as long as Commercial Code Article 12 covers the situation.

The practical result of the court's decision is not desirable, however. In order to safeguard his self-interest, a third party will need to investigate the Commercial Register every time he enters into a commercial transaction with a merchant. Thus, he will no longer be able to rely on the fact that a particular person was recently elected to be a representative director of the corporation because that person may have resigned and that fact may have been entered in the Commercial Register. This imposes an excessive burden on the third person and unnecessarily threatens the security and efficiency of the underlying transactions. The question then arises: Is the court's decision desirable? Does it appropriately address the potential conflicts of interest between the merchant and the third person?

Most scholars who have commented on the decision have questioned the appropriateness of its result and have formulated their own interpretations of the law designed to protect the bona fide third person. The most widely supported of these formulations relies on an expansive interpretation of Article 262 of the Commercial Code, which states:

> A company shall be liable to a bona fide third person for any act done by a director *invested with any title* such as president, vice-president, chief director or managing director from which it may be assumed that he has authority to represent the company even in cases where such person has no power of representation. [emphasis added].

In this formulation, the phrase "invested with any title" is construed broadly to encompass the situation in which the company was aware of the unauthorized use of the title but did not complain about it. Had the Supreme Court used this formulation, it might have found in favor of the third party, X.

In any case, while courts and scholars agree that Article 262 is applicable notwithstanding Article 12, they place themselves in an analytic bind. Since their constructive notice interpretation of Article 12 assumes that a person who is able to investigate the Commercial Register has notice of what is in it, there is no room for application of Article 262, which requires proof that the person was ignorant of the information. Article 262 was enacted into law in 1938, when Article 12 was already on the books. Scholars maintain that the former supersedes the latter and they base this opinion on either of the following two theories: (1) Article 262 is an exception to Article 12, or (2) reliance on external appearance of authority constitutes a "reasonable cause" under Article 12. Neither theory is entirely satisfactory.

With respect to the first, or so-called exception theory, the question arises: Since both Articles 262 and 112 are intended to protect reliance on the external appearance of authority, why is not Article 112 also considered an exception to Article 12? Even more troublesome is the fact that if the exception theory does extend to Article 112, and subsequently to every other provision that protects the reliance on external appearances, the question arises: What is the purpose for having Article 12 at all?

With respect to the second, or so-called external appearance theory, the question arises: Why does not Article 112 also fall within the "any reasonable cause" defense of Article 12? * * *

Questions and Discussion Points

1. *Purpose of the Commercial Register system*: In the excerpt above, Hamada criticizes the Supreme Court's constructive notice theory with regard to Section 12 of the Commercial Code. She also describes the competing theory that Section 262 of the Commercial Code permits one engaged in a commercial transaction some degree of reliance on external appearances. On the one hand, the constructive notice theory does seem to burden commercial transactions with a duty to inspect the Commercial Register. On the other, if one permits parties the latitude reasonably to rely on external appearances, one undermines much of the rationale for having a Commercial Register. How should this dilemma be resolved?

2. *Actual use of the Commercial Register*: The constructive notice concept established under Japanese law has to some extent found expression in Japanese business practice. Registry information is available to the public at local offices under the Ministry of Justice. Before entering into transactions in which matters covered by registry information are a concern, parties sometimes obtain relevant information themselves or hire judicial scriveners (*shihō shoshi*) to do so for them. In more complex transactions, lawyers (*bengoshi*) sometimes perform this function in connection with the issuance of opinion letters.

II. Directors' Duties to Third Parties

In Part B of this chapter we discussed the Commercial Code duties of loyalty and care that directors of Japanese companies have to their companies. Section 266-3 of the Commercial Code also imposes on directors of Japanese companies a duty to third parties.

ROBERT DZIUBLA, ENFORCING CORPORATE RESPONSIBILITY: JAPANESE CORPORATE DIRECTORS' LIABILITY TO THIRD PARTIES FOR FAILURE TO SUPERVISE*

18 Law in Japan 55
57-71 (1986)

1. Representative Directors

[The] seminal case concerning a director's liability to third parties is *Izuo Kōzai K.K. v. Mutō*.[20] In that case, [defendant] Mutō * * * had three occupations (patent attorney, veterinarian, and member of the prefectural assembly) when he was asked to become the president and representative director of Kikusui Kōgyō K.K., a manufacturing concern that had fallen on hard times. Although he had no

*From Robert Dziubla, "Enforcing Corporate Responsibility: Japanese Corporate Directors' Liability to Third Parties for Failure to Supervise," 18 *Law in Japan: An Annual* 55 (1986), at 57-71. Reprinted by permission.

experience with and little interest in the products made by Kikusui, Mutō agreed at the end of November 1951 to assume the offices of president and representative director. This assumption of office was registered on February 12, 1952. Mutō also retained his three other jobs, and during the time when the facts at issue were occurring he was on a trip abroad.

The business operations of Kikusui were run virtually single-handedly by the senior managing representative director (*senmu daihyō torishimariyaku*), Sakitarō Kōketsu. Because Mutō had only enough time to drop by the company two or three times per week at most, he entrusted his seal to Kōketsu and had Kōketsu promise verbally to get Mutō's approval for the issuance of checks and notes over ¥100,000 issued in Mutō's name. Kōketsu, however, did not keep his promise, and that is how the instant case arose.

Kōketsu, as a representative director of Kikusui, ordered sixteen tons of steel materials from the plaintiff, Izuo Kōzai K.K. * * * , for a total price of ¥720,000. In payment for this steel, Kōketsu issued a promissory note under Mutō's name as the president and a director of Kikusui. Izuo Kōzai duly presented the note for payment, but Kikusui refused payment on the grounds that the transaction had been cancelled. Izuo filed the instant suit for damages on the grounds that Mutō and Kōketsu, acting together, had deceived Izuo Kōzai and swindled it out of the steel. Kōketsu settled and the suit proceeded against Mutō alone.[21]

The Osaka District Court found that although Mutō and Kōketsu had not acted together to perpetrate an unlawful act (*fuhō kōi*), Mutō was liable under article 266-3(1) because he grossly neglected his duty to supervise Kōketsu and because he neglected his duty of care (*chūi gimu*) as a usual honest director.[22] The Osaka High Court dismissed Mutō's *kōso* [first] appeal.

In his reasons for the *jōkoku* [second] appeal,[23] Mutō argued that the lower courts had ignored the fact that he was a representative director for less than a month and a half: Mutō's assumption of office was registered on February 12, 1952, and he gave his notice of resignation on March 16, thereafter severing all ties with Kikusui. The resignation, however, was not registered by the company until May 10, and it was during this time that Kōketsu issued the promissory note (with a due date of May 2) on March 4.

Mutō also argued that he was diligent in the performance of his duties because even though he entrusted both his personal seal and his seal as president of Kikusui to Kōketsu, Mutō continually asked Kōketsu if any notes were being issued and Kōketsu denied any issuance, including that of the instant note. Thus, Mutō was diligent and used his best efforts to supervise Kōketsu who had the power as a representative director to act independently on behalf of Kikusui. In conclusion, Mutō claimed that he was stabbed in the back by Kōketsu.

The Supreme Court, in an eleven-to-four Grand Bench decision, rejected the *jōkoku* appeal in a wide-ranging and somewhat contradictory opinion that considered both the legislature's expansion of directors' liability under article 266-3 and the issue of whether a third party has to show that a director's bad faith or gross negligence was directed at the third party. With regard to the former point, the

Court first remarked that a director, as a mandatory, has both the duty of diligence of a conscientious manager (*zenryō na kanrisha no chūi gimu*) under Commercial Code article 254(3) and Civil Code article 644, and the duty of loyalty (*chūjitsu gimu*) under Commercial Code article [254-3]. The Court then said that although the director must obey these duties by reason of his relationship to the company with regard to the performance of his own tasks, he has "no such relationship to a third party, and even though a third party is harmed by a director's violation of these duties, the director has no duty *per se* to pay damages."[24]

The Court, however, then found that in light of the important role of stock corporations in the economy and the need for corporations to be able to rely on the directors' performance of their duties:

> From the standpoint of protecting third parties, the law provides that when a third party suffers harm because a director has violated his duties due to wrongful intent or gross negligence, so long as a proper causal relationship exists between the director's act of neglecting his duties and the harm to the third party—without regard to whether it is a situation where the result of the harm to the company, because of this negligence, produces in turn a harm to a third party or whether it is a situation where a third party suffers harm directly—the said director should bear the responsibility of paying damages directly to the third party.[25]

In short, if proper causation exists, an injured third party can collect directly from the offending director.

The Court based this reasoning on the legislature's expansion of directors' liability. While an earlier version of article 266-3(1) had stated that directors were responsible for damage caused by contravention of the law or the corporate charter, the amendment "expanded the old provision to embrace actions in contravention of a director's duties to his company."[26] Thus, concluded the Court, "[i]f the third party who has been injured because of the director's negligence in his duties pleads and proves only the director's wrongful intent or gross negligence, the third party need not go so far as to plead and prove intent or negligence with regard to the damages against himself."[27]

Turning to the issue of the allocation of duties when there are two representative directors, the Court said that in such a situation one representative director has no duty to supervise the other representative director unless the corporate charter so provides. Because a representative director is the representative of the company externally, however, and is responsible for the performance of all work internally, he must pay broad attention to the entire spectrum of the company's business. Thus, concluded the Court:

> [W]hen a representative director completely entrusts all of the corporate duties to the other representative director and to other people and it comes about that he takes no care whatsoever in the performance of his duties and ultimately shuts his eyes to the

> unlawful actions or neglect of duty by those other people, we find that the representative director himself also has neglected his duties because of wrongful intent or gross negligence.[28]

Applying this reasoning to the instant case, the Court affirmed the findings of the court below that Mutō breached his duty "to prevent in advance the gross negligence or unlawful actions of the other representative director," and that as a result of this breach Izuo Kōzai was damaged. An important fact that helped the Court reach this conclusion was that Mutō previously had been informed by a third party that Kōketsu was dishonoring other promissory notes and for that very reason Mutō eventually decided to resign as the representative director. * * *

Less than a year later the Supreme Court clarified *Izuo Kōzai* in a case involving article 30-3 of the Limited Corporations Act (*Yūgengaishahō*), which is an identical counterpart to article 266-3 of the Commercial Code. In *Maruyoshi Kōzai K.K. v. Satō*,[29] the non-party Masanori Hosoya was the sole proprietor of a welding supplies limited corporation. In order to increase the external confidence in the company, Hosoya persuaded the defendant Satō to become a dummy director in the company. Upon assuming office, Satō promptly entrusted all real power in the company to Hosoya, who ran the company at his sole discretion. Satō did not participate in the management of the company at all. [When the limited corporation went bankrupt, Maruyoshi Kōzai K.K. lost more than ¥4 million because of credit sales to the limited corporation.] The plaintiff filed suit against Satō claiming that Hosoya managed the welding supplies company so poorly that it went bankrupt and that Satō had grossly neglected his duties to the company by entrusting his seal as representative director to Hosoya and by neglecting his duty to supervise Hosoya. The Tokyo District Court ruled in favor of the plaintiff,[30] but the Tokyo High Court reversed.[31]

The plaintiff filed a *jōkoku* appeal which the Supreme Court dismissed because of insufficient proximate cause between the defendant's conduct and the plaintiff's loss. The Court first cited its conclusion in *Izuo Kōzai* with approval but then clarified the need for proximate cause:

> In order for this liability [of a representative director] to arise, however, * * * a proper causal relationship between the director's act of neglecting his duties and the third party's injury must exist; and even if the third party is damaged in any case, unless the third party pleads and proves facts that can confirm the existence of this proper causal relationship, he clearly cannot claim compensation for his damages.[32]

Because the Court found that a proper causal relationship did not exist, the appeal was dismissed.

The Supreme Court relied heavily on the findings and analysis of the Tokyo High Court in reaching this conclusion, and it is the latter court's comments that are most instructive. That court found that although Hosoya did not conduct a credit check on his usual customers and did not require the posting of security in credit sale transactions, he did run a credit check through a bank at the start of each new transaction. Moreover, although the company's monthly sales were about ¥13 million and although its total debts were ¥12 to 13 million at the time of the announcement of insolvency, by the time of the announcement of bankruptcy, the company had recovered about ¥2 million of the total credit sales of ¥3 million.

The court thus concluded that:

> Although we can find that there was an expectation of recovering several hundreds of thousands of yen, there is no material at all that shows whether there was any kind of important connection between, on the one hand, the two points that the usual credit checks were insufficient and that security was not posted, and, on the other hand, the fact, which we can find from the testimony, that the company's difficulty in collecting money was the reason for the bankruptcy. With regard to the issue of security, whether the company should have had the buyers post security is a business matter that should be decided based on various factors such as the scope of the transaction, the credit rating of the customers, and the course of dealing; there is no reason why the buyers should always have to post security because the transaction is a credit sale.[33]

Therefore, said the court, there was an insufficient causal relationship between the plaintiff's damages and the defendant's admitted neglect of his duties. * * *

2. Regular Directors

a. Supreme Court Precedent

* * * In * * * *[Kobayashi] v. Hashimoto*,[34] Asano individually ran an electrical appliance store. In order to establish an electrical appliance repair service, Asano (a defendant in the court of first instance) joined forces with Hashimoto and Matsuzaki (defendants, *kōso* appellants, *jōkoku* appellants), who already were operating such a service. These three men recruited Horikō (defendant, *kōso* appellant) and established Maruzen K.K. in 1967. Of the ¥1,000,000 in capitalization, Asano contributed ¥950,000 and Horikō ¥50,000. Asano became the representative director, Hashimoto and Matsuzaki became regular directors, and Horikō became the auditor.

Maruzen's operations were divided into a sales section and a repair section. Hashimoto and Matsuzaki devoted themselves full-time to the affairs of the repair section, while entrusting the entire management of the company to Asano. From the start Asano convened neither shareholders' meetings nor board of directors' meetings; he handled corporate matters at his sole discretion, and he did not have Horikō audit the company books. At first Maruzen's business involved only the repair of electrical appliances, but Asano, without conferring with the other directors, decided to expand into automobile repairs. To obtain the capital necessary for that expansion, Asano issued a promissory note for ¥900,000. This note came into the plaintiff's possession by way of endorsement. Maruzen went bankrupt before paying this note, and the plaintiff filed suit under article 266-3(1) against Asano as the representative director, against Hashimoto and Matsuzaki as directors who failed to supervise Asano, and against Horikō for negligence in auditing the company. The plaintiff alleged that these failures caused Maruzen's bankruptcy and hence the plaintiff's inability to collect on the note.

The court of first instance found all of the defendants jointly liable to the plaintiff,[35] and Hashimoto, Matsuzaki and Horikō filed *kōso* appeals. The court of second instance, citing *Izuo Kōzai*, dismissed the appeal by the two directors on the grounds that if they had actively performed their duties, they could have prevented Asano's reckless issuance of the instant note.[36] The court, however, quashed the judgment against Horikō because no proper causal relationship existed between Horikō's alleged negligence and the plaintiff's loss: there were no corporate books for Horikō to audit because of the directors' failure to keep any records or books and, therefore, *a fortiori* there could be no negligence in auditing. Hashimoto and Matsuzaki filed *jōkoku* appeals arguing that they could have neither foreseen nor prevented the plaintiff's loss and that no proper causal relationship existed between their failure to oversee Asano and the issuance of the instant note.

The Supreme Court rejected the *jōkoku* appeal in a brief and pithy unanimous opinion:

> It is appropriate for us to find that because the board of directors of a corporation is in the position of supervising the administration of the company, the directors who constitute the board, with regard to their company, should not stop at supervising only the matters raised before the board. They should in general supervise the representative director's performance of his duties, and if the necessity arises they should convene the board themselves or demand that the board be convened. They have a duty to function through the board so as to fulfill the duties of their office properly.[37]

The decision laid to rest a long-standing split among the lower courts and among scholars as to whether directors had a duty to supervise only matters raised before the board, the so-called duty of passive supervision (*judōteki kanshi gimu*), or whether their duties extended to matters not raised before the board, the so-called duty of active supervision (*nōdōteki kanshi gimu*). Under the rule adopted in [*Kobayashi*], directors have both an active and a passive duty of supervision, which includes the duty to supervise the representative director's performance of his duties. And their means of control is to convene the board of directors. * * *

b. Subsequent Lower Court Cases

Notwithstanding the Supreme Court's clear directive, lower court cases after these two leading Supreme Court cases have shown a strong tendency to absolve both full-time and dummy regular directors of liability under article 266-3(1). The most famous of these cases and the one most frequently cited by the district courts is the Osaka High Court decision in *K.K. Kōfuku Sōgō Ginkō v. Ōtani.*[38]

In *Ōtani*, the defendant was the head of the production department (*seizōbuchō*) of Yamato K.K., which was a "one-man" company under the exclusive control of Kumagi from the time of its founding until its bankruptcy. The defendant agreed, at the request of Kumagi, who was the representative director and, presumably, president of Yamato, to become a director of the company so as to round out the number of directors.[39] That is, he became a full-time regular director. The defendant Ōtani had never graduated from high school, and before he joined Yamato he had helped his wife at a mah-jongg parlor for about ten years. He had no experience concerning bank financing, current accounts, or note and check transactions. The defendant's salary did not increase after he became a director, and he and the rest of the employees passively followed the orders of Kumagi and of Kasui, who was the most senior employee in the company, the third director of the corporation, and a defendant in the court of first instance. Not surprisingly, there were no meetings of the board of directors, no conferences with Kumagi or Kasui, and no reports or account books concerning the financial condition of Yamato.

During the time that the defendant Ōtani was a director, Kumagi persuaded the plaintiff bank to discount a deficient promissory note issued by Yamato by doctoring the company books and by concealing its pre-bankruptcy financial condition. When Yamato went bankrupt, the plaintiff sued both Ōtani and Kasui[40] under article 266-3(1), and the court of first instance found for the plaintiff. Ōtani appealed, claiming that he did not possess the statutorily required wrongful intent or gross negligence, and the Osaka High Court reversed.

The court first reviewed in detail the defendant's lack of education and financial experience, as well as the autocratic control exercised by Kumagi and Kasui over the defendant and the other employees and the financial skulduggery perpetrated by them. The court then articulated the test that it believed should apply in cases involving regular directors:

> Because a regular director cannot participate in business matters that are not raised before the board, a third party has the duty to prove, with regard to the illegal actions of the representative director or other directors that are not based on resolutions of the board of directors, that: (1) the regular director against whom liability is sought knew of the representative director's or other directors' illegal actions; or (2) he carelessly overlooked the illegal actions even though he could easily have known about them

> without considerable attention * * * and, therefore, (3) despite there having been the possibility of board supervision before the fact, intent, or negligence corresponding to intent (gross negligence), existed with regard to the regular director's not having taken the necessary steps to exercise his right of supervision.[41]

Applying this test to the facts at bar, the court, acknowledging that Ōtani might have been slightly negligent, found no gross negligence.

Rather, suggested the court, the plaintiff's loss resulted from a combination of the plaintiff's own conference with Kumagi, by which the plaintiff came to believe that the company's affairs were in order, and Kumagi's autocratic control of the company, which would have effectively prevented any action by Ōtani, who was outvoted on the board by Kumagi and Kasui. Thus, the court concluded that Ōtani had no liability to the plaintiff.

Questions and Discussion Points

Recall the situation of Newco and its directors sent from A.Co and J.Co. Given the joint venture relationship between A.Co and J.Co, how likely is it that all of the directors will take an active role in overseeing the affairs of Newco? How likely is it that when A.Co and J.Co agree upon courses of action for Newco that technically require approval of Newco's board of directors, the board will always in fact be convened to cast the necessary votes? What about, as discussed in the previous section, directors who compromise the interests of Newco in order to further those of A.Co or J.Co? Might directors of Newco who are inattentive to the company's affairs or who compromise Newco's interests in promoting those of A.Co or J.Co be exposing themselves to liability to any third-party creditors of Newco?

III. Disregard of the Corporate Entity

In Japan, as in the United States, there are cases in which courts have "pierced the corporate veil" and disregarded the formal existence of a corporation when it has been judged that the corporate form has been used for improper purposes. In addition, in Japan there are specific Code provisions providing for the dissolution of entities that have been set up for the clear purpose of defrauding creditors.[42]

Consider contract or tort creditors of Newco. Should such creditors be able to reach the assets of A.Co and J.Co directly if those of Newco are not sufficient to satisfy a claim? Should their ability to do so be greater if A.Co and J.Co have, between themselves, not operated Newco according to all Commercial Code requirements, *e.g.*, if they have implemented decisions regarding Newco without the formal authority of Newco's board or one of its representative directors? Consider these issues in approaching the cases that follow.

Translation by Yanagida Nomura & Akai

Yamayoshi Shōkai K.K. v. Hoshihara
23 Minshū 511
(Sup. Ct, P.B., Feb. 27, 1969)

REFERENCES:

Commercial Code, § 504

FACTS:

On February 20, 1961, Hoshihara, plaintiff-appellee, rented a building to Yamayoshi Shōkai K.K. (Y.S.), defendant-appellant, whose representative director, Kishi, ran an electronics store at the site. Five years later, Hoshihara requested termination of the rental agreement and, on February 20, 1966, Kishi submitted to Hoshihara a written consent that he would vacate the premises by August 21st of that year. Kishi signed his own name on the consent and made no reference to Y.S.

When Kishi did not vacate by the agreed date, Hoshihara filed suit. At the recommendation of the court, Hoshihara and Kishi reached a compromise (*wakai*, *see* Chapter 11, Part D) on March 4, 1967, the essence of which was that Kishi was to vacate the building by January 31, 1968. Following the compromise, however, Kishi contended that Y.S. was renting the store space, that he had already vacated the 4-1/2 *tatami* mat space he had been using on an individual basis, and that there was no obligation on the part of Y.S. to vacate the portion it was using. Hoshihara filed suit once more, this time against Y.S., again seeking the vacation of the premises.

Hoshihara argued that Y.S. was the lessee, that both the February 20, 1966, consent agreement and the compromise agreement were made by Kishi as the representative of Y.S., and that Y.S. was thus the party that had agreed to terminate the lease and vacate the premises. Kishi alleged that he had signed both documents in his individual capacity and noted that in executing the compromise agreement Hoshihara had been represented by two lawyers (Kishi had acted on his own behalf). Both the Tokyo District Court and High Court found in favor of Hoshihara. Among the reasons given by the District Court for its decision was that:

> At the time of the foregoing compromise agreement, the fact that the name of the lessee of the store set forth in the lease contract was Y.S. was not considered by the parties. Kishi himself, the representative director of Y.S., did not consciously distinguish between Kishi the individual and Kishi the representative director of Y.S., and he did not exclude his qualification as the latter when he agreed to the compromise.

The High Court, in affirming the decision, noted that the terms of the compromise agreement, which included penalty provisions if Kishi did not vacate by the agreed date and "vacation compensation" to him if he did, simply did not make sense unless Y.S. were also taken to be bound by the obligation to vacate.

JUDGMENT:

The appeal is dismissed.

REASONS:

It is axiomatic that in the case of a legal entity, the juristic person and its members have separate personalities under the law. This holds even where there is only one member of the legal entity. It must also be understood, though, that the granting of juristic status to an association is a matter of legislative policy, resulting from the assessment that there is merit in recognizing such association. Only after determining that an association is worthy of recognition as a holder of rights is the association granted, by various legal techniques, juristic status. Accordingly, in instances where the juristic status granted to an association operates as nothing more than an utter shell, or when it is abused so as to avoid application of the law, then the recognition of juristic status should not be allowed, in light of the original intent in awarding juristic status. In connection with this point, in the case of corporations we must be especially cognizant of the circumstances next described.

Upon meeting certain legal requirements, it is easy to establish a corporation under the law. Moreover, incorporation is possible even for so-called one-man corporations. Thus, it sometimes happens that a corporate form is nothing more than a straw man. In such a case, the corporation is the individual, and the individual is the corporation; and the essence of the corporation is identical with an individual business enterprise. In such a situation, it is necessary to protect parties contracting with the corporation who may not be able to determine whether a transaction is being made with the corporation or with the individual. Therefore, we hold that when situations arise where it is necessary to grasp the individual underlying the legal entity, even if transactions have been undertaken in the name of the corporation, the other party may disregard the juristic status of the corporation and deem the transaction to have been made with the underlying individual, in order to pursue the individual's responsibility. Furthermore, even if acts are undertaken by a corporation in the name of an individual, the other party, without having to rely upon Section 504 of the Commercial Code, may treat such acts as those of the corporation. In our opinion, if acts are not interpreted in this fashion, it would be possible for an individual to utilize a corporate form to impose unwarranted injuries upon the interests of other parties.

In the instant case, the court below * * * found the following facts. * * * Y.S. was set up for the purpose of reducing the tax burden on the "Electronics Store" that Kishi had been operating. Kishi himself was the representative director of Y.S., and in essence Y.S. was nothing more than the individual enterprise operated by Kishi. Hoshihara even believed that he was renting the space to Kishi's "Electronics Store." * * *

Considering the findings of fact in light of the doctrine set forth above, even though Y.S. had obtained juristic status, Hoshihara could claim rent from Kishi for the store and was able to file a lawsuit against Kishi the individual for vacation of the store because the leasing entity was, in essence, nothing other than Kishi, as the individual underlying the corporation Y.S. We must evaluate the *res judicata* effect of the judgment separately, however. Even though it was adjudged that Kishi must vacate the store, the effect of that judgment does not extend to the appellant corporation. While it is true that the compromise agreement before the court was made between Hoshihara and Kishi in his own name, Kishi's act may be interpreted as that of Y.S. Thus, it is proper to say that Y.S. should have vacated the store by January 31, 1968.

[T]his Court unanimously renders its decision as stated in the judgment [and pursuant to Section 401 of the Code of Civil Procedure, which allows a court to dismiss a *jōkoku* appeal without hearing oral arguments if it considers the appeal to be without merit after having reviewed the briefs of the parties].

MISAO TATSUTA, A PARENT CORPORATION'S LIABILITY FOR ITS SUBSIDIARY'S OBLIGATIONS*

Cases and Materials on Japanese and U.S. Business Corporation Law, Vol. 1, pg. 3-11 3-11 to 3-14 (1994)

CASE A:

Petition for provisional disposition of payment of back wages, Sendai Dist. Ct., First Civil Division, decision of March 26, 1967, aff'd, 588 *Hanrei Jihō* 38.

CASE B:

Petition to suspend execution of a provisional attachment, Sendai Dist. Ct., First Civil Division, decision of March 26, 1967, dis'd, 588 *Hanrei Jihō* 52.

FACTS:

[One-hundred eleven employees (the Employees) of a steel frame processing company, Subsidiary K.K., a wholly-owned subsidiary of a steel frame construction company, Parent K.K., were dismissed by Subsidiary with back wages left unpaid. The Employees brought two actions.

The first action was against Subsidiary for provisional attachment of specified property on Subsidiary's work site. The second action, Case A above, was against Parent and claimed that, based on the doctrine of disregard of the corporate entity, Parent should be held liable for the back wages owed by Subsidiary.

In the first action, the Employees obtained a favorable ruling, but it turned out that the subject property was actually owned by Parent. This led Parent to bring a third-party action against the Employees in which it challenged the validity of its property being attached through a proceeding in which Subsidiary was the named respondent.

For procedural reasons, the foregoing third-party action brought by Parent

*Adapted from Misao Tatsuta, "Jūzoku kaisha no chingin saimu ni kansuru shihai kaisha no sekinin" ("A Parent Corporation's Liability for Its Subsidiary's Obligations"), 602 *Hanrei Jihō* 138 (1970), translated in Misao Tatsuta & Richard O. Kummert, *Cases and Materials on Japanese and U.S. Business Corporation Law*, Vol. 1 (Temp. Ed. 1994), at 3-11 to 3-14. Reprinted by permission.

would not prohibit the Employees from disposing of the attached property. Parent thus brought a further action against the Employees, Case B above, in which it sought suspension of execution of the provisional attachment pending Parent's challenge to the validity of that attachment.]

The issues common to Cases A and B were (i) whether obligations of a subsidiary could be asserted against its parent under the doctrine of disregard of the corporate entity; and (ii) whether there was sufficient unity (*ittaisei*) between Parent and Subsidiary to permit application of the doctrine in this case.

The following facts were not disputed between the parties:

Parent acquired all of Subsidiary's shares in May 1964. From that time forward, Subsidiary was a wholly-owned subsidiary of Parent. Parent's * * * representative and senior managing director served concurrently as Subsidiary's representative director. Employees of companies affiliated with Parent were directors of Subsidiary. Moreover, employees were transferred from Parent and affiliated companies to Subsidiary as department chiefs, section chiefs and lower-level managers. In the September 1966 reporting period, Parent reported profit realized from ownership of Subsidiary that represented 29.69% of Parent's total investment in Subsidiary. That rate of return was 3.9 times the average return for subsidiaries of major iron and steel corporations. During the same period, Subsidiary's accumulated deficit exceeded ¥50,000,000. Despite this deficit, Parent did not provide financing to Subsidiary after April 1967. Yet Parent was simultaneously receiving lease payments from Subsidiary of ¥2,000,000 per month and concluding contracts that allowed it to demand evacuation of leased factories without formal demand for Subsidiary's performance whenever Subsidiary defaulted. During the March 1967 settlement of accounts, Parent also set off its liability to Subsidiary for construction work against credit it had previously extended to Subsidiary.

The judgment also found from [the evidence] that (i) the General Affairs Department of Parent's head office gave instructions regarding hiring and firing of Subsidiary's section chiefs and managers, and regarding compensation of Subsidiary's employees; (ii) * * * Parent's business information brochures read as if Subsidiary was a [factory directly controlled by Parent]; and (iii) * * * Subsidiary was required to report to Parent whenever Subsidiary purchased items equal to or more than a fixed amount (¥1,000 originally, then ¥10,000).

The Employees asserted that, to minimize risk and facilitate steel construction orders, Parent would construct factories in regions where there was work, operate them by leasing them to subsidiaries, and then abandon the operation in favor of other regions whenever there was no longer any work (the so-called "commercial caravan method"). The Employees asserted that Subsidiary was subjected to this policy and dissolved as a result. The Employees also asserted that Parent had abused the right to dissolve Subsidiary because Parent was attempting to conceal unfair labor practices. The Employees alleged that in 1964 labor unions of Parent's affiliated companies organized a joint conference, with the result that Subsidiary's labor union became Parent's main union. The Employees alleged that Subsidiary's deficit arose because Parent had siphoned off Subsidiary's profits and that Subsidiary's dissolution was designed to lay off all union employees.

SUMMARY OF JUDGMENT:

Case A: All aspects of Subsidiary's management, ranging from decisions concerning personnel, salary and labor relations to decisions concerning Subsidiary's day-to-day production goals and management tactics, were conducted under Parent's consolidated direction. * * *

Active application of the doctrine of disregard of the corporate entity is necessary to achieve justice, the *raison d'etre* of Japanese corporation law and the ultimate objective of the Japanese legal system. At the same time, active application of the doctrine does not deviate from the principle of maintaining viable corporations which runs through the corporation law. In view of these principles, it must be said that Parent's position would sacrifice the interests of creditors of the subsidiary in the name of legal stability and would inflexibly operate to benefit only the interests of its shareholders. * * *

[W]henever corporate shareholders and investee corporations economically and socially form a single enterprise, disregard of the corporate entity of an investee corporation is not repugnant to general corporate principles. Even if the entity of an investee corporation is disregarded, limited liability still exists for individual shareholders of the corporate shareholder. * * *

For the sake of generally recognized social benefits, the law accepts the principle of limited liability even though the interests of creditors of the corporate entity may be sacrificed. The law does not accept, however, the notion that limited liability may be enjoyed in excess (*i.e*, by doubling or tripling of limited liability) by individual shareholders at the expense of creditors. Active approval of excessive use of limited liability risks contradiction of the law's central purpose, which is equity. Therefore, the doctrine of disregard of the corporate entity should more readily be applied to subsidiary corporations owned by parent shareholding companies than to corporations owned by individual shareholders. In the case of parent-subsidiary corporations, the doctrine may be asserted without calling into question the shell-like nature of a corporation itself.

* * * Two factors determine whether, and the extent to which, the corporate entity of a subsidiary corporation should be disregarded: first, the parent corporation's shareholdings must be sufficient for it to possess effective control of the business and assets of the subsidiary, and that control must be exercised by parent-directed management of the corporate activities of the subsidiary; and second, the creditors asserting the doctrine must be in a passive position in relation to the subsidiary (unless the evidence shows that the parent corporation formed or used the subsidiary in order to abuse corporate or general legal principles). Whenever the required control relationship between parent and subsidiary corporations exists, it is reasonable to hold that the obligations of the subsidiary to passive creditors should, without more, be borne by the parent corporation. These results are consistent with the general legal principle: "where there is control, there is liability."

* * * In the current situation, the Employees were passive creditors whose

destinies were controlled by the unilateral wishes of Subsidiary. The obligation to pay the claims for wages asserted by the Employees should be borne by Parent under the doctrine of disregard of the corporate entity * * * [and it is clear that the necessity of provisional protection of the claims exists.]

[*Case B*: The court repeated the substance of its reasoning in Case A and held that, as a result of application of the doctrine of disregard of the corporate entity, Parent was not a third-party that could object to the validity of the provisional attachment of the subject property on Subsidiary's work site. The implication was that Parent would lose its challenge to the validity of the provisional attachment so it should not be granted an order to suspend execution of the attachment.]

Questions and Discussion Points

1. *The Yamayoshi case*: This decision of the Supreme Court ushered the corporate disregard doctrine into Japanese law. Given this, was Yamayoshi relying entirely on a formalistic argument of the sort no longer credible after the decision in this case, or was there any substantive merit to Yamayoshi's position?

2. *The corporate disregard doctrine and the P.C.*: For what purposes did A.Co and J.Co choose to structure their joint venture through Newco? Might a creditor of Newco have an argument that one purpose of establishing Newco was to try to shield the actual parties in interest, A.Co and J.Co, from potential liabilities? The analytical problem is that limited liability is an inherent goal of most business corporations. How does one then draw a line between legitimate and illegitimate recourse to such limitation? If Newco was established for completely legitimate business reasons, but happens to operate for A.Co and J.Co as a shield against certain potential liabilities to third parties, should the doctrine of corporate disregard be applied?

Since the sweeping generalities in terms of which the court expresses its rationale for disregarding the corporate form give little guidance to the applicability of the doctrine, particular attention must be paid to the evidentiary criteria suggested by the court. These criteria may differ from those familiar to observers accustomed to the American rules on "piercing the corporate veil." In the United States, the focus has generally been on factors such as disregard of formalities, commingling of funds, lack of business purpose, thin capitalization, or fraud. These and other similar factors give rise to an inference of bad faith, of an intent to use the corporation as a "mere alter ego." Though the general terms in which U.S. courts express the harm that they seek to mitigate seem similar to the general language used by the Japanese courts, the criteria may differ. As we have seen, in the parent-subsidiary context, Japanese courts may not require evidence of bad faith or lack of business purpose. They may look to objective criteria of corporate control such as percentage of shareholding and appointment of directors.

PART D: Validity of Shareholder Agreements

Introduction

In Part D we consider a corporate law issue of fundamental importance for joint venture corporations: the freedom of the shareholders to agree among themselves to modify rules made applicable by the Commercial Code. This concerns a legal issue we approached as a general matter in Chapter 2 in our overview of Japan's civil law system: the question of how to determine which Code provisions are compulsory and which are discretionary and thus subject to modification by private agreement. After considering this issue generally, we will look at it in the context of shareholder agreements on provisions relating to control of joint venture corporations.

I. Contracting Out of Code Provisions

Joint venturers who create a joint venture corporation to be equally and solely owned by them envision a corporation that will be operated in a manner quite distinct from that in which a large publicly traded corporation is operated. Nevertheless, a joint venture corporation formed as a public corporation (*kabushiki kaisha*) is subject to the same provisions of the Commercial Code as the typical publicly traded corporation. It is the latter type of corporation that appears to be contemplated by many of the *kabushiki kaisha* sections of the Commercial Code. For instance, Section 204 of the Commercial Code makes clear the basic principle that shares should be freely transferable. In the typical joint venture corporation, however, neither party wants the other to be able unilaterally to transfer its shares, and there are several other provisions of the Commercial Code that joint venturers might find cumbersome when applied to their joint venture corporation.

The selection that follows argues that the Japanese approach to these issues follows from the highly formalistic way in which the Civil Code is applied in the context of transactions covered by more specific legislation. Following the selection are two cases in which Japanese courts ruled on efforts to contract out of Code provisions concerning corporate governance.

DONALD P. SWISHER, USE OF SHAREHOLDER AGREEMENTS AND OTHER CONTROL TECHNIQUES IN JAPANESE JOINT VENTURE CORPORATIONS AND THEIR VALIDITY UNDER JAPANESE CORPORATE LAW*

9 International Lawyer 159
160-163 (1975)

In attempting to assess the efficacy of various devices under the Japanese legal system, it is first necessary to cope with the compartmentalization of the Japanese legal system. In Japanese law, not only is there a basic distinction between public and private law, under which agreements in violation of public law provisions may still be enforceable as a matter of private law,[43] but there is also a rather complete segregation of the discrete sections of private law.[44] Thus, the mere fact that a particular technique for achieving the interests of one party in a joint venture corporation cannot be exercised through a provision in the Articles of Incorporation does not necessarily invalidate the technique when made part of a contract. This segregation or dichotomy between basic contract concepts in the Civil Code, on the one hand, and matters of the law of corporations found in the Commercial Code, on the other hand, leads to the widespread belief that an agreement between shareholders to accomplish a given objective will be valid, at least between the parties, even though the result runs contrary to provisions of corporate law. It also leads to a compartmentalization of thinking among the scholars, so that the corporate law scholar rarely considers the role of agreements as they might affect corporate relations, and the contract law specialist rarely applies his knowledge to determine the effects of contracts in separate fields of study not specifically enumerated in the Civil Code.

Looking to the field of contract law, one starts with the basic concept of freedom of contract, applied with greater vigor in Japan than in the United States. If applied in full force to agreements which allocate power among shareholders or bind them to make certain decisions on behalf of the joint venture corporation, this principle would lead to the conclusion that such agreements are fully enforceable. In actual fact, although there is frequently little evidence upon which to base the conclusion, such agreements may be valid and effective within amazingly broad limits. Some of these limits are those generally recognized in the Japanese Civil Code, primarily as built into articles 1, 90, and 91.

Article 1 probably could pose a barrier to freedom to contract in the context of the present type of situation. It sets forth essentially three principal doctrines: (1) public welfare, (2) good faith, and (3) the abuse of rights doctrine. Although the first of these three potentially could cause some difficulty when a party seeks to enforce a shareholder agreement, this principle is primarily aimed at protecting rights of the public from being destroyed by private party agreement,[45] and there-

*From Donald P. Swisher, "Use of Shareholder Agreements and Other Control Techniques in Japanese Joint Venture Corporations and Their Validity Under Japanese Corporate Law," 9 *International Lawyer* 159 (© 1975 American Bar Association), at 160-163. Reprinted by permission.

fore does not appear appropriate where, as here, there are no outside parties affected by the agreement. Of course, if there were other shareholders in the corporation and they did not adhere to the contract, this principle *might* apply to invalidate the agreement to the extent that they were affected. The same result might also be achieved via the abuse of rights principle. However, at least where there are but two shareholders and no third party interests are involved, it seems doubtful that article 1 will provide a significant barrier to the validity of a contract between two shareholders who own all outstanding shares of the corporation.

Article 90 states that a juristic act (including the making of a contract) "which has for its object such matters as are contrary to public policy or good morals is null and void."[46] Superficially it would appear that an attempt to accomplish by shareholder agreement what the Commercial Code would prohibit if included in the articles would run contrary to a well-defined public policy. However, the courts have not fully developed this concept, and it has been narrowly limited. Wagatsuma indicates that this provision generally would apply only to the following types of situations: (1) juristic acts contrary to morality (such as contracts sustaining immoral relationships), (2) juristic acts contrary to the principles of justice (such as a contract to commit a crime or payment in exchange for not doing a bad act), (3) juristic acts taking unfair advantage of another's distress (such as usury), (4) excessive restrictions on an individual's freedom (usually involuntary servitude types of situations), (5) limitations on freedom to conduct economic enterprises (unreasonable covenants not to compete, contracts between competitors which create monopolies or restraints of trade), (6) acts which dispose of one's basic means of livelihood (*seizon no kisotaru zaisan o shobun suru koto*), and (7) excessively speculative acts.[47] Thus, most provisions in a shareholders' agreement of the type contemplated in this article probably are not precluded by article 90, even though some individual shareholder agreements might clash with that article (such as prohibited limitations on one's freedom to conduct economic enterprises).

Article 91 probably provides the firmest foundation for recognizing the validity of shareholder agreements in the context of this paper. That section provides as follows: "If the parties to a juristic act have declared an intention which differs from any provisions of laws or ordinances which are not concerned with public policy, such intention shall prevail."

Thus, even where the codes indicate that, for example, restrictions on share transfers must be in the articles to be valid, so long as it would not violate public policy, the shareholders among themselves can agree to restrictions on share transferability and have the agreement enforceable among themselves. A problem arises, however, in that the Japanese recognize a distinction between required provisions (*kyōkō hōki*) and optional provisions (*nin'i hōki*), and article 91 applies only when an optional provision is involved. Thus, before it can be said that a particular legal provision is not binding when the contract has a contrary clause, it may be necessary to determine (1) whether the particular provision is mandatory or optional, and, if mandatory, (2) whether the mandatory nature of a legal provision governing the corporation will also affect a contract to which the corporation is not a party.

As can be seen from the above, one's conclusions concerning the efficacy of shareholder agreements under the Japanese Civil Code depend on answers which must be based upon an assessment of the impact of Commercial Code provisions governing the corporation when the corporation itself is not a party to the particular agreement. In this shadowy valley between the two codes, very little Japanese scholarly light has been shed.

- - - - - - - - - - -

Translation by Yanagida Nomura & Akai

Meisei Kensetsu Kōgyō K.K. v. Ogami
1325 Hanrei Jihō 140
(Kyoto Dist. Ct., Feb. 3, 1989)

REFERENCES:

Commercial Code, § 204
Civil Code, §§ 90 and 91

FACTS:

Defendant Ogami was an employee of Plaintiff Meisei Kensetsu Kōgyō K.K. (Meisei), an unlisted stock company. At the time of Ogami's retirement from the company in 1984, all shares in Meisei were owned by directors or employees of Meisei, although by 1988 there were several Meisei shareholders that were neither directors nor employees of the company. When Ogami retired, he owned 6,000 shares of common stock of the company, the aggregate face value of which was ¥3,000,000.

Upon Ogami's retirement, Meisei requested that he sell all his shares in the company at their face value, alleging that there existed an agreement between Meisei and its directors and employees that each of them must transfer to Meisei his or her shares in the company (at their face value) when leaving his or her position as director or employee. Ogami asserts that there is no such agreement, and that even if such an agreement exists, because the value of the stock owned by Ogami amounts to ¥84,000,000, *i.e.*, twenty-eight times its face value, the agreement should be found void as jeopardizing the public order or violating good morals by so severely limiting Ogami's recovery of his investment.

JUDGMENT:

Held for Meisei.

REASONS:

I. [Omitted.]

II. [Omitted—In this section, the court finds that there was an agreement of the type alleged by Meisei (the Agreement).]

III. [Omitted.]

IV. 1. [Omitted.]

2. It is true that an agreement such as the present one restricts operation of the Commercial Code principle of free transferability of stock. On the other hand, when a stockholder consents to the terms of such an agreement, the principle of freedom of contract is to be applied. Therefore, we consider it reasonable to hold that the Commercial Code, in any event, does not deny the enforceability of such

an agreement and that it would make such an agreement void only if the contents of the agreement were so unreasonable as to prevent a stockholder from recovering his or her capital investment.

Based upon the following evidence [omitted], we find that the actual par value of the Meisei stock owned by Ogami was, as of November 11, 1984, ¥14,492. Relying upon this fact alone, however, it cannot be said that special circumstances exist [to render the Agreement void]. On the other hand, we find that since the articles of incorporation of Meisei provide that a shareholder cannot transfer its shares without obtaining the approval of the board of directors, Meisei shares are not expected to be sold or purchased freely. Further, we find that Ogami acquired all his Meisei shares at their face value and that from 1967, when he acquired the shares, to 1984, when he retired, he had received annual dividends at rates of 15 - 30%, which are considered high.

Based upon the foregoing findings, even though Ogami cannot sell his shares at their actual value, it cannot be said that he is unable to recover his capital investment. Rather, it should be said that he has already recovered his capital investment and profited from the high dividend rates. Therefore, the Agreement is not unreasonable and does not jeopardize the public order or violate good morals.

V. - VI. [Omitted.]

- - - - - - - - - -

Translation by Yanagida Nomura & Akai

Maruyama v. K.K. Miruton
1316 Hanrei Jihō 139
(Osaka Dist. Ct., Nov. 30, 1988)

REFERENCES:

Commercial Code, § 254(3)
Civil Code, § 651(1)

FACTS:

Plaintiff Maruyama was one of the five directors of defendant K.K. Miruton and, as such, was registered in the Commercial Register. On January 21, 1988, Maruyama sent K.K. Miruton a letter stating his intention to resign from his position as director. The company, however, did not accept his resignation, alleging that there existed an agreement among the five directors to the effect that no director could resign without obtaining the other directors' approval. Maruyama requested in his complaint that the court order K.K. Miruton to proceed with the registration of his resignation.

JUDGMENT:

Held for Maruyama.

REASONS:

I. [Omitted.]

II. * * *

The relationship between a stock company and its directors is governed by the provisions concerning mandate (Com. Code, § 254(3)). Since the parties to a mandate contract may terminate the contract at any time (Civ. Code, § 651(1)), we consider it reasonable that a director of a stock company may resign from his office at any time. Furthermore, taking into consideration that a stock company may remove a director from office at any time by a resolution of a general shareholders' meeting (Com. Code, § 257(1)), that a director must assume special liabilities to the company (Com. Code, § 266(1)), and that a director is restricted from certain acts (Com. Code, §§ 264 and 265(1)), it is reasonable to hold that an agreement restricting a director's freedom to resign is void. Therefore, even if the agreement asserted by K.K. Miruton does, in fact, exist, Maruyama's resignation became effective when he expressed his intention to resign to Miruton.

III. [Omitted.]

Questions and Discussion Points

1. *The Meisei case*: What was Meisei trying to accomplish by the share transfer agreement? What alternative arguments are there for a holding that the agreement between Meisei and Ogami should not have been enforceable?

2. *The Maruyama case*: What was the purpose of the alleged agreement amongst the K.K. Miruton directors? How did it differ from the purpose behind the *Meisei* agreement?

3. *Distinguishing the cases*: What factors moved the *Meisei* court to uphold an agreement modifying the Commercial Code and the *Maruyama* court not to? In light of factual differences in the cases, how do these factors illuminate the interplay between analysis of the Codes and consideration of underlying policy goals?

4. *Mandatory and permissive Code provisions*: What is the relationship between Sections 90 and 91 of the Civil Code?

Based on the discussion in the Swisher selection and the holdings in the two cases, is it clear how to distinguish Commercial Code rules that can be modified from those that cannot be? Suppose in the P.C. that A.Co and J.Co wished to dispense with the formality of having to act through the board of directors of Newco and thus sought to agree in the JVA that Newco would have no board of directors (but that Newco would have two directors to represent it in dealings with third parties). Should such an agreement be permissible? Whose interests might be harmed? What public policies might be affected? Which provisions of the Civil Code and the Commercial Code would be relevant, and how would the interplay of those provisions affect the legal result?

II. Shareholder Agreements on Control Mechanisms

When parties seek to modify the effect of Commercial Code provisions by private agreement, they are often motivated by a desire to protect their respective abilities to exercise control over corporate affairs. They may consider the protection afforded by the usual corporate provisions insufficient to cope with the risks involved in the joint venture. They may, for example, seek to require super-majorities for any decision of consequence made at the company's shareholders' or directors' meeting. Such requirements prevent either venturer from exercising unilateral control. The following selection discusses common mechanisms for exercising control over corporations and whether the mechanisms are available under the Commercial Code and other relevant law. Following the selection is a chart showing which of the mechanisms discussed in the selection are utilized in the P.C. Agreements.

DONALD P. SWISHER, USE OF SHAREHOLDER AGREEMENTS AND OTHER CONTROL TECHNIQUES IN JAPANESE JOINT VENTURE CORPORATIONS AND THEIR VALIDITY UNDER JAPANESE CORPORATE LAW*

9 International Lawyer 159
163-170, 173-177, 181 (1975)

[I.] Voting Agreements, Including Pooling Agreements, Voting Trusts, and Irrevocable Proxies

There are several types of voting agreements recognized in American law, of which pooling agreements, voting trusts, and irrevocable proxies are the most common.

1. Pooling Agreements

A pooling agreement is one in which all or a portion of the shareholders of a corporation agree to pool their votes and to vote all of them in favor of designated directors. In the context of a Japanese-American joint venture corporation with all shares held by two shareholders, such an agreement would, for example, require both parties to vote for a full slate of candidates, half nominated by the Japanese shareholder and half by the American shareholder. * * *

In Japan, there is no specific provision in the Commercial Code dealing with pooling devices. The Code does specify, however, that each shareholder shall have one vote for each share,[48] and it has been pointed out that this is mandatory law, so that any provision in the articles to the contrary will be void unless expressly permitted by statute. Thus, a provision in the articles allowing pooling of rights arguably has no validity.

It would appear, however, that regardless of whether such a provision can be inserted in the articles, a shareholder agreement by which the parties agree to restrict their votes would be valid. Scholarly opinions are split on the subject, with some feeling these are void, and others indicating they would be valid. Most indicate, however, that even if such agreements are valid and enforceable, if a shareholder exercises his voting rights in violation of the agreement, his vote would still be valid as cast. On the practical side, as well, there is evidence these agreements are

*Excerpts from Donald P. Swisher, "Use of Shareholder Agreements and Other Control Techniques in Japanese Joint Venture Corporations and Their Validity Under Japanese Corporate Law," 9 *International Lawyer* 159 (© 1975 American Bar Association), at 163-170, 173-177 and 181. Reprinted by permission.

considered valid. Several authors have suggested that agreements regarding division of directors in a joint venture corporation should routinely be included. Thus, these types of agreements would appear to be a viable means of committing the parties to a pre-determined organization of the board of directors, even though a vote in violation of the agreement would not be invalidated. * * *

[II.] High Voting and Quorum Requirements, Including Express Veto Powers, and Special Requirements for Amending the Articles, Authorizing the Issuance of Stock and Fundamental Corporate Acts

Veto Powers

In the United States, it is often possible to include an express veto power in the articles or by-laws. This veto can be in the form of a requirement of shareholder unanimity or an equivalent requirement for director action. Express veto provisions have also been included in shareholder agreements, although (it has been argued that) this method is much more risky than a charter or by-law provision. Ordinarily these provisions are included only if all shareholders are parties to the agreement, and even then they might not be enforceable, especially as against the corporation.

In Japan there is no express statutory prohibition against the veto power concept. While certain minimum requirements for passing resolutions of shareholders are set out in the Commercial Code, there is no prohibition on making these more stringent.[49] Note, however, that scholarly opinion is split on whether the two-thirds requirement of article 343, which applies to several fundamental corporate decisions,[50] can be raised by a provision in the articles. * * * The Commercial Code also has specific provisions regarding voting requirements for directors' decisions, with article [260-2] permitting a more stringent requirement to be placed in the articles.[51] However, there are many who feel that a veto-type provision would be void, including one by which the vote of a particular director must be included in those favoring a proposition. Thus, even though there is some authority which would recognize a veto power provision in some situations, the issue is sufficiently beclouded to raise a warning that such a provision is not advisable. * * *

Assuming that an explicit veto-type provision in the articles risks being considered invalid, it is next necessary to determine if a unanimity provision or a veto provision inserted in a shareholders' agreement would be acceptable. Such a provision has rarely been considered in Japan. Based upon the Japanese legal distinction between corporate law and contract law, theoretically, at least, such a provision in a shareholders' agreement should be valid between the shareholders. One should be concerned, however, that this might be one place where article 1 of the Civil Code might be applied to nullify such a provision, either on the basis of "public welfare" or as an "abuse of rights." In inserting these kinds of provisions in shareholder agreements, the parties are in effect surreptitiously altering the apparent decision-making structure of the corporation, so that the public policy behind the Commercial Code provisions requiring certain votes in the corporation is circumvented, a factor likely to be weighed adversely by a court which finds that the corporation's interests in policing its own voting procedures have been thwarted by a contract giving veto power to a foreign minority. So long as the corporation is considered a third party as to this contract, a provision which in effect amends a provision of its articles (in contrast to one merely agreeing among the shareholders as to how they will vote) may be attacked both due to the interference with public interests regarding the operation of the corporation and because the shareholders have abused their rights in ways affecting seriously the operation of the third party corporation. Although no explicit authority for this proposition can be found, the general tenor of legal authorities would seem to support it.

Special Voting and Quorum Requirements

In the United States, it is common for the articles to contain higher voting requirements for shareholder decisions than required by law, and this custom is expressly sanctioned in the statutes of many states. In addition, the statutes require a greater majority for certain fundamental acts, even without a provision in the articles. The quorum can be freely set in the articles, although low quorums are impractical where a high percentage of total issued shares must approve a decision. Likewise, quorum and voting requirements for directors can be freely raised by provisions in the articles or by-laws of the corporation. These same matters probably can be accomplished by a shareholder agreement, as in the case of agreements regarding unanimity or veto powers, but this method appears to be rarely if ever used.

In Japan, the Commercial Code already provides the structure for higher quorum and voting requirements for certain fundamental acts, and these provisions of themselves are often sufficient to protect the interests of substantial minorities, so long as the articles include express pre-emptive rights provisions.[52] However, often in the case of certain ordinary decisions of shareholders or the election of directors, express arrangements may be desirable. This result can be readily achieved by a provision inserted in the articles.[53] Likewise, the quorum and voting requirements for director action can be made more stringent through a provision in the articles.[54] Thus, the kind of protection for minority shareholders which we seek can best be attained by the existing statutory requirements plus statutorily authorized provisions in the articles. This solution often can be every bit as effective as any attempt to obtain a requirement of unanimity or an express veto right, and for this reason, this method is decidedly preferable to an attempt to use the other techniques.

Since arrangements for higher quorum and voting requirements can be adequately handled without resort to a shareholder agreement, there usually will be little reason for resorting to the latter technique for this purpose. Moreover, an attempt to raise quorum or voting requirements by shareholder agreement probably would encounter many of the same problems that were explored in discussing contract provisions regarding veto powers. * * *

[III.] Employment and Management Contracts: Agreements as to Who Will Be Officers

A number of shareholder agreements in the United States contain provisions naming the persons to occupy some or all corporate offices or giving certain contracting parties the right to name certain officers. Although increasingly accepted, these types of provisions have been attacked on [various] grounds. * * * Management contracts are agreements between the corporation and others entrusting aspects of its management to particular individuals or corporations. * * * Employment contracts between the corporation and a given key employee, whether a shareholder or not, have been used in the United States, but, like management contracts, their validity beyond a short period of time is quite speculative. * * *

In Japan much the same type of statutory problem must be faced. The Commercial Code requires the directors both to administer the affairs of the company and to appoint the representative director(s).[55] However, shareholder agreements regarding designation of officers and other key employees are considered to be a natural matter of legitimate concern in joint venture corporations, and they do not appear to have been seriously challenged. Such shareholder agreements appear to be valid; however, they probably are not enforceable against the corporation, should its board of directors choose to exercise its powers without regard to the shareholder agreement. A close analogy can be drawn to pooling agreements already discussed. On the other hand, any attempt to shift the actual formal designation from the board of directors to the shareholders probably would be invalid as contrary to the Commercial Code.[56]

Attempts to set up management contracts or similar employment contracts would also have to be channeled through the directors to be effective, as these can be formalized only by making the corporation a party to them. Considering the extent to which there is controversy over the scope to which the board can delegate authority to the representative directors and other officials on a regular basis, it would be reasonable to conclude that any long-term delegation of authority or any excessive delegation of significant authority beyond this immediate circle of officials would likely be struck down as an evasion of the provisions of article 260.

[IV.] Restrictions on Salaries of Directors and Officers

In a close corporation where a shareholder with a sizeable minority interest is basically an outsider regarding day-to-day management, the majority insiders can establish high salaries for themselves and thereby increase their return while reducing the return to the minority through dividends. One method of preventing this tactic in the United States involves inclusion of a provision in the articles or by-laws concerning the method for fixing compensation. Restrictions on compensation can also be included in shareholder agreements.

In Japan the Commercial Code requires that the compensation of directors as directors be fixed in the articles or by resolution of the shareholders.[57] Since the Code clearly indicates that this decision belongs to the shareholders, it should be possible for the shareholders to agree among themselves concerning what the salaries should be, and for such an agreement to be valid. If combined with a higher than majority voting requirement for shareholder resolutions, minority shareholders can usually be adequately protected in this way. When it comes to the salaries of officers or director-officers, however, the problem is more complex. Since directors are charged with the administration of the affairs of the corporation,[58] there is a valid argument that this is a matter solely for the directors' discretion. However, the prevailing opinion apparently supports the view that the shareholders can set the salaries of directors working in other capacities, both where the directors are working in these capacities primarily because they are directors, and where their employment in the position is not related to the fact that they are directors. In both cases, this subject would be appropriate for inclusion in a shareholder agreement. The salaries of other employees, however, probably should not be handled through a shareholder agreement, as this responsibility would ordinarily fall solely upon the directors, and any such agreement would only be binding upon the corporate parents. Thus, even if technically valid, an agreement setting the salaries of ordinary employees would be ineffective should the directors choose to ignore it.

[V.] Restrictions on Dividends

One of the most frequent causes of controversy in close corporations is its dividend policy. This problem is often most acute where one side is running the corporation and deriving substantial salary and other remuneration, while the other can derive benefits solely via the extraction of dividends. On the other hand, especially in a multi-national corporation, the parties may disagree on dividend policies due to different views on fundamental policies, different tax considerations, and different national customs. In the United States, parties often have attempted to control dividend policies by shareholder agreements, but these still are frequently struck down in many states as an unjustified interference with the powers of the directors.

In Japan, a shareholder agreement regarding a corporation's dividend policy would probably be valid and effective. This conclusion is based primarily upon the different locus of power regarding dividends. The Japanese Commercial Code leaves the actual approval of dividends to the shareholder meeting, even though in reality the shareholders merely have the opportunity to pass upon what has already been decided by the directors.[59] The formality of placing the dividend decision in the hands of the shareholders may mean little in the average corporation; however, this provision does afford a reasonable basis for holding that a shareholder agreement regarding dividends does not interfere with any decision-making power of the directors, thus eliminating one of the principal objections to these agreements in the United States. Primarily for this reason, shareholders in Japanese corporations probably are free to agree among themselves that they will only approve dividends of a certain amount or will refrain from approving dividends not meeting certain criteria. This type of agreement, however, although useful to block certain dividends contrary to the agreement, probably cannot be effective to compel a recalcitrant shareholder to approve dividends which meet the criteria of the agreement.

[VI.] Pre-Emptive Rights

Many effective methods for protecting minority rights require the minority to have a significant block of stock. Usually the minority must have at least one-third of the total shares to be assured of effective checks upon majority actions.[60] Thus, it is necessary to assure that such a percentage of shareholding can be maintained. Perhaps the most effective tool for preserving this position is to guarantee pre-emptive rights to existing shareholders.

* * * In Japan, unless the articles otherwise specify, it is a director decision whether there will be pre-emptive rights upon the issuance of new shares, and, if so, under what terms and conditions. Thus, the articles should set out these matters in detail sufficient to guarantee a meaningful opportunity for the minority to protect itself by exercise of pre-emptive rights. If for some reason it is undesirable to place all of these details in the articles, the Code permits a corporation to leave the matter of pre-emptive rights to the shareholders by including a provision in the articles stating that matters relating to pre-emptive rights are to be determined by shareholder resolution. This Code provision opens the possibility that the scope of pre-emptive rights can be the subject of a shareholder agreement spelling out the form of such rights and the various details concerning their operation. In fact, this approach appears to be generally acceptable in joint ventures in Japan, and a shareholder agreement is a common method of handling the preemptive rights problem, where, for some reason, a more detailed article provision is not desired.

* * * In summary, even though many forms of shareholder agreements may be valid, their effectiveness may leave much to be desired. Not only will an act done in breach be considered valid, but the contract is only operative among and between the actual parties. Furthermore, it will frequently be difficult to obtain an effective remedy when the contract is breached or about to be breached. This dilemma points out the need to include in the contract appropriate means for settlement of the dispute which rely primarily upon other than lawsuit-based remedies.

- - - - - - - - - -

Several of the control mechanisms discussed in the preceding selection are utilized by A.Co and J.Co in the JVA or in the Articles of Incorporation of Newco. Consider whether any of the control provisions in the P.C. are inconsistent with the Commercial Code, and, if so, whether the provisions should nevertheless be enforceable between A.Co and J.Co.

Control Mechanism	Relevant Provisions in Articles or JVA	Relevant Sections in Com. Code
Pooling Agreements		
–for voting for directors	JVA §§B-7(b)	241(1)
–for voting for auditors	JVA §§B-9(b)	241(1)
Veto Powers		
–as to shareholder resolutions	Article 16, JVA §B-4(a)	239(1), 343
–as to board resolutions	Articles 27 & 28, JVA §B-10	260-2(1)
Cumulative Voting	Article 20	256-3
Restricting Share Transfer	JVA §B-6	204
Stipulating Officers and Representative Directors	Article 22, JVA §B-8(a)	260(1), 261(1)
Restricting Directors' and Officers' Salaries	Article 23, JVA §B-8(c)	269
Restrictions on Dividends	Article 32	281-293
Preemptive Subscription Right to New Shares	Article 7, JVA §B-4(c)	280-2

PART E: Deadlock and Dissolution of Close Corporations

Introduction

In joint venture corporations such as Newco, each venturer has effective veto power as to any matter requiring shareholder or board approval. Therefore, any serious matter which cannot be agreed upon between the two venturers may lead to corporate deadlock of the joint venture company. Here in Part E we assess strategies for resolving potential deadlock that would be available to parties when drafting their JVA. We then consider Japanese law on resolution of corporate deadlock by means of judicially-enforced dissolution of the joint venture company.

I. Drafting Strategies

In the JVA contemplated in the P.C., no specific strategy is designated for resolving any corporate deadlock that might arise between A.Co and J.Co. The JVA simply provides for termination by agreement of A.Co and J.Co (§I-1) or for breach by either party (§I-2). In the event of termination, Newco is to be dissolved and the net assets of Newco are to be distributed to A.Co and J.Co (§I-4(c)). If A.Co and J.Co cannot agree to terminate the JVA, any dispute resulting in deadlock could be resolved by arbitration (§H-7).

For some joint venture corporations, however, the venturers agree in advance on specific approaches to resolving corporate deadlock. Consider the merits of each of the approaches below, all of which come from actual agreements. Note that in each excerpt the joint venture company is referred to as "Newco" and the venturers by names indicating their corporate citizenship.

1. **Requiring extended discussions and mediation**

(a) In case a difference of opinion between Japan Co. and U.S. Co. in respect of any material and serious matter relating to the operation of Newco results in the failure to convene a general meeting of shareholders or meeting of the Board of Directors of Newco and/or in a failure by either party to approve a reasonable and valid proposal of the other party, the parties hereto shall try to resolve said dispute as follows:

(i) each party hereto shall submit documents explaining the opinion of the party and negotiate with the other party about the dispute;

(ii) if the parties hereto still fail to resolve the difference of opinion, the parties hereto shall form a committee of four members (the Committee), two each of whom shall be appointed by each party hereto, to resolve the dispute; and

(iii) if the parties hereto fail to resolve the dispute in the Committee, the Committee shall entrust the mediation of the dispute to a third party agreed upon by the parties hereto; provided, however, that the mediation by such third party shall not legally bind the parties hereto.

(b) If the parties have no expectation of being able to resolve the dispute even by use of the procedures of this Article or if the dispute is not resolved within six (6) months after the start of the procedures specified in this Article, each party hereto shall have the right to terminate this Agreement.

2. **Right to request liquidation**

If a difference of opinion between Japan Co. and U.K. Co. in respect to any material matter relating to the operation of Newco results in the failure to convene a meeting of the Board of Directors or shareholders of Newco and/or in a failure to approve a reasonable and valid proposal or motion of either party hereto, and the parties after good faith negotiation are unable to resolve the difference of opinion within a period of three (3) months, and irreparable injury to either of the parties hereto shall thereby be caused or threatened, either party (hereinafter called the "Electing Party") hereto shall have the right to request liquidation of Newco and the other party (hereinafter called the "Other Party") hereby agrees to proceed with such liquidation. Notwithstanding the foregoing, if the Other Party hereto elects to continue the activities as engaged in by Newco, the Electing Party shall, at the request of the Other Party, discuss in good faith with the Other Party the transfer of the shares of Newco owned by the Electing Party, and if the parties fail to reach agreement, the Electing Party shall have the right to sell to a third party the shares of Newco owned by it under terms and conditions more favorable than those offered by the Other Party.

3. **Forcing a buy-sell option**

If a difference of opinion between the parties hereto with respect to any material matter relating to the operation of Newco results in the failure to convene a general meeting of the shareholders or of the directors of Newco and/or in a failure to approve a reasonable and valid proposal or motion of one of the parties hereto, and the parties, after good faith negotiation, are unable to resolve the difference of opinion within a period of six (6) months, and irreparable injury to any of the parties hereto shall thereby be caused or threatened, either party hereto shall have the right to designate a price per share and the other party shall within two (2) weeks of such designation elect either to buy all of the shares of the first party in Newco at such price per share or sell all of its shares in Newco to the other party at such price, and the parties shall thereafter in good faith negotiate any remaining matters concerning the buying party's continuance of the operation of Newco.

What rights and duties are created by each of the above provisions? A.Co and J.Co have essentially left resolution of any protracted deadlock to *ad hoc* determination. What are the merits of such an approach? The demerits? In considering these questions, it is important to bear in mind the costs that would be involved if the parties were to be forced to resort to the statutory remedy provided by Japanese law, discussed in the following section.

II. Court-Ordered Dissolution

What if two joint venturers remain in protracted deadlock and cannot agree even upon whether to liquidate their joint venture company? One solution is to seek court-ordered dissolution. The brief selection and the case below explain basic Japanese law on the right of shareholders to seek court-ordered dissolution.

DENNIS S. KARJALA, THE CLOSELY HELD ENTERPRISE UNDER JAPANESE LAW*

7 Boston University International Law Journal 229
245-247 (1989)

Minority participant oppression is as much a problem in Japan as in the United States, and it stems from the same basic sources. Normally no market exists for the equity interests in a closely held enterprise, but the controlling parties can insure a return on their investment through salaries and other perquisites of office. If the minority participant has neither protected his employment position nor required a policy of paying dividends through advance planning, or if the law prohibits such planning, his investment may be locked in without return indefinitely. In the United States, following the British legislative example, most commentators have found the solution to oppression problems in liberal judicial dissolution provisions. Such provisions authorize the courts to consider a wide range of equitable remedies to fairly balance all parties' interests. This section considers the possibilities for using the judicial dissolution remedy in Japan in a similar way.

The Corporations Code [by which the author refers to the portion of the Commercial Code, Sections 165 to 456, relating to *Kabushiki Kaisha*] and the Limited Liability Company Act provisions on dissolution are essentially identical. Therefore, there is no advantage under current law for choosing the limited liability company with respect to this crucial issue. In addition to judicial dissolution, both statutes provide that a company is dissolved upon the occurrence of any reason specified in the articles of association, as well as by resolution of the general meeting.[61] These provisions appear to permit article provisions granting power to a minority participant to dissolve at will, or at least upon the occurrence of a stated event, such as the minority participant's termination as a company employee or the company's failure to declare a dividend for some stated time period. Moreover, a shareholders voting agreement achieves the same result, if all shareholders have agreed to vote in favor of a resolution to dissolve upon the occurrence of stated circumstances.[62] Although advance planning is required to take advantage of these provisions, they are surprisingly liberal. Unfortunately, it appears that few Japanese or their lawyers are using these options, as they do not figure in the cases or much of the commentary.

In any event, many businesspersons do not plan in advance. When a business is getting started, the participants are usually friends and optimistic about business prospects. It is difficult to predict what will eventually cause them to fall out, but the fact remains that disputes, sometimes bitter disputes, develop frequently. When such disputes break out, what are the remedies available to the participant out of power?

Both the Corporations Code and the Limited Liability Company Act provide for judicial dissolution at the insistence of a 10% equity participant where "un-

*From Dennis S. Karjala, "The Closely Held Enterprise Under Japanese Law," 7 *Boston University International Law Journal* 229 (1989), at 245-247. Reprinted by permission.

avoidable reasons" exist and either (1) the company is suffering or is threatened with irreparable injury due to a crisis in management of the company's business or (2) the company's existence is endangered by grossly improper management or disposition of the company's property.[63] These are obviously very severe restrictions on the right to seek judicial dissolution. A number of justifications have been advanced in defense of these restrictions, such as upholding the basic principle of majority rule, preventing abuse by minority participants, and the effect dissolution has on third parties like employees. The result, however, is to deny a judicial remedy based on the particular circumstances of an oppressed minority participant. Therefore, a minority participant in a going concern, in which the controlling parties are paying themselves healthy salaries rather than distributing profits as dividends but there is no deadlock or waste of assets, would probably not be entitled to relief under these provisions, regardless of whether the entity is a corporation or a limited liability company.

- - - - - - - - - -

Translation by Yanagida Nomura & Akai

Kimura et al. v. K.K. Land Ace
843 Kin'yū Shōji Hanrei 46
(Tokyo Dist. Ct., July 18, 1989)

REFERENCES:

Commercial Code, §§ 112 and 406-2

FACTS:

Defendant K.K. Land Ace, a real estate broker, developer and management company, is a stock corporation established in 1970. It was established with capital of ¥30 million represented by 60,000 shares evenly divided between two families and held by various members of those families. Until around April 1984, the plaintiffs, several members of the Kimura family, held their 30,000 shares as follows: the late Rin'ichirō Kimura owned 6,000 shares; his wife, plaintiff Yoshi Kimura, 6,000 shares; and his sons, plaintiffs Shintarō, Kimifumi and Nobuya Kimura, 6,000 shares each. The other 30,000 shares were owned by members of the Kijima family as follows: intervenor on the side of Land Ace, Takaaki Kijima, owned 20,000 shares; his mother, Kei Kijima, 8,000 shares; and his wife, Mitsuko Kijima, 2,000 shares.

Land Ace was set up so that management and participation in profits would be shared equally by the Kimura and Kijima families. The representative directors of Land Ace were, from the Kimura family, the late Rin'ichirō Kimura, and from the Kijima family, Takaaki Kijima. Equal numbers of directors were appointed from each family. Profits, rather than being distributed in the form of dividends, were equally paid out to each family in the form of payment of remuneration to the directors.

The two families appear to have operated Land Ace harmoniously until representative director Rin'ichirō Kimura died on June 14, 1984, following which disagreement arose as to disposition of the shares he had held. On the Kimura family side, it is alleged that the shares were inherited by Kimura family members and that they had agreed that the shares were to be equally distributed to each of Rin'ichirō Kimura's sons. On the Kijima family side, Takaaki Kijima alleges that Rin'ichirō Kimura, on May 9, 1984, assigned to him the 2,000 shares that the agreement among the Kimura family members designated as having been inherited by plaintiff Nobuya Kimura (the Disputed Shares).

Takaaki Kijima held a general meeting of shareholders of Land Ace on February 28, 1985, without giving any notice to members of the Kimura family, and at that meeting the Kijima family (acting on their view that they now held 32,000 shares) passed resolutions to the effect that Shintarō and Yoshi Kimura be discharged from their respective positions as director and auditor of Land Ace and that Eriko Kijima be appointed to fill the vacated directorship.

The Kimura family plaintiffs allege that since Rin'ichirō Kimura's death Takaaki Kijima has ignored their position regarding the Disputed Shares, has not allowed them to inspect the books of account or company records of Land Ace, has led the Kijima family shareholders in voting to raise the remuneration paid to the directors of Land Ace (now all Kijima family members), and has paid a retirement allowance of ¥30 million to former director Kei Kijima, without doing so on Rin'ichirō Kimura's behalf to his heirs. In response, Takaaki Kijima alleges that, even prior to the death of Rin'ichirō Kimura, he was the one who substantially and successfully conducted the business of Land Ace. He further alleges that the reason the Kimura family has been left out of the management of Land Ace is that they have been uncooperative since the death of Rin'ichirō Kimura, their being left out is the natural result of their minority stake in Land Ace, and the payment of the retirement allowance to Kei Kijima was reasonable.

The Kimura family plaintiffs further allege that Takaaki Kijima caused Land Ace in February 1988 to sell at the price of ¥300 million a building valued at ¥1 billion to K.K. Winning, a company for which Takaaki Kijima is the representative director. They further allege that Takaaki Kijima caused Land Ace to borrow a total of ¥7.16 billion from banks and other institutions and to loan ¥6.6 billion of such funds to Winning, and that because Winning made no payments of principal or interest on the loan, and because of general mismanagement by Takaaki Kijima, Land Ace is in default to banks and other institutions and faces bankruptcy.

The Kimura family argues that because distrust between the two families has become so severe that it is impossible for them jointly to manage Land Ace, and because it is apparent that if Takaaki Kijima were to continue to manage Land Ace irrevocable damage would be inflicted upon the company, Land Ace should be ordered by the court to be dissolved. Takaaki Kijima counters that even if no agreement concerning management of Land Ace could be reached between the two families, the deadlock could be resolved by one side's purchasing the shares of the other, by an assignment of the assets of Land Ace, or by some other means, and, therefore, that it is not the case that the only way to resolve the difficulties of Land Ace is to dissolve the company.

In separate actions, Nobuya Kimura was successful in obtaining declaration of his ownership of the Disputed Shares and invalidation of the Land Ace shareholder resolutions of December 17, 1985, by which members of the Kijima family were reelected as directors, the remuneration of the directors was raised to ¥30 million, and that of the auditor was raised to ¥5 million. Also in a separate action, Shintarō Kimura was successful in obtaining invalidation of the Land Ace shareholder resolutions of March 18, 1987, by which members of the Kijima family were reelected as directors, the remuneration of the directors was further raised to ¥50 million, and that of the auditor was further raised to ¥10 million.

JUDGMENT:

Land Ace shall be dissolved.

REASONS:

I. 1. [Omitted.]

2. [Omitted—In this section the court states that it finds to be true that Land Ace sold the building to Winning, Takaaki Kijima was the representative director of Winning, and the outstanding liabilities of Land Ace are as stated by the Kimura family plaintiffs.]

II. [On the issue of the Disputed Shares, the court makes various findings of facts and concludes as follows:] Therefore, it is reasonable to conclude that, in order for the Kijima family to monopolize the management of Land Ace, Takaaki Kijima fabricated the story of the assignment of the Disputed Shares to himself from Rin'ichirō Kimura.

III. According to the findings as stated above in Sections I and II, it is determined that while Land Ace was a joint corporation to which the Kimura family and the Kijima family made equal capital contributions and regarding which they jointly assumed they would share equally in the management and profits, Takaaki Kijima, after the death of Rin'ichirō Kimura, began making false assertions that he had been assigned the Disputed Shares by Rin'ichirō Kimura, and then, based on the alleged majority holding of the Kijima family, orchestrated the elimination of the Kimura family from the management and sharing of profits of Land Ace. Putting together all the foregoing findings and the tenor of the oral arguments, it is determined that the distrust between the Kimura family and the Kijima family is extremely strong and, therefore, it can hardly be expected that the two families could manage Land Ace in a cooperative manner. With each family owning 50% of the shares of Land Ace, it would be impossible by a general shareholders' meeting to constitute the company's board of directors, which is the decisionmaking body of Land Ace. Thus, given that Takaaki Kijima has striven to eliminate the Kimura family from the management of Land Ace, has arbitrarily managed Land Ace for the benefit of Winning, a corporation managed by himself, and has driven Land Ace into insolvency, it is obvious that Land Ace is in a state of management deadlock and that irreparable injury to it is threatened.

Additionally, in accordance with the following evidence [omitted], it is found that Land Ace became insolvent as of the end of March 1989, and that the main causes therefor are the facts that Takaaki Kijima has failed to cause Winning to repay the loan and interest due to Land Ace and that K.K. K&T, another company for which Takaaki Kijima is the representative director, has failed to remit to Land Ace the proceeds earned by a Shinjuku capsule hotel it has been managing on behalf of Land Ace. Furthermore, it can be anticipated that Land Ace will need immediately to bring suit against Takaaki Kijima for damages due to his violations of his duties as a director. In view of this situation, it is also necessary for the plaintiffs to have brought this action seeking a judgment for dissolution of Land Ace, so that the court could appoint a liquidator for Land Ace (*see* Com. Code, §§ 430(1), 122 and 94(vi)).

IV. Therefore, the claim of plaintiffs is found to be just and, accordingly, we hold in favor of the plaintiffs, with Article 89 of the Code of Civil Procedure applied to the bearing of court costs.

Questions and Discussion Points

1. *The Land Ace case and the standards for court-ordered dissolution*: Consider the statutes referenced in the case and the discussion of the court. Under what standards will a court order dissolution?

Suppose that in the *Land Ace* case: 1) Kijima had in fact been assigned the shares by Rin'ichirō Kimura, 2) all the transactions initiated by Takaaki Kijima had been on terms fair to Land Ace and had not resulted in any damage to Land Ace, and 3), as actually did occur in the case, the Kijima family had used its majority of shares to remove all Kimura family members from the Land Ace board of directors and to channel earnings into directors' compensation. Under this set of circumstances, should the court grant a petition by the Kimura family plaintiffs for dissolution? If not, is there any other relief that would, or should, be available to the Kimura family?

In assessing drafting strategies for A.Co and J.Co, consider the relevance of the criteria required for judicial dissolution in Japan to the concerns these joint venturers have for their respective interests. In this connection, one should note that the dissolution issue has also been a matter of considerable concern in U.S. law and has given rise to judicial and legislative efforts to consider the position of shareholders, as well as the objective question of the well-being of their company. In Japan proposals have been advanced to modify the dissolution provisions of the Code to give courts greater latitude in instances of oppression of minority shareholders, but none was included in the 1991 or 1993 amendments to the Commercial Code.

2. *The enforceability of shareholder agreements taking away the right to petition for dissolution*: Recall our discussion of the enforceability of shareholder agreements modifying applicable provisions. Should agreements taking away the right of shareholders to petition for court-ordered dissolution be enforceable?

Consider this question in the contexts both of the P.C. and of the mandatory buy-sell option provision reviewed above. In the P.C., §H-7 of the JVA requires A.Co and J.Co to resolve disputes by means of arbitration. If dispute between A.Co and J.Co has led to protracted deadlock in Newco, and if A.Co or J.Co seeks court-ordered dissolution of Newco, should the other have a right to prevent this by relying on the prior agreement to arbitrate all disputes?

A similar dilemma is presented by the mandatory buy-sell option. In the event of corporate deadlock, if one party invokes the provision and the other party responds by filing an action for court-ordered dissolution, should the first party be able to block the dissolution proceeding and have the buy-sell agreement enforced?

FURTHER READING

Intercorporate Relations

J. Mark Ramseyer, "Legal Rules in Repeated Deals: Banking in the Shadow of Defection in Japan," 20 *Journal of Legal Studies* 91 (1991).

Paul Sheard, "The Main Bank System and Corporate Monitoring and Control in Japan," 11 *Journal of Economic Behavior and Organizations* 399 (1989).

Corporate Law and Corporate Governance

James C. Abegglen and George Stalk, Jr., *Kaisha, The Japanese Corporation.* New York: Basic Books, 1985.

Masahiko Aoki, *Information, Incentives, and Bargaining in the Japanese Economy.* Cambridge: Cambridge University Press, 1988.

Michael L. Gerlach, *Alliance Capitalism: The Social Organization of Japanese Business.* Berkeley: University of California Press, 1992.

Ronald J. Gilson & Mark J. Roe, "Understanding the Japanese Keiretsu: Overlaps Between Corporate Governance and Industrial Organization," 102 *Yale Law Journal* 871 (1992).

Dan F. Henderson, "Threshold Advice to American Incorporations in Japan," in John Owen Haley, ed., *Current Legal Aspects of Doing Business in Japan and East Asia*, pp. 76-92. Chicago: American Bar Association, 1978.

Toru Ishiguro, "Japan," in Joseph CF Lufkin & David Gallagher, eds., *International Corporate Governance*, pp. 153-170. London: Euromoney Books, 1990.

Japan External Trade Organization, *Setting Up a Business in Japan.* Tokyo: Japan External Trade Organization, 1989.

Note, "Japan's Company Law and the Promotion of Corporate Democracy: A Futile Attempt?," 27 *Columbia Journal of Transnational Law* 195 (1988).

Colin McKenzie and Michael Stutchbury, eds., *Japanese Financial Markets and the Role of the Yen.* North Sydney: Allen & Unwin in association with Australia-Japan Research Centre, Australian National University, 1992.

J. Mark Ramseyer, "Columbian Cartel Launches Bid for Japanese Firms," 102 *Yale Law Journal* 2005 (1993).

Lawrence Repeta, "Declining Public Ownership of Japanese Industry: A Case of Regulatory Failure," 17 *Law in Japan: An Annual* 153 (1984).

Mark J. Roe, "Some Differences in Corporate Structure in Germany, Japan, and the United States," 102 *Yale Law Journal* 1927 (1993).

Paul Sheard, ed., *International Adjustment and the Japanese Firm.* Sydney: Allen & Unwin, 1992.

NOTES TO CHAPTER EIGHT

1. Commercial Code, art. 261, para. 1. Representative directors are those with authority to represent the company. They usually have a title such as president, executive vice-president, senior managing director or managing director. To protect bona fide third parties, the Commercial Code provides that a company shall be liable to a bona fide third person for any act done by an apparent representative director. *Id.* art. 262. An apparent representative director is a director with a title from which it may be assumed he has authority to represent the company, although he actually has no such power. * * *

2. Commercial Code, art. 260, para. 2. The four subjects which the board as a whole must decide upon are: (1) disposal or acquisition of substantial assets; (2) borrowing in substantial amount; (3) appointment or removal of a manager or other senior employee; and (4) substantial organizational changes.

3. *Id.* art. 260, para. 3. While normally only representative directors would be in a position of responsibility requiring such reports back to the board, this provision places the duty to report on all directors, thus anticipating occasions where other directors might be in positions of such responsibility. * * *

4. *E.g.*, article 264 of the Commercial Code used to provide that a director who planned to effect a personal transaction in competition with the company must first obtain the approval of the shareholders by a majority vote of at least two-thirds of the outstanding stock. Because in practice this approval was difficult to achieve in companies whose stocks were widely dispersed, both companies and the courts would construe the competitive transaction in a narrow sense in order to obviate the need for shareholder approval. * * * The new Code requires the director to disclose all the material facts relating to the competitive transaction at a meeting of the board of directors and obtain its approval. This will make it easier to obtain approval, but also will result in a stricter scrutiny of the transaction. Because under the new law approval is obtained from the board, the individual director involved will still be liable if any damage results. * * * In cases where a director does not get board approval, there is a presumption that the damage to the company resulting from such a competitive transaction is the amount of the profit obtained by the director or a third person from the transaction. Commercial Code, art. 266, para. 4.

5. *E.g.*, under the new Code any director has the power to demand that a meeting of the board of directors be called when the director designated to call such meetings refuses to do so. Commercial Code, art. 259. * * *

6. Article 254-2 of the new Code reads:

The following persons may not be directors:

(1) An interdict or a quasi-interdict;

(2) A person who was declared bankrupt and has not yet been reinstated;

(3) A person who was subject to any penalty on account of having committed any crime set forth in this Code, the Law regarding Exceptional Rules of the Commercial Code concerning Auditing, etc., of Stock Corporations, or the Law of Limited Corporations, where two years have not yet elapsed since the date on which the execution thereof is completed or the date on which the execution thereof is discontinued; or

(4) A person who was subject to penalty of imprisonment or of a severer nature on account of having committed any crime other than that set forth under the preceding item, where the execution thereof is yet to be discontinued; provided, however, that the restriction hereunder shall not apply to a person under probation. * * *

7. Commercial Code, arts. 254, 280; Special Audit Law, art. 18. "*Kansayaku*," also translated as "Statutory auditor." Because auditors are individuals who usually work solely for the company in question and often were previously employed by that company in other capacities, they are also known as "inside auditors."

8. Retiring directors who have some particular expertise that their company desires will also sometimes be retained nominally as part-time auditors.

9. Some of these powers apply only to auditors of "large" and "medium" corporations. * * * The powers and duties of auditors of "small" companies are limited. Special Audit Law, arts. 22, 25.

10. [T]he auditor's role in the company is sometimes so insignificant that some Japanese, instead of saying "*kansayaku*" ("auditor"), jokingly make a play on words and say "*kansanyaku*," which translates as "official of leisure." * * *

11. Commercial Code, art. 274, para. 2. A director has the duty to immediately report to an auditor facts which give rise to an apprehension that significant damage may be incurred by the stock company. *Id.* art. 274-2.

12. [H]owever, in a 1982 survey of 669 listed companies, only 19.3% responded that they thought the amendments would be effective at strengthening and improving audits done by auditors, while 58.4% responded that the quality of audits depends upon the efforts of those conducting the audits and that the change in the law cannot be expected to significantly affect this. * * *

13. [T]he requirement of having two auditors in large companies presents little problem in practice, as over 99% of listed companies and 87% of large but unlisted companies already had two or more auditors before the law was passed. * * * There is a problem, however, in determining when a company has a "full-time" auditor. According to one survey the ratio of "part-time" to "full-time" auditors in listed companies is 1 to 1.76. * * * However, many of these companies are making a distinction between being merely an "auditor" (*kansayaku*) and a "regular auditor" (*jōnin kansayaku*). The latter term designates a higher rank but does not necessarily mean that the auditor in question has the expertise or is spending the time necessary to be considered a "full-time" auditor as the term is used in the new law. * * * While the actual qualifications required for the new "full-time" auditors are open to interpretation and must eventually be clarified, * * * the amendments decree that many companies will have to expand the role played by their auditors. * * * Uncertainties also surround the role of "part-time" auditors.

14. For example, where the dismissal of an accounting auditor is considered at a shareholders' meeting, the accounting auditor may speak directly to the shareholders so that the shareholders do not have to rely solely on the opinions of the directors and inside auditors. Special Audit Law, arts. 6-2, 6-3. Accounting auditors may have no other associations with the company. *Id.* art. 4, para. 2, item 2. The amendments to the Special Audit Law add criteria for the disqualification of accounting auditors which are stricter than those found in either the Certified Public Accountants Law or Securities Exchange Law of Japan. * * * *See* Special Audit Law, art. 4, para. 2.

15. The accounting auditor shall be jointly and severally liable for damage caused to the company due to negligence in performance of his duties. Special Audit Law, art. 9. Accounting auditors are also liable for damage to third parties due to false statements in the auditing report. *Id.* art. 10.

16. The corporation may issue either par value or no par value shares, or both. Commercial Code, arts. 199, 242.

17. *Id.* art. 256-3, paras. 1 & 2. The Commercial Code as adopted in 1950 by SCAP allowed any shareholder to demand cumulative voting. Even if the articles of incorporation provided otherwise, any shareholder or group of shareholders holding 25% or more of the issued shares could demand cumulative voting. *Id.* art. 256-4 (1950). In practice, Japanese almost never used cumulative voting. * * * However, there were fears that foreign shareholders might take advantage of the right to cumulative voting. In 1974 the Code was amended to delete art. 256-4, and to change art. 256-3 to its present form, providing that a company may prohibit cumulative voting.

18. Article 284, which provided as follows, was deleted by the 1981 amendments to the Commercial Code:

If a contrary resolution will not have been adopted within two years after an ordinary general meeting will have given the approval mentioned in paragraph 1 of the preceding Article, the company shall be deemed to have released the directors and auditors from any liability; provided, however, that this shall not apply where there has occurred some dishonest act on the part of any of the directors or auditors.

19. [Taniguchi v. Aikawa Golf K.K.,] 28 Minshū 368 (Sup. Ct., 2nd P.B., March 22, 1974).

20. 23 Minshū 2150 (Sup. Ct., G.B., Nov. 26, 1969). For scholarly discussion of the historical context of *Izuo Kōzai,* see, *e.g.*, Ueyanagi, *Shōhō ni-roku-roku-jō no san dai-ikkō zendan no hōi* (The legal intent of Commercial Code article 266-3(1)), *Jurisuto: Bessatsu* (No. 63) 106 (April 1979).

21. Although the case does not indicate, I assume that Kikusui Kōgyō was not made a party defendant because it had gone bankrupt. The majority of the cases under article 266-3(1) involve situations where the directors are sued because their company itself has become bankrupt.

22. 23 Minshū 2202 (Osaka Dist. Ct., Jan. 25, 1963).

23. 23 Minshū 2214 (Osaka High Ct., July 16, 1963).

24. 23 Minshū at 2153.

25. *Id.*

26. *Id.*

27. *Id.* at 2154. The Court also noted that a third party's ability to seek damages from a director under article 266-3(1) is not limited to cases where, premised on the director's wrongful intent or gross negligence, the company itself bears a duty to pay damages to the third party under Civ. Code article 44.

28. *Id.* at 2154-55.

29. 24 Minshū 1061 (Sup. Ct., 1st P.B., July 16, 1970).

30. 24 Minshū 1070 (Tokyo Dist. Ct., April 25, 1967).

31. 24 Minshū 1074 (Tokyo High Ct., July 31, 1968).

32. 24 Minshū at 1063.

33. *Id.* at 1076.

34. 27 Minshū 655 (Sup. Ct., 3d P.B., May 22, 1973).

35. It is interesting to note that the court of first instance apparently agreed with Justice Matsuda's dissenting opinion in *Izuo Kōzai,* for it found that Maruzen K.K. was a mere facade. The court disregarded the corporate entity and imposed joint liability on all the defendants under the partnership provisions of the Civil Code. *Id.* at 662.

36. *Id.* at 666. The court of second instance specifically found the defendants liable under article 266-3(1), rather than under the partnership provisions of the Civil Code (via the doctrine of disregarding the corporate entity), because the note was issued by the corporation. *Id.*

37. *Id.* at 656.

38. Hanrei Jihō (No. 897) (Osaka High Ct., April 27, 1978), *jōkoku* appeal filed.

39. Commercial Code, art. 255 (requires that a company have at least three directors).

40. The case does not state whether Kumagi settled with the plaintiff out of court or was judgment-proof, or whether the plaintiff simply decided not to sue him for some other reason.

41. Hanrei Jihō (No. 897) at 98.

42. *See* Article 424 of the Civil Code and Articles 141 and 147 of the Commercial Code. Note, however, that the foregoing Commercial Code provisions are not applicable to *kabushiki kaisha.*

43. [There are various] cases holding contracts valid even when they violate provisions of laws. A good general discussion of the public-private law dichotomy can be found in 1 J. Tanaka, *Gyōseihō Kōgi* (Lectures in administrative law) 109-118 (1965).

44. The basic provisions relating to contract law are found within Chapter II of Book III of the Civil Code, as part of the law of claim or obligation (*saiken*), while the corporate law, governing corporations, is found as Chapter IV of Book II of the Commercial Code. Legal scholarship in Japan deals with these as compartmentalized and discrete fields of study, with the corporate law specialist rarely, if ever, delving into the realm of contract law in his analysis. A typical example of this is T. Ishii, *Kaishahō* (Corporate law) (1967) [hereinafter cited as Ishii]. A rather exhaustive study of most of this two-volume work discloses that the topic of shareholder agreements is discussed only with regard to the efficacy of shareholder agreements restricting transfer of shares. *See* 1 *id.* at 168-73.

45. *See* S. Wagatsuma, *Mimpō Sōsoku* (General provisions of the Civil Code) 33-34, 38-39 (1965) [hereinafter cited as Wagatsuma]. As an example, he mentioned a private right to float logs on a river or canal, indicating that this right cannot interfere with the public's rights related to electrical power, public water systems, and similar uses. *Id.* at 38-39.

46. Civil Code, art. 90.

47. Wagatsuma, *supra* note [45], at 270-282.

48. Commercial Code, art. 241(1).

49. *See* Commercial Code, arts. 239 & 243. * * *

50. Commercial Code, art. 343. This article requires that certain shareholder resolutions be adopted by "two-thirds or more of the votes of the shareholders present who hold shares representing more than one-half of the total number of the issued shares." Ishii lists 14 decisions for which the requirements of article 343 apply. *See* 1 Ishii, *supra* note [44], at 267-269. For the most part, these come within the American understanding of fundamental corporate decisions, and are clearly enumerated in various parts of the Commercial Code.

51. Commercial Code, art. 260-2. The basic voting requirement is an affirmative vote of a majority of the directors present, with a quorum consisting of a majority of all directors.

52. *See, e.g.,* Commercial Code, art. 343. * * *

53. Commercial Code art. 239 expressly authorizes higher requirements for ordinary resolutions, while art. 256-2 does the same for the election of directors. Inclusion of such a provision governing election of directors is essential, as the Code only requires a quorum of one-third.

54. Commercial Code, art. 260-2.

55. Commercial Code, arts. 260 and 261.

56. *See* * * * Commercial Code, art. 230-2, [which reads] as follows: "The resolution shall be adopted by a general meeting [of shareholders] as to only the matters provided for in this Code or the articles of incorporation." This article was added in the 1950 revision of the Code and was designed to narrow the scope of decision-making power of the shareholders.

57. Commercial Code, art. 269.

58. Commercial Code, art. 260.

59. Commercial Code, arts. 281-283.

60. *See* Commercial Code, art. 343, with its two-thirds majority requirement for certain major decisions, and note that it extends, *inter alia,* to amendments of the articles [of incorporation] under art. 342.

61. Commercial Code, arts. 94, 404; Limited Liability Company Act, art. 69(1).

62. There may be a problem with specific enforcement of such agreements, however. * * *

63. Commercial Code, art. 406-2; Limited Liability Company Act, art. 71-2.

NINE

Intellectual Property Law

Introduction

We begin by investigating private technology licenses and the government regulation of patent and know-how licensing. Later, following a summary of the forms of intellectual property in Japan we turn to a detailed examination of the law governing know-how, patents, and trademarks.

PART A: Licensing

I. Technology Licensing

A. Patents and know-how

Most technology licenses concern know-how and patents. Patents are granted for inventions or processes and give the patent holder the exclusive right to use the invention or process for the life of the patent. Both Japan and the U.S. have patent statutes that define patent rights clearly. In both countries, patent applications must contain considerable detail about the invention or process for which a patent is sought, and in Japan patent grants tend to be quite narrowly defined.

Know-how (also known as trade secrets) is far more ambiguous. The term refers to information which is not patentable, or for which a patent has not been sought. Some know-how is not patentable because it lacks sufficient inventiveness or novelty; other know-how is not patentable because it concerns a type of knowledge not considered patentable (*e.g.*, business plans).

Even if unpatentable, know-how can still be valuable. Some U.S.-based securities firms, for example, have succeeded in Japan by exploiting their private know-how in arbitrage strategies. In the manufacturing sector, know-how typically concerns ways to design and manufacture products, and is often related to patent rights. As a result, when one company licenses another to use a patented process or manufacture a patented product, it often also trains the licensee in the related know-how.

Patents and know-how differ most sharply in the security their holder has in each. A patent right gives the holder a property right to prevent others from using the patented process or from manufacturing and selling the patented product. By contrast, the principal security in know-how is its secrecy. If a third party learns the know-how, the original developer may have no recourse.

B. Level of technology licensing

(1) **NUMBER OF TECHNOLOGY INDUCTION CONTRACTS**

Year	*Number of Contracts*
1970	1,768
1975	1,836
1980	2,142
1985	2,436
1990	3,211

Source: Adapted from Science and Technology Agency Analysis of Trends in Technology Imports for 1991, at 60. Reprinted by permission.

(2) **TECHNOLOGY INDUCTION CONTRACTS BY COUNTRY (COUNTRIES FROM WHICH MORE THAN 50 TECHNOLOGY INDUCTION CONTRACTS WERE EXECUTED IN 1991)**

	Number of Contracts			
Country	**1981**	**1986**	**1991**	**% of '91 total**
U.S.A.	977	1,354	2,002	63.1
E. & W. Germany	226	182	170	5.4
U.K.	175	149	213	6.7
France	224	212	205	6.5
Switzerland	89	84	102	3.2
Holland	74	60	86	2.7
Italy	119	109	73	2.3
Canada	15	26	68	2.1
Singapore	2	32	50	1.6

Source: Adapted from Science and Technology Agency Annual Report for 1981, at 31, and for 1986, at 33; and Science and Technology Agency Analysis of Trends in Technology Imports for 1991, at 61-62. Reprinted by permission.

(3) BALANCE OF PAYMENTS ON TECHNOLOGY IMPORT AND EXPORT CONTRACTS

Year	Receipts (In millions of $US)	Payments	Receipts as % of Payments
1950	0.0	2.6	—
1960	2.3	94.9	2.4
1965	17	166	10.2
1970	59	433	13.6
1975	161	712	22.6
1980	378	1,439	26.3
1985	746	2,522	29.6
1990	2,582	6,004	43.6

Source: Adapted from Science and Technology Agency Analysis of Trends in Technology Imports for 1991, at 17. Reprinted by permission.

(4) TECHNOLOGY INDUCTION CONTRACTS BY INDUSTRY

Industry	1981	1986	1991	% of '91 total
Computer, High Tech. Elect.	219	663	1,614	50.8
Consumer Elect.	71	86	148	4.7
Textiles	167	152	106	3.3
Medical Products	77	98	102	3.2
Transport Related Mach.	78	82	75	2.4

Source: Adapted from Science and Technology Agency Analysis of Trends in Technology Imports for 1991, at 9. Reprinted by permission.

II. Technology Licensing Agreements and the P.C.

Recall that in the P.C.'s Technical Agreement, A.Co licenses its technology to Newco, and in the Manufacturing Agreement, Newco hires J.Co to use the technology to manufacture the excavator.

Consider the questions below.

Questions and Discussion Points

1. *The subject of the technology license*: Exactly what has A.Co licensed to Newco? The central licensing clause of the TechA is §B-1. How does TechA §B-1 limit the ways Newco can use the Licensed Patents and the Technical Data, Technical Improvement Data and Technical Assistance?

2. *The status of Newco and J.Co*: Compare the basic terms of A.Co's license to

Newco in TechA §B-1 with those for Newco's hiring of J.Co in MA §§B-1 to 3. How do the provisions of the MA limit J.Co's use of A.Co's technology? How do Newco's and J.Co's status differ? Given that Newco has no capacity to manufacture Licensed Products, what is the purpose of Newco? Why is the technology license not simply structured between A.Co and J.Co?

3. *Accomplishing the technology transfer*: TechA §§E-1 to 7 and F-1 and 2 detail how A.Co's technology is to be made available to Newco, and MA §§C-1 to 3 and E-1 detail how the information is to be made available to J.Co. Under these clauses, how should the technology transfer take place? How might the transfer in the real world differ from what the agreements suggest?

4. *Protection of know-how*: What interests do a know-how transferor and transferee have in maintaining the know-how's secrecy?

Analyze TechA §E-8, MA §§C-2 and 5, and JVA §D-1 to understand the secrecy obligations of the parties to the P.C. Agreements. What obligations do the agreements impose on Newco, J.Co, and A.Co?

5. *Inventions and future patent rights*: In any technology license agreement, both the licensor and licensee will have a strong interest in improvements made on the know-how, in new inventions related to the licensed technology, and in the new patents available for such new inventions. What specific obligations might a licensor and a licensee want to extract from each other?

What are the rights and obligations of A.Co, Newco, and J.Co with respect to new know-how and patents? Consider TechA §§B, C, and E, and MA §§C and D.

How does TechA §E-12 relate to the issue of improvements and what is the function of this clause within the technology licensing framework of the P.C. Agreements?

6. *The interests of the licensor and the licensee*: In a technology licensing arrangement, what are the possible gains and losses to the licensor and licensee? What common and what antagonistic interests might they have? What contractual pro visions might each seek where their interests are antagonistic? How successful were A.Co and J.Co in protecting their interests in the P.C. Agreements?

III. Government Control of Technology Licensing

The terms under which parties license technology are not merely the product of private agreement. Laws and regulations can also affect technology licensing by encouraging or prohibiting certain transactions. For instance, regulations in the licensor's country may ban some technology transfers, or those in the licensee's country may ban the importation of some technologies. Other regulations may circumscribe the terms under which licensing may take place or the ways in which licensees may pay their foreign licensors.

In Japan, the main rules on technology licensing are in the Foreign Exchange and Foreign Trade Control Act (FECA), which we examined in Chapter 6, and the Antimonopoly Act, which we will consider in Chapter 10.

A. Control through the FECA

MITSUO MATSUSHITA AND THOMAS J. SCHOENBAUM, JAPANESE INTERNATIONAL TRADE AND INVESTMENT LAW*

186-188 (1989)

Before 1980, the old [Foreign Exchange and Foreign Trade] Control Law [FECA] and the Foreign Investment Law [were] used by governmental authorities both to restrict international technology transfers and to effect the most beneficial terms possible for the Japanese parties involved. At the present time, however, with the enactment in 1979 of the new [FECA, and with subsequent amendments to that Act], Japan no longer exercises any significant degree of substantive restraint on technology transfer except with respect to export controls on weapon, nuclear, and certain other technologies for national security purposes. Nevertheless, there are significant reporting provisions that must be complied with in concluding any technology transfer contract. These reporting requirements have been greatly simplified and rationalized.

First, the new [FECA] requires any technology induction contract to be reported [by the resident party within 15 days] of concluding the contract [through] the Bank of Japan (BOJ) [to the Ministry of Finance and any other] appropriate governmental ministry. This reporting requirement is normally carried out by filing an appropriate form with the Foreign Department of the BOJ.

The notification forms require the following information: (1) the names, addresses, and type of business of the reporting parties; (2) the type of technology; (3) the period of the contract; (4) the payment scheme; (5) an outline of the agreement; (6) the content of the technology; (7) the purpose of the agreement; (8) a summary of the industrial property rights involved; and (9) the production plans. In addition, for [certain] designated technologies * * * the BOJ will generally request a complete copy of the technology transfer contract. * * *

The purpose of this reporting requirement is primarily information gathering, although the government has authority to restrict or suspend transactions that imperil the national security, disturb the public order, or adversely affect domestic business. * * *

Outbound technology transfer is also subject to [an after-the-fact] notification requirement. [A permission-license pursuant to FECA §25] is not required, however, unless the technology falls within the scope of those strategic items that MITI has designated as subject to export controls. Those are primarily nuclear and defense technologies and other important high-technology systems.

B. Control through the Antimonopoly Act

The Antimonopoly Act requires a firm to notify the Japan Fair Trade Commission (JFTC) whenever it enters into an international agreement (regulations ex-

*From Mitsuo Matsushita and Thomas J. Schoenbaum, *Japanese International Trade and Investment Law* (University of Tokyo Press, 1989), at 186-188. Reprinted by permission.

empt from this notice requirement simple agreements such as purchase and sell contracts and other agreements considered not to be a threat to competition). This requirement enables the JFTC to review international agreements to determine whether they violate the Section 6(1) ban on agreements that "contain such matters as constitute unreasonable restraints of trade or unfair trade practices." As we will see in Chapter 10, in 1977 the JFTC investigated whether the P.C. Agreements violated the unfair trade practices ban of Section 6(1) of the Antimonopoly Act. The provisions in questions were TechA §§C-1 and 2; MA §§B-3(a) and D-1 and 2(a) and (c); and DA §F.

In 1968, the JFTC announced Guidelines for International Technology Induction Agreements, on which it relied when it reviewed international contracts filed under Section 6 of the Antimonopoly Act. In 1989, the JFTC issued a revised set of guidelines, the Guidelines for the Regulation of Unfair Trade Practices with Respect to Patent and Know-How Licensing Agreements (the Licensing Guidelines). In considering the questions below, review the 1989 Licensing Guidelines, which appear in the Appendices.

Questions and Discussion Points

1. *The structure of the Licensing Guidelines*: How much guidance do the Licensing Guidelines really give? How can one learn how the Licensing Guidelines will be applied in practice?

2. *The Guidelines and the P.C. Agreements*: If the Licensing Guidelines had existed in their current form at the time of the P.C., would the terms of the P.C. Agreements have met the requirements of the Licensing Guidelines?

C. The technology control system in the P.C.

1. The interests of licensors and licensees

When a technology licensor such as A.Co grants rights to its patents and know-how, it earns profits. It also, however, helps create a long-term competitor. For this reason, a technology licensor may try to impose various limits on how the licensee can use the transferred patents and know-how. This attempt to control the licensee's use of the licensed patents and know-how may inhere in the idea of a license agreement. After all, if the licensor cared only about the money it could make by providing its technology to another firm, it could simply sell its patents and train the buying firm in the know-how. By contrast, a license agreement generally creates a series of commitments between the licensor and licensee. Typically, the licensor will want commitments that constrain the licensee's competitive use of the technology against the licensor.

The licensee usually has adverse interests, of course. Ordinarily, it will want to improve its technological capabilities on a long-term basis. For this, it will want as few restrictions as possible. In negotiating the license agreement, the licensor and licensee thus have several fundamentally opposing preferences. Common areas of conflict include the following: Can the licensee sell the products it makes with the licensed technology in markets where the licensor already does business? If the licensor improves the know-how during the term of the agreement, must it make these improvements available to the licensee? What if the licensee improves the know-how? Can the licensee continue to use the licensor's know-how after the termination of the license agreement? If not, how can the licensor determine which knowledge held by the licensee is its own knowledge and which knowledge it obtained from the licensor?

2. Relevant provisions of the P.C. Agreements

The following provisions of the P.C. Agreements concern the respective interests of A.Co, Newco and J.Co in the technology involved in the P.C.:

TECHNICAL AGREEMENT

(§A) *Definitions.* See paragraphs 5-10.
(§B) *Grants.* See paragraphs 1, 3, 4, 6.
(§C) *Disclosure of Inventions.* See paragraphs 1, 2.
(§E) *Supply of Data.* See paragraphs 1-3, 8, 12c.
(§F) *Supply of Technical Assistance.* See paragraphs 1, 2.

MANUFACTURING AGREEMENT

(§B) *Appointment of J.Co.* See paragraphs 1-3.
(§C) *Supply of Technical Data.* See paragraphs 1, 5.
(§D) *Inventions and Patents.* See paragraphs 1, 2.
(§F) *Supply of Technical Assistance.* See paragraph 1.

JOINT VENTURE AGREEMENT

(§D) *Ownership and Protection of Data.* See paragraph 1.

Under the TechA, A.Co grants Newco an exclusive license to use certain patents and the Technical Data to manufacture the Licensed Products for Newco Territory (TechA §B-1). Newco, however, does not actually use the Licensed Patents or Technical Data nor undertake to manufacture the Licensed Products itself. Rather, through the MA it hires J.Co as a subcontractor to manufacture the Licensed Products (MA §§B-1 and 2).

In order for A.Co to convey to J.Co proprietary information related to the manufacture of the Licensed Products, the TechA has several provisions concerning documents and drawings that A.Co will provide Newco. It also provides for consultations and visits between personnel of A.Co and J.Co (the latter in its capacity as Newco's subcontractor) (TechA §§E and F). In turn, the MA provides that Newco will then convey the documents and information to J.Co (MA §§C and E).

The documents specify that the reason for the license of its patents and know-how by A.Co to Newco lies in the manufacture of Licensed Products (TechA §B-1). Newco is not to disclose the Technical Data to any third party, except to have the Licensed Products manufactured (TechA §E-8). J.Co is to use the Technical Data solely to manufacture the Licensed Products (MA §B-2). It, too, is not to disclose the Technical Data to any third parties (MA §C-5). In addition, Newco is not to allow J.Co to change the Technical Data, unless A.Co consents (TechA §E-12(c)).

Improvements and inventions related to the Licensed Products stay within the same system. A.Co is to disclose to Newco related improvements and inventions. These will then be incorporated into A.Co's license. Newco is to disclose to A.Co any improvements or inventions made by it or its subcontractors or sublicensees (TechA §C-2). In turn, J.Co has a separate obligation to disclose to A.Co any improvements or inventions it makes (MA §D-1). Any patent rights related to the Licensed Products that Newco obtains are subject to a free nonexclusive license to A.Co (TechA §B-4). Any related patent rights J.Co obtains are to be granted to Newco or A.Co (MA §D-2).

3. The P.C. Agreements and the Licensing Guidelines

Consider again the Antimonopoly Act Licensing Guidelines in light of the control system in the P.C. Particularly problematic provisions of the P.C. Agreements include the following:

(1) MA §§D-2(a) and (c) may fall within subparagraphs (5) or (6) of the "highly likely" category of the Guidelines because they give A.Co exclusive rights in any patents resulting from improvements.

(2) TechA §§C-1 and 2 and MA §D-1, along with MA §§D-2(a) and (c), may fall within subparagraph (3) of the "may" category of the Guidelines because they impose unequal obligations on the licensor, A.Co, and the substantive licensee, J.Co.

(3) MA §B-3(a) probably does not fall under the "unlikely" category, but it may fall within subparagraph (1) of the "may" category or subparagraph (3) or (4) of the "highly likely" category.

(4) DA §F possibly falls within subparagraph (1) of the "may" category or subparagraph (3) or (4) of the "highly likely" category.

(5) If A.Co's technology has become publicly known, then Amending Agreement No. 15 §§A-1(b) and 2 fall under subparagraph (4) of the "highly likely" category. (Amending Agreement No. 15 is discussed later in this chapter.)

PART B: Know-How

I. The Know-How Issue in the P.C.

A. Presentation of the issue

About three and one-half years after entering into the P.C. Agreements, J.Co notified A.Co that it had developed a new hydraulic excavator that was smaller than the products for which A.Co had licensed technology. J.Co said it wanted to sell this new model, designated the 10-H, as its own product, rather than as a Newco product. J.Co's letter and A.Co's response are reprinted below. In reading these, try to identify what issues J.Co's plans present under the P.C. Agreements. Imagine you represent A.Co and must help it formulate a reply.

- - - - - - - - - -

[J.Co letterhead]
October 23, 1973

Mr. A. J. Rose, Director
International Operations
A.Co
[Address omitted]

Subject: Development of Small Size Hydraulic Excavator by J.Co

Dear Mr. Rose:

This will confirm our telephone conversation of October 20 concerning the manufacture of the small size (250 liter) hydraulic excavators by J.Co.

J.Co intends to manufacture hydraulic excavators that it has designed and that have the following basic specifications:

Dipper size	.2 - .25 cu. meter
Working weight	8,000 kg
Digging depth	3,500 - 4,000 mm

We propose that the model name for these small size hydraulic excavators be "10-H." The 10-H is required for water and gas pipe laying purposes at narrow job sites, especially streets in urban areas. Furthermore, the lighter working weight of the 10-H would substantially reduce transportation costs.

The 10-H is necessary because the Licensed Products are too large and too heavy for use at such narrow job sites. By offering a broader line of products, we believe we will eventually expand sales of the 15-H and 20-H excavators (the Licensed Products). We are now conducting an analysis on the market for these small excavators; and we will relay the results to you as soon as they are available.

As stated in the above-referenced telephone conversation, we are entirely confident that the 10-H will not compete with the Licensed Products, as it was developed for entirely different purposes.

Your prompt response to this matter will be highly appreciated.

Yours sincerely,
[signed]

N. Obayashi
Executive Managing Director
J.Co

- - - - - - - - - -

[A.Co letterhead]
December 8, 1973

Mr. N. Obayashi
Executive Managing Director
J.Co
[Address omitted]

Subject: Development of Small Size Hydraulic Excavator by J.Co

Dear Mr. Obayashi:

Please accept our apologies for the delay in answering your letter of October 23rd. The delay was caused by the absence from the office of some of our officers.

We believe that the development by J.Co of any size of excavator would conflict both with the word and the spirit of the JVA. With the spirit, because we always looked upon Newco as a JV formed by A.Co and J.Co to fill the excavator needs of the Japanese market as well as those of other countries in Asia. With the word, because such action on J.Co's part would conflict with § B-3(a) of the Manufacturing Agreement.

It is our considered opinion, based on world-wide experience selling machines of this size and type, that any excavator with (1) hydraulic system, (2) hoe front-end, and (3) main front-end machinery integrated in design (as distinguished from tractors in which the front-end is merely mounted as auxiliary equipment) will inevitably (a) compete with any other immediately larger or smaller excavator having such character, and (b) be based on common know-how and design considerations.

Apart from the legal issues, we think that Newco's and A.Co's interests might be affected because in border-line cases, when a customer is undecided between a 250 liter machine (such as the proposed 10-H) and the 15-H (the 375 liter Licensed Product), J.Co's staff would naturally favor the sale of their own product. This would deprive Newco of its share of the mark-up and A.Co of a royalty. Furthermore, we feel that in developing such a 250 liter machine, J.Co would inevitably use know-how acquired from us under the JVA, for which we should be compensated.

However, having regard for J.Co's interests as well as for the foregoing, we would be prepared to agree to J.Co developing the proposed 10-H under the following conditions:

1. It meets the general specifications listed in your October 23 letter.
2. J.Co would pay A.Co a royalty at the rate of 2% on the 10-H models shipped with the standard 250 liter dipper. If, for special applications, machines are equipped with a larger dipper, the normal royalty of 5% would apply.

We believe the above proposal is a fair compromise. The mechanism for formalizing this arrangement (by amendment to the JVA) should be considered carefully, and we have asked our attorney, Mr. Holmes, for his recommendations. We will be writing to you further on this point. Your comments will be appreciated.

Yours very truly,
[signed]

A.J. Rose
Director,
International Operations
A.Co

B. The know-how dispute

First, note that the two principal issues in the letters above are: 1) whether the new model 10-H competes with the Licensed Products and thus violates MA §B-3(a), and 2) whether it incorporates A.Co's know-how. In this section, we address the second issue: whether the 10-H incorporates A.Co's know-how. We will discuss the competition issue in Chapter 10. Second, note that this know-how dispute did not involve patent rights. All the patents licensed in the P.C. had either expired or were narrowly enough defined that J.Co could avoid their scope.

Questions and Discussion Points

1. *Identifying A.Co's know-how*: Under the MA, A.Co licensed its "Technical Data," "Technical Improvement Data," and "Technical Assistance." Consider carefully the definitions of these terms in Section A of the MA. Do the definitions help determine whether model 10-H incorporates A.Co's know-how? Below is an excerpt from a document A.Co prepared in connection with its dispute with the Japan Fair Trade Commission (which is discussed in Chapter 10). In the excerpt, A.Co identifies its know-how as follows:

> Technology for a single model typically consists of hundreds of general, assembly, and detailed engineering drawings (showing the dimensions of, and the interrelationship of, component parts of a machine), engineering lists and bills of materials, a thorough description of materials specifications, details concerning heat treatment and stress relieving of castings, test procedures, and a detailed description of the methods and procedures to be used in the manufacturing process (including drawings of jigs, fixtures, and special tools). * * *
>
> Technology cannot simply be given to a manufacturer with the expectation that the manufacturer will be able to produce the machine. There must also be in-depth discussions between engineering and manufacturing personnel of the parties (A.Co and J.Co). In these discussions, the discloser's (A.Co's) personnel provide a detailed explanation of the interrelationships among the various elements of the technology and impart to the disclosee's (J.Co's) personnel the benefit of the discloser's experience gained over many years in the production of the machines. Assistance must also be given in adapting the technology to the disclosee's manufacturing facilities. Disclosures of the kind described and follow-up disclosures have continued on an active basis since the agreements were executed in 1970.

2. *Basic design concept*: In its letter, A.Co states that any excavator incorporating specified basic characteristics would "inevitably * * * be based on common know-how and design considerations." In other letters, A.Co developed

this logic into its "basic design concept" argument, *i.e.*, that the new model 10-H excavator, which J.Co claimed to have developed independently, incorporated the "basic design concept" expressed in A.Co's know-how.

Should a "basic design concept" be considered know-how?

3. *Evaluating the claims of A.Co and J.Co*: A.Co also argued in its letter that, "in developing [the new 10-H excavator], J.Co would inevitably use know-how acquired from us under the JVA." A.Co claimed that, because J.Co did not manufacture hydraulic excavators before entering into the JVA, J.Co could not plausibly have developed the new excavator without using A.Co's know-how. Whom do you believe?

In analyzing each company's claims, consider the practice of reverse engineering—the process of disassembling a product to determine how to make a competing product without directly using the same technology. Is reverse engineering legal? Is it relevant to the know-how dispute between A.Co and J.Co?

4. *The connection to the non-competition issue*: Note that A.Co refers to MA §B-3(a) and the non-competition issue. Is the clause relevant?

C. The compromise

A.Co and J.Co negotiated for almost two years before resolving their dispute over the 10-H. Their agreement is expressed in Amending Agreement No. 15 (AA-15). Review AA-15 to understand the nature of the compromise. Focus in particular on the third "Whereas" clause and paragraphs A-1; B-1 and 2; and C. Below is the cover letter A.Co sent with AA-15.

- - - - - - - - - -

[A.Co letterhead]
July 20, 1975

Mr. Taro Kawada, President
J.Co
[Address omitted]

Subject: Model 10-H
Hydraulic Excavator

Dear Mr. Kawada:

I have reviewed with some concern the matter of the 10-H hydraulic excavator, and would like to outline in this letter my views as to the best way to handle this subject under the Joint Venture Agreement (JVA).

First, the following important matters of principle are involved:

(1) The proposed 10-H model raises the question as to how we are to handle under the JVA a machine designed by J.Co (rather than by A.Co) that is competitive with Newco products because it is of the same type, close in size, and similar in general design, and that is developed jointly by or based on common know-how of A.Co and J.Co. It is important that we decide now how we will treat this type of product, which I will call a "Related Licensed Product."

(2) Since the Manufacturing Agreement between J.Co and Newco expressly prohibits J.Co from "directly or indirectly being concerned in the manufacture, sale or handling of any items competitive with Newco," it is clear that such manufacture or sale by J.Co requires the consent of both parties to the JV and should be documented by an appropriate Amending Agreement to the JVA.
(3) Such amendment to the JVA should not be limited to the 10-H, but should govern other "Related Licensed Products" in similar future situations, so that a sound approach developed now will be available to avoid confusion and needless negotiations in the future.
(4) It is fundamental to the JV that, if a machine otherwise prohibited by the Manufacturing Agreement is to be produced at all, it be produced and sold within the framework of the JVA as a Related Licensed Product complementary to the line of Newco Products. Otherwise, we would have great confusion in the marketplace as well as many administrative complications within the JV itself.

We propose to treat the 10-H as a Related Licensed Product within the framework of the JVA under the attached Amending Agreement 15. The basic features of the Amending Agreement are as follows:

(1) The model 10-H would be incorporated into the JVA structure as a "Related Licensed Product."
(2) "Related Licensed Products" would be defined as J.Co excavators/cranes and parts and components thereof that are similar in design to Licensed Products, being developed jointly by, or based on common know-how of, A.Co and J.Co.
(3) A.Co would, in addition to its related know-how already furnished and utilized in the 10-H, continuously furnish to Newco and J.Co know-how in the form of Technical Assistance, especially as to review of designs, quality standards, training and technical matters.
(4) Newco would thus be a licensee and J.Co a sublicensee with respect to such know-how.
(5) J.Co would pay Newco and Newco would pay A.Co a 2% Technical Assistance Fee, but no minimum fee and no disclosure fee.
(6) Sales in Japan would be exclusively handled by J.Co. Sales outside Japan in Newco Territory and A.Co Territory would be handled through Newco and A.Co as in the case of Licensed Products.

Amending Agreement No. 15 is enclosed. We also propose immediate discussions regarding the sale of the 10-H abroad in A.Co Territory where we feel there is a potential market.

Sincerely yours,
[signed]

P.E. Berger
President

Questions and Discussion Points

1. *The know-how issue*: To exactly what have A.Co and J.Co agreed?

2. *Distinctions in the technology transfer*: In the P.C. Agreements, the technology transfer is effected by a license from A.Co to Newco (TechA §B-1) and then by Newco's hiring J.Co as a contractor (MA §B-1). How are Related Licensed Products treated in AA-15? Why was this new structure used?

3. *Resolving know-how disputes*: In the above letter, A.Co states that it intends AA-15 to serve as a model for future machines designed by J.Co. Might this approach be successful in resolving future disputes?

II. Protection of Know-How

Suppose A.Co and J.Co were not able to agree on the know-how issue and that the MA did not impose a non-competition obligation on J.Co. If J.Co proceeded with the independent manufacture of the new model, what claims might A.Co have? Suppose further that J.Co conveyed A.Co's know-how to a third party. What recourse would A.Co have against this third party?

These questions go to the issue of whether there are enforceable rights in know-how. The selections and case below set out the Japanese law on point.

A. Protection under contract and by criminal sanctions

JAY DRATLER, TRADE SECRETS IN THE UNITED STATES AND JAPAN: A COMPARISON AND PROGNOSIS*

14 Yale Journal of International Law 68

100-104 (1989)

[1.] **Contractual Protection of Information**

Japanese law appears to provide adequate protection against direct misappropriation of a trade secret by an individual in contractual privity with the trade secret owner. The leading decision is *Yūgen Kaisha Foseco Japan Ltd.*[1] Upon beginning employment, two employees had been paid a special allowance and had signed a special nondisclosure and non-competition agreement with their employer, which was to last for two years after termination of employment. Both worked for the company for more than ten years. After their retirement, they became directors of a newly-established company, which began manufacturing and marketing the same products as their former employer and soliciting the former employer's customers. When the former employer sued, the court awarded it a provisional injunction prohibiting the two employees from manufacturing or marketing products similar to their former employer's products for the duration of the two-year term of the agreement.

---

*From Jay Dratler, "Trade Secrets in the United States and Japan: A Comparison and Prognosis," 14 *Yale Journal of International Law* 68 (1989), at 100-104. Reprinted by permission.

In awarding injunctive relief to prevent direct misappropriation of information received and used in violation of special nondisclosure and noncompetition agreements, this decision is unremarkable. But its reasoning is more interesting than its result. In enforcing the special agreements, the Nara District Court relied in part upon the defendants' receipt of specific technical information, or "property with objective value," as the court described it, that was not generally available. By concluding that the employees' knowledge of this information rendered the special agreement enforceable, the court appeared to imply that the contract might *not* be fully enforceable if the information did not have "objective value." * * *

A second relevant decision involved the copying and sale of a confidential customer list while in the possession of a subcontractor.[2] In an action against the subcontractor, the Tokyo District Court found that the information in the list was useful and had competitive value. It also found that the terms of the subcontract required the subcontractor, upon completion of its work, to return the list to the contractor. The court ruled that the subcontractor had a duty as a bailee not only to preserve the list from physical loss or destruction, but also to maintain information in the list in confidence and to avoid reducing the value of that information as a trade secret. Finding that the subcontractor had violated that duty, the court awarded "consolation money" in an amount greater than the plaintiff's claim, although it refused to award direct damages for lost profits due to failure of proof.

Three points about this case are worth noting. First, the actual misappropriator (apparently an unknown employee) was not before the court. Second, the third party that purchased and used the information also was not before the court. Finally, in noting that the information * * * had competitive value, the Tokyo District Court appeared to be applying the same "objective value" theory as the court in the *Foseco* case.

Although of doctrinal interest, the apparent requirement that information have objective economic value in order to enjoy contractual protection in Japan is unlikely to have great practical effect. Most information worth fighting about probably will satisfy this test. * * *

[2.] Criminal Sanctions

Reported Japanese cases also indicate that Japan has useful criminal sanctions for willful misappropriation of trade secrets. In several such cases, Japanese courts have imposed criminal sanctions under theories of embezzlement, breach of trust, larceny, and receiving stolen property.

Perhaps the most comprehensive decision of this kind is *Tōyō Rayon Co.*[3] There an engineer, who was vice-chief of the manufacturing technology division of a chemical plant, received confidential documents relating to his company's new products and sold them to a competitor through two brokers. He and the two brokers were convicted on charges of embezzlement in the performance of business, and the competitor's employees who received the stolen documents were convicted of purchasing stolen property. * * *

Embezzlement convictions are not the only criminal sanctions for trade secret misappropriation in Japan. In *Dainippon Insatsu*,[4] a manager hired a private investigator to determine whether his company's trade secret had been disclosed to a competitor, but the private investigator attempted to play both ends against the middle by intimidating executives of the competitor. Among other things, he claimed he had been hired to spy on the competitor, tried to extort money from the competitor, and induced an employee of the competitor to give him the competitor's secret documents, which he then sold to the manager at the company that had hired him. The employee supplying the documents was convicted of larceny, and both the private investigator and the manager who had hired him were convicted of receiving stolen property.

These criminal cases all have one thing in common: they involve sanctions against individuals, not against the firms for which they worked. As in the United States, these criminal sanctions have practical disadvantages, such as the requirement of proof of criminal culpability and dependence on the prosecutorial machinery of the state. More important, however effective these sanctions may be against individuals, they do not operate directly on the firm that obtains the benefit of the misappropriation, nor do they prevent use of the misappropriated trade secret by that firm. It is the unique province of tort law to provide effective relief against use of a secret by a third party that benefits from the misappropriation. Therefore, in Japan as in the United States, it is tort law to which a trade secret owner must turn for complete relief.

B. Protection without privity of contract

JAY DRATLER, TRADE SECRETS IN THE UNITED STATES AND JAPAN: A COMPARISON AND PROGNOSIS

14 Yale Journal of International Law 68

104-108 (1989)

In theory, Japanese tort law is broad enough to support legal protection for trade secrets or know-how. Article 709 of the Japanese Civil Code contains a very general definition of the concept of tort, translated into English as follows:

A person who intentionally or negligently violates the rights of another is obligated to compensate for damages arising therefrom.

In practice, however, there is some doubt whether trade secrets and know-how are the sort of "rights" that this provision seeks to protect. The question is reminiscent of the dispute between the "property" and "breach of confidence" schools of thought in the United States and flows from the same source, the weakness of trade secret protection, which makes courts in all nations uncomfortable comparing rights in trade secrets with those in patents and copyrights.

---

*Excerpt from Jay Dratler, "Trade Secrets in the United States and Japan: A Comparison and Prognosis," 14 *Yale Journal of International Law* 68 (1989), at 104-108. Reprinted by permission.

One decision suggests that Japanese tort law may provide a *damage* remedy against a third party, at least where the third party is a legal entity set up by the actual misappropriators. The case involved defections from Sanrei-Yamako, a mail-order firm.[5] Toyama, a director of the firm, induced an employee of the firm to take its customer list and other secret materials for use in starting a similar mail-order business under the name of Colm Trading Co. Toyama had established Colm while still a director of Sanrei-Yamako, but he resigned before engaging in competitive business. Colm then produced imitations of Sanrei-Yamako's catalogues and sent them to customers on the stolen mailing list.

Upon suit by Sanrei-Yamako, the Kobe District Court held both Toyama and Colm liable for damages for violation of Articles 1.1 and 1.2 of the Unfair Competition Prevention Law [currently codified in Section 2 of the Unfair Competition Prevention Act of 1993, reproduced in the Appendices], and for tort. On appeal, the Osaka High Court upheld the judgments against Toyama and Colm on both theories, noting that Toyama had carried on a business based on an improperly obtained customer list. It upheld an award of damages in an amount it deemed to be a reasonable license fee for use of the customer list and other secret materials taken. Apparently there was no claim for injunctive relief.

The *Sanrei-Yamako* decision suggests that a third party may be liable in damages under a tort theory for misappropriation of trade secrets in Japan. Yet for two reasons the case provides only weak authority for this proposition. First, the Osaka High Court mentioned the tort theory only in passing, but did not discuss it. The claim for unfair competition appeared more substantial, occupied more of the court's attention, and undoubtedly was sufficient by itself to support the award of damages. Second, the "third party" in this case—Colm Trading Co.—was in fact an alter ego of the individual defendants. Had the defendant been a truly "arm's length" third party, the result might have been different.

As for injunctive relief, the only reported case directly on point casts great doubt on the practical availability of injunctions for misappropriation of trade secrets in Japan[, at least prior to 1990 amendments to the Unfair Competition Prevention Act and the complete revision of that Act discussed in Section C below.] That case is *Deutsche Werft A.G. v. [Chūetsu Waukesha] Y.G.*

- - - - - - - - - -

Translation by Yanagida Nomura & Akai

Deutsche Werft A.G. v. Chūetsu Waukesha Y.G.
464 Hanrei Jihō 34
(Tokyo High Ct., Sept. 5, 1976)

REFERENCES:

Code of Civil Procedure, § 760

Civil Code, §§ 415 and 719

FACTS:

Claimant Deutsche Werft A.G. (D.W.), a Germany company, granted an American company, Waukesha Bearings Co. (Waukesha), a license to use D.W.'s know-how in the manufacture of oil-lubricated bearings for ship propellers (the "products"). The license restricted the use of this know-how by Waukesha to the United States and Canada. Waukesha and a Japanese company, K.K. Chūetsu, later established a joint venture company in Japan, the respondent Chūetsu Waukesha Yūgen Gaisha (C.W.), in which Waukesha held a 45 percent share. C.W. began to manufacture and sell the products in Japan, using know-how that had been disclosed to Waukesha under its license agreement with D.W.

D.W. petitioned the Tokyo District Court for a temporary injunction enjoining C.W. from manufacturing and selling the products. The District Court dismissed the petition. D.W. has appealed the District Court's decision to this court, arguing that as C.W. is only an "alter ego" of Waukesha, C.W.'s acts should be deemed to be acts by Waukesha. Accordingly, it argues, C.W.'s use of the know-how disclosed by D.W. to manufacture the products in Japan constitutes a breach of contract. D.W. further alleges that even if C.W. is regarded as an independent legal entity, C.W. and Waukesha should be held to have jointly and tortiously infringed D.W.'s know-how.

JUDGMENT:

The appeal by D.W. is dismissed.

REASONS:

* * * Regardless of its current legal status, know-how clearly has proprietary value. Yet such value is still not recognized as a right in the eyes of the law. A party receiving assistance under a know-how agreement (a technical assistance agreement) naturally assumes an obligation not to disclose that know-how beyond the scope prescribed in the agreement. This obligation is a contractual one, and the obligor who discloses such know-how in violation of the contract is liable for damages and other relief under contract law. However, if a third party acquires the know how accidentally or from the contractual obligor, and if such third party then incorporates the know-how into its manufacture, the law does not provide a way to halt such third party's manufacture of products that use that know-how.

Although know-how does have proprietary value, it does not carry rights that bind third parties (regardless of whether it is an intellectual property right or a contractual right). Know-how can only be protected by its holders, who must labor to keep it from being disclosed to third parties.

In the instant case, the respondent C.W. counts among its shareholders such a contract obligor as described above, Waukesha. Waukesha contributed about 45% of the equity capital of C.W. Moreover, two of C.W.'s directors are sent from Waukesha. As D.W. has acknowledged, despite these circumstances, C.W. must legally be considered a third party to the above-mentioned contract.

C.W. may have injured D.W. by collaborating with Waukesha in the latter's failure to perform its contractual obligation not to disclose the know-how. Nonetheless, * * * and leaving aside the question of whether C.W. is liable in damages, the interest which D.W. desires to protect through this petition for a temporary injunction has not been accompanied by a preliminary showing sufficient to warrant such action. Moreover, it is unreasonable to allow a security deposit to substitute for a preliminary showing.

Thus, the original decision dismissing D.W.'s petition for a temporary injunction is correct.

Questions and Discussion Points

1. *The holding of the court in Waukesha*: Is the court's holding sensible? Is it inevitable given the relevant law?

2. *Effect of the holding in Waukesha*: Does the holding let licensees use dummy third parties to route the know-how they receive under license agreements?

C. Recent statutory reform

In 1990, the Diet amended the old Unfair Competition Prevention Act (Law No. 14 of 1934) to cover know-how. In 1993, the Diet replaced that Act with a new Unfair Competition Prevention Act (the UCPA, Law No. 47 of 1993), which carried over the provisions regarding know-how. The UCPA, which appears in the Appendices, prohibits various deceptive practices and provides remedies against, *inter alia*, those who use another's trade name or falsely indicate the place products were manufactured.

Analyze Section 2, Subsection 1, Items (iv) through (ix) and Section 2, Subsection 4 of the UCPA to determine whether, if they had been in effect when the *Waukesha* case was heard, the result would have been different. Consider also the effect of Section 4.

PART C: Statutory Intellectual Property

I. Overview: Traditional Intellectual Property Right Categories

The forms of intellectual property traditionally recognized by statute in Japan are patents, utility models, designs, trademarks, and copyrights. The following section briefly summarizes salient characteristics of these intellectual property forms.

1. Patents

Patents are governed by the Patent Act (Law No. 121 of 1959) and administered by the Patent Office, which is a division of MITI. Patents can be granted for products or processes which meet the requirements of novelty, utility, and inventiveness. During the life of a patent—the shorter of 15 years from the date of publication of the patent application and 20 years from the date of filing of the application—the patent holder has the exclusive right to work the patent.

2. Utility models

Utility models, which do not exist under U.S. law, are essentially a lesser form of patent. They are governed by the Utility Model Act (Law No. 123 of 1959), which basically parallels the Patent Act, and are also administered by the Patent Office. Utility model registrations can be obtained for inventions that involve less of an inventive step than that required for patent registrations, but their life is five years shorter than that of patents.

3. Designs

Design registrations are available under the Design Act (Law No. 125 of 1959). During their 15-year life, designs provide their holders an exclusive right to the commercial use of the shape, pattern, color, or combination of the foregoing of an object.

4. Trademarks

Trademark registrations are available under the Trademark Act (Law No. 127 of 1959) for "letters, figures, or signs, or any combination of these and colors" that are used on goods or in connection with services by a person who, "as a business," "produces, processes, certifies or assigns" such goods or "renders or certifies" such services. Unlike in the U.S., a trademark registration must designate the type of goods or service for which the trademark will be used. Trademarks last for 10 years and can usually be renewed. That renewal is subject, however, to certain requirements, including that the trademark holder or its licensee actually use the trademark during the three years before the renewal request.

5. Service marks

Until amendments to the Trademark Act that became effective in 1992, trademark protection was available only for marks used on goods, *i.e.*, the Act did not provide for the registration of symbols identifying service companies, such as package delivery or life insurance companies. These symbols, called service marks, could often be protected, however, under the Unfair Competition Prevention Act (UCPA). The UCPA bans deceptive practices that confuse consumers about the origin of goods and allows a firm to enjoin an "infringing" party from using a well-known mark, symbol, or name. Even with the amendment to the Trademark Act, the UCPA (which, as discussed above, was itself revised in 1993) still provides important additional protections for marks, such as protections for certain items that do not qualify as trademarks or that do qualify but were not registered, and protections against those who in effect copy a company's trade name registered pursuant to the Commercial Code.

6. Copyrights

The Copyright Act (Law No. 48 of 1970) offers protection for "works of authorship" such as literary works, musical works, paintings,and photographic works, and, as of amendments in 1985 and 1986, computer programs, data bases, and cable technology data. Derivative works, such as translations or the movie version of a copyrighted book, are protected independently of the original works, but this protection does not prejudice the rights of the authors of the original works.

Copyright protection extends to works of authorship that are produced by Japanese nationals (including legal entities), are first published in Japan or published in Japan within 30 days of being first published elsewhere, or must be given protection due to a treaty obligation. Copyrights ensue from the moment of creation and last until, in the case of natural persons, 50 years following death, and in the cases of legal persons and all copyrights for cinematographic and photographic works, 50 years from publication (or, if not published, from creation).

The contents of Japanese copyrights are similar to those of other developed countries. However, the Copyright Act operates to allow the commercial lending of phonograms (CD's, cassette tapes, LP's, etc.) (*see* the *Miyagi* case, Chapter 5, Section III.A.2.). The producer of a phonogram has the exclusive right to lend the phonogram publicly for only one year from publication; after that rental shops may offer phonograms, though the producer may collect royalties through a collection organization.

II. Patents

A. The Patent Act[6]

1. Patents versus utility models

Often, it will not be clear whether an invention qualifies as a patent or only as a utility model. This ambiguity creates a strategic decision. The inventor must decide whether to obtain a utility model registration (an easier process) or to file for a patent (and obtain longer protection). Apparently, Japanese and foreign companies calculate the odds differently—at least, if one assumes both groups of companies have relatively equal levels of knowledge about the respective forms. According to a 1977 Japanese Patent Office report, 57% of invention filings by Japanese were for utility models while only 6% of those by foreigners were.[7] We will not discuss utility models in the rest of this chapter. Nonetheless, because the Utility Model Act parallels the Patent Act, much of the basic law explained below for patents applies to utility models.

2. The first-to-file system

In Japan, the party entitled to obtain a patent is the first party to file an application (Patent Act, §39), while in the U.S. the right inheres in the inventor. Two things should be noted about this difference. First, the U.S. is the only major industrial country to use the first-to-invent rule. Second, under Japan's Patent Act, an inventor who fails to make a timely filing and finds that someone else has obtained the patent does not necessarily lose the right to work the invention (*see* Patent Act, §79).

3. Patent applications and the laying-out system

Applications for Japanese patents must disclose enough detail to enable someone reading the application to work the invention. Unless an application is withdrawn, eighteen months after it is filed the substance of its contents will be made publicly available (Patent Act, §65-2). The virtue of this system is that it discourages duplicate research by giving everyone access to the most recent knowledge. The patent applicant, of course, is not trying to disclose his or her invention but to obtain an exclusive right to work it. The excerpt below explains the *quid pro quo* to the patent applicant for having the substance of the application made public.

SADANAO AMEMIYA AND KIKUO NISHIMOTO, PATENTS AND UTILITY MODELS*

4 Doing Business in Japan
Part 6, §2.06[4] (1994)

In return for the automatic disclosure of the contents of his application, an applicant is given a *conditional* right to collect a reasonable royalty from anyone who works his invention, but he does not have the right at this stage to halt another's working of the invention. One such condition is that the right vanishes *ab initio* if no patent ever issues on the application or if an issued patent is later canceled. A second condition is that, in view of the relatively large number of such laid open applications published each month, the right to a royalty from a user of the invention begins only after the user actually knows of the laying open. In practice, the applicant sends such a user a simple warning letter which includes a copy of the laid open application to establish proof of the user's knowledge. A third condition is that no court action may be brought to exercise the right until the application has progressed to the point where it has been published for opposition (*kōkoku*), currently about four years after laying open.

In view of these restrictions, the conditional right is of limited value. However, where the applicant has good reason to suspect that his invention is or will be used in Japan by a particular party, he should investigate and send a warning letter. The only drawback in sending such a letter is that the recipient will then surely be aware of the application and be likely to submit copies of relevant prior art for the use of the examiner or to file an opposition when the application is published for opposition.

The only way an applicant can prevent laying open is by early abandonment (*hōki*) or withdrawal (*torisage*) of his as yet secret application. * * *

Abandonment without laying open leaves the applicant's claims citable against the claims of later applications. However, in the case of withdrawal without laying open, the application is treated as if it had never been filed, permitting a later filing by the same applicant or another.

- - - - - - - - - -

*Reprinted with permission from Sadanao Amemiya and Kikuo Nishimoto, "Patents and Utility Models," in Zentaro Kitagawa, general ed., 4 *Doing Business in Japan*, at Part 6, §2.06[4].

4. Request for examination by the Patent Office

Unlike in the U.S., patent applications in Japan are not reviewed substantively by the Patent Office until a request is made for examination (Patent Law, §48-2). If no request is made within seven years of an application's being filed, the application is treated as having been withdrawn (Patent Act, §48-3(4)). Even if the applicant requests review, the process does not move rapidly. Because of backlogs at the Patent Office, applicants must often wait three or four years before the Patent Office actually begins its examination. The examination itself then adds several more years to the process.

5. Publication for opposition system

In the U.S., if the Patent Office concludes that an invention merits a patent, it issues one. In Japan, an initial favorable decision by the Patent Office instead leads simply to the publication of the patent application. At that point, others have three months to file objections with supporting evidence (Patent Act, §55(1)). Only if no one objects (or the Patent Officer rejects the objections) does the applicant receive the patent.

Nonetheless, once a patent application is published for opposition, the applicant obtains a provisional patent right. At this point, the applicant can enjoin others from using the invention and collect damages from such infringers (Patent Act, §52-2). Because the applicant's right is only provisional, if the patent is not ultimately granted, the applicant must indemnify anyone from whom it has obtained royalties and pay damages to anyone it has enjoined (Patent Act, §52(4)).

6. Scope of patent grants

The scope of patent grants under Japanese law has been a subject of considerable contention. American parties have often claimed that Japanese patent grants are so narrow that other parties can effectively circumvent the patent by obtaining their own patents for minor changes in the invention. Some (admittedly ambiguous) evidence for this claim exists in the number of filings made; in recent years there have been about 900,000 patent and utility model applications each year in Japan (about 30,000 by American applicants), but only about 100,000 patent applications in the U.S. (about 20,000 by Japanese applicants).[8]

B. Validity challenges and infringement suits

A major difference between U.S. and Japanese patent law concerns the relationship between infringement suits and challenges to the validity of a patent. In the U.S., the defendant in an infringement suit can challenge the validity of the subject patent in court. By contrast, in Japan the Patent Office has the exclusive original jurisdiction on the validity of patents. As a result, defendants in infringement suits cannot directly challenge a patent's validity in court. Instead, under Section 123 of the Patent Act, a defendant challenging the validity of a patent must file a separate invalidation suit at the Patent Office and then (under Section 168) stay the infringement suit pending the outcome of the Patent Office suit. The problem with this strategy is simply delay: an invalidation action at the Patent Office can take a very long time.

NOBUHIRO NAKAYAMA, PATENT INFRINGEMENT SUITS AND PUBLICLY KNOWN TECHNOLOGY*

98 Hōgaku Kyōkai Zasshi 115

1115-1116, 1136-1137 (1981)

After rigorous examination by the Patent Office, patent rights should be granted to any technology that exceeds the technology publicly known at the time of filing. In practice, however, it is impossible to expect the Patent Office to conduct the complete, error-free examination of the novelty and inventiveness of the technology required by Section 29 of the Patent Act. A complete examination of "inventions described in publications distributed in foreign countries," as required by Section 29(1)(iii), would be particularly hard.

Despite the system of opposition filing * * * (called the "publication for opposition system"), many issued patents may lack novelty and inventiveness. Although such patents are invalid (*see* §123(1)(i)), they do not immediately become invalid. Instead, they are only potentially subject to an invalidation hearing (§123(1)). A patent right that has reason to be held invalid [*e.g.*, one that lacks novelty] is treated as valid in Japan, as in Germany, until [the Patent Office] rules otherwise. Even a court cannot hold such a patent invalid. Not only can one not sue in court to have a patent held invalid, one cannot even argue in an infringement suit for damages that a patent is invalid. This view appears consistently in court decisions and is almost unanimously supported by scholars. If in an infringement suit a defendant thinks that a patent is invalid, the defendant must petition for an invalidation hearing at the Patent Office.

Although the law provides ways to coordinate the two legal actions [the infringement suit and the invalidation hearing] (*see* §168), the redundant processes of litigation and hearing can place a great burden on the parties, particularly upon the allegedly infringing party. The current hearing process takes far too long, usually many years from the filing to a final ruling. If the infringement trial is put on hold and then begun again after the ruling in the invalidation hearing, it is not rare for the court to reach a decision on the infringement issue only after the patent right has expired. In a time of rapid technological progress, such time-consuming litigation becomes pointless for patent disputes. The more important a dispute, the more the parties will try to avoid litigation.

In both Germany and Japan, some scholars and courts have advocated allowing alleged infringers some right to contest the validity of a patent in an infringe-

*Excerpts from Nobuhiro Nakayama, "Tokkyo Shingai Soshō to Kōchi Gijutsu" ("Patent Infringement Suits and Publicly Known Technology"), 98 *Hōgaku Kyōkai Zasshi* 1115 (1981), at 1115-1116, 1136-1137 (translated by Yanagida Nomura & Akai). Reprinted by permission.

ment suit. These scholars and courts have found the case particularly compelling where the patent right contains publicly known technology and is infringed.

In Japan, courts have taken the initiative. * * *

The first line of decisions follows the theory appearing in a [1964 Supreme Court case (18 *Minshū* 1319, Aug. 4, 1964)]. In these cases, the courts interpret the scope of the patent claim as narrowly as possible. They thus reach a substantively reasonable result by holding that the defendant has not infringed the plaintiff's patent right. By assuming that courts cannot rule on the validity of a patent right, these decisions try to resolve the matter by making the issue turn on the patent right's scope. Therefore, even though the patent involved publicly known technology, it remained valid in theory—any party using technology identical to the claim infringes the patent. In reality, however, in order to secure a substantively reasonable result, the courts effectively invalidate part or all of the patent under the pretext of interpreting its scope.

The second line of decisions recognizes that if the patent is based entirely on publicly known technology, the court cannot allow the patent holder legal protection. These courts presume that the patent itself is valid unless determined otherwise by an invalidation trial, but refuse to permit the exercise of the patent right. Two cases (2 *Mutaireishū* 612, Osaka Dist. Ct., Nov. 30, 1970, and 852 *Hanrei Jihō* 95, Nagoya Dist. Ct., Nov. 26, 1976) base rulings to this effect on the legal principle of abuse of rights. Whether the principle properly applies here, the courts do reach reasonable results without making the unreasonable interpretations that the first group of courts made. This second group of cases does not question whether the allegedly infringed technology falls within the scope of the patent. Instead, the cases hold that an exercise of the right cannot be permitted since all the claims consist, in fact, of publicly known technology.

III. Basic Features of the Trademark Act

A. Registrability of trademarks

Sections 3 and 4 of the Trademark Act determine which types of marks are registrable. Much trademark litigation, whether before the Patent Office (which administers the trademark system) or the Tokyo High Court (which hears appeals from the Patent Office), concerns whether particular marks should qualify for registration. The first case below illustrates a typical issue under Section 3; the second is typical of the often more contentious cases that arise under Section 4.

K.K. Shiseidō v. Director-General of the Patent Office*
(Tokyo High Ct., Sept. 13, 1974)

FACTS:

The plaintiff applied for registration, on June 5, 1970, of a trademark which

*Translation by Teruo Doi, *Trademark and Unfair Competition Law of Japan: Digest of Court Decisions*, Vol. 1, pp. 51-53 (AIPPI Japan, 1980). Reprinted by permission.

consisted of flower and arabesque designs of oval shape in golden color against a light green background for tooth paste, soaps and cosmetic products including perfumes.

Plaintiff's trademark

Upon refusal of registration by the examiner on April 1, 1971, the plaintiff demanded a trial hearing, but the Patent Office upheld the examiner's refusal on November 1, 1973, on the ground that the plaintiff's trademark did not possess a distinctive character. The Patent Office held as follows:

> In the field of cosmetic products for women, ornamental arrangements of flower and arabesque designs are frequently used in order to stress feminine beauty and elegance. The plaintiff's trademark consists solely of such arrangement of designs and lacks any portion which plays a distinctive function. And, therefore, when the plaintiff's trademark is used for the designated goods, including cosmetic products, traders and consumers simply understand the plaintiff's trademark as an ornamental design of the containers, and hence, the plaintiff's trademark falls under Article 3(1)(vi) of the Trademark Law.

The plaintiff brought this action in the Tokyo High Court for the cancellation of the Patent Office decision. * * *

JUDGMENT:

The plaintiff's trademark is registrable and the Patent Office decision shall be canceled.

REASONS FOR JUDGMENT:

The Patent Office erred in finding that the plaintiff's trademark lacked distinctive function and, therefore, its decision is [contrary to the law].

The plaintiff's trademark consists of a combination of flower and arabesque designs with a background color. These designs are arranged in oval shape and painted in gold color on a light green background. It is proper to find that the plaintiff's trademark, when looked at as a whole, possesses the quality to distinguish the plaintiff's product from the products of others.

The Patent Office reasoned that an ornamental arrangement of flower and arabesque designs was frequently used for women's cosmetic products, and, therefore, the plaintiff's trademark did not possess any portion which drew consumers' attention. This finding is not correct. Flower and arabesque designs are some of the elements of the plaintiff's trademark. Although individual elements of a given trademark lack distinctive quality, their arrangement, combination or coloring may create a distinctive quality. It is also erroneous for the Patent Office to find that the plaintiff's trademark is understood by traders and consumers to be no more than an ornamental design of the container.

The decision of the Patent Office shall be canceled.

- - - - - - - - - -

*Maruman K.K. v. Director-General of the Patent Office** (Tokyo High Ct., July 21, 1970)

FACTS:

The plaintiff applied for a trademark registration of a word "*supairarukareji*" in *katakana* letters for papers and stationery on July 29, 1965. Upon refusal of registration by the examiner on May 26, 1967, the plaintiff demanded a trial hearing, but the Patent Office rendered a decision that there was no ground for the demand on June 24, 1968. The Patent Office stated the ground for upholding the examiner's refusal as follows:

> The trademark under application is a word "*supairarukareji*" in *katakana* letters which consists of two parts *supairaru* and *kareji*. The *supairaru* part derives from an English word "spiral," which means a helix shape or coiled wire, and is used in Japan as a word to describe the shape or quality of certain products. More specifically, notebooks and photo albums are among the goods falling under the class of papers and stationery, and those bound by spiral wires are called "*supairaru-nōto*" (spiral notebooks) or "*supairaru-arubamu*" (spiral albums).
>
> Accordingly, the *supairaru* part of the plaintiff's mark under application is understood by traders and the consuming public to mean the method of binding, and the part which should have a distinctive function must be the *kareji* part.
>
> The trademark cited by the examiner as a conflicting trademark registered for the goods of the same class under earlier application is "*kareji*" in *katakana* letters. The plaintiff's mark and the cited trademark have a common sound and are similar and conflicting when applied to the designated goods. Accordingly, the plaintiff's trademark is unregistrable under Article 4(1)(xi) of the Trademark Law, which makes unregistrable a trademark which is identical with or similar to a trademark registered in accordance with an earlier application for goods of the same class.

The plaintiff brought this action for the cancellation of the Patent Office decision in the Tokyo High Court, alleging as follows:

> Although it is admissible that the word *supairaru* has the meaning stated by the Patent Office, the plaintiff's trademark

*Translation by Teruo Doi, *Trademark and Unfair Competition Law of Japan: Digest of Court Decisions*, Vol. 1, pp. 36-39 (AIPPI Japan, 1980). Reprinted by permission.

"*supairarukareji*" should not be separated into *supairaru* and *kareji* parts.

The plaintiff's trademark was created by combining a word "*supairaru*" which connotes an English word "spiral" (helix) and a word "*kareji*" which connotes another English word "college" (school) and is, as a whole, understood as meaning "spiral-college." The plaintiff's trademark consists of nine *katakana* letters and is written horizontally from left to right in the same style and size, and the two components should not be separated.

The Patent Office points out that the word *supairaru* is descriptive of the quality of certain products and, therefore, lacks distinctive quality. Such a finding has no ground, in view of the fact that the word *supairaru* is registered for papers and stationery (Registration No. 593935). Thus, the Patent Office erred in finding that the plaintiff's trademark is similar to the registered trademark "*kareji*" cited by the examiner. * * *

JUDGMENT:

The decision of the Patent Office shall be upheld.

REASONS FOR JUDGMENT:

The plaintiff's contention has no ground. It is a fact undisputed by the plaintiff that the *supairaru* part of the plaintiff's mark derives from an English word "spiral" and is used by stationery manufacturers and dealers to mean a kind of method of binding notebooks and photo albums. The natural conclusion from this fact is that when the plaintiff uses the mark under application for notebooks and albums that are bound, consumers and traders will understand that [the] *supairaru* part of the plaintiff's mark represents the quality or method of binding of the plaintiff's products. Thus, the portion of the plaintiff's mark which has a distinctive function is the *kareji* part. The plaintiff contends that the mark should be regarded as an inseparable whole.

We are not persuaded by the evidence to hold that it should be treated as inseparable when used in connection with the above products. Although the word *supairaru* is registered for papers and stationery, we should not make a hasty conclusion that this word has a distinctive quality in view of its use in the stationery industry.

Thus, the court considers that the dominant part of the plaintiff's mark is the *kareji* part and this part is in conflict with the registered trademark cited by the Patent Office.

B. Classes of goods, associated marks, and defensive marks

A registration must specify the class or classes of goods or services to which the trademark applies. A registration applicable to sportswear, for example, might not offer protection against the mark's use on sporting equipment. For the sportswear trademark holder to protect the mark against its use on equipment, he or she could either pursue dual registration covering both classes of goods or seek an associated mark registration or a defensive mark registration. These last two categories are described in the following selection.

KAZUKO MATSUO, TRADEMARKS*

4 Doing Business in Japan

Part 6, §§3.01[3][b], [c] (1994)

[1.] Associated Trademark Registrations

As the purpose of the Trademark Act is to protect the goodwill which the user has created or will create with respect to the trademark, as well as to protect the general public's expectation that all goods [or services] bearing the same mark have the same origin and quality, a later trademark identical with or similar to one with prior rights cannot be registered. However, since 1909, an exception has been made in the event such later trademark belongs to the same person as the one with prior rights; in this case the later mark can be registered as an associated trademark, and both the prior and the later trademarks become associated trademarks.

According to Article 7 of the Trademark Act, when the owner of a registered trademark later wishes to register a similar trademark which is used in connection with the same goods [or services] as those of the registration, or when he later wishes to register the same trademark or a similar trademark in connection with goods [or services] similar to those described in the already existing trademark registration, he can do so only when he files for an associated trademark. The associated trademark application can be filed * * * in association with [either] a prior existing trademark registration or [an] application. An application can be filed from the beginning as an associated trademark application, or an independent application can be converted to an associated application on the applicant's own initiative or after receiving a preliminary notice of rejection from the Patent Office based on the same owner's prior registration or application [§11(2)]. In either instance, the Patent Office's decision on the registrability of a trademark as an associated trademark is final. Once the decision has become final, an application cannot later be changed either to an independent trademark application or to an associated trademark application, respectively [§11(3)].

An associated trademark must meet the same substantive registration requirements as an independent trademark, such as distinctiveness, dissimilarity to third parties' trademarks, and dissimilarity of the goods [or services] to those of prior third parties using marks of like appearance, etc.

The scope of an associated trademark is determined as if it were an independent trademark, and the associated trademark registration enjoys the same full effect as an ordinary registered trademark. However, in order to avoid confusion

*Reprinted with permission from Kazuko Matsuo, "Trademarks," in Zentaro Kitagawa, general ed., 4 *Doing Business in Japan*, at Part 6, §§3.01[3][b] and [c].

among the public as to the origin of the goods [or services], an associated registration can only be transferred together with the transfer of the other associated trademark registration, although a license to use an associated trademark can be separately granted from a right to use the other associated trademark [§24(2)]. Furthermore, a trademark which is associated with other registered trademarks is renewable even if it has not been used, provided that its associated trademark has been used. In such case, the registrant who wants to renew the non-used associated trademark has to file evidence of use of the other associated trademark which has been used.

By availing himself of the associated trademark system, a registrant may expand the exclusiveness of his original trademark right to similar goods [or services] and similar trademarks, keeping his registrations up to date with developments in actual trademark use.

[2.] Defensive Mark Registrations

The defensive mark registration system was adopted in 1959 to give broader protection to a widely known trademark.

A defensive registration is one that can be obtained only by the owner of a registered trademark so "widely known" among consumers as indicating the designated goods [or services] relating to his business that a third party's use of the same trademark, even in connection with goods [or services] dissimilar to those listed in the widely known trademark's registration, would cause "confusion as to the origin of the second party's goods [or services]" [§64]. In other words, a defensive mark is obtainable (1) for a trademark identical with the applicant's already widely known registered trademark and (2) for goods [or services] dissimilar to those listed in the widely known trademark's registration, but (3) only when confusion as to the origin of the goods [or services] is likely. There are no other requirements, such as that the defensive mark must be a coined word or invented word, and no requirement that the registrant himself will use the mark in connection with the goods [or services] listed in the defensive registration. * * *

To date, there have been very few defensive mark registrations granted, probably owing to the difficulty of persuading an examiner to recognize the "widely known" status of an applicant's registered trademark. In this connection, traders and practitioners have urged the Patent Office to switch to a more attainable standard of commercial fame.

C. The first-to-file system

Like the Patent Act, the Trademark Act bases the right to hold a trademark on the first-to-file rule. And on this point, trademark law in the U.S. diverges in the same manner as patent law—in the U.S. prior use creates the trademark right. This first-to-file rule, combined with the fact that the Trademark Act does not require that an applicant actually use the mark, creates considerable potential for free riders to register marks others have developed. The trademark registrant can then demand compensation from a "legitimate" user. If the two parties cannot agree, the trademark holder can bring an infringement suit. These suits present the courts with a dilemma: whether to enforce the letter of the law and preserve the first-to-file system, or to do what they perceive to be substantive justice in the particular case.

Osaka Sankei K.K. v. Ox K.K.*
(Osaka Dist. Ct., Feb. 24, 1976)

FACTS:

The plaintiff Osaka Sankei K.K. is the owner of a registered trademark (No. 536992) consisting of an English word "POPEYE," its *katakana* equivalent "*popai*" and Popeye's standing figure in sailorman's outfit for clothing, handkerchiefs, buttons, pins, etc. The plaintiff's application was filed on June 26, 1958, and the registration was effected on June 12, 1959. The plaintiff's registered trademark appears as follows:

Plaintiff's registered trademark

The defendant is engaged in the manufacture and distribution of undershirts which bear A mark or B mark shown below. * * *

Defendant's A mark

Defendant's B mark

[Undershirts omitted.]

*Translation by Teruo Doi, *Trademark and Unfair Competition Law of Japan: Digest of Court Decisions*, Vol. 1, pp. 126-129 (AIPPI Japan, 1980). Reprinted by permission.

The plaintiff brought this action for an injunction against trademark infringement in the Osaka District Court. The plaintiff contended that A and B marks were similar to the plaintiff's trademark and that the defendant's products, undershirts bearing A or B mark, fell under the designated goods for which the plaintiff's trademark was registered, and, therefore, the manufacture and sale by the defendant of these undershirts infringed upon the plaintiff's registered trademark.

The defendant contended that its use of Popeye's comic figure together with the letters "Popeye" on the undershirts in question was simply an ornamental use or a use for a design purpose of Popeye's comic figure and not the use as a trademark as generally understood in the society, and hence such use did not raise a problem of trademark infringement.

The defendant further asserted that King Features Syndicate was the owner of [the] copyright in the United States for The Thimble Theatre, first published on January 1, 1929, and was entitled to national treatment in Japan under the Universal Copyright Convention, and that the defendant was engaged in the manufacture and sale of children's undershirts using the cloth manufactured by Treebig, not a party in this action, who printed Popeye's character and name on the cloth under a license granted by King Features in 1972, and, therefore, the defendant's act was an exercise of copyright which superseded the plaintiff's trademark right and did not constitute an infringement of the plaintiff's trademark under Article 29 of the Trademark Law.

POINT AT ISSUE:

Whether or not the defendant's undershirts bearing the word "POPEYE" or its *katakana* equivalent "*popai*" and Popeye's comic figure infringe upon the plaintiff's registered trademark "POPEYE."

JUDGMENT:

The defendant's use of the word "POPEYE" and Popeye's comic figure is not a trademark use in view of the labels attached to the defendant's undershirts that bear the defendant's trademark.

REASONS FOR THE JUDGMENT:

1. * * * Article 37 of the Trademark Law provides that an act of a third party of using a trademark which is similar to the registered trademark on the designated goods is regarded as an infringement upon such trademark right.

The court now examines whether the act of the defendant of attaching A and B marks on its undershirts falls under the definition of infringement under Article 37.

The plaintiff's registered trademark and A and B marks have in common comic figures of Popeye as their respective dominant part, but these figures [differ] in shape and setting. However, the plaintiff's registered trademark and A and B marks have the same meaning "Popeye a comic character," since the plaintiff's trademark and the defendant's A and B marks bear Popeye's figure and the name "POPEYE." Thus, A and B marks have pronunciation and meaning identical with those of the plaintiff's registered trademark.

When a registrable trademark (Art. 3) is registered through the required procedure, a trademark right is created with respect to the designated goods (Art. 18), and the owner of the trademark right (exclusive licensee when an exclusive right to use (*senyō-shiyōken*) is established with respect to such trademark right) enjoys an exclusive right to use the registered trademark for the designated goods. When a third party commits an act of infringement or is likely to infringe upon the registered trademark, he can claim suspension or prevention of the infringing act. The Trademark Law aims at giving legal protection to the economic function of registered trademarks.

"A trademark in its true meaning" is attached to the goods of one's business in order to distinguish them from the goods of another. This is the primary purpose of attaching a trademark. "A trademark in its true meaning" possesses, as its economic functions, the function to guarantee the quality of the goods and the function of advertising the goods, in addition to the function of indicating the source of the goods. Protection of trademarks under the Trademark Law is designed to protect the indication-of-source function of "a trademark in its true meaning" from being illegally obstructed.

2. According to some Popeye comic books published by the King Features Syndicate Co., which are before this court as exhibits, the comic character Popeye appeared for the first time in 1929 as the principal actor in a comic entitled "Thimble Theatre" by E.C. Seager originally published in 1919, and since then, it has become well-known throughout the world including Japan.

According to the fashion books and magazines submitted to the court as exhibits, it appears that comic characters, letters, animal figures, players of rugby, soccer and other sports, etc., are printed on the front or back portion of shirts in order to make them more appealing to the consuming public. The use of comic characters and letters on undershirts is for the purpose of promoting sales rather than to make them play a trademark function.

The defendant's use of the character and letters in question on its undershirts is also aimed at promoting sales rather than indicating the source of the goods.

"A trademark in its true meaning," which is a symbol to distinguish the source, also plays the advertising and guarantee functions. A trademark, because of its functions, is usually indicated on the tags and wrapping bags of the goods. A trademark in its true meaning may sometimes be shown on the front or back of shirts, but it is not printed so large as to cover the entire surface of the front or back portion of the shirts no matter how well-known it is throughout the world.

Each one of the defendant's undershirts for children bears a tag on the neck portion, which indicates a trumpet and the letters "AIRCOTT" and *katakana* letters "*pibusu*." The upper neck portion of the defendant's shirts bears the letters "DAIWABO aircott" and "*kashimiron*." It is evident that these signs are the defendant's trademarks.

A and B marks on the defendant's undershirts do not possess essential functions of trademarks (the function to distinguish one's products from the products of another and the function to guarantee the quality of the goods), and are not intended to distinguish the source of the products.

The defendant's use of A and B marks cannot be said to infringe upon the plaintiff's registered trademark. Accordingly, the plaintiff's claim has no ground.

- - - - - - - - - -

_Lee Sen Ming Co. v. Sankyō Seikō K.K._*
(Osaka Dist. Ct., Feb. 24, 1976)

FACTS:

The plaintiff Lee Sen Ming Co., of 6 North Bridge Road, Singapore, is the owner of the following registered trademark consisting of the letters "Crocodile" and the figure of a crocodile in a rectangular frame:

Date of application: April 27, 1959. * * *

Plaintiff's registered trademark

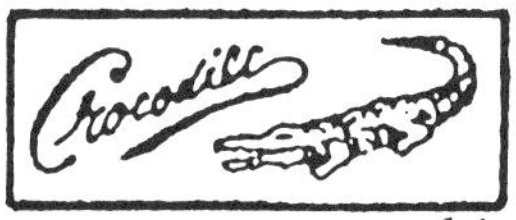

The defendant is a trading company engaged in the sale of clothing and is selling sports shirts bearing on their breast portion A or B mark together with vinyl bags bearing C mark. A, B and C marks are shown as follows:

A mark

[B and C marks omitted]

The plaintiff brought this action in the Osaka District Court to enjoin the defendant from selling these sports shirts and to recover from the defendant damages in the amount of 1,000,000 yen calculated on the basis of royalty to be paid by the defendant for its use of the plaintiff's trademark for 10,000 or more sports shirts already sold by the defendant, alleging that the use by the defendant of A, B and C marks infringes upon the plaintiff's registered trademark.

The defendant admits that it has been engaged in the import and sale of sports shirts manufactured by the world famous La Chemise Lacoste of France, including sports shirts bearing A mark. * * * The defendant contends that import and sale of sports shirts bearing Lacoste's marks do not infringe upon the plaintiff's registered trademark on the following grounds:

(1) Lacoste's sports shirts that the defendant imports and sells bear (a) mark on a label attached to the inside neck portion and (b) mark on the breast portion. (b) mark consists of a figure of a crocodile in green color and the letters "Lacoste" written in black. (a) mark consists of a combination of (b) mark and the letters "CHEMISE LACOSTE" written horizontally above (b) mark.

[Marks omitted]

The bags for these sports shirts bear (c) mark that consists of a combina-

*Translation by Teruo Doi, *Trademark and Unfair Competition Law of Japan: Digest of Court Decisions*, Vol. 1, pp. 108-113 (AIPPI Japan, 1980). Reprinted by permission.

tion of the letters "La chemise LACOSTE" and the figure of a crocodile in green color. (c) mark is, therefore, not a simple figure of a crocodile.

[Mark omitted]

(2) The plaintiff's registered trademark consists of the figure of a crocodile and the letters "Crocodile" and, therefore, it is not a crocodile figure alone.

At the time of filing of an application for registration of the plaintiff's trademark, there were many trademarks already registered for goods belonging to Class No. 36 which related to *wani* (a Japanese word meaning the crocodilians), including the following:

(1) *tsukiwani* (moon-crocodile) (Reg. No. 530290)
(2) ALLIGATOR (Reg. No. 404219)
(3) *wanidori* (crocodile-bird) (Reg. No. 412298)
(4) CROCODILE-HILL (Reg. No. 425094)
(5) *chikyūwani* (earth-crocodile) (Reg. No. 440949)
(6) *wanikai* (crocodile-shell) (Reg. No. 442946)
(7) *hoshiwani* (star-crocodile) (Reg. No. 456089)
(8) *okanwani* (crown-crocodile) (Reg. No. 516986)

All of these trademarks, except (2) and (4), consist of a combination of the figure of *wani*, the figure of other objects and letters and not the figure of *wani* alone. Each one of these trademarks has a meaning and pronunciation of such combination. On the other hand, a trademark "ALLIGATOR" has the meaning of an alligator. These trademarks are distinctive from (2) mark "ALLIGATOR."

In view of these trademarks, it can be said that the plaintiff's trademark was registered as possessing distinctive quality since it consists of a combination of a figure and letters. If it consists of the figure alone, it is in conflict with (2) mark. If it consists of the letters only, it is in conflict with (2) and (4) marks. Although the registrability of the plaintiff's trademark is still doubtful, registration was effected on the assumption that the plaintiff's trademark does not have a meaning and pronunciation of *wani* alone.

(3) (a), (b) and (c) marks used by the defendant consist of the letters "LACOSTE" as their dominant part and have the meaning of Lacoste's crocodile, and do not give rise to the meaning of crocodile alone. Hence, they are not similar to the plaintiff's registered trademark in both appearance and meaning. * * * Therefore, the plaintiff's action for trademark infringement has no ground.

(4) La Chemise Lacoste Inc. was established in 1933 by René Lacoste, the world tennis champion of 1926-27. It adopted a crocodile mark for its major products, sports wear. Crocodile was the nickname of René Lacoste. After World War II, Lacoste's sports wear attained a world-wide reputation with their high quality and now they are exported to eighty countries. Lacoste's trademark consisting of the figure of a crocodile was first registered in France in 1933, and it is presently registered in more than fifty countries.

The sale of Lacoste's sports shirts in Japan has been steadily increasing since the defendant, as Lacoste's sole distributor, began to import them in large quantity in 1968. Thus, the crocodile mark attached to the breast portion of sports shirts has become well-known as indicating Lacoste's products.

As Lacoste's crocodile mark has become well-known throughout the world, the plaintiff intended to conduct a free ride on its reputation, and applied for trademark registration in Japan as well as in various countries of Southeast Asia. The plaintiff's trademark, since its registration, had not been used for about ten years until recently. At the time of bringing this action, the plaintiff began an extensive advertisement and sale of sports shirts manufactured by Yamoto Shirts K.K. in Japan, using its registered trademark thereon and saying that the plaintiff is in cooperation with Crocodile Co. of England. Such conducts of the plaintiff are nothing but free riding on the reputation of Lacoste's crocodile mark.

Although the defendant and Lacoste have no legal right to exclude the plaintiff's free riding in Japan because of the territorial nature of trademark protection, the plaintiff's conducts which take advantage of the formality and technicality of a trademark should not be permitted as an abuse of right. * * *

JUDGMENT:

Lacoste's marks attached to the defendant's sports shirts are not similar to the plaintiff's registered trademark and, therefore, do not infringe upon the latter.

REASONS FOR THE JUDGMENT:

In view of the facts that the plaintiff's trademark consists of a combination of the letters "Crocodile" and the figure of a crocodile and that there exist a number of trademarks which relate to crocodile or alligator, it should be said that the plaintiff's trademark has its distinctive feature only in such combination of the letters and the figure.

When the plaintiff's registered trademark, being looked at as a whole, is compared with (a), (b) and (c) marks, the latter are not similar to the former. The use by the defendant of these marks, therefore, does not infringe upon the plaintiff's trademark right.

Questions and Discussion Points

1. *Strategy for protecting the legitimate mark user:* In each of the two preceding cases, how was the court able to protect the original user of the mark? Why might many developers of marks be very wary of the "ornamental use" approach the court takes in the "Popeye" case? Does the "abuse of rights" approach of the court in the "crocodile" case present similar or other serious concerns?

2. *Subsequent developments with the "Popeye" marks:* The plaintiff in the "Popeye" case, Osaka Sankei (OS), several years later brought another suit based on its "Popeye" marks, this time against K.K. Matsudera, a wholesaler buying from a legitimate sub-licensee of a legitimate licensee of King Features Syndicate (KFS), the holder in the U.S. and elsewhere of rights connected to the character Popeye. Matsudera had been distributing scarves with "Popeye" written on them in Roman

letters (Mark A), attached to which were sales tags that included the word and a drawing of Popeye (Mark B).

Notwithstanding its ruling in the first "Popeye" case, as to Mark A the Osaka District Court rejected the "ornamental use" and other arguments made by Matsudera. For Mark B, however, it refused to grant an injunction or damages, holding that because the drawing of Popeye was covered by a prior *copyright* held on the side of the legitimate users of the Popeye mark, Trademark Act §29 prohibited OS from asserting its trademark right against such users with respect to the drawing. The High Court sustained the judgment, but the Supreme Court (44 *Minshū* 876 (1990)) reversed with respect to Mark A.

Rather than relying on the "ornamental use" approach of the District Court in the first "Popeye" case, however, the Supreme Court based its ruling on the "abuse of rights" doctrine, holding that enforcing the trademark rights that had been held by OS (before the case reached the Supreme Court, OS had transferred rights in the subject marks to a third party) would subvert the purposes of the Trademark Act, given that OS had taken advantage of the popularity of KFS's Popeye mark free of charge (*mushō riyō*).

In the most recent of the "Popeye" line of cases, KFS and its Japanese licensees went on the offensive, bringing suit against OS, Matsudera (which, in either a reckless or cautious move, had obtained licenses from both sides) and another party to enjoin their use of OS's "Popeye" trademarks and related marks. All of the KFS plaintiffs sought relief under the UCPA, and KFS alone made an alternative claim for injunctive relief based on its Popeye copyrights and Trademark Act §29. The Tokyo High Court (1431 *Hanrei Jihō* 62 (1992)) granted the KFS plaintiffs injunctions pursuant to the UCPA, and additionally ruled that KFS could also obtain injunctions based on its copyrights, though only as to OS marks using the character of "Popeye" (as opposed to marks using the name "Popeye" written in English or Japanese script).

3. *Rationale for the first-to-file system*: In protecting actual first-users and parties granted rights by actual first-users, are the courts undermining the first-to-file system? Are they conducting the sort of inquiry into first-use that the first-to-file system nominally avoids?

IV. The Role of the Unfair Competition Prevention Act

As discussed briefly above, the UCPA long helped fill the gap left by the fact that registration of service marks had not been available under the Trademark Act, and it continues to offer protections to some marks that the amended Trademark Act does not cover. Both cases below, the first of which concerns service marks and the second of which explores the relationship between the UCPA and other intellectual property statutes, arose before the inclusion of "service marks" in the Trademark Act and before the thorough revision of the UCPA in 1993.

*Hokkoku Shōji K.K. v. Eikō Shōji K.K. and Tsutsui**
(Tokyo Dist. Ct., Nov. 27, 1972)

FACTS:

Tamotsu Aoike, representative of the plaintiff Hokkoku Shōji K.K., opened a restaurant to sell *Sapporo ramen* (a kind of Chinese noodles) in Ryōgoku, Tokyo, in 1967. The plaintiff adopted "Sapporo Ramen Dosanko" as its service mark, and displayed this mark on its signboards, curtains, and *chōchins* [lanterns] in a very distinctive way. The words "Sapporo Ramen Dosanko" were written both horizontally and vertically in white, yellow or black on the red ground, together with a drawing of the map of Hokkaido in black line, on which the city of Sapporo is indicated by a black dot. The plaintiff's *Sapporo ramen* sale was so successful that he opened four more restaurants within three months.

Aoike then started a franchise business, in order to overcome the limited financial resources to meet his rapidly expanding business. Under this franchise system, Aoike collects membership fees from his franchisees and gives them in return technical and managerial assistance and guidance in the manufacture of *Sapporo ramen.*

Aoike sells to his franchisees noodles and seasonings that he manufactures, and exercises necessary control and supervision over the taste and quality as well as the price of *Sapporo ramen* sold by the franchisees.

The first franchise agreement was made in September 1967. In the following year, Aoike established the plaintiff company, and Aoike's franchise business was succeeded by the plaintiff company. At the end of September 1969, the number of franchisees reached one hundred and fifty. These franchisees' restaurants were almost identical with the plaintiff's directly operated restaurants in their appearance, interior decorations, layout, etc., and were using the same signboards, curtains and *chōchins* as those used by the plaintiff's own restaurants.

The daily supply of noodles, raw materials of *Sapporo ramen*, to these franchisees was about an amount for 60,000 persons at the end of September 1969, and the plaintiff's sale of such noodles reached ¥25,000 per month. The monthly consumption of flour in the Tokyo metropolitan area was about 3,500 bags of 25 kilograms each. The plaintiff also sold bowls and chopsticks of uniform design to his franchisees.

The defendants Tsutsui and Eikō Shōji jointly began a business of selling *ramen* in Asagaya, Suginami-ku, Tokyo, using a mark similar to the plaintiff's mark on their signboards, curtains and *chōchins*, and on October 7, 1969, the defendants made a trade name registration (*shōgō tōki*) at the Suginami branch office of the Tokyo regional office of the Justice Ministry. The defendants' registration consists of the following matters: type of business—sale of noodles; place of business—No. 58-1, 3 chome, Asagaya Minami, Suginami-ku, Tokyo-to; Trade name—"Dosanko."

The plaintiff brought this action in the Tokyo District Court for an injunction against the use of a mark, signboards, curtains, *chōchins*, etc., which are similar to

*Translation by Teruo Doi, *Trademark and Unfair Competition Law of Japan: Digest of Court Decisions*, Vol. 1, pp. 155-158 (AIPPI Japan, 1980). Reprinted by permission.

the plaintiff's mark, signboards, curtains, *chōchins*, etc.; for cancellation of the defendants' trade name registration; and for damages, under Article 1(1)(ii) of the [old] Unfair Competition Prevention Law. [That provision is carried over in Section 2(1)(ii) of the new UCPA.] * * *

JUDGMENT:

Injunction is granted. * * *

REASONS FOR THE JUDGMENT:

The signboards, curtains, *chōchins*, etc., which bear the plaintiff's mark "Sapporo Ramen Dosanko" are "marks * * * well-known in the territory in which this Law is in force" within the meaning of Article 1(1)(ii) of the Unfair Competition Prevention Law, and are "indications of the business" of the plaintiff. Franchisees themselves are independent business proprietors, and the use of such signboards, curtains, *chōchins*, etc., by such business proprietors cannot be said to be the use of an indication which represents the plaintiff's business alone.

But those who sell *Sapporo ramen* under such signboards, curtains, *chōchins*, etc., are regarded to be persons who sell such products as integral parts of the organization of a single business enterprise. In fact, the plaintiff, acting as the franchisor, exercises a certain degree of control over these independent proprietors and maintains the unity of these independent proprietors and maintains the unity of a business organization under the mark. Thus, plaintiff, the plaintiff franchisor, and his franchisees form a kind of an organized body, which functions as a single business enterprise under the plaintiff's control. Therefore, such signboards, curtains, *chōchins*, etc., used by these franchisees must be regarded as indications of the plaintiff's business within the meaning of Article 1(1)(ii) of the Unfair Competition Prevention Law.

The defendants' use of similar marks on similar signboards, curtains, *chōchins*, etc., must be said to be an act which causes confusion with the business establishment and activities of the plaintiff, and the plaintiff is likely to suffer damages by such conduct of the defendants. The plaintiff should be entitled to an injunction and can demand the defendants to remove all such signboards, curtains, *chōchins*, etc. * * *

- - - - - - - - - -

*National Football League Properties, Inc., and Sony Kigyō K.K. v. Marutake Shōji K.K.**
(Osaka Dist. Ct., Oct. 6, 1976)

FACTS:

The claimant National Football League Properties, Inc. (NFLP) is a California corporation organized on February 20, 1963, for the purpose of acquiring a right to use commercially the symbol mark of each member football team (club) of the National Football League (NFL) and to grant to third parties licenses to use these

*Translation by Teruo Doi, *Trademark and Unfair Competition Law of Japan: Digest of Court Decisions*, Vol. 1, pp. 184-189 (AIPPI Japan, 1980). Reprinted by permission.

marks for commercial purpose. There are at present twenty-[six] member clubs [and two conferences] in the League and their symbol marks appear as follows:

[NFL marks omitted]

In the United States, NFLP has been engaged in the business of licensing merchandising rights of the symbol marks to various manufacturers of textile products, sheets, curtains, stationery, games, accessories, watches and sundries and the amount of transaction[s] reach[es] 30,000,000,000 dollars [presumably a mistaken figure] annually.

On October 2, 1973, another claimant, Sony Kigyō K.K., entered into a contract with NFLP and obtained from the latter an exclusive license to operate a business of merchandising NFLP's symbol marks under an obligation to pay royalty to NFLP and to grant sublicenses to various manufacturers in Japan. The contract provided Sony Kigyō's obligation to file various reports with NFLP, to keep records, and to exercise quality control over various products bearing the symbol marks, as well as detailed conditions for sublicensing. The contract also provided that sublicense contracts should contain a provision to enable the licensor, Sony Kigyō, to exercise complete control over the quality of the goods for which these symbol marks are used under sublicenses. Sony Kigyō extensively advertised its merchandising business under the contract with NFLP.

The respondent Marutake Shōji has been engaged in the manufacture and sale of portable wardrobes, the vinyl covers of which bear NFL symbol marks. * * *

[Photographs omitted]

NFLP and Sony Kigyō jointly filed a petition for a temporary injunction prohibiting the respondent from using NFL symbol marks on their portable wardrobes under Article 1(1)(i) of the [old] Unfair Competition Prevention Law [which is equivalent to Section 2(1)(i) of the new Unfair Competition Prevention Act]. * * *

JUDGMENT:

Temporary injunction is granted on a condition that the claimants post 500,000 yen as a security.

REASONS FOR THE JUDGMENT:

1. The symbol marks in question consist of drawings of intellectual creation bearing the name of each member team (club) of the National Football League.

In view of the increasing popularity of the American type football game in Japan, the claimants planned to establish a merchandising business in Japan with a view to exploiting the goodwill attached to the symbol marks, and the sublicensees have been engaged in the merchandising business of using the symbol marks for those goods agreed upon with the licensor. The symbol marks, therefore, constitute an indication of the business of a group of sublicensees under the claimants, and this fact has become well-known in Japan.

It is clear that the respondent's use of the symbol marks causes confusion with the claimants' merchandising business of these marks.

The respondent contends that if the claimants' exclusive right to use the symbol marks were considered unlimited regardless of whether they are used as trademarks or designs, and [regardless] of the purpose, place and method of use, as well as of the kinds of goods for which they are used such as clothing, shoes, foodstuffs, cakes and electric appliances, it would become an extremely strong right equal to a trademark right, design right and copyright combined together, and that such an extremely strong monopolistic right should never exist under the Japanese legal system.

However, the claimants are not petitioning [on] the basis of an exclusive right in the symbol marks, regardless of whether they are well-known in Japan and [of whether confusion is likely to result from] the respondent's use of the symbol marks with the goods or business activities of the claimants and their licensees.

The claimants in their petition before this court mention copyright, a right to one's name, a merchandising right and a right to publicity. But they are not seeking injunction on the basis of these rights. They are claiming that the symbol marks are intellectual creations of the member teams and possess goodwill and economic value when they are attached to goods sold in the market, and that these marks cannot be left for free use by third parties, rather they are interests entitled to legal protection, and, further, that the claimants are engaged in the merchandising business under lawful license from the owners, and the symbol marks are indications of the claimants' business activities.

2. The Unfair Competition Prevention Law aims at establishing and maintaining a fair competitive order. Article 1(1)(i) and (ii) [Sections 2(1)(i) and (ii) in the new UCPA] prohibit acts of using an indication identical with or similar to a well-known indication of goods (item (i)) or business (item (ii)) of another and thereby causing confusion with the goods or business establishment or activities of such person, and the Law gives a person whose business interest is likely to be harmed by such prohibited act a claim for injunction.

When a particular indication has become well-known in Japan as indicating the goods or business of a person, an act of a third party of using an indication identical with or similar to such well-known indication and thereby [likely to] cause confusion with the goods or business establishment or activities of such person is prohibited by the Law, regardless of whether the indication is a work entitled to protection under the Copyright Law, a mark entitled to trademark registration or a design entitled to design registration. [This is b]ecause such act goes beyond the freedom of business activities and destroys the competitive order and is contrary to honest business practices (Article 10 *bis* (2) of the Paris Convention).

The Unfair Competition Prevention Law provides that a person whose business interest is likely to be harmed by an act of unfair competition can claim injunction against such act. This remedy amounts to giving the claimant an absolute exclusive right in this well-known mark under the substantive law, but it is merely a reflected result [*hanshateki na kekka*, *i.e.*, an incidental consequence of the operation of the law]. In order to obtain remedy under Article 1(1) of the Unfair Competition Prevention Law, it is of course [not] necessary to have an absolute right under the substantive law such as copyright, trademark right or design right.

The word "another" [*tanin*] used in Article 1(1)(i) and (ii) means the legitimate [person] whose business is represented by the well-known indication. When the indication is licensed by the [person] to one or more [other persons who] engage in a business of merchandising, such [persons] also fall under [the term] "another."

Questions and Discussion Points

1. *The Sapporo Ramen case*: Why was this case brought under the UCPA instead of the Trademark Act? Does the amendment of the Trademark Act to provide for registration of service marks mean that the subject mark in this case would no longer need protection under the UCPA?

2. *The UCPA as creating an all-inclusive right*: Consider the defendant's argument in the NFL case that the ruling sought by the plaintiff would give the plaintiff a combined trademark right, design right, and copyright? How does the court respond? How should the "Popeye" and "crocodile" cases come out under the UCPA?

3. *Subsequent developments in the NFL case*: The claimants in the NFL case subsequently brought suit seeking to enjoin the respondent's manufacture of the wardrobes with the NFL marks and seeking damages. This suit reached the Supreme Court in 1984 (38 *Minshū* 920). Among the issues that confronted the Court were the meaning of "another" in UCPA §1 (*tanin*; translated as "another person" in the Appendices) and whether the fact that the respondent had obtained a design right for the wardrobes precluded recovery by the claimants.

In ruling for the claimants, the Supreme Court held on the first of the above issues that "another" in Section 1 can mean a "group," *i.e.*, a licensor, licensee(s) and sub-licensee(s) who have the common goal of protecting a symbol mark's function (*kinō*), and that "acts causing confusing" in the provision could thus mean acts causing people to believe that the respondent was a member of the claimants' merchandising group. With this approach, the claimants could clearly prevail notwithstanding that there was no competition between the claimants and respondents with respect to wardrobe manufacturing.

On the second issue above, the Supreme Court relied on the abuse of rights doctrine. Noting, among other considerations, that the respondent had clearly sought to make use of the popularity of the NFL marks and that it had applied for its design right only after having received a letter from the claimants requesting it to cease use of the NFL marks on its wardrobes, the Court held that it would amount to an abuse of right to enforce the respondent's design right.

4. *Advising foreign businesses*: Suppose you represent a rapidly growing U.S. company that has no current plans to enter the Japanese market but thinks it may begin expanding overseas in five or ten years. What patent and trademark advice would you give?

FURTHER READING

Teruo Doi, *Intellectual Property Protection and Management: Law and Practice in Japan*. Tokyo: Waseda University Institute of Comparative Law, 1992.

Teruo Doi, "The Role of Intellectual Property Law in Bilateral Transactions between Japan and the United States," in Gary Saxonhouse and Kozo Yamamura, eds., *Law and Trade Issues of the Japanese Economy: American and Japanese Perspectives*, pp. 157-192. Seattle: University of Washington Press, 1986.

Akira Goto and Ryuhei Wakasugi, "Technology Policy," in Ryutaro Komiya, Masahiro Okuno, and Kotaro Suzumura, eds., *Industrial Policy of Japan*, pp. 183-204. Tokyo: Academic Press, 1988.

Ken'ichi Imai, "Industrial Policy and Technological Innovation," in Ryutaro Komiya, Masahiro Okuno, and Kotaro Suzumura, eds., *Industrial Policy of Japan*, pp. 205-229. Tokyo: Academic Press, 1988.

Dennis S. Karjala and Keiji Sugiyama, "Fundamental Concepts in Japanese and American Copyright Law," 36 *American Journal of Comparative Law* 613 (1988).

Note [Carter Mackley], "The Role of the Patent System in Technology Transfer—The Japanese Experience," 26 *Columbia Journal of Transnational Law* 131 (1987).

Hugh Patrick, ed., *Japan's High Technology Industries: Lessons and Limitations of Industrial Policy*. Tokyo: University of Tokyo Press, 1986.

Roger D. Taylor, C. Larry O'Rourke and Chris Marchese, "A Comparison of International Intellectual Property Licensing Guidelines in the United States and Japan," 9 *UCLA Pacific Basin Law Journal* 104 (1991).

Yoichiro Yamaguchi, "Japanese Design Law and Practice," 19 *University of Baltimore Law Review* 416 (1989).

NOTES TO CHAPTER NINE

1. 624 Hanrei Jihō 78 (Nara Dist. Ct., Oct. 23, 1970). * * *

2. Japan Reader's Digest, 713 Hanrei Jihō 83 (Tokyo Dist. Ct. Feb. 19, 1973). A contractor had agreed to deliver a magazine in Japan using a list of information about the magazine's subscribers. It hired a subcontractor to assist it, and a copy of the list was made and sold to a third party while the list was in the subcontractor's possession.

3. 1012 Hanrei Jihō 35 (Kobe Dist. Ct., Mar. 27, 1981).

4. 419 Hanrei Jihō 14 (Tokyo Dist. Ct., June 26, 1965).

5. Sanrei-Yamako, 1084 Hanrei Jihō 122 (Osaka High Ct., Mar. 3, 1983).

6. This section has been developed in part with materials specially prepared by Sadanao Amemiya, Esq.

7. As reported in Sadanao Amemiya and Kikuo Nishimoto, "Patents and Utility Models," in Zentaro Kitagawa, general ed., 4 *Doing Business in Japan* (Matthew Bender, 1994), Part 6, §2.04[1][a][ii].

8. Figures from English translation of Sadanao Amemiya, "Patent Law: Comparative Study of Japan/U.S. Patent Law" (unpublished outline prepared in 1990), at 1.

Ten

The Antimonopoly Act

Introduction

Japan's Act Concerning the Prohibition of Private Monopoly and the Maintenance of Fair Trade (Law No. 54 of 1947; the Antimonopoly Act) had a dramatic impact on the P.C. Our introduction to the Antimonopoly Act will come in the same way it came to A.Co: through letters from Newco and the Japanese Fair Trade Commission (the JFTC). We will proceed much as the attorneys for A.Co did: first, learning about the Antimonopoly Act and the JFTC, and second, studying how the JFTC became interested in the P.C. Finally, we will ask whether the P.C. Agreements violate the statute and survey the antitrust procedures relevant to the P.C.

I. The Antitrust Issues in the P.C.

[Newco letterhead]
June 9, 1977

Mr. James A. Theory
Vice President
A.Co
[address omitted]

Subject: Joint Venture Agreement
Official Notice "KO-KEI-KOKU No. [XXX]"

Dear Mr. Theory:

Referring to our telex N77-237 on this subject, we enclose an original copy of the captioned notice accompanied by its English version translated by the original signer.

The Japanese version was prepared in triplicate addressed to the presidents of the related parties—J.Co, A.Co and Newco—and was delivered this morning. We have been requested to transmit to you the Japanese version together with the aforementioned English translation.

In this connection, please be advised that the officials of the JFTC recommended that we take prompt remedial measures. If you have any questions or need further information on this matter, please let us know.

Yours very truly,

(signed)

A. Hirayama
Director & General Manager
Newco, K.K.

- - - - - - - - - -

P.E. Berger, President
A.Co
[address omitted]

KO-KEI-KOKU No. [XXX]
June 9, 1977
Director General of
Economic Department,
Fair Trade Commission

We refer to the Joint Venture Agreement entered into between J.Co and A.Co and the collateral Agreements thereof on which, in compliance with Paragraph 2, Section 6, of the "Act Concerning the Prohibition of Private Monopoly and the Maintenance of Fair Trade," J.Co has reported to the Japanese Fair Trade Commission on January 28, 1977. We hereby ask that you take prompt measures to remedy the following provisions in the said Agreement and collateral Agreements. These provisions are seen as suspected unfair business practices under the provisions of said Act:

1. Paragraphs C-1 and C-2 of the Technical Agreement.
2. Paragraphs D-1, D-2(a), and D-2(c) of the Manufacturing Agreement.
3. Paragraph B-3(a) of the Manufacturing Agreement.
4. Paragraph F of the Distributor Agreement.
5. Paragraphs A-1(b) and A-2 of the Amending Agreement No. 15.

Questions and Discussion Points

1. *Response of A.Co:* What is the JFTC's concern? How should A.Co respond?
2. *Response of J.Co:* Assume you represent J.Co. What initial advice might you have?

II. Background on the Antimonopoly Act

The selection below discusses the history of the Antimonopoly Act and two of the three types of conduct it prohibits: private monopolization and unreasonable restraints of trade. The third area of prohibited conduct, unfair trade practices, is discussed later in the chapter. Note that the Japanese term for "unfair trade practices" is often translated as "unfair *business* practices," as in the letter above from the JFTC and in some of the materials used in the rest of this chapter.

MITSUO MATSUSHITA, THE ANTIMONOPOLY LAW OF JAPAN*

11 Law in Japan 57
57-68 (1978)

[1.] Historical Sketch

In the period before the Second World War, there existed in Japan no legislation to prohibit the formation of monopolies and cartels. In fact, a great deal of prewar legislation permitted—indeed encouraged—a monopolistic system. During the occupation of Japan by American forces following the war, the notion of a system of free enterprise was introduced to Japan, and accordingly the Japanese Antimonopoly Law (*Dokusen kinshi hō*) was enacted in 1947, a fundamental piece of legislation for the development of industry in Japan.

The development of the Law in the years following its enactment in 1947 has been marked by considerable fluctuation in the degree of rigidity in its enforcement. The early period—to which we may set as boundaries the years from 1947 to 1952—was marked by energetic enforcement of the terms of the Law. This was in large part due to the support of the Occupation Force, a vigorous proponent of strict enforcement. In the following years, however, from 1952 to the middle of the next decade, enforcement of the Law was significantly relaxed. In 1952 the Law was amended, resulting in the elimination of several important provisions such as the provision which held cartels to be illegal *per se* and the provision which provided for the dissolution of a large business simply because of its size. Furthermore, provisions were added which exempted certain cartels (specifically, depression cartels and rationalization cartels) and allowed for resale price maintenance.

For a variety of reasons, the Law has been enforced with renewed vigor since the mid-1960s. Among the factors contributing to this resurgence must be numbered the continuous inflation during this period, the rise of consumerism, the liberalization of trade and capital transactions, and a shift in the goals of economic policy from high growth to welfare. The year 1977 was a landmark in the history of Japan's Antimonopoly Law. In that year, the Law was again amended, but this time with an eye toward the strengthening of its provisions and tougher enforcement.

American ideology and the ideas of free enterprise exercised a considerable influence upon the formation of Japan's Antimonopoly Law; to a great extent the Law was modelled after the United State's antitrust laws. However, the history of the Law in the thirty years since its enactment demonstrates that there is some difference in the manner of its enforcement as compared with its American coun-

*From Mitsuo Matsushita, "The Antimonopoly Law of Japan," 11 *Law in Japan: An Annual* 57 (1978), at 57-68. Reprinted by permission.

terpart. For example, in Japan private suits for damages on the basis of the Antimonopoly Law have yet to play a large role, despite the fact that there have been a few criminal prosecutions against violators. In the main, Japan's Antimonopoly Law has been enforced by an administrative agency, the Fair Trade Commission (FTC).

Differences of opinion, and sometimes conflict, have arisen in the administration of antimonopoly policy by the FTC and in the industrial policy of the Ministry of International Trade and Industry (MITI). During the 1960s, it was the policy of MITI to encourage mergers in order to build up enterprises large enough to compete with those of the United States and Europe, while at the same time the FTC was making an effort to control mergers by means of the Antimonopoly Law. Excessive concentration of industries, according to the FTC, would result in oligopoly and thereby deprive the economy of viable competition. However, * * * this attempt on the part of the FTC was often futile.

In the 1970s, the situation has been significantly altered. The previous policy, with its heavy emphasis upon the concentration and development of industry, has been subjected to considerable criticism, and, as noted above, greater emphasis has been laid upon antimonopoly policy.

In the future, business interests in Japan may anticipate tighter regulation in the three main areas covered by the Law: private monopolization, unreasonable restraint of trade and unfair business practices. * * *

[2.] **Private Monopolization**

Definition

"Private monopolization" is defined in the Law in article 2(5) as follows: "The term 'private monopolization' as used in this Law shall mean such business activities by which any entrepreneur, individually, by combination or conspiracy with other entrepreneurs, or in any other manner, excludes or controls the business activities of other entrepreneurs, thereby causing, contrary to the public interest, a substantial restraint of competition in any particular field of trade."

Examples

The exclusion of the business activities of other entrepreneurs may take various forms. Consider, for example, the case of an entrepreneur who maintains a policy of predatory pricing which discriminates on the basis of geographical distribution or the kinds of customers, or a dominant entrepreneur who sells below cost so as to drive out competitors. Such actions may be held to constitute "exclusion" under the definition of private monopolization if the net result is the creation of a situation where competition has effectively ceased to exist. Certain forms of restrictive contracts which deny access to market channels or sources of raw materials to other entrepreneurs may be held to be exclusion if competition is substantially restrained. To give an example, if a dominant manufacturer enters into a series of agreements with several distributors and imposes upon them restrictions of such a kind that these distributors can no longer purchase and resell the products of competing manufacturers, then the dominant manufacturer may be accused of engaging in the exclusion of the business activities of other entrepreneurs.

In the *Snow Brand* case,[1] two dominant manufacturers of dairy products conspired with a dominant financial institution and a federation of farmers' cooperatives in the Hokkaido area. The financial institution was persuaded to issue loans to dairy farmers on the condition that they agreed not to supply milk to the competitors of the two manufacturers. Those dairy farmers who borrowed money were thus obligated to refuse to supply milk to the manufacturers' competitors, whose business was thereby badly damaged. After the FTC had decided that this constituted private monopolization, it proceeded to take action against the four parties to the conspiracy and held that the two manufacturers had committed an act of private monopolization.

Control

Control of the business activities of other entrepreneurs may be both direct and indirect. Any exertion of power by a strong entrepreneur against a weaker entrepreneur which directs, restricts or prohibits the activities of the weaker party is considered direct control. Stock holding, restrictive covenants, and financial pressure are some of the means by which pressure is exerted but there are others. * * * In the *Noda Soy Sauce* case,[2] the leading manufacturer of soy sauce in Japan directed retailers to charge a certain "suggested" retail price so as to bring about resale price maintenance at the retail level. In fact the manufacturer used coercive measures to maintain this price level. Because of the tightly-regimented oligopolistic structure of the industry and the problem of product differentiation, the smaller manufacturers were left with no choice but to recommend retail prices at the same level. As a result, on each occasion that Noda raised the retail prices of its own products, the other manufacturers were compelled to follow suit. The FTC and the courts held that maintenance of retail prices by Noda in this way had the effect of giving Noda "indirect control" over the pricing decisions of competing entrepreneurs and constituted a private monopolization.

At this point, it must be noted that smaller businesses operating in some types of oligopolistic markets cannot possibly conduct their business activities (especially pricing decisions) in a manner different from the leading manufacturer. When the leading firm sets its price, its competitors in the market have little choice but to adjust their prices accordingly. In this way, the pricing decisions of the leading firm in an oligopolistic market often set off a chain reaction of parallel pricing moves by other firms, which inevitably results in uniformity of price in the market. * * *

Public Interest and a Particular Field of Trade

According to article 2(5) of the Law, private monopolization exists if the conduct of an entrepreneur in either excluding or controlling the business activities of other entrepreneurs is the cause of a substantial restraint of competition in a particular field of trade. Three concepts are central to this provision. The first is that the restraint be "contrary to the public interest"; the second is that it must be a "substantial restraint of competition"; and the third is that it must involve "a particular field of trade."

Opinion is divided as to the meaning of the public interest in matters concerning the Antimonopoly Law. There are, however, two theories which are most important. The prevailing opinion among the FTC, the courts, and legal scholars is that the public interest as far as the Antimonopoly Law is concerned is the maintenance of competition for its own sake, and that therefore the public interest is harmed whenever free competition is substantially restrained in any market. On the other hand, another school of thought, which finds favor among some officials of MITI and among business groups, maintains that the public interest is not necessarily served by the maintenance of free competition. According to the adherents to this theory, the public interest should be interpreted to mean the maintenance of a balance between the interests within the national economy. * * *

[3.] **Unreasonable Restraint of Trade**

Definition

The definition of "unreasonable restraint of trade" is given in article 2(6) of the Law as follows: "The term 'unreasonable restraint of trade' as used in this Law shall mean such business activities by which entrepreneurs by contract, agreement, or any other concerted activities mutually restrict or conduct their business activities in such a manner as to fix, maintain, or enhance prices; or to limit production, technology, products, facilities, or customers or suppliers, thereby causing, contrary to the public interest, a substantial restraint of competition in any particular field of trade."

According to the definition given above, unreasonable restraint of trade consists of collusion on the part of entrepreneurs which results in a substantial restraint of trade in a particular field of trade contrary to the interests of the public. "Unreasonable restraint of trade" is synonymous with "cartel."

Cases of Unilateral Restriction

In the *Asahi Shinbun* case,[3] the FTC found fault with agreements between a newspaper publisher and retail newspaper sellers in which the retailers were assigned exclusive territories for their sales activities. The Tokyo High Court ruled that only an agreement which imposed mutual restrictions upon participants ought to be considered an unreasonable restraint of trade. According to these terms, an agreement between a publisher and retail vendors, such as that in the *Asahi Shinbun* case, is not considered unreasonable restraint of trade. The reasoning behind this decision was that, according to the requirements of the statute, an unreasonable restraint of trade exists only when entrepreneurs "mutually" restrict their activities and that an agreement in which territories are assigned to retailers by a manufacturer (or publisher) is unilateral rather than mutual. * * *

Proof of the Existence of a Cartel

Proving that a cartel does in fact exist is one of the most important problems in the enforcement of the Antimonopoly Law with regard to unreasonable restraint of trade. It is also one of the most difficult. A cartel is an agreement which puts an end to competition among the participants. Before the FTC can proceed against a cartel, it must first prove that an agreement has actually been entered into by the participants. However, when tacit communication takes place in an oligopolistic market and an agreement is reached among large-scale entrepreneurs concerning prices, quantities, and other terms of business, it is often difficult to detect and to prove. In such cases, material evidence, such as contracts, letters, or records of meetings, is often difficult to secure, if in fact it exists. * * *

Restrictions on Trade Associations

Article 8(1) of the Law bars certain restrictive activities of trade associations. Often a trade association which is composed of entrepreneurs in an industry functions in a manner quite similar to that of a cartel. Trade associations exist in most of the major industries in Japan. If a program establishing restrictive terms of business which are to be observed by the members is adopted by an association following a resolution of the executive committee, then the members will cease to compete among themselves. Consider, for example, the case of an association which adopts a resolution establishing specific limits in the quantity of the commodity to be produced by the members of the association. In such a situation, the activity of the association is scarcely distinguishable from that of a cartel. * * *

Exemptions

The Antimonopoly Law and other laws contain provisions which permit cartels under certain circumstances. In the Antimonopoly Law itself, there are two such provisions, article 24-3 and article 24-4. Article 24-3 provides an exception for a depression cartel agreement arrived at by manufacturers when the price of their product drops below the average production cost and it would be hard to overcome this difficulty through rationalization. Those entrepreneurs who want to enter into a depression cartel are obliged to first resort to limiting the quantity of production. Only after a limitation of the quantity of production has been shown to be incapable of overcoming the depression will permission be granted to fix the price.

Article 24-4 permits rationalization cartels. If a group of entrepreneurs wishes to agree on terms for rationalization (*e.g.*, a specialization agreement, or an agreement to build a common transportation facility), they may file a request with the FTC for permission, and, once it is granted, they may proceed to put it into effect.

There are a considerable number of laws that permit certain types of cartels. The Export and Import Transactions Law is one. It authorizes the creation of an export and import cartel under the supervision of the MITI. The Marine Transportation Law, which authorizes tariff agreements entered into by shipping companies, is another. The so-called shipping conferences are permitted under this legislation, which reposes the power of authorization with the Ministry of Transportation. The Small and Medium Business Organization Law authorizes agreements entered into by small and medium enterprises, and the Insurance Business Law permits insurance companies to enter into agreements which unify the contents of insurance policy contracts. An agreement is exempted from the provisions of the Antimonopoly Law if it is specifically authorized by one of these statutes.

The Order to Eliminate

The FTC takes necessary steps to eliminate any illegality when a cartel is found to be in violation of existing laws. An order issued by the FTC may take various forms depending upon the particular type of violation involved. For example, if a cartel has been created to fix prices, the order requires the cancellation of the cartel agreement, and usually that some form of general announcement be made to consumers to the effect that the agreement has been cancelled. * * *

Dealing with International Cartels

The prohibition of international cartels and unfair international business practices is provided for in article 6 of the Antimonopoly Law, which reads as follows: "No entrepreneur shall enter into an international agreement or an international contract which contains such matters as constitute an unreasonable restraint of trade or unfair business practices."

The *Tōyōbō* case[4] is an interesting illustration. An agreement was made between German manufacturers and their Japanese counterparts according to which both parties agreed to refrain from exporting into each other's "traditional market." The agreement was discovered and determined to be in violation of article 6 of the Law. Before action was taken in Japan, the German Cartel Authority had already proceeded against the German participants and held that this agreement was in violation of the German Cartel Law. This case is an excellent example of two governments cooperating in an effort to control restrictive international business practices.

III. Section 6 Reporting of International Agreements

In the letter from the JFTC, note the reference to Paragraph 2 of Section 6 of the Antimonopoly Act. The selection below explains some of the reporting requirements under this section.

JAMES L. HILDEBRAND AND MITSUO MATSUSHITA, ANTIMONOPOLY LAW OF JAPAN—POTENTIAL CONSEQUENCES OF INTERNATIONAL CONTRACT VIOLATIONS UNDER ARTICLE 6*

6 NYU Journal of International Law and Politics 215
223-227 (1973)

Under Article 6(2) of the [Antimonopoly] Law, * * * an entrepreneur who has entered into an international agreement or contract must file a report thereof with the FTC within thirty days after the date of the formation (*seiritsu*) of said agreement or contract. The form of such report has been [prescribed by the FTC]. This reporting duty falls generally upon the Japanese party to the agreement, although there is no indication in the Antimonopoly Law that the word "en-

*From James L. Hildebrand and Mitsuo Matsushita, "Antimonopoly Law of Japan—Potential Consequences of International Contract Violations Under Article 6," 6 *NYU Journal of International Law and Politics* 215 (1973), at 223-227. Reprinted with permission of the NYU Journal of International Law and Politics.

trepreneur" (*jigyōsha*) as it appears in Article 6(2) is necessarily limited to domestic entrepreneurs. * * *

[Under related FTC regulations,] the reporting duty does not apply to an international agreement or contract with respect to a single transaction[,] * * * or to an agreement or contract merely creating an agency relationship in business matters (with the exception of agreements or contracts containing conditions that restrict the business activities of the other party or parties)[, or, since amendments made to the regulations in 1992, to contracts or agreements concerning only (i) transfer of rights in technology, (ii) licensing of technology rights to non-"major" domestic parties (*i.e.*, ones controlling 10% or less of their product markets and not being one of the three largest producers in their field) (as long as such licenses do not contain price or resale price provisions), (iii) sales by non-"major" domestic parties, (iv) joint ventures with small domestic parties, or (v) transfer or licensing of trademarks or copyrights other than those involving software programs]. * * *

It is the current practice of the FTC to require a new report to be filed in case of renewal of an international agreement or contract upon expiration thereof and in case of modification of the contents of an existing agreement or contract. In both of these cases the FTC deems it proper to consider that a new international agreement or contract has been concluded. * * *

During the first half of 1971 a total of 1,542 international contracts were reported to the FTC, which represents a 78.3 percent increase over the comparable period of the previous year. * * * Of [those] 1,542 cases * * *, 48.2 percent or 741 cases involved United States companies, and 140 cases involved British and West German companies. [Reporting must now be made for inbound and outbound international contracts. In 1985, 2,551 inbound contracts (1,394 with the U.S.) and 2,013 outbound contracts (305 with the U.S.) were reported. In 1990, the corresponding figures were 3,470 (1,983 with the U.S.) and 2,258 (334 with the U.S.). As a result of the amendments described above, the figures for 1992 decreased dramatically to 357 (U.S. 168) and 781 (U.S. 80), respectively.]

International contracts reported to the FTC are screened on the basis of the standards discussed previously. As a result of the screening of the 1,542 cases reported during the first half of 1971, 51 cases (62 cases for the comparable period of the previous year) were subjected to informal "administrative guidance" (*gyōsei shidō*) by the FTC because of possible Antimonopoly Law violations. Most of those provisions of international agreements or contracts which the FTC deems to be objectionable as unreasonable restraints of trade or unfair business practices are stricken out of the agreements or contracts pursuant to the informal "administrative guidance" before any formal proceedings are initiated. In the past the number of cases for which guidance was required increased in proportion to the increase in the number of cases reported. However, the most recent statistics show that even though the total number of cases reported has been increasing rapidly, the percentage of cases requiring "administrative guidance" has been decreasing.

* * * * *

	Number of cases reported	Number of cases guided	Percentage of occurrence
First half of 1970	865	62	7.2%
Second half of 1970	774	38	4.9%
First half of 1971	1,542	51	3.3%
[1985	4,564	159	3.5%]
[1990	5,728	279	4.9%]
[1992	1,138	50	4.4%]

Source: Omitted.

* * * * *

This trend may indicate the effectiveness of the FTC's Guidelines [for International Technology Induction Agreements, discussed in Chapter 9, Part A, Section III.B]. Of the 51 cases which required guidance during the first half of 1971, a United States company was party to the contract in 22 cases (43.1 percent), a West German company in nine cases (17.6 percent) and English and Swedish companies in 5 cases (9.8 percent). [The corresponding statistics for later years are not reported by the FTC.]

Questions and Discussion Points

1. *Reporting international agreements*: Why does the antitrust statute require the reporting of international agreements?

2. *Reporting of the P.C. agreements*: When did J.Co report the P.C. Agreements to the JFTC as required by Antimonopoly Act §6(2)? Why?

3. *Effect of late reporting*: Should the fact that the P.C. Agreements were reported to the JFTC almost seven years after the agreements took effect have any legal effect on the JFTC's handling of the case?

IV. Unfair Trade Practices

A. The General Designation

Although the JFTC letter provides no detail on how the provisions of the P.C. Agreements may violate the Antimonopoly Act, it claims that they may constitute "unfair business [or trade] practices." To give some guidance on what constitutes an unfair trade practice, the JFTC has promulgated a "General Designation on Unfair Trade Practices." At the time the antitrust issues arose in the P.C., an earlier version of the General Designation was in effect. The chart below offers a simple comparison of the two versions. After the chart, we include a selection explaining the practices banned by the 1982 General Designation.

HIROSHI IYORI AND AKINORI UESUGI, THE ANTIMONOPOLY LAW OF JAPAN*

265-270 (1983)

Comparison of 1982 General Designation on Unfair Trade Practices (New Designation) and 1953 General Designation (Old Designation)

New Designation (Notification No. 15 of 1982)	Old Designation (Notification No. 11 of 1953)
(Concerted Refusal to Deal) 1. Without proper justification, taking an act specified in one of the following paragraphs concertedly with another entrepreneur who is in a competitive relationship with oneself (hereinafter, referred to as a "competitor"): (i) Refusing to deal with a certain entrepreneur or restricting the quantity or substance of a commodity or service involved in the transaction with a certain entrepreneur; or (ii) Causing another entrepreneur to take an act which comes under the preceding paragraph.	1. Unjustly refusing or restricting supply of commodity, fund, or another kind of economic benefit from or to a certain entrepreneur.
(Other Refusal to Deal) 2. Unjustly refusing to deal, or restricting the quantity or substance of a commodity or service involved in the transaction with a certain entrepreneur, or causing another entrepreneur to take any act which comes under one of these categories.	
(Discriminatory Pricing) 3. Unjustly supplying or accepting a commodity or service at prices which discriminate between regions or between the other parties.	2. Affording without proper justification, substantially favorable or unfavorable treatment to a certain entrepreneur in regard to the terms or execution of a transaction.
(Discriminatory Treatment on Transaction Terms, etc.) 4. Unjustly affording favorable or unfavorable treatment to a certain entrepreneur in regard to the terms or execution of a transaction.	3. Excluding a specific entrepreneur from a concerted activity or from a trade association, or unduly discriminating against a specific entrepreneur in the concerted activity or the trade association, thereby causing to the entrepreneur undue disadvantage with respect to his business activities. 4. Supplying or accepting, without proper justification, a commodity, fund, or any other kinds of economic benefit at a price which discriminated between regions or between other parties.

*Adapted from Hiroshi Iyori and Akinori Uesugi, *The Antimonopoly Law of Japan* (Federal Legal Publications, Inc., 1983), at 265-270. Reprinted by permission.

New Designation (Notification No. 15 of 1982)	Old Designation (Notification No. 11 of 1953)
(Discriminatory Treatment in a Trade Association, etc.) 5. Unjustly excluding a specific entrepreneur from a trade association or from a concerted activity, or unjustly discriminating against a specific entrepreneur in a trade association or a concerted activity, thereby causing difficulties in the business activities of the said entrepreneur.	
(Unjust Low Price Sales) 6. Without proper justification, supplying a commodity or service continuously at a price which is excessively below cost incurred in the said supply, or otherwise unjustly supplying a commodity or service at a low price, thereby tending to cause difficulties in the business activities of other entrepreneurs.	5. Supplying a commodity, fund or another kind of economic benefit at an unjust low price or receiving supply of them at an unjust high price.
(Unjust High Price Purchasing) 7. Unjustly purchasing a commodity or service at a high price, thereby tending to cause difficulties to the business activities of other entrepreneurs.	
(Deceptive Customer Inducement) 8. Unjustly inducing customers of a competitor to deal with oneself by causing them to misunderstand that the substance of a commodity or service supplied by oneself, or terms of the transaction, or other matters relating to such transaction are much better or much more favorable than the actual one or than those relating to the competitor.	6. Inducing or coercing, directly or indirectly, customers of a competitor to deal with oneself by offering unjust advantages or by threatening unjust disadvantages in the light of normal business practices.
(Customer Inducements by Unjust Benefits) 9. Inducing customers of a competitor to deal with oneself by offering unjust benefits in the light of normal business practices.	
(Tie-in Sales, etc.) 10. Unjustly causing another party to purchase a commodity or service from oneself or from an entrepreneur designated by oneself by tying it to the supply of another commodity or service, or otherwise coercing the said party to deal with oneself or with an entrepreneur designated by oneself.	

New Designation (Notification No. 15 of 1982)	Old Designation (Notification No. 11 of 1953)
(Dealing on Exclusive Terms) 11. Unjustly dealing with the other party on condition that the said party shall not deal with a competitor, thereby tending to reduce transaction opportunities for the said competitor.	7. Without proper justification, dealing with the other party on condition that the said party shall not supply commodities, funds, or other kinds of economic benefits to, or shall not accept commodities, funds, or other kinds of economic benefits from, a competitor of oneself.
(Resale Price Restriction) 12. Supplying a commodity to the other party who purchases the said commodity from oneself while imposing, without proper justification, one of the restrictive terms specified below: (i) Causing the said party to maintain the sales price of the commodity that one has determined, or otherwise restricting the said party's free decision on sales price of the commodity; or (ii) Having the said party cause an entrepreneur who purchases the commodity from the said party to maintain the sales price of the commodity that one has determined, or otherwise causing said party to restrict the said entrepreneur's free decision on sales price of the commodity.	8. Dealing with the other party on conditions which, without proper justification, restrict any transaction between the said party and a supplier of a commodity, fund, or another kind of economic benefit to him or between the said party and any person receiving supply of those from him, or any relationship between the said party and his competitor.
(Dealing on Restrictive Terms) 13. Other than any act coming under the preceding two paragraphs, dealing with the other party on conditions which unjustly restrict any transaction between the said party and his transacting party or other business activities of the said party.	9. Dealing with a company on condition, without proper justification, that the appointment of officers of that company (meaning those as defined by Subsection 3 of Section 2 of the Act Concerning Prohibition of Private Monopoly and Maintenance of Fair Trade) shall be subject to prior direction or approval by oneself.
(Abuse of Dominant Bargaining Position) 14. Taking any act specified in one of the following paragraphs, unjustly in the light of the normal business practices, by making use of one's dominant bargaining position over the other party: (i) Causing the said party in continuous transaction to purchase a commodity or service other than the one involved in the said transaction, (ii) Causing the said party in continuous transaction to provide for oneself money, service, or other economic benefits, (iii) Setting or changing transaction terms in a way disadvantageous to the said party,	10. Trading with the other party on conditions which are unjustly disadvantageous in the light of normal business practices by making use of one's dominant bargaining position over the said party.

New Designation (Notification No. 15 of 1982)	Old Designation (Notification No. 11 of 1953)
(iv) In addition to any act coming under the preceding three paragraphs, imposing a disadvantage on the said party regarding terms or execution of a transaction, or (v) Causing a company which is one's other transacting party to follow one's direction in advance, or to get one's approval, regarding the appointment of officers of the said company (meaning those as defined by Subsection 3 of Section 2 of the Act Concerning Prohibition of Private Monopoly and Maintenance of Fair Trade).	
(Interference with a Competitor's Transaction) 15. Unjustly interfering with a transaction between another entrepreneur who is in a domestic competitive relationship with oneself or with the company of which one is a stockholder or an officer and the other party to such transaction, by preventing the formation of a contract, or by inducing the breach of a contract, or by any other means whatsoever.	11. Unjustly interfering with a transaction between another entrepreneur who is in a domestic competitive relationship with oneself or with the company of which one is a stockholder or an officer and the other party to such transaction, by preventing the formation of a contract, or by inducing the breach of a contract, or by any other means whatsoever.
(Interference with Internal Operations of a Competing Company) 16. Unjustly inducing, abetting, or coercing a stockholder or an officer of a company which is in a domestic competitive relationship with oneself or with the company of which one is a stockholder or an officer, to take an act disadvantageous to such company by the exercise of voting rights, transfer of stock, divulgence of secrets, or any other means whatsoever.	12. Unjustly inducing, abetting, or coercing a stockholder or an officer of a company which is in a domestic competitive relationship with oneself or with the company of which one is a stockholder or an officer, to take an act disadvantageous to such company by the exercise of voting rights, transfer of stock, divulgence of secrets, or any other means whatsoever.

MITSUO MATSUSHITA WITH JOHN D. DAVIS, INTRODUCTION TO JAPANESE ANTIMONOPOLY LAW*

55-65 (1990)

[1.] Unreasonable Discrimination

The General Designations

Article 2(9) paragraph (i) [of the Antimonopoly Act] provides that unreasonable discrimination exercised by an enterprise is an unfair business practice, and the FTC is authorized to designate unfair business practices in this area. The FTC has announced 5 general designations under this heading: (1) boycott, (2) individual refusal to deal, (3) price discrimination, (4) discriminatory dealing, and (5) discrimination in a trade association. We will deal with only [(1) and (3) among] these designations.

The Boycott

General designation No. 1 states that a collective refusal to deal by agreement among competing enterprises is unlawful in principle. This is the prohibition of a boycott and includes a secondary as well as a primary boycott. A boycott is regarded as unlawful in principle and only in those cases in which justifiable cause is proven is it regarded as lawful. The question then, is, what factors justify a boycott?

When a collective refusal to deal is exercised in self-defense, it is probably justified. On one occasion a trade association of soy sauce brewers requested the FTC's opinion regarding the legality of an association decision to the effect that members would not submit to certain business terms employed by large supermarkets pressuring them to contribute money to and purchase certain commodities from the supermarkets.

In the *Clearing House* case,[5] the issue was the legality of a rule in the bank-established clearing house that member banks should refuse to deal with customers issuing bad cheques twice in a six-month period. A customer who had been thus refused claimed that the rule amounted to a boycott and sought damages to compensate for losses caused by the refusal. The Tokyo High Court decided that the rule of the clearing house was justified since it was necessary to maintain credibility in the banking system using such cheques. * * *

Price Discrimination

General designation No. 3 states that unreasonable price discrimination is an unfair business practice. According to the designation, both offering a commodity or service at different prices to different customers or territories and accepting such terms are included in this category. However, under what circumstances price discrimination should be deemed "unreasonable" is by no means clear.

It is generally understood that business activity of this kind is unreasonable

---

*From Mitsuo Matsushita, with John D. Davis, *Introduction to Japanese Antimonopoly Law* (Yūhikaku, 1990), at 55-65. Reprinted by permission.

only when it is detrimental to competition, a situation which only arises when there is a tendency for competition to be restrained and an anti-competitive impact is felt by the majority of enterprises in the market. * * *

[2.] Unreasonable Price

Sale Below Cost

Article 2(9) paragraph (ii) provides that unreasonable pricing is an unfair business practice and directs the FTC to designate specific conduct in this area. Under this heading, the FTC announced general designation Nos. 6 and 7. The former deals with sale below cost and the latter unreasonably high pricing. However, the former is far more important than the latter and, therefore, only designation No. 6 will be discussed below.

A sale below cost of production or purchase, as the case may be, is an unfair business practice in principle if the price charged is substantially below such cost level and is carried out by an enterprise on a continual basis. "Cost" in this context is understood to be the sum of the cost of production or purchase plus general overhead expenses.

In the *Maruetsu-Haromato* case,[6] two competing supermarkets cut the retail price of milk. The cost of purchasing a carton of milk wholesale was 160 yen, but the two supermarkets continued to sell milk at 100 yen. This was held to be unfair pricing.

In principle, cost is based on actual expenses incurred by the producer or seller of a product. In the event special circumstances exist, however, they should be taken into consideration. One problem here is how to calculate cost when a seller is assisted by another enterprise. In the *Chūbu Yomiuri Shinbun* case,[7] Chūbu, a newspaper company, sold daily newspapers at the price of 500 yen a month. Chūbu was heavily subsidized by Yomiuri Shinbun Newspaper Company, one of the leading newspaper publishers in Japan, although the relationship did not involve stock ownership or interlocking directorships.

The FTC applied to the Tokyo High Court for a temporary injunction to stop this pricing practice while the case was awaiting an FTC administrative hearing. In granting a temporary injunction, the Tokyo High Court stated that the cost of production in this case should not be the cost actually incurred by Chūbu since Chūbu was subsidized by another company, and the cost actually incurred did not reflect that which would have been incurred had Chūbu carried on its business independently. Therefore, the Tokyo High Court tacked on a certain amount to the alleged cost of producing the newspaper and stated that if the sales price were set below this "constituted" price, then it would be regarded as unreasonably lower than production cost.

[3.] Unreasonable Inducement or Coercion of Customers

Unreasonable Inducement

Article 2(9) paragraph (iii) states that "unreasonably inducing or coercing a competitor's customers to deal with oneself" is an unfair business practice. With regard to unreasonable inducement, the FTC has issued designation No. 8 which deals with deceptive inducement and inducement with economic advantage. No. 8 envisages such conduct as false advertising and misrepresentation and designation No. 9 aims to regulate sales with excessive premiums.

As regards designations Nos. 8 and 9, however, a special law has been enacted to supplement such provisions, the "Law Prohibiting Unreasonable Premiums and Representations and Other Matters" (hereafter referred to as the "Premium Law"), which regulates representations and premiums as they affect consumers. Practically speaking, the Premium Law is far more important than Article 2(9) paragraph (iii) and the general designations issued thereunder, and will therefore be discussed briefly below.

Control of Unreasonable Representations and Excessive Premiums

The Premium Law regulates both false and deceptive representations and sales with excessive premiums. With regard to false and deceptive advertising, not only a false representation but also a misleading one is subject to regulation. For example, the use of the term "England" on a product which was manufactured by a machine imported from England but not made in the United Kingdom was held to be a misleading representation.

Under the Premium Law, the FTC is authorized to designate permissible levels for premiums offered in connection with the sale of goods or services, which are indicated as a percentage of the value of the item sold.

One important feature of the Premium Law is the enforcement procedure. Under this law, whenever there is a violation the FTC conducts a hearing and then issues an order prohibiting the representation or premium in question. Compared with regular [Antimonopoly Act] procedure, enforcement is prompt and efficient. If a person to whom the order is directed objects, he can file a complaint with the FTC, which must then initiate a formal hearing under the [Antimonopoly Act]. Thereafter, the case is dealt with according to regular procedures under the [Antimonopoly Act] and the court system.

Fair competition "codes" are permitted under the Premium Law. For example, if enterprises in an industry agree to set limits on the value of premiums they offer or restrict the use of certain kinds of representation, such agreement is filed with the FTC. After reviewing whether the agreement is effective in preventing excessive premiums or misleading representations, the FTC can grant permission to use the agreed terms, and enterprises in such industry can use such terms with immunity from application of the [Antimonopoly Act]. Therefore, such enterprises can enforce the agreement against violators using private law remedies.

Unreasonable Coercion (Tie-in Clause)

General designation No. 10 provides that unreasonable coercion (or a tie-in clause) is an unfair business practice. If one party to a transaction imposes on the other party (in which the former offers a commodity or service, *i.e.*, a tying product) the condition that the latter must purchase a different commodity or service (a tied product) as a condition of purchasing such commodity, this is known as a tie-in clause. For example, if a manufacturer of computers conditions its sale of computers upon the buyer's purchase of computer cards used together with the computer, then this is a tie-in contract.

Such tie-in contracts are not unlawful in principle. However, if the party offering the tying product enjoys a powerful economic position in the market for such product, the purchaser is forced into purchasing the tied product which it may not wish to purchase. Such contract may be regarded as unreasonable coercion of the customer and an unfair business practice. * * *

[4.] Unreasonable Restriction of Business Activities

In General

Article 2(9) paragraph (iv) provides that "trading with another party on such conditions as will unreasonably restrict the business activities of such party" is an unfair business practice and directs the FTC to designate unfair business practices in this category. The FTC has designated exclusive dealing, resale price maintenance, and other types of unreasonable restrictions as unfair business practices, each of which is discussed below.

Exclusive Dealing Arrangement

General designation No. 11 provides that if a party prohibits the other party to a transaction from dealing with the former's competitors and thereby unduly reducing business opportunities for such competitors, such exclusive dealing arrangement would amount to an unfair business practice. Exclusive dealing can be a contract between a manufacturer and a dealer whereby the former prohibits the latter from handling products or services of its competitors, or it can be a contract in which a powerful distributor obligates suppliers to provide products or services only to such distributor. This latter practice may also be called a "sole agency agreement."

Exclusive dealing is not unlawful in principle; however, it may become so if employed by a powerful enterprise. For example, in the *Mutō Kōgyō* case,[8] a powerful manufacturer of drawing instruments with a market share of approximately 70% imposed a condition on its dealers that they should refrain from handling competing products. The FTC ruled that this requirement amounted to an unreasonable exclusive dealing arrangement. * * *

Resale Price Maintenance

Resale price maintenance is typically a requirement imposed by a manufacturer on its wholesalers and/or retailers to the effect that such wholesalers or retailers, as the case may be, must maintain wholesale or retail prices at levels indicated by the manufacturer. It is usually a requirement that wholesalers or retailers set their prices at or above the level set by the manufacturer. In unusual cases, however, a manufacturer may direct its dealers to sell at or below a certain maximum price when they resell products supplied by the manufacturer.

General designation No. 12 provides that resale price maintenance is in principle unlawful if parties reselling the product are bound by a directive of the manufacturer. However, there must be a binding obligation that the reselling parties must adhere to price levels set by the manufacturer. Therefore, a mere "suggested price" or "recommended price" does not amount to resale price maintenance. The rationale for holding resale price maintenance unlawful in principle is that such activity can only be carried out in situations where the manufacturer is able to impose such terms on distributors, and in such situations the product in question enjoys a monopolistic position due to the fact that the product market in question is highly differentiated or an oligopolistic structure exists at the manufacturer's level. * * *

Although unlawful in principle, resale price maintenance agreements are exempt from the [Antimonopoly Act] in certain cases. The first exemption category is concerned with copyrightable books and published material under Article 24-2. In addition, the FTC is authorized to designate items for exemption from the [Antimonopoly Act]. If the FTC designates an item for such purpose, the item is exempt from the [Antimonopoly Act] as far as resale price maintenance is concerned. There are currently two items exempted by FTC designation, cosmetics and pharmaceuticals. * * *

[5.] Abuse of Dominant Position

Relevant Provisions

Article 2(9) paragraph (v) states that "dealing with another party by unwarranted use of one's bargaining position" is an unfair business practice and directs the FTC to designate specific conduct under this heading. The FTC has issued general designation No. 14, which provides that to engage in the activities enumerated in the designation by unreasonably utilizing superior bargaining position is an unfair business practice.

General designation No. 14 specifies the following five activities to be unfair business practices: (1) requiring the party to a continuous transaction to purchase goods or services other than those which are the subject of the transaction; (2) requiring the party to a continuous transaction to offer money, services or other kinds of economic benefit to oneself; (3) setting or changing business terms which are disadvantageous to the other party to a transaction; (4) disadvantaging the other party to a transaction with regard to the terms and enforcement of the transaction other than the above 3 items; and (5) requiring the other party to a transaction to follow a directive or to obtain one's approval concerning the selection of such other party's directors.

What Is "Dominant Position"?

General designation No. 14 applies when an enterprise with bargaining power, *i.e.*, with a dominant position, unduly utilizes such position thus resulting in unreasonable disadvantage to the other party to a transaction. The question here is the meaning of "dominant position." Although no definition is provided in the [Antimonopoly Act], it is generally understood that the term does not mean dominant position in a market, but rather dominant position in a particular transaction. Therefore, even if a party is a relatively small enterprise, it can be in a dominant position if the other party to the transaction is comparatively smaller and, therefore, the dominant party is able to impose unreasonable terms, such as unduly high sales prices. In the *Miyagawa* case [which appears later in this chapter], a small business cooperative (a relatively small organization) loaned money on the condition that the party taking out the loan deposit a large sum of money as a fixed term deposit. The Supreme Court held that this amounted to an abuse of dominant position.

What Is "Abuse of Dominant Position"?

If there is a difference in bargaining power between the parties to a transaction, naturally the weaker party is forced to accept terms disadvantageous to it. To hold that any disadvantage incurred by a weaker party to a transaction is an abuse of dominant position by the more powerful party would certainly be an excessive intervention of law into the freedom of contract doctrine. Therefore, whether an "abuse" exists or not should depend upon the particular circumstances of the case at hand.

While there is no clear answer to the question "what constitutes an abuse?", it would seem that suppressive or intimidating conduct would be required; for example, if a dominant party intimidates the other party to a transaction to the extent that the stronger party will refuse to deal with the weaker party if it declines to accept such disadvantageous business terms.

A well-known case in this area is the *Mitsukoshi* case.[9] The respondent Mitsukoshi chose to settle in accordance with the consent decision procedure and, therefore, this case has little precedent value. Nevertheless, the facts of this case provide a good illustration of abuse of dominant position. At the time, Mitsukoshi was the largest retailer in Japan and enjoyed tremendous prestige. Suppliers of products clamored for the opportunity to sell products to Mitsukoshi, since this would give them credibility and prestige as suppliers. In this sense, Mitsukoshi was in a dominant position *vis-à-vis* its suppliers.

Using its economic advantage, Mitsukoshi demanded that suppliers purchase certain luxury items such as paintings and jewels, contribute money for festivals sponsored by Mitsukoshi to promote its business, and bear the costs of repairing and renovating Mitsukoshi retail stores without guaranteeing that products supplied by suppliers contributing such funds would be exhibited there. The FTC claimed that if a powerful purchaser such as Mitsukoshi made a request, suppliers had no choice but to comply and, therefore, the mere fact that Mitsukoshi made such proposals constituted an abuse of dominant position.

Mitsukoshi countered that there must be specific evidence of abuse in order to challenge such practices. This would have been an interesting case had both parties argued the legal points and a formal ruling been made. Unfortunately, however, the case was terminated and resolved by a consent decision.

B. The P.C. Agreements and the General Designation

The provisions of the P.C. Agreements identified by the JFTC as possible unfair trade practices were TechA §§C-1 and 2; MA §§B-3(a), D-1 and 2(a) and (c); DA §F, and AA-15 §§A-1(b) and 2.

TechA §C-1: This provision requires A.Co to disclose to Newco any improvements related to the Licensed Products. More precisely, the obligation covers any "invention, improvement, modification or design, whether patented, patentable or not, * * * actually utilized by A.Co."

TechA §C-2: This provision imposes a similar obligation on Newco to disclose improvements to A.Co. Newco's obligation explicitly extends to improvements developed by its subcontractors or sublicensees (including J.Co), but does not include the requirement that Newco actually use the improvement.

MA §B-3(a): This provision is a non-competition provision. It prohibits J.Co from manufacturing, selling or handling items that compete with the Licensed Products.

MA §D-1: This provision requires J.Co to disclose improvements to both Newco and A.Co. In essence it is identical to A.Co's disclosure obligation, but it does not require that J.Co use the improvement for the disclosure obligation to take effect.

MA §D-2: This provision stipulates what rights the parties will have in improvements. MA §D-2(a) states that all improvements disclosed by J.Co to Newco or A.Co will become the property of Newco, and MA §D-2(c) states that any patents arising from such improvements will be the property of Newco.

DA §F: This provision is also a non-competition provision. It prohibits J.Co from selling products "of the same nature as or similar to" the Licensed Products.

AA-15 §§A-1(b) and 2: These provisions identify the Related Licensed Products, *i.e.*, those developed with the know-how of both A.Co and J.Co.

In the letter below, J.Co explains what it understands the JFTC's concerns over the cited provisions to be.

- - - - - - - - - -

[J.Co. letterhead]

February 3, 1978

Mr. James A. Theory
Vice President
A.Co
[address omitted]

Dear Mr. Theory:

Thank you for your telex dated January 23, 1978. We are prepared to meet with you on any day except Wednesdays, when we hold top management meetings. We are awaiting a schedule of your plans to visit Japan, and hope that you will agree to discuss the antitrust problem. Let me again address the legal aspects of this problem.

The Japanese Antimonopoly Act prohibits "unfair business practices" (Section 19) and international agreements containing such "unfair business practices" (Section 6(1)). Certain business practices are considered "unfair business practices" if they meet the following three conditions:

(A) The practice falls within any of Paragraphs 1 through 6 of Section 2(9),

(B) The practice tends to impede fair competition, and

(C) The practice is designated by the Fair Trade Commission as an "unfair business practice."

Consider now our joint venture. Paragraphs C-1 and C-2 of the Technical Agreement and Paragraph D-1 of the Manufacturing Agreement fall within General Designation 10. These provisions concern the disclosure of improved technology. They require Newco to disclose to A.Co *all* inventions and improved technology which Newco or its subcontractor has made with respect to licensed products. By contrast, A.Co must disclose to Newco only those inventions and improved technology that A.Co actually uses. J.Co too must disclose to A.Co and to Newco all inventions and improved technology with respect to licensed products. Such unequal business relationships do not exist in normal business arrangements.

Paragraph D-2(a) of the Manufacturing Agreement falls under General Designation 7. This paragraph makes technology produced by J.Co the property of Newco. However, J.Co should be able to determine for itself to whom its improved technology will belong. By limiting J.Co's discretion, the paragraph violates the Antimonopoly Act's ban on "exclusive trade practices."

Paragraph D-2(c) of the Manufacturing Agreement falls under General Designation 5 or 8. This paragraph prescribes that upon A.Co's written request, all patentable inventions and improved technology made and disclosed pursuant to paragraph D-1 of the Manufacturing Agreement by J.Co shall be assigned to A.Co. As pointed out above, J.Co should be able to determine what entity receives the benefit of J.Co inventions and technology. By forcing J.Co to assign its own inventions and technology to a specific third party, this paragraph falls within General Designation 8.

Paragraph B-3(a) of the Manufacturing Agreement and Paragraph F of the Distributorship Agreement fall under General Designations 7 and 8. Paragraph B-3(a) of the Manufacturing Agreement prohibits J.Co from manufacturing, selling and dealing with products competing with Licensed Products, with the exception of J.Co's tractors and the tractor shovels. Paragraph F of the Distributorship Agreement prohibits J.Co from keeping in stock, offering, selling or manufacturing any product resembling the Licensed Products. By reducing the scope of allowable competition, Paragraph B-3(a) and Paragraph F fall under General Designation 7.

Paragraphs A-1(b) and A-2 of Amending Agreement No. 15 fall under General Designation 7. These paragraphs prescribe that the products jointly developed by A.Co and J.Co based on common know-how become the property of Newco. Hence, they fall under General Designation 7 for the reasons set forth above.

Best regards,
[signed]

A. Kurokawa
General Manager

V. Enforcement of the Antimonopoly Act

A. The JFTC and enforcement procedures

HIROSHI IYORI AND AKINORI UESUGI, THE ANTIMONOPOLY LAW OF JAPAN*

119-127 (1983)

[1.] The Fair Trade Commission

The Structure of the Fair Trade Commission

The FTC was created to implement the purposes of the Antimonopoly Act, and is composed of a Chairman and four Commissioners (Sections 27(1) and 29(1)). Although the FTC belongs administratively to the jurisdiction of the Prime Minister (Section 27(2)), it is an Extra-Ministerial Agency attached to the Prime Minister's Office under the National Government Organization Act. The Chairman and the Commissioners perform their duties independently (Section [28]). In order to assure their independence, Section 31 fully guarantees their status.

The Chairman and the Commissioners are appointed by the Prime Minister with the consent of both Houses of the Diet from individuals who are considered experts in law or economics. The appointment or dismissal of the Chairman is attested by the Emperor (Section 29(2) and(3)). The term of office for the Chairman and the Commissioners is five years (Section 30(1)); and they must be at least 35 years of age at the time of their appointment (Section 29(2)). Retirement at age 65 is compulsory (Section 30(3)).

Staff Office

The Staff Office executes the FTC's day-to-day operations (Section 35). The number of personnel in the Staff Office, including typists, secretarial clerks, etc., was fixed at [493 as of March 31, 1994]. The Staff Office is located in Tokyo and is composed of the Secretariat, Economic Bureau, Trade Practice Bureau and the Investigation Bureau (Section 35-5). * * * The Staff Office maintains local branch offices in: Sapporo, Sendai, Nagoya, Osaka, Hiroshima, Takamatsu and Fukuoka (Section 35-6).

Powers

The FTC has, as an independent administrative agency, the power to exercise a quasi-legislative and quasi-judicial power, in addition to its administrative power.

The FTC, as part of its administrative powers, has such powers of investigation as are necessary for performing its function as the enforcement agency under the Act. In addition, it has the duty to receive and approve various reports filed with the FTC, to authorize depression cartels, to approve stockholdings by a financial company and to consult with other ministries.

---

*From Hiroshi Iyori and Akinori Uesugi, *The Antimonopoly Law of Japan* (Federal Legal Publications, Inc., 1983), at 119-127. Reprinted by permission.

As a quasi-legislative power, the FTC has rulemaking power to designate commodities for which resale price maintenance is permissible (Section 24-2), and to define unfair business practices (Section 72). It also establishes the procedures for handling cases brought before it and determines the form of reports required to be filed with the FTC (Section 76).

As a quasi-judicial power, Division 2 of Part VIII of the Act provides the procedures to be followed by the FTC when handling cases it has found to violate the Act. With the exception of very ordinary matters, such as a suit asking for the revocation of "designations," which would be referred to the district courts, appeal of an FTC decision lies exclusively in the Tokyo High Court. This is exceptional in Japanese jurisprudence and reflects the importance attached to the expertise of the FTC in antimonopoly cases. * * *

[2.] Administrative, Civil and Criminal Procedures

Administrative Procedures

The FTC will conduct investigations, hold hearings and issue a cease and desist order if it finds a violation of the Act. The ordinary procedural format is:

(a) Preliminary investigation;
(b) Compulsory investigation;
(c) Recommendation to the respondent;
(d) If the recommendation is rejected, the issuance of a complaint;
(e) Trial type hearing;
(f) Initial decision;
(g) Final (formal) decision.

Preliminary Investigation

The Investigation Bureau engages in a preliminary investigation, either upon a complaint from entrepreneurs or other interested parties, or upon its own initiative. Any person may request the FTC to institute an investigation, with respect to any matters which are suspected of falling under any prohibition stipulated in the Act (Section 45(1)). * * *

Compulsory Investigation

The FTC is empowered to take the following compulsory measures when, after a preliminary investigation, there are grounds to believe a violation of the Act may have occurred (Section 46(1)):

(a) Order to give testimony or to produce documentary evidence;
(b) Order to give expert testimony;
(c) Order persons holding financial records and other relevant documents to submit the same, and to retain the documents submitted;
(d) Entering any place of business, or other necessary premises of the persons concerned with a case, and inspecting said business operations and property, financial records, documents and other materials. * * *

Recommendation System

When the FTC finds that there exists a violation of the Act, it can recommend that the party concerned take appropriate remedial measures, as specified by the

FTC (Section 48(1)). The party must ["promptly"] notify the FTC whether it accepts the recommendation (Section 48(3)). When the recommendation is accepted, the FTC will normally issue a decision in keeping with what it has recommended, without resorting to a formal hearing procedure (Section 48(4)). When rejected, or if no notice from the party has been filed, the FTC will issue a complaint against the party and open a formal hearing procedure. * * *

Formal Hearing Procedure

The FTC may conduct a hearing, but usually hearing examiners are designated for this purpose (Section 51(2)). Normally, a tribunal of three examiners is formed for each case.

When the FTC will directly hear a case, the Chairman and no fewer than two Commissioners shall attend it (Section 34(1)). Representatives for the respondent are not limited to attorneys if prior approval is obtained from the FTC (Section 52(2)). Therefore, it is not unusual for a Managing Director and a Secretary for a trade association to represent the company or the trade association. * * *

Initial Decision

Hearing examiners must prepare an initial decision within 30 days from the conclusion of the hearing, and must submit it with all records of the case to the FTC. The transcript of the decision is served on the respondent, and he is entitled to file an objection in writing against the initial decision within two weeks. * * *

Consent Decision

The FTC may render a consent decision when the respondent: (1) submits a written statement setting forth that he admits both the findings of fact and the application of law as described in the complaint; (2) states that he intends to accept a decision without resorting to subsequent proceedings; and (3) files a plan with respect to the specific measures to be taken in order to eliminate the violation, in accordance with what the FTC considers appropriate remedial measures (Section 53(3)).

Therefore, a consent decision does contain facts as well as the application of law, and thus can be used as evidence to show a violation of the Antimonopoly Act in a civil damage suit in accordance with Section 25. However, the defendants can argue in court that although they admitted the facts and application of law for the purpose of concluding a consent decision, it does not mean that there was in fact a violation. * * *

Any person who does not comply with the decision [may be] punished by an administrative fine or penal servitude (Sections 90(iii), 95 and 97).

Temporary Injunction

The Tokyo High Court may, upon application of the FTC when it deems it of urgent necessity, order the person doing an act suspected of violating the Act, to temporarily cease the said act (Section 67), and any person who does not comply with this order shall be liable to fine (Section 98).

The FTC must specify possible grave injury to fair competition, if such acts are not enjoined at the time of the request, and show that ordinary FTC procedure for taking remedial measures cannot restore competitive conditions effectively.

The execution of the temporary injunction order may be stayed by depositing such bonds or security as the court may fix from time to time. However, no stay of injunction has so far been ordered.

Civil Procedures

Any person dissatisfied with the decision of the FTC may file a suit for revocation of the decision with the Tokyo High Court (Sections 77 and 87). If the findings of fact by the FTC are supported by substantial evidence, the Court shall be bound by such facts (Section 80).

B. Problems of service of process and standing

Before the JFTC can institute any proceedings, it must have personal jurisdiction over the party it wants to investigate. On what basis can the JFTC assert jurisdiction over a foreign party such as A.Co?

Suppose that because of the difficulty in asserting jurisdiction over a foreign party, the JFTC were to proceed only against the domestic party in a case of a suspected violation of Section 6(1) of the Act. If the JFTC were to rule on the agreement, what impact would this have on the foreign party to the agreement? In the case that follows, the JFTC had proceeded against only the domestic party and issued a "recommendation order," which was in essence a consent decision, ordering it to delete certain provisions of its international agreement. The Supreme Court's resolution of the response of the foreign party follows.

Translation by Yanagida Nomura & Akai

Novo Industri S.A. v. Japan Fair Trade Commission
800 Hanrei Jihō 35
(Sup. Ct., P.B., Nov. 28, 1975)

REFERENCES:

Antimonopoly Act, §§ 6, 48, 54 and 77

Administrative Case Litigation Act, § 9 ("Only one with a legally-protected interest may institute an action for revocation of a disposition or revocation of a decision.")

FACTS:

Novo Industri S.A. (Novo), a Danish chemical manufacturing company, entered into a distribution agreement (the Agreement) with Amano Pharmaceutical Company (Amano), a Japanese company. Under the Agreement, Amano became Novo's exclusive distributor in Japan for "Alkalase," a chemical cleaning agent. The following three provisions were included in the Agreement: 1) a resale price maintenance obligation on the part of Amano; 2) a prohibition against Amano handling competitive products during the term of the Agreement and for three years after its expiration; and 3) a prohibition against Amano manufacturing competing products during or after the term of the Agreement.

Two years after the Agreement was executed, Amano reported it to the Japan Fair Trade Commission (JFTC) pursuant to §6(2) of the Act Concerning the Prohibition of Private Monopoly and the Maintenance of Fair Trade (Antimonopoly Act). Pursuant to §48(1) of the Act, the JFTC then recommended that Amano delete the above provisions on the grounds that they violated §6(1) of the Act. Amano agreed and, pursuant to §48(4) of the Act, the JFTC issued such a recommendation order. During the time of the investigation by the JFTC, the Agreement was terminated. Accordingly, only the provisions imposing post-termination obligations on Amano remained relevant, and thus the JFTC's final order did not refer to the resale price maintenance requirement.

Novo was not issued any recommendation order by the JFTC nor included in the JFTC's proceedings. Novo therefore sued in the Tokyo High Court to have the JFTC's recommendation decree vacated. The High Court held that Novo lacked standing to sue the JFTC. Novo appealed.

JUDGMENT:

The appeal by Novo is hereby dismissed.

REASONS:

According to the record, this case was initiated by Appellant Novo, which has its principal office in Copenhagen, Denmark. Novo sought to have the January 12, 1970, recommendation order (the Order) issued against Amano by Appellee JFTC pursuant to §48(4) of the Antimonopoly Act dismissed. In the Order, the JFTC ordered Amano to delete Articles 3 and 4 and the latter part of Article 10 of the Agreement regarding the sale of an alkaline bacterial protein decomposing enzyme called "Alkalase." According to the JFTC, these articles, which prohibit Amano's manufacture, sale and handling of competitive products after termination of the Agreement, violated §6(1) of the Antimonopoly Act. It issued the Order after Amano had accepted its recommendation pursuant to §48(1) of the Antimonopoly Act. The court below dismissed Novo's complaint, holding that Novo did not have standing to sue or any legally recognized interests at stake. It held that the Order to delete the articles of the Agreement was in the form of an order to only Amano, and thus Novo's rights and legal entitlements were not directly infringed by the Order.

In contesting the judgment below denying its standing and grounds for suit, Novo argues that the court below misconstrued §77 of the Antimonopoly Act and §9 of the Administrative Case Litigation Act. However, the JFTC may issue a so-called recommendation order pursuant to §48 of the Antimonopoly Act whenever it finds that a person has violated the Antimonopoly Act and the person accepts the JFTC's recommendation that he take appropriate measures to correct the violation (Corrective Measures). The person does so before the JFTC initiates any formal hearing proceedings, and the order itself issues without formal hearings and prescribes the same actions as the prior recommendation made by the JFTC.

In principle, Corrective Measures are to be undertaken after hearings where evidence is examined and violations are found (*see* Antimonopoly Act, §54(1)). Nonetheless, the Antimonopoly Act provides that the JFTC may issue recommendation orders without a formal hearing if the person voluntarily agrees to take Corrective Measures. By doing so, the Act facilitates the enforcement process. Therefore, a formal order following hearings is based on a finding of a violation proven by evidence, while a recommendation order is based solely on the respondent's agreement to accept the recommendation voluntarily.

In light of the purpose and nature of a recommendation order, as long as it is based on the respondent's voluntary acceptance, such an order duly binds the respondent. The recommendation order binds regardless of whether an objective violation actually existed and regardless of whether the Corrective Measures recommended are appropriate. The recommendation order does not, however, bind third parties. Indeed, it has no legal consequence to such a third party at all—for example, it neither establishes that the acts in question constitute violations of law nor justifies any actions taken by the respondent in accordance with the recommendation order. Therefore, absent special circumstances, the rights and legal interests of third parties are not adversely affected by a recommendation order.

The Order was issued to Amano on the basis of Amano's acceptance of the prior recommendation. It was not issued to Novo. Although it ordered Amano to delete certain provisions in the Agreement and although Novo was a party to the Agreement, Novo was not the addressee of the Order. Novo is merely a third party to the Order, and unless there exist special circumstances, its rights and legal interests cannot be adversely affected by it. * * *

If Amano breaches or defaults on the Agreement because of the Order, this breach or default constitutes a voluntary and unilateral breach or default by Amano. It is not as the result of coercion based on the Order. This is because Amano's having become bound by the Order is the result of Amano's exercise of its free choice in accepting the recommendation of the JFTC. * * *

The conclusion of the court below that Novo does not have standing to seek revocation of the Order is proper. There is no error in the original judgment, and Novo's arguments are rejected.

Questions and Discussion Points

1. *Subsequent breach suit*: Following the case, if Novo were to sue Amano for breach of contract, how should the court rule?

2. *Service of process in the P.C.*: Since the *Novo* case, the JFTC's policy concerning Antimonopoly Act investigations pursuant to Section 6(1) has been to serve both the domestic and the foreign party. Pursuant to this policy, in the actual case on which the P.C. is based, the JFTC tried to serve A.Co. As can be seen above, it attempted this by having Newco forward its letter to A.Co.

Should this form of service on A.Co be considered adequate? Assume that you are advising A.Co on how to respond to the JFTC's letter. Should A.Co challenge the adequacy of service, or should it submit to the JFTC's jurisdiction and focus on the substantive issues? How might consideration of the *Novo* case affect your advice to A.Co?

In the case on which the P.C. is based, A.Co chose to challenge the adequacy of the service of process by the JFTC. The first several hearings before the JFTC, which took several months, involved only this issue. Eventually, A.Co and the JFTC agreed to discuss substantive issues, but only on condition that it would not prejudice A.Co's right to raise the service of process issue later.

VI. Enforceability of a Contract in Violation of the Antimonopoly Act

Suppose that the JFTC had not intervened in the P.C., but that J.Co, frustrated by what it perceived to be unfair contract terms, decided to breach the agreements. If A.Co were then to sue, J.Co might argue that the agreements were void because they violated the Antimonopoly Act. If the court agreed that the agreements violated the Act, it would then have to decide whether, notwithstanding the violation, the contract remained enforceable. The case below addresses that issue.

Translation by Yanagida Nomura & Akai

K.K. Miyagawa v. Gifu Commercial & Industrial Credit Assoc.
856 Hanrei Jihō 3
(Sup. Ct., P. B., June 20, 1977)

REFERENCES:

Antimonopoly Act, § 19
JFTC General Notification No. 11 of 1953, Item 10
Civil Code, § 90
Interest Rate Restriction Act, § 1

FACTS:

Plaintiff K.K. Miyagawa, a small corporation engaged in the manufacture and sale of paper lanterns and screens, defaulted on loans made by defendant credit union Gifu Commercial & Industrial Credit Association pursuant to a complex series of loan agreements.

Under these loan agreements, Gifu Credit had made two loans to Miyagawa totaling ¥11,500,000. The loans were contingent on Miyagawa mortgaging properties valued at ¥5,660,000, obtaining guarantees from five other parties, and meeting the following two conditions:

(1) make time deposits at Gifu Credit totaling ¥6,000,000 (Miyagawa earned minimal interest on these time deposits and, because Miyagawa was required by Gifu Credit to pledge the deposits against the repayment of the loans, Miyagawa could not withdraw the funds from the time deposit accounts); and

(2) pay the interest on the loans in advance.

Because of these conditions and of the additional fees charged by Gifu Credit, the actual amount Miyagawa received from Gifu Credit was ¥4,445,850.

After defaulting on the loans, Miyagawa sued for a declaration that the loan agreements were unenforceable. It alleged that the loans were sufficiently secured by its mortgages and the guarantees. Notwithstanding that security, Gifu Credit used its superior bargaining power to impose on Miyagawa the conditions concerning the time deposits, the prepayment of the interest on the loans and the deductions for various fees. These conditions enabled Gifu Credit, Miyagawa argued, to obtain an effective interest rate in excess of that permitted under the Interest Rate Restriction Act. Hence, Miyagawa continued, the loan agreements violated §19 of the Antimonopoly Act as unfair trade practices and violated Item 10 of JFTC General Notification No. 11 of 1953 as a misuse by Gifu Credit of its superior bargaining position. The loan agreements consequently were void under §90 of the Civil Code, which outlaws practices contrary to good morals and the public order.

The Gifu District Court held that because the loan agreements violated the Antimonopoly Act *ab initio*, the agreements were void. On appeal by Gifu Credit, the Nagoya High Court held that the loan agreements were enforceable. Even though the agreements violated the Antimonopoly Act, it explained, the violation was not so serious as to render the agreements void. Miyagawa then appealed to the Supreme Court.

JUDGMENT:

Such part of the judgment of the Nagoya High Court as was rendered against Appellant Miyagawa is hereby vacated, and the case is remanded to the Nagoya High Court for further proceedings.

REASONS:

[The court confirmed the factual findings by the High Court and concluded that the amount of the time deposits should be deducted from the principal amount received by Miyagawa. As a result, it found that Miyagawa had paid an effective interest rate of 17.18%.]

The effective interest [charged to Miyagawa] was about 17.18%, which is above the 15% maximum allowed under §1 of the Interest Rate Restriction Act. We thus find that, at the least, Gifu Credit imposed the conditions above on Miyagawa in order to gain unlawfully high interest on the actual principal of ¥5,500,000.

These loan terms should be considered "conditions unduly disadvantageous to the other party in the light of normal business practice." They were imposed by Gifu Credit "taking advantage of its superior position in the transaction." Accordingly, we find that Gifu Credit used unfair trade practices as defined in §19 of the Antimonopoly Act and Item 10 of [JFTC] General Designation [No. 11 of 1953].

An agreement that violates §19 of the Antimonopoly Act is not void *per se*. Instead, it is void only if it is also deemed contrary to the public order and good morals. * * * Moreover, even though the effective rate of interest in the instant case violates the Interest Rate Restriction Act because of the various conditions imposed on the transaction, that illegal result can be corrected as detailed above [*i.e.*, by declaring certain default penalties illegal, which the High Court was directed to determine how to do on remand]. In light of this fact and given the circumstances, the loan agreements cannot be considered to be against the public order and good morals clause of §90 of the Civil Code. Therefore, the judgment of the court below that the loan agreements are valid is reasonable.

Questions and Discussion Points concerning the Miyagawa case

1. *Holding in the case*: Is the Supreme Court's analysis of the public order and good morals issue convincing?

If the Interest Rate Restriction Act had not existed (*i.e.*, if the law did not impose maximum interest rate restrictions) but the rates charged were unusually high, would the Supreme Court have decided the case differently?

2. *Miyagawa and the P.C.*: What is the significance of the *Miyagawa* case to the issues presented by the P.C.? Assuming that the P.C. Agreements do, in fact, violate the Antimonopoly Act, would their enforcement violate the public order and good morals?

VII. Civil and Criminal Sanctions under the Antimonopoly Act

JAMES L. HILDEBRAND AND MITSUO MATSUSHITA, ANTIMONOPOLY LAW OF JAPAN—POTENTIAL CONSEQUENCES OF INTERNATIONAL CONTRACT VIOLATIONS UNDER ARTICLE 6*

6 NYU Journal of International Law and Politics 215
239-241 (1973)

[1.] Action for Damages Under Article 25 of the Antimonopoly Law

Whenever damage to property results from a violation of the Antimonopoly Law, the person (or legal entity) who sustains such damage may institute a claim for recovery in the Tokyo High Court pursuant to Article 25 of the Law, which provides:

(1) Any entrepreneur who has effected private monopolization or unreasonable restraint or who has employed unfair business practices, shall be liable for indemnification of damages to the person or party injured.

(2) No entrepreneur may be exempted from the liability as prescribed in the preceding paragraph by showing the non-existence of willfulness or negligence on his part.

* * * However, in order for the "injured party" to bring such a * * * claim, one of the three types of decrees [*i.e.*, recommendation decree, consent decree, or regular decree] must have been issued by the FTC with regard to the case in question. In other words, under the Antimonopoly Law the injured party must wait until the decision of the FTC has become final and conclusive with respect to the illegal act of the entrepreneur in question before instituting [such a suit]. When a decision has been rendered by the FTC with regard to a particular case, the decision may serve as conclusive evidence of illegality in a subsequent tort claim action brought against the respondent. The right to claim compensation for

*From James L. Hildebrand and Mitsuo Matsushita, "Antimonopoly Law of Japan—Potential Consequences of International Contract Violations under Article 6," 6 *NYU Journal of International Law and Politics* 215 (1973), at 239-241. Reprinted with permission of the NYU Journal of International Law and Politics.

damages terminates three years from the date the FTC's adjudication becomes final and conclusive (Article 26(2)).

* * * It has also been argued by some legal commentators that Article 35 of the Antimonopoly Law does not preclude the injured party from bringing a [tort] suit against the entrepreneur on the basis of the general clause of Article 709 of the Civil Code, in case such injured party cannot bring a suit under Article 25 due to the FTC's non-action or delay in issuing a decree. In such a case, however, the litigation would be more difficult, since the plaintiff would have the burden of proving the illegality of the conduct of the defendant.

A suit under Article 25 must be brought before the Tokyo High Court, which exercises exclusive jurisdiction over such matters (Article 85, Item 2). The court must seek the opinion of the FTC with respect to the amount of damages caused by the alleged illegal act of the entrepreneur (Article 84(1)). * * *

The "injured party" can be the other party to the contract, or some third party. For example, in the case where a restrictive provision of an international licensing agreement prohibiting the licensee from engaging in competitive activity is found by the FTC to be illegal as an unfair business practice, the licensee may subsequently sue the licensor for damages under Article 25 of the Antimonopoly Law. It is interesting to note that in the case of *FTC v. Taishō Seiyaku Kabushiki Kaisha,*[10] which did not involve an international agreement or contract, a non-competition clause imposed by a large Japanese manufacturer of pharmaceutical products on more than three thousand retail drugstores in Japan was held illegal by the FTC. Subsequently, one of the retail drugstores sought (under Article 25) to recover damages, which had been caused by the suspension of trade by the defendant manufacturer, such suspension having been found illegal by the FTC. The case was eventually settled and the court issued a settlement judgment. * * *

[2.] Criminal Sanctions

Private monopolization and unreasonable restraint of trade are criminal offenses and are punishable by a fine or imprisonment or both, pursuant to Article 89 of the Antimonopoly Law. It should be noted, however, that Article 90, Item 1, makes a violation of Article 6(1) a crime only when such violation is committed by the conclusion of an international agreement or contract which contains therein any matter coming under an "unreasonable restraint of trade." Therefore, entrepreneurs who enter into international agreements or contracts provisions which are deemed to constitute only "unfair business practices" will not be subject to criminal sanction under Article 89 of the Antimonopoly Law.

Nevertheless, in any case where an FTC "recommendation decree," "consent decree" or regular "decree" is issued, and becomes final and conclusive, an entrepreneur who does not comply with such FTC adjudication may be penalized by imprisonment for not longer than two years or a fine of not more than three million yen, pursuant to Article 90, Item 3 of the Law. In criminal proceedings in which the Tokyo High Court has exclusive jurisdiction, the FTC has the exclusive power to bring a complaint (*kokuhatsu*) against the violator before the Procurator-General * * *. It should be noted, however, that such criminal action can be taken only after such an accusation has been made (Article 96). It should be noted, further, that such criminal actions have rarely been brought in Japan.

J. MARK RAMSEYER, THE COSTS OF THE CONSENSUAL MYTH: ANTITRUST ENFORCEMENT AND INSTITUTIONAL BARRIERS TO LITIGATION IN JAPAN*

94 Yale Law Journal 604
616-618 (1985)

Although the Japanese Antimonopoly Act created a Fair Trade Commission (FTC) as an analogue to the [U.S.] Federal Trade Commission and gave it the power to enforce the Act through criminal and civil sanctions, Japanese and American antitrust enforcement could hardly differ more. While the Antimonopoly Act does provide prison terms for price-fixers, it permits fines of only up to [¥3 million], and its civil penalties include only consent decrees, cease-and-desist orders, and a surcharge [calculated at rates, following recent amendments, of 1% for wholesalers, 2% for retailers, and 6% for all others] of a cartel's gross earnings. Although the FTC does initiate a fair number of administrative actions each year to which it generally obtains consent decrees and although it regularly sues to recover the surcharge, neither a consent decree nor the surcharge can significantly deter price-fixing. Nevertheless, public antitrust enforcement has proceeded no further. The FTC has initiated only six criminal prosecutions in the thirty-seven-year history of the Antimonopoly Act, only two against cartels.[11]

If public antitrust enforcement has been sparse, private enforcement has been almost nonexistent. Although the Antimonopoly Act grants the victims of a cartel a strict liability cause of action for actual damages, the private damage actions brought to date demonstrate the extent to which private Japanese antitrust litigation is a fiction. Private parties apparently have filed only seven antitrust damage suits. The plaintiffs in two of these cases settled; all others lost. Other than the plaintiffs who settled, no plaintiff collected any compensation. No private antitrust damage claimant has ever prevailed in court in Japan.

In two of the five private damage actions decided by a court, the FTC had not undertaken administrative actions against the defendants. Although the Antimonopoly Act authorizes private actions, a plaintiff may sue under the Act only if the FTC has issued a final administrative order against the defendant. In neither of these two cases had the FTC issued a final order. Thus, the courts faced the issue of antitrust liability only in three cases: *Kai v. Nippon Sekiyu K.K.*,[12] *Satō v. Sekiyu Renmei K.K.*,[13] and *Ōkawa v. Matsushita Denki Sangyō K.K.*[14] In all three cases, plaintiffs' claims were ultimately rejected.

---

*From J. Mark Ramseyer, "The Costs of the Consensual Myth: Antitrust Enforcement and Institutional Barriers to Litigation in Japan," 94 *Yale Law Journal* 604 (1985), at 616-618. Reprinted by permission of The Yale Law Journal Company and Fred B. Rothman & Company from *The Yale Law Journal*, Vol. 94, pp. 604-645.

VIII. Actual Disposition of the Case in the P.C.

A.Co and J.Co held a series of meetings to try to agree on modifications of the P.C. Agreements. J.Co argued that the provisions constituted clear violations of the Antimonopoly Act and that it was thus necessary to delete most of the substance of the provisions. A.Co argued that the provisions did not constitute serious violations and that only minor modifications were necessary. A.Co and J.Co remained deadlocked on this issue. Finally, on November 13, 1977, the JFTC began formal proceedings against A.Co, J.Co, and Newco to determine whether the cited provisions constituted violations of the Antimonopoly Act. The proceedings lasted over three years. Eventually, A.Co and J.Co settled their differences and terminated the P.C. Agreements. At that point, the antitrust issues became moot and the JFTC terminated its proceedings without final resolution.

FURTHER READING

General Explanations of the Antimonopoly Act

Eleanor Hadley, *Antitrust in Japan.* Princeton, NJ: Princeton University Press, 1970.

Mitsuo Matsushita, *International Trade and Competition Law in Japan.* Oxford: Oxford University Press, 1993.

J. Mark Ramseyer, "The Antitrust Pork Barrel in Japan," *Antitrust*, Summer 1992.

The Oil Cartel Cases

John O. Haley, "Oil Cartel Cases: The End of an Era," 15 *Law in Japan: An Annual* 1 (1982).

Note [J. Mark Ramseyer], "Trustbusting in Japan: Cartels and Government-Business Cooperation," 94 *Harvard Law Review* 1064 (1981).

J. Mark Ramseyer, "Japanese Antitrust Enforcement After the Oil Embargo," 31 *American Journal of Comparative Law* 395 (1983).

Lawrence Repeta, "The Limits of Administrative Authority in Japan: The Oil Cartel Criminal Cases and the Reaction of MITI and the FTC," 15 *Law in Japan: An Annual* 24 (1982).

Enforcement of the Antimonopoly Act

John O. Haley, "Antitrust Sanctions and Remedies: A Comparative Study of German and Japanese Law," 59 *Washington Law Review* 471 (1984).

Antitrust and U.S./Japan Relations

Comment, "Japan Fair Trade Commission Guidelines Concerning Distribution Systems and Business Practices: An Illustration of Why Antitrust Law Is a Weak Solution to U.S. Trade Problems with Japan," 1993 *Wisconsin Law Review* 921.

Joel Davidow, "Keiretsu and U.S. Antitrust," 24 *Law and Policy in International Business* 1035 (1993).

NOTES TO CHAPTER TEN

1. In re Yukijirushi K.K. et al., 8 Kōsei Torihiki Iinkai Shinketsushū [*FTC*] 12 (1956). * * *

2. In re Noda Shōyu K.K., 7 *FTC* 108 (1950) and Noda Shōyu K.K. v. FTC, 10 Kōsai minshū 743 (1957). * * *

3. Asahi Shinbun et al. v. FTC, 6 Kōsai minshū 435 (1953).

4. In re Tōyōbō K.K. et al., 19 *FTC* 124 (1972).

5. 690 Kin'yū Shōji Hanrei 4 (Tokyo High Ct., Nov. 17, 1983).

6. 29 *FTC* 13 (1982).

7. FTC v. Chūbu Yomiuri Shinbun K.K., 776 Hanrei Jihō 30 (1975).

8. In re Mutō Kōgyō, 21 *FTC* 148 (1974).

9. 29 *FTC* 31 (1982).

10. 7 *FTC* 99 (1955).

11. *See* Japan v. Idemitsu Kōsan K.K., 985 Hanrei Jihō 3 (Tokyo High Ct., Sept. 26, 1980), *translated in* Ramseyer, *The Oil Cartel Criminal Cases: Translations and Postscript*, 15 *Law in Japan* 57, 66 (1982), *aff'd in part and rev'd in part*, 1108 Hanrei Jihō 3 (Japan Sup. Ct., Feb. 24, 1984); Japan v. Sekiyu Renmei, 983 Hanrei Jihō 22 (Tokyo High Ct., Sept. 26, 1980), *translated in* Ramseyer, *supra*, at 57; Japan v. K.K. Miai Tochi, *unreported case* (Tokyo High Ct., Jan. 29, 1971); Japan v. Ōkawa Gōmei Kaisha, *unreported case dismissed under amnesty proclaimed with the U.S.-Japan Peace Treaty* (Tokyo High Ct., May 12, 1952); Japan v. Yamaichi Shōken K.K., *unreported case, prosecution withdrawn* (Tokyo High Ct., Dec. 28, 1951); Japan v. Nōrin Renraku Kyōgikai, *unreported case* (Tokyo High Ct., April 27, 1951), *aff'd, unreported* (Sup. Ct., Dec. 5, 1961). There have been no criminal prosecutions filed under the Antimonopoly Act since 1974.

By contrast, from 1945 to 1969, the U.S. Department of Justice filed criminal prosecutions in over 350 cases. *See* Posner, *A Statistical Study of Antitrust Enforcement*, 13 *J.L. & Econ.* 365, 385 (1970).

12. 32 Gyōsei jiken saibanreishū 1099 (Tokyo High Ct., July 17, 1981), *aff'd*, 41 Minshū 785 (Sup. Ct., July 2, 1987).

13. 997 Hanrei Jihō 18 (Yamagata Dist. Ct., March 31, 1981), *aff'd*, 1147 Hanrei Jihō 19 (Sendai High Ct., March 26, 1985), *aff'd sub nom.* Satō v. Nippon Sekiyu K.K., 43 Minshū 1259 (Sup. Ct., Dec. 8, 1989).

14. 863 Hanrei Jihō 20 (Tokyo High Ct., Sept. 19, 1977).

ELEVEN

Dispute Resolution

Introduction

In this chapter we will discuss some of the basic features of arbitrating, litigating, and settling disputes in Japan. Part A considers the dispute in the P.C. and whether A.Co's and J.Co's attempts to resolve the dispute embody distinctive American and Japanese attitudes toward renegotiation of agreements. Part B concerns litigation in Japan generally, and Part C, arbitration. In Part D, we will discuss dispute settlement in Japan, the actual settlement reached in the P.C., and whether the Japanese are expecially averse to formal, contentious means of resolving disputes and especially predisposed toward the amicable settlement of disputes.

PART A: Dispute and Termination in the P.C.

I. The Dispute

In our studies of know-how and antitrust, we saw the outbreak of the dispute between A.Co and J.Co. In this chapter, we trace the evolution of that dispute and explore its resolution.

Recall that the dispute began when J.Co developed the small 10-H excavator and proposed that it market it as its own product. After negotiations that took close to two years, A.Co and J.Co agreed in Amending Agreement No. 15 to treat the 10-H as a Related Licensed Product—*i.e.*, a product recognized as incorporating both J.Co's and A.Co's know-how and manufactured by J.Co on a sublicense basis rather than on the subcontract basis used for the manufacture of Licensed Products.

Within two years after executing Amending Agreement No. 15, J.Co began complaining to A.Co about various other aspects of the joint venture. Eventually A.Co, too, began to express certain dissatisfactions, though the dialogue continued to be principally characterized by J.Co complaining and A.Co responding. Amid this developing contention between A.Co and J.Co came the investigation by the JFTC pursuant to the Antimonopoly Act.

J.Co's basic complaint was that the venture with A.Co was losing money. From 1970 to 1977, J.Co claimed to have lost ¥3.53 billion, while A.Co had received income of ¥3.38 billion in royalties and Newco dividends.

A.Co was unsympathetic. It responded that any losses J.Co suffered were either "paper losses" or the result of costs that J.Co had agreed to bear. A.Co disputed J.Co's figures because they were unverified, based on information within the control of J.Co, and based on accounting methods A.Co did not accept. It argued that any real losses J.Co suffered were J.Co's responsibility because they derived from product modifications for which J.Co was responsible under the agreements.

II. The Issue of Renegotiation

A. The attitudes of A.Co and J.Co

The negotiations between the two companies led to the following exchange of letters.

- - - - - - - - - -

[J.Co letterhead]

April 27, 1976

Mr. James A. Theory
Vice President and Secretary
A.Co
[Address omitted]

Dear Mr. Theory:

At the time of our talks here in Tokyo (Feb. 22, 23), several important problems relating to our business were discussed. Your proposal that the scope of the function of Newco should be expanded and the capital increased in the face of growing competition in the export market was noted and received with interest.

Our Agreements regarding the Newco joint venture were executed more than six years ago. It goes without saying that market conditions have changed radically since that time.

Under our Agreements, Newco, as A.Co's licensee, has the manufacturing and sales rights for Newco products. J.Co acts as the manufacturer and distributor for Newco. In actuality, however, J.Co has not only participated in the manufacture of the products, but has also suggested many design changes and improvements. In the area of sales, J.Co acts not as Newco's distributor, but as would a sub-licensee.

We feel that both parties fully realize that the effective utilization of J.Co's engineering, manufacturing and sales capabilities regarding excavators has contributed greatly to the development of Newco's business. We feel strongly that there is no need to duplicate in Newco the capabilities already developed in J.Co. This should be strictly avoided. It is J.Co, after all, that actually participates in the market and is able to listen and respond to customers' requests and feedback.

Accordingly, we believe that the Agreements should be modified to conform more closely to prevailing conditions and expected developments. In order to begin this modification process to our mutual benefit, we propose a series of meetings for drafting a new contractual arrangement.

[In an omitted section, J.Co proposes the following: 1) J.Co's distributors in South Korea, Taiwan, and the Philippines be designated Newco's distributors for these territories, 2) Indonesia be added to Newco Territory and J.Co's distributor be designated Newco's distributor for Indonesia, 3) no increase be made in the capitalization of Newco, and 4) the formula in §F of the JVA be adjusted to reflect the reality of J.Co's role as actual manufacturer and seller and of Newco's role as "managing the joint venture agreements."]

There is no doubt in our minds that we have your full recognition and understanding of the issues outlined in this letter, and that you are in general agreement with what we propose.

Sincerely yours,
[signed]

Takashi Shiraki
Executive Director
J.Co

- - - - - - - - - -

[A.Co letterhead]

May 18, 1976
Mr. Takashi Shiraki
Executive Director
J.Co
[Address omitted]

Dear Mr. Shiraki:

Thank you for your letter of April 27, 1976. Although we appreciate the frankly expressed views of J.Co with respect to the JVA, we feel that these matters, which have been the subject of exhaustive correspondence over the past year, should now be resolved promptly. Our views follow.

I.

We feel that the fundamental organization and terms of the Joint Venture should not be subject to continuous renegotiation. A.Co does not feel it is appropriate to continuously raise topics that were fully negotiated and resolved when the agreements were executed. A.Co is, however, willing to consider constructive suggestions for growth of Newco within the present framework of the JVA.

In considering such constructive suggestions we regard certain assumptions as implicit and fundamental to the continuation and success of the Joint Venture:

A. Long-Term Association

The Joint Venture was intended to be a long-term association of the parties, and since entering the JVA in 1970 the parties have acted in reliance on this assumption.

B. Basic Framework

The basic framework of the Joint Venture is sound and, to insure continued growth and success, the parties should continue to operate within that framework. Vital features which A.Co is not willing to change (A.Co would otherwise never have entered into the Joint Venture) include the following:

(1) The established formulas for financial compensation, fees (including royalties), and division of profits;
(2) A.Co Territory and J.Co Territory and the respective responsibilities of the parties with respect to such territories;
(3) Powers of Newco Board of Directors; and
(4) Exclusivity of engineering, manufacturing, and selling rights of the parties (to avoid unnecessary duplication and chaos in the marketplace).

C. Established Responsibilities of the Parties

The established rights, contributions and responsibilities of the parties are fundamental to the Joint Venture. We feel these should again be briefly summarized and reviewed:

(1) *Role of A.Co*

(a) *Supply of Engineering*

One of the essential contributions of A.Co to the Joint Venture is the exclusive supply of the designs that form the basis of the Licensed Products, subject only to relatively minor modifications to suit the Japanese market. It would defeat the whole concept of the Joint Venture if J.Co were to attempt to duplicate these design efforts.

(b) *Export Sales into A.Co Territory*

Another fundamental contribution by A.Co to the Joint Venture is the sale of the Licensed Products in A.Co Territory exclusively through A.Co's world-wide distributor network. It is fundamental that A.Co's sales efforts in A.Co Territory should not be duplicated by J.Co, just as the sales efforts in Newco Territory are not duplicated by A.Co.

(2) *Role of J.Co*

(a) *Manufacturing*

J.Co (as subcontractor of Newco for the Licensed Products, and as sublicensee for the Related Licensed Products) is the manufacturer of products for Newco.

(b) *Domestic Sales in Japan*

J.Co is the exclusive selling channel in Japan for the Licensed Products, just as A.Co performs a similar role in A.Co Territory.

(3) *Role of Newco*

Under the JVA Newco is not only the formal agent for controlling all operations under the JVA, but also the principal contractor for appointing subcontractors and distributors in Newco Territory, and has a vital responsibility for export sales and service.

II.

We believe that our difficulties can be resolved within the foregoing framework. We propose, as we have previously suggested, that we agree to take immediate steps to increase Newco's capital by capitalizing retained earnings and to support export sales and other growing activities of Newco by recruiting and training competent personnel.

III.

In conclusion, I hope this letter will serve to clarify A.Co's position as to the Joint Venture so that action on a constructive "family basis" within the present framework of the Joint Venture can be taken.

With kind personal regards.

Sincerely,
[signed]

James A. Theory
Vice President & Secretary
A.Co

Questions and Discussion Points

1. *Reversing the position of A.Co and J.Co*: If Japanese and Western parties tend to have a fundamentally different attitude toward renegotiation, and if J.Co and A.Co embody these attitudes, then we should expect that if A.Co and J.Co switched substantive positions (*i.e.*, if J.Co had been licensing technology to A.Co), the dispute would have developed differently. If the roles of J.Co and A.Co were reversed (but with an identical legal regime), how might A.Co have raised its objections and how might J.Co have responded?

2. *Drafting in anticipation of requests for renegotiation*: Assuming there is a considerable distinction in Western and Japanese attitudes toward renegotiation, what should the Western party do in the contract drafting phase? Should the Western party try to prevent the Japanese party from requesting renegotiation, or should it accept this as one of the realities of doing business in Japan? Is the foregoing assumption valid?

B. The doctrine of changed circumstances

The article below explores whether Japanese law recognizes the right to demand contractual modifications in cases such as that which the P.C. encountered.

PAUL WAER, FRUSTRATION OF CONTRACTS IN JAPANESE LAW: THE DOCTRINE OF CHANGED CIRCUMSTANCES*

20 Law in Japan 187

191-199 (1987)

There are four generally accepted prerequisites justifying application of the doctrine of changed circumstances. They are as follows:

1) The circumstances at the origin of the juristic act changed substantially.
2) Such change was not and could not reasonably be foreseen.
3) Such change was not attributable to the parties themselves.
4) As a consequence of the changed circumstances, execution or continuation of the original obligations would substantially violate good faith and fairness.

It seems appropriate to examine each of these four requirements in more detail.

[1.] The First Requirement: Substantial Change in Circumstances at the Time of Formation of the Juristic Act

First, one should be careful in deciding whether there has been a "substantial change" in circumstances. Too rash a judgment could jeopardize legal predictability. The change in circumstances should be "certain." Second, one should judge the circumstances at the origin of the legal act "objectively." Subjective circumstances relating to the parties cannot be taken into account. In one decision, for example, the court found that the destruction of numerous houses in Osaka as a consequence of acts of war constituted a "substantial change" in the housing situation. Such fact constituted an "objective" change in circumstances. On the contrary, the court held that the loss in the war of the particular house in which the seller lived could not constitute a "change in circumstances" justifying rescission of the sale of another house. This fact was deemed a purely "subjective" circumstance relating to the seller. So far as this was not an express resolutory condition (*kaijo jōken*) contained in the agreement, the fact that the house in which the seller lived was lost in the war could [not] be taken into account. Otherwise, the buyer would suffer an unpredictable disadvantage. Although some scholars approve this decision in general, they nevertheless point to the fact that in agreements between non-merchants such personal factors are often decisive and argue that the courts should take into account changes occurring as a result of exceptional facts such as fire.

Other examples of facts held to constitute "certain" and "objective" substantial changes in circumstances include the following: a hundredfold increase in the value

---

*From Paul Waer, "Frustration of Contracts in Japanese Law: The Doctrine of Changed Circumstances," 20 *Law in Japan: An Annual* 187 (1987), at 191-199. Reprinted by permission.

of immovable property after conclusion of a sales contract in 1944; a unilateral promise of sale with fixed price and a term of 10 years concerning an immovable property, the value of which increased several hundred times; a considerable increase in the value of immovable property resulting from the high inflation caused by the defeat in the war, which was the object of a compromise agreement concluded in 1942; the impact of the yen after 1945 in relation to a promise of resale of an immovable property against a fixed price with an undetermined term; and the increase in the yen value of a piece of land from [550 yen per] *tsubo* (*i.e.*, about 36 square feet) in 1948, to 20,000 yen per *tsubo* by April 1956. * * *

In contrast, in the following cases the courts have deemed the facts not to constitute a substantial change in circumstances: in *Kyōei K.K. v. K.K. Kōryū Yōkō*,[1] a tenant asked his landlord for reimbursement of expenses incurred for work on the property, arguing that as the economic circumstances had changed, the amount thereof should be increased. The Tokyo District Court, however, ruled that the economic circumstances in Japan had not changed to the same extent as "the terrible inflation in Germany after the First World War." Moreover, the court noted, the claim originated in July 1945 at the end of the war and the subsequent changes were not of such nature that they were not anticipated nor could be foreseen by the parties. Further, although the tenant had, under Civil Code article 608, the right to claim the necessary expenses "immediately," he had not done so. Instead, he "slept on his right" so he could not be allowed to claim a higher amount afterward when the value had risen. * * *

[2.] The Second Requirement: Unforeseeability

The second prerequisite is that the change in circumstances could not be foreseen with "normal knowledge and prudence."

In *Suzuki v. Kawanoue*,[2] for example, the Supreme Court held that at the moment of conclusion of a sale on November 12, 1944, one could foresee that under wartime conditions houses in a city like Fukui could be destroyed as a result of air attacks. In other towns such destruction was foreseen but nevertheless quite a few houses were being sold. Commentators on the Supreme Court decision have criticized this rationale. It has been argued that the Supreme Court at least should have supported the decision with more concrete facts.

An example in which this was done is a decision by the Osaka High Court that holds that at the moment of conclusion of a compromise agreement (*wakai*) relating to a disputed lease in October 1943, the drastic deterioration of the housing situation was not particularly bad. Quite a few houses in and outside of Osaka were still available. By the beginning of 1945, however, the situation had changed drastically with numerous homes destroyed in air attacks. Although for some months after the war the situation was not so bad, housing in and around Osaka became very scarce. Even by 1952, despite signs of improvement, the housing problem had not yet been solved.

The courts have held that a change in circumstances was not foreseeable in a number of other extraordinary cases. In one, the court held that, in concluding a resale agreement with a fifteen- to twenty-year term for a tract of land in 1935, the parties could have foreseen some change in value, but not a 620 percent increase. Similarly, the parties to a ten-year preliminary contract (*i.e.*, option) for purchase of real property in 1942 for a fixed price could not have foreseen a several hundred-fold rise in values. In another instance the court held that the parties could not have reasonably foreseen the postwar inflation at the time they concluded a compromise in 1942. Similarly, in a case involving a compromise entered into in 1943 to settle a dispute over real property, the Kumamoto District Court reasoned that at the time the Japanese people still believed in certain victory and no one could have reasonably foreseen the defeat and consequent social turmoil or the ensuing inflation. In other decisions district courts have viewed the drastic inflation between 1944 and 1950, the depreciation of the yen after 1945, and the rise in land prices between 1948 and 1956 to have been unforeseeable. In a more recent case, the Fukuoka District Court held that, in granting an option to acquire immovable property in 1963, the parties could not have foreseen a 1969 decision by the government to construct a ["bullet train"] line. * * *

[3.] The Third Requirement: Nonattributability

Because the doctrine of changed circumstances is based on the principle of "good faith," the nonattributability of the change to the parties themselves is an obvious requirement. If the circumstances change as a result of acts or omissions by a party, the doctrine does not apply. There have been few, if any, problems with this requirement in Japanese decisional law. It is obvious, for example, that postwar inflation was not attributable to the parties themselves.

[4.] The Fourth Requirement: Substantial Violation of Good Faith and Fairness in Performance or Continuation of the Original Obligation

The General Rule

The fourth prerequisite purports to ensure that the circumstances are examined from different angles and the interests of *both* parties are taken into account in order to prevent a possible abuse of the right of rescission (*kaijoken*) on the basis of changed circumstances.

In most cases it is hard to determine whether this requirement is fulfilled. One criterion is whether the changed circumstances upset the balance of the agreement and as a result there exists a great discrepancy in the neutrality of the obligations of the parties. In a number of cases, after establishing the *disequilibrium between the respective obligations*, the courts have concluded without further elaboration that performance or continuation of the original obligation would substantially violate good faith and fairness. However, in one case involving a dispute over a mining concession, the Supreme Court has held that, although there was a great difference in the value of the yen between May 1936 and October 1952, this fact itself was not sufficient to justify adjustment of the provisions of the agreement. Something more was necessary.

In other cases, however, the courts have found such justification in pointing out that one of the parties did not act in "good faith." The Nagasaki District Court, for example, held that, with respect to a promise to sell with an undetermined term and fixed price, a party does not act in "good faith" if it lets time go by, disregarding the depreciation of the currency and the growing damage to the other party, but nevertheless later on demands performance against the original fixed price.[3] Similarly, the Osaka District Court has held that if a sharp increase in the value of land (from 550 yen per *tsubo* to 20,000 yen per *tsubo*) has occurred during delay in payment by the buyer, seeking enforcement of the original agreement against the seller would be unfair and contrary to "good faith."[4] * * *

Default and "Good Faith"

Because the doctrine of changed circumstances is based on the "good faith" principle, certain problems occur if the person who invokes the doctrine was in default because of delay (*rikō chitaichū*).

The Supreme Court first considered this problem in *Hirai v. Shibata.*[5] In July 1945, the plaintiff's predecessor contracted for the purchase of a house from the defendant. Part of the price was paid immediately. It was agreed, however, that the remainder would be paid after the defendant fulfilled the formalities for registration for transfer of ownership. In January 1946, the defendant requested payment from the plaintiff because he intended to complete the registration procedure. The plaintiff sent a representative, but because of procedural problems registration could not be completed. In September of the same year, the plaintiff urged the defendant to act, but the defendant replied by demanding an increase in the sales price of 240,000 yen. Afterward the plaintiff commenced a proceeding for specific performance of the contract. In response, the defendant invoked the doctrine of changed circumstances.

In the first instance and on *kōso* appeal, the courts held for the plaintiff. They found that because of the postwar inflation and housing shortage, the current value of the house, as compared to its value at the time of conclusion of the agreement, had risen considerably and that the original price was very low. Both courts then concluded that these facts could constitute a "change in circumstances." They further found such change in circumstances to be neither foreseeable nor attributable to the defendant. The defendant could only invoke such changed circumstances, however, if the plaintiff's claim for enforcement of the original agreement violated the standards of good faith. The rise in value of the house was, however, a change in circumstances that had occurred during default as a result of delay in performance of the registration obligation by defendant. Had the defendant performed his obligations he would not have received the benefit of the change in circumstances. If one ruled that the defendant in such case could invoke the changed circumstances, the end result would be to permit a party to benefit from the doctrine by not performing his obligation, contrary to "good faith." Therefore, the arguments of the defendant were rejected. The Supreme Court affirmed this decision.

III. Termination and Related Issues

Although A.Co made some concessions to allow J.Co to recover larger amounts for its manufacturing and selling costs and to pay a lower overall royalty, these did not resolve the dispute. Instead, the dispute persisted, with A.Co arguing that its concessions were sufficient and J.Co that they were inadequate. Indeed, the dispute over the determination of J.Co's manufacturing costs for the JVA, the §F price determination formula, was so severe that for two years running A.Co and J.Co would not agree on these figures. Meanwhile, Newco remained in corporate deadlock.

In 1978, J.Co announced its intent to begin manufacturing and selling back-hoes independently. A.Co argued that the back-hoes competed with the Licensed Products and thus could not be sold without A.Co's consent. For that consent, A.Co demanded 2 percent royalties from J.Co. J.Co, naturally, claimed that the back-hoes did not compete with the Licensed Products.

Letters were exchanged and meetings were held, but the dispute persisted. To A.Co, J.Co seemed to be putting less and less effort into the joint venture business. J.Co continued to manufacture and sell the Licensed Products, but refused A.Co's suggestions for adding new models to the Newco product line, for increasing Newco's capitalization, or for responding to export bid requests of Asian governments.

Eventually, J.Co sent the following letters to Newco and A.Co.

- - - - - - - - - -

[J.Co letterhead]

December 26, 1979
Mr. H. Ishii, President
Newco K.K.
[Address Omitted]

Dear Mr. Ishii:

As we suggested at the meeting with your company and A.Co held on October 22, 1979, we hereby notify you that we choose not to renew the April 24, 1970, Manufacturing Agreement entered into by your company and our company, and that we terminate the following two agreements effective July 24, 1980:

1. The Distributorship Agreement entered into by your company and our company dated April 24, 1970, and

2. The Amending Agreement No. 15 entitled "Agreement Concerning Related Licensed Products" entered into by your company, A.Co and our company dated September 29, 1975.

Please be advised that we have concurrently sent A.Co a similar notice to terminate. The Selling Agreement entered into by your company, A.Co and our company dated April 24, 1970, shall automatically terminate upon the termination of the Joint Venture Agreement on July 24, 1980.

Sincerely yours,
[signed]

Taro Kawada
President
J.Co

- - - - - - - - - - -

[J.Co letterhead]

December 26, 1979
Mr. B.W. Summer
President and Chief Operating Officer
A.Co
[Address Omitted]

Dear Mr. Summer:

Please be advised that today we sent the enclosed letter to Mr. Ishii, as suggested at our meeting on October 22, 1979, and more recently in our telex to you of December 7, 1979.

Consequently, we hereby notify you that we have chosen to terminate the following three agreements on July 24, 1980:

1. The Joint Venture Agreement between your company and our company dated April 24, 1970, as amended,

2. The Trademark Agreement between your company and our company dated April 24, 1970, and

3. The Amending Agreement No. 15 entitled "Agreement Concerning Related Licensed Products" entered into by your company, Newco K.K. and our company dated September 29, 1975.

Accordingly, the Selling Agreement entered into by your company, Newco K.K. and our company dated April 24, 1970, shall automatically terminate on July 24, 1980.

Very truly yours,
[signed]

Taro Kawada
President
J.Co

Questions and Discussion Points

1. *Terminability of the JVA and constituent agreements*: Consider the duration and termination clauses of each of the MA, DA, JVA, and Amending Agreement No. 15. J.Co chose not to renew the MA with Newco and to terminate the DA and AA-15 with Newco and the JVA, Trademark Agreement, and AA-15 with A.Co. On what basis did J.Co terminate the JVA? The DA? The Trademark Agreement? The Amending Agreement No. 15? What happens to the TechA? What is likely to be A.Co's position on these issues? What should A.Co do if J.Co has terminated an agreement A.Co believes it has no authority to terminate?

2. *Post-termination manufacture by J.Co*: Assume that the JVA and constituent agreements have been effectively terminated. If J.Co then wants to manufacture and sell excavators, is there anything to prevent it from doing so?

Consider the non-compete clause, MA §B-3. Does this clause have any validity after the termination of the MA? Consider whether any of the following clauses has any impact on the post-termination manufacture of excavators by J.Co.: MA §§C-5(a), D-1, D-2, D-3, H-7(c); JVA §§D-1, I-4(e); or TechA §I-6.

PART B: Litigation

I. Transnational Litigation

A. Strategic Issues

By terminating the joint venture, J.Co raised several issues: whether the termination was effective, whether J.Co had breached its contractual obligations, and whether it could now manufacture products similar to the Licensed Products and Related Licensed Products.

The possibility of litigation between A.Co and J.Co raised several further questions. Suppose A.Co wished to sue J.Co for contractual and tort damages and also wanted to prevent J.Co from manufacturing products with A.Co's know-how. Threshold questions for A.Co would include the following: Could it sue in the United States? Would a U.S. court have jurisdiction over J.Co? If a U.S. court did have subject matter and personal jurisdiction, would it apply Japanese substantive law, or might it instead apply U.S. substantive law? What if J.Co instituted parallel proceedings in Japan? Does J.Co have assets in the United States against which A.Co could enforce a favorable judgment? Could an American judgment be enforced against J.Co in Japan? Which substantive law would most favor A.Co? Could A.Co obtain injunctive relief in Japan? Declaratory relief? How would A.Co find legal counsel in Japan? How much would a lawsuit in Japan cost?

Given the constraints of these materials, we confine our investigation below to a single issue: the recognition of foreign judgments. We will then survey some of the basic features of Japanese civil litigation.

B. Recognition of foreign judgments

The process for enforcing foreign judgments in Japan is straightforward: with the favorable foreign ruling in hand, a plaintiff files suit in the appropriate Japanese court for recognition of the ruling. Once recognized, its effect is the same as if the Japanese court had made the ruling itself. Nonetheless, the materials below illustrate just how complex this can become.

TAKAO SAWAKI, BATTLE OF LAWSUITS: *LIS PENDENS* IN INTERNATIONAL RELATIONS*

23 The Japanese Annual of International Law 17
17-18 (1980)

In 1968, an accident happened at Seattle, Washington, and [between then and] 1977 seven judgments were delivered in relation to the accident, four in the state of Washington and three in Japan.

[The] circumstances were as follows: Y [Kansai Iron Works Ltd.] was a Japanese company engaged in the manufacture and sale of various machines, and M [Marubeni-Iida] was a Japanese company engaged in internal and international trade. In 1966, Y sold one of [its] power press machines to M under the term *ex* warehouse Kobe (JAPAN), and subsequently this machine was resold to X [Marubeni America Co.], which is a New York company and a subsidiary of M in the United States. X then sold the machine to a United States company W, which sold it to another United States company B doing business in Seattle. While operating the machine at B's plant, D, an employee of B, met the above-mentioned accident, in which his left-hand fingers were cut off. D brought a lawsuit against W, X and Y in a Washington state superior court to recover damages caused by the accident (U.S. Case No. 1), [the] summons and complaint [for which were] not served [on] Y. X also filed a lawsuit, as a third party action, against Y before the same state court in order to get indemnification from Y if [it] lost (U.S. Case No. 2). By way of judicial assistance, [the] summons and complaint were served [on] Y in September 1970. Y appeared to contend a lack of jurisdiction, but the Washington state court dismissed the contention. Upon *certiorari*, the Supreme Court of the State of Washington examined the issue and remanded the case for further proceeding to the superior court, holding that courts of the State of Washington had jurisdiction over Y (*in personam* jurisdiction) under the state's long-arm statute.[6]

On September 17, 1974, the Washington State Superior Court delivered a judgment as to U.S. Case No. 2, which held that Y should pay the sum of 86,000 U.S. dollars to X, and this became conclusive on October 17 of the same year.

Opposing these lawsuits pending in the Washington state court, Y brought a lawsuit against X in Japanese court seeking a judgment declaring the non-existence of the right of indemnification that had been claimed against [it] in the United States based on product liability. On October 9, 1973, the Osaka District Court, by

*From Takao Sawaki, "Battle of Lawsuits: *Lis Pendens* in International Relations," 23 *The Japanese Annual of International Law* 17 (1980), at 17-18. Reprinted by permission.

an interlocutory judgment (JAPAN Case No. 1), rejected X's plea in abatement with respect to the jurisdiction. It was held as one of the opinions of the court that:

> [A]lthough [X] contends that the institution of this lawsuit is illegal because it turns out to be double action (Article 231 of the Code of Civil Procedure) with respect to the U.S. Case No. 2, which has been pending in the United States, this contention of [X]'s is groundless, because the word "court" in said article should be construed to mean court of our country and not to include a foreign court.

On October 14, 1974, about one month after the United States No. 2 case judgment, the same court in Japan delivered a judgment to the effect that Y was under no obligation to indemnify X for damages due to the accident claimed (Japan Case No. 2).

In 1976, X filed a lawsuit against Y in the same Japanese court, requesting permission [for] execution in virtue of the Washington state court judgment (U.S. Case No. 2). On December 22, 1977, the Osaka District Court dismissed the request [in the opinion reproduced below].

Following these developments, the battle of lawsuits seems to [have] come to an end, ten years after the accident, with the disastrous result of a conflict of *res judicata.*

----

*Marubeni America Co. v. Kansai Iron Works Ltd.**
361 Hanrei Taimuzu 127
(Osaka Dist. Ct., Dec. 22, 1977)

STATUTORY REFERENCES

Civil Procedure Code, § 200

TEXT OF JUDGMENT

1. The claim is dismissed. * * *

OPINION OF THE COURT

I. Regarding the Claim of the Plaintiff.

A. There is no dispute between the parties [that] the Court of Appeals of King County in the State of Washington held on September 17, 1974, in the case between the parties (Case No. 713245) that the [Defendant] shall pay $86,000 to the [Plaintiff] and that this decision became final on October 17, 1974.

B. According to the evidence [omitted], which is not in dispute, the Osaka District Court held on October 14, 1974, in the case between the parties (Case No. 668, 1970) regarding the claim for a judgment confirming non-liability for damages that despite the decision of the Court of Appeals of King County in Washington (Case No. 713245), the Defendant is not liable to pay the Plaintiff ¥97,000,000 in indemnification as ordered by the Washington court. It is evident by the entire

*Translation from 23 *The Japanese Annual of International Law* 200 (1980). Reprinted by permission.

tenor of the oral proceeding that this decision had become final before the beginning of the suit before us.

C. According to the facts, which are not in dispute, and to the court's findings, at the time the Plaintiff brought the present suit for enforcement of the Washington judgment, there already existed a Japanese final judgment, based on the same set of facts, which judgment conflicted with the Washington judgment.

Now we come to examine whether each of the requirements of Article 200 of the Code of Civil Procedure of Japan is satisfied. It should be evident that to recognize a foreign judgment contrary to a Japanese judgment, in which the parties are the same and which is based on the same set of facts, is contrary to the order of the judicial system and against Article 200(3) of the Code, which requires "that the judgment of a foreign court must not be contrary to the public policy in Japan," regardless of whether the former was brought, held or finalized earlier than the latter, since to recognize a foreign judgment that is inconsistent with a domestic judgment disturbs the order of our entire legal system.

Therefore, the U.S. judgment before us cannot be recognized for it does not satisfy Article 200(3) of the Code of Civil Procedure. Thus the claim of the Plaintiff is without merit and we need not examine the rest of the points at issue. * * *

[II.] Conclusion

Therefore, both the claim and the counterclaim are dismissed. Applying the Code of Civil Procedure Article 89 to the litigation, we render the judgment stated in the Text of Judgment. * * *

WILLIAM T. JORDEN, BEYOND JINGOISM: SERVICE BY MAIL TO JAPAN AND THE HAGUE CONVENTION ON THE SERVICE ABROAD OF JUDICIAL AND EXTRAJUDICIAL DOCUMENTS IN CIVIL OR COMMERCIAL MATTERS*

16 Law in Japan 69

69-84 (1983)

[1.] Introduction

In 1970, Japan formally ratified the Hague Convention on the Service Abroad of Judicial and Extrajudicial Documents in Civil or Commercial Matters (hereinafter the "Convention"). As stated in its Preamble, the primary purposes of the Convention were to establish means by which the tribunals and litigants of a signatory state could be assured of assistance in another signatory state with respect to service of legal documents in the latter state, and to assure that defendants in foreign litigation be given reasonably certain notice of such litigation. [The Convention provides:]

*From William T. Jorden, "Beyond Jingoism: Service by Mail to Japan and the Hague Convention on the Service Abroad of Judicial and Extrajudicial Documents in Civil or Commercial Matters," 16 *Law in Japan: An Annual* 69 (1983), at 69-84. Reprinted by permission.

> *Article 10*
> Provided the State of destination does not object, the present Convention shall not interfere with:
> (a) the freedom to send judicial documents by postal channels, directly to persons abroad.[7]

Among Japan's designations and declarations made at the time of its ratification was the following: "It is declared that the Government of Japan objects to the use of the methods of service referred to in subparagraphs (b) and (c) of Article 10." It would seem, therefore, that in choosing not to object to subparagraph (a) of article 10, Japan wished to leave the other ratifying states with the impression that service of process by mail was unobjectionable as a matter of Japanese public policy. Moreover, foreign parties, or their attorneys, could very easily be given the impression that any default judgment obtained abroad based on service mailed to Japan would not be unenforceable in Japan as a foreign judgment because of improper service, and that it would not be necessary to rely on the other time-consuming service mechanisms involving the Central Authority. To date, no Japanese court has directly addressed the implications of article 10(a) of the Convention. * * *

[2.] **The Hague Convention**

A close reading of the Convention would reveal that its purpose is not one of furthering international cooperation alone. Articles 15 and 16 * * * are clearly concerned with assuring fair treatment for defendants served in compliance with the *lex fori.* Article 15(1) provides that a court of a ratifying state may enter a default judgment if a) the defendant was served in accordance with the internal law of the state of destination, or b) a "writ of summons or an equivalent document" was "actually delivered" to the defendant by a method provided for in the Convention. Article 15(2) further provides that, regardless of failure to satisfy the criteria of article 15(1), if a) the documents in question were "transmitted" in accordance with the Convention, b) a period of time (not less than 6 months) considered adequate by the judge in question has passed, and c) the party requesting service has made every reasonable effort to obtain a certificate of service or delivery from the state of destination, a default judgment may be entered, provided the state of the rendering court has made a formal declaration to the effect that its courts are permitted to enter default judgments in such circumstances (both Japan and the United States have made such declarations).

Service by mail could come under either of the paragraphs of article 15. However, if there were no proof of actual delivery (*e.g.*, a receipt signed by the defendant) as required under article 15(1), a plaintiff might have to satisfy all the conditions of the second paragraph, including the article 15(2) certification requirement. Arguably, this certification requirement can only be fulfilled through use of the service mechanisms involving the Central Authority appointed by the state of destination under articles 2 through 6.

By placing limitations on default judgments, the drafters must have intended that such default judgments have international effect: it would seem bizarre indeed for a ratifying state, like Japan, to countenance default judgments enforceable not only in the state of origin but also in third states, while denying enforceability in Japan. Japan presumably is interested in protecting Japanese nationals whatever the forum, and not merely in Japan.

There is no evidence that Japan's representatives to the Hague Conference considered articles 15 and 16 to be a threat to Japanese nationals. Indeed, the legislative history of Japan's ratification of the Convention makes it clear that protection of Japanese defendants in foreign litigation was a major reason for Japan's ratification.
* * *

[3.] Japanese Law

It is a settled principle of Japanese constitutional law that treaty provisions take precedence over domestic statutory law. If my analysis of article 10(a) is correct, it would follow that a Japanese court would be required to recognize the adequacy of any method of service permitted under the Convention in connection with an action in Japan to enforce a foreign judgment, regardless of what the relevant rules of Japanese domestic law concerning the recognition and enforcement of foreign judgments might be. Those rules, however, provide an independent argument for the validity and enforceability in Japan of foreign judgments based on service of process mailed to Japan.

The basic Japanese statutory provision relating to the recognition and enforcement of foreign judgments is article 200 of the Code of Civil Procedure. * * *

At first sight, article 200(2) would appear to permit any form of service of process (as "service of process" is defined in the foreign jurisdiction) on a Japanese national, provided that substituted service by publication was not used and that there was proof that the defendant actually received such process. An authoritative commentary on the Code of Civil Procedure, *Chūkai Minji Soshōhō,* seems to support such an interpretation when it states that, "With respect to the manner of service, there is of course no requirement that the requirements for service of process under the Code of Civil Procedure be followed. * * * "[8]

[A]rticle 17 of the U.S.-Japan Consular Convention (and article 8 of the [Hague] Convention) permit U.S. consular officers to serve judicial documents on any person (American or Japanese) in Japan. [Yasuhiro] Fujita[, with whom Jorden is disagreeing in this article,] has no difficulty with this threat to Japanese dignity, since it involves an express permission by the Japanese government. And I am very much in agreement that service of process effected on Japanese territory by U.S. consular officials without such consent would indeed represent a violation of Japanese sovereignty in much the same way that a U.S. attempt to exercise criminal enforcement jurisdiction on Japanese territory would represent a violation of sovereignty. Because a state has a legitimate interest in minimizing potential dangers inherent in serving process by limiting the right to personally deliver summons and complaints to public officials, arguments founded on sovereignty seem defensible with respect to personal service. With respect to notice by mail, however, a state's interest in minimizing the risks of violence does not seem involved to the same extent. A reasonable reading of article 200(2) would recognize that its primary focus is on protecting Japanese defendants, not Japan's dignity. This view is borne out in the only recorded case (to my knowledge) in which (by way of *dicta*) the validity of a foreign judgment was denied on article 200(2) grounds.

The 1976 case of *Daiei K.K. v. Bragoewich*[9] involved an action for a declaratory judgment under the Japanese Bankruptcy Law brought by a plaintiff's receiver in bankruptcy against a putative creditor of the plaintiff, in which the plaintiff sought a judgment to the effect that it had no outstanding debts in relation to the defendant. The defendant, a resident of France, did not appear, and the court, per Judge Kurata of the Tokyo District Court, awarded a default judgment to the plaintiff under article 140 of the Code of Civil Procedure. Service on the French defendant was apparently effected in accordance with the Convention and the Supreme Court Rules concerning International Service, and the Japanese complaint was apparently accompanied by a French translation. However, in conducting an "investigation" permitted to a judge under Japanese law ("*shokken chōsa*"), the court inferred from the plaintiff's complaint that there had been an earlier judgment in France against the plaintiff in the Japanese action in which the summons and complaint had been sent directly by mail to the Tokyo District Court (though not mentioned by the court, clearly a contravention of Japan's formal declaration concerning subparagraphs (b) and (c) of article 10 of the Convention) and, in turn, sent by the District Court to the Japanese defendant. The court stated in *dicta* that, inasmuch as the judicial documents sent in connection with the original French suit were in French and not translated into Japanese, the Japanese defendant did not have a fair opportunity to understand the contents of the French summons. Thus the French judgment would not be recognized in Japan because of article 200(2) of the Code of Civil Procedure.

The court did not address the issue of whether a direct request to a Japanese court in connection with foreign litigation represented an affront to the dignity of the court, much less a violation of the Convention. Of course, I have argued above that to the extent that Japan has not formally filed a declaration at the Hague requiring all documents served under article 10 of the Convention to be translated into Japanese, either French or English should be satisfactory. *Bragoewich* suggests that a Japanese translation might be required for article 200(2) purposes. It must be stressed, however, that *Bragoewich* was a default judgment against a foreign (non-Japanese) party who had no opportunity to, or chose not to, argue in Japan for the validity of the French judgment. In sum, *Bragoewich* should not be seen as a particularly authoritative treatment of the parameters of article 200(2).

Under article 200, Japanese defendants are provided with a number of defenses that do not require resort to an unnecessary conceptualistic analysis of "*sōtatsu*" [*i.e.*, service].

First, if the facts so warranted, a defendant could claim that he did not receive actual notice, as required under article 200(2).

Second, article 200(1) denies validity to foreign judgments based on exorbitant exercises of jurisdiction. It is not within the scope of this article to delve deeply into the complexities of the concept, *saibanken* (general competence), as it is used in article 200(1). Suffice it to say that it is not necessarily synonymous with the general venue (*futsū saibanseki*) or special venue (*tokushu saibanseki*) required for a Japanese court to assert jurisdiction in domestic litigation. Japanese courts have on at least one occasion permitted themselves considerable latitude to apply their own notions of fairness (*jōri*) or "principles of international law" to justify a finding that foreign assertion of jurisdiction in a given case was exorbitant.[10] There can be little doubt that under article 200(1), for example, a Japanese court would deny enforcement to an American judgment based on transient jurisdiction. * * *

As for article 200(3), [it] is technically correct [to] argu[e] that, other than in the context of a conflict between a domestic and foreign judgment, this provision has never been applied by a Japanese court in denying enforceability to a foreign judgment. However, in at least two cases, Japanese courts have countenanced arguments to the effect that enforcement would represent a violation of public policy. In one case, the Tokyo High Court admitted that extrinsic fraud, if proven, would constitute an article 200(3) defense to enforcement of a District of Columbia judgment, but found on the merits that no fraud had in fact taken place. In the other, a Tokyo District Court decision, enforcement of a California money judgment was ordered in spite of the underlying transaction's having been in contravention of Japanese foreign exchange regulations. (The court in the latter case also found it necessary to examine the entire foreign opinion, and not merely the *shubun* (decree or formal holding), the supposed impermissibility of which Fujita uses as a premise for the argument that article 200(3) is of little use with respect to foreign money judgments against Japanese defendants. In so arguing, Fujita seemed to be implying that article 200(2) must be read expansively, since article 200(3) is of so little use.)

On the basis of the foregoing, it emerges that, leaving aside item (4) of article 200 concerning reciprocity, items (1) and (3) afford Japanese courts considerable authority to protect Japanese (and, dare we say, some non-Japanese residents of Japan) against exorbitant or unfair foreign judgments, without having to resort to arguments based on sovereignty. Accordingly, jurisprudential legerdemain is *not* required to protect Japanese defendants and the focus of 200(2) can be limited to assuring that defendants receive *actual* notice in substance, not form.

Questions and Discussion Points

1. *Strategic implications*: Suppose that J.Co had sufficient presence and assets in the U.S. for A.Co to conclude that suing in the U.S. could be feasible. What impact, if any, might the holding in *Marubeni America Co. v. Kansai Iron Works Ltd.* have on A.Co's determination of whether to sue J.Co in the U.S.?

What impact, if any, might the case have on J.Co's determination of how to respond to a suit initiated by A.Co in the U.S.?

2. *A foreign judgment including punitive damages*: In Japan, courts do not

award punitive damages. Under Section 200 of the Code of Civil Procedure, should a Japanese court enforce a foreign judgment that includes punitive damages? For discussion of a recent Japanese court decision refusing to enforce a California punitive damages award, see Dan Fenno Henderson, "Comparative Law in the Japanese Courts: Punitive Damages," 24 *Law in Japan: An Annual* 98 (1991).

II. Litigating in Japan

A. The nature of civil trials

JOHN O. HALEY, COMMERCIAL LITIGATION–ARBITRATION*

2 Japan Business Law Guide
¶80-700 (1988)

Ordinary civil trial proceedings in contemporary Japan continue to reflect continental law patterns despite the introduction of some of the adversarial features of common law trials as part of the post World War II legal reforms. The salient differences from common law trials include the prolonged, fragmented process of the Japanese lawsuit, the absence of a jury, and the more active participation by judges.

The Japanese civil "trial" follows the continental pattern of a discontinuous series of hearings. Instead of the familiar concentrated or continuous proceedings of common law jurisdictions, trial sessions in Japan are held piecemeal. Even the testimony of an individual witness may be interrupted and rescheduled to resume several weeks later. * * * [D]elay is chronic. * * * A number of factors contribute, [but a]bove all, Japanese judges and lawyers are burdened by extraordinary caseloads. In 1974, for example, Japanese courts adjudicated a total of 1,708 civil and criminal cases per judge. In 1984, approximately 946 new civil actions were filed per judge in Japan. Moreover, because of normal career rotation within the career judiciary, usually at 3 year intervals, frequently proceedings must be interrupted and begun anew as judges are transferred to other courts. Thus a relatively simple case involving only two or three witnesses may take one to two years from filing to final judgment and another one to two years on appeal, not counting delay in execution.

There is no jury or other form of lay participation in civil or criminal proceedings, except in separate conciliation proceedings (*chōtei*). As fact-finder the judge takes an active role and has an obligation to clarify facts and issues (*shakumeiken*) (see CCP [Code of Civil Procedure] Arts. 127, 135). The judge's failure to exercise this role can constitute reversible error. Nonetheless, the judge is bound by the claims the parties make, the issues they raise and the evidence they present (CCP

*From John O. Haley, "Commercial Litigation—Arbitration," in Mitsuo Matsushita, ed., 2 *Japan Business Law Guide* (CCH International, 1988, © CCH Australia Limited), at ¶80-700. Reprinted with the permission of CCH Australia Limited.

Art. 186). There are few restrictions on admissible evidence, and what rules do exist are rarely applied.

There is no pretrial discovery * * *, but the fragmented nature of the proceedings, the opportunity for retrial of the facts on first appeal (*kōso* appeal * * *) and liberal rules on amendment of claims preclude much if any gain from surprise.

* * * Depending upon the importance and complexity of the case, either a single judge or a panel of three judges is appointed. In the case of a three-judge panel, one judge, not necessarily the presiding judge, is designated as the judge in charge, who is then responsible for managing the case, including drafting an initial judgment for the panel. In especially complex cases, the court may require preliminary or preparatory proceedings (*jumbi tetsuzuki*) held either in chambers or in open court to expedite the trial by reviewing the issues and anticipated evidence in an attempt to clarify points in contention and narrow the issues. Otherwise the case proceeds to "oral proceedings" (*kōtō benron*), a technical term for the main trial proceedings in open court.

The oral proceedings begin with a series of brief sessions directed with questions and instructions by the presiding judge in which the parties submit their pleadings, written briefs with arguments, exhibits and summaries of the facts of the case, as well as formal requests to the court for evidence, including the witnesses to be summoned (*yobidashi*) by the court. In the sessions that follow, witnesses testify in response to questions by counsel on both sides and the court. At the conclusion of testimony, the presiding judge, or, in the case of a three-judge panel, the judge in charge, holds one or more conferences with the parties to attempt to mediate a judicial compromise (*saibanjō no wakai* * * *). If this effort fails, the parties submit final written arguments, which are followed by the written judgment from several weeks to several months later.

- - - - - - - - - -

An initial constraint on the filing of civil cases is the filing fee, which is based on the amount of damages claimed. Following an amendment effective October 1, 1992, the fee starts at 1 percent for the first ¥300,000 of damages claimed, drops to 0.8 percent of the amount claimed between ¥300,000 and ¥1 million, and then progressively down to 0.2 percent of amounts claimed over ¥1 billion. Using an exchange rate of ¥110 to US $1, the plaintiff would have to pay a nonrefundable filing fee of over $4000 in order to file a suit claiming $1 million in damages. (Until the addition in 1993 of subsection 4 to Section 267 of the Commercial Code, there had been contention over the filing fee requirements for a shareholder derivative action. One view was that the fee should be calculated as in any standard civil action for damages, *i.e.*, based on the amount of the claim. The opposing view was that a derivative claim involves rights other than rights to payment or in property (*zaisan-ken*), and, as such, should be deemed for filing fee purposes to be a claim for ¥950,000 (*see* Act concerning Fees for Civil Actions, etc., §4(2)). The 1993 amendment expressly provides that shareholder derivative actions are not *zaisan-ken* claims. Accordingly, they are deemed to be claims for ¥950,000, and thus are subject to a filing fee of ¥8,200.) The following excerpt describes another practical constraint: scheduling of hearings.

SCHEDULING OF ORAL ARGUMENTS*

61 Hōgaku Kyōshitsu 178
178-179 (Oct. 1985)

From the date of a valid filing till the first court date, on average it takes about 35 days (but that can range up to 60 days for the Tokyo District Court and other crowded courts). The initial "hearing" lasts two to three minutes, basically for checking on the schedules of parties and counsel. (These figures are based on a 1974 survey by the Japan Federation of Bar Associations, but reportedly remain about the same today.)

Between the first and second court date, it takes an average of about thirty-eight days. At the second court date, if the points of controversy are clear, the parties indicate what evidence they want the court to examine, and the court decides what witness(es) it will examine at the next hearing. The second hearing also lasts only two to three minutes per case.

The next hearing is usually an evidentiary session. Due to the need to adjust the witnesses' schedules and for the parties to prepare for the hearing, the periods between the second court date and the first evidentiary hearing (and the periods between evidentiary hearings) are longer. On average it takes seventy-three days between hearings, but in the Kyoto District Court, for instance, the period can last anywhere from fifty to one hundred and fifty days. Each of these witness investigation hearings typically lasts from thirty minutes to one hour.

Between the closing arguments and final judgment, on average it takes forty-six days, but some courts average over one hundred days (with some cases taking over a year).

Based on statistics from 1982, about half of all district court cases (a total of 103,426 cases) ended within the first two court dates (the brief scheduling dates), either through withdrawal of the case, settlement, or failure of one of the parties to appear. The average number of court dates per case was 4.9, plus an average of 1.1 dates for extensions and continuances (for a total of six court dates). About 5 percent of the cases required over sixteen court dates for resolution.

As of 1983, the average time for resolution at the district court level was 13.4 months. From 1965 on, this average has been about 12-13 months, except for a peak at over 16 months in the mid-1970s. [More complete statistics are provided later in this chapter.]

---

*From "Minji Soshō Hō 1: Kōtō Benron Kijitsu" ("Civil Procedure Law 1: Scheduling of Oral Arguments [in Civil Cases at District Courts in Japan]"), 61 *Hōgaku Kyōshitsu* 178 (Oct. 1985) (translated by Daniel H. Foote), at 178-179. Reprinted by permission.

B. Proof-taking in civil trials

Consider the factual issues raised in any case between A.Co and J.Co. J.Co's defense against a breach of contract claim will rest in part on its allegation of severe losses relating to the venture, and A.Co will thus require access to J.Co's records. A.Co's claims about J.Co's post-termination manufacturing would involve A.Co's know-how, and J.Co's defense would therefore involve documents internal to A.Co. In the United States, the gathering of evidence takes place principally in the discovery phase of a civil action. By contrast, in Japan trials proceed almost immediately to a hearing before a judge. The selection below details the principal means of proof-taking in Japanese civil trials. Consider what information A.Co and J.Co may want to obtain from each other and whether they will be able to do so.

TAKAAKI HATTORI AND DAN F. HENDERSON, CIVIL PROCEDURE IN JAPAN*

¶7.05 [4], [6], [9]-[11] (1985)

[1.] Proof-taking—General Remarks

Admissibility of Evidence

In principle, there are few restrictions on the admissibility of evidence, and almost all kinds of statements, documents, and other tangible things may be used as evidence as long as they have relevancy.

Adversary (or Autonomy) Principle

As a general principle, each party must produce evidence to prove his allegations, or, in other words, the court may not take evidence, unless it is tendered by a party.

However, there are several exceptions to this general principle. A court may take evidence *ex officio* in the following instances: (1) it may require necessary information from government offices; (2) it may require an expert opinion from a government office; (3) it may inquire as to the authenticity of an official document; (4) it may examine expert witnesses during the course of inspection; (5) it may examine parties; and (6) it may order perpetuation of evidence during the pendency of an action.

The court is not compelled to take all evidence tendered by parties; whether particular evidence tendered by a party will be admitted depends upon the reasonable discretion of the judge. However, it may not refuse to accept evidence tendered by a party if it is his only evidence available.

Time and Place of Proof-taking

As a general rule, proof-taking occurs in the courtroom on the date of the

---

*From Takaaki Hattori and Dan F. Henderson, *Civil Procedure in Japan* (Transnational Juris Publications, 1985), at ¶7.05 [4], [6] and [9]-[11]. Reprinted with the permission of Transnational Juris Publications, Inc., Irvington, New York.

hearing. If necessary, however, the judge may take evidence out of court; for example, he may go to the place to inspect land in dispute or examine a sick witness at the hospital. Alternatively, the judge may have a commissioned judge or requisitioned judge take proof. Although parties have the right to be present, the judge may proceed with proof-taking, if they fail to appear.

Types of Evidence

Evidence may take the form of testimony of witnesses, expert witnesses or parties, and documentary evidence or evidence by inspection (tangible evidence). * * *

[2.] The Obligation to Serve as a Witness of Facts

All persons present in Japan, whether Japanese nationals or foreigners, except those exempt from Japanese jurisdiction, have the obligation to serve as a witness.

The Duty to Appear in Court

As a rule, a subpoena (*yobidashijō*) commanding a witness to appear in court is prepared by the clerk and served on the witness, though he may appear voluntarily upon informal request of a party. The subpoena must contain the date and place of examination, the names of the parties, a brief description of the subject upon which testimony from the witness is desired, and notice of the legal sanction prescribed for failure to appear. If a subpoenaed witness fails to appear without good reason, the court may charge him with the cost occasioned by his non-appearance, and impose upon him a non-penal or penal fine and/or detention. Such a witness may also be forcibly brought to court by court order. * * *

The Duty to Testify and Privileges

As a general rule, a witness may not refuse to testify. Sometimes, he may be required to write Japanese characters in his own hand, or do such other acts as may be found necessary by the judge. However, a witness may refuse to testify in certain limited instances.

First, civil servants and public office holders, active or retired, must refuse to testify as to official secrets unless they have approval of the authorities concerned. Similarly, judges and retired judges must always keep secret their deliberations (*hyōgi*) on collegial courts. Second, professionals, such as doctors, dentists, apothecaries, druggists, mid-wives, lawyers, notaries public, and clergy, may refuse testimony as to the knowledge obtained in their professional capacity, unless they have been released from the obligation of secrecy. Witnesses may also refuse to disclose their technical or professional secrets. Third, witnesses may refuse testimony likely to incriminate themselves or others protected by law, or likely to bring disgrace upon them. If a witness refuses testimony without cause, he is subject to the same punishment as for failure to appear. * * *

[3.] Expert Witnesses

The role of the expert witness is to assist the judge by testifying about his special knowledge or giving his expert opinion. Expert witnesses are always selected by the judge from among appropriate persons of knowledge or experience. An expert witness selected must testify, and if he fails to appear he may be punished in the same manner as an ordinary witness. However, unlike ordinary witnesses, an expert may not be brought forcibly to court, because ordinarily he can be replaced by another expert.

Before examination, the expert witness must take an oath, administered by his reading the written oath by which he swears to give his opinion conscientiously and faithfully. The judge may require the expert's opinion either orally or in writing. He may require several expert witnesses to render joint or separate opinions. The expert witness is entitled to reasonable compensation for his services, in addition to travel and lodging expenses plus a daily allowance.

Besides expert witnesses, the judge may, *ex officio*, request government offices, domestic or foreign, or juristic persons to furnish expert opinions. In this case, the same rules for expert witnesses apply, except that the oath is not required. * * *

[4.] Party Testimony

Party testimony in civil cases may be given by parties themselves and their legal representatives, and, when juristic persons, associations, or foundations are parties, the testimony is given by directors or administrators representing the entities in the action.

The judge may examine the parties to obtain evidence only if he is unable to reach a decision after taking all other evidence. This policy derives from the notion that party testimony is less reliable than third person testimony, and that it is unfair to force the parties to testify against their interests. However, in practice, judges rarely reject an application to examine a party even though all other evidence is not in. Such deviations are probably explained by judicial belief, contrary to that of the Code's draftsmen, that party testimony is often a very important and convenient way to find the truth. * * *

[5.] Documentary Evidence

General Remarks

Documents may be used as evidence in two ways. When the meaning or idea contained in a document is used as evidence, it is considered to be documentary evidence. On the other hand, when the physical form or condition of a document is regarded as evidence, it is taken to be an object for inspection (tangible evidence).

Under present practice, any document is admissible as evidence. In the past, the court denied admission to documents prepared after filing of the complaint on the matter at issue. Also inadmissible were documents (or affidavits) prepared by the party (or others) for the purpose of dispensing with a witness. These restrictions on admissibility of documents have been removed by later cases.

Documentary evidence is tendered by a party by actually presenting the document at the session or by applying for an order to produce it addressed to the person in possession. A document may also be tendered by demanding that the holder forward it to the court. Documents must be presented in the form of the original (*genpon*), an exemplification (*seihon*), or a certified copy (*ninshō aru tōhon*).

Order for Production of a Document

The judge may, on application, order the holder of a document to produce it, but only if he is legally bound to do so. The holder may not refuse to produce it: (1) if as a party he has cited the said document in the action; (2) if the party applying for the order is entitled to have or see it; or (3) [if] the document was executed for the benefit of the applicant or with respect to a legal relation between him and the holder. In addition, a party who is a merchant may not refuse to produce his trade books (*shōgyō chōbo*). If the application is in order, the judge must order the holder to produce the designated document.

Third persons failing to comply with a production order may be liable to a non-penal fine. Also, if the party so ordered refuses to produce, the judge may deem the allegation of the other party relating to such document to be true. The same assumption is warranted if a party, with the intention of preventing its use by his opponent, destroys or defaces a document which he is bound to produce.

Questions and Discussion Points

1. *Absence of discovery*: In the case between A.Co and J.Co, how does the absence of U.S.-style discovery affect each party?
2. *Proof-taking at trial*: What types of information would A.Co and J.Co likely want from the other? What rules discussed in the selection might frustrate either party?

C. Remedies

Although A.Co would probably be pleased with any damages it could win, it will likely be even more interested in injunctive relief. If available, a preliminary injunction against J.Co's manufacturing excavators using A.Co's know-how (defined broadly) would for A.Co be tantamount to winning a final judgment. Armed with such a ruling, it could probably extract a settlement from J.Co on very favorable terms.

Preliminary relief of the kind A.Co would want is available under Japanese law (though A.Co might not have a good substantive claim that J.Co was actually using its know-how). There are two main forms of preliminary relief available under Japanese law: provisional attachment and provisional disposition.

Provisional attachments are designed for situations where a debtor might try to dispose of property otherwise available for satisfying a judgment. Under this procedure, the debtor's property is attached until a judgment on the merits is rendered. Provisional dispositions resemble preliminary injunctions under U.S. law. The selection below explains their use in more detail.

In late 1989, the Civil Preservation Act (*Minji Hozen Hō*, Law No. 91 of 1989) was passed. That Act, which took effect on January 1, 1991, substantially revised the standards governing provisional relief. (The new Act completely replaced the sections on provisional relief that had been contained in the Code of Civil Procedure, which were deleted.) The primary reforms concerned the procedures for obtaining relief, rather than the substantive standards. Accordingly, the following selection, although it was written prior to passage of the Civil Preservation Act, remains accurate.

TAKAAKI HATTORI AND DAN F. HENDERSON, CIVIL PROCEDURE IN JAPAN*

¶6.06[1] (1985)

[T]here are two types of provisional dispositions: (1) provisional disposition with respect to the subject matter in dispute, and (2) provisional disposition temporarily fixing the state of affairs with respect to the legal relations in dispute.

Provisional disposition relating to the subject matter in dispute is, like provisional attachment, a procedural device to ensure satisfaction of a future judgment. It is, however, a remedy to be utilized only by a creditor who has a claim against specific property, other than money, that is not subject to provisional attachment. For example, a creditor who has a claim for the transfer of title to specific real property may bring an action against the debtor demanding the transfer. However, if the debtor were to transfer the property or title to a third person while the action was pending, the judgment in the creditor's favor would be ineffectual. To prevent such an occurrence, the creditor, before or during the action, may apply for a provisional disposition which temporarily prohibits the debtor from transferring the property to a third person and orders him to preserve the status quo with respect to the property until the time of the judgment. Specific property subject to provisional disposition may be real property or personal property, a debtor's claim against a third person, or industrial property (*e.g.*, patents, trademarks, or copyrights). To obtain this kind of provisional disposition, the creditor must demonstrate that execution on a favorable future judgment would be difficult because of an existing danger that the property in issue will be transferred or damaged by the debtor or other persons.

Provisional disposition temporarily fixing the state of affairs with respect to a legal relation in dispute differs considerably from a provisional disposition relating to the subject matter in dispute. By this second type of provisional disposition, which may be granted either prior to the action or during its pendency, the court establishes an interim legal relation and essentially grants a creditor all or part of the specific relief sought while the action is pending. Such dispositions are granted only when necessary to forestall substantial damage to the [interests of the rightsholder]. For example, a court may temporarily enjoin a defendant from engaging in conduct that is alleged to infringe on a patent or from using a trade name. A court, through a provisional disposition, may also appoint a third person as an interim director, if the director's position is the subject of dispute. If a continuing legal relation such as an employment contract is in dispute, the court may order

*From Takaaki Hattori and Dan F. Henderson, *Civil Procedure in Japan* (Transnational Juris Publications, 1985), at ¶6.06[1]. Reprinted with the permission of Transnational Juris Publications, Inc., Irvington, New York.

the employer to continue to pay wages temporarily if it finds upon examination of the employee's application that his wages are necessary to avoid imminent hardship.

Questions and Discussion Points

1. *Requirements for obtaining a provisional disposition*: To obtain a provisional disposition, an applicant must show a need for the order and evidence offering reasonable support for the underlying claim. Except in the most urgent cases, the court will hold a hearing on the matter and give the party against whom the provisional disposition is sought a chance to show why it should not be granted. Courts usually also require the applicant to post security, even where it seems clear that the applicant's position is quite strong. The security is available to satisfy any damages suffered by the responding party if the applicant party does not succeed on the merits.

2. *Permanent injunctions*: As to A.Co's obtaining a permanent injunction against J.Co, consider the following excerpt:

JOHN O. HALEY, COMMERCIAL LITIGATION–ARBITRATION*

2 Japan Business Law Guide
¶81-400 (1988)

The remedial and enforcement powers of the courts in Japan are considerably weaker than those in common law and most other civil law jurisdictions. The judicial power as defined in Japanese legal theory and practice does not encompass anything akin to the powers of English equity courts. Japanese judges do not have the authority to fashion remedies to assure adequate relief or to retain jurisdiction over a case once they render a final judgment. Unable to monitor or police compliance over time, they do not exercise authority to grant prospective or on-going relief, such as permanent injunctions. A court's formal involvement with an action in effect ceases once its judgment becomes irrevocable. Enforcement actions and even retrials are in form and effect new separate actions usually adjudicated by different judges.

Japanese courts do not have contempt power. Nor does Japanese criminal law provide for analogous penalties as in many continental systems. The maximum penalty for most violations of a judicial order is a non-penal fine recently raised from 5 to 100 thousand yen, still less than [US $1000]. In terms of formal sanctions, at least, many parties can ignore judicial orders with impunity. Compliance is thus more a result of self-help and social constraints than effective legal controls.

*From John O. Haley, "Commercial Litigation—Arbitration," in Mitsuo Matsushita, ed., 2 *Japan Business Law Guide* (CCH International, 1988, © CCH Australia Limited), at ¶81-400. Reprinted with the permission of CCH Australia Limited.

D. Appeals

JOHN O. HALEY, COMMERCIAL LITIGATION–ARBITRATION*

2 Japan Business Law Guide
¶¶81-300 to 81-340 (1988)

[1.] General considerations

Japanese law provides for several forms of appeal (*jōso*) corresponding to the type of decision being reviewed. Final judgments are subject to two levels of appellate review. The first is the *kōso* appeal of both law and fact; the second is the *jōkoku* appeal only on questions of law. A final judgment of a district court is therefore subject to review on *kōso* appeal by the appropriate high court and on *jōkoku* appeal by the Supreme Court. Similarly, final judgments by summary courts are reviewed on *kōso* appeal by the appropriate district courts and on *jōkoku* appeal by high courts. Because constitutional issues are in all cases to be appealed to the Supreme Court (CCP [Code of Civil Procedure] Art. 409-2), a second *jōkoku* appeal from final judgments by summary courts is possible. All appeals from final judgments are a matter of right. Japanese courts, including the Supreme Court, do not exercise the discretion to select cases for review from appropriately filed appeals. As final judgments, partial as well as complete judgments are subject to appeal. Japanese law allows review of interlocutory judgments, however, in the context of an appeal from the subsequent final judgment (CCP Arts. 360, 362).
* * *

Appeals have twofold effect. First and foremost, once appealed a judgment ceases to be irrevocable and therefore is not enforceable without further process. * * * Second, with transfer of the case record, the appeal results in the transfer of the action to the appellate court (CCP Art. 369). The result is that even if only a segment of the judgment is appealed, all portions become unenforceable.
* * *

[2.] *Kōso* appeals

The *kōso* appeal is in effect a continuation of the prior proceedings (*zokushin*) or a second trial. Review is not in any manner restricted to the record. As an appeal on law and fact in most particulars, both the appellant (*kōsonin*) and the appellee (*hikōsonin*) may introduce new arguments, evidence and claims and may even add a new cause of action (CCP Arts. 378, 232). Relevant events that occurred after conclusion of oral proceedings in the first instance up to the time of conclusion of oral proceedings on appeal are regularly taken into account and may be determinative.

Nevertheless, oral proceedings on appeal need not be held unless one of the

*From John O. Haley, "Commercial Litigation—Arbitration," in Mitsuo Matsushita, ed., 2 *Japan Business Law Guide* (CCH International, 1988, © CCH Australia Limited), at ¶¶81-300 to 81-340. Reprinted with the permission of CCH Australia Limited.

parties wishes to add to the prior record (CCP Art. 377). Nearly two-thirds of all civil *kōso* appeals require three or more trial sessions. * * *

At the conclusion of the proceedings, the appellate court must dismiss the appeal if it finds the holding or disposition of the court below to be justified (CCP Art. 384(1)), although not necessarily for the reasons given in the judgment (CCP Art. 384(2)). Otherwise, the appellate court must quash (*haki*) or revoke (*torikeshi*) the judgment as to any portion it finds unreasonable (CCP Art. 385-386) or in contravention of law (CCP Art. 387). The court may not change the judgment to the disadvantage of the appellant, however, unless there has been a cross-appeal (CCP Art. 377). The appellate court must remand the case to the court below if it revokes a judgment dismissing the original action (CCP Art. 388) or if it deems further oral proceedings to be necessary (CCP Art. 389(1)). If the court dismisses the appeal for improper jurisdiction, it must transfer by judgment the case to the competent court (CCP Art. 391).

[3.] *Jōkoku* appeals

A second or *jōkoku* appeal from final judgments is available by right for review solely for errors of law (CCP Art. 394). In most cases, the *jōkoku* appeal involves review by the Supreme Court of the judgment on *kōso* appeal from a high court. However, Japanese procedure permits, with the consent of the parties, a "jumping" *jōkoku* appeal (*hiyaku jōkoku*) directly from the original judgment by passing the *kōso* appeal (CCP Arts. 393(2), 360). The *jōkoku* appeal is heard by a high court if the original judgment was rendered by a summary court. In such instances, as noted, a second *jōkoku* appeal to the Supreme Court on constitutional issues is available (CCP Art. 409-2). * * *

The grounds for reversal for error on *jōkoku* appeal include material misinterpretation and misapplication of relevant provisions of law, including the Constitution, statutes and administrative regulations (CCP Art. 394).

Despite the absence of a doctrine of *stare decisis*, inconsistency with judicial precedents, particularly Grand Bench decisions of the Supreme Court, is a ground for reversal on the theory that precedent provides an authoritative interpretation of the law.

The principal procedural errors are set out in the Code of Civil Procedure (CCP Art. 395):

1. Unlawful constitution of the court.
2. Disqualification of a judge as a result of a criminal offense related to the case or where participation was otherwise precluded by law.
3. Defective power of attorney or lack of authority by a legal representative.
4. Case within the exclusive jurisdiction of another court.
5. Contravention of provision for public proceedings.
6. Failure to state reasons for judgment or inconsistent statement of reasons.

The first three are also grounds for retrial (*see* CCP Art. 420 * * *).

Most cases before the Supreme Court are assigned at random to one of three petty benches, each comprising five justices. The justices review the cases with the assistance of research judges (*chōsakan*) in chambers and generally reach a decision based on the record. Oral argument is available, but it tends to involve formal summaries of the written arguments of counsel. If the case raises significant new issues of law, especially pertaining to constitutional interpretation, it would usually be decided *en banc* by all fifteen justices.

PART C: Arbitration

I. Arbitration Clauses in International Agreements

Many agreements between Japanese and U.S. parties require disputes to be resolved by means of arbitration. In this section, we will first examine issues relating to the drafting of arbitration clauses and then evaluate the enforceability of what is drafted and the nature of arbitration in Japan.

A. Choosing the site and rules

The principal decisions to be made in drafting an arbitration clause are what rules should guide any arbitration between the parties and where any arbitration should take place. Various institutions offer their own sets of rules. Leading arbitration institutions include, in the U.S., the American Arbitration Association, and, in Japan, the Japan Commercial Arbitration Association, as well as such international institutions as the International Court of Arbitration of the International Chamber of Commerce. One way to designate the rules is simply to choose one of these institutions and its rules. The choice of site would then be constrained by the options offered by that institution.

In the P.C., A.Co and J.Co took a different approach. Consider §H-7 of the Joint Venture Agreement, which refers to the "Japanese-American Trade Arbitration Agreement." That Agreement, which is frequently specified in the arbitration clauses of agreements between U.S. and Japanese parties, follows. What does it mean for A.Co and J.Co to be "bound" by it?

AGREEMENT BETWEEN THE
JAPAN COMMERCIAL ARBITRATION ASSOCIATION AND THE
AMERICAN ARBITRATION ASSOCIATION
TO FACILITATE THE USE OF COMMERCIAL ARBITRATION IN TRADE
BETWEEN JAPAN AND THE UNITED STATES OF AMERICA

Being convinced that a wider use of commercial arbitration would lend confidence and stability to commercial transactions between firms in Japan and in the United States of America, the Japan Commercial Arbitration Association and the American Arbitration Association are agreed henceforth to recommend that firms engaged in such trade should insert in their contracts the following clause:

[language essentially identical to JVA §H-7]

1. Arbitration to be held in Japan shall be conducted under the rules of the Japan Commercial Arbitration Association; arbitration to be held in the United States of America shall be conducted in accordance with the rules of the American Arbitration Association.

2. If the place where the arbitration is to be held is not designated in the contract, or the parties fail to agree in writing on such place, the party demanding arbitration shall give notice to the Arbitration Association of the country in which the party resides. That Association shall notify the parties that they have a period of about 14 days to submit their arguments and reasons for preference regarding the place to a Joint Arbitration Committee of three members, two appointed by the respective Associations, and the third, to act as Chairman, to be chosen by the other two. The third member shall not be a member of either Association. The seats of the two Committees shall be in Tokyo and in New York. The determination of the place of arbitration by the Joint Arbitration Committee shall be final and binding upon both parties to the controversy.

3. The Associations each agree to establish such International Panels of Arbitrators as may be necessary to carry out the provisions of this agreement.

* * *

Questions and Discussion Points

What appears to be the main purpose of the Japanese-American Trade Arbitration Agreement? (Consider the relationship between Articles 1 and 2 of the agreement.) According to what standards is the Joint Arbitration Committee to choose whether arbitration is to be conducted in the United States or Japan? Given the nature of the dispute in the P.C., if J.Co or A. Co were to initiate arbitration, would the Joint Arbitration Committee be more likely to choose Japan or the United States as the site for arbitration?

Another way to choose the rules and site for arbitration is to use a "finger-pointing" clause:

> The arbitration shall be conducted according to Rules of Conciliation and Arbitration of the International Chamber of Commerce. If the party initiating the arbitration is U.S.Co., the arbitration shall be held in Tokyo, and if the party initiating the arbitration is Japan Co., the arbitration shall be held in New York.

Such clauses have become increasingly popular in recent years. What advantages and disadvantages does such a clause have as compared to §H-7 of the JVA in the P.C.? Does the prospect of arbitration in the other party's country make arbitration more or less likely to be initiated?

B. Other drafting choices

The rules of the major arbitration institutions typically are sufficiently comprehensive to address nearly any matters that may arise with respect to the arbitration. An arbitration clause in an agreement thus needs only to designate a set of rules and a site (or a mechanism like a "finger-pointing" clause for making these choices). But while arbitration rules are designed to be comprehensive, they usually are liberal in allowing the parties to agree in advance to deviations from the rules.

Many arbitration clauses thus contain more than simply a designation of a set of rules and a site. In agreements between American and Japanese parties, the most common additional provision concerns the number of arbitrators and how to choose them. Language such as the following is frequently used:

> The arbitration shall be brought before three (3) arbitrators. Each party shall appoint one (1) arbitrator and the two (2) arbitrators so selected shall choose the third arbitrator within fourteen (14) days after they have both been appointed. [Sometimes added: Such third arbitrator shall be neither a U.S. national nor a Japanese national.]

Because arbitration clauses usually require the parties to solve all their disputes by arbitration rather than litigation, arbitration clauses also sometimes include the following language:

> The foregoing shall not preclude either party from applying for any preliminary or injunctive remedies available under applicable laws for the purpose of facilitating the subsequent enforcement of an arbitration award.

Whatever provisions in addition to choices of a set of rules and a site are made in drafting an arbitration clause, it is imperative to insure that the rules chosen permit the desired deviations and are practical. Failure to conduct appropriate research before drafting and agreeing to an arbitration clause may lead to serious problems.

II. Enforcing Arbitration Agreements

Before executing an agreement with an arbitration clause, one should investigate whether the courts will later enforce it. This involves three principal issues: First, will courts enforce the arbitration clause? If one party sues in court and the defendant raises the arbitration agreement, will the court stay the suit? Second, will courts recognize the arbitration clause as severable from the contract? If one party terminates the contract, is the arbitration clause of the contract still enforceable? Third, will courts enforce awards made by arbitral bodies?

A. The New York Convention

The enforceability of court judgments across national boundaries is governed by longstanding principles of international law such as comity and sovereignty. These principles are reflected in such national laws as the Japanese Code of Civil Procedure provisions discussed in Part B of this chapter. In contrast, when seeking to enforce arbitral awards across national boundaries, the ready bases for enforcing court judgments were not traditionally available. This problem has been addressed by the United Nations Convention on the Recognition and Enforcement of Foreign Arbitral Awards (1957) (the "New York Convention"). The New York Convention is the starting point for understanding the transnational enforcement of arbitral awards.

The New York Convention sets forth the basic obligation of contracting states to recognize and enforce foreign awards upon the presentation to a court of the authenticated award and the arbitral agreement. Many countries, including Japan and the United States, have entered the Convention subject to the reservation that they will apply the Convention only to awards made in the territory of other contracting parties. Though the Convention thus limits the scope of arbitral awards that must be enforced, Japanese courts have also sometimes relied on deference to party autonomy to enforce on a discretionary basis awards that do not fall under the Convention.[11]

The simplified procedure provided by the New York Convention sometimes makes a foreign arbitral award easier to enforce than a foreign court judgment. The enforcement obligation under the Convention, however, is not unqualified. The key limitations on enforceability are contained in Article V:

Article V

> 1. Recognition and enforcement of the award may be refused, at the request of the party against whom it is invoked, only if that party furnishes to the competent authority where the recognition and enforcement is sought, proof that:
>
> (a) The parties to the agreement * * * were, under the law applicable to them, under some incapacity, or the said agreement is not valid under the law to which the parties have subjected it or, failing any indication thereon, under the law of the country where the award was made; or
>
> (b) The party against whom the award is invoked was not given proper notice of the appointment of the arbitrator or of the arbitration proceedings or was otherwise unable to present his case; or
>
> (c) The award deals with a difference not contemplated by or not falling within the terms of the submission to arbitration, or it contains decisions on matters beyond the scope of the submission to arbitration, provided that, if the decisions on matters

submitted to arbitration can be separated from those not so submitted, that part of the award which contains decisions on matters submitted to arbitration may be recognized and enforced; or

(d) The composition of the arbitral authority or the arbitral procedure was not in accordance with the agreement of the parties, or, failing such agreement, was not in accordance with the law of the country where the arbitration took place; or

(e) The award has not yet become binding on the parties, or has been set aside or suspended by a competent authority of the country in which, or under the law of which, that award was made.

2. Recognition and enforcement of an arbitral award may also be refused if the competent authority in that country where recognition and enforcement is sought finds that:

(a) The subject matter of the difference is not capable of settlement by arbitration under the law of that country; or

(b) The recognition or enforcement of the award would be contrary to the public policy of that country.

Questions and Discussion Points

1. *Comparison with enforcement of court judgments*: In what ways would a foreign arbitral award rendered in a contracting state be easier to enforce in Japan than a foreign court judgment? In what ways would it be more difficult?

How do the limitations on enforceability contained in Article V of the New York Convention differ from Code provisions limiting the enforceability of foreign court judgments? What are the practical implications of these differences?

2. *Extent of party autonomy*: What is the role of the parties' arbitral agreement in determining the scope of enforceability? How is this affected by public policies inherent in Japanese law? How would such enforceability issues affect your drafting of an arbitral clause?

B. Judicial attitudes toward enforcement of agreements to arbitrate

Historically, common law judges were antagonistic toward arbitration. They often refused to enforce agreements to arbitrate, and only through recent statutory changes and judicial rulings has the uncertainty over whether courts would enforce arbitration clauses largely disappeared. By contrast, Japan's civil law system offers clear support for agreements to arbitrate (*see* Civil Code §§786-805).

Japanese courts have consistently enforced agreements to arbitrate. The following selection offers a brief summary of their approach. Although written over twenty years ago, the essay's conclusions remain accurate.

DAN FENNO HENDERSON, FOREIGN ENTERPRISE IN JAPAN: LAWS AND POLICIES*

333-335 (1973)

[1.] Court Assistance under the U.S.-Japanese FCN Treaty and Auxiliary Statutes

Under the Japanese law, there is adequate legal support to enforce contracts obligating the parties to arbitrate either in Japan or in the U.S. There are several postwar Japanese lower court cases enforcing arbitration contracts, though Supreme Court cases are lacking on this point. In the *Kobayashi*[12] case, the seller failed to ship goods from Australia; therefore, the Japanese buyer cancelled the contract and sought damages through a clause in the contract calling for arbitration in Japan. The defendant refused to appoint an arbitrator or otherwise participate. The plaintiff went to court, and the court granted an order appointing an arbitrator on defendant's behalf and rejected defendant's *force majeure* defense for nonperformance, holding that it went to the merits and was to be presented only to the arbitrator later.

A little different kind of support was lent to an arbitration clause in *Rose Int'l Corp. v. Japan Commercial Arbitration Ass'n.*[13] Appellant Rose, an American motion picture company, chartered a ship from the complainant. Under the charter, disputes over the charter hire were to be settled by arbitration in Japan. Rose refused to pay the charter hire, so the shipowner commenced the arbitration proceeding. Rose, refusing to participate, sought a court injunction against the arbitration association to prevent it from administering the arbitration proceeding. Finding Rose's court action without merit, the court refused the injunction, and presumably the association appointed an arbitrator and proceeded with the arbitration, ending in an award or settlement.

Perhaps even more specifically useful, however, is the enforcement procedure built into the AAA [the American Arbitration Association] and JCAA [the Japan Commercial Arbitration Association] rules incorporated into the Arbitration Agreement. These rules provide that when a party fails to perform his duty to appoint an arbitrator and to arbitrate, the competent association in either country will automatically, after due notice and lapse of a proper period of time, appoint an arbitrator for him. This is a convenient and generally effective method of insuring that, when a dispute arises, the arbitration will progress efficiently to an award, despite the bad faith of an opponent. Once such an award is rendered, the scope of challenge is quite restricted. For example, in *G.M. Casaregi Compagnia di Navigazione e Commèrcio, S.P.A. v. Nishi Shōji K.K.*,[14] plaintiff Casaregi, an Italian shipowner, contracted to sell a ship to Nishi, a Japanese buyer, for $162,000 (U.S.), and Nishi agreed to use its best efforts to obtain an approval from the Japanese government;

---

*Reprinted from *Foreign Enterprise in Japan: Laws and Policies*, by Dan Fenno Henderson, at pages 333-335.

such approval was required before Nishi could make a foreign-exchange payment in dollars. The approval was not obtained, and Casaregi sought London arbitration under English law, as provided in the contract, to recover for the loss occasioned by failure of the sale. Nishi refused to appoint an arbitrator; thus, under the English Arbitration Act of 1950, Casaregi's arbitrator became legally the sole arbitrator. Defendant failed to appear on the appointed date though he had been given adequate notice; therefore, under the English law, the arbitrator was empowered to proceed to an award without Nishi's presence. Casaregi was awarded damages (20,966 pounds), based on a finding by the arbitrator that Nishi breached its duty to use its best efforts to obtain government approval. When the award was presented to the Tokyo District Court for enforcement, the court enforced it, despite the fact that Nishi had not been represented at the London arbitration proceedings.

These holdings will, of course, go a long way toward establishing the point that in Japan failure to participate in an agreed arbitration for various make-weight reasons can be done only at one's own peril.

[2.] Dismissal of Litigation

The second problem in enforcing arbitral clauses is presented when either a U.S. company or Nippon K.K. files a suit in the U.S. or Japan instead of resorting to arbitration as agreed. Will the courts in the U.S. or Japan dismiss the suit or stay the litigation? Or enjoin a suit in another court pending arbitration?

In the U.S., despite its negative common-law history, the federal courts can be expected to stay a suit that has been brought in violation of an agreement to arbitrate in Japan. Similar support is becoming the rule in U.S. state courts as well. Dismissal of Japanese suits in violation of an agreement to arbitrate in London, New York, and elsewhere may also be expected.

In an early postwar case, a Panama shipowner, Compania, agreed to carry 8,280 tons of wheat from the Columbia River to Japan for defendant, Mataichi, which failed to deliver the cargo. Plaintiff sued in Tokyo for lost freight and Mataichi defended with a clause calling for New York arbitration. Despite plaintiff's plea that a foreign arbitration clause could not prevent a suit against a Japanese in Japan, because a foreign award would not be enforceable, the court dismissed. Note that the Japanese courts do not "stay" litigation contrary to arbitral clauses. The Japanese lower courts have been true to this holding ever since, although there has been no postwar Supreme Court holding on the point.

In *Hinode Kagaku Kōgyō K.K. v. Sankō Kisen K.K.*,[15] plaintiff Hinode, an importer of phosphorus for fertilizer, contracted for defendant to transport 8,000 tons of raw phosphorus material from Egypt to Japan. Leakage caused loss to the cargo in transit, and plaintiff sued in Osaka despite a clause for London arbitration. The court dismissed in favor of arbitration, rejecting plaintiff's argument that a clause for arbitration in a place foreign to both parties and all phases of the contract as well were void and that an award resulting from such an arbitration would be unenforceable in Japan. Note that the law of the forum (Japan), not the law of the contract (New York), has been held to govern the method of relief to be granted where an arbitration clause was asserted as a defense to a Japanese suit requesting dismissal.

C. The U.S.-Japan FCN Treaty

A final source of law relevant to enforcing agreements to arbitrate between American and Japanese parties is the U.S.-Japan Treaty of Friendship, Commerce and Navigation (FCN Treaty).[16] Article IV(2) of the FCN Treaty provides:

> Contracts entered into between nationals and companies of either Party and nationals and companies of the other Party, that provide for the settlement by arbitration of controversies, shall not be deemed unenforceable within the territories of such other Party merely on the grounds that the place designated for the arbitration proceedings is outside such territories or that the nationality of one or more of the arbitrators is not that of such other Party. Awards duly rendered pursuant to any such contracts, which are final and enforceable under the laws of the place where rendered, shall be deemed conclusive in the enforcement proceedings brought before the courts of competent jurisdiction of either Party, and shall be entitled to be declared enforceable by such courts, except where found contrary to public policy. When so declared, such awards shall be entitled to privileges and measures of enforcement appertaining to awards rendered locally. It is understood, however, that awards rendered outside the United States of America shall be entitled in any court in any state thereof only to the same measure of recognition as awards rendered in other states thereof.

III. Arbitrating in Japan

Consider the report below from one U.S. attorney involved in one arbitration proceeding in Japan. Which problems that he notes might have been averted by careful drafting? Which are problems that a Japanese party would face in the U.S.?

CHARLES RAGAN, ARBITRATION IN JAPAN: CAVEAT FOREIGN DRAFTER AND OTHER LESSONS*

7 Arbitration International 93

97-98, 101-111 (1991)

[1.] Volume of Arbitrations

It is so well-publicized as to be axiomatic that Japanese parties do not like

*From Charles Ragan, "Arbitration in Japan: Caveat Foreign Drafter and Other Lessons," 7 *Arbitration International* 93 (1991), at 97-98 and 101-111. Reprinted by permission.

litigation. Part of this tradition may fairly be attributed to some commonly held views of Japanese culture. For example, in Japan, disagreement in public is to be avoided; harmony in interpersonal relationships is paramount; to admit that a personal relationship has failed (as one must in alleging a breach of contract or other dispute that cannot be resolved amicably) will cause a loss of face; and conflicts are usually dealt with indirectly. Thus, it should not be a surprise that the JCAA [the Japan Commercial Arbitration Association] has had a lower volume of arbitrated disputes than, for example, the ICC [the International Chamber of Commerce].

During a recent five-year period the JCAA had no more than seven international arbitration cases filed with it in any year, and only 16 international cases were pending at the end of 1989. This is shown in the following table, prepared on the basis of figures supplied by the JCAA in response to written questions from the author:

Newly Filed International Cases		Pending At Year-End
1985	7	12
1986	7	11
1987	4	12
1988	4	12
1989	7	16
Total	29	

Virtually all JCAA arbitrations during the above period involved at least one non-Japanese party.

The Japan Shipping Exchange, Inc. handled even fewer arbitrations; no more than five international arbitration cases were filed with it each year during the same period as above, as shown by the following table:

Newly Filed International Cases		Pending At Year-End
1985	5	0
1986	3	0
1987	3	0
1988	4	2
1989	4	1
Total	19	

By comparison, the numbers of cases handled during calendar year 1989 by the major American and European arbitration institutions were as follows: The American Arbitration Association had 54,677 domestic cases and 142 international cases filed with it; the ICC Court of Arbitration had 309 international cases filed with it; the London Court of International Arbitration had approximately 70 international cases filed with it. * * *

[2.] From the Inside Looking Out, and Back Again

In Western Europe and the United States, there are perhaps two principal hallmarks of modern international arbitration procedure: (1) party autonomy and, when the parties cannot agree, (2) procedural decisions by the tribunal which treats each side fairly. I expected some form of these principles existed in arbitrations with Japan.

Without going into great detail, the specific source of most of the author's early experience with arbitration in Japan was a dispute between an American client and a major Japanese trading house over an alleged breach of an exclusive distributorship agreement. During contract negotiations (in which my firm was not involved), it was agreed that any dispute would be resolved by arbitration under the JCAA Rules in Tokyo, and that California law would govern. The contract was silent as to the number of arbitrators and the language of the arbitration.

Based on prior experience and our review of published materials, we expected that the Japanese arbitral experience would be similar in many respects to modern international arbitration practice elsewhere, but that there might be a greater emphasis on achieving an early resolution through conciliation or other consensual means. At a minimum, we expected that it would entail a neutral and fair process—where each side was treated evenly and had an opportunity both to present its case and to understand the case of the opposition; where the facts and the law would be considered objectively; and where the result would be achieved with reasonable efficiency and economy. Although the amount in dispute was (depending upon one's perspective) approximately in the low eight-figure range, we expected that the proceedings would be concluded in about three years. We were continually surprised—and in some instances, astonished—at the reality which unfolded during more than 30 arbitral sessions spread over the next 56 months!

Before proceeding, I hasten to note our experience may have been aberrational. In at least one sense it clearly appeared to be: the Japanese party commenced the proceeding. Alternatively, the volume of international arbitration cases in Japan may be so slight that there are no norms. In any event, a word to the wise is sufficient; the following should be more than enough.

Selection of arbitrator(s)

Once an arbitration is commenced, the first order of business is to select the arbitrator(s). The ability to have a voice in this selection process and [the ability] to choose specialists as "judges" are often said to be major benefits distinguishing arbitration from litigation.

As noted, the agreement in our case was silent on the number of arbitrators. Under JCAA Rules (Rules 17 and 18), absent agreement by the parties, there is a bias in favour of a single arbitrator. Rule 16, however, provides that the parties may agree on the number and method of selecting arbitrators. This seems abundantly fair.

Not unlike other arbitral institutions, the JCAA takes responsibility for forwarding the initial arbitral pleading to the respondent (Rule 8(2)). In our case, that transmittal letter which the JCAA mailed to our client advised the respondent of

Rule 16, and specified that unless the Association received notice of an agreement by the parties *within 30 days of the date of the letter*, the number of arbitrators would be one.

About six weeks after the letter was mailed by the JCAA, it reached the attention of our client's general counsel. He promptly wrote to the claimant and the JCAA, and suggested that, because the contract was in English and California law governed the novel questions raised by the arbitration, it would be prudent to have a panel of three, one of whom might be a Californian. The claimant rejected the suggestion as untimely, and expressed its preference to leave selection of an arbitrator to the JCAA. The JCAA's reply followed, stating that, because its time limit had expired, it could not extend the period without claimant's consent.

If this experience were normative (but see earlier caveats), it would imply two clear messages for foreigners arbitrating in Japan before the JCAA. First, the JCAA apparently applies its Rules stringently, even if a suggestion for variance appears logical and rational to its presenter. Second, if one has contracts providing for JCAA arbitration, and one receives mail from the JCAA, be prepared to act on it immediately.

The next lesson learned was the natural follow-on to the first experience and will come as no surprise to some readers. The Rules require that JCAA arbitrators reside in Japan at the time of appointment (Rule 15). In addition, the Association maintains a panel of approximately 110 persons whom it may appoint. As of November 1989, the nationalities of the individuals on the JCAA panel were as follows:

Japan	103
New Zealand	1
USA	3
West Germany	3

The panel included a number of practicing attorneys specializing in international commercial and/or intellectual property law. In our case, however, the Association appointed a Japanese professor of civil procedure as the sole arbitrator to resolve novel and complex questions of California law relating to distribution of and license rights to sophisticated technology. The lessons we learned from this selection also were simple. First, if a contract involves specialized or technical goods or services, it is wise to consider (a) providing in the contract for three arbitrators so one can exercise the right to have a voice in the selection of at least one arbitrator, or (b) obtaining a copy of the JCAA panel, and suggesting the appropriate expertise for candidates. Second (and as before), move fast.

Language

Although the contract (and all its precedents) were written in English, the agreement did not specify the language of the arbitration. In many arbitral regimes, if there is no agreement of the parties, the tribunal determines the language or languages to be used in the proceedings.

The JCAA Rules do not specifically cover the question. They do state that the award shall be written in Japanese, but, where there has been a request by one of the parties, the award shall be written in both Japanese and English and both versions shall be authentic (Rule 37). The Rules further provide for interpretation or translation if the Tribunal has so ordered, or there has been a request by one of the parties (Rule 29). Finally, the Rules provide that, absent an order from the Tribunal, the cost of various expenses (including interpretation and translation) shall be borne by the requesting party. These rules in the aggregate have the appearance of reasonableness.

In our case, there was *no* interpretation through more than two years of proceedings. Although the American party was permitted to submit initial responsive pleadings and briefs in English, all oral proceedings (and there were about 10 sessions in that time period) were conducted in Japanese. House counsel for the American party complained that he was never quite certain in these sessions that he had a complete grasp of what was unfolding before him.

During the evidence-taking, because of obvious irregularities in some interpretation services,[17] we experimented with tape recordings, simultaneous translation, consecutive translation, and finally consecutive translation with stenographers for both languages. No ideal solution was found. Similar problems also occurred in the exchange of briefs: whenever one opponent submitted a brief, we had it translated into English; before responding, we then sought to determine the adequacy and sufficiency of the translation, and whether there were any special clues or messages 'between the lines' of the opponent's brief. The perils and costs of this process are obvious.[18]

From this experience it seems fair to conclude that: (i) The language determination is parochial. (ii) The parties are not treated equally. (iii) The foreign party does not have an equal chance to present its case without being subject to substantial additional costs.

Trial counsel

The ability to be represented in an international arbitration by the counsel of a party's choice is another feature of international arbitration that is often trumpeted as a major advantage over litigation of international disputes in national courts. In international arbitration, clients frequently and understandably prefer to employ counsel from their home base, as it may be more convenient and economical to develop the facts of the case. (In our case, this decision seemed even more logical since California law governed.)

The JCAA Rules appear to recognize and incorporate this common sense principle. They state:

> A party may be represented by a lawyer or such other person as shall be recognized to be justified in taking procedures under these Rules (Rule 6).

The Rules also provide for the submission of powers of attorney (Rule 7). This in itself is not surprising, because it is typical for lawyers who appear in Japan to submit powers of attorney, and a similar practice often obtains in Europe.

I made my first trip to Japan in October 1987, shortly before the evidence-taking phase was to begin. The objective was to develop, before the evidence-taking or "trial" began, a good working relationship between Japanese local counsel and my firm, which the client had always regarded as lead strategists and trial counsel. In advance of that trip, one of my partners inquired of the JCAA about the kind of power of attorney we should present. I have preserved the response, which was short but (I was soon to learn) most meaningful: "It is very difficult to answer through the phone."[19] When I arrived in Tokyo, however, I was informed that I could not attend the scheduled arbitration session.

The reason for this was that, until very recently, the JCAA and the Japanese bar have interpreted the Lawyers' Law to prohibit *all* foreign lawyers from acting as arbitration counsel of record. This view in fact derived from two separate laws. Article 801 of the Japanese Code of Civil Procedure provides that an arbitration award may be cancelled where the "parties were not represented in accordance with the law." Article 72 of the Lawyers' Law prohibits, as unauthorized practice of law, the participation for remuneration of an unlicensed lawyer in an arbitration proceeding. The coupling of these two laws makes it impracticable for a foreign lawyer, who is not licensed to practice in Japan, to take on the exclusive representation of any party in a Japanese arbitration. The reason is simple: a knowledgeable Japanese party may hold the traditional view as a trump card, with which it would seek to upset an unfavourable award.

In our case, we did not appear as counsel of record. We attended approximately 20 arbitral sessions as a "guest"; we participated in the preparation of all fact and law submissions; with the consent of the arbitrator and opposing party, we made numerous comments (some might say "arguments"), but these comments were in English and, for the reasons mentioned above, may not have been effective even after translation. In any event, we were not permitted to examine any witness directly.

The law was also unclear as to whether the many foreign lawyers recently granted limited licenses to serve as foreign legal consultants in Japan may represent a party at an arbitration. Recently, the Japanese Federation of Bar Associations (the "Nichibenren") voted to allow foreign legal consultants (or "*Gaikokuhō jimu bengoshi*") to represent parties in Japanese arbitrations where the lawyer is qualified to practice the governing or applicable substantive law of the arbitration.

To date, however, no Japanese court has endorsed such representation (and the Nichibenren's interpretation makes clear that the foreign legal consultant acting as arbitration counsel is *not* permitted to file a motion in a Japanese court or appear before a public agency). No foreign lawyer has attempted to represent a party in an arbitration without qualified local counsel, and it is unlikely that one will attempt to do this when the possibility of the cancellation of an award remains. Moreover, the Nichibenren's recent promulgation concludes with the observation "it is desirable that [a *gaikokuhō jimu bengoshi* representing a party in a Japanese arbitration] will [nonetheless] have a [Japanese] *bengoshi* participate in the arbitration proceedings held in Japan."

Thus, even with the recent bar association vote, the implications of the restrictive Japanese rules on the practice of law are profound: The foreigner can either flout the law and risk having a favourable award upset, or maintain an appearance of parochial propriety and incur substantially greater legal costs than his Japanese opponent.

Hearing (or trial) procedures * * *

[As described in the following:]

> The JCAA arbitration proceeds in three stages: (1) presentation and delineation of facts and claims, accompanied with exchanges of documents; (2) examination of witnesses; and (3) preparation of the award by the arbitrators. At the first stage, documents are often exchanged four or five times, a process resembling the customary ritual of exchanging *junbi shomen* (preparatory documents) in the courts.

There are two important messages here: first, the JCAA first stage is like the practice in Japanese courts; second, it continues for an unspecified number of exchanges. In our case, the exchange of position papers continued for two years. It included more than two dozen submissions (excluding numerous documents submitted as evidence but including extensive opinions from each side providing background information on California law). In short, it *was* a ritual but not one calculated to achieve a prompt, amicable settlement. * * *

Trial Schedule

Perhaps the rudest shock to the American client came as the trial schedule unfolded with what the JCAA might term "the greatest expedition possible." It has been written that:

> Hearings are held, on the average, ten times per case. * * * When a witness from a foreign country is examined, hearings go on without interruption in mornings or afternoons for a week or so.

In our case, arguments to compress the hearing schedule in the interests of speed and economy—either by witness or by issue—were rejected continually. Invariably, the reason given was: that is not how we do it here in Japan. Thus, evidence-taking spanned another 25 months. As a result, the "record"—all evidence (testimonial and documentary) and briefs, which the parties argued in their concluding liability briefs—stood about *three meters* high. The cost of repetitive preparations and ferrying American witnesses and counsel to Tokyo was astonishing; the correlative cost to the Japanese party must have been minuscule. Equally important were the unknowable costs of arguments we made but which were lost on the arbitrator solely due to the passage of time. But, perhaps more important, there were enormous, not fully quantifiable, costs to the American party which, because of prevailing cultural norms, was impeded from doing business in Japan throughout the pendency of the arbitration, even in unrelated lines of business.

Aversion to Orders

When Japanese authorities speak about arbitration, they talk glowingly about its "amicable texture." They also note "a deeply ingrained abhorrence of confrontation and the resolution of disputes through enforceable means which Japanese people share." Thus, to "order" a party to do something is regarded as incompatible with the arbitration process in Japan.

What happens when these two phenomena converge in the context of a procedural dispute may not be readily apparent to Westerners accustomed to arbitration as an alternative dispute resolution technique according to law. Briefly stated, when the arbitrator wants the parties to agree (perhaps because he shares the Japanese party's cultural aversion to decisions imposed by third parties), but the parties cannot agree, and the arbitrator declines to make a decision which will offend one of the parties, arbitral paralysis sets in. Issues which would seem to require minutes or seconds to consider take hours to discuss. Exasperation (or worse, anger) are natural Western reactions, which must be resisted. * * *

Settlement

The final arbitral procedure with which I have specific experience in Japan is settlement or "reconciliation." On this point, it has been observed that JCAA tribunals appear positively to commend settlement.[20] The general practice in JCAA arbitrations may not be unique in current arbitral practice, but is certainly different from Western arbitration or litigation practices. Basically, after the evidence-taking and briefing is concluded, but before the preparation of an award (*i.e.*, between * * * examination of witnesses and * * * preparation of award * * *), the arbitrator serves as a conciliator/mediator in an effort to obtain a settlement. In this capacity, the arbitrator may meet *ex parte* with the opposing sides, and discuss case values and the merits. If the parties fail to reach a settlement, he will then proceed to decide the case. With the Japanese party especially, however, the arbitrator's recommendation of an amicable settlement will carry great force. * * *

[3.] Conclusions

From the foregoing "war stories," several disturbing conclusions emerge.

(1) Arbitrating in Japan can be very expensive for foreigners.

(2) The "default" for procedural issues on which the parties disagree is an arcane Japanese civil procedure.

(3) Rather than a decision under a specific governing law, the conclusion of a lengthy arbitration in Japan may be a settlement arranged by the tribunal appointed to decide the case and influenced by its notions of general fairness.

Questions and Discussion Points

1. *Arbitrating the dispute in the P.C.*: Which of the problems above might arise in any arbitration between A.Co and J.Co?

2. *Comparison to litigation*: What advantages does Japanese arbitration have over Japanese litigation? Which process would A.Co and J.Co likely prefer?

PART D: Settlement

A.Co and J.Co eventually resolved their dispute through a negotiated settlement. We will consider why they did this and on what terms. Before doing so, though, we will examine first the legal framework for dispute settlement in Japan, and then the popularly held view that the Japanese are particularly averse to litigation and arbitration.

I. The Legal Framework for Settlement of Disputes

JOHN O. HALEY, COMMERCIAL LITIGATION–ARBITRATION*

2 Japan Business Law Guide

¶81-500 (1988)

In civil actions either party may * * * invoke the provisions for formal conciliation (*minji chōtei*) under the separate Civil Conciliation Law (*Minji-chōtei-hō*), Law No. 222, 1951 (hereinafter abbreviated "CCL"), and Supreme Court Civil Conciliation Rules (*Minji chōtei kisoku*), Supreme Court Rule No. 8, 1951 (hereinafter abbreviated "CCR"). Frequently used to settle small claims and relatively minor noncommercial disputes in summary court, formal conciliation is designed to foster equitable resolution of disputes by compromise (CCL Art. 1). To institute the proceedings, a party petitions the court where an action is pending or in the other party's general forum (domicile) or place of residence (CCL Art. 3). The parties may also [petition] the court by agreement (CCL Art. 3). The petition may be oral or in writing (CCR Art. 3). The court where an action is pending may also institute conciliation on its own motion (CCL Art. 20).

Conciliation begins with the court's appointment of a Conciliation Committee, usually comprising one judge and two lay conciliation commissioners (*minji chōtei nin*) (CCL Arts. 5, 6, 7). The court may also appoint a single judge to mediate (CCL Art. 5(1)).

The procedures are flexible. The Conciliation Committee is authorized to permit interested parties to intervene (CCL Art. 11), to stay execution and to enjoin other acts that might interfere with a settlement (CCL Art. 12). The Committee may also terminate the proceedings whenever it decides that a settlement is not possible (CCL Art. 14).

Although the settlement must be voluntary, the court with the advice of the Conciliation Committee is also empowered to impose by ruling at least a temporary settlement within the scope of the parties' petitions (CCL Art. 17). The ruling loses effect, however, if either party objects (CCL Art. 18(2)). Special provisions on conciliation in commercial cases permit the Committee to stipulate the terms of

*From John O. Haley, "Commercial Litigation—Arbitration," in Mitsuo Matsushita, ed., 2 *Japan Business Law Guide* (CCH International, 1988, © CCH Australia Limited), at ¶81-500. Reprinted with the permission of CCH Australia Limited.

settlement so long as the parties agree in writing to comply (CCL Art. 31(1)). If a settlement is reached in commercial cases, the Committee prepares a protocol for the parties to sign and affix their seals. The protocol establishes the terms of the settlement and has the effect of an in-court compromise (CCL Arts. 16, 31(2)).

- - - - - - - - - -

Letter to U.S. client explaining the conciliation system

The following is a letter from a Japanese attorney to an in-house attorney of a U.S. company. The U.S. company's wholly owned subsidiary in Japan had recently become involved in a dispute with one of its Japanese distributors.

- - - - - - - - - -

February 14, 1989
VIA FACSIMILE
Mr. Ronald W. Royster, III, Esq.
Associate General Counsel
International Legal Divisions
Gizmo, Inc.
U.S.A.

Re: Oshiro Case

Dear Mr. Royster:

The purpose of this letter is to advise you of developments in the Mr. Yoshio Oshiro case.

Oshiro filed with the Summary Court of Tokyo for a Conciliation Procedure with Gizmo, Inc. In filing for the Conciliation Procedure, Oshiro is seeking confirmation that he holds the rights with respect to the Gizmo distributorship which has been in dispute. The first day of the Conciliation Procedure will be March 6, 1989.

The following is a brief explanation of the Conciliation Procedure as it applies to the Oshiro case.

1. The Conciliation Procedure, which is subject to the Civil Conciliation Act, will be performed by a Conciliation Committee composed of three members, one judge and two citizen conciliators. One of the two citizen conciliators is usually a lawyer and the other usually has not been legally trained but has rich experience in public life.

2. The Conciliation Committee will hear statements from both Gizmo, Inc. and Oshiro, and will organize and summarize such statements in order to facilitate discussion and settlement of the dispute.

The Conciliation Committee may, on its own authority, investigate facts concerning the dispute and take evidence from the parties or from experts and administrative agencies.

The Conciliation Procedure is not open to the public.

3. In the event that an agreement is reached by Gizmo, Inc. and Oshiro and is approved by the Conciliation Committee, it shall be deemed that a Conciliation has been accomplished. Appropriate records will be drawn up by a court clerk and the Conciliation will have the same effect as a final court judgment.

On the other hand, if the Conciliation Committee deems an agreement reached between Gizmo, Inc. and Oshiro to be inappropriate or if there is no possibility of agreement between the parties, the Conciliation Committee may terminate the Conciliation Procedure and declare that Conciliation has not been accomplished. Should this occur, either party would be free to pursue the matter in court.

As should be clear from the above, the Conciliation Procedure is designed to facilitate agreement by the parties. Neither party can be forced into agreement, nor is either party bound by any opinions or conclusions issued by the Conciliation Committee to which that party has not agreed.

As we learn more about this matter, we will keep you informed. If you have any questions or comments, please do not hesitate to contact us.

Very truly yours,
[signed]

N. Enomoto

II. The Judicial Attitude Toward Settlement

Are Japanese judges more likely to promote settlement than American judges? Consider the following excerpt from a speech by a Japanese judge.

SHUNKŌ MUTŌ, CONCERNING TRIAL LEADERSHIP IN CIVIL LITIGATION: FOCUSING ON THE JUDGE'S INQUIRY AND COMPROMISE*

12 Law in Japan 23
23-28 (1979)

1. The Course of Civil Lawsuits[21]

As you well know, civil lawsuits have two means of resolution. One is a court decision and the other is compromise. When a civil lawsuit ends with a decision, its course is distinguished by three stages in the following order: (a) issue definition, (b) investigation of evidence and (c) decision. When a civil lawsuit ends in compromise, [it may be] concluded at any of the above stages. * * * Since the

*From Shunkō Mutō, "Concerning Trial Leadership in Civil Litigation: Focusing on the Judge's Inquiry and Compromise," 12 *Law in Japan: An Annual* 23 (1979), at 23-28. Reprinted by permission.

investigation of evidence must largely await the activities of attorneys, the three tasks mainly carried out through the activities of judges are issue definition, decision and compromise.

That is the reason I often refer to the "three joys of civil judges." The first is to conduct a full judge's inquiry and to define the issues succinctly, the second is to write a decision which is persuasive, and the third is to create a compromise which is satisfactory, both to the litigants and to yourself (the judge). Even if it may be unsatisfactory when seen from the eyes of another, when a result is obtained concerning these three about which you yourself can think "it was pretty good," it is a very enjoyable feeling, even though you don't receive praise from anyone. Since a civil judge receives a decent salary, although it is not all that large, since his work itself is of some benefit to mankind and his country, and additionally since he himself can obtain these three "joys," I think that it is not a bad occupation at all. * * *

[2.] **Compromise (*Wakai*)**

* * * There is no mistaking that the great majority of litigants usually desire a compromise. When I was an assistant judge, * * * I thought that since the parties brought the dispute to court they naturally wanted a court decision, * * * so I promptly made a decision with almost no effort at reaching a compromise. However, at that time I once was told by a lawyer that "You reach a decision too quickly. Even if a party wants a compromise he is embarrassed to broach the matter by himself." I thought, "that might well be so," and from that time on I said, "How about a compromise?" at the conclusion of the case. When I did so there were in fact litigants who took an interest, and at that time I came to think that "Compromise might be good, at that." * * * [T]hat the parties desired a compromise * * * is natural if you think about it.

Litigants come to the court requesting a resolution of the dispute, and one that is a final resolution, not a tentative one. A trial court decision is only a tentative resolution, and furthermore, considerable time is required until there is a decision of the highest court; the defeated party is dissatisfied and successful execution of the judgment is doubtful. In contrast to this, compromise requires only a few concessions, obtains a final resolution, no antagonism (between the parties) remains and execution is prompt and certain. * * * It is often said that there are some cases appropriate for compromise and some inappropriate for compromise, but I think that the overwhelming number of cases belong to the former category. * * * Speaking in a somewhat exaggerated manner, I've come to think that rendering a court decision indicates an inadequacy in the persuasive powers of the judge. * * * However, even if I say to strive for a compromise, of course it is useless to do so haphazardly. Here, the timing and method are important.

First taking timing, the first opportunity is after the definition of issues and prior to beginning the examination of witnesses. If it is a simple case where the facts are understood by glancing at the complaint and answer * * * it is proper to begin compromise procedures immediately, as long as it is the wish of the parties. But in the usual case I think it is better not to initiate compromise before the definition of issues is completed. This is because when both parties say they want a compromise and compromise procedure is immediately entered into under the urging of the parties, the arguments of the parties will not be clarified and accordingly neither the court nor the parties have a clear outlook concerning the case. This can easily result in wasting time. * * * [W]hen issue definition is completed, documents have been presented, and the court has come to hold a tentative view concerning the case, this view should be frankly stated to both parties. For example, one might speak about the state of the case, saying, "In this lawsuit, if this point is proven, it will probably turn out like this. If that point is proven, there is a strong possibility it will turn out like that, but it may well be difficult to prove that point in the light of this documentation. In spite of that, if Mr. X gives some money, some solution may possibly be achieved. What if we call in Mr. X and try talking it over?"

However, when the parties do not wish to initiate a compromise at this stage, unreasonable efforts should not be made. * * * In this case I make an attempt at compromise once again at the stage when useful witnesses have been examined concerning the important issues and I have formed a tentative belief about the case. When you have come this far, very often one of the parties desires a compromise, but thinks that if he speaks out by himself it will cause him some loss, and in many cases he secretly hopes for an initiative by the court.

Finally, another opportunity for compromise occurs following the examination of evidence prior to concluding the trial. At this stage the court already has a belief [concerning the case] and the parties are predicting their respective chances of winning. It is the final chance for compromise in the trial court. Therefore, it is easy to reach a compromise by advancing the discussion premised on this fact. However, since no compromise was possible up to this stage, it can also be said that it will be as difficult to obtain a compromise as before. Also, in a rare case there may be an attempt at compromise after conclusion of the trial. In this case I make an exception and postpone assignment of a date for the announcement of the decision, and if the compromise attempt fails I immediately assign a date for announcement of the decision.

Next, taking the method of attempting a compromise, I always have the litigants themselves come to court. This is because first hand information can be obtained from the litigants and because only they can make the final decision. Few litigants are audacious enough to entrust everything to their attorneys. As a place for compromise, I try not to use the judges' room, where other people are present, but rather to pick an isolated room such as a compromise room. In this so-called secret room there will be only the judge, the litigant and his attorney, and I hear information directly from the litigant. I have the litigant repeat what he told his attorney at his attorney's office and I listen to this. It seems that when people are separated from others and you have a heart-to-heart talk they generally tell the truth. Especially when considering that the other person is a judge, it seems that litigants who meet a judge for the first time often reveal the whole truth. Sometimes the attorney says "I haven't heard that" concerning what the litigant is saying, and the litigant says, "I haven't even told this to my attorney . . . " and proceeds to discuss even facts which hurt his position. Indeed, it may be that he speaks the truth since he feels that even if he tells a lie it will be discovered by the opposing litigant who is also in the courtroom at my request.

Another benefit is that the litigant apparently has a sense of satisfaction in having the judge listen to him. Sometimes there are simple people who are satisfied just by having the judge listen to their entire story and who don't care what happens afterwards, so that a compromise can be reached on the spot. Therefore, even if I think the litigant keeps harping on the same trivial subject, I endure and listen to it without interrupting to demand that he end his story and quickly state his terms. And thus if I listen for about ten minutes the litigant is satisfied, and even from a seemingly trivial story the true situation of the case often emerges.

Another by-product of listening to the stories of both the litigants in their own words is that even if compromise negotiations stall and it is suggested that we return to oral arguments, *de facto* examination of the litigants has already been completed. This is a powerful trump card for the court; the likelihood is that, since there are no other valid witnesses to question, the compromise procedure continues and easily achieves success.

After listening to the litigant's story, I next hold a discussion with the litigant and his attorney. This discussion is not fundamentally different from that with the attorney at the time of the initial judge's inquiry. For example, I say something like "Your argument goes like this, but considering it from the viewpoint of general common sense it is strange that this conclusion should be reached despite the existence of this and that fact. And although these documents are evidence for this point they probably can't be said to be evidence for that point." In that way I explain my outlook on the case. It is best if the litigant says "I see, that makes sense," but even if it doesn't go that far it will certainly reach the point where he thinks "if that's what the court thinks about it, it can't be helped." If by this time witnesses have been examined and a tentative belief about the case has been formed, I think this may be expressed after explaining that it is only a tentative belief. Also, when the discussion makes no progress because only hypothetical arguments are produced concerning some point, I sometimes suspend the compromise discussion and examine witnesses on only that point. Doing it this way shows sincerity and zeal on the part of the judge, and in any case if you persuade them with reasoning based on the evidence many of the litigants are persuaded.

Thus, when the court and both parties come to have some level of common perception of the case, at this point [potential settlement] terms first emerge. Of course, depending on the case a litigant may first state terms and then provide an explanation. In either case I discuss it with the litigant; I must understand why this proposal is put forward. It serves no purpose to simply transmit a proposal from one party to the other or to strive to split the difference between the proposals from both sides. Therefore, even when I listen to proposals from both sides, I do not take them whole to the other side; rather I examine them based on the discussion up to

[that] point * * * and transmit them to the opposing party after increasing or reducing them to an appropriate point as much as possible.

[Also,] I indicate what matters and terms should be investigated by each party prior to the next session. Occasionally there are unscrupulous litigants who come and feign ignorance saying "Did you really say something like that last time?" or who think nothing of presenting a lower amount than was discussed before. In such a case I am indignant and say "Don't trifle with the court!" Ultimately, many of the cases turn out unfavorably for a litigant who does something like that.

When the proposals of the plaintiff and defendant are far apart it is probably best for the court to put forward its own proposal. Also in this situation there is no splitting the difference (between the parties' proposals). Unless it is a proposal which can be explained on a clear basis the parties will not be satisfied. * * * I put forward proposals based on the strength of my belief about the case. For example, I might say "In this claim for repayment I think you have a 60-40 advantage. Therefore if a judgment is made in the trial court you will win everything, but in the appellate court you have a 40% chance of losing everything, so how about accepting 60% of the amount of money claimed?" However, when finally working out the terms it is no time for theory; it is necessary to appeal to emotion. Also, when there is a difference of 100,000 yen or so it is necessary to press for a resolution which splits the difference down the middle. In either case, once a proposal of the court has been put forward it must not be changed unnecessarily. Changing the proposal in favor of one party because he is intransigent negates the purpose of the court's proposal. [Y]ou must have the intention to break off the compromise procedure if the court's proposal is unacceptable. Also, when you show such a resolve an agreement is often reached. I think that a method which centers on logic and evidence and which adds to this an appropriate appeal to emotion is the most satisfactory for all including the court itself.

In this way, I think the court should strive for a compromise with zeal, but never force things unreasonably. * * * Even when with great pains and effort you enter into compromise procedure, if there is no progress because the parties lack enthusiasm or are obstinate and won't concede anything it is best to immediately call a halt. * * * You must not make further efforts which would lead the parties to believe that you are attempting to achieve a compromise because you do not wish to render a judgment. [W]hen the parties are obstinate and there is no hope, I instead quickly render a decision. * * * [W]hen compromise procedure is initiated following conclusion of the trial, I have sometimes completed a rough draft of a decision, told this to the parties and then achieved a compromise. In this case, the contents of the decision must be the same as the belief concerning the case expressed during compromise proceedings. Thus, I display an attitude that "The court never imposes a compromise. It is quite simple to write a judgment. I attempted a compromise for the sake of the parties, and I frankly expressed my belief about the case." When you do this, at the very least the lawyers understand the attitude of the court and will become very cooperative in the next case, and they also convey this to other lawyers.

- - - - - - - - - -

Note: The rate of settlement of litigation: Of 122,904 ordinary civil cases processed in 1992 by the Japanese district courts as cases of first instance, 46.8% ended in a court judgment, 33% ended in settlement, and 16.5% of the cases were withdrawn (presumably many of these were settled by the disputants). Of 12,621 ordinary civil cases processed in the same year by Japanese high courts, 55% ended in a judgment, 35% ended in settlement, and 10.3% were withdrawn.

III. Institutional Incapacity and Dispute Resolution

One commonly held view is that the Japanese are particularly averse to asserting their rights through litigation. It is often said that the Japanese have a similar aversion to formal arbitration. The following two articles challenge the notion that such a cultural predisposition best explains the low level of litigation in Japan. Consider whether the arguments also apply to arbitration.

JOHN O. HALEY, THE MYTH OF THE RELUCTANT LITIGANT*

Journal of Japanese Studies, Vol. 4, No. 2, pg. 359
366-373, 378-389 (1978)

[1.] The Myth Reconsidered

Is there, then, any evidence of an unusual Japanese aversion towards lawsuits that leads a party to accept a settlement less beneficial than one he anticipates he would gain by suing? The answer, I believe, is negative. What little evidence there is suggests the opposite—that most Japanese are willing to go to court in such circumstances. The recent pollution cases and thalidomide case are illustrative.

A recently published inquiry into the decisions to litigate in the pollution cases documents a variety of cultural factors causing the litigants to hesitate to sue. These included a sense of "shame" for physical and mental deformity, constraints on individual initiative and "selfish" behavior imposed by the demands of community unity and group consciousness, and hostility against an association with what was perceived to be—correctly, I believe—a leftist, antigovernment cause reflected in the politics of the lawyers who dominated the conduct of these trials. This experience was paralleled in part in the thalidomide case, where the apparent reason for reluctance to sue was a fear of public exposure of the children's deformities. "In a society strongly prejudiced against deformity," one of the plaintiffs' lawyers wrote, "it took considerable courage to sue." In each of these cases the plaintiffs filed suit only reluctantly and as a last resort. The reluctance, however, was based on a variety of factors related to the particular circumstances and nature of the disputes, not an unwillingness to sue in general.

*From John O. Haley, "The Myth of the Reluctant Litigant," *Journal of Japanese Studies,* Vol. 4, No. 2, pg. 359 (1978), at 366-373 and 378-389. Reprinted by permission.

The one arguable exception was the attitude that bringing an action for damages reflected socially unacceptable "selfishness." At first blush this would appear to be a cultural barrier to litigation in general. It was overcome in these instances, however, by justifying the lawsuit as a means of bringing wrongdoers to justice, coupling compensation with a desire to prevent others from inflicting similar harm. But such justifications are among the principal policies behind damage awards and private tort actions, and few plaintiffs would find similar rationalization of their motives difficult. Moreover, the success of the initial suits in these cases has produced others as well as a significant change in the standards being applied in private settlements of similar disputes.

The few direct surveys of Japanese attitudes that have been made provide further support for rejecting the orthodox view. For example, in the survey by Sasaki Yoshio * * *, when asked, "What would you do if a civil dispute arose and despite discussions with the opposite party you could not settle it?," 64% of the 2,098 respondents replied that they would willingly go to court.

Even more persuasive, however, is the pattern of litigation in Japan from 1890 to the present. As indicated in * * * Table [11-1], litigation has been *less* frequent in absolute numbers in the postwar years than the period from 1890 to the outbreak of the Sino-Japanese War in 1937. Relative to population, the contrast is even more startling. In 1934, for example, 302 new civil cases involving formal trial proceedings were initiated in courts of first instance per 100,000 persons, while in 1974 there were 135 such cases per 100,000 persons—2.2 times as many per capita in 1934 than there were in 1974.

By and large this pattern holds true for all categories of cases. While there is a slight variation in the frequencies of certain types of suits in some years, overall, over longer periods, there is a parallel rise or fall in the rate of litigation in each category. Nor do statistics reveal any aberration resulting from the prevalence of a particular type of suit during the prewar period, such as rural tenancy cases.

There was a greater frequency of litigation in absolute numbers in the prewar years in almost every category. (In the postwar period the increase in use of automobiles has led to a significant increase in personal injury actions.) Table [11-2], for example, shows the actual number of new filings for civil trials in courts of first instance for selected categories of cases in 1926 and 1969. The categories selected represent, with the exception of divorce actions, the standard bread and butter fare of litigation and the most numerous types of actions filed in both years. Again, in absolute numbers in 1926, several years prior to the prewar peak in 1934, there was far more litigation than in 1969. Since Japan's population increased by 40% during the interval, on a per capita basis there was only a slight increase in divorce actions and suits relating to land in 1969 and, if we discount traffic accidents as peculiar to the postwar environment, no significant increase in damage actions.

Moreover, the conclusion reached after a trend analysis of the series of trial actions filed from 1891 through 1941 and from 1949 through 1974 is that there is no discernible trend *upwards* or *downwards* during either of these periods. * * *

It is apparent that these patterns are inconsistent with conventional ideas about the reluctance of Japanese to litigate; moreover, they contradict the widely held belief that there has been a greater willingness to sue in the postwar period. In short, most of what is said or written about Japanese attitudes toward the legal process is myth. But as with many myths, it contains an important element of truth.

Although, at least since the middle of the Meiji Period and perhaps even earlier, the Japanese in general may not have been unusually reluctant to litigate, the evidence points to the conclusion that to do so was offensive to some—that is, those who wished to maintain a paternalistic order based on a hierarchical submission to authority. As [Dan Fenno] Henderson has detailed in his often cited (but apparently seldom read) study of conciliation in Japanese law, Tokugawa officialdom had constructed a formidable system of procedural barriers to obtaining final judgment in the Shogunate's courts. The litigant was forced each step of the way to exhaust all possibilities of conciliation and compromise and to proceed only at the sufferance of his superiors. We can only marvel at the endurance and perseverance of those who eventually prevailed. Conciliation was coerced—to use Henderson's phrase "didactic"—not voluntary. Yet, as Henderson tells us, litigation increased. * * *

[2.] The Reality of Institutional Incapacity

If the Japanese are not particularly averse to litigation, how then can we explain why they appear to use their courts far less frequently than do Americans and perhaps others? Why has litigation decreased since the war (and continues to do so)? Also, what accounts for the pervasive acceptance by Japanese themselves that they are unusually "nonlitigious"? And how do such explanations relate to the efficacy of the judicial model in Japan? To answer these questions, we should first reconsider the paradigm process of dispute resolution.

Typically, the parties to a dispute will move through stages—from direct negotiation, to third party mediation and finally to litigation—as a result of failure in the preceding stage to agree to an acceptable resolution. In this process, a relative lack of litigation can be explained by several factors.

One is the effectiveness of third party intervention. The availability of suitable third parties who are willing and able to perform this role reduces the need to invoke formal judicial intervention. At the outset, mediation requires the presence of persons who, because of position or personal relationships, command respect and are able to exercise some measure of authority. In other words, to be effective, the mediator must be someone who can command the parties' trust and their obedience to the settlement.

One would thus anticipate that suitable third parties are more readily available in a stable, closely-integrated and hierarchical society like Japan, than in a more geographically mobile, less cohesive society like the United States in which individual autonomy and social equality are emphasized. Societal expectations and habits are equally relevant. The role of the mediator becomes increasingly legitimate for both the mediator and the parties to disputes where there is repeated reliance on third parties to settle disputes. A contrast in police attitudes in Japan and the United States pointed out by David H. Bayley is especially interesting in this respect. Japanese commonly rely on the police for assistance in settling disputes. But despite similar popular demand in the United States, "what is different," says Bayley, "is that American police organizations have not adapted willingly to perform this function." Another Japanese example is the mediating service some companies provide for employees involved in traffic accidents. In short, the Japanese may be more successful in avoiding litigation because of social organization and values more conducive to informal dispute resolution through mediation.

The tendency of the Japanese to mediate does not necessarily impair the effectiveness of the judiciary, however. As we have seen, the judicial model does not depend on the actual frequency of litigation, but rather the influence of the perceived outcome of the litigation on the mediated settlement.

Resort to court is, however, reduced by another set of factors that do inhibit or enhance the utility of the judicial model as a vehicle for social control and development.

First, for courts to have an impact through decisions in individual cases beyond those persons immediately affected in those cases, information about the courts and these decisions must be disseminated in order that parties to similar disputes are sufficiently aware of the legal norm for it to influence informal resolution of their disputes. This does not mean the judicial model cannot work unless people are fully aware of what the courts will do. But people must be generally cognizant that the courts do provide an available option, and they must have the means to become informed about what the probable outcome will be in the specific case. Thus in societies where illiteracy rates are high or little is communicated about the courts, the judicial model will be less successful. A lack of law-trained persons and the absence of published reports of court decisions, for example, are serious barriers to the effectiveness of the judiciary.

There must also be meaningful access to the courts. Access can be denied directly by jurisdictional barriers that prevent the courts from adjudicating certain types of disputes altogether. Bond-posting requirements that may place an intolerable burden on the parties seeking relief illustrate another form of conscious policy designed to prevent resort to courts. Limited institutional capacity also inhibits access. There must be a sufficient number of courts, of judges and of lawyers, to insure that the costs and delays of litigation do not preclude lawsuits as a realistic option. * * *

Assessing the effectiveness of Japanese courts in terms of these criteria, one finds first that lack of information in Japan is not a particular problem. Law is among the most popular fields of undergraduate study. The newspapers and other media cover the courts and regularly report judicial decisions. There is also in Japan an amazing abundance of legal journals and books on the law, including a plethora of layman's *Handobukku* for particular legal problems to advise the average person. But evidence of other institutional barriers to litigation is ample.

The courts in Japan are even more strained to capacity than in the United States. Superior courts in California in 1971-72, for example, disposed of 964 cases per judge. In 1974, United States District Courts had a caseload of only 325 cases per judge. These caseloads are considered to be excessively high. Yet District Courts in Tokyo and Osaka disposed of 1,525 cases per judge in 1969 and the total Japanese caseload in 1974 was 1,708 cases per judge. This results from a lack of judges. As indicated in Table [11-3], the number of judges in Japan has grown but little for the entire period from 1890 to the present. Thus as the population has grown, the ratio of judges to the population has declined from one judge to 21,926 persons in 1890 to one judge to 52,800 persons in 1926 and one judge to 56,391 persons in 1969.

As a result of overcrowded courts, aggravated by the form of trials in Japan that (as in other civil law jurisdictions) involve recurring hearings typically spaced at one month intervals, delay is acute. The simplest trial can take over a year at the district court level, and the average is two years. If there are appeals, the case will take about five years (Table [11-4]), but proceedings that continue for eight to ten years are not uncommon.

The relationship of delay and a lack of lawyers to frequency of litigation is revealed rather starkly in analysis of litigation in prewar Japan. [F]or the period between 1891-1941, the percentage change in new civil actions filed in any given year was best predicted by a model in which a rise in actions filed in one year tended to predict a rise in the next year, but a fall in the third year. Such a trend can be explained in terms of legal institutions that are very responsive to "market" forces. As the availability of judicial relief becomes known, more lawsuits are filed. As the number of lawsuits increases so the number of lawyers also increases, resulting in even greater information about and access to the courts. If, however, the number of judges is not expanded to meet such increases, there will be greater delay as caseloads per judge become heavier. Such delay contributes in turn to a decrease in litigation. * * *

The failure of Japan to provide more judges and lawyers has been clearly a matter of governmental policy. As to lawyers, since the mid-1930s, entry has been limited by a strictly enforced examination system. * * * In the postwar system, with few exceptions, all members of the legal profession have had to complete an apprenticeship under the Legal Training and Research Institute (*Shihō Kenshū Sho*). To enter, a person must pass the national judicial examination (*shihō shiken*). As can be seen from the data in Table [11-5], the number of applicants has increased tenfold, while the number of those who pass has been limited to about 500. The most common reason given is budgetary constraint—those who attend the Institute receive governmental stipends. For purposes of comparison—and to put to rest any doubts about contemporary Japanese attitudes toward the legal profession—the number per capita of Japanese taking the judicial examination in 1975 was slightly higher than that of Americans taking a bar examination. Since in the United States 74% passed compared to 1.7% in Japan, the desire to become a lawyer on the part of Japanese may be significantly higher than Americans if self-selection is considered.

TABLE [11-1]
NEW CASES FOR FORMAL TRIAL PROCEEDINGS (SOSHŌ)
FILED [1892-1990]

1892	118,474	(293)
1896	79,546	(189)
1900	104,739	(239)
1904	127,004	(275)
1908	90,570	(189)
1912	117,049	(231)
1916	159,351	(298)
1920	129,152	(233)
1924	208,774	(358)
1928	248,406	(400)
1932	255,157	(387)
1936	180,501	(274)
1940	88,160	(123)
1950	68,488	(82)
1954	133,595	(157)
1958	162,786	(184)
1962	132,191	(140)
1966	169,979	(173)
1970	175,164	(170)
1974	149,688	(135)
1978	156,505	(136)
1982	244,069	(205)
1986	335,679	(276)
1990	210,178	(170)

Sources: [Omitted.]

Note: [The table is abbreviated from the original to include only every fourth year, and updated to include years after 1974.] These statistics represent actions involving ordinary trial procedures in civil cases. * * * The statistics for the postwar period include administrative suits, precluded for the prewar courts by jurisdictional limitations. * * * The figures in parentheses indicate the number of new cases filed per 100,000 persons in Japan. * * *

TABLE [11-2]
COMPARISON OF CASES DOCKETED FOR FORMAL TRIAL PROCEEDINGS (SOSHŌ) IN COURTS OF FIRST INSTANCE, 1926, 1969, and 1990

Subject of Action		1926	1969	1990
a.	Divorce	1383 (Dt. Cts. only)	2935 (same)	5450 (same)
b.	Actions relating to land	6894 Dt. Ct.-2890 Ward Ct.-4004	15,151 Dt. Ct.-10,193 Summ. Ct.-1958	21,137 Dt. Ct.-17,936 Summ. Ct.-3381
c.	Evictions & Actions for delivery of buildings	10,315 Dt. Ct.-757 Ward Ct.-9558	7073 Dt. Ct.-4063 Summ. Ct.-3010	20,824 Dt. Ct.-18,002 Summ. Ct.-2822
d.	Actions for contract price	41,731 Dt. Ct.-2634 Ward Ct.-38,597	30,639 Dt. Ct.-11,362 Summ. Ct.-19,277	9,766 Dt. Ct.-3707 Summ. Ct.-6059
e.	Actions for money lent	64,796 Dt. Ct.-4852 Ward Ct.-59,944	20,960 Dt. Ct.-12,215 Summ. Ct.-8754	42,531 Dt. Ct.-10,486 Summ. Ct.-32,045
f.	Actions for damages	5991 Dt. Ct.-2215 Ward Ct.-3776	20,071 Dt. Ct.-18,006 Summ. Ct.-2065 (Traffic Accidents = 10,968	23,111 Dt. Ct.-17,607 Summ. Ct.-5504 7026)

Sources: [Omitted]. [Updated to include figures for 1990.]

TABLE [11-3]
THE LEGAL PROFESSION IN JAPAN 1890-1994

Year	Judges	Public Procurators	Private Attorneys	Private Attorneys per 1 million persons
1890	1,531	481	1,345	33.7
1900	1,244	473	1,590	36.3
1910	1,125	390	2,008	40.8
1920	1,134	570	3,082	55.6
1930	1,249	657	6,599	103.3
1940	1,541	734	3,498	70.7
1950	2,261	1,673	5,862	70.5
1960	2,367	1,761	6,439	70.2
1970	2,605	1,983	8,868	86.2
1980	2,747	2,092	11,438	97.8
1990	2,823	2,092	14,171	114.3
1994	2,852	2,092	15,209	N/A

[The table is abbreviated from the original to include only every tenth year, plus latest year available (1994). Updated to include years after 1970. Note and source are omitted.]

TABLE [11-4] COURTS AND PROCEDURE
Average Time Required for Disposition of Civil Cases
(not including administrative cases)

A. Cases First Brought In Summary Courts
The Period from Filing in the Court of First Instance to Decision

Year	Summary Courts	District Courts *(kōso)*	High Courts *(jōkoku)*
1960	4.9 months	22.4 months	42.8 months
1965	5.7	31.6	50.7
1970	4.8	36.2	53.9
1980	4.1	40.7	60.5
1982	3.4	38.6	59.3

B. Cases First Brought In District Courts
The Period from Filing in the Court of First Instance to Decision

Year	District Courts	High Courts *(kōso)*	Supreme Court *(jōkoku)*
1960	12.6 months	38.2 months	67.5 months
1965	12.1	40.4	67.7
1970	12.8	40.0	66.0
1980	12.8	43.8	67.5
1982	11.5	42.7	67.5

Source: Hideo Tanaka, *The Japanese Legal System: Introductory Cases and Materials* (Tokyo: University of Tokyo Press, 1976), p. 476. [Updated through 1982; statistical reporting form changed thereafter.]

TABLE [11-5]
THE JAPANESE NATIONAL LAW EXAMINATION

Year	Applicants	Persons passing final examinations (and entering the LTRI)	Percentage of successful applicants
1950	2,755	269	9.8%
1955	6,306	264	4.2%
1960	8,302	345	4.2%
1965	13,681	528	3.9%
1970	20,160	507	2.5%
1975	27,791	472	1.7%
1980	28,656	486	1.7%
1985	23,855	486	2.0%
1990	22,900	499	2.2%

[The table is abbreviated from original to include only every fifth year, and updated to 1990. Source is omitted.]

J. MARK RAMSEYER AND MINORU NAKAZATO, THE RATIONAL LITIGANT: SETTLEMENT AMOUNTS AND VERDICT RATES IN JAPAN*

18 Journal of Legal Studies 263
266-273, 278-281 (1989)

[1.] The Debate Over Japanese Litigation Rates: Culture, Costs, and Predictability

The Possible Primacy of Culture

Most observers of Japanese disputes use two basic arguments to explain what they see.[22] First, they claim that litigation threatens a fundamental Japanese concern for consensus and harmony. Japanese define themselves, they explain, by reference to the network of particularistic relationships within which they live and work. Accordingly, Japanese cultural norms place a premium on maintaining peace within those relations. By making disagreements public and compromise difficult, litigation threatens this social order. Out of deference to such considerations, Japanese potential plaintiffs avoid the courts. Second, these observers argue that law does not structure Japanese social relations. The universalistic principles embodied in modern law contradict the more particularistic and status-based principles of Japanese culture. Because modern law clashes with their cultural structures, Japanese ignore it. Instead, they live their lives according to indigenous communal values.

As the above summary implies, champions of this traditional approach often bring to their work a basic distrust of all models that assume that people maximize their short-term financial gain. [Many skeptics thus] attack these models as being far too closely tied to the occidental culture whence they derive. Notions of rational, maximizing humans, [anthropologist Marshall Sahlins] argues, are but "a bourgeois construction"; whatever the case in the West, people elsewhere do not necessarily maximize their claims over scarce resources. Instead, they do so only if their culture projects a sense of scarcity and proffers maximization as a viable ethical option. Japanese culture, many analysts claim, does not present maximization as a legitimate strategy—and strategies that people cannot perceive, they cannot employ.

The Possible Primacy of Costs

Whatever the real effect of Japanese culture, these traditionalists have at least one fact right: Japanese litigate fewer cases per capita than people in most common-law countries. Over ten years ago, however, several revisionist scholars began to suggest that various institutional features of the Japanese legal system (primarily its alleged costs, ineffectiveness, and delays) explain the low Japanese litigation rates within standard rational choice models.[23] If Japanese plaintiffs avoid litigation, they argue, they avoid it because it does not pay. Although these scholars offer a new explanation for Japanese litigation rates, many leave unchallenged the traditional

*From J. Mark Ramseyer and Minoru Nakazato, "The Rational Litigant: Settlement Amounts and Verdict Rates in Japan," 18 *Journal of Legal Studies* 263 (1989), at 266-273, 278-281.

account of the role that law plays in Japan. Because people cannot realistically invoke the courts to solve their disputes (so the revisionists argue), the law cannot be structuring the way they live their lives. Some revisionist scholars even characterize the legal system as a failure. After all, if the courts are so slow, powerless, and expensive, then the system must be denying victims effective relief. After interviewing several such scholars, a *New York Times* reporter recently adopted what has almost become a new academic orthodoxy: the Japanese legal system is "bankrupt."

The Possible Primacy of Predictability

There is a third alternative. Japanese disputants could also be settling such a high percentage of their disputes because they find it relatively easy to agree on how courts would adjudicate their disputes. That, in turn, would suggest that Japanese are settling their disputes in light of their expected litigated outcomes. If so, then the traditional and revisionist theories are both wrong: wealth-maximizing models apply, plaintiffs recover damages, and law structures Japanese behavior.

To see why this third alternative might explain Japanese litigation rates, recall that high levels of agreement on expected outcomes will generate high settlement and low litigation rates. In Japan, as in other societies, litigation costs * * * generally exceed settlement costs. * * * As a result, most rational parties try to settle out of court. Whether they are able to do so depends in part on how nearly their estimates of the litigated outcome * * * converge. If their estimates are close, they usually settle to their mutual advantage. Thus, plaintiffs accept any amount that earns them at least their expected net gain from litigating the dispute. * * * In turn, defendants pay any amount that costs less than their expected total burden from litigating it. * * * For example, a plaintiff who estimates recovery at 100, litigation costs at 25, and settlement costs of 5, will settle for any sum greater than [100-25+5=] 80. A defendant who estimates recovery at 90, litigation costs at 25, and settlement costs at 5, will settle for any sum under [90+25-5=] 110. At these numbers, the parties will have a settlement range of 80-110. If this defendant estimates the likely outcome of litigation at 50, however, then he or she will offer only 70. Because the plaintiff demands 80, litigation may ensue. The more nearly the parties' estimates of the outcome of litigation converge, in short, the greater the likelihood of settlement. More generally, if (i) the total net costs that the parties expect to save through settlement exceed (ii) the difference between the plaintiff's (greater) and defendant's (lower) estimates of the outcome of suit, then settlement is possible. If the costs they expect to save are less than the difference in their estimates, it is not. * * *

At stake, therefore, is the ability of Japanese parties to agree on the litigated verdict. Reasons why they might agree more readily than American disputants are easy to find. First, the absence of juries decreases the uncertainty introduced by amateur fact finders. Attorneys can, instead, try their cases before professional judges who take pride in uniformity over time and whose past decisions lawyers can often discover. Second, the use of discontinuous trial sessions spaced over a long period gives Japanese judges a better chance to explain their views to the parties before the trial ends. Many judges even consider it their duty to offer such explanations. Once a judge has revealed his or her plans, few parties will have any reason to finish the trial. Third, as part of a program to standardize their decisions, Japanese judges use detailed, clear, and public formulae to calculate comparative negligence percentages and the victim's damages—whether for death, disability, or simple injury. Although judges need not follow the formulae, most apparently do. Attorneys can thus rely on the formulae when they negotiate settlements. Given the array of how-to books (including how-to comic books) on accident law in most Japanese bookstores, even lay people can use them. Last, Japan maintains only one national (as opposed to over fifty states and federal) body of law. Gone, as a result, are both the elaborate American conflicts-of-law questions and the confusion introduced by courts in one state interpreting the law of another.

Each of these aspects increases the predictability of the Japanese judicial system. In a world of rational and mathematically sophisticated parties, of course, unpredictability should not raise litigation rates. After all, if rational parties have the same information, they should settle by reference to the same expected mean, no matter how great the variance. In fact, however, information is rarely symmetrical, and seldom does either party possess enough calculating prowess to process correctly all the relevant information. In a world of asymmetric information and "bounded rationality," parties are far more likely to make similar estimates of the litigated outcome under the relatively clear and unified Japanese system than under the plastic and fragmented American one.

[2.] Empirical Evidence From Traffic Accident Disputes

The Hypotheses Proposed

We can test these alternative hypotheses about why Japanese settle their disputes. Suppose, first, that the traditional culture-based hypothesis about Japan is true: that community norms about group harmony and consensus do induce disputants to act in ways inconsistent with the simple, wealth-maximizing manipulation of legal rules. If so, then one of the following would necessarily also be true: either (a) prospective plaintiffs abandon claims (do not even negotiate settlements) when they can profitably litigate them, (b) prospective plaintiffs settle their claims out of court for amounts less than their anticipated net litigated recoveries, or (c) prospective defendants settle claims for amounts greater than their total anticipated litigated costs. If any of these propositions hold, then the disputants are not promoting their short-term economic advantage, and the law is not structuring the resolution of disputes. If none of them holds then the traditional notions about the importance of harmony and consensus in Japan could still be true. They would also, however, be redundant. Models of rational, wealth-maximizing actors who manipulate legal rules to their immediate advantage would also predict Japanese behavior.

Suppose, next, that the revisionists correctly characterize the Japanese judicial system as a costly failure. If so, then many prospective plaintiffs should be abandoning legitimate legal claims entirely or settling them for trivial amounts. According to the revisionist argument, they would be doing so because they face such high litigation costs and such a low return from litigation that they cannot credibly threaten to sue. Because they cannot make a credible threat, defendants rarely offer them more than nominal settlements. As a result, losses would lie as they fell rather than as the law assigned them. Once again, law would not structure human affairs.

Litigation rates alone simply do not disclose whether either of these hypotheses is true—or whether disputants instead reach out-of-court settlements that closely reflect litigated judgments. Low litigation rates are consistent (i) with ethical norms that effectively discourage any recourse to courts and any reliance on legal rules, (ii) with a society of plaintiffs who abandon their claims in the face of overwhelming litigation costs and tiny litigation returns, and (iii) with a society of disputants who face more modest litigation costs and more effective legal relief but who find it relatively easy to agree on the expected litigated outcome and can therefore settle by reference to that outcome. To test these three possibilities, one must instead compare out-of-court settlements with expected litigated verdicts. How often do aggrieved parties assert claims? If they assert them, do they settle them for a more-than-nominal out-of-court payoff? And if they obtain a significant payoff, is it both (a) more than the net recovery they could expect to obtain in court and (b) less than the total expense the potential defendant could expect to incur in court? Unfortunately, for most disputes, no observer will have any idea whether any of this occurs.

For disputes over traffic accidents, however, data close to the information required are available. Government statistics cover almost all serious automobile accidents. They disclose both the number of deaths from such accidents and the number and amounts of the claims that insurers pay. Other records detail the size of court judgments in litigated cases. As a result, one can accurately compare (i) the number of deaths from accidents with the number of wrongful death claims paid and (ii) the average amounts insurers pay in settlement with the amounts courts award in litigation.

True, one cannot generalize from traffic accident disputes to all others or from negotiations with insurance companies to those with neighbors or business partners. Liability insurers are generally more sophisticated than most disputants and do not deal with any particular claimants (the decedent's heirs) on a repeated basis. Yet these disputes may be less idiosyncratic than they initially seem. First, precisely because they are so extraordinarily common, they constitute as "typical" a kind of dispute as might be found. Second, they involve relatively simple legal issues. Third, because Japanese consumers insure against a wide variety of contingencies, negotiations with insurers occur in many different kinds of disputes. Finally, although a claimant may negotiate with the insurer, he or she can direct the negotiations only by threatening to sue the tort-feasor driver. The insurance dispute thus not only originates in a private dispute, it also remains private in at least this critical respect.

The Claims Asserted

The insurance data show that heirs to accident victims almost always assert their legal claims against tort-feasors. To demonstrate this point, Table [11-6] compares the number of deaths from traffic accidents in Japan (col. A) with the number of wrongful death claims paid by insurers over such accidents (col. B); the final column expresses the numbers in column B as percentages of those in column A. According to both the traditional and the revisionist views, the numbers in column A should exceed those in column B substantially—many tort victims should elect to suffer losses unrecompensed.

Table [11-6] shows that nothing of the sort occurs. According to the table, families of accident victims file claims and successfully recover damages in 80-95 percent of all deaths. By contrast, studies in Anglo-American negligence jurisdictions generally find that fewer than half (admittedly not just in fatal accidents) of the traffic accident victims or their heirs recover compensation in tort. Note that the number of deaths in Table [11-6] includes both single-car accidents and multicar accidents where the victim was the only party at fault. The high rate of successful claims thus suggests that neither ethical values nor high costs dull the willingness of victims to assert their legal rights. * * *

The Size of the Settlements: The Evidence

To test the various hypotheses about Japanese litigation rates, Table [11-7] compares average trial rulings on the value of human life in disputes over fatal traffic accidents (col. A) with average insurer payments in such disputes (col. B). The final column expresses column B as a percentage of column A.

Although Table [11-7] may seem to show initially that claimants settle their claims for much less than they could earn in court, such is not the case. Consider the effects of comparative negligence, potential nonrecovery, and underinsurance. First, column A does not represent the amount plaintiffs actually received in court. Instead, it shows how courts valued human life. Before awarding damages to a victim's heirs, the courts subtracted from this value an amount commensurate with the victim's own negligence. Japanese courts appear to reduce awards for comparative negligence in litigated wrongful death cases by slightly less than one-third.

Second, when rational disputants negotiate settlements, they will adjust the amounts in column A for the possibility of nonrecovery. Claimants will not settle by reference only to what a court will likely award them if they win; they will first discount that amount by the possibility that they might lose. Third, 40-50 percent of Japanese drivers purchase only the statutorily required minimum liability insurance policies. In recent years, the insurer's maximum liability under these policies has fallen far short of the litigated value of human life. As a result, insurers are often contractually liable for much less than the amount given by column A.

Adjusted for these conclusions, Table [11-7] shows that Japanese tort claimants do very well out of court. In most years, they receive 55-75 percent of the litigated value of human life. Discounted for comparative negligence at one-third (and with appropriate caveats about the nonrandom character of litigated disputes), these figures suggest that they recover, on average, about 80-110 percent of the amount they would earn if they sued and won against a fully insured defendant. If so, they seem to do at least as well as their American peers. A recent Rand Corporation study, for example, found that American claimants in automobile accidents settle their general damage claims for an average of about 84 percent of the litigated awards. The surprising aspect of Table [11-7], therefore, may be how *high* the out-of-court settlements are. Although some scholars still argue that cultural norms or various procedural faults of the legal system induce Japanese plaintiffs to eat their losses, Table [11-7] suggests that little of the sort occurs.

Table [11-7] includes drivers covered by liability policies more generous than the statutorily required minimum policies. For settlements involving drivers who carried only the latter, turn to Table 3 [omitted]: comparisons between the statutorily required minimum coverage for death (col. A) and the average amounts paid to wrongful death claimants in automobile accidents on behalf of drivers who carried only the statutory minimum policies (col. B). With respect to the insurer, if these disputes reached the courts, the statutory amount would (with minor adjustments) be the maximum amount it could owe; where the decedent's life was legally worth less than the statutory minimum, the insurer would, of course, owe even less. Again, the table shows that settlements follow the anticipated court awards closely; the claims paid averaged 70-90 percent of the statutory minimum.

TABLE [11-6]
NUMBER OF INSURANCE CLAIMS
PAID IN FATAL TRAFFIC ACCIDENTS

Year	A. Deaths from Traffic Accidents	B. Insurance Claims Paid	Col. B/Col. A (%)
1960	13,429	8,269	61.6
1962	13,756	8,569	62.3
1964	16,764	12,102	72.2
1966	17,979	13,743	76.4
1968	18,454	15,465	83.8
1970	21,535	17,334	80.5
1972	20,494	18,259	89.1
1974	15,448	14,574	94.3
1976	13,006	11,521	88.6
1978	12,030	10,081	83.8
1980	11,752	10,146	86.3
1982	12,377	10,431	84.3
1984	12,432	10,529	84.7

[Sources and odd-numbered years omitted.]

TABLE [11-7]
COURT AWARDS AND INSURER PAYMENTS
IN FATAL TRAFFIC ACCIDENTS
(All Insurance Policies)

Year	A. Litigated Value of Human Life (Million Yen)	B. Average Insurer Payments (Million Yen)	Col. B/Col. A (%)
1969	6.86	3.88	56.6
1970	7.13	5.21	73.1
1971	7.90	5.09	64.4
1972	8.89	5.16	58.0
1973	10.29	5.61	54.5
1974	11.77	8.90	75.6
1975	13.77	11.41	82.9
1976	18.29	13.21	72.2
1977	19.01	13.68	72.0
1978	23.91	14.77	61.8
1979	24.92	16.17	64.9
1980	28.95	17.02	58.8
1981	33.79	17.95	53.1
1982	37.34	18.62	49.9
1983	37.25	18.78	50.4
1984	35.81	19.49	54.4

[Sources omitted.]

Questions and Discussion Points

1. *The institutional incapacity theses*: If Japanese are not culturally predisposed to avoid litigation, but instead are deterred by institutional incapacity, why has there not been protest about the institutional incapacity?

2. *The reluctant party to arbitration*: Note that Haley's argument concerns only litigation, not arbitration. Do similar arguments about institutional incapacity apply with respect to arbitration in Japan?

3. *Pressures on A.Co and J.Co to settle*: Aside from the factors discussed in the selections above, are there particular pressures that might encourage A.Co or J.Co strongly to seek settlement rather than pursue arbitration or litigation?

IV. The Settlement Between A.Co and J.Co

Ultimately, A.Co and J.Co settled their dispute. They agreed that they would liquidate Newco, and that A.Co would sell to J.Co all rights to its technical data. The Settlement Agreement and Termination Agreement follow:

SETTLEMENT AGREEMENT

AGREEMENT dated March 31, 1981, made by and between A.Co * * * and J.Co. * * *

WHEREAS:

A. For the purpose of carrying out in Japan the business of manufacturing and selling excavators which incorporate technology of A.Co, A.Co and J.Co entered into a joint venture agreement and established in Japan Newco K.K. (hereinafter called "Newco") on August 30, 1970, by making a joint investment.

B. The shares in Newco owned by A.Co and J.Co respectively have been in the past, and are at present, as follows:

Shareholder	Number of Shares	Par Value	Shareholding Ratio
A.Co	90,000	¥45,000,000	50%
J.Co	90,000	¥45,000,000	50%

C. Attached to the JVA are the following Agreements: [recitation of the Agreements omitted.]

D. Various amendments and changes have been made to the JVA and the attached agreements listed above by certain Letter Agreements and Amending Agreements among the relevant parties. The JVA and the agreements attached thereto and listed above, as amended by such Letter Agreements and Amending Agreements, shall hereinafter be collectively called the "JVA Agreements."

E. Up until July 24, 1980, J.Co, as subcontractor and distributor of Newco or as sublicensee of Newco, as the case may have been, had manufactured in Japan and distributed mostly in Japan certain models of excavators which incorporated technology supplied by A.Co to J.Co through Newco (hereinafter called the "JVA Models"). For the JVA Models and parts and components therefor manufactured and sold on or before July 24, 1980, J.Co paid to Newco the due amount payable for such manufacture and sale under the JVA Agreements.

F. A disagreement has arisen between A.Co and J.Co concerning the termination and terminability of the JVA Agreements. J.Co has interpreted the JVA Agreements as being subject to termination by it, effective July 24, 1980, while A.Co has interpreted such agreements as not subject to unilateral termination by any party thereto as of such date.

G. The parties hereto desire to resolve the disagreement described above in a way satisfactory to both of them and to Newco and for this purpose have been negotiating vigorously for a long time. As a result, a Termination Agreement (hereinafter called the "Termination Agreement") setting forth the termination of the

JVA Agreements and the dissolution of Newco was entered into as of the date hereof by and among A.Co, J.Co and Newco.

NOW, THEREFORE, in consideration of the premises and of the mutual covenants and agreements hereinafter set forth, the parties hereto agree as follows:

Article 1. ***(Termination of JVA Agreements)***

The parties hereto confirm that the JVA Agreements remained valid and effective on and after July 25, 1980, and terminated effective upon the execution of the Termination Agreement.

Article 2. ***(Dissolution of Newco)***

As shareholders of Newco, the parties hereto shall cooperate in bringing about Newco's dissolution as provided in the Termination Agreement and Newco's expeditious liquidation in accordance with the Commercial Code of Japan and the Termination Agreement.

Article 3. ***(Technical Assistance and Improvement Fees)***

3.1 J.Co shall pay to Newco prior to or at the Closing defined in Paragraph 4.1 hereof the entire amount payable under the JVA Agreements from J.Co to Newco for the manufacture and sale by J.Co of the excavators, and parts and components therefor, during the period from July 25, 1980, through the date hereof. It is agreed and understood that said amount shall include the Technical Assistance and Improvement Fees (hereinafter called "Fees") payable under the JVA Agreements from Newco to A.Co for the said manufacture and sale by J.Co during the said period, *i.e.*, One Billion and One Hundred Million Yen (¥1,100,000,000). It is also agreed and understood that the above amount of Fees includes the best estimate of those payable for the month of March 1981 available as of the date hereof, that that estimate is completely satisfactory to J.Co, Newco and A.Co, and that for the difference, if any, between the estimated amount of Fees and the actual amount of Fees for the month of March 1981, no adjustment shall be required with respect to the payment from J.Co to Newco under this Paragraph 3.1 and to the payment from Newco to A.Co under Paragraph 3.2 below.

3.2 The parties hereto shall cause Newco to pay to A.Co at the Closing defined in Paragraph 4.1 hereof the Fees in the amount of One Billion and One Hundred Million Yen (¥1,100,000,000) described in Paragraph 3.1 above, less the due amount of withholding tax payable from Newco for A.Co to the Japanese tax authorities in connection with this payment.

3.3 [Mode of payment omitted.]

Article 4. ***(Purchase and Sale of A.Co Technical Information)***

4.1 Subject to the completion of the filing with the Japanese Government required under the Japanese Foreign Exchange and Foreign Trade Control Act, which filing shall be completed as promptly as possible after the date hereof, and to the terms and conditions hereof, J.Co shall purchase and accept from A.Co, and A.Co shall sell, convey, and deliver to J.Co, A.Co's entire right, title and interest in and to the Technical Data and Technical Improvement Data comprising the documents defined in Paragraphs A-8 and A-9 and Schedule VI of the Technical Agreement ("TechA") that pertain to Models 15-H, 20-H, 20-HT, 10-H and 12-H excavators and were furnished to J.Co through Newco (such Technical Data and Technical Improvement Data being hereinafter collectively called the "Data"), at the closing (hereinafter called the "Closing"), which shall be no later than one month after the completion of the above filing and shall be determined and communicated by J.Co to A.Co and Newco reasonably in advance. J.Co shall have the sole and exclusive right to use said Data throughout the world for whatever purposes including but not limited to the manufacture and sale of the models of excavators enumerated above and any other types or models of excavators, to convey rights in the same, and to enforce proprietary interests therein, and promptly after the Closing A.Co shall destroy any copies of the Data in its possession. A.Co further agrees that after the Closing it will not manufacture any of Models 15-H, 20-H, 20-HT, 10-H and 12-H excavators producible from the Data, and J.Co agrees that the Data does not cover or extend to other machinery of A.Co that is currently under development, or that may be developed in the future.

4.2 As the purchase price, J.Co shall make a lump sum payment to A.Co at the Closing in the amount of Three Billion Yen (¥3,000,000,000). [Mode of payment omitted.]

4.3 [Discussion of applicability of Japanese withholding tax omitted.]

4.4 No other fees or other amounts shall be payable by J.Co to A.Co by reason of any future manufacture or sale by J.Co anywhere in the world of excavators or parts or components therefor embodying the Data conveyed herein.

4.5 A.Co warrants, represents and covenants to J.Co that A.Co has retained the Data in a confidential status and that A.Co shall continue to retain such confidence until the delivery and thereafter.

Article 5. ***(Return of A.Co Technical Information)***

At the Closing, J.Co shall return to A.Co through Newco all the Technical Data and the Technical Improvement Data (as defined in the TechA) furnished by A.Co to J.Co through Newco under the JVA Agreements, excluding the Data to be purchased by J.Co from A.Co.

Article 6. ***(Terminability of This Agreement)***

6.1 This Agreement shall not be subject to termination under any circumstances by either party hereto.

6.2 If, for any reason, J.Co and A.Co are unable to close this Agreement on or before May 15, 1981, by payment from J.Co to A.Co and to Newco, respectively, and payment from Newco to A.Co of the respective amounts provided herein and transfer by A.Co to J.Co of the Data pursuant hereto, then (i) this Agreement shall become null and void on such date, (ii) as between J.Co and A.Co the Termination Agreement shall become null and void, and (iii) J.Co and A.Co shall cause Newco to remain as a going concern (with an appropriate shareholders meeting resolution under the Commercial Code of Japan, if necessary) and also cause the Joint Venture Agreements to be reinstated.

Article 7. ***(Assignability of This Agreement)***

This Agreement shall not be assigned to any party by either party hereto, whether in whole or in part.

Article 8. ***(Confidential Nature of This Agreement)***

This Agreement shall not be disclosed to any third party except pursuant to the order of a court of competent jurisdiction or the order or request of any competent government authorities, or pursuant to the rules and regulations of any competent government authority or any stock exchange on which the stock of either party is listed.

Article 9. ***(Miscellaneous)***

It is agreed and confirmed between J.Co and A.Co that there exists no unresolved disagreement between them or no unresolved breach or unfulfilled obligation on the part of either party under or relating to any prior representations, negotiations or agreements with respect to the subject matter of this Agreement and the Termination Agreement, including those agreements terminated by the Termination Agreement, and that neither party has any rights against or obligations to the other party other than those provided in this Agreement, the Termination Agreement and any Letter Agreements entered into on the same day as this Agreement.

IN WITNESS WHEREOF, the parties hereto have caused this Agreement to be duly executed and delivered by their respective authorized representatives as of the day and year first above written.

A.Co	J.Co
By [signed]	By [signed]
Title: CHAIRMAN AND CHIEF EXECUTIVE OFFICER	Title: PRESIDENT

- - - - - - - - - -

TERMINATION AGREEMENT

THIS AGREEMENT is made among A.Co * * *, J.Co * * *, and Newco K.K. * * *

WHEREAS:

[Recitations similar to those in the preceding agreement omitted.]

NOW, THEREFORE, in consideration of their mutual promises and their benefits to be derived herefrom,

IT IS AGREED AS FOLLOWS:

1. Pursuant to Paragraph I-1 of the JVA and the applicable provisions, if any, of the Collateral Agreements providing for termination, the PARTIES and Newco hereby agree to terminate the JVA and the Collateral Agreements effective as of the date hereof. All provisions of the JVA and the Collateral Agreements which by their terms continue in effect after termination shall remain in effect as provided therein.

2. The last three lines of Paragraph G-3(b) of the Technical Agreement notwithstanding, the Technical Assistance and Improvement Fees for the Fee-bearing excavators, parts and components which accrued pursuant to said Paragraph of the Technical Agreement during the last half of 1980 and the first quarter of 1981 shall be payable from Newco to A.Co no later than May 15, 1981.

3. Newco shall, and the PARTIES shall cause Newco to, hold its annual general shareholders' meeting for the fiscal year of 1980 on March 31, 1981, at which Newco shall, and the PARTIES shall cause Newco to, be liquidated as expeditiously as possible in accordance with the relevant provisions of the Japanese Commercial Code. The proceeds from the liquidation of Newco shall be distributed among the PARTIES on a pro-rata basis proportionate to their respective shareholdings pursuant to the Japanese Commercial Code. During the period from the date hereof through May 15, 1981, Newco's function shall be limited to dealing with the termination of the JVA and the Collateral Agreements.

4. This Agreement shall take effect upon its execution.

IN WITNESS WHEREOF, the PARTIES and Newco have caused these presents to be duly executed in the manner appropriate on each of the dates respectively set forth below.

J.Co	A.Co
By [signed]	By [signed]
Attest: ____________	Attest: ____________
Date	Date
Newco K.K.	
By [signed]	
Attest: ____________	
Date	

Questions and Discussion Points

1. *The terms of settlement*: What did each of A.Co and J.Co gain and give up in the settlement?

Why did A.Co agree to give up all rights in the technical data for the specified excavators?

Why did J.Co agree to pay such a huge sum for the technical data that it has been saying was not valuable and that it would not be using in the future?

2. *Terms contemplating possible failure of the settlement*: Consider Article 6.2 of the Settlement Agreement between A.Co and J.Co. How might the settlement fail?

FURTHER READING

On the Level of Litigation in Japan

John O. Haley, "Sheathing the Sword of Justice in Japan: An Essay on Law without Sanctions," *Journal of Japanese Studies*, Vol. 8, No. 2, pg. 265 (1982).

John Owen Haley, *Authority without Power: Law and the Japanese Paradox*. New York: Oxford University Press, 1991.

Takeyoshi Kawashima, "Dispute Resolution in Contemporary Japan," in Arthur T. von Mehren, ed., *Law in Japan: The Legal Order in a Changing Society*, pp. 41-72. Cambridge, MA: Harvard University Press, 1963.

J. Mark Ramseyer, "The Costs of the Consensual Myth: Antitrust Enforcement and Institutional Barriers to Litigation in Japan," 94 *Yale Law Journal* 604 (1985).

J. Mark Ramseyer, "Reluctant Litigant Revised: Rationality and Disputes in Japan," 14 *Journal of Japanese Studies* 111 (1988).

Takao Tanase, "The Management of Disputes: Automobile Accident Compensation in Japan," 24 *Law & Society Review* 651 (1990).

Litigation and Procedure in Japan Generally

"Courts and Procedure," Chpt. 6, pp. 444-548, in Hideo Tanaka, ed., *The Japanese Legal System*. Tokyo: Tokyo University Press, 1988.

John Kakinuki, "Dispute Resolution in Japan: Choosing the Right Alternative," 9 *East Asian Executive Reports* 5 (1987).

Takeshi Kojima, ed., *Perspectives on Civil Justice and ADR: Japan and the U.S.A.*, Series of the Institute of Comparative Law in Japan 18. Tokyo: The Institute of Comparative Law in Japan, Chuo University Press, 1990.

Litigating in Japan

Masaru Itō, "Diary of the Plaintiffs' Attorneys' Team in the Thalidomide Litigation," 8 *Law in Japan: An Annual* 136 (1975).

Japanese Civil Procedure

Yasuhiro Fujita, "Japanese Rules of Jurisdiction," 4 *Law in Japan: An Annual* 55 (1970).

Kōji Harada, "Civil Discovery Under Japanese Law," 16 *Law in Japan: An Annual* 21 (1983).

Attitudes of the Judiciary

Takeo Hayakawa, "The Japanese Judiciary in the Whirlwind of Politics," 7 *Kobe University Law Review* 15 (1971).

J. Mark Ramseyer and Frances McCall Rosenbluth, *Japan's Political Marketplace.* Cambridge, MA: Harvard University Press, 1993.

Conciliation and Settlement

Dan Fenno Henderson, *Conciliation and Japanese Law, Tokugawa and Modern.* 2 vols. Seattle: Published for the Association for Asian Studies by University of Washington Press, 1965.

Yoshirō Kusano, "A Discussion of Compromise Techniques," 24 *Law in Japan: An Annual* 138 (1991).

Tetsuya Obuchi, "Role of the Court in the Process of Informal Dispute Resolution in Japan: Traditional and Modern Aspects, with Special Emphasis on In-Court Compromise," 20 *Law in Japan: An Annual* 74 (1987).

Joel Rosch, "Institutionalizing Mediation: The Evolution of the Civil Liberties Bureau in Japan," 21 *Law & Society Review* 243 (1987).

Hiroshi Wagatsuma and Arthur Rosett, "The Implications of Apology: Law and Culture in Japan and the United States," 20 *Law & Society Review* 461 (1986).

Arbitration in Japan

Teruo Doi, "The Effect of an Arbitration Clause in a Voidable Contract: Separability Doctrine Adopted by the Supreme Court of Japan," in Institute of Comparative Law, Waseda University, ed., *Law in East and West*, pp. 609-621. Tokyo: Waseda University Press, 1988.

Hiroshi Hattori, "Arbitration," in Zentaro Kitagawa, ed., 7 *Doing Business in Japan*, pp. XIV 4-1 to 4-32. New York: Matthew Bender, 1994.

Takeshi Kojima, "Arbitration System in Japan," in Institute of Comparative Law in Japan, ed., *Conflict and Integration: Comparative Law in the World Today*, pp. 327-348. Tokyo: Chuo University Press, 1989.

Robert Bennett Lubic, "International Commercial Arbitration in Japan: Background and Suggestions," 2 *American Review of International Arbitration* 87 (1991).

Toshio Sawada, "International Commercial Arbitration—Practice of Arbitral Institutions in Japan," 30 *The Japanese Annual of International Law* 69 (1987).

NOTES TO CHAPTER ELEVEN

1. 1 Kakyū minshū 475, 487 (Tokyo Dist. Ct., April 4, 1950).

2. 8 Minshū 234, 236 (Sup. Ct., Jan. 28, 1954).

3. Deguchi v. Ishikawa, 3 Kakyū minshū 791, 795 (Nagasaki Dist. Ct., June 9, 1952).

4. Wada v. Kamei, 10 Kakyū minshū 1812, 1819 (Osaka Dist. Ct., Aug. 29, 1959).

5. 5 Minshū 36, 37 (Sup. Ct., Feb. 6, 1951).

6. Deutch v. West Coast Machinery Co., Marubeni-Iida, Inc. (Respondent), Kansai Iron Works, Ltd. (Petitioner), 497 P.2d 1311 (Wash. Sup. Ct. 1972).

7. Subparagraphs (b) and (c) of article 10 provide as follows:

> (b) the freedom of judicial officers, officials or other competent persons of the State of origin to effect service of judicial documents directly through the judicial officers, officials or other competent persons of the State of destination,
>
> (c) the freedom of any person interested in a judicial proceeding to effect service of judicial documents directly through the judicial officers, officials or other competent persons of the State of destination.

8. *Chūkai minji soshōhō* 352 (H. Saitoh ed. 1973).

9. Daiei K.K. v. Bragoewich, 352 Hanrei Taimuzu 246 (Tokyo Dist. Ct., Dec. 21, 1976).

10. Le Gimex, S.A. v. Hōei Shōji K.K., 667 Hanrei Jihō 47 (Tokyo Dist. Ct., May 2, 1972), denied enforcement to a French judgment against a Japanese defendant concerning a contract admitted to be performed in France, even though under article 5 of the Code of Civil Procedure, a Japanese court would have special competence under similar circumstances. The court argued that *jōri* and "principles of international law" (as evidenced by the *Draft* Hague Convention on Enforcement of Judgments) militated in favor of denying enforcement of the French judgment inasmuch as the Japanese defendant in the original action had no physical presence in France and since defending the French action would have proved burdensome for the Japanese party. The court admitted that if a similar contract action were brought in Japan, the Japanese court would appear to have jurisdiction under article 5 of the Code, but went on to argue, in *dicta*, that venue under the Code is not sufficient to constitute competence in international cases, and that therefore, in the interests of fairness to the foreign defendant, a Japanese court ought to refuse jurisdiction in such circumstances.

I have been able to find no other cases in which Japanese venue rules were *not* applied in solving issues of international competence. * * *

11. *See, e.g.*, American President Lines v. Soubra K.K., 10 Kakyū minshū 2232 (Tokyo Dist. Ct., Jan 25, 1959). On the policy in favor of deference to party arbitral clauses, see also Compagnia de Transportes del Mar S.A. v. Mataichi K.K., 4 Kakyū minshū 502 (Tokyo Dist. Ct., April 10, 1953).

12. K.K. Kobayashi Shōten v. Kenlick Far East K.K., 9 Kakyū minshū 111 (Tokyo Dist. Ct., 25 Jan. 1958).

13. 13 Kakyū minshū 338 (Tokyo High Ct., 5 Mar. 1962).

14. 10 Kakyū minshū 1711 (Tokyo Dist. Ct., 20 Aug. 1959).

15. 10 Kakyū minshū 970 (Osaka Dist. Ct., 11 May 1959).

16. April 2, 1953, 4 U.S.T. 2063.

17. The quality of interpreter services provided by the JCAA was uneven. Often, there would be long and apparently significant exchanges in Japanese which either went untranslated or had such abbreviated translations as to leave one with concern about the adequacy of the translation. It does not seem reasonable to expect local Japanese counsel to serve as local counsel and interpreter during these proceedings. Lawyers are paid to be counsel.

18. At the conclusion of the arbitration, the Rules of the JCAA were interpreted to require that the American party bear the cost of English interpretation and translation, and to share the cost of Japanese stenographers, in the arbitration. Total costs to the American client for translation and interpretation, in and outside the arbitration chamber, approached $100,000.

19. At the time, I considered myself moderately knowledgeable about international arbitration but basically ignorant about Japanese business or culture. Based on the available literature, I (wrongly) assumed the former was sufficient. I was later enlightened as to the linguistic significance of the JCAA response. I discovered that "If someone allows that something is difficult, it is a good bet that he is really saying 'forget it'." *NY Times*, "Some Japanese (One) Urge Plain Speaking" (March 27, 1989), at 3.

20. * * * The suggestion that one reason for this is that JCAA arbitrators are only paid for the time they actually attend arbitral sessions, and are not compensated for pre-hearing study or the drafting of an award, initially shocked me, but has been confirmed by knowledgeable sources.

21. The civil law system is based on a more active role for judges than the passive "umpire" of the common law. "Judge's inquiry" (*shakumei*) is a general term used for those activities in which the judge takes the initiative. It includes "issue definition," in which issues are defined not only through pleadings but also through the judge's questioning of the parties, and also includes the judge's questioning of witnesses during the investigation of evidence.

22. [The most prominent observer to make this point was Takeyoshi Kawashima, one example of whose work was excerpted in Chapter 7, Section IV.]

23. [*See* John Haley's work, excerpted immediately above.]

TWELVE

Publicly Traded Corporations

Introduction

The discussion of Japanese corporate law in Chapter 8 concerned corporate issues applicable both to closely held and to publicly held corporations. The issues selected, however, are often of greater concern in the closely held context, where the lack of a ready market for shares makes it difficult for shareholders to walk away when matters become unsatisfactory. This lack of liquidity therefore puts a greater premium on the importance of intra-corporate mechanisms for risk allocation and corporate control.

Different issues assume significance for shareholders and management in the context of a securities market. The effects of this different context are the subject of this chapter. Of course, just as the Code provisions studied in Chapter 8 generally apply both to publicly held and closely held corporations, the Code provisions considered in this chapter apply to shareholders in both types of corporations.

In Part A we will focus on the role of shareholders in publicly traded companies in Japan, an issue we considered in general terms in Chapter 3. Looking at the practical means by which Japanese shareholders seek to effectuate their rights can help us understand what those rights and resulting expectations entail. Our discussion of this issue will start by focusing on the role of gangsters in the corporate world. Beginning with this topic does not mean that corporate gangsters constitute the only, or even the dominant, form of shareholder activity. Nevertheless, such activity has long been a common feature of the Japanese corporate system. Because the gangster activity seems so different from that to which North American and European observers are accustomed, that activity provides a good test case for considering how the seemingly more familiar provisions of corporate law actually work in the Japanese context.

We then turn to the headline-grabbing dispute between U.S. investor T. Boone Pickens, famous for his involvement in a number of contested takeover bids in the United States, and a Japanese manufacturing company in which he acquired a substantial block of shares. The Pickens case juxtaposes sharply the assumptions underlying the Japanese approach with those that U.S. shareholders often take for granted. The Pickens case will also introduce us to the topic of Japanese mergers and acquisitions (M&A), the subject of Part B of this chapter. Japanese rules and practices with respect to M&A reflect the legal system's response to the questions of policy that are implicit in the Pickens case.

PART A: The Role of Shareholders

I. Shareholder Control

JAMES C. ABEGGLEN AND GEORGE STALK, JR., KAISHA: THE JAPANESE CORPORATION*

185-186 (1985)

[W]hen the shareholder's claim to a return on his investment is met by the Japanese company, the shareholder has little or no further voice in corporate affairs. The board of directors of the Japanese company consists almost entirely of inside board members, that is, of the senior management of the company. They achieve board member status as they move up in the executive ranks; they are career employees. To the extent that they might be seen as representatives of a constituency, their constituency is the career employees of the company itself. * * *

A recent and colorful case was an interesting exception to these rules of continuity and control from inside the company. Shigeru Okada was dismissed as president of the Mitsukoshi Department Store through the offices of an outside director. Mitsukoshi has long been Japan's most prestigious department store group. * * * Its special prestige stems largely from its being the source of the fortunes of the Mitsui family, the initial firm in what became the Mitsui Group, once Japan's largest combination of companies.

Okada assumed the presidency of Mitsukoshi in the early 1970's, and soon established a reputation as both a flamboyant and a one-man operator. His one-man style was evident as executives began to leave the company for other firms (in itself very unusual) and his flamboyance was displayed in his rental of the Versailles Palace for a night, with guests flown to Paris to celebrate the fame and position of Mitsukoshi.

The trigger for Okada's downfall in 1982 was a store-sponsored display for Persian treasures, many of gold, and many of which turned out to be fakes produced in a workshop not far from Tokyo. With the press in full outcry, management rose up and removed him, reportedly by a unanimous vote of the sixteen directors, on the grounds of the ruinous inventory position of the store. Most of the excess, unsaleable inventory had been supplied to the store by companies organized by Okada's mistress. This proved to be the last straw in a long sequence of mismanagement.

The Okada case is of interest in this discussion in two regards. First, it has been widely reported as the first in recollected Japanese history where a chief executive has been voted out of office by his board of directors in direct confrontation. In

*From James C. Abegglen and George Stalk, Jr., *Kaisha: The Japanese Corporation* (Basic Books, 1985), at 185-186.

itself, the rarity of this case supports the view of succession, continuity, and lack of shareholder control as being the Japanese pattern.

Second, other players in this drama are of interest. The coup that unseated Okada was engineered by Goro Koyama, retired executive of and still advisor to the Mitsui Bank. Koyama served on the Mitsukoshi board as banker and group representative and arranged the overturn to defend the financial interests of its bank and department store. Even so, some reports indicated that the actual vote to dismiss Okada was close, despite the appearance of unanimity.

A final observation on the Mitsukoshi case is important. Okada's successor was not an outsider brought in to clean up the situation, nor a bank executive sent to defend the interests of the Mitsui Bank. The successor was another company officer who had been running Mitsukoshi's Nagoya store, and thus was not involved with Okada's operations. For all of the drama, the final note was the continuity and integrity of the organization.

II. Shareholders and Gangsters

A. Introduction to the *sōkaiya*

SURVEY, CORPORATE GOVERNANCE IN JAPAN: THE POSITION OF SHAREHOLDERS IN PUBLICLY HELD CORPORATIONS*

5 University of Hawaii Law Review 135

170-171 (1983)

[A] major reason for the lack of shareholder participation has been the presence at meetings of "professional shareholders" known as "*sōkai-ya*." The *sōkai-ya* are hired by management to attend meetings to ensure that no debate takes place, that no embarrassing questions are asked, and that the meeting runs smoothly and ends quickly. These men each own a few shares to gain entrance to the meeting, and are paid handsomely from corporate funds funneled through some nondescript account. * * * *Sōkai-ya* also make money by posing as a threat to management. * * * [In the words of one observer,] "They make a living out of extortion; managements pay for their silence on such matters as pollution, etc."[1] * * *

[In 1981, the Diet enacted amendments to the Commercial Code designed to control the activities of *sōkaiya*.] Article 294-2, which prohibits a corporation from giving "any person any benefit estimable in terms of properties with respect to the exercise of the rights of a shareholder," is the main provision in the new Code [the 1981 amendments] attacking the activities of *sōkai-ya*. Thus a company may not

---

*From Survey [Christopher Lee Heftel], "Corporate Governance in Japan: The Position of Shareholders in Publicly Held Corporations," 5 *University of Hawaii Law Review* 135 (1983), at 170-171. Reprinted by permission.

give cash or property to a shareholder in order to induce or prevent the shareholder's exercise of his rights, nor may a company bestow such benefits on a nonshareholder to prevent him from acquiring stock. The recipient of any such benefit is liable for its return to the company. In addition, there are criminal penalties of a maximum jail sentence of six months and a maximum fine of 300,000 yen * * * which can be enforced against any director, auditor or employee of the company who gives such benefits, any recipient with knowledge or any person who directs that such benefits be given to a third person.

In order to alleviate the difficulty of proof, the Code dictates that the benefits will be presumed to have been made to influence the exercise of shareholder rights any time the company has transferred property to a shareholder without consideration or for grossly inadequate consideration. However, such presumption does not exist in the case of transactions between the company and nonshareholders.

DAVID E. KAPLAN AND ALEC DUBRO, YAKUZA: THE EXPLOSIVE ACCOUNT OF JAPAN'S CRIMINAL UNDERWORLD*

169-173 (1986)

Japan's underworld showcase of extortion * * * is not in the "water business" [bars, hostess clubs, etc.], or even in the *sarakin* [loan-sharking]. It thrives among a remarkably brazen, professional class of corporate racketeers whose activities have traditionally centered around the company shareholders' meeting: the *sōkaiya*. The word translates directly as "shareholders' meeting men" or "specialists," but the *sōkaiya* gangs have been variously described in English as "financial racketeers," "general meeting mongers," "black gentlemen in the shadow," and "rent-a-thugs."

For years, virtually every company listed on Japan's stock exchanges dealt with them. They could be seen forming large queues in front of the general affairs bureau of any bank or securities firm. Most wore light-colored business suits similar to those of ordinary employees; others sported loud jackets adorned with wide neckties. At the larger banks, they would check to ensure their names were still officially listed in a special registry, enabling them to receive payoffs at least twice annually. Some made daily rounds through Japan's business districts, visiting several hundred corporations each year. At one major shipping firm, as many as eighty *sōkaiya* visited each morning. They would be serviced by a company official who had been paying off *sōkaiya* for twenty-five years. At another firm, a leading bank, some 2,000 persons, including known gangsters and rightists, were registered to receive twice-annual payments of typically between $20 and $200; certain callers were quietly handed as much as $15,000.

Although not operating as overtly as it once did, Japan's *sōkaiya* industry is alive and well. And if they are not queueing up for corporate payoffs each morning,

---

*From David E. Kaplan and Alec Dubro, *Yakuza: The Explosive Account of Japan's Criminal Underworld* (Addison-Wesley, © 1986 by the Center for Investigative Reporting), at 169-173. Reprinted by permission.

these racketeers are still blackmailing the country's largest businesses out of millions of dollars.

Why are these extortionists paid off? Largely to leave the companies alone, to stop disrupting the staid world of Japanese businesses. Typically, the groups operate by buying several shares of a company's stock, digging up scandalous information, and then demanding hush money. They ferret out embarrassing facts about the company's top management: high-ranking officials who cheat on their income tax, ignore safety rules in their plants, or keep mistresses. If the corporation refuses to pay up, at its next general meeting the *sōkaiya* will appear armed with these unpleasant revelations and loudly berate the company management. The executives, highly concerned over losing face before their employees and the public, have traditionally anted up. As one police official put it, "It's not threats of violence that scare corporate executives. They're more afraid of damage to the reputations of friends and family members. We live in a culture of shame."

The larger *sōkaiya* groups play both sides of the game by also selling companies their services as strong-arm guards to ensure that shareholder meetings run without serious questions being asked. Dissident stockholders who dare protest company policy usually find themselves shouted down—and often beaten up—by the boisterous troop of *sōkaiya* on hand. Occasionally, the larger companies have played one *sōkaiya* group against another, at times with violent consequences. But most frequently, the result is to render the Japanese shareholder meeting useless, a highly staged, sometimes farcical performance that usually lasts less than twenty minutes.

* * *

Among the leading bosses of the *sōkaiya* world was, until his death, Yoshio Kodama. He is said to have systematically advanced into *sōkaiya* circles after 1965, starting his own racketeering groups and making alliances with others. Taking their lead from Kodama, the mainstream *yakuza* [gangster] syndicates began moving heavily into the field around 1972, and the *sōkaiya* business started to boom, increasing fourfold between 1972 and 1977. At their peak in 1981, a police survey revealed 6800 *sōkaiya* in 500 separate groups extorting as much as $400 million annually.

Police today estimate that some 70 percent of the *sōkaiya*'s annual take ends up in the hands of *yakuza* syndicates. A survey by the NHK public broadcasting network (Japan's equivalent of Britain's BBC) reported that one out of every four *sōkaiya* is in fact a *yakuza* gang member. Other reports put the number of *yakuza* far higher. At least one *sōkaiya*, though, was careful to mark the distinction between the two crime groups. "I don't like people to use the terms '*sōkaiya*' and '*yakuza*' interchangeably," said Jiro Morimoto, boss of a thirty-member *sōkaiya* group. "*Yakuza* are inheritors of the old *bushidō*, the *samurai* spirit, who stick to one principle. On the other hand, *sōkaiya* could tell a story in ten different ways."

The scams devised by the *sōkaiya* over the years are as ingenious as they are lucrative. Often they pose as legitimate consultants from "economic research institutes," gathering corporate intelligence and, with the help of private detectives, maintaining dossiers on leading executives—down to the names and addresses of their mistresses. Many pose as publishers of small magazines and newsletters who are only too happy to accept money for "subscriptions" and "advertising" in exchange for not printing scurrilous stories. Management views such scandalous press with the same horror as threats against its general meetings. The contents of such stories are typically leaked to the company before the issue is distributed, and the company buys up all the copies, often at premium rates. * * *

The practitioners of these varied exploits fall into several classes. Those who run sophisticated organizations—working at times closely with company management—receive salaries comparable to the best-paid corporate executives. They are chauffeured around town in limousines and maintain powerful political connections. Most *sōkaiya*, though, are petty thugs hoping for an easy payoff. Their members come from varied walks of life: taxi drivers, tradesmen. There are even the reputed "bartender *sōkaiya*," former barmen who switched to extortion after listening to conversations between top executives over drinks. Also in the lower ranks of the business is the so-called *banzai sōkaiya*, who walks around company offices shouting the exclamation "*Banzai*!" When questioned, he states that he has just become a shareholder and is merely expressing his joy and desire to encourage greater worker productivity. Several thousand yen is usually enough to convince him that his joy is better expressed elsewhere.

So lucrative is the field that many corporate officials who once dealt regularly with *sōkaiya* have switched roles and turned up as *sōkaiya* at company meetings—much to the surprise of management. The *sōkaiya*'s rationale, like that of the *yakuza* in general, is that they play a critical role in society. "The stockholders' meeting is a solemn function," one *sōkaiya* told the newspaper *Yomiuri*. "We help it proceed smoothly and protect the interests of the innocent shareholders. We are the prop men of modern capitalism."

B. Selected cases

Translation by J. Mark Ramseyer

Japan v. Hobo
23 Keishū 1359
(Sup. Ct., P. B., Oct. 16, 1969)

REFERENCES:

Commercial Code, §§494 (amount of fine increased in 1981), 294-2 (added in 1981), 497 (added in 1981).

FACTS:

The company at issue planned to market color television sets that it had bought from another firm. Toward that end, it contracted for sets from a supplier. Unbeknownst to it, however, its supplier simply bought the sets from another maker and raised the voltage on the sets to increase the brilliance of the screen. For a time, the company's stock price rose as rumors about the screen's brilliance circulated. It fell again, though, once observers began to have doubts about the set.

Given those doubts, the company's managers tried to learn the content of its supplier's technology. When the supplier stonewalled, they rescinded the contract. Apparently worried about questions at the next shareholders' meeting, they met with the defendant *sōkaiya* at a restaurant, asked for help, and paid the *sōkaiya* in cash.

The defendants were prosecuted for violating the criminal provisions of the Commercial Code. The trial court acquitted but (the state being able to appeal acquittals in Japan) the High Court reversed.

JUDGMENT:

The appeal is dismissed.

REASONS:

* * * Shareholders may hold stock for their personal profit, but the corporation is an entity separate from its shareholders with its own interests. To protect that corporate interest and prevent its infringement, shareholders must be able to debate issues fairly at the shareholders' general meeting, and must pass resolutions fairly. Therefore, officers (and others) of the company violate the Commercial Code §494 ban on "unlawful solicitations" if, in order to escape criticism for their own managerial improprieties or failures, they (a) ask some shareholders to prevent others from fairly speaking or fairly exercising their vote at the shareholders' general meeting, and (b) compensate those shareholders with property in connection with that assignment. As the trial court noted, the officers of the corporation in the present case had as managers failed to develop a new product. They thus expected the shareholders to try to hold them responsible for that failure at the next regular shareholders' general meeting. Such officers violate the ban [in §494] on "unlawful solicitations" if they (i) ask so-called *sōkaiya* shareholders or their agents to prevent other shareholders from speaking on the floor of the general meeting and to monitor the progress of the business at the meeting so that all resolutions pass in the form in which the company proposed them, and (ii) compensate the *sōkaiya* or their agents. * * *

- - - - - - - - - -

Translation by J. Mark Ramseyer

Chisso K.K. v. Gotō
736 Hanrei Jihō 20
(Osaka Dist. Ct., March 28, 1974),
aff'd, 945 Hanrei Jihō 23 (Osaka High Ct., Sept. 27, 1979)

REFERENCE:

Commercial Code, §247.

FACTS:

The following excerpt, from David E. Kaplan & Alec Dubro, *Yakuza: The Explosive Account of Japan's Criminal Underworld,* at 174-177,* describes the background of this case.

> For over a generation, the Chisso Corporation dominated the political and economic life of Minamata, a country town of 36,000

*(Addison-Wesley, © 1986 by the Center for Investigative Reporting). Reprinted by permission.

on Japan's southern island of Kyushu. The long-established fertilizer company had grown since the war into a leading manufacturer of petrochemicals. From its Minamata plant—a huge, gray complex of pipes, towers, and tanks—the company had for years routinely dumped its lethal by-products into the heavily fished waters of Minamata Bay.

The Chisso Corporation had run into pollution problems before. Three times—in 1926, 1943, and 1954—the company paid local fishermen for losses caused by its dumping practices. But by 1953, the early effects of a far more serious development could be seen—the outbreak of one of the world's largest environmental poisoning disasters.

In their book about environmental problems in Japan, *Island of Dreams*, authors Norrie Huddle and Michael Reich describe the chilling progression of what would be called "Minamata Disease":

> Birds seemed to be losing their sense of coordination, often falling from their perches or flying into buildings and trees. Cats, too, were acting oddly. They walked with a strange rolling gait, frequently stumbling over their own legs. Many suddenly went mad, running in circles and foaming at the mouth until they fell—or were thrown—into the sea and drowned. Local fishermen called the derangement 'the disease of the dancing cats,' and watched nervously as the animals' madness progressed.

Soon the malady spread to the fishermen and their families. The symptoms of the disease were horrible to watch. Although it was still undiagnosed, physicians knew the disease attacked the central nervous system and the brain, crippling its victims and eventually rendering them bedridden and incoherent. Forty percent of those poisoned died. Autopsies showed that their brains had become spongelike as cells were eaten away. Hundreds of families were affected, while medical authorities warned that thousands more were in danger.

By 1958, the victims and their families, treated as pariahs by a fearful public, demanded compensation and better pollution control at the Chisso plant. The company, however, resolutely denied that its operations were responsible, as it would for the next fifteen years. Yet, as early as 1959, Chisso knew from its own secret tests that its massive discharges of organic mercury were the cause of the Minamata disease. A long-overdue official government report would much later reveal that for thirty-three years—until 1965—Chisso dumped 80 tons of mercury into the shallow waters of Minamata Bay, mixed in with 600,000 tons of sludge.

To local fishermen, who had watched the number of victims grow as their catch steadily declined, Chisso's conduct was inexcusable. In a series of protests, they stormed the factory, at one point holding the executive director hostage overnight and causing extensive damage to company buildings. After the Japanese press picked up the story, the company eventually agreed to pay a small amount in compensation money to those affected. The Chisso Corporation, however, never admitted any responsibility in the matter. * * *

In September 1968, fifteen years after the poisonings first appeared, the Japanese government officially recognized organic mercury as the cause of Minamata Disease. Before another year would pass, Minamata victims * * * filed suit against Chisso. Supporters of the Minamata group, however, went a full step farther. They took their cause directly to Chisso's corporate headquarters and stockholders' meetings in Tokyo and Osaka. This was as good as a declaration of war to Chisso, and the company promptly enlisted the help of two groups closely associated with the underworld—the *sōkaiya* and the *hoshō kaisha*, or "security companies."

Borrowing a tactic from the *sōkaiya*, Minamata victims and supporters began purchasing single shares of the company's stock, entitling them to attend Chisso's general meetings and introduce motions. Although some 500 members of the Minamata delegation arrived at the company's meeting in November 1970, few got much farther than the front door. The activists were barred by a line of guards who looked as if they'd been recruited from the seediest realms of the Tokyo underworld. One protester who did make it inside found his attempts at amending a management proposal futile. Waiting for the man were a host of *sōkaiya*, who easily drowned him out with a chorus of jeers and promptly called the meeting to a close. Total time of Chisso's shareholder meeting: five minutes.

The company's next general meeting, in May 1971, took place in an atmosphere of increasing tension. Minamata victims and their supporters grew increasingly frustrated as their lawsuit dragged through the courts. Chisso, meanwhile, stood as resolute as ever, and came to its stockholders' meeting prepared to do battle.

In a replay of the November meeting, the protesters were met at the door by a menacing line of guards, *sōkaiya*, and members of local ultra-nationalist gangs, and were again shouted down. The meeting lasted twelve minutes.

Outraged by the abrupt conclusion this time, the protesters

> remained at the site, arguing fiercely with company shareholders and *sōkaiya.* Suddenly, about twenty guards stormed into the hall and attacked the Minamata contingent, smearing the green seats of the auditorium with blood. Within two minutes they were gone, leaving behind a shaken and battered group, and sending one badly injured youth to a hospital emergency room.
>
> Police until now had stood by, letting Chisso and the protesters fight it out. But such a blatant attack—with wide press coverage and serious injuries—prompted a raid on the offices of Chisso's specially hired guard services. That Chisso's guardsmen had strong underworld ties should not have surprised the police. The *yakuza*-dominated security companies were a suspect lot, frequently called on by firms to harass striking workers during labor disputes.
>
> Chisso's next shareholders' meeting took place in November 1971. This time, both sides came prepared. Nearly 300 protesters, each owning one share of Chisso stock, slept on the concrete outside the convention hall the night before. At about 8:15 A.M., company supporters, including a mass of *sōkaiya* and what one newspaper described as "18 members of a local rightist group," were allowed into the hall through two back doors. The main entrance, where the protesters stood assembled, remained locked. As Chisso corporate officials arrived, skirmishes broke out between protesters and the company's hired musclemen barring the entrance. Some 200 riot police moved in and broke up the fighting, evicting protesters from the entrance and making a number of arrests.
>
> Meanwhile, inside the building, the handful of protesters who had made it in were unable to introduce motions, or even be recognized by the chair. Frustrated, they threw their bodies together and stormed the stage, shouting "Murderer!" and "You swallow mercury!" The burly troops of *sōkaiya* lining the front rows responded, and as in a lopsided football scrimmage, the activists were violently thrown back.
>
> Shielded from the battle below him, the chairman called for a vote on the company's audit report, and a "unanimous" approval echoed through the hall. With no more items on the agenda, the proceedings were promptly adjourned. Total duration of Chisso's forty-fourth shareholders' meeting: nine minutes.

As Kaplan and Dubro explain, the protesters had organized a "One Share" movement, in which they each bought a share of Chisso and attended its shareholders' meeting. The company usually had at most 120 shareholders attend its annual meetings, but for the 1970 meeting expected 1000. Although it reserved a larger hall for the occasion, 300 shareholders were unable to enter it. At the beginning of the meeting, plaintiff Gotō shouted out his motions, waved his arms, and scattered various leaflets on which he had printed his motions. The company ignored him and concluded the meeting quickly. Twenty-six shareholders moved to rescind the annual meeting on the grounds that the procedures were illegal and grossly unfair. The District Court found for the plaintiffs.

JUDGMENT:

The decision of the District Court is affirmed.

REASONS:

[The District Court opinion, as incorporated into the High Court opinion, held:] From the time motions were introduced at the general shareholders' meeting until they were decided, there was an almost constant uproar. Yet there were no microphones or other equipment in the hall by which shareholders could communicate with the chairman. Because defendant Chisso personnel prevented plaintiff Gotō from climbing onto the stage, Gotō went directly below it. There, near the place where the chairman and his assistants (*e.g.*, officers and executive personnel) sat, Gotō shouted that he wanted to introduce motions to amend, held leaflets printed with his motions in his right hand, and waved the leaflets around in a manner visible from the stage. From these facts, it is reasonable to hold that Gotō introduced his motions. Furthermore, from [evidence omitted], we conclude that the company expected that shareholders might raise questions and introduce motions, and that the chairman may well have been aware of Gotō's actions. Even if he did not notice those actions, the other executive personnel should have noticed them and told the chairman. Chisso officers had an obligation to clarify what Gotō wanted and to take measures to deal with his demands. As noted above, Gotō attempted to introduce his motions before the chairman had concluded the meeting. Because Chisso personnel made no effort to deal with Gotō's demands when the circumstances were such that it was possible for them (including the chairman) to have noticed his actions, we are forced to conclude that the measures they took at the present meeting were grossly unfair—regardless of whether Chisso personnel *actually* noticed Gotō.

[On this point, the High Court held:] Therefore, we hold that there existed an important defect in the steps taken at the meeting, especially in the failure to recognize appellee Gotō's motions to amend.

[The District Court opinion, as incorporated into (and amended by) the High Court opinion, further held:] As noted above, only about 1110 shareholders were able to enter the hall, and about 300 were kept out. It is clear that these excluded shareholders could not ask questions, make motions, or otherwise discuss the proposals or exercise their participatory rights. Chisso had a duty to give all shareholders who sought to attend the shareholders' general meeting an opportunity to exercise their participatory rights. Even if physical circumstances made that impossible in this case on the scheduled date, Chisso does not escape responsibility. It should instead have noted explicitly that some shareholders could not enter the hall and have taken action to transmit their opinions. Alternatively, it should have changed the date of the annual meeting, extended it, or continued it at a later date. Chisso was required to make certain that the excluded shareholders had an opportunity to participate. The law has as its purpose the recognition of shareholder participatory rights through such means. Because these measures were possible but not taken, we conclude that the meeting violated that statutory purpose.

Questions and Discussion Points

1. *Function of* sōkaiya: Are the *sōkaiya* providing firms with a wanted (if perhaps antisocial) service, or are they blackmailing the managers of the firm? How would one tell the difference?

Some *sōkaiya* argue that they serve a policing function that in fact benefits other shareholders and society as a whole. Is there any basis for this claim, or is it simply a self-serving justification?

2. *Abolish annual meetings?*: Suppose the *sōkaiya* are blackmailing the firms. If annual meetings were abolished, would that end the blackmail? What would you do if you were a blackmailing *sōkaiya* and the annual meetings disappeared?

3. *Position of dissident shareholders*: Suppose the *sōkaiya* are providing firms with a service. Why would managers want the service? Why would they care whether shareholders ask questions at the meetings? How much would a manager pay to avoid having to respond to shareholder questions at the annual meeting? Suppose you were a dissident shareholder. If annual meetings were abolished, what would you do? If a shareholder has serious doubts about the managers of his or her firm, what should the shareholder do?

4. *Aims of legislation*: What do the questions above suggest about the 1981 amendments aimed at controlling *sōkaiya*?

Other than the embarrassment of disrupted meetings, what is the source of pressure on executives from shareholders that leads some companies to resort to the *sōkaiya*? What alternatives are currently available to shareholders? Publicizing information about company practices can discipline executives by affecting the price of their company's shares. Is such discipline relevant to Japanese corporate governance? Such questions of the relationships among the interests of Japanese executives, the options open to dissident shareholders, and the impact of the equities market should be kept in mind when considering the debate between T. Boone Pickens and the management of Koito Manufacturing K.K.

III. The Pickens-Koito Dispute

A. Competing views of the firm's constituency

In April of 1989 it was revealed that U.S. investor T. Boone Pickens had, through his Boone Company, acquired approximately 20% of the issued and outstanding shares of Koito Manufacturing K.K., a company that makes automobile lighting systems, primarily for supply to Toyota Motor K.K. There followed a highly publicized dispute between Pickens and the management of Koito.

T. BOONE PICKENS, SECRETS KOITO HOPED TO HIDE BY KEEPING ME OFF ITS BOARD*

The Wall Street Journal

March 28, 1990

As the largest shareholder of one of the major suppliers of Toyota, I have been learning first hand just how Japan's *keiretsu* (kay-ret-su) system operates, and the threat these interlocking relationships among corporations and their suppliers, distributors, bankers and insurers pose to America's free market.

A year ago, my investment company, Boone Co., bought a 20% interest in Koito Manufacturing Co., which makes auto lighting systems primarily for Toyota. We have since increased our stake to 26%.

We purchased the Koito stock to share in the long-term growth and management of a Japanese company. We had no intentions of taking over Koito, which is virtually impossible anyway, because between 60% and 65% of Koito's stock is locked up by Toyota's *keiretsu.* (Toyota itself owns 19% of Koito; Nissan Motor, 5.9%; Matsushita Electric, 5.3%; Nippon Mutual Life, 4.1%; Dai-Ichi Mutual Life, 3.3%; Matsushita Real Estate, 2.5%; Japan Securities Finance, 2.3%; and Mitsubishi Bank, Sumitomo Bank and Dai-Ichi Kangyo Bank each own 1.5%.)

All we asked for as Koito's major shareholder was four seats on the 20-member Koito board of directors. We also asked for detailed financial records of the company, a right afforded by Japanese law to any shareholders who own 10%. Both requests have been repeatedly refused. Boone Co. has now filed suit in Tokyo District Court for the financial information.

Koito's management could always outvote us on the board. So, why don't they want me? The only answer I can figure is that they have something to hide. They don't want me or any outsider to see the inner workings of their cartel.

For example, we have reason to believe that Toyota forces Koito to restrict its profit margin when Toyota wants to increase its profits. (This may reveal a great deal about how Toyota has built up its incredible cash position: Toyota reportedly has reserves of $25 billion in liquid assets, which puts the company at a decided advantage in world-wide auto manufacturing competition.) We also believe that some of Koito's top managers, most of whom are former Toyota employees, enjoy certain benefits that they would find quite embarrassing if revealed to their workers. For example, Koito's president—a 31-year Toyota veteran—enjoys a $1 million country club membership purchased by the company and lives in a beautiful house on the club grounds.

In the Japanese press, there have been reports that if we do succeed in getting on Koito's board, Toyota will cut off purchases from the company. Managers of other auto parts suppliers have complained anonymously in the Japanese press about their *keiretsu*'s dictatorial ways.

The Japanese claim their *keiretsu* system is deeply embedded in their culture

*From T. Boone Pickens, "Secrets Koito Hoped to Hide by Keeping Me off its Board." This article appeared in *The Wall Street Journal,* Issue of March 28, 1990.

and history. To me and a lot of other businessmen around the world who have come up against the *keiretsu* system, they look and act just like old-fashioned cartels. These cartels permit Japanese corporate managers to develop their famous "long-term" growth and market domination strategies. With approximately 65% to 75% of a company's stock secured by fellow members of a *keiretsu*, corporate managers don't have to worry about responding to the wishes of shareholders.

When I criticized the *keiretsu* system in a recent speech to the Japan Society in New York, someone asked how I could disagree with an economic system that has been so efficient and successful. My response was that as an economic system, indentured servitude also was very efficient and successful. It was also wrong.

Their cartels force Japanese consumers to pay more for the goods they produce than foreigners do. A Toyota car costs $15,000 more in Japan than it does in the U.S. A Sony television costs two and one-half times as much in Japan as in the U.S.

Criticism of the *keiretsu* system cannot be dismissed as "Japan bashing." Several recent economic studies, by what cannot be considered anti-Japanese groups, have focused on these cartels as the root of the world's trade problems with Japan. Even the Japanese press and some government officials have started to criticize the cartels' domination of the Japanese economy.

An October 1989 study by the Organization for Economic Cooperation and Development called the *keiretsu* system a major impediment to world trade and economic competition. A similar study released at the same time by the Institute for International Economics in Washington points out that Japanese manufacturers in the U.S. tend to buy more from their traditional Japanese suppliers, while European manufacturers have an open competitive situation with their suppliers in the U.S.

But the *keiretsu* system's final victim may be Japan itself. The Japanese stock market is highly inflated. Since most of the corporate stock is locked up by the *keiretsu*, Japanese shares trade at price-to-earnings ratios 10 times higher than American corporate shares. The Dow Jones industrial average would be 25,000 if American companies traded at the same multiples.

Meanwhile, the average dividend yield on Japanese stocks is less than one-half of 1%. To get to a 3% yield, the American average, Japanese stock prices would have to fall 84%. The spreading realization among international investors that the Japanese stock market is overvalued has a lot to do with its recent volatility.

I am not opposed to Japanese investment in the U.S. I am opposed to Japanese cartels in our markets. If the Japanese are to continue to invest in the U.S., the *keiretsu* system must be dismantled, just as American monopolies were. Until the Japanese lift their foreign investment restrictions, we should consider the reciprocity legislation now pending in Congress. The U.S. would then have the power to adopt restrictions similar to those Americans are facing in Japan.

TAKAO MATSUURA, HOW A JAPANESE FIRM FOILED T. BOONE PICKENS*

The San Francisco Chronicle

January 8, 1990

[Koito's president, Takao Matsuura, offered his own perspective on Pickens and his assault on the Japanese company:]

June 29 was the longest day of my life. Texas takeover artist T. Boone Pickens had just acquired 20 percent of the shares in my firm, Koito Manufacturing Co., Japan's leading automotive lighting maker. That day he showed up at our stockholders' meeting demanding three seats on the board of directors.

Pickens later called it the "most unusual shareholders' meeting" he had ever attended. It was for me, too.

The first hint of trouble came two years ago. One day in July 1987, my administrative manager, Tamotsu Aoyama, pointed out that since May, Koito stocks had risen from $4.13 per share, where they had been for some time, to $4.82. More than 1 million Koito shares were being traded daily, he said.

I saw no cause for alarm but, just to be on the safe side, I asked Aoyama to find out which brokerage firm was acting on behalf of the speculator.

Koito had just recovered from the recession caused by the strong yen, which had nearly doubled in value against the dollar since 1985. Orders were picking up. "Investors have re-evaluated our performance and that's pushed up the value of our stocks," I said optimistically.

But Koito shares climbed past $6.89 and continued to rise. By December 1987, they had hit $11.37. We were either in the midst of a takeover bid or someone was trying to "greenmail" us—force Koito to buy back the stock at the higher price.

I immediately set up a task force under my personal direction to deal with the acquisition attempt. There were about a dozen of us, including vice presidents, senior managing directors, finance executives, company lawyers and underwriters. Our first meeting was December 17. In early 1988, task force members visited large shareholders and asked them not to sell Koito stock.

But, the question was, who was raiding us? * * *

On Feb. 15, 1988, we finally learned the raider's identity. Azabu Jidosha K.K., an auto importer, called requesting a meeting. That afternoon, I sent three executives to see Kitaro Watanabe, Azabu Jidosha's president.

"We bought the Koito stock to speculate with," Watanabe told the trio bluntly. "The Azabu Jidosha financial group owns 23 million shares, and a friend of mine has 17 million." Then without batting an eyelash, he added, "Do you have anything to say to your largest shareholder?"

When my deputies reported back, I didn't understand Watanabe's question. The meaning soon became clear. On February 23, Watanabe called Aoyama, offer-

*From Takao Matsuura, "How a Japanese Firm Foiled T. Boone Pickens," Japan Translation Series Staff, The Asia Foundation. This article appeared in *The San Francisco Chronicle* on January 8, 1990. Reprinted by permission of the Japan Translation Series Staff, The Asia Foundation.

ing to resell Koito 20 million shares at $19.37 each. Aoyama replied tersely that Watanabe should sell the shares where he bought them—on the stock market.

Watanabe has a reputation for backdoor wheeling and dealing. In fact, his direct approach to Koito seemed out of character. The market value of our equities was then $17. Had we taken the bait, Azabu Jidosha would have bled us dry. No management in its right mind would fall for such a scam.

Three months passed. Then on May 25, Watanabe showed up at our Tokyo office. He told Executive Vice President Junsuke Kato, "If Koito doesn't want the shares, get Toyota Motor to buy them." Kato gave him a polite but firm "no."

That was the last we heard from Watanabe. I made no effort to contact him. Later I heard rumors that he had gone to the United States to unload the stock. * * *

[Then], on March 31, Aoyama burst into my office, his face pale and taut. "Our stock transfer agent telephoned to say Boone Co. has just acquired 32 million Koito shares. If it's true, Boone now has 20.2 percent of our stock. That makes him our biggest shareholder."

"Boone?" I said quizzically. "As in T. Boone Pickens," Aoyama replied. "The takeover artist."

Pulling myself together, I decided there was not time for hesitation. I contacted Nishimura & Sanada, a law firm known for its expertise in mergers and acquisitions. They agreed to take the case.

On April 10, I received a letter from Pickens requesting a meeting. I reserved a suite at a hotel near our Tokyo head office and, together with Aoyama and two lawyers, met the Texan there on April 20. He was accompanied by Sidney L. Tassin, his vice president in charge of finance, and two other Boone officials.

My first impression of Pickens was of a sharp, cool operator. He smiled only once, when we first shook hands. We sat down on opposite sides of the table. Pickens made the first move. The Boone Co.'s philosophy, he said, is to put the stockholders' interests first. By that I supposed he meant that Koito should comply with any Boone Co. demands.

"In our case," I replied, "we have to consider the interests of our employees, our clients and the local communities where we operate, as well as the shareholders."

Vice President Tassin broached the subject of board representation. The request took me by surprise. In Japan, the first meeting is usually reserved for introductions and getting to know each other. "If you send us a formal written proposal, we will consider it," I said.

The meeting lasted about an hour. Three days later, Pickens' letter arrived asking for three seats on the board. I responded in writing that we thought Pickens should tell us what arrangements he had with Watanabe for repurchase of the shares or other financial guarantees.

On May 20, about 160 auto parts manufacturers under contract to Toyota gathered at a golf course in Toyota City, Aichi Prefecture. We meet on the links annually to socialize and swap information. I had momentarily forgotten about Pickens and played a good game, working off some of the stress from April.

At the party after the game, Shoichiro Toyoda, president of Toyota Motor, buttonholed me. "What are you going to do about Boone?" he asked.

"Boone Co. doesn't know anything about our operations," I said with conviction. "I don't see how I can honor the request." That was the only time I ever discussed the issue with Toyota's top management.

For weeks before the annual meeting, trade negotiators, investors, and the public on both sides of the Pacific had anticipated Pickens' intervention. Media overkill turned his quest for board seats into a *cause célèbre*. The tension in the hall of Tokyo's Shinagawa Prince Hotel that day was palpable. * * *

I took the chair in the Prince Hotel's conference room at 9:57 a.m. Including 20 board members, there were 231 people present, twice the usual number.

Pickens sat facing me in the second row. Next to him was a lawyer, who also was an interpreter.

I brought the assembly to order at 10 a.m. sharp. The auditor certified that the financial statement for the year ahead was correct, and I reported on Koito's overall performance. I then turned to the 40 questions Boone Co. had submitted in advance. Three Koito senior executives responded to each of the items.

Next, at a little past 11 a.m., we opened the floor to questions. Pickens and several others immediately raised their hands. I promptly recognized Pickens. I had decided earlier to confront the issue squarely and let the man have his say.

A hush fell over the assembly. Suddenly, someone grabbed the microphone and began bellowing. Another man jumped to his feet and glowered at me. I supposed they were "*sōkaiya*," professional stockholders who own a few shares and often disrupt shareholders' meetings.

Pickens looked surprised. "May I ask a question?" he said. Then, looking nervously at a man standing behind him, he sat down.

I was determined to let Pickens speak. "Silence!" I yelled in my most stentorian voice. Ending the meeting without hearing Pickens would only add to the acrimony over U.S.-Japan trade and investment practices. Koito would be accused of discriminating against foreign investors. I could just see the headlines.

The confrontation with the "*sōkaiya*" lasted only about two minutes, but to me it seemed like more than an hour. When Pickens finally took the floor and began asking questions in a loud, clear voice, I sagged in my chair with relief.

The questions were what we had expected. But I was surprised when he moved to admit himself and two other Boone Co. executives to the board of directors. We knew next to nothing about the other two. None of them, including Pickens, had any experience in the automobile industry or international business.

Pickens was new and outnumbered. With only 20 percent of the stock, he must have known he would lose. Predictably, the motion was rejected.

The request was probably for dramatic effect. Rebuffed, Pickens could later say Koito overrode its biggest shareholder because he was not Japanese. In a recent statement, he accuses me of having a "closed mind" and representing "the cartel mentality that dominates business in Japan."

Pickens was also incensed that Koito had hired private financial advisors to assess Boone Co. When an unknown investor suddenly acquires a 20 percent stake in our company, we want to know with whom we are dealing.

The American was on the floor for about 30 minutes. When he concluded, I asked him if all his questions had been answered. I wanted to be sure that he had the opportunity he wanted to make his points. He said yes.

After more talk from "*sōkaiya*," the session finally adjourned at 1:17 p.m. It was one of the longest I can remember, lasting more than three hours. In Japan, as in the United States, most shareholders' meetings end in 15 or 20 minutes.

But we accomplished our main goal: to let Pickens speak. No one can accuse us of breaking our own rules.

On July 11, Pickens took his case to Washington. Before the Senate's Commerce, Science and Transportation Committee, he characterized Koito's rejection as symbolic of Japan's closed economic structure. Unless Japan makes serious attempts to open its markets, he said, its "continued economic prosperity will undoubtedly suffer—if not of stagnation from within, perhaps of retaliation from without. . . . Investment between our two countries is not a two-way street." * * *

At the committee hearing, Pickens also criticized many large stockholders for giving Koito proxy to cast their votes at the annual meeting. That charge is without foundation. All 47 leading corporate investors were represented by senior executives. Only one firm voted by proxy.

Questions and Discussion Points

1. *Conception of the role of shareholders*: What are Pickens' and Matsuura's respective conceptions of the role of shareholders in public corporations? To what extent is Pickens making a claim for vindication of legal rights and to what extent is he making a policy-based criticism of the Japanese corporate system?

2. *Pickens' demand for seats on the board of directors*: What is the legal basis for Pickens' demand for four seats on the board of directors of Koito?

Matsuura criticizes Pickens for having no experience in the auto parts supply industry or in international business in general. Is this a valid reason for rejecting his membership on the board? What kinds of expertise are desirable on a board of directors? Is the kind of "experience" that Matsuura stresses experience in auto parts, or is there a broader institutional and personal aspect to his concerns?

3. *Views of other shareholders*: Are other shareholders of Koito likely to be pleased or upset by Pickens' acquisition?

B. Disclosure requirements and Pickens' abandoned bid

In the June 1990 shareholder meeting, Pickens and management of Koito again clashed. Pickens and 32 other American shareholders (whose way Pickens paid from the U.S., according to the Japanese press) were cordoned off, given only cursory responses by Koito management to their questions, and heckled repeatedly by *sōkaiya*. After three hours they stormed out of the meeting.

Pickens called the meeting "a farce." Koito management countered that if Pickens were knowledgeable about Japanese shareholders' meetings, he could have avoided misunderstanding, and hinted that the *sōkaiya* might actually have been hired by Pickens in order to create the impression that he was being mistreated.

In 1990 amendments were made to the tender offer provisions of the Securities Exchange Act (discussed further in Part B), which are similar to the U.S. tender offer statute, the Williams Act. Among the modifications were new disclosure requirements for those holding more than 5% of the shares of publicly traded companies.

Throughout the ordeal, Koito management had been calling upon Pickens to disclose the nature of his ownership of the shares in Koito, as it was rumored that he was merely the nominal owner and that Watanabe had retained actual control over the shares. The disclosure filings did in fact reveal that one of Watanabe's companies had lent Pickens the funds to purchase the Koito shares and that the shares were the collateral for the loan.

Following many accounts in newspapers about the loan from Watanabe, Pickens announced his intention to return the shares in Koito to Watanabe and published the following article.

T. BOONE PICKENS, THE HECK WITH JAPANESE BUSINESS–WHY I'M NOT INTERESTED IN TRYING TO COMPETE IN A CARTEL SYSTEM*

The Washington Post

C1, April 28, 1991

Okay, Toyota, okay, Koito, I give up. After more than two years as the largest shareholder in Koito Manufacturing, it has become clear to me that you will never grant my request for representation on Koito's board. And I'm not interested in being a 26-percent owner in a company in which I have no influence.

As an oil man I've drilled my share of dry holes, but I've always prided myself in knowing when to plug them. I have decided to sell Boone Co.'s stake in Koito back to its former owner. Koito is known as one of the world's premier auto-lighting manufacturers and I had hoped to make it still more profitable. But now I realize that I can't fight Japan's cartel system that keeps Koito—and many others like it—captive.

I won't realize a profit on the deal, but I have learned an important lesson. It is this: as good as it is, Japan's industry is not necessarily smarter, more agile and more efficient than ours—it is simply based on business practices that America spurned almost a century ago when we outlawed trusts, monopolies and cartels.

*From T. Boone Pickens, "The Heck With Japanese Business—Why I'm Not Interested In Trying to Compete in a Cartel System," *The Washington Post*, April 28, 1991, at C1. Reprinted by permission.

We never said those practices didn't work—the question was, work for whom and at what cost?

* * * Cartels may be good for business, but ultimately they limit consumer choices and increase prices. Unfortunately, since the competitors have to be squeezed out first—and while the squeezing is going on, prices often fall sharply—consumers are the last to recognize what is happening.

* * * We'd requested meetings with Koito's major shareholders and other prominent business and government leaders to present our case. Tokyo's airport must have been busy that day, because every one of them claimed to be out of town. The few Japanese businessmen who met with us led us through narrow alleys to basement pubs of the Roppongi district where they shared their experiences fighting *keiretsu* from within Japan.

One brave Japanese businessman, who wrote to me supporting Boone Co.'s efforts, later testified before the U.S. House Judiciary Committee. Positioned behind a screen to protect his identity, he told how his auto parts business started out making parts for a number of companies. One company gradually became his largest customer and offered to "improve" his supply process, sending quality control officers, then auditors, then board directors. Eventually his company was held captive—its profit margins set by the *keiretsu* along with every other facet of the business. Asked why he didn't break away, he explained, "No one else would buy from me. All my family wealth is in my company. It would be economic suicide." Even more alarming for our own economy is that his story is similar to one told to me by a Chicago manufacturer. His company, having previously sold parts in Japan with some success, approached a large Japanese auto "transplant" company in the Midwest in hopes of securing a contract. The Japanese company required the American to enter into a joint venture with one of its Japanese suppliers. Quickly the plant was overloaded with four times the expected orders from the transplant. This may appear at first blush to be a high-class problem, but the Japanese company had put him right where they wanted him. He either had to put in new capital or go bankrupt. Now that he had been sucked in, the cram-down could be enforced and his profit margin shrank to a pittance. "Get out," a Japanese friend told him. "This is how they work. In the end they control you, because you can't get out without suffering economic disaster."

Questions and Discussion Points

1. *The relationship between Pickens and Watanabe*: Why did Pickens and Watanabe enter into the arrangement that they did? Why did they end it?

2. *Disclosure requirements*: Was the agreement between Pickens and Watanabe a legitimate concern of Koito management? Of other Koito shareholders? Of investors who might become Koito shareholders?

3. *Cram-downs: U.S. and Japan*: Compare the concerns expressed by Pickens in the last paragraph of his second article with the Tokyo Bed and other cases discussed in *The Daily Yomiuri* article in Chapter 1. What's the difference?

4. *Cartelization*: Where is the cartel to which Pickens refers?

PART B: Mergers and Acquisitions

In Part B, we first consider the incidence of takeovers in Japan. We then turn to several explanations for the apparently low level of hostile acquisitions. After exploring the legal provisions governing such acquisitions, we conclude with two cases on takeover defenses.

I. The Incidence of Takeovers

HIROSHI OKUMURA, STOCK CORNERING, TAKEOVERS AND TENDER OFFERS: THE ECONOMICS OF STOCK ACQUISITIONS*

Foreword (1989)

Up to now there have been almost no hostile takeovers in Japan, and never once has one of the country's big businesses been acquired by another company, as frequently happens in the United States. Leveraged buyouts have not been used as a takeover tool, nor have companies been acquired for the purpose of selling off their assets. Even takeover bids have been few and far between. * * *

Mergers, by contrast, are relatively common. Those reported to the Fair Trade Commission rose notably during the 1960s, eventually reaching 1,000 a year, and have since remained at that level, albeit with some fluctuation from year to year. Yet even here there are distinctive Japanese patterns. Most mergers are between small or medium-sized firms capitalized at less than ¥1 billion. Since around 1970, when the Yawata and Fuji steelmakers joined to form the gigantic Nippon Steel, mergers of big companies have been tapering off. These major deals, moreover, generally take place between parent companies and their subsidiaries or between two companies in the same corporate group. Such mergers rarely have a major impact on the economy. * * *

*From Hiroshi Okumura, *Kaishime, Nottori, TOB: Kabushiki Shutoku no Keizaigaku (Stock Cornering, Takeovers and Tender Offers: The Economics of Stock Acquisitions)* (Tokyo: Shakai Shisosha, 1989) (translation by Yanagida Nomura & Akai), at Foreword. Reprinted by permission.

II. Reasons for the Low Level of Hostile Acquisitions

A. Ideology of the firm

JAMES C. ABEGGLEN, WHY JAPAN MISTRUSTS MERGERS*

Mergers & Acquisitions 16-18 (Winter 1983)

Why are there so few acquisitions in Japan? Shareholders in Japan surely enjoy making profits through capital gains as much as do shareholders in other countries. We know that Japanese companies are as interested in rapid and low-risk diversification as are companies in other countries. And Japanese companies undoubtedly have businesses they would like to divest, just as companies in other countries do.

From my experience as a business consultant in Japan, I would say the answer lies mainly in the areas of personnel and human relations. At a very general level, it might be argued that in Japan the concept of The Company is different than it is in the West. That is, the Japanese company is seen as integrally including the people who compose it. Therefore, the purchase or sale of a business or company in Japan has the flavor of the purchase or sale of people. It is, in short, considered immoral. The owners and managers of the company have certain unstated, implicit, yet strong obligations to all of the members of the company.

In contrast (and with some overstatement), it might be said that The Company in the West is seen as a collection of assets: facilities, technology, brand identity and even human resources. These assets have a market value. If buyer and seller agree on the value of the assets, they may then be traded or sold.

Whereas most American managers believe that their companies belong to shareholders—a view supported in corporate charters and state and federal laws—the Japanese view is different. The Japanese manager believes that the shareholders provided the capital that made the company possible, and therefore are entitled to a return on that capital. However, ultimately the Japanese company exists for the employees, to ensure their well-being and their future. Thus, sale of the company is not a decision for the shareholders but is rather a decision for the entire workforce of the company. (Similarly, unusual profits in Japan are seldom paid out in the form of a higher or extra dividend, but rather in extra wages and bonuses.)

---

*From James C. Abegglen, "Why Japan Mistrusts Mergers," *Mergers & Acquisitions*, Winter 1983, at 16-18. Reprinted by permission.

B. The prevalence of cross-shareholding

HIROSHI OKUMURA, STOCK CORNERING, TAKEOVERS AND TENDER OFFERS: THE ECONOMICS OF STOCK ACQUISITIONS*

29-30 (1989)

Why do so few takeovers occur in Japan? Why are there so many instances of Japanese-style stock cornering? The answer to these questions is found in the practice of cross-shareholding. This is a system whereby each company seeks to secure shareholder stability by placing large blocks of its stock in the hands of friendly companies. These so-called stable shareholders include the members of the company's corporate group and the banks and firms the company does business with. * * * Nearly all the presidents of listed companies consider it to be a part of their duties to seek out stable shareholders.

When a majority of the outstanding stock of a company is in the hands of friends who agree not to trade it, the firm cannot be taken over either through cornering operations or through a tender offer. At the same time, the company can ask its friendly shareholders for help if it needs to regain control over the stock held by a greenmailer. The greenmailer cannot hope to ever acquire a majority stake in the company, but an equity position of 20% or 30% will give it the right to inspect company books and make other bothersome demands. The mediation of politicians allied with the greenmailer can also cause trouble. The result is that targeted companies prefer to reacquire their stock and place it with their friends. Japanese-style cornering has become rampant as a way of exploiting this practice. Without these stable shareholders, companies would find it much harder to buy back their stock.

1. Development of cross-shareholding

JEFF USCHER, UNFRIENDLY TAKEOVERS: A RETURN TO TRADITION**

Hoare Govett Investment Strategy Comment

Oct. 14, 1985

During the period 1949-1953, many companies sold shares formerly registered in the names of their directors and employees to other business corporations which were, more often than not, fellow members of the now defunct *zaibatsu*. This trend was accelerated by the "Yowa Real Estate incident" shortly after the reopening of the Tokyo Stock Exchange in 1949.

---

*From Hiroshi Okumura, *Kaishime, Nottori, TOB: Kabushiki Shutoku no Keizaigaku* (*Stock Cornering, Takeovers and Tender Offers: The Economics of Stock Acquisitions*) (Tokyo: Shakai Shisōsha, 1989) (translation by Yanagida Nomura & Akai), at 29-30. Reprinted by permission.

**From Jeff Uscher, "Unfriendly Takeovers: A Return to Tradition," *Hoare Govett Investment Strategy Comment* (Oct. 14, 1985). Reprinted by permission.

The Mitsubishi *zaibatsu* had come in for particularly rough treatment by the Occupation authorities. For example, Mitsubishi Corporation was broken up into 120 separate companies (the company had regrouped into its prewar/present form by 1953) while all of the Mitsubishi group's land assets were divided between two real estate companies. One company, Yowa Real Estate, held all of the Mitsubishi land in the Marunouchi district of central Tokyo, the very heart of the Mitsubishi group. One individual who had managed to save some of his personal assets at the end of the war, Mr. Kuniro Fujizuna, was able to buy 35% of the shares outstanding in Yowa Real Estate within weeks of the reopening of the stock exchange, literally holding the entire Mitsubishi group hostage. After protracted negotiations with various Mitsubishi group representatives, Mr. Fujizuna sold his shares back to the group for an undisclosed sum. The "Yowa Real Estate incident" convinced Japanese managers of the importance of stable shareholders which resulted in the system of mutual corporate shareholdings that is so familiar today.

One of the most aggressive Japanese corporate raiders was Toyota Motor, which established shareholdings in most of its extensive group of auto parts suppliers during the period 1966-1972. Toyota did not actually have to gain a majority shareholding in order to subjugate another company's management. Toyota became the largest shareholder in Hino Motors with a 6.7% stake in October 1966 (Toyota now owns 11.3% of the shares outstanding) and bought a 5.74% stake (now 14.7%) in Daihatsu in November 1967. Toyota was able to offer the managers of these companies the ability to survive as nominally independent, small automobile assemblers in an increasingly competitive market.

Although there was little resistance to Toyota in the cases of Hino and Daihatsu, Toyota fought a losing battle with the Mitsubishi group for control of Japan Storage Battery during 1971-1972, attempted to prise Tokiko from the Hitachi group in 1971, nearly wrested Ichiko Kogyo from Nissan in 1972 and actually succeeded in fighting off MEI, Nissan and Sanko Steamship to gain control of Koito Seisakusho in 1972. During this period, Toyota also established major shareholdings in Kansai Paint, Futaba Sangyo and Toyo Radiator. Very few of these moves were made with the prior knowledge let alone the consent of the takeover target. Evidence of past battles may be seen in the list of major shareholders of Kayaba Kogyo (Toyota 11.3%, Nissan 9.5%) and Akebono Brake (Bendix 15.2%, Nissan 14.7%, Toyota 14.5%).

Banks have also used shareholdings to cement relationships with their customers, even if the customer feels that the relationship is not in its best interests. A case in point is Sumitomo Bank's attempt to take over C. Itoh and merge it with Sumitomo Corporation in 1972-1973. C. Itoh had always had close relations with the Sumitomo group and, at the time, Sumitomo bank was the largest shareholder with a stake of some eight per cent. The problem with Sumitomo Bank's plan was that C. Itoh management felt in the event of a merger, it would not be able to maintain its independence from Sumitomo Corporation's managers. While all of this was going on, Dai Ichi Bank (now Dai Ichi Kangyo Bank) had lost its group trading company, Nissho, in a merger with Iwai Sangyo of the Sanwa Bank group to form today's Nissho-Iwai. Dai Ichi Bank was the third largest shareholder in C.

Itoh and was not about to lose yet another trading company to a corporate raider.

As Sumitomo Bank increased its shareholding in C. Itoh, Dai Ichi Bank was aggressively buying C. Itoh shares on the market, quickly surpassing the Bank of Tokyo to become the second largest shareholder in the disputed trading firm. On October 1, 1972, Dai Ichi Bank merged with the Kangyo Bank, which happened to be the tenth largest shareholder in C. Itoh, making the new company, Dai Ichi Kangyo Bank, the largest shareholder in C. Itoh and effectively putting an end to Sumitomo Bank's attempt to fully absorb C. Itoh into the Sumitomo group.

As is evident from the examples above, unfriendly takeovers and forced mergers have been largely responsible for the highly developed system of mutual shareholdings and bank centered financial groups we see today. Seen in historical perspective, the destruction of the *zaibatsu* left an economic power vacuum which had to be filled in order to avoid the kind of chaos that could be wrought by astute opportunists such as Mr. Fujizuna. That vacuum was eventually filled by the new economic powerhouses such as the banks and rapidly growing industrial companies such as Toyota. That tradition is being carried on today by aggressive, high technology companies including Minebea and Kyocera.

2. Limitations of the cross-shareholding explanation

J. MARK RAMSEYER, TAKEOVERS IN JAPAN: OPPORTUNISM, IDEOLOGY AND CORPORATE CONTROL*

35 UCLA Law Review 1

21-25 (1987)

In a wide variety of Japanese firms, managers have sought to prevent takeovers by exchanging large portions of their firm's stock with other firms through cross-shareholding agreements. Not infrequently, firms have undertaken the agreements with the implicit or even explicit understanding that neither firm will tender the other's shares in a hostile takeover bid. Indeed, Japanese law reviews occasionally publish "how-to" articles on the subject. The articles describe ways to circumvent the legal limitations on cross-shareholding arrangements and thereby insure the "stability" of a firm's stock. The larger the number of target shares not tendered in an acquisition, of course, the greater the percentage of available shares an acquiror will need to purchase to gain control. The greater the percentage the acquiror must purchase, the higher the premium the acquiror will need to pay.

Unfortunately, revisionist writers eager to avoid culture-based explanations of the corporate control market have occasionally overstated the impact of these cross-shareholding arrangements. "Due to crossholding of shares among Japanese corporations," explains one author, "control of public corporations is generally not for sale. . . ." Yet the cross-shareholding agreements are rarely that effective. First,

*From J. Mark Ramseyer, "Takeovers in Japan: Opportunism, Ideology and Corporate Control," 35 *UCLA Law Review* 1 (1987), at 21-25.

the agreements usually do not apply to a majority of a firm's shares. Accurate estimates of corporate shares held under cross-shareholding arrangements are, of course, impossible to make. The percentage in most cases, however, almost certainly is less than the cross-shareholding percentages of the famed diversified corporate groups. The cross-shareholding in those groups averages approximately twenty percent. Target managers will raise the premium a would-be acquiror will need to pay by putting twenty percent of target stock in the hands of non-tendering shareholders. By taking these steps, however, managers generally will not make a tender offer bid impossible.

Second, if an acquiror initiates a tender offer bid, a firm holding target stock under a cross-shareholding agreement will not necessarily refuse to tender. The managers of such a firm instead face a curious dilemma. To be sure, if shareholding firm S tenders and the acquisition fails, firm S loses both the premium and target T's goodwill, and perhaps suffers a blemish on its reputation in business circles. If firm S does not tender but the acquisition succeeds, however, firm S likewise forgoes the tender offer premium and loses T's (now under the new management of acquiror A) goodwill. And if firm S does tender and the acquisition succeeds, S gains both the premium and the goodwill of the new T management. T's goodwill is important even if S is not a business partner of T, for T is a shareholder of S. The loss of T's goodwill thus destroys the stability of S's own stock. Moreover, there is a society-wide prisoner's dilemma to the tender/hold back choice: The shareholders of one firm may be able to tender without destroying the general effectiveness of cross-shareholding agreements. Yet if all firms suspect that all others may behave opportunistically in a tender offer, then few will adhere to the terms of any cross-shareholding agreement. Because all managers defect from the cooperative solution, all lose.

As most analysts note, many Japanese firms try to consolidate their relationship with their business partners by holding the partners' stock. Many of these firms apparently would not readily sell their partners' stock to a hostile bidder. As a result, the tendency of Japanese firms to invest in the stock of their partners may likewise raise the cost of hostile takeovers.

Unfortunately, these analysts too often assume that firms would *never* sell the stock of their partners. The analysts make that assumption because they ignore the calculations such firms would need to make to respond to a tender offer bid. In order to decide whether to tender, the shareholding firms must at least implicitly weigh (a) the profitability of their existing business relations with the target, (b) the size of the premium offered, and (c) the likelihood that the takeover will succeed. For example, if shareholder firm A maintains business relations with issuer firm B, A will try to maximize its *total* return from all transactions with B. A's shareholders will expect this of A and A's managers will attempt to do so since they thereby maximize the marginal product they provide the firm (and thus their own compensation). If A obtains a *sub*-market return on its investment in B stock, for instance, A will expect to obtain a *supra*-market return from its other relations with B. Similarly, if A would lose its business with B as a result of a takeover but would earn a premium on its stock, A may still sell its B stock if A could be certain the bid would succeed and the premium offered exceeded the sum of (x) the present value of any *supra*-market profits from its trades with B that A anticipated losing as a result of the takeover and (y) any general (*e.g.*, reputational) losses A would suffer. In fact, however, if the takeover succeeds and Japanese firms are even half as concerned with "personal relationships" as the stereotypes suggest, A may *not* lose its business with B. B now will be under new management and A will have shown its willingness to cooperate with that management. On the other hand, if A did not tender but the takeover nonetheless succeeded, A would have shown an *un*willingness to cooperate with the new management. A could then lose its business with B precisely because A did not tender.

Questions and Discussion Points

1. So why are there few hostile tender offers in Japan?
2. Do shareholders gain or lose in tender offers?
3. Do employees gain or lose (in the long term) from the availability of tender offers?

III. The Law of Acquisitions

A. The tender offer provisions of the Securities Exchange Act

MISAO TATSUTA, PROXY REGULATION, TENDER OFFERS, AND INSIDER TRADING*

Japanese Securities Regulation 159
175-186 (1983)

[I.] Definition

A *kōkai kaitsuke* (tender offer) is defined as a public offer to buy or a public solicitation to sell or exchange share certificates, or such other securities as may be prescribed by Cabinet order, outside the securities market. Thus, cash and exchange offers for outstanding securities are both regulated in the same way.

The Cabinet order brings within this definition any stock certificate, subscription warrant, or convertible debenture issued by a corporation subject to the periodic reporting requirements of the Securities Exchange Law. Accordingly, regulated tender offers are those made in connection with securities issued by listed

*From Misao Tatsuta, "Proxy Regulation, Tender Offers, and Insider Trading," in Louis Loss, Makoto Yazawa & Barbara Banoff, eds., *Japanese Securities Regulation* (Tokyo: University of Tokyo Press, 1983), pp. 159-195, at 175-186. Reprinted, with updates for revisions in tender offer system, by permission of the Japan Securities Research Institute.

corporations, by corporations whose securities are registered as over-the-counter stock with the Japan Securities Dealers Association, and by corporations that have filed a registration statement in connection with a public offering of new or outstanding securities and that are not exempt from the requirement of filing a periodic report.

Tender offers are exempt from regulation if the offeror and its affiliates will acquire beneficial ownership of less than [5] percent of the total shares outstanding[, a 1990 amendment having lowered the percentage triggering the registration requirement from 10 to 5 percent]; if the offer is made for the purpose of redemption of shares; and in such other cases as may be prescribed by ministerial ordinance.

[II.] Disclosure

1. Advance Review

Except for the exempted tender offers mentioned above, a tender offer may not be made unless the offeror has filed a tender offer registration statement with the Minister of Finance and the registration has become effective. [Pursuant to a 1990 amendment, a requirement that the registration be filed ten days before the commencement of the tender offer was abolished. Under the revised system, the tender offeror may purchase shares by taking out a public notice in a national newspaper and filing a registration statement with the Minister of Finance on the day of such public notice. That registration statement becomes effective upon acceptance by the Minister, rather than ten days later, as was the case previously.]

2. Contents of the Registration Statement

The contents of the tender offer registration statement are prescribed by ministerial ordinance. The statement must set forth:

(1) the purpose of the tender offer,
(2) the duration of the offer,
(3) the number of shares to be purchased, and the existence or nonexistence of withdrawal rights,
(4) the offer price,
(5) the amount and the source of the funds,
(6) a description of the offeror and its affiliates, and
(7) the number of shares in the target company held by these persons.

3. Dissemination

Immediately after the tender offer registration statement becomes effective, the offeror must publish, in two or more daily newspapers reporting current affairs, those portions of the registration statement prescribed by Ministry of Finance Ordinance. Any post-effective amendment must also be published. The purpose of the publication requirement is to afford to all shareholders of the target company an opportunity to learn of the offer and its terms and to accept it if they desire. * * *

The offeror must also deliver a written explanation of the tender offer to the target's security holders before the shares are purchased. This explanation corresponds to the prospectus used with a public offering. * * *

4. Notification to the Target

No tender offer may be made unless a copy of the registration statement has been sent to the target company. This requirement of advance notification is similar to that of some U.S. state statutes. However, since the statute does not specify how far in advance notice must be given, notification just before the effective date of the registration statement is sufficient. * * *

* * *

6. Side Deals

Japanese law does not require disclosure of any agreement or understanding between the tender offeror and the target company and its management unless the target's management expresses an opinion on the tender offer. Since management recommendations are not mandatory, such side deals frequently will not be disclosed. * * *

[III.] Substantive Regulation

Japanese law regulates the substantive terms of tender offers, requiring that they conform with the provisions of a Cabinet order with respect to the duration of the offer, the purchase price, withdrawal rights, delivery and liquidation, and other matters considered necessary for the regulation of purchases.

1. Price

The terms of the offering must be uniform. The requirement that the purchase price or exchange ratio be uniform means that it might be illegal to give offerees a choice between cash and a security or between different classes of securities.

The purchase price must be paid without delay after the offer period has expired, and a notice, similar to a sales confirmation, must be transmitted to the tendering shareholders. If tenders are not accepted, the tendered share certificates must be returned as quickly as possible.

2. Duration

A tender offer may not begin until after an announcement has been published. The offer must be open for at least 20 days and for no longer than [60] days from the date the public announcement is made. [The 1990 amendments extended the maximum time that an offer might remain open from 30 to 60 days.] * * *

3. Withdrawal

A shareholder who has accepted a purchase offer, or who has offered to sell, may revoke the contract or withdraw the offer[, following the 1990 amendments, at any time during the tender offer period.]

On the other hand, the tender offeror may not revoke the contract or withdraw the offer, unless it has reserved the right to do so if (1) the business or financial condition of the target company is subject to a change of circumstances that would make it very difficult to attain the objectives of the offer and (2) such a change has in fact taken place. This provision restricts an offeror's waiver of the tender, and it appears that a tender offer may not be revoked on the basis of the doctrine of frustration, unless the above-mentioned conditions have been expressly attached to the offer.

[Pursuant to the 1990 amendments, however, the tender offeror is authorized to freely change the terms of purchase except where the change would be prejudicial to the interests of shareholders who have subscribed. Prohibited prejudicial changes would include a cut in the purchase price, a reduction in the number of shares to be purchased, etc.]

B. Other legal considerations

J. MARK RAMSEYER, TAKEOVERS IN JAPAN: OPPORTUNISM, IDEOLOGY AND CORPORATE CONTROL*

35 UCLA Law Review 1

(1987)

Mergers Law

To effect a merger in Japan, the managers of the two companies first conclude a merger agreement (Com. Code § 408(a)). If the boards of directors recommend that the merger proceed (*i.e.*, call a shareholders' meeting to consider the contract, Com. Code § 231), the shareholders of both corporations must then ratify that decision by a two-thirds vote (Com. Code §§ 408(c), 343). The meeting must be attended by representatives (including proxy holders) of one-half of the issued and outstanding shares (Com. Code § 408(c)).

A major asset sale requires a similar procedure. If a firm intends to sell all or substantially all of its assets, its managers negotiate a sales contract. After the selling firm's board approves the sale, its shareholders must ratify that decision by a two-thirds vote, and the meeting must be attended by representatives of the owners of one-half of the issued and outstanding shares (Com. Code §§ 245(a), 343). The same provisions apply to a transferee corporation if it receives all of the transferor's assets (Com. Code § 245(a)(iii)).

Antitrust Law

First, the Antimonopoly Act (AMA) prohibits a firm from acquiring the stock of any corporation if the acquisition "would substantially restrict competition in any field of trade" (AMA § 10(a)). There is little case law construing this provision.

*Adapted by the author from J. Mark Ramseyer, "Takeovers in Japan: Opportunism, Ideology and Corporate Control," 35 *UCLA Law Review* 1 (1987).

A leading Japanese antitrust scholar argues that an acquiror violates this provision if, as a result of the acquisition, it acquires *any* market power. The Japanese FTC has indicated that it will review merger notifications (mergers are also subject to the "substantial restraint" test) with special care if, *inter alia*, one of the firms or both firms together (a) have a 25% market share, (b) have the largest market share and have a 15% market share, (c) have the largest market share and that share is considerably larger than that of either of the two firms having the next largest market shares, or (d) have one of the three largest market shares and the firms with the three largest market shares together have at least a 50% market share.

Second, the AMA prohibits any stock acquisition that constitutes an "unfair trade practice" (§§ 10(a), 4(a)). The FTC has interpreted this ban to encompass the "undue solicitation" of a competitor's stock to the detriment of the competitor. Prior to 1982, the FTC also had arguably considered the purchase of stock at an unduly high price to be an unfair trade practice.

Third, the AMA bans holding companies (§ 9). Because the statute defines a holding company as a firm whose primary business is that of controlling domestic corporations through stock ownership, however, acquirors can avoid its reach through reasonably careful planning.

Fourth, the AMA prohibits financial firms from holding more than 5% of the stock of any domestic firm (§ 11). Fifth, the AMA prohibits a large non-financial firm from acquiring additional stock if the value of the stock it already holds exceeds the greater of its capital and the net value of its assets (§ 9-2).

Sixth, although a tender offer does not formally involve a merger or the purchase of a business, target management could attempt to use the antitrust restrictions against mergers and business acquisitions even in the case of a tender offer. The management would argue that the restrictions applied either because the tender offer constituted the functional equivalent of a merger or business acquisition or because the acquiror allegedly intended to merge the target into another firm after the stock acquisition (*see* AMA §§ 15(a), 16). The AMA prohibits mergers and business acquisitions if either they would "substantially restrict competition in any field of trade" or the acquiror's methods constituted an "unfair trade practice."

IV. Selected Cases on Takeover Defenses

Translation by Yanagida Nomura & Akai

Shūwa K.K. v. K.K. Chūjitsuya
1317 Hanrei Jihō 28
(Tokyo Dist. Ct., July 25, 1989)

REFERENCES:

Commercial Code, §§ 280-2(2), 280-10 and 343

FACTS:

In October 1987, Shūwa K.K., a major real estate development and investing company, began to purchase a large number of listed shares of supermarket chains K.K. Chūjitsuya and K.K. Inageya. At that time, the number of outstanding shares of Chūjitsuya was approximately 90,300,000 (its stated capital was about ¥12,560,000,000), and the number of outstanding shares of Inageya was approximately 50,900,000 (its stated capital was about ¥8,250,000,000).

Until December 1987, the market price of Chūjitsuya's stock hovered around ¥900 to ¥1,200 per share, and that of Inageya's stock around ¥820 to ¥1,150 per share. In February 1988, however, due to Shūwa's purchases, the market price of Chūjitsuya shares jumped to about ¥4,000, and that of Inageya shares to about ¥2,000 (it reached ¥3,000 in June 1988). From that time until July 1989 (when the share issues in question were authorized by the boards of directors of both Chūjitsuya and Inageya), the market price of Chūjitsuya shares was not less than ¥4,000, and Inageya shares did not fall below ¥3,000. By July 1989 Shūwa had become the largest shareholder in both Chūjitsuya (33.4% of the issued shares) and Inageya (21.4%).

In the course of purchasing the shares in Chūjitsuya and Inageya, Shūwa proposed to the two companies that they merge with a third company, K.K. Life Store. Chūjitsuya and Inageya rejected this proposal, and as a defense against Shūwa's takeover attempt they entered into a business cooperation agreement. On July 10, 1989, in accordance with this cooperation agreement, Chūjitsuya's board of directors resolved to issue 22,000,000 new shares (an amount equal to 19.5% of its outstanding shares) at the price of ¥1,120 per share and to allot all of the new shares to Inageya; and Inageya's board of directors resolved to issue 12,400,000 new shares (equal to 19.5% of its outstanding shares) at the price of ¥1,580 per share and to allot all of the new shares to Chūjitsuya.

Shūwa seeks a provisional disposition to enjoin Chūjitsuya and Inageya from proceeding with their issues of new shares. Shūwa alleges that since the new shares are to be issued at a specially favorable price to persons other than current shareholders, such issues will violate § 280-2(2) of the Commercial Code, because the necessary two-thirds majority resolution of a general shareholders' meeting has not been obtained, and that since the purpose of the planned issues is to dilute the shareholding percentage of Shūwa, the planned issues are grossly unfair and, therefore, prohibited by § 280-10 of the Commercial Code.

(Below are the judgment and reasons for *Shūwa v. Chūjitsuya.* An essentially identical holding was reached in *Shūwa v. Inageya.*)

JUDGMENT:

Chūjitsuya is provisionally enjoined from issuing the 22,000,000 new shares in compliance with the resolution of its Board of Directors of July 10, 1989.

REASONS: * * *

II. First, we discuss whether the issue price of the new shares in question is a specially favorable price under § 280-2(2) of the Commercial Code.

The fair issue price of new shares is to be determined so as to achieve fairness between the existing shareholders and the purchaser of the new shares. In the event that a listed company issues new shares, as in the case before the court, the market price of shares in that company on the stock exchange, where ordinary investors freely sell and purchase shares, serves as a standard for determining the fair issue price. This is proper since the market price of a stock is based upon the objective value of the company as determined by ordinary investors' evaluations of the company's assets, profitability, and future business prospects.

Even in the event that a company's stock becomes the target of speculative investment and the prices of its shares thus rise, the fair issue price of new shares in such company is still determined basically in accordance with the market price, though an appropriate adjustment should be made. This is true since in the public market, where shares are the objects of transactions, the role of speculation by investors in the formation of market prices of shares cannot be ignored. Thus, when a company's stock becomes the target of speculation by investors and the market price of its shares rises suddenly, the inflated price cannot be eliminated as a factor in the determination of a fair issue price for new shares.

In the event, however, a company's stock becomes the target of extreme speculation by investors and the market prices of its shares greatly exceed the objective value of the company—provided that such speculative market prices are ephemeral—such prices should not be taken into account in determining the fair issue price for new shares.

In the case before the court, as described above [in an omitted section], the market price of Chūjitsuya shares exceeded ¥3,000 for 17 months and ¥4,000 for a year. Thus, the market price remained at a high level for a considerable period of time. Although it can be said that Shūwa's purchase of a large number of the shares was a cause of the rise in share price, it cannot be denied that the company's stock was also a target of speculation by ordinary investors. In light of the above-mentioned increase in the market price of Chūjitsuya shares, and especially the fact that the price remained at a high level for a considerable period of time, it is not reasonable to eliminate the market price of Chūjitsuya shares as a basis for determining the fair issue price for its new shares.

Therefore, since the issue price in question of ¥1,120 per share was determined without regard for the market price and was far different from the market price at that time, it is deemed a specially favorable issue price, as defined in § 280-2(2) of the Commercial Code. Accordingly, Chūjitsuya's issuance of new shares at such price was illegal since it was not approved by a special resolution of a general shareholders' meeting, as required by § 280-2(2).

III. Next, we shall consider whether the share issue in this case would constitute an unfair issue.

The Commercial Code has eliminated the preemptive rights of shareholders and recognizes the principle of free allocation. Thus, in a case where the purpose of the new issue requires allocation to third parties, such allocation, when based on the judgment of the directors in the exercise of their managerial authority, is permitted. As a result, even if the proportionate shareholding of existing shareholders is reduced, one cannot say on that basis alone that the new issue is unfair. However, in a case where there is a dispute over the control of a company and new shares are issued to a third party in a number that has a grave impact on the shareholding ratios of existing shareholders, and when a major purpose of such issue is to reduce the shareholding ratio of a particular shareholder, such issue of new shares must be said to constitute an unfair issue. Even if such cannot be said to be a major purpose of an issue, when the issue is undertaken with the knowledge that it will result in a marked drop in the shareholding ratio of a particular shareholder, unless there is a rational reason sufficient to justify the same, such an issue must also be said to constitute an unfair issue.

In the case before the court, as described above [in an omitted section], we find that Chūjitsuya and Inageya had never held serious negotiations concerning business cooperation [prior to Shūwa's merger proposal], even though they had considered there to be a certain probability of cooperation some day. We find further that their agreement concerning business cooperation was effected as a defense to Shūwa's takeover attempt only after they refused Shūwa's proposal of a merger of Chūjitsuya, Inageya and Life Store; that there has not been a sufficient preliminary showing to demonstrate that it is necessary for Chūjitsuya to allot such a large number of new shares to Inageya; and that most of the capital obtained by selling the new shares in question to Inageya would be spent in the acquisition of Inageya's new shares, even though Chūjitsuya would reserve a balance of ¥5,000,000,000 of such newly acquired capital. There has been, however, no preliminary showing to demonstrate that Chūjitsuya has a particular business plan for such ¥5,000,000,000. Finally, there has been no preliminary showing to demonstrate that Shūwa's participation in the business operations of Chūjitsuya would have any seriously detrimental effect on Chūjitsuya.

Upon the foregoing, we hold that the primary purposes of Chūjitsuya's issuance of the new shares in question were to reduce Shūwa's shareholding ratio and to maintain the existing directors' control over the company; that the issue of new shares was undertaken, at a minimum, with the knowledge that it would result in a marked drop in Shūwa's shareholding ratio; that there is no reason to justify the issuance of such a large number of new shares; and, therefore, that Chūjitsuya's issuance of the new shares was a grossly unfair issue.

- - - - - - - - - -

Translation by Yanagida Nomura & Akai

Mizuno v. Ariyoshi, et al.
1188 Shōji Hōmu 36
(Tokyo High. Ct., July 3, 1989)

REFERENCES:

Commercial Code §§ 210, 211-2 (enacted in 1981 subsequent to the filing of this case), 266(1)(v) and 267

FACTS:

Plaintiff Mizuno is a shareholder of Mitsui Kōzan K.K. (M.K.), a mining company whose shares are listed on the stock exchange. Defendants were all M.K. directors and several of them were representative directors who constituted the company's Executive Officers Committee (*Jōmukai*).

Mizuno instituted this action on behalf of M.K. under § 267 of the Commercial Code, demanding that defendants compensate M.K. for the damages for which they were liable under Commercial Code § 266(1)(v).

Mizuno's argument was as follows:

> M.K. is one of the companies of the Mitsui Group. In October 1975, the largest shareholder in M.K. was an individual investor, Toguri, who owned 15.5 million (25.5%) of the 60 million outstanding shares, although he had no relationship with the Mitsui Group. At that time M.K. was proceeding with its merger with Mitsui Cement K.K. (M.C.), a cement manufacturer and also a company of the Mitsui Group. As Toguri opposed the merger, however, there was a high probability that M.K. would not obtain the necessary two-thirds vote at a general shareholders' meeting to proceed with the merger.
>
> M.K. planned to purchase all of Toguri's shares in M.K. through its wholly owned subsidiary, Mitsui Kaihatsu K.K. (Kaihatsu), a real estate development company, and to sell them through Kaihatsu to several companies of the Mitsui Group and several clients of M.K. This plan was adopted either by a resolution of M.K.'s Board of Directors held in November 1975 or by the unanimous approval of the *Jōmukai* in December 1975.
>
> In accordance with M.K.'s plan, in December 1975 Kaihatsu purchased all of Toguri's shares at the price of ¥530 per share, the total price of which amounted to ¥8.215 billion. Kaihatsu then sold the shares to Mitsui Corporation, the Mitsui Bank Ltd., other companies of the Mitsui Group, and some of M.K.'s clients at an average price of ¥300 per share, the total of which amounted to ¥4,663,400,000.
>
> Kaihatsu thus suffered a loss of ¥3,551,600,000, representing the difference in the purchase prices and the sale prices of the shares. Since Kaihatsu is a wholly owned subsidiary of M.K., Kaihatsu's loss should be deemed a loss of M.K.
>
> In light of M.K.'s 100% ownership of Kaihatsu, the acquisition by Kaihatsu of M.K.'s shares violated § 210 of the Commercial Code, which prohibits a stock company from acquiring its own shares except in certain specified cases.
>
> Therefore, the members of M.K.'s Board of Directors who voted affirmatively for the purchase from Toguri by Kaihatsu of shares in M.K., or at least the members of the *Jōmukai*, who unanimously approved the same, should be jointly liable to compensate M.K. for the abovementioned loss for the reason that they acted in violation of the law.

The defendants argued that Kaihatsu's purchase of shares in M.K. did not violate § 210 because Kaihatsu was a separate legal entity from M.K. Moreover, the intent of § 210 was not violated because M.K. had Kaihatsu acquire the shares for the legitimate reasons of facilitating a smooth merger with M.C. and of obtaining stable shareholders, because M.K. intended Kaihatsu's obtaining of M.K.'s shares to be only temporary, *i.e.*, for the sole purpose of immediate resale, and because Kaihatsu, in fact, completed such resale within a very short period.

The District Court found that although M.K.'s Board had not adopted a resolution authorizing Kaihatsu to purchase the M.K. shares from Toguri, the same decision was effected at a *Jōmukai* held in December 1975, at which all members were present and approved making the purchase; that Noguchi, a director of M.K., arranged the share purchase; and that in the purchase and resale of the shares Kaihatsu suffered the loss alleged by plaintiff. The court further held that the loss of Kaihatsu should be deemed a loss of M.K. and that the members of the *Jōmukai* and Noguchi should be liable to M.K. for the loss.

In interpreting § 210, the District Court held that if, on the basis of a case-by-case review, it were found that a company had acquired its own shares as a matter of necessity in achieving an important interest or avoiding a detrimental loss, such an acquisition would not violate the statute. The court concluded, however, that in the present case there existed no such necessity for M.K. The defendants appealed.

JUDGMENT:

The judgment of the court below is affirmed.

REASONS:

* * * The appellants assert in their first defense that even if the purchase by Kaihatsu of the shares were deemed an acquisition by M.K. of its own shares, such an acquisition would not violate the intent of § 210. We shall address this assertion.

If a company issues shares on the stock market, it is theoretically possible for the company to acquire its own stock on the market. Such action would, however, have the following harmful effects: the company's capital assets would be jeopardized; the interests of shareholders and/or ordinary investors would be jeopardized by corporate control of the market price of the company's shares or by speculative sales and purchases in reliance on inside information; the principle of equal treatment of shareholders would be offended by the purchase of shares from a particular shareholder; and the current directors could indirectly abuse their authority to manage the company by purchasing shares from a particular shareholder.

Therefore, in light of such societal viewpoints, § 210 of the Commercial Code prohibits a company from acquiring its own shares, except in four specified cases for which there exists no probability of the abovementioned harmful effects. Furthermore, in the event the directors violate the § 210 prohibition, § 489(ii) of the Commercial Code provides that such directors may be jailed for not more than five years or fined not more than ¥300,000 (which figure was amended to ¥2,000,000 by Law No. 74 of 1981).

It is obvious to this court that, notwithstanding frequent requests from the business world for a loosening of the prohibition under § 210, the amendments to the Commercial Code effected by Law No. 74 of 1981 (enacted after the purchase by Kaihatsu) did not loosen the prohibition, even though they partially relaxed the restriction on companies accepting their own shares as pledges.

In view of the literal wording of § 210 and the abovementioned legislative history, the provision must be interpreted to prohibit a company from acquiring its own shares, except in the four cases specified therein, and in certain other cases in which it is obvious that there are none of the abovementioned harmful effects. Such other cases would include, for example, the acquisition by a company of its own shares at no cost and the acquisition of its own shares by a company engaged in the brokerage business in the course of a transaction as an intermediary. We hold that the exceptions under § 210 should be strictly limited as described above and that, even when it is alleged that circumstances make the acquisition by a company of its own shares necessary to achieve an important interest or to avoid a detrimental loss, such a claim shall not constitute an exception nor be entitled to review.

* * * If we granted the directors of a company the discretion to determine whether the company has a justifiable reason to acquire its own shares, considerable abuse and misuse of such discretion, as well as evasion of § 210 due to ignorance of its intent, would occur.

Accordingly, it is obvious that the purchase of shares in question violated the intent behind § 210, even if such purchase was, in fact, made under the circumstances alleged by the appellants. Therefore, we do not accept the appellants' request to overturn the opinion of the court below.

Questions and Discussion Points

1. How do you suppose other shareholders responded to the cross-shareholding arrangement in *Shūwa*?
2. What effect would a 19.5 percent cross-shareholding arrangement have?
3. Suppose there are 800 shares of stock outstanding at ¥4000 per share. The company issues 200 more shares, to a selected investor, at ¥1100 per share. What will happen to the price of the original 800 shares?
4. Section 210 of the Commercial Code bans the repurchase by a company of its own shares. What is the section's statutory "intent"? Do you find the court's discussion convincing?

FURTHER READING

Walter Lansing Ames, "Buying a Piece of Japan, Inc.: Foreign Acquisitions in Japan," 27 *Harvard International Law Journal* 361 (1986).

Harald Baum, "Japanese Capital Markets: New Legislation," 22 *Law in Japan: An Annual* 1 (1989).

Harald Baum and Ulrike Shaede, "Institutional Investors and Corporate Governance in Japanese Perspective," pp. 609-664, in Theodor Baums, Richard M.

Buxbaum, and Klaus J. Hopt, eds., *Institutional Investors and Corporate Governance.* Berlin: W. de Gruyter, 1993.

Toru Ishiguro, "Japan," pp. 153-170, and Aron Viner, "Mergers, Acquisitions and Corporate Governance in Japan," pp. 27-32, in Joseph CF Lufkin and David Gallagher, eds., *International Corporate Governance.* London: Euromoney Books, 1990.

Kanji Ishizumi, *Acquiring Japanese Corporations.* Tokyo: Japan Times, 1988.

W. Carl Kester, *Japanese Takeovers: The Global Contest for Corporate Control.* Boston: Harvard Business School Press, 1991.

Note [Tomoko Akashi], "Regulation of Insider Trading in Japan," 89 *Columbia Law Review* 1296 (1989).

Note [Merit E. Janow], "Mergers and Acquisitions in Japan: A New Option for Foreign Companies?," 26 *Columbia Journal of Transnational Law* 573 (1988).

Aron Viner, *Inside Japanese Financial Markets.* Homewood, IL: Dow Jones-Irwin, 1988.

NOTES TO CHAPTER TWELVE

1. H. Stokes, *The Japanese Competitor* 11 (1976).

Appendix A
The Principal Case Agreements

Table of Contents

*Amending Agreements No. 1 to No. 14 are omitted.

JOINT VENTURE AGREEMENT
(A.Co-J.Co)

Contents

F. DISCOUNTS AND MARK-UPS
1. Determination of SELLING PRICES
2. Determination of COSTS
3. Determination of Trade Discounts
4. Determination of Mark-Ups
5. Adjustment of Estimated COSTS
6. Other Activities of Newco

G. TRADEMARKS AND NAMES
1. Use of Name "A.Co"
2. Change of Corporate Name
3. Use of Trademarks and Names by J.Co
4. Use of Trademarks and Names by Newco

H. GENERAL PROVISIONS
1. Disclaimer of Agency
2. Non-Assignment of Agreement
3. Entire Agreement
4. Applicable and Supervening Law
5. Governmental Approvals
6. Access to Accounts
7. Arbitration
8. Waivers
9. Notices
10. Schedules and Exhibits
11. Titles

I. TERMINATION
1. By Agreement
2. For Breach
3. For Insolvency, etc.
4. Effect
5. Other Remedies

J. EFFECTIVE DATE
1. Definition
2. Notifications

SCHEDULES

I A.Co TERRITORY
II Newco TERRITORY
III COSTS OF J.CO (C_1)
IV COSTS OF Newco (C_2)

EXHIBITS

A ARTICLES OF INCORPORATION
B TECHNICAL AGREEMENT
C TRADEMARK AGREEMENT
D MANUFACTURING AGREEMENT
E SELLING AGREEMENT
F DISTRIBUTOR AGREEMENT

JOINT VENTURE AGREEMENT

AGREEMENT made between [A.Co and J.Co.]

WHEREAS: [Recitals omitted.]

NOW, THEREFORE, in consideration of the premises and the mutual benefits to be derived herefrom,

IT IS AGREED AS FOLLOWS:

A. DEFINITIONS

The following terms where used in this Agreement shall have the following meanings:

1. EXCAVATOR
   A power-operated excavator that constitutes a LICENSED PRODUCT and/or LICENSED PRODUCT IMPROVEMENT as defined in the Technical Agreement attached hereto as Exhibit B, with all materials, tools, equipment, accessories, and other items pertaining thereto, except PARTS and COMPONENTS.

2. PART
   A finished part, unit or subassembly of an EXCAVATOR.

3. COMPONENT
   An unfinished PART.

4. MACHINERY
   EXCAVATORS, PARTS and COMPONENTS.

5. PARTY
   A.Co or J.Co.

6. BUYER
   An individual, firm, company, or governmental department, whether a USER, or DISTRIBUTOR or other intermediary,
   (a) From which an inquiry is received and with which a contract is likely to be made, or
   (b) From which an order is received.

7. USER
   Any individual, firm, company or governmental department which inquires about or purchases any MACHINERY.

8. [Omitted.]

9. DISTRIBUTOR
   Any individual, firm or company regularly appointed or approved by A.Co or Newco to act as a distributor for MACHINERY.

10. TERRITORY
    A.Co TERRITORY — as specified in Schedule I attached hereto.

    NEWCO TERRITORY — as specified in Schedule II attached hereto.

11. RELATED CORPORATION
    A parent corporation or wholly-owned subsidiary corporation of a PARTY, or any wholly-owned subsidiary corporation of such parent corporation.

12. FAIR SHARE VALUE
    The value of a share of Newco which the CERTIFYING AUDITOR of Newco shall, on application of a PARTY, certify in writing to be the fair value of such share, for the purpose of Paragraph B-6(a) hereof.

13. SELLING PRICE
[See §F.]

14. COSTS
[See Schedules III and IV.]

B. FORMATION OF NEWCO KABUSHIKI KAISHA

1. *New Company*
The PARTIES shall, within ninety (90) days after the EFFECTIVE DATE of this Agreement as defined in Paragraph J-1, cause to be incorporated as a Joint Stock Corporation (Kabushiki Kaisha) under the Commercial Code of Japan a company which shall:
(a) Be called "Newco Kabushiki Kaisha" (hereinafter "Newco");
(b) Have authorized capital of 360,000,000 yen, or such other sum as shall be agreed by the PARTIES, divided into shares of 500 yen par value each; and
(c) Have Articles of Incorporation in the form attached hereto as Exhibit A.

2. *Purpose*
The purpose of Newco shall be:
(a) The manufacture, sale and distribution of excavating and material-handling equipment of all kinds and related products and parts therefor; and
(b) At the outset Newco shall primarily engage in arranging for the manufacture and sale in Japan for resale and use in Newco TERRITORY of MACHINERY of A.Co design and related activities.

3. *Life*
The duration of Newco shall be perpetual, unless earlier dissolved by agreement of the PARTIES or as provided herein.

4. *Capital Subscriptions*
(a) At the time of incorporation of Newco the PARTIES shall each subscribe to one-fourth (1/4th) of the authorized shares of Newco as follows:
A.Co 90,000 shares (50%) (45,000,000 yen)
J.Co 90,000 shares (50%) (45,000,000 yen)
(b) The subscribed shares shall be acquired for cash, and shall be fully paid in.
(c) Thereafter, each PARTY shall have an obligation and preemptive right to subscribe from time to time to such additional shares as Newco shall determine to issue, provided, that:
(1) Such additional shares shall be issued to the PARTIES so that A.Co and J.Co shall hold respectively 50% and 50% of such additional shares; and
(2) Such additional shares shall not be issued unless A.Co shall, with respect to its additional shares, obtain guarantees of remittance of dividends and of repatriation of capital under Japanese law.

5. *Organization*
[Provisions concerning formation of Newco omitted.]

6. *Transfer of Shares*
(a) In the event that a PARTY or RELATED CORPORATION of such PARTY desires to sell or transfer all or any of its shares in Newco, it shall first offer by written notice to sell such shares to the other PARTY at a price equal to the FAIR SHARE VALUE of such shares at said date.
(b) If a PARTY to which an offer under Subparagraph (a) above is made does not accept it in writing within sixty days from the date of receipt thereof, then the prospective transferor may during the next six months sell or transfer the offered shares to a third party.

(c) An offer under Subparagraph (a) above shall be non-assignable by any PARTY to which it is made, except to a RELATED CORPORATION, and must be accepted by such PARTY, or by such RELATED CORPORATION, with respect to all shares offered to such PARTY by the prospective transferor. The purchase price of the shares shall be payable in cash upon transfer of the shares. Any transfer of shares shall be subject to the approval of the Japanese Government, if required, and shall not become effective until such approval has been obtained.
(d) Subparagraph (a) above shall not apply with respect to any shares in Newco of a PARTY or RELATED CORPORATION where one of the following conditions is first satisfied with respect to such shares:
  (1) The sale or transfer is by a PARTY to a RELATED CORPORATION of such PARTY;
  (2) The sale or transfer is by a RELATED CORPORATION to its PARTY or to any other RELATED CORPORATION of such PARTY; or
  (3) The sale or transfer is by one PARTY and made with the prior written consent of the other PARTY.
(e) The provisions of Subparagraphs (a) through (d) above shall apply *mutatis mutandis* to any pledge of shares in Newco.

7. *Directors*
(a) Newco shall have a Board of Directors which shall consist of six directors.
(b) A.Co and J.Co shall each have the right to nominate three directors; and the PARTIES agree to cause their shares and the shares of their RELATED CORPORATIONS to be voted to elect such directors.
(c) [Omitted.]

8. *Management*
(a) Newco shall have a President (*Shachō*) and an Executive Managing Director (*Senmu Torishimariyaku*) who shall be appointed representative directors of Newco, and J.Co shall be entitled to nominate the President and A.Co shall be entitled to nominate the Executive Managing Director.
(b) [Omitted.]
(c) The President and the Executive Managing Director may be compensated as determined by Resolution of the Board of Directors.

9. *Auditors*
(a) Newco shall have two Statutory Auditors.
(b) Each PARTY shall have the right to nominate one Statutory Auditor; and the PARTIES agree to cause their shares and the shares of their RELATED CORPORATIONS to be voted to elect such auditors.
(c) [Omitted.]
(d) Newco shall have an outside accountant, which shall be an independent certified public accounting firm having offices in Japan nominated by A.Co, and which shall also be the CERTIFYING AUDITOR of Newco.
(e) and (f) [Omitted.]

10. *Matters Requiring Approval by Board of Directors*
Except as otherwise provided in this Agreement, the following matters and powers shall not be determined or exercised by Newco or by the Directors, the President, or the Executive Managing Director of Newco without the authority of a general or specific resolution of the Board of Directors of Newco:
(a) Adoption or amendment of the By-Laws;
(b) Borrowing or lending of money;
(c) Acquisition or disposition of:
  (1) Real property,
  (2) Stock or securities of any other corporation, or
  (3) Patent or trademark rights;

(d) Initiating or ceasing production of any model of machinery;
(e) Disclosure by sale or otherwise of technical data;
(f) Fixing remuneration of Directors or Statutory Auditors;
(g) Formation of any subsidiary;
(h) Appointment of any subcontractor, sublicensee or distributor;
(i) Capital expenditures;
(j) Amendment, termination, or extension of any of the Agreements referred to in Paragraph C of this Agreement; and
(k) Other matters or powers for the determination or exercise of which a resolution of the Board of Directors of Newco is required by law, the Articles of Incorporation or By-Laws of Newco, or the provisions of this Agreement or any Exhibit thereof, as from time to time amended.

C. AGREEMENTS BETWEEN PARTIES AND NEWCO

1. *Technical Agreement*
A.Co shall grant patent rights and supply certain TECHNICAL DATA and TECHNICAL ASSISTANCE to Newco in accordance with the Technical Agreement between A.Co and Newco attached hereto as Exhibit B; and J.Co hereby jointly and severally guarantees the performance by Newco of its obligations to A.Co under said Technical Agreement.

2. *Trademark Agreement*
A.Co shall grant trademark rights to Newco in accordance with the Trademark Agreement attached hereto as Exhibit C; and J.Co hereby jointly and severally guarantees the performance by Newco of its obligations to A.Co under said Trademark Agreement.

3. *Manufacturing Agreement*
J.Co shall manufacture LICENSED PRODUCTS for Newco in accordance with the Manufacturing Agreement attached hereto as Exhibit D.

4. *Selling Agreement*
A.Co, Newco and J.Co shall sell products of Newco in accordance with the Selling Agreement attached hereto as Exhibit E; and J.Co hereby jointly and severally guarantees the performance by Newco of its obligations to A.Co under said Selling Agreement.

5. *Distributor Agreement*
J.Co shall distribute products of Newco in accordance with the Distributor Agreement attached hereto as Exhibit F.

6. *Approval of Agreements*
The agreements attached hereto as Exhibits B to F inclusive shall be appropriately approved and ratified by Resolution of the Board of Directors of Newco immediately following execution of this Agreement, and a certified copy of the ratifying resolution shall be sent to the PARTY or PARTIES involved.

D. OWNERSHIP AND PROTECTION OF DATA

1. *Non-Disclosure by J.Co*
J.Co agrees that any technical data or other information made available to it by Newco or by A.Co shall be for temporary use only, and that it shall not acquire any right to or in said technical data, or other information, or supply or disclose the same to anyone to any extent whatsoever other than as provided herein or by previous written agreements or by the Agreements attached hereto.

2. *Non-Disclosure by Others*
Before or at the time of supplying or disclosing any such technical data or other information to any third party, J.Co shall require such third party to enter into an agreement not to supply or disclose any such data or information other than as provided herein.

E. OFFERS, SALES AND SERVICE

1. *Distribution in Newco TERRITORY*
   (a) Newco shall be responsible for the sale in Newco TERRITORY of MACHINERY manufactured by or for Newco, in accordance with the Selling Agreement attached hereto as Exhibit E.
   (b) Newco shall appoint J.Co as exclusive DISTRIBUTOR in Japan of MACHINERY manufactured by or for Newco in accordance with the Distributor Agreement attached hereto as Exhibit F, and shall supervise and direct the activities and performance of service by J.Co for USERS and others.

2. *Distribution in A.Co TERRITORY*
   (a) Newco may sell MACHINERY of its manufacture for delivery into A.Co TERRITORY with the approval of A.Co on a case by case basis.
   (b) A.Co, or a RELATED CORPORATION of A.Co designated by A.Co, shall be the General Distributor in A.Co TERRITORY of MACHINERY manufactured by or for Newco, in accordance with the Selling Agreement attached hereto as Exhibit E.
   (c) As such General Distributor of MACHINERY manufactured by or for Newco, A.Co, or such RELATED CORPORATION, may appoint non-exclusive or exclusive DISTRIBUTORS in A.Co TERRITORY of MACHINERY manufactured by or for Newco, and shall supervise and direct the activities and performance of service by such DISTRIBUTORS for USERS and others.

3. *Shipments*
   In view of J.Co's role as subcontractor for Newco under the Manufacturing Agreement in Exhibit D hereof, and as DISTRIBUTOR of Newco under the Distributor Agreement in Exhibit F hereof, any shipment of MACHINERY by J.Co to a BUYER or other purchaser or lessee shall, except as otherwise expressly agreed in writing, be deemed to be a shipment by Newco to such BUYER, purchaser or lessee.

4. [Omitted.]

5. *Prohibited Transactions*
   Newco and its appointed subcontractors, sublicensees or DISTRIBUTORS, including J.Co, shall not directly or indirectly sell, deliver or disclose MACHINERY or other goods, technical data or information, in or to any country where such sale, delivery, or disclosure by A.Co would be prohibited by the U.S. Trading with the Enemy Act, or any similar law or regulation imposing restrictions on U.S. trade with foreign countries.

6. *Rights of A.Co*
   Except as provided for in the Technical Agreement attached hereto as Exhibit B, nothing contained herein or in the Agreements constituting Exhibits hereto shall restrict the right of A.Co to sell MACHINERY of its manufacture throughout the world.

F. DISCOUNTS AND MARK-UPS

1. *Determination of SELLING PRICES*
   Unless otherwise provided by Resolution of the Board of Directors of Newco:
   (a) The SELLING PRICES of MACHINERY sold to Newco by J.Co, as subcontractor to Newco under this Agreement and the Manufacturing Agreement attached hereto as Exhibit D, shall be determined from time to time by the formula:

$$SP_1 = C_1 + M_1$$

where:

SP_1 = Said SELLING PRICE of J.Co for such MACHINERY.

C_1 = COSTS of J.Co allocable hereunder to the MACHINERY so sold.

M_1 = Mark-up allocable to such MACHINERY, as determined and allowable hereunder to J.Co.

(b) The SELLING PRICES of MACHINERY manufactured by or for Newco and sold by Newco to J.Co or other BUYERS as DISTRIBUTORS shall be determined from time to time by the formula:

$$SP_2 = SP_1 + C_2 + M_2 + D$$

where:

SP_2 = Said SELLING PRICE of Newco for such MACHINERY.

SP_1 = The SELLING PRICE of J.Co for such MACHINERY, as determined under Paragraph F-1(a).

C_2 = COSTS of Newco allocable hereunder to such MACHINERY sold by Newco, excluding SP_1 and D.

M_2 = Mark-up allocable to such MACHINERY, as determined and allowable hereunder to Newco.

D = Trade Discount determined and allowable hereunder to such DISTRIBUTOR by Newco on the sale of such MACHINERY to the DISTRIBUTOR.

2. *Determination of COSTS*
   (a) COSTS of J.Co (C_1) allocable to Models and items of MACHINERY from time to time sold to Newco by J.Co, as subcontractor to Newco hereunder, shall be such costs as are:
      (1) Reported, in accordance with standard accounting practices, by J.Co in writing to Newco and A.Co at such times and in such form and detail as may be specified by Resolution of the Board of Directors of Newco; and
      (2) Certified to be true and correct and in accordance with this Agreement by the CERTIFYING AUDITOR of Newco.
   (b) COSTS of Newco (C_2) allocable to models and items of MACHINERY from time to time manufactured by or for Newco and sold by Newco to J.Co or other DISTRIBUTORS shall be such costs as are:
      (1) Reported, in accordance with standard accounting practices, by Newco in writing to the PARTIES at such time and in such form and detail as may be specified by Resolution of the Board of Directors of Newco; and
      (2) Certified to be true and correct and in accordance with this Agreement by the CERTIFYING AUDITOR of Newco.
   (c) J.Co agrees to report and the PARTIES agree to cause Newco to report the COSTS C_1 and C_2 as specified in this Paragraph F-2, and to establish and maintain accounting policies to that end. The effective date and periods for the application of costs C_1 and C_2 reported and certified hereunder shall be fixed by Resolution of the Board of Directors of Newco.

3. *Determination of Trade Discounts*
   Unless otherwise provided by Resolution of the Board of Directors of Newco, the Trade Discounts (D) allowable by Newco to J.Co or other DISTRIBUTORS on the sale by Newco to such DISTRIBUTORS of MACHINERY manufactured by or for Newco shall be in accordance with the Distributor Agreement in Exhibit F.

4. *Determination of Mark-ups*
   (a) The total Mark-up ($M_1 + M_2$) allocable to MACHINERY manufactured by J.Co, as subcontractor for Newco, and sold to Newco shall be fixed annually by Resolution of the Board of Directors of Newco in such detail with respect to Models and items as determined by the Board in said Resolution.

(b) Subject to Subparagraph (c) below, and unless otherwise provided by Resolution of the Board of Directors of Newco, the total Mark-up determined under Subparagraph 4(a) above shall be applied as follows for the purposes of determining SELLING PRICES under Paragraph F-1 hereof:

(1) 66≈ % of said total Mark-up to Mark-up of J.Co (M_1); and

(2) The remaining 33⅓% of said total Mark-up to Mark-up of Newco (M_2).

The resulting allowance (i) to J.Co of a total of 83⅓% of Newco's profits (instead of a portion (50%) proportionate to its share ownership in Newco) and (ii) to A.Co respectively of only 16≈ % (instead of 50%) of Newco's profits, is in order to compensate J.Co for J.Co's risk of incurring excess start-up costs over and above normal start-up costs allowable under Schedule III, Paragraph 4(a)(4) of this Agreement.

(c) For any fiscal year in which the total Mark-up ($M_1 + M_2$) of Newco for all MACHINERY by Model is established by resolution of the Board of Directors under Paragraph F-4(a) hereof to be:

(1) Greater than zero, then such total Mark-up shall be applied as specified in Paragraph F-4(b) hereof;

(2) Zero, then the total allowable COSTS (C_1) for such year shall be adjusted and fixed to equal $SP_2 - C_2 - D$, in accordance with Paragraph F-1 hereof, and accordingly the only items of profit or loss of Newco that shall be credited or charged to surplus shall be items of profit or loss (if any) not attributable to manufacture or sale of such MACHINERY manufactured by or for Newco and sold by Newco to J.Co or other BUYERS (such as sales commissions received by Newco from A.Co); or

(3) Less than zero, then such negative Mark-up shall be borne as follows:

(i) 66≈ % of such total negative Mark-up by J.Co as a reduction of SP_1; and

(ii) The remaining 33⅓% of said total negative Mark-up shall be charged, first to items of profit or loss (if any) not attributable to manufacture or sale of such MACHINERY manufactured by or for Newco and sold by Newco to J.Co or other BUYERS, and second to surplus of Newco.

(d) The effective dates and periods for application of Mark-ups (M_1, M_2) determined hereunder shall be fixed from time to time by Resolution of the Board of Directors of Newco.

5. *Adjustment of Estimated COSTS*

(a) COSTS of J.Co (C_1) and COSTS of Newco (C_2) shall, for purposes of determining estimated SELLING PRICES (SP_1 and SP_2) and fixing preliminary Mark-ups (M_1 and M_2), be initially reported by J.Co and Newco on an estimated basis.

(b) At the end of each fiscal year, upon ascertainment of actual costs with respect to such fiscal year, appropriate adjustments shall be made for any differences between estimated and actual costs, and the allowable COSTS (C_1 and C_2) shall be finally determined, reported and certified hereunder for such fiscal year in accordance with Schedules III and IV hereof.

(c) On the basis of such finally determined allowable COSTS (C_1 and C_2), Mark-ups (M_1 and M_2) for the fiscal year shall be finally determined in accordance with Paragraph F-4 hereof, and appropriate adjustments made to SELLING PRICE (SP_1) for such fiscal year in accordance with Paragraph F-1 hereof.

6. [Omitted.]

G. TRADEMARKS AND NAMES

[See Trademark Agreement.]

H. GENERAL PROVISIONS

1. *Disclaimer of Agency*

   This Agreement shall not constitute Newco or any PARTY the legal representative or agent of any other PARTY or Newco for any purpose whatsoever, and neither Newco nor any PARTY nor any DISTRIBUTOR of either shall have the right or authority to assume, create or incur any liability or obligation of any kind, express or implied, against, in the name or on behalf of such other PARTY, a RELATED CORPORATION thereof, or Newco.

2. *Non-Assignment of Agreement*

   Except as otherwise provided herein, this Agreement and the rights and obligations of the PARTIES hereunder are personal and shall not be capable of assignment whether voluntary or otherwise, provided that, if a PARTY shall desire to assign all its rights and obligations hereunder to a bona fide RELATED CORPORATION, the other PARTIES will not unreasonably withhold their consent to such assignment.

3. *Entire Agreement*

   (a) This Agreement sets forth the entire agreement and understanding between the PARTIES as to the subject matter hereof.

   (b) No modifications, amendments, or supplements to this Agreement shall be effective for any purpose unless in writing signed by each of the PARTIES. Approvals or consents required hereunder of a PARTY shall also be in writing.

4. *Applicable and Supervening Law*

   This Agreement shall be subject to and construed in accordance with the laws of Japan, provided, however, that if any provision of this Agreement shall contravene the laws of, or require the approval of any governmental authority in, Japan or the U.S.A., the same shall be ineffective to the extent it is in contravention of such laws, or until such approval shall have been obtained, without invalidating the remaining provisions hereof.

5. *Governmental Approvals*

   (a) This Agreement is subject to the issuance, and to A.Co's obtaining satisfactory documentation, of Japanese Government approval of this Agreement and/or the Agreements attached hereto as Exhibits B to F inclusive, as may be required, including Japanese Government approval of unrestricted payment in U.S. dollars of all fees, dividends, and other payments or remittances in accordance with this Agreement and the Exhibits hereof.

   (b) [Omitted.]

   (c) The rights granted to Newco and/or J.Co under this Agreement and the Agreements attached hereto as Exhibits B to F inclusive are based on the assumption that no laws or governmental regulations or any other intervening hindrance shall impede Newco or J.Co from carrying out their respective obligations under said Agreements. If Newco or J.Co should be so impeded, A.Co and/or Newco by acts approved by Resolution of its Board of Directors shall be at liberty, independently of such rights, to take any steps which it considers advisable toward protecting, for the time that may be involved, the market interests of A.Co and/or Newco in Newco TERRITORY.

6. *Access to Accounts*

   [PARTIES to make available to each other and the CERTIFYING AUDITOR "all books, accounts, vouchers and documents relating to the subject matter of this Agreement, and all agreements hereunder, to check statements and reports rendered by a PARTY hereunder." A.Co and J.Co to have "equal access to the books of account and records of Newco."]

7. *Arbitration*
Unless otherwise settled by the PARTIES, all disputes, controversies, or differences which may arise between the PARTIES out of, in relation to or in connection with this Agreement, or for breach thereof, shall be finally settled by arbitration pursuant to the Japan-American Trade Arbitration Agreement of September 16, 1952, by which each PARTY hereto is bound.

8. *Waivers*
The waiver by either PARTY of any right hereunder, or of the failure to perform or breach by the other PARTY, shall not be deemed a waiver of any other right hereunder or of any other breach or failure by said other PARTY, whether of a similar nature or otherwise.

9. *Notices*
Any notice hereunder, by one PARTY to any other PARTY, shall be in writing and shall be deemed served if sent by registered mail, with return receipt requested, addressed to such other PARTY to the attention of its President, at its principal office and address designated herein, or at such other address as such other PARTY may designate by the means herein described for giving notice.

10. *Schedules and Exhibits*
Schedules I to IV inclusive and Exhibits A to F inclusive attached hereto are incorporated herein and made a part hereof to the same effect as if set forth herein in full.

11. *Titles*
The titles to Paragraphs, Schedules and Exhibits of this Agreement are for convenience of reference only and this Agreement is not to be construed by reference thereto.

I. TERMINATION

1. *By Agreement*
This Agreement shall continue in effect until terminated by agreement of the PARTIES, unless terminated as hereinafter provided.

2. *For Breach*
(a) In the event of a substantial breach of this Agreement by A.Co, this Agreement may be terminated by J.Co forthwith upon ninety (90) days prior written notice to A.Co specifying the reason for termination.
(b) In the event of a substantial breach of this Agreement by J.Co, or of the Technical Agreement in Exhibit B hereof, or the Selling Agreement in Exhibit E hereof, by Newco, then this Agreement may be terminated by A.Co forthwith upon ninety (90) days prior written notice to J.Co specifying the reason for termination.
(c) Said termination under either Subparagraph (a) or (b) shall become effective at the end of said ninety (90) day period unless the breach is cured within said period.

3. *For Insolvency, etc.*
In the event of bankruptcy, insolvency, receivership, or liquidation of a PARTY, this Agreement may be terminated by the other PARTY forthwith upon written notice to the other PARTY.

4. *Effect*
Upon termination of this Agreement:
(a) No PARTY shall be discharged of any antecedent obligation to the other PARTY, except that the PARTIES shall not be liable for special or consequential damages;
(b) The PARTIES shall continue to be bound by the provisions of Paragraphs B-5, B-6, B-9, B-10, D, G, H-6 and H-7 hereof;
(c) Newco shall be dissolved and its net assets distributed as promptly as reasonably possible;

(d) The Agreements attached hereto and made a part hereof as Exhibits B to F inclusive shall become terminated except as otherwise expressly agreed now or hereafter in writing by the PARTIES or by the provisions of said Agreements; and

(e) Newco and J.Co shall reassign all their rights in and return, and secure the return by any subcontractor of Newco or J.Co, to A.Co and discontinue the use of, and cease manufacture of MACHINERY under, all TECHNICAL DATA, TECHNICAL IMPROVEMENT DATA and written information supplied to Newco and J.Co under Exhibits B and D hereof, subject to the temporary rights of Newco and J.Co respectively under Exhibit B, Paragraph I-6(c) and Exhibit D, Paragraph H-7(c) hereof.

5. *Other Remedies*

Nothing in this Agreement shall prevent either PARTY from enforcing the provisions hereof by such remedies as may be available to it in lieu of termination.

J. EFFECTIVE DATE

1. *Definition*

This Agreement shall become effective on the date at which all governmental approvals and rulings specified in Paragraph H-5(a) hereof are finally issued.

2. *Notification*

J. Co and Newco shall promptly:

(a) Notify A.Co in writing of the filing of applications for and the obtaining of the governmental approvals and rulings specified in Paragraph H-5(a) hereof; and

(b) Furnish A.Co satisfactory documentation of such governmental approvals and rulings and the date of issuance thereof.

IN WITNESS WHEREOF, the PARTIES have caused these presents to be duly executed in manner appropriate to each and their corporate seals hereunto affixed on the dates respectively set forth below.

American Heavy Equipment, Inc.

By: ______________________

President

Attest: ______________________

Secretary

Date: ______________________

Japan Construction Machinery K.K.

By: ______________________

President

Attest: ______________________

Secretary

Date: ______________________

SCHEDULE I

A.Co TERRITORY

Countries outside Newco TERRITORY, except:
A. The United States of America
B. Panama Canal Zone

SCHEDULE II

Newco TERRITORY

A. Japan
B. Republic of Korea (Southern)
C. Taiwan
D. Philippines

SCHEDULE III

COSTS OF J.CO (C_1)

COSTS of J.Co (C_1) allowable hereunder with respect to MACHINERY from time to time manufactured by J.Co and sold by J.Co to Newco under this Agreement and the Manufacturing Agreement attached hereto as Exhibit D shall, for the purposes of Paragraph F of this Agreement, be determined in accordance with the following principles and provisions:

1. GENERAL PRINCIPLE
   As Manufacturer of such MACHINERY, J.Co will have certain COSTS C_1 which it will be allowed to recover hereunder. For its efforts and investment, it will also be allowed to recover a profit determined and allowed hereunder in the form of a Mark-up M_1.

2-4. [Accounting guidelines for determining COSTS C_1 omitted.]

5. ALTERNATIVE SIMPLIFIED DETERMINATION OF COSTS OF J.CO (C_1)
   (a) *General*
   In order to simplify determination of COSTS of J.Co (C_1) under this Agreement, COSTS C_1 may be fixed for any fiscal year in accordance with this Paragraph 5 and if so fixed shall be deemed to be the finally determined allowable COSTS C_1 under Paragraph F-5 of this Agreement.
   (b) and (c) [Omitted.]
   (d) *Definition of AGREED MANUFACTURING COSTS*
   AGREED MANUFACTURING COSTS of J.Co (*i.e.*, direct labor plus direct material plus manufacturing overhead), for purposes of determining COSTS C_1 under this Paragraph 5 shall, for machines and variable equipment produced for Newco by J.Co and sold by Newco in each fiscal year, be:
   (1) * * * approved by Newco Board Resolution in the November preceding such fiscal year; and
   (2) The Newco Board, in its determination and approval of each AGREED MANUFACTURING COST of J.Co, shall take into consideration for the same or most nearly comparable Model:

(i) J.Co's actual and estimated costs (excluding excess costs);
(ii) Newco's actual and estimated selling price and margin;
(iii) Selling prices of competitive machines manufactured in Japan;
(iv) A.Co's comparable standard costs; and
(v) Other relevant economic and commercial factors.

SCHEDULE IV

COSTS of Newco (C_2)

COSTS of Newco (C_2) allowable hereunder with respect to MACHINERY from time to time manufactured by Newco, by itself or by subcontract with J.Co under the Manufacturing Agreement attached hereto as Exhibit D, or otherwise, and sold by Newco to BUYERS, shall, for the purposes of Paragraph F of this Agreement, be determined in accordance with the following principles and provisions:

1. GENERAL PRINCIPLE
As Manufacturer and Seller of such MACHINERY, Newco will have certain COSTS (C_2) which, in addition to J.Co's SELLING PRICE (SP_1), it will be allowed to recover hereunder. For its efforts and investment, it will also be allowed to recover a profit determined and allowed hereunder in the form of a Mark-up M_2.

2.-4. [Accounting guidelines for determining COSTS C_2 omitted.]

5. ALTERNATIVE SIMPLIFIED DETERMINATION OF COSTS OF NEWCO (C_2)
In order to simplify determination of COSTS of Newco (C_2) properly allocable to MACHINERY manufactured by or for Newco under this Agreement, agreed allowable COSTS C_2 may be fixed for any fiscal year by Newco Board Resolution in the November preceding such fiscal year. * * *

EXHIBIT A
ARTICLES OF INCORPORATION of NEWCO K.K.

Chapter I
General Provisions

Article 1. Corporate Name

The name of the Company shall be "NEWCO KABUSHIKI KAISHA" (in English "NEWCO K.K.").

Article 2. Object

The object of the Company shall be to engage in the following business:

(1) Manufacture, sale and distribution of excavating and material handling equipment of all kinds and related products and parts therefor; and

(2) Operation of business related to the preceding item.

Article 3. Location of Head Office

[Tokyo.]

Article 4. Method of Public Notices

Public notices of the Company shall be made in the Official Gazette (*Kampō*).

Chapter II
Shares

Article 5. Total Number of Shares

The total number of shares authorized to be issued by the Company shall be seven hundred and twenty thousand (720,000) shares.

Article 6. Par Value Shares

All shares to be issued by the Company shall be par value shares and the par value of each share shall be five hundred (500) yen.

Article 7. Right of Preemption

The shareholders of the Company shall have the preemptive right to subscribe to all future share issues of the Company.

Article 8. Denomination of Share Certificates

[Omitted.]

Articles 9.-12

[Rules concerning registering with the company shares and share transactions omitted.]

Chapter III
General Meeting of Shareholders

Article 13. Holding of General Meeting of Shareholders

The ordinary general meeting of shareholders shall be held in February of each year and an extraordinary general meeting shall be held whenever necessary.

Article 14. Calling of General Meeting

The convening of general meetings of shareholders and place of the meetings shall be determined by the Board of Directors.

[Provisions concerning notices for meetings omitted.]

Article 15. Chairman of General Meetings

One of the directors shall act as chairman as determined by resolution of the Board of Directors.

Article 16. Requisites for Resolutions

Unless otherwise provided by law, all resolutions of general meetings of shareholders shall be adopted by a three-fourths (3/4) vote by the shareholders present at the meeting in person or by proxy, which shareholders shall hold shares representing in the aggregate at least three-fourths (3/4) of the total number of issued shares.

Each shareholder shall have one (1) vote for each share.

Article 17. Voting by Proxy

A shareholder may exercise his vote through a proxy. * * *

Article 18. Minutes of General Meetings

The substance of proceedings at a general meeting of shareholders and the results thereof shall be recorded in the minutes of the meeting * * * and shall be preserved in the Company's head office. * * *

Chapter IV
Directors and Auditors

Article 19. Number of Directors and Auditors

There shall be six (6) directors of the Company and there shall be two (2) auditors.

Article 20. Election

The directors and the auditors shall be elected at a general meeting of shareholders.

Article 21. Term of Office

The term of office of the directors shall [be two years], and the term of office of the auditors shall [be one year].

Article 22. Election of Representative Directors and Directors with Specific Powers

The Board of Directors shall appoint by resolution one (1) President (*Shachō*) and one (1) Executive Managing Director (*Senmu Torishimariyaku*), and one (1) or more managing directors (*Jōmu Torishimariyaku*), as the Board may determine.

The President and Executive Managing Director shall represent the Company.

Article 23. Remuneration and Retirement Allowances

The remuneration of directors and of the auditors shall be determined by resolution of the shareholders in a general meeting of shareholders.

Chapter V
Board of Directors

Article 24. Person to Call Meetings

Meetings of the Board of Directors may be called by any director.

Article 25. Notice of Meetings of Board of Directors

[Provisions concerning notices for Board meetings omitted.]

Article 26. Chairman

The director calling a meeting shall act as chairman at meetings of the Board of Directors.

Article 27. Resolutions

Resolutions at a meeting of the Board of Directors shall be adopted by the unanimous vote of the directors present who shall constitute at least four (4) directors.

Article 28. Composition of Quorum

The four (4) directors required for a resolution of the Board of Directors under Article 27 shall include at least one (1) director nominated and elected by each of the original corporate promoters of the Company or their respective related transferees.

Articles 29 and 30.

[Provisions concerning minutes of Board meetings and the possibility of adopting by-laws omitted.]

Chapter VI
Accounts

Article 31. Business Year

[Omitted.]

Article 32. Procedures for Disposal of Profit

The profit for each business year of the Company, added to the amount carried forward from the preceding business year, shall be disposed of in the manner provided below; provided, however, that a certain amount may, if necessary, either be set aside as reserves or be carried forward to the succeeding business year:

(1) Legal reserve out of profit,
(2) Dividends to shareholders.

Article 33. Payment of Dividends to Shareholders

Dividends shall be paid to the shareholders or registered pledgees appearing on the register of shareholders as of the closing of accounts for each business year.

Dividends to shareholders shall bear no interest.

Chapter VII
Supplementary Provisions

Article 34. Shares Issued at the Time of Incorporation

The number of shares issued by the Company at the time of incorporation shall be one hundred and eighty thousand (180,000) common par value shares, and the issuing price shall be five hundred (500) yen per share.

Articles 35 and 36.

[Omitted.]

The undersigned promoters for the purpose of incorporation of NEWCO K.K. have made these Articles of Incorporation in accordance with the provisions of the Commercial Code and have hereunto affixed their signatures or names and seals, with their respective addresses, this the

__________ day of __________, 1970.

1. ______________________________
2. ______________________________
3. ______________________________
4. ______________________________
5. ______________________________
6. ______________________________
7. ______________________________

EXHIBIT B

TECHNICAL AGREEMENT

(A.Co-Newco)

Contents

8. Confidential Data
9. Data Import Permits
10. Warranty and Disclaimer
11. Patent Indemnity
12. Quality Standards and Control

F. SUPPLY OF TECHNICAL ASSISTANCE
1. Training of Personnel
2. Consultation
3. Permits
4. Terms and Conditions of Service of A.Co Technical Representatives and Product Specialists

G. FEES AND COMPENSATION
1. Initial Disclosure Fees
2. Subsequent Disclosure Fees
3. Technical Assistance and Improvement Fees
4. Minimum Fees
5. Method of Payments
6. Taxes
7. Fee Statements
8. Charges for Provision of A.Co Technical Representatives
9. Charges for Newco Technical Representatives Who Visit A.Co

H. GENERAL PROVISIONS
1. Non-Assignment of Agreement
2. Entire Agreement
3. Applicable and Supervening Law
4. Governmental Approval
5. Suspension of Performance
6. Arbitration
7. Waivers
8. Notices
9. Schedules

I. TERMINATION
1. By Agreement
2. For Breach
3. For Insolvency, etc.
4. For Termination of Joint Venture Agreement
5. For Governmental Disapproval
6. Effect
7. Other Remedies

J. EFFECTIVE DATE AND DURATION OF AGREEMENT
1. Effective Date
2. Duration

SCHEDULES

I A.Co TERRITORY
II Newco TERRITORY
III EXCAVATOR Covered by Initial Grant
IV EXCAVATOR Subject to Option
V LICENSED PATENTS

TECHNICAL AGREEMENT

AGREEMENT made between [A.Co and Newco].

WHEREAS: [Recitals omitted.]

NOW, THEREFORE, in consideration of the premises and the mutual benefits to be derived herefrom,

IT IS AGREED AS FOLLOWS:

A. DEFINITIONS
The following terms where used in this Agreement shall have the following meanings:
[Definitions identical to those in the JVA omitted.]

5. LICENSED PRODUCTS
A.Co EXCAVATOR licensed under this Agreement pursuant to Paragraph B-1 hereof and listed in Schedule III hereof, and any other A.Co EXCAVATOR that may be licensed under this Agreement pursuant to paragraph B-2(a) hereof; and PARTS and COMPONENTS of such EXCAVATOR.

6. LICENSED PRODUCT IMPROVEMENTS
All product refinements and improvements to LICENSED PRODUCTS resulting from normal product development and improvement activities of A.Co and owned and applied by A.Co in its general production in the U.S.A. to the same EXCAVATOR Models as are included in LICENSED PRODUCTS.

7. LICENSED PATENTS
The patents and applications listed in Schedule V hereof, and any other patents or applications that may be brought under this Agreement pursuant to Paragraph B-2(c) hereof, and all other patents, patent applications and patent rights in Newco TERRITORY owned by A.Co during the life of this Agreement and directly relating to LICENSED PRODUCTS and LICENSED PRODUCT IMPROVEMENTS and to materials and methods used in their manufacture pursuant to this Agreement.

8. TECHNICAL DATA
Data directly relating to, and regularly used by A.Co to manufacture, LICENSED PRODUCTS, and supplied to Newco hereunder; said data, collectively as to each EXCAVATOR Model, consisting of reproducible copies of the items listed in Schedule VI hereof.

9. TECHNICAL IMPROVEMENT DATA
Data directly relating to, and regularly used by A.Co to manufacture, LICENSED PRODUCT IMPROVEMENTS, and supplied to Newco hereunder; said data, collectively as to each EXCAVATOR Model, consisting of the applicable items listed in Schedule VI hereof.

10. TECHNICAL ASSISTANCE
Advice and service of technical personnel of A.Co regarding design, manufacture, sale, use, repair and maintenance of LICENSED PRODUCTS and LICENSED PRODUCT IMPROVEMENTS.

11. PARTY
A.Co or Newco.

12. A.Co TERRITORY
The territory specified in Schedule I attached hereto.

13. Newco TERRITORY
The territory specified in Schedule II attached hereto.

14. NET SELLING PRICE
Gross selling price f.o.b. factory, less applicable trade and cash discounts, and excluding price of the truck and parts thereof in the case of truck-mounted MACHINERY.

B. GRANTS

1. *License*
Subject to the terms and conditions of this Agreement, A.Co hereby grants to Newco for the duration of this Agreement with respect to each Model under Paragraph J-2 hereof an exclusive license to manufacture, use and sell in Newco TERRITORY LICENSED PRODUCTS and LICENSED PRODUCT IMPROVEMENTS under and in accordance with the:
(1) LICENSED PATENTS,
(2) TECHNICAL DATA and TECHNICAL IMPROVEMENT DATA, and
(3) TECHNICAL ASSISTANCE
respectively licensed, supplied and rendered to Newco hereunder.
A.Co agrees to execute and do and procure to be executed and done by all necessary parties all such documents and things as may be requisite to vest in and secure to Newco the rights and benefits granted to Newco hereunder, the documents evidencing such rights to be delivered, upon request, in recordable or fileable form.

2. *Option*
(a) If, during the first five years of the life of this Agreement, Newco notifies A.Co in writing of its election to manufacture in Newco TERRITORY any Model of the A.Co EXCAVATORS listed in Schedule IV attached hereto, A.Co shall extend the Grant under Paragraph B-1 above to include such EXCAVATOR Model, and PARTS and COMPONENTS thereof, as LICENSED PRODUCTS, provided:
(1) That the Model in question is then in production by A.Co in the U.S.A., and
(2) That A.Co and Newco are mutually satisfied that sufficient market then exists in Newco TERRITORY to justify such manufacture in Newco TERRITORY.
(b) If A.Co should determine that a Model of EXCAVATOR listed in Schedule IV hereof, but not then included as a LICENSED PRODUCT, is ready for service in Newco TERRITORY and that sufficient market exists for such Model in Newco TERRITORY, A.Co may so notify Newco in writing, giving Newco access to complete data and specifications to permit Newco to study the general design manufacture of such Model; and if Newco does not, within one year from the date of said notice by A.Co, notify A.Co that Newco elects to manufacture said Model in Newco TERRITORY as a LICENSED PRODUCT, said Model shall then be dropped from future consideration as a LICENSED PRODUCT and shall be deleted from Schedule IV hereof.
(c) A.Co agrees that any patent or patent application in Newco TERRITORY not listed in Schedule V hereof, for an invention owned by A.Co at the date of signing of this Agreement and relating to a LICENSED PRODUCT, may on written notice by Newco to A.Co be considered as included among the LICENSED PATENTS.

3. *A.Co Inventions*
(a) Upon the written request and at the expense of Newco, A.Co shall, in any country in Newco TERRITORY designated by Newco, file application or applications for and use its best endeavors to obtain, in the name of A.Co, patents for any invention, improvement, modification or design disclosed to Newco pursuant to Paragraph C-1 hereof.
(b) Every patent so obtained, and every patent disclosed to Newco pursuant to Paragraph C-1 hereof, shall, upon the issuance or such disclosure thereof, be considered as

included among the LICENSED PATENTS and subject, for the duration of this Agreement, to the exclusive license granted to Newco in Paragraph B-1 hereof.

4. *Newco Inventions*
   (a) Any patents obtained by Newco on the basis of any invention, improvement, modification or design disclosed to A.Co pursuant to Paragraph C-2 hereof shall be the sole property of Newco, and A.Co shall be granted the right to use such patents free of charge for the duration of this Agreement.
   (b) Upon the written request of A.Co, Newco shall, in any country or countries designated by A.Co, file application or applications for, and use its best endeavors to obtain, patents for any such invention and the like, in the name of Newco.

5. *Execution of Documents*
   [Provision concerning obligation to execute necessary documents for obtaining patent rights omitted.]

6. *Product Changes*
   A.Co reserves the right, with respect to any LICENSED PRODUCT or LICENSED PRODUCT IMPROVEMENT, to:
   (a) Cease production thereof,
   (b) Make changes in design, or
   (c) Add improvements without liability to Newco or any third party.

7. *Prohibited Transactions*
   Newco and its appointed subcontractors, sublicensees or DISTRIBUTORS shall not directly or indirectly sell, deliver or disclose MACHINERY or other goods, technical data or information, in or to any country where such sale, delivery or disclosure by A.Co would be prohibited by the U.S. Trading with the Enemy Act, or any similar law or regulation imposing restrictions on U.S. trade with foreign countries.

8. [Omitted.]

9. *Sales of MACHINERY by A.Co*
   Nothing contained in this Agreement shall restrict the right of A.Co to sell MACHINERY of its manufacture throughout the world.

C. DISCLOSURE OF INVENTIONS

1. *By A.Co*
   A.Co shall promptly disclose in writing to Newco any invention, improvement, modification or design, whether patented, patentable or not, made, developed or acquired by A.Co and relating to and actually utilized by A.Co in its then current manufacture of any LICENSED PRODUCT or LICENSED PRODUCT IMPROVEMENT, and shall fully disclose to Newco the nature and manner of performing or utilizing the same.

2. *By Newco*
   Newco shall promptly disclose to A.Co in writing, and review at least annually in writing with A.Co, any invention, improvement, modification or design, whether patented, patentable or not, made or developed, either independently or jointly with A.Co, or made, developed or acquired by Newco or by any of its subcontractors or sublicensees and relating to any LICENSED PRODUCT or LICENSED PRODUCT IMPROVEMENT, and shall fully disclose to A.Co the nature and manner of performing or utilizing the same.

3. *Excluded Disclosures and Grants*
   Neither PARTY shall be required to make any disclosure or grant hereunder, if it is prohibited or prevented by governmental act or regulation from, or any third party is entitled to prohibit or prevent such PARTY from, making such disclosure or grant. * * *

D. PROTECTION OF PATENTS

1. [Newco maintenance obligation omitted.]

2. *Validity*

(a) Newco hereby agrees and admits that it will not at any time directly or indirectly dispute or jeopardize the validity or enforceability of any LICENSED PATENT.

(b) A.Co shall not be held responsible by Newco for the validity or enforceability of any LICENSED PATENT should such validity or enforceability be contested by third parties or such PATENT be prematurely terminated for any cause whatsoever.

3. *Marking*

[Newco and J.Co must place on excavators manufactured by them a metal plate indicating that the manufacture took place under a license from A.Co.]

4. *Infringement*

[Newco has the right to take action against infringers of any LICENSED PATENT, but if it does not do so, A.Co may.]

E. SUPPLY OF DATA

1. *Initial Disclosure*

Within 60 days after the receipt by A.Co of the Disclosure Fee under Paragraph G-1(a) hereof, A.Co shall ship to Newco one complete set of reproducible copies of TECHNICAL DATA relating to each Model listed in Schedule III hereof.

2. *Subsequent Disclosures*

[A.Co also to supply TECHNICAL DATA for any additional models listed in Schedule IV that are brought within the scope of the JVA.]

3. *Disclosures of TECHNICAL IMPROVEMENT DATA*

A.Co shall from time to time promptly, after release of the same for general production in the U.S.A., ship to Newco one set of applicable TECHNICAL IMPROVEMENT DATA, not previously supplied to Newco, which relates to LICENSED PRODUCT IMPROVEMENTS.

4.–7. [Omitted.]

8. *Confidential Data*

(a) The TECHNICAL DATA and TECHNICAL IMPROVEMENT DATA furnished or disclosed hereunder to Newco by A.Co is confidential and derives a major part of its value from the fact that it is confidential. The exclusive rights of Newco to use TECHNICAL DATA and TECHNICAL IMPROVEMENT DATA within Newco TERRITORY does not include any right in Newco or in any person deriving either limited or unlimited rights in such TECHNICAL DATA and TECHNICAL IMPROVEMENT DATA from Newco either immediately or remotely to make any reproduction, use, sale or disclosure of such TECHNICAL DATA or TECHNICAL IMPROVEMENT DATA that would impair or tend to impair the ownership by A.Co of such TECHNICAL DATA and TECHNICAL IMPROVEMENT DATA outside of Newco TERRITORY. The ownership by A.Co of such TECHNICAL DATA and TECHNICAL IMPROVEMENT DATA outside of Newco TERRITORY similarly does not, except as provided in Paragraphs B-8 and B-9 hereof, include any right to reproduce, use, sell or disclose such TECHNICAL DATA or TECHNICAL IMPROVEMENT DATA in such a way as to impair or tend to impair the exclusive rights hereunder of Newco in such TECHNICAL DATA and TECHNICAL IMPROVEMENT DATA within Newco TERRITORY.

(b) All TECHNICAL DATA and TECHNICAL IMPROVEMENT DATA furnished or disclosed hereunder to Newco by A.Co shall be deemed confidential and shall not be disclosed by Newco during or after termination of this Agreement except as may be permitted in Subparagraph (a) above or as required for manufacture of LICENSED PRODUCTS and LICENSED PRODUCT IMPROVEMENTS in Newco TERRITORY.

(c) Newco further agrees to take any steps, including suitable marking of all copies of drawings and other data, necessary to prevent its employees, subcontractors, sublicensees and vendors from disclosing, and to preserve the confidential nature of, any confidential data disclosed to them by Newco as aforesaid. Disclosure as aforesaid shall not relieve such TECHNICAL DATA and TECHNICAL IMPROVEMENT DATA of its confidential nature.

(d) Subcontractors, sublicensees or vendors of Newco to whom said TECHNICAL DATA and TECHNICAL IMPROVEMENT DATA is disclosed for manufacture of LICENSED PRODUCTS and LICENSED PRODUCT IMPROVEMENTS shall produce such products only for use of or sale by Newco, except as may from time to time be mutually agreed by A.Co and Newco.

9. [Omitted.]

10. *Warranty and Disclaimer*

(a) A.Co warrants to Newco that the TECHNICAL DATA and TECHNICAL IMPROVEMENT DATA supplied to Newco under this Agreement are and will be such as are then used by A.Co in the manufacture, assembly, sale and maintenance of LICENSED PRODUCTS and LICENSED PRODUCT IMPROVEMENTS.

(b) If any errors are found by A.Co or by Newco in any of said TECHNICAL DATA and TECHNICAL IMPROVEMENT DATA, A.Co will promptly notify Newco of corrections to be made.

(c) Although A.Co will take great care to prevent any errors, A.Co cannot guarantee that none will occur, and, in such event, does not assume any responsibility for any consequences that could be attributed to these errors.

(d) A.Co makes no warranty, express or implied, that MACHINERY built in accordance with said TECHNICAL DATA and TECHNICAL IMPROVEMENT DATA is patented, or will be free from defects or from patent infringement, or will perform to the satisfaction or meet the requirements of any particular purchaser thereof.

11. *Patent Indemnity*

Newco agrees not to sue, and agrees to indemnify, A.Co with respect to any liability or claim for patent infringement resulting from the manufacture, use or sale of LICENSED PRODUCTS and LICENSED PRODUCT IMPROVEMENTS by Newco or by any subcontractor or sublicensee of Newco.

12. *Quality Standards and Control*

[(a) and (b), concerning obligation of Newco and its subcontractors to follow A.Co's quality control procedures in manufacture and service, omitted.]

(c) Newco agrees not to make, or allow any subcontractor or sublicensee to make, any change in the design or materials of LICENSED PRODUCTS or LICENSED PRODUCT IMPROVEMENTS or to vary from the quality standards as established by A.Co. The following procedures shall apply with respect to A.Co's approval of changes in engineering design or material. * * * [Detailed procedures for Newco or J.Co staff communicating desired changes to A.Co staff omitted.]

F. SUPPLY OF TECHNICAL ASSISTANCE

1. *Training of Personnel*

To assist Newco (or any subcontractor or sublicensee of Newco) in the manufacture and sale of LICENSED PRODUCTS and LICENSED PRODUCT IMPROVEMENTS, A.Co shall:

(a) Furnish, upon request from Newco (or J.Co), the services of qualified technical representatives, in the number and for the time as mutually agreed by A.Co and Newco (or J.Co), to train employees of Newco (or J.Co) on the job, for which Newco shall pay (or require J.Co to pay) A.Co charges in accordance with Paragraph G-8 hereof;

(b) Train, at the facilities and expense of A.Co, and subject to Paragraph G-9 hereof, technical representatives of Newco (or J.Co), such training to be scheduled in advance by Newco (or J.Co) and to be such as Newco (or J.Co) may reasonably require for its aforesaid manufacture; and

(c) [Omitted.]

2.–4. [Omitted.]

G. FEES AND COMPENSATION

1. *Initial Disclosure*

On or immediately after the effective date of this Agreement, Newco, in consideration of A.Co's grant under Paragraph B-1 hereof, shall pay to A.Co the sum of $300,000.

2. *Subsequent Disclosures*

[Newco to pay J.Co disclosure fees listed in Schedule IV for additional models brought into the scope of the JVA.]

3. *Technical Assistance and Improvement Fees*

(a) For the TECHNICAL DATA and TECHNICAL IMPROVEMENT DATA supplied to it hereunder, Newco shall pay to A.Co, in U.S. dollars converted at the then official exchange rate of authorized foreign exchange banks of Japan, Technical Assistance and Improvement Fees in an amount equal to five per cent (5%) of the NET SELLING PRICES of all LICENSED PRODUCTS and LICENSED PRODUCT IMPROVEMENTS manufactured by or for, or under sublicense from, Newco, and sold or leased by Newco or by any sublicensee of Newco, as the case may be.

(b) Except as provided in Subparagraph (c) below, said Technical Assistance and Improvement Fees shall accrue on the date when the fee-bearing MACHINERY shall have been initially shipped or initially invoiced by Newco (or by any sublicensee of Newco), whichever is earlier, to a BUYER. * * *

(c) [Omitted.]

4. *Minimum Fees*

(a) The Technical Assistance and Improvement Fees referred to in Paragraph G-3 above represent the only method that A.Co has of receiving compensation for the costs of maintaining the TECHNICAL DATA supplied to Newco with respect to LICENSED PRODUCTS and LICENSED PRODUCT IMPROVEMENTS.

(b) To assure A.Co that it will recover the costs of product refinements and improvements relating to LICENSED PRODUCTS and LICENSED PRODUCT IMPROVEMENTS, the Minimum Fees specified in Schedule VII hereof shall apply to cover the actual costs to A.Co of maintaining such TECHNICAL DATA and TECHNICAL IMPROVEMENT DATA. * * *

5. *Method of Payment*

[Omitted.]

6. *Taxes*

[Omitted.]

7. *Fee Statements*

(a) Newco shall at all times keep, and cause any sublicensee to keep, an accurate account by Model and Attachment of all sales, leases, and shipments of LICENSED PRODUCTS and LICENSED PRODUCT IMPROVEMENTS hereunder, and shall, on or before the payment date for each semiannual fee, render to A.Co a summarized statement thereof, in sufficient detail * * * to enable A.Co to determine the correctness of such fee payment. * * *

(b) and (c) [Omitted].

8. *Charges for Provision of A.Co Technical Representatives*
[A.Co to be paid all traveling and living expenses plus *per diem* fee to be agreed upon from time to time.]

9. *Charges for Newco Technical Representatives Who Visit A.Co*
[Newco responsible for all costs.]

H. GENERAL PROVISIONS
[Essentially the same as for JVA, with the addition of:]
5. *Suspension of Performance*
(a) Except for payment obligations hereunder, neither PARTY shall be liable for failure of performance hereunder occasioned by any cause beyond the control of such PARTY.
(b) Suspension of performance by reason of this Paragraph H-5 shall be limited to the period during which such cause of failure exists, but shall not affect the running of the term of this Agreement or any extension thereof.

I. TERMINATION
1. *By Agreement*
This Agreement shall continue in effect until terminated by agreement of the PARTIES, unless terminated as hereinafter provided.

2. *For Breach*
(a) This Agreement may be terminated by either PARTY by 90 days prior written notice to the other PARTY, specifying the reason for termination, in the event of a substantial breach by said other PARTY.
(b) Said termination shall become effective at the end of said 90 day period unless the breach or adverse effect is cured within said 90 day period.

3. *For Insolvency, etc.*
[Same language as in JVA]

4. *For Termination of Joint Venture Agreement*
Upon termination of the Joint Venture Agreement between A.Co and J.Co of even date, this Technical Agreement shall become terminated.

5. *For Governmental Disapproval*
If continuance of all or any part of this Agreement is disapproved by the Government of the United States of America or of Japan, this Agreement shall become terminated.

6. *Effect*
Upon termination of this Agreement, however occasioned:
(a) Neither PARTY shall be discharged of any antecedent obligation to the other PARTY, except that the PARTIES shall not be liable for special or consequential damages;
(b) The PARTIES shall continue to be bound by the provisions of Paragraphs B-6 to B-9 inclusive, E-6, E-8, E-10, E-11, E-12, G-2 to G-9 inclusive, H-3, H-6, H-7 and I hereof; and
(c) Newco shall reassign to A.Co all its rights in, and return to A.Co and discontinue the use of, all TECHNICAL DATA and TECHNICAL IMPROVEMENT DATA supplied by A.Co hereunder, and all copies thereof, including but not limited to copies in the possession of subcontractors, sublicensees, or vendors of Newco; provided, however, that Newco shall have the right to retain temporarily, but not longer than six months after termination, TECHNICAL DATA and TECHNICAL IMPROVEMENT DATA necessary to permit it, or its subcontractors or sublicensees, to complete manufacture of MACHINERY in process as of termination of this Agreement, and shall have the right to sell in Newco TERRITORY such MACHINERY and MACHINERY in stock as of such termination. Newco shall reassign to A.Co all its rights in, and shall discon-

tinue the use of, all TECHNICAL DATA and TECHNICAL IMPROVEMENT DATA covered by LICENSED PATENTS.

7. *Other Remedies*
   [Same language as in JVA.]

J. EFFECTIVE DATE AND DURATION OF AGREEMENT

1. *Effective Date*
   This Agreement shall be effective, with respect to MACHINERY of each Model listed in Schedule VIII hereof, as of the applicable effective date stated in said Schedule VIII.

2. *Duration*
   This Agreement shall, except as otherwise provided herein, continue in effect, with respect to MACHINERY of each Model listed in Schedule VIII hereof, for a period of 10 years from the applicable effective date stated in said Schedule VIII, and for successive one-year periods thereafter unless and until terminated at the end of the initial or any successive period by either PARTY, not less than 90 days before the end of such initial or successive period, by giving to the other PARTY written notice of such termination.

IN WITNESS WHEREOF, the PARTIES have caused these presents to be duly executed in manner appropriate to each and their corporate seals hereunto affixed on the dates respectively set forth below.

\merican Heavy Equipment, Inc.

By: ______________________
President

Attest: ______________________
Secretary

Date: ______________________

Newco K.K.

By: ______________________
President

Attest: ______________________
Secretary

Date: ______________________

SCHEDULE I

A.Co TERRITORY

Countries outside Newco TERRITORY, except:
A. The United States of America
B. Panama Canal Zone

SCHEDULE II

Newco TERRITORY

A. Japan
B. Republic of Korea (Southern)
C. Taiwan
D. Philippines

SCHEDULE III

EXCAVATORS Covered by Initial Grant

The following A.Co EXCAVATORS, and PARTS and COMPONENTS thereof, constitute LICENSED PRODUCTS for which TECHNICAL DATA is initially granted and supplied under Paragraphs B-1 and E-1 of this Agreement.

Model	*Disclosure Fee*
15-H Hydraulic Excavator	$300,000
20-H Hydraulic Excavator	$300,000

[Other models deleted from list.]

SCHEDULE IV

EXCAVATORS Subject to Option

The following A.Co EXCAVATORS, and PARTS and COMPONENTS thereof, may by option be included as LICENSED PRODUCTS for which TECHNICAL DATA is subsequently granted and supplied under Paragraphs B-2 and E-2 of this Agreement.

Model	*Disclosure Fee*
25-H Hydraulic Excavator	$100,000
30-H Hydraulic Excavator	$100,000

[Other models deleted from list.]

SCHEDULE V

LICENSED PATENTS

(a) *Patents*

Country	*Patent No.*	*Date of Grant*	*Inventor*	*Title*

[Omitted.]

(b) *Patent Applications*

Country	*Patent No.*	*Date of Grant*	*Inventor*	*Title*

[Omitted.]

SCHEDULE VI

TECHNICAL DATA ITEMS*

As to each EXCAVATOR Model:

1. Engineering general, assembly and detail drawings;
2. Engineering lists and bills of material;
3. General and detailed specifications, including specifications and performance data of purchased items;
4. Analyses of material;
5. Heat treatment and other special manufacturing procedures;
6. Details of manufacturing operations and planning, including:
   Routing cards,
   Performance data;
7. Drawings of jigs, fixtures and special tools;
8. Sales and service bulletins and instructions;
9. Other relevant instructions, data and information owned and regularly used by A.Co to manufacture MACHINERY of said MODEL and complete in detail in accordance with the then production practice of A.Co.

*Media such as, but not limited to, microfilms, wall charts, training films, photostats, photographic negatives or prints, etc., other than prints of engineering drawings and multilith or blueprint copies of the items listed herein, will be furnished to Newco at prices to be agreed by the PARTIES at the time such media are requested.

SCHEDULE VII

MINIMUM FEES FOR EACH MODEL

[Omitted.]

SCHEDULE VIII

APPLICABLE EFFECTIVE DATES OF AGREEMENT BY MODEL

[Omitted.]

Note on TRADEMARK AGREEMENT

In the actual case on which the P.C. is based, the name of the joint venture company was a hyphenated combination of the name of each venturer (i.e., "J.-A.Co" rather than "Newco"). The U.S. venturer thus required a trademark license agreement by which it licensed to the joint venture company the right to incorporate the U.S. venturer's name into the trademark bearing the joint venture company's name. The Trademark Agreement (and JVA §6) therefore reference Newco's incorporating the A.Co trademark into its own trademark.

EXHIBIT C

TRADEMARK AGREEMENT

(A.Co and Newco)

THIS AGREEMENT, made between [A.Co and Newco].

WHEREAS, A.Co is the proprietor of the trademark "American Heavy Equipment, Inc.", which trademark has been registered in Japan, Reg. No. [x]; and

WHEREAS, Newco desires to obtain a nonexclusive license to use said trademark in Japan,

NOW, THEREFORE, in consideration of the foregoing and of the mutual covenants and undertakings hereinafter set forth, A.Co hereby grants to Newco, for the life of this Agreement, the nonexclusive right to use the said trademark in Japan in connection with the goods covered by said registrations, subject to the following conditions and provisions:

1. No right, title or interest in the said trademark and any registrations thereof, except the right to use said trademark in Japan on the goods covered by said registrations, is transferred by this Agreement to Newco.

2. Newco agrees to limit its use of the said trademark to:

(a) Goods substantially identical to and of quality and workmanship not inferior to goods manufactured by A.Co, and manufactured in accordance with designs, plans, and specifications prescribed or approved by A.Co;

(b) Utilization, upon or in connection with said goods, as a part of the name "Newco" and in a form or forms approved in writing by A.Co prior to such use; and

(c) Utilization in Japan and the remainder of Newco TERRITORY, as defined in the Technical Agreement of even date between the PARTIES.

3. Except as provided in Paragraph 2(b) hereof, Newco shall not have the right to use said trademark in combination with any other trademark, word, symbol, letter or design.

4. and 5. [Omitted.]

6. Newco agrees to notify A.Co, in writing, of any conflicting uses of, and of any application or registration for, said trademark, alone or in conjunction with any other word, or any similar trademark, or of any acts of infringement or of unfair competition involving said trademark, promptly after such matters are brought to its attention or it has knowledge thereof.

7. * * * Infringement or unfair competition proceedings shall be entirely within the discretion of A.Co.

8. Newco hereby acknowledges that said trademark and the goodwill relative thereto are the property of A.Co and agrees that it will not in any way dispute or impugn the validity of said trademark * * * both during the life of this agreement and thereafter, and that it will not at any time, unless it be at A.Co's request, file an application on its own behalf in Japan or any other country for said trademark either alone or in combination with any other word, symbol, letter or design.

9. A.Co reserves the right to use said trademark in any country and also reserves the right to license other parties to use said trademark.

10. Either party shall have the right to terminate this Agreement at any time by giving not less than 90 days notice in writing to the other party to that effect.

11. A.Co shall have the right to terminate this Agreement upon not less than 30 days written notice to Newco, in the event of any change in the legal form of Newco's organization or in the event of Newco's going into bankruptcy, winding-up, consolidation, merger, or any sequestration by any Governmental authority.

12. Upon the termination of this Agreement, however occasioned, Newco agrees to:
    (a) Discontinue immediately the use of said trademark or any colorable imitation of said trademark, alone or in combination with any other word, letter, symbol or design;
    (b) Amend its corporate or business name to remove therefrom said trademark; and
    (c) [File necessary documents with the appropriate authorities to remove all references to the trademark, etc.]

13. [Upon termination, A.Co may take appropriate actions at the Patent Office of Japan to cancel the registration of the agreement.]

14. This Agreement shall not be assignable by Newco.

15. This Agreement shall be effective as of the date of Japanese Governmental approval of said Technical Agreement of even date between the PARTIES hereto, and shall be interpreted according to the laws of the State of New York, U.S.A., or Japan, at the option of A.Co.

16. [A.Co and Newco agree to execute necessary documents at the Patent Office of Japan to register the agreement and to prosecute any infringement action.]

IN WITNESS WHEREOF, the PARTIES have caused these presents to be duly executed in manner appropriate to each and their corporate seals hereunto affixed on the dates respectively set forth below.

American Heavy Equipment, Inc.

By: ______________________________

President

Attest: ______________________________

Secretary

Date: ______________________________

Newco K.K.

By: ______________________________

President

Attest: ______________________________

Secretary

Date: ______________________________

EXHIBIT D

MANUFACTURING AGREEMENT

(Newco-J.Co)

Contents

F. CONDITIONS OF SALE
   1. Subcontract Sales to Newco
   2. [Omitted]

G. GENERAL PROVISIONS
   1. Non-Assignment of Agreement
   2. Entire Agreement
   3. Applicable and Supervening Law
   4. Suspension of Performance
   5. Waivers

H. TERMINATION
   1. By Agreement
   2. For Breach
   3. For Insolvency, etc.
   4. For Termination of Joint Venture Agreement
   5. For Termination of TECHNICAL AGREEMENT
   6. For Governmental Disapproval
   7. Effect
   8. Other Remedies

I. EFFECTIVE DATE AND DURATION OF AGREEMENT
   1. Effective Date
   2. Duration

MANUFACTURING AGREEMENT

AGREEMENT made between [Newco and J.Co.]

WHEREAS: [Recitals omitted.]

NOW, THEREFORE, in consideration of the premises and the mutual benefits to be derived herefrom,

IT IS AGREED AS FOLLOWS:

A. DEFINITIONS
The following terms where used in this Agreement shall have the following meanings: [Definitions contained in previous agreements omitted.]

B. APPOINTMENT OF J.Co

1. *Manufacture of LICENSED PRODUCTS*
Newco hereby appoints J.Co, subject to the terms and conditions of this Agreement, manufacturer for or under Newco in Newco TERRITORY for all LICENSED PRODUCTS.

2. *Conditions of Manufacture*
Except as provided in Paragraph F-2 hereof, J.Co shall manufacture LICENSED PRODUCTS only as subcontractor to the order of and for sale to, or with the prior written consent of, Newco; and agrees that its manufacture of LICENSED PRODUCTS shall not be subcontracted without the prior written approval of Newco, and shall be in accordance with the designs, plans, specifications, technique and procedures and instructions prescribed or approved from time to time by Newco, or by A.Co in accordance with the provisions of TECHNICAL AGREEMENT and TRADEMARK AGREEMENT between Newco and A.Co.

3. *Other Products*
   (a) J.Co shall not at any time during this Agreement manufacture, sell or handle, or directly or indirectly be concerned in the manufacture, sale or handling of any items competitive with LICENSED PRODUCTS, except that J.Co may, at its discretion, continue the manufacture, sale and handling of tractors, tractor shovels and tractor hoes, and other clearly non-competitive tractor-mounted, tractor-drawn or tractor-operated equipment.
   (b) J.Co shall, insofar as practicable, conduct its manufacturing operation hereunder so that the materials, supplies and LICENSED PRODUCTS involved therein are separated from other materials, supplies and products manufactured or handled by J.Co.

4. and 5. [Omitted.]

6. *Access to Accounts*
   J.Co shall make available to representatives of Newco and A.Co, and to auditors appointed by either, all books, accounts, vouchers and documents relating to the subject matter of this Agreement and orders thereunder, and to the statements and reports rendered by J.Co and the accounting relationship between the PARTIES.

C. SUPPLY OF TECHNICAL DATA

1. *Initial Use*
   For each Lot of MACHINERY consisting of a specified number of EXCAVATORS and/or PARTS of a specified Model, ordered from J.Co by Newco, Newco shall furnish or cause to be furnished to J.Co a set of complete reproducible copies of TECHNICAL DATA covering such Model for a period sufficient to permit J.Co to manufacture such Lot.

2. *Return or Renewal*
   Upon completion of manufacture of such a Lot, the TECHNICAL DATA covering it and all copies thereof shall be returned to Newco, unless J.Co obtains written permission from Newco for the renewed use of such TECHNICAL DATA for an additional Lot.

3. *Revisions*
   With such permission for renewed use, Newco shall concurrently furnish J.Co all revised TECHNICAL DATA relating to the MACHINERY involved since the TECHNICAL DATA for the preceding Lot was furnished, in order to bring such TECHNICAL DATA up to date.

4. [Omitted.]

5. *Confidential Data*
   (a) All TECHNICAL DATA furnished hereunder to J.Co by Newco, or by A.Co at the request of Newco, shall remain the property of Newco or A.Co respectively, shall be deemed confidential and shall not be disclosed by J.Co during or after termination of this Agreement, except as may be required for manufacture of LICENSED PRODUCTS, including necessary disclosures to employees, subcontractors, and vendors who supply material, and as may be required for sale, use and service of LICENSED PRODUCTS.
   (b) J.Co further agrees to take any necessary steps to prevent such employees, subcontractors, and vendors from disclosing any confidential material disclosed to them by J.Co as aforesaid. Disclosure as aforesaid shall not relieve such TECHNICAL DATA of its confidential nature.
   (c) Subcontractors or vendors of J.Co to whom said TECHNICAL DATA is disclosed for manufacture of LICENSED PRODUCTS shall produce such products only for use of or sale by J.Co, except as may from time to time be mutually agreed by Newco and J.Co.

6. *Product Changes*
Newo and A.Co reserve the right, with respect to any LICENSED PRODUCTS, to:
(a) Cease production thereof,
(b) Make changes in design, or
(c) Add improvements,
without liability to J.Co or any third party.

7. *Translation of Data*
[All TECHNICAL DATA to be supplied in English, with any translation to be at J.Co's expense.]

8. *Warranty and Disclaimer*
(a) Newco warrants to J.Co that the TECHNICAL DATA supplied to J.Co under this Agreement is and will be such as are used by Newco and/or A.Co in the design, manufacture, assembly, sale and maintenance of MACHINERY designated herein as LICENSED PRODUCTS.
(b) If any errors are found by J.Co or by Newco in any of said TECHNICAL DATA, Newco will promptly notify A.Co of corrections to be made.
(c) Although Newco will take great care to prevent any errors, Newco cannot guarantee that none will occur, and, in such event, does not assume any responsibility for any consequence that could be attributed to errors.

D. INVENTIONS AND PATENTS

1. *Disclosure of J.Co Inventions*
J.Co shall promptly disclose in writing to, and review at least annually in writing with, Newco and A.Co any invention, improvement, modification or design, whether patented, patentable or not, made or developed, either independently or jointly with Newco and/or A.Co, or acquired by J.Co, relating to any LICENSED PRODUCT, and shall fully disclose to Newco and A.Co the nature and manner of performing or utilizing the same.

2. *Ownership and Patenting of J.Co Inventions*
(a) Every invention, improvement, modification or design disclosed to Newco or A.Co pursuant to Paragraph D-1 hereof shall, subject to the provisions of TECHNICAL AGREEMENT between A.Co and Newco, be the property of Newco.
(b) Upon the written request of Newco or A.Co, J.Co shall, at Newco's expense (Newco reserving the right to designate the agents therefor), in any country or countries designated by Newco or A.Co, file application or applications for, and use its best endeavors to obtain, patents for any such invention and the like, in the name of J.Co.
(c) Every patent so obtained shall forthwith upon the issuance thereof be assigned to Newco, or, upon the written request of A.Co, to A.Co.

3. *Validity*
(a) J.Co hereby admits and covenants that it will not at any time directly or indirectly dispute or jeopardize the validity or enforceability of any LICENSED PATENT now or hereafter obtained.
(b) Newco shall not be held responsible by J.Co for the validity or enforceability of any LICENSED PATENT should such validity or enforceability be contested by any third party or such patent be prematurely terminated for any cause whatsoever.

4. *Marking*
[Omitted.]

E. SUPPLY OF TECHNICAL ASSISTANCE

1. *Training of Personnel*
J.Co shall from time to time be entitled:

(a) To send technical representatives to receive training at the facilities of A.Co in accordance with Paragraph F-1(b) of TECHNICAL AGREEMENT between Newco and A.Co; and

(b) To require A.Co to furnish technical representatives to train employees of J.Co in accordance with Paragraph F-1(a) or for consultation under Paragraph F-2 of said TECHNICAL AGREEMENT.

2. *Terms and Conditions of Service of A.Co Technical Representatives*
J.Co agrees that the services of A.Co technical representatives rendered, under Paragraph E-1 hereof and Paragraphs F-1 and F-2 of said TECHNICAL AGREEMENT, to J.Co as subcontractor of Newco shall be subject to the Terms and Conditions of Paragraph F-4 of said TECHNICAL AGREEMENT applied *mutatis mutandis* to J.Co in place of Newco.

3. *Charges for A.Co Technical Representatives*
J.Co shall pay A.Co all charges under said TECHNICAL AGREEMENT with respect to such training of, or consultation with, J.Co personnel under this Agreement and Paragraph G-8 of said TECHNICAL AGREEMENT.

4. [Omitted.]

F. CONDITIONS OF SALE

1. *Subcontract Sales to Newco*
Except as provided in Paragraph F-2 hereof, J.Co shall manufacture LICENSED PRODUCTS only as subcontractor of Newco and only to the order of and for sale to Newco, and all orders and subcontracts hereunder for J.Co's manufacture and sale to Newco of LICENSED PRODUCTS shall be subject to the following terms and conditions:

(a) *Price*
The sale prices of MACHINERY sold by J.Co to Newco shall be determined in accordance with the provisions of Paragraph F of the Joint Venture Agreement of even date.

(b) *Warranty*
J.Co warrants that the MACHINERY furnished will be as specified therein, and free from defects of materials and workmanship, and will function properly.

(c) *Inspection*

(i) All materials and workmanship shall be subject to Newco's and A.Co's inspection and tests at all times and places, and when practicable, during manufacturing * * * J.Co's manufacturing plant * * * shall at all times be subject to inspection by representatives of A.Co or Newco.

(ii) [Omitted.]

(d) *Acceptance and Rejection of MACHINERY*

(i) MACHINERY shall not be deemed finally accepted (notwithstanding payment or inspection) until it shall have been finally accepted by customers or users of the MACHINERY.

(ii) All rejected material against any order shall be held at J.Co's risk and expense subject to J.Co's advice as to disposition. Unless otherwise agreed, all rejected material will be returned and charged back, including all transportation and handling costs.

(iii) Final acceptance shall not bar claims based on defects not evident during inspection.

(iv) J.Co's acceptance of MACHINERY returned because of defect disclosed by tests shall constitute J.Co's acceptance of results of such tests and assent to Newco's or A.Co's destruction of test samples.

(e) *Tools, Dies, Patterns, Drawings, etc.*
Any tools, dies, patterns, drawings or other equipment furnished or paid for by Newco shall continue to be the property of Newco and subject to Newco's disposition at any time, shall be held by J.Co at J.Co's risk and replaced by J.Co if lost or destroyed, and shall be used exclusively in the production of LICENSED PRODUCTS.

(f) *Delivery*
J.Co shall not be responsible for delays or defaults of deliveries occasioned by wars, strikes, fires, Acts of God or public enemy, labor or transportation difficulties or other cause beyond the control of J.Co.

2. [Omitted.]

G. GENERAL PROVISIONS

1. *Non-Assignment of Agreement*
Except as otherwise provided herein, this Agreement and the rights and obligations of the PARTIES hereunder are personal and shall not be capable of assignment whether voluntary or otherwise, except that J.Co may, with the prior written approval of Newco, engage subcontractors to manufacture PARTS or COMPONENTS for assembly by J.Co into EXCAVATORS or Units or Sub-assemblies of EXCAVATORS of J.Co's own manufacture for Newco.

2.–6. [Other general provisions essentially the same as in JVA and TECHNICAL AGREEMENT §H-5.]

H. TERMINATION

1. *By Agreement*
This Agreement shall continue in effect until terminated by agreement of the PARTIES, unless terminated by expiration or otherwise as hereinafter provided.

2. *For Breach*
(a) This Agreement may be terminated by either PARTY by ninety (90) days prior written notice to the other PARTY, specifying the reason for termination, in the event of a substantial breach by said other PARTY.
(b) Said termination shall become effective at the end of said ninety (90) day period unless the breach or adverse effect is cured within said period.

3. *For Insolvency, etc.*
[Same language as in JVA.]

4. *For Termination of Joint Venture Agreement*
Upon termination of the Joint Venture Agreement of even date between A.Co and J.Co, this Agreement shall become terminated.

5. *For Termination of TECHNICAL AGREEMENT*
Upon termination of the TECHNICAL AGREEMENT between A.Co and Newco, this Agreement shall become terminated.

6. *For Governmental Disapproval*
[Same language as TECHNICAL AGREEMENT §I-5.]

7. *Effect*
Upon termination of this Agreement, however occasioned:
(a) Neither PARTY shall be discharged of any antecedent obligation to the other PARTY, except that the PARTIES shall not be liable for special or consequential damages;
(b) The PARTIES shall continue to be bound by the provisions of Paragraphs B-5, B-6, C-5, D-3 and G-3 hereof;
(c) J.Co shall return to Newco and discontinue the use of all TECHNICAL DATA sup-

plied by Newco and/or A.Co hereunder, and all copies thereof, including but not limited to copies in the possession of subcontractors or vendors of J.Co; provided, however, that J.Co shall have the right temporarily to retain TECHNICAL DATA necessary to permit it to complete manufacture and sale as subcontractor hereunder as the case may be of MACHINERY in process or in stock as of termination of this Agreement; and

(d) Newco shall be entitled, with the written consent of A.Co, to appoint such other manufacturer as it may deem fit to manufacture LICENSED PRODUCTS in Japan.

8. *Other Remedies*
[Same language as in JVA.]

I. EFFECTIVE DATE AND DURATION OF AGREEMENT

1. *Effective Date*
The effective date of this Agreement shall be the date of Japanese Government approval of said TECHNICAL AGREEMENT.

2. *Duration*
This Agreement shall, except as otherwise provided herein, continue in effect for a period of 10 years from its effective date and for successive one-year periods thereafter unless and until terminated at the end of the initial or any successive period by either PARTY, not less than 90 days before the end of such initial or successive period, giving to the other PARTY written notice of such termination.

IN WITNESS WHEREOF, the PARTIES have caused these presents to be duly executed in manner appropriate to each and their corporate seals hereunto affixed on the dates respectively set forth below.

Newco K.K.

By: ______________________
President

Attest: ______________________
Secretary

Date: ______________________

Japan Construction Machinery K.K.

By: ______________________
President

Attest: ______________________

Date: ______________________

EXHIBIT E

SELLING AGREEMENT

(A.Co-Newco-J.Co)

Contents

SCHEDULES

SELLING AGREEMENT

AGREEMENT made among [A.Co, Newco and J.Co.]

WHEREAS: [Recitals omitted.]

NOW, THEREFORE, in consideration of the premises and the mutual benefits to be derived herefrom,

IT IS AGREED AS FOLLOWS:

A. DEFINITIONS
The following terms where used in this Agreement shall have the following meanings:
[Definitions contained in previous agreements omitted.]

10. UNAUTHORIZED INTERMEDIARY
An individual, firm or company, not a DISTRIBUTOR, making an inquiry for MACHINERY for resale by it to a USER which is not its subsidiary, parent or associate and for which it is not a regularly appointed buying office or agent.

11. PRINCIPAL CONTRACTOR
A.Co or Newco or J.Co, whichever PARTY is legally responsible to the BUYER for satisfactory performance of the contract.

12. MANUFACTURER
Newco.

13. TERRITORY
[Omitted.]

14. DISTRIBUTOR'S COMMISSION
The amount payable, under a DISTRIBUTOR's agreement, to the DISTRIBUTOR by a PARTY on the sale of MACHINERY by the PARTY to a purchaser other than the DISTRIBUTOR (whether or not referred to as a "penalty" in such agreement).

15. DISTRIBUTOR'S DISCOUNT
The trade discount allowable, under a DISTRIBUTOR's agreement, to the DISTRIBUTOR by A.Co or Newco on the sale of MACHINERY by A.Co or Newco to the DISTRIBUTOR.

16. RELATED CORPORATION
    [Omitted.]

B. OFFERS, SALES AND SERVICE

1. *General Principle*
   (a) The offer and sale of MACHINERY shall be conducted based on the principle of obtaining the maximum amount of acceptable business, primary consideration being given in each individual transaction to making the offer that will be most acceptable to the USER, with due regard to his preferences and needs, to economic and commercial circumstances at the time and to available facilities for effective maintenance service.
   (b) To this end, A.Co and Newco may each seek orders from, and authorize its DISTRIBUTORS to seek orders from and/or purchase for resale to, BUYERS in its TERRITORY (other than persons known by it to be UNAUTHORIZED INTERMEDIARIES acting for USERS in the other's TERRITORY) for MACHINERY.
   (c) All such orders on a PARTY shall be subject to acceptance by it at its home office and neither the other PARTY nor its distributors shall have any authority to conclude sales on behalf of the PARTY to whom the order is addressed.

2. *Appointment and Supervision of DISTRIBUTORS*
   (a) Except as otherwise provided herein, A.Co and Newco shall each appoint the DISTRIBUTORS in its TERRITORY as exclusive or non-exclusive distributors of MACHINERY, and shall supervise and direct their activities and the performance of service for USERS and others.
   (b) Newco shall appoint J.Co such exclusive DISTRIBUTOR in Japan.
   (c) Newco and its appointed DISTRIBUTORS may sell MACHINERY of its manufacture for delivery into A.Co TERRITORY only on a case by case basis and with the written approval of A.Co.

3. *Administration of Sales*
   For orderly and effective sales administration, and in order to best serve USERS, wherever located,
   (a) Except as provided in Subparagraph (c) below, Newco shall refer to A.Co for negotiation, correspondence, service and other handling by A.Co and its distributors all inquiries received from:
      (1) BUYERS in A.Co TERRITORY for use anywhere, and
      (2) BUYERS in Newco TERRITORY who are persons known by Newco to be UNAUTHORIZED INTERMEDIARIES acting for USERS in A.Co TERRITORY.
   (b) Except as provided in Subparagraph (c) below, A.Co shall refer or cause to be referred to Newco, for negotiation, correspondence, service and other handling by Newco and its DISTRIBUTORS all inquiries received by A.Co from:
      (1) BUYERS in Newco TERRITORY for use anywhere, and
      (2) BUYERS in A.Co TERRITORY who are persons known by A.Co to be UNAUTHORIZED INTERMEDIARIES acting for USERS in Newco TERRITORY.
   (c) and (d) [Omitted.]

4. *Contracts*
   Except where circumstances make it desirable to otherwise fix contract responsibility, Newco shall:
   (a) Act as PRINCIPAL CONTRACTOR,
   (b) Establish the governing contract conditions, prices and terms of payment,
   (c) Assume the credit risk, and
   (d) Be responsible for all risks involved in its standard conditions of tender and any modification thereof to which it has consented.

5.–9. [Omitted.]

10. *Prohibited Transactions*
Newco and J.Co and their appointed subcontractors, sublicensees and DISTRIBUTORS shall not, directly or indirectly, sell, deliver or disclose MACHINERY or other goods, technical data or information in or to any country where such a sale, delivery or disclosure by A.Co would be prohibited by the U.S. Trading with the Enemy Act or any similar law or regulation imposing restrictions on U.S. trade with foreign countries.

C. COMMISSIONS
1. *Transactions Subject to Commission*
Newco shall pay a commission to A.Co on all MACHINERY supplied by Newco or J.Co to:
(a) BUYERS in A.Co TERRITORY for use anywhere,
(b) BUYERS in Newco TERRITORY for use in A.Co TERRITORY * * *.

2. and 3. [Provisions concerning calculations and method of payment of commissions omitted.]

4. *Commission Rate*
The amount of commission payable hereunder on MACHINERY shall be the following applicable percentage of the f.o.b. works selling price of such MACHINERY:

MACHINERY Model	*Applicable Percentage*
EXCAVATORS	2%
PARTS and COMPONENTS	15%

D. GENERAL PROVISIONS
[Provisions essentially the same as for JVA.]

E. TERMINATION
1. *For Breach*
(a) This Agreement may be terminated by any PARTY by 90 days prior written notice to the other PARTIES, specifying the reason for termination, in the event of a substantial breach by either of said other PARTIES.
(b) Said termination shall become effective at the end of said 90 day period unless the breach or adverse effect is cured within said 90 day period.

2. *For Insolvency, etc.*
[Same language as in JVA.]

3. *For Termination of Joint Venture Agreement*
Upon termination of the Joint Venture Agreement of even date between A.Co and J.Co, this Selling Agreement shall become terminated.

4. *For Termination of Technical Agreement*
Upon termination of the Technical Agreement of even date between A.Co and Newco, this Agreement shall become terminated.

5. *For Governmental Disapproval*
[Same language as Technical Agreement §I-5.]

6. *Effect*
Upon termination of this Agreement, however occasioned:
(a) No PARTY shall be discharged of any antecedent obligation to any other PARTY, except that the PARTIES shall not be liable for special or consequential damages, and
(b) No PARTY shall be liable hereunder for any commission or discount on account of any orders or sales obtained or concluded after such termination.

7. *Other Remedies*
[Same language as in JVA.]

F. EFFECTIVE DATE AND DURATION

1. *Effective Date*
   The effective date of this Agreement shall be the date of Japanese Government approval of said Technical Agreement.

2. *Duration*
   This Agreement shall continue in effect until terminated by agreement of the PARTIES, unless terminated as provided in Paragraph E hereof.

IN WITNESS WHEREOF, the PARTIES have caused these presents to be duly executed in manner appropriate to each and their corporate seals hereunto affixed on the dates respectively set forth below.

American Heavy Equipment, Inc.

By: ______________________________
President

Attest: ______________________________
Secretary

Date: ______________________________

Newco K.K.

By: ______________________________
President

Attest: ______________________________

Date: ______________________________

Japan Construction Machinery K.K.

By: ______________________________
President

Attest: ______________________________

Date: ______________________________

SCHEDULE I

A.Co TERRITORY

Countries outside Newco TERRITORY, except:
A. The United States of America
B. Panama Canal Zone

SCHEDULE II

Newco TERRITORY

A. Japan
B. Republic of Korea (Southern)
C. Taiwan
D. Philippines

SCHEDULE III

[Omitted.]

EXHIBIT F

DISTRIBUTOR AGREEMENT

(Newco-J.Co)

Contents

DISTRIBUTOR AGREEMENT

AGREEMENT made between [Newco ("COMPANY") and J.Co. ("DISTRIBUTOR")].

WHEREAS: [Recitals omitted.]

NOW, THEREFORE, in consideration of the premises and the mutual benefits to be derived herefrom,

IT IS AGREED AS FOLLOWS:

A. DEFINITIONS

The following terms in capital letters where used in this Agreement shall have the following meanings:

1. MACHINERY
   The products or any of the products manufactured by or for COMPANY described in Schedule I hereto as revised from time to time pursuant to Paragraph B hereof.

2. DISTRIBUTOR'S TERRITORY
   Japan

3. MANUFACTURER
   COMPANY.

4. DISCOUNT
   The amount allowed hereunder by COMPANY to DISTRIBUTOR as a deduction from the selling price of MACHINERY sold by COMPANY to DISTRIBUTOR for resale in accordance herewith.

5. COMMISSION
   The amount paid hereunder by COMPANY to DISTRIBUTOR on a sale of MACHINERY by COMPANY otherwise than to DISTRIBUTOR.

6. STANDARD RATE
   The applicable rate of DISCOUNT or COMMISSION specified in Schedule I hereto as revised from time to time pursuant to Paragraph B hereof.

7. CUSTOMER
   A purchaser or lessee of MACHINERY for use, either from COMPANY or DISTRIBUTOR, as distinguished from a distributor purchasing for resale.

B. AMENDMENT OF SCHEDULES
The parties hereto may amend Schedule I by mutual written agreement. Any Model that may be brought under the Technical Agreement of even date between American Heavy Equipment, Inc. and Newco, pursuant to Paragraph B-2 thereof, shall be added by amendment to Schedule I hereof, as of the date of grant with respect to such Model under said Paragraph B-2.

C. RIGHTS AND RESPONSIBILITIES OF DISTRIBUTOR

1. *Purchase for Resale*
   Subject hereto, DISTRIBUTOR shall have the right to purchase MACHINERY from COMPANY for resale to any CUSTOMER residing or located in DISTRIBUTOR'S TERRITORY.

2. *COMPANY's Right to Make Changes in Design*
   [Omitted.]

3. *Sales Promotion and Service*
   DISTRIBUTOR shall use its best endeavors to promote the sale of MACHINERY in DISTRIBUTOR'S TERRITORY. * * * DISTRIBUTOR shall provide full and complete service in connection with MACHINERY located in DISTRIBUTOR'S TERRITORY, and shall take such measures as may be necessary to retain the goodwill of CUSTOMERS and otherwise safeguard COMPANY's interests in DISTRIBUTOR'S TERRITORY.

4. *Disclaimer of Agency*
   DISTRIBUTOR is not the agent of COMPANY for any purpose whatsoever and agrees not to describe itself as such. * * *

D. ASSISTANCE PROVIDED BY COMPANY

1. *Supply of Printed Matter*
   [COMPANY to supply promotional material free of charge.]

2. *Technical Assistance*
   [At its sole discretion, COMPANY may supply assistance by its staff.]

E. PRICES
The prices to be paid by DISTRIBUTOR shall be the published or quoted list prices of COMPANY, current for DISTRIBUTOR when the order is placed, less a DISCOUNT as provided in Paragraph H hereof. * * *

F. COMPETING GOODS
DISTRIBUTOR shall not directly or indirectly keep in stock, offer, sell, or be interested in the sale or manufacture of, any article of the same nature as or similar to MACHINERY, unless it has been obtained from COMPANY. DISTRIBUTOR shall not without the written consent of COMPANY act as distributor or agent or in any other capacity for any other concern that manufactures or sells such articles.

G. SALES INTO OTHER TERRITORIES

1. *Sales by DISTRIBUTOR*
   DISTRIBUTOR shall not sell MACHINERY for delivery outside DISTRIBUTOR'S TERRITORY without the prior written consent of COMPANY. * * * If any MACHINERY sold by DISTRIBUTOR in the belief that it is for initial use in DISTRIBUTOR'S TERRITORY is discovered within two years of the date of its sale to have found its way

unused into any other territory, DISTRIBUTOR shall refund to COMPANY any portion of the DISCOUNT or COMMISSION allowed or paid to DISTRIBUTOR in excess of the amount that would have been allowed or paid to DISTRIBUTOR had the circumstances been known at the time of sale.

2. *Sales by COMPANY*
[Corresponding obligation of COMPANY to pay COMMISSION to DISTRIBUTOR for sales of MACHINERY that come within two years to be used in DISTRIBUTOR'S TERRITORY.]

H. DISCOUNTS AND COMMISSIONS

1. *Conditions of Allowance*
On each order for MACHINERY, COMPANY shall, except as otherwise provided herein, allow DISTRIBUTOR a DISCOUNT on an order by DISTRIBUTOR to COMPANY, or pay DISTRIBUTOR a COMMISSION on a direct order by a CUSTOMER to COMPANY, at the applicable STANDARD RATE, provided that the order is:
(a) From DISTRIBUTOR to COMPANY for resale, or secured by DISTRIBUTOR from CUSTOMER to COMPANY for MACHINERY for initial use in DISTRIBUTOR'S TERRITORY, and
(b) Accepted in writing by COMPANY during the term of this Agreement.

2. *Divided or Reduced DISCOUNT or COMMISSION*
COMPANY may, at its option, allow or pay no DISCOUNT or COMMISSION, or may allow or pay such DISCOUNT or COMMISSION as in its judgment may be warranted in the light of the services performed or to be performed by DISTRIBUTOR, in instances where:
(a) CUSTOMER has a permanent office and/or permanent operation outside DISTRIBUTOR'S TERRITORY,
(b) The negotiation or sale is conducted or made outside of DISTRIBUTOR'S TERRITORY by COMPANY, by another distributor or otherwise, for shipment to and installation in DISTRIBUTOR'S TERRITORY,
(c) A direct order by a CUSTOMER to COMPANY is secured partially or entirely through the efforts of COMPANY, or
(d) COMPANY considers the circumstances to be unusual.

3. *Basis of DISCOUNT or COMMISSION*
[Accounting guidelines omitted.]

4. *Method of Payment*
[Omitted.]

5. [Omitted.]

I. PAYMENT
[Provisions concerning methods of payment and record keeping omitted.]

J. DELIVERIES
(a) [*Force majeure* clause protecting COMPANY when delayed in making shipments.]
(b) Acceptance by DISTRIBUTOR or CUSTOMER of any shipment shall constitute a waiver of all claims for damages by reason of any delay or for loss or damage in transit.

K. WARRANTY
All MACHINERY supplied hereunder is sold subject to the provisions of this Paragraph K and in making a resale of any MACHINERY, DISTRIBUTOR shall expressly use such provisions or provisions of DISTRIBUTOR's own not imposing greater liability.

(1) MANUFACTURER warrants the MACHINERY and all spares, replacements and auxiliary equipment now or hereafter furnished by it therefor to be built in a workmanlike manner, of sound high grade material, and to operate properly under normal use and with proper attention. Any claim made under this warranty must be presented in writing to MANUFACTURER at Tokyo, Japan, within twelve months after delivery (ex works) of MACHINERY by MANUFACTURER (except in the case of sales to DISTRIBUTOR for stock, in which event the claim must be presented within six months after release from stock by DISTRIBUTOR) but in no event later than six months after receipt of the MACHINERY by the eventual CUSTOMER. MANUFACTURER's liability in no event shall exceed the replacement value of the defective element F.O.B. MANUFACTURER's works. In the case of units or parts purchased by MANUFACTURER, MANUFACTURER's liability shall not exceed the settlement which can be obtained by them from their supplier. MANUFACTURER shall have the option of requiring the return of any alleged defective part transportation charges prepaid (which will then become the property of MANUFACTURER if it so desires) before recognizing any claim. MANUFACTURER is to have a reasonable time after recognition of claim in which to remedy any proved defect or replace any part proved to be defective. No liability will attach to MANUFACTURER without MANUFACTURER's written consent. If parts other than of the original manufacturer are used in replacement without MANUFACTURER's written consent, or if the said CUSTOMER falls in arrears in making any payment, or if without MANUFACTURER's written consent the MACHINERY is repaired or altered in such a way as in MANUFACTURER's judgment to reduce its stability or reliability, or if the MACHINERY is subjected to misuse, negligence or accident, all warranties are thereby waived.

(2) The foregoing warranty is in lieu of all tort liability, and all other warranties or representations express or implied by MANUFACTURER whatsoever. No agent, distributor or other person is authorized to give any other warranty or to assume any other liability.

(3) MANUFACTURER is not to be liable for any indirect, special or consequential damages, and DISTRIBUTOR shall save it harmless from all damages to third parties in tort, contract, or otherwise howsoever.

L. USE OF TRADEMARKS AND NAMES

[Omitted.]

M. SALES DATA, REPORTS AND RECORDS

1. *Records*

DISTRIBUTOR shall maintain accounting records that will at all times accurately reflect the financial condition of DISTRIBUTOR's business and enable DISTRIBUTOR to furnish reports and statements hereunder.

2. *Statements*

DISTRIBUTOR shall, when requested by COMPANY, furnish COMPANY for its confidential use, in form satisfactory to COMPANY, statements showing:

(a) DISTRIBUTOR's current financial condition, and

(b) DISTRIBUTOR's inventory of MACHINERY and PARTS on hand as of any date specified by COMPANY.

N. GENERAL PROVISIONS

[Provisions essentially same as for JVA omitted.]

Sub-Distributors

DISTRIBUTOR shall not appoint agents or subdistributors for the sale of MACHINERY without the written consent of COMPANY, and then only subject to the terms of that consent.

O. TERMINATION

1. *Basis*

   This Agreement may be terminated in any of the following ways:

   (a) By either party by giving the other party at least ninety days prior written notice of such termination for any cause whatsoever or without cause;

   (b) By either party immediately upon written notice to the other party for breach of any provision by the other party; or

   (c) By either party immediately upon written notice to the other party in the event of bankruptcy or receivership or substantial change in ownership of the other party.

2. *Notice*

   [Omitted.]

3. *Effect*

   Upon termination of this Agreement, however occasioned:

   (a) Neither party shall be discharged from any antecedent obligation; but COMPANY may, at COMPANY's option, cancel any or all unfilled orders accepted from DISTRIBUTOR, except orders with respect to which DISTRIBUTOR has firm resale commitments in writing;

   (b) COMPANY shall credit DISTRIBUTOR with the DISCOUNTS and/or COMMISSIONS to which DISTRIBUTOR is entitled hereunder on orders accepted by COMPANY prior to the date of termination, as and when such DISCOUNTS and/or COMMISSIONS would have become due if termination had not occurred;

   (c) DISTRIBUTOR shall pay COMPANY all amounts owed by DISTRIBUTOR to COMPANY, as and when such payments would have become due if termination had not occurred; and

   (d) DISTRIBUTOR shall comply with the reasonable instructions of COMPANY regarding disposition of all COMPANY's property then in DISTRIBUTOR's possession or custody and shall return to COMPANY all printed matter, drawings, data, parts lists, photographs, price books and supplies furnished or loaned by COMPANY to DISTRIBUTOR.

4. *Other Remedies*

   [Same language as in JVA.]

P. EFFECTIVE DATE AND DURATION

1. *Effective Date*

   This Agreement shall be effective on the effective date of the Selling Agreement of even date between American Heavy Equipment, Inc. and Newco and shall apply to all offers, sales and shipments made thereafter, whether or not such offers, sales, or shipments relate to negotiations prior to such effective date.

2. *Duration*

   This Agreement shall continue in effect until terminated as provided in Paragraph O hereof or by agreement of the PARTIES.

IN WITNESS WHEREOF, the PARTIES have caused these presents to be duly executed in manner appropriate to each and their corporate seals hereunto affixed on the dates respectively set forth below.

Newco K.K.

By: ________________________
President

Attest: ________________________

Date: ________________________

Japan Construction Machinery K.K.

By: ________________________
President

Attest: ________________________

Date: ________________________

SCHEDULE I

DISCOUNTS AND COMMISSIONS

COMPANY'S PRODUCTS

	STANDARD RATE	
	Discount	*Commission*
1. *Machines* [Omitted.]	5%	5%
2. *Equipment Assemblies and Units when for Machines*	5%	5%
3. *Repair Parts*	35%	5%
4. *Dragbuckets when for Machines*	5%	5%

AMENDING AGREEMENT NO. 15

AGREEMENT CONCERNING RELATED LICENSED PRODUCTS

(A.Co-Newco-J.Co)

WHEREAS, American Heavy Equipment, Inc. ("A.Co") and Japan Construction Machinery Kabushiki Kaisha ("J.Co") entered into a Joint Venture Agreement ("JVA") and various collateral agreements, signed 1970 and subsequently validated by the Japanese government, providing *inter alia* for the operation of a jointly owned Japanese corporation called "Newco K.K." ("Newco"); and

WHEREAS, Newco handles certain LICENSED PRODUCTS; and

WHEREAS, the PARTIES desire to provide for Newco's handling of certain products that are related to the LICENSED PRODUCTS and are developed jointly by, or based on common know-how of, A.Co and J.Co.,

NOW, THEREFORE, the PARTIES mutually covenant and agree as follows:

A. "RELATED LICENSED PRODUCTS"

1. The term "RELATED LICENSED PRODUCTS" or "R.L. Products" where used in this Agreement shall mean EXCAVATORS and PARTS and COMPONENTS thereof that are:
   (a) Similar in design to LICENSED PRODUCTS, being developed jointly by, or based on common know-how of, A.Co and J.Co, and
   (b) Listed in Schedule III of JVA, Exhibit B, as RELATED LICENSED PRODUCTS for which TECHNICAL ASSISTANCE is supplied under Paragraphs B-1 and F of said Exhibit B.

2. JVA, Exhibit B, Schedule III, is hereby amended by inserting at the end thereof the following words:

   "The following EXCAVATOR, and PARTS and COMPONENTS thereof, constitute RELATED LICENSED PRODUCTS for which TECHNICAL ASSISTANCE is supplied under Paragraphs B-1 and F of this Agreement:

   Model
   10-H."

3. JVA, Exhibit B, Schedule VIII, is hereby amended by inserting at the end thereof the following paragraph (e):

   "(e) *Models licensed by Amending Agreement No. 15*
   10-H Effective Date of Amending Agreement No. 15."

4. Except as otherwise provided in this Amending Agreement, all provisions of said JVA and its collateral agreements applicable to LICENSED PRODUCTS shall apply *mutatis mutandis* to RELATED LICENSED PRODUCTS.

B. TECHNICAL ASSISTANCE

1. *Supply of TECHNICAL ASSISTANCE*
   A.Co shall render TECHNICAL ASSISTANCE with respect to RELATED LICENSED PRODUCTS to Newco, as licensee, and to J.Co, as sublicensee, under the applicable provisions of JVA, Exhibit B.

2. *Technical Assistance Fees*
   The Technical Assistance and Improvement Fees payable by Newco to A.Co under Paragraph G-3 of JVA, Exhibit B, shall be two per cent (2%) of the NET SELLING PRICES of all RELATED LICENSED PRODUCTS.

3. *Payment of Technical Assistance Fees*
J.Co, as sublicensee hereunder, shall pay to Newco the Technical Assistance Fees, and other payments or charges payable by Newco to A.Co applicable to sublicensee sales by J.Co, *mutatis mutandis,* in accordance with the provisions of Paragraphs G-3, G-5, G-8, and G-9 of JVA, Exhibit B, and shall render to Newco and A.Co fee statements as required by Paragraph G-7 of said Exhibit B.

4. *Disclosure Fees*
No Disclosure Fees shall accrue or be payable under Paragraphs G-1 and G-2 of JVA, Exhibit B.

C. SUBLICENSEE OF RELATED LICENSED PRODUCTS
J.Co shall, as sublicensee of Newco, have the exclusive right to manufacture in Japan and sell RELATED LICENSED PRODUCTS, subject to:
1. Subparagraphs (a) through (f) of Paragraph F-1 of JVA, Exhibit D, which shall apply *mutatis mutandis* to a J.Co sale to or for Newco, or to or for BUYERS or USERS outside Japan; and
2. Paragraph B-3 hereof.

D. TRADEMARK AND MARKING
[Omitted.]

E. QUALITY STANDARDS AND CONTROL
1. J.Co, as sublicensee hereunder, shall be primarily responsible for, and assume the expense of engineering design of, RELATED LICENSED PRODUCTS, and shall insure that RELATED LICENSED PRODUCTS are not inferior in quality and performance to comparable LICENSED PRODUCTS, and are produced in accordance with quality standards and quality controls of A.Co applicable to LICENSED PRODUCTS.

2. J.Co, as sublicensee hereunder, upon written request of A.Co with respect to RELATED LICENSED PRODUCTS specified in such request, shall supply A.Co without charge one complete set of TECHNICAL DATA in the form used by J.Co in the production of such RELATED LICENSED PRODUCTS.

3. A.Co shall, as a part of its TECHNICAL ASSISTANCE hereunder, review such TECHNICAL DATA and consult and cooperate with J.Co, as reasonably required, for purposes of instruction, information and advice with respect to any problem of design, manufacture, quality standards and quality control for RELATED LICENSED PRODUCTS.

F. SALES
1. *Newco TERRITORY*
(a) Newco shall be responsible for the sale in Newco TERRITORY of RELATED LICENSED PRODUCTS manufactured by J.Co as sublicensee, in accordance with the applicable provisions of JVA, Exhibit E, and this Amending Agreement, and shall appoint J.Co as exclusive DISTRIBUTOR in Japan of such RELATED LICENSED PRODUCTS.
(b) J.Co, as such sublicensee, shall have the right to sell, and appoint its distributors for, RELATED LICENSED PRODUCTS in Japan.
(c) Newco and A.Co shall refer or cause to be referred for handling and negotiation to J.Co, as sublicensee, PRINCIPAL CONTRACTOR and exclusive DISTRIBUTOR of Newco in Japan, all inquiries for RELATED LICENSED PRODUCTS received from buyers in Japan.

2. *A.Co TERRITORY*
(a) A.Co, as general DISTRIBUTOR in A.Co TERRITORY of RELATED LICENSED PRODUCTS manufactured by J.Co as sublicensee hereunder, shall be responsible in cooperation with J.Co for the sale in A.Co TERRITORY of such RELATED LICENSED

PRODUCTS, and shall supervise and direct the activities and performance of service for such RELATED LICENSED PRODUCTS in A.Co TERRITORY, in accordance with applicable provisions of JVA, Exhibits D and E.

(b) As such general DISTRIBUTOR, A.Co may appoint non-exclusive and exclusive DISTRIBUTORS in A.Co TERRITORY for such RELATED LICENSED PRODUCTS, and shall supervise and direct the activities and performance of service of such DISTRIBUTORS.

G. EFFECTIVE DATE

The effective date of this Amending Agreement and of JVA, Exhibit B, with respect to each model of MACHINERY constituting a RELATED LICENSED PRODUCT, shall be the date of Japanese Government approval of this Amending Agreement with respect to such model.

H. CONFIRMING AMENDMENTS TO JVA

The PARTIES agree to make appropriate applicable amendments to the JVA and its collateral agreements, to include therein the substance of this Amending Agreement, and to insert new pages in said Agreements, which pages shall be corrected and retyped by A.Co as required by this Amending Agreement.

IN WITNESS WHEREOF, the PARTIES have caused these presents to be executed on the dates respectively set forth below.

American Heavy Equipment, Inc.

By ______________________________

Newco K.K.

By ______________________________

Japan Construction Machinery K.K.

By ______________________________

Appendix B
Statutory Materials

Table of Contents

Note: The statutory translations contained herein are for reference purposes only. It goes without saying that the original Japanese statutes, rather than any translation, control in the event of any actual dispute. In nearly all instances, moreover, we have included only selected provisions, rather than the full text of the statutes.

1. THE CONSTITUTION OF JAPAN

November 3, 1946
Source: The Supreme Court, Japan, *The Constitution of Japan.*

Preamble

We, the Japanese people, acting through our duly elected representatives in the National Diet, determined that we shall secure for ourselves and our posterity the fruits of peaceful cooperation with all nations and the blessings of liberty throughout this land, and resolved that never again shall we be visited with the horrors of war through the action of government, do proclaim that sovereign power resides with the people and do firmly establish this Constitution. Government is a sacred trust of the people, the authority for which is derived from the people, the powers of which are exercised by the representatives of the people, and the benefits of which are enjoyed by the people. This is a universal principle of mankind upon which this Constitution is founded. We reject and revoke all constitutions, laws, ordinances, and rescripts in conflict herewith.

We, the Japanese people, desire peace for all time and are deeply conscious of the high ideals controlling human relationship, and we have determined to preserve our security and existence, trusting in the justice and faith of the peace-loving peoples of the world. We desire to occupy an honored place in an international society striving for the preservation of peace, and the banishment of tyranny and slavery, oppression and intolerance for all time from the earth. We recognize that all peoples of the world have the right to live in peace, free from fear and want.

We believe that no nation is responsible to itself alone, but that laws of political morality are universal, and that obedience to such laws is incumbent upon all nations who would sustain their own sovereignty and justify their sovereign relationship with other nations.

We, the Japanese people, pledge our national honor to accomplish these high ideals and purposes with all our resources.

Chapter I
The Emperor

Article 1. *(Status of the Emperor; people's sovereignty)*
The Emperor shall be the symbol of the State and of the unity of the people, deriving his position from the will of the people with whom resides sovereign power.

Article 2. *(Succession to the Imperial Throne)*
The Imperial Throne shall be dynastic and succeeded to in accordance with the Imperial House Law passed by the Diet.

Article 3. *(Imperial Acts of State; Cabinet advice and approval)*
The advice and approval of the Cabinet shall be required for all acts of the Emperor in matters of state, and the Cabinet shall be responsible therefor.

Article 4. *(Limitation of the Emperor's authority)*
1. The Emperor shall perform only such acts in matters of state as are provided for in this Constitution and he shall not have powers related to government.
2. The Emperor may delegate the performance of his acts in matters of state as may be provided by law.

Article 5. *(Regency)*
When, in accordance with the Imperial House Law, a Regency is established, the Regent shall perform his acts in matters of state in the Emperor's name. In this case, paragraph one of the preceding article will be applicable.

Article 6. (Imperial Acts of State: Appointment of Prime Minister and Chief Justice)

1. The Emperor shall appoint the Prime Minister as designated by the Diet.
2. The Emperor shall appoint the Chief Judge of the Supreme Court as designated by the Cabinet.

Article 7. (Other Imperial Acts of State)

The Emperor, with the advice and approval of the Cabinet, shall perform the following acts in matters of state on behalf of the people:

1. Promulgation of amendments of the constitution, laws, cabinet orders and treaties.
2. Convocation of the Diet.
3. Dissolution of the House of Representatives.
4. Proclamation of general election of members of the Diet.
5. Attestation of the appointment and dismissal of Ministers of State and other officials as provided for by law, and of full powers and credentials of Ambassadors and Ministers.
6. Attestation of general and special amnesty, commutation of punishments, reprieve, and restoration of rights.
7. Awarding of honors.
8. Attestation of instruments of ratification and other diplomatic documents as provided for by law.
9. Receiving foreign ambassadors and ministers.
10. Performance of ceremonial functions.

Article 8. (Giving and receiving of property by the Imperial Household)

No property can be given to, or received by, the Imperial House, nor can any gifts be made therefrom, without the authorization of the Diet.

Chapter II
Renunciation of War

Article 9. (Renunciation of war; nonmaintenance of weapons of war)

1. Aspiring sincerely to an international peace based on justice and order, the Japanese people forever renounce war as a sovereign right of the nation and the threat or use of force as means of settling international disputes.
2. In order to accomplish the aim of the preceding paragraph, land, sea, and air forces, as well as other war potential, will never be maintained. The right of belligerency of the state will not be recognized.

Chapter III
Rights and Duties of the People

Article 10. (Conditions of Japanese nationality)

The conditions necessary for being a Japanese national shall be determined by law.

Article 11. (Possession of fundamental human rights as eternal and inviolate)

The people shall not be prevented from enjoying any of the fundamental human rights. These fundamental human rights guaranteed to the people by this Constitution shall be conferred upon the people of this and future generations as eternal and inviolate rights.

Article 12. (Duty to maintain and utilize freedoms and rights; ban on abuse)

The freedoms and rights guaranteed to the people by this Constitution shall be maintained by the constant endeavor of the people, who shall refrain from any abuse of these freedoms and rights and shall always be responsible for utilizing them for the public welfare.

Article 13. (Respect as individuals)

All of the people shall be respected as individuals. Their right to life, liberty, and the pursuit of happiness shall, to the extent that it does not interfere with the public welfare, be the supreme consideration in legislation and in other governmental affairs.

Article 14. (Equality under the law; ban on peerage; presentation of decorations)

1. All of the people are equal under the law and there shall be no discrimination in political, economic or social relations because of race, creed, sex, social status or family origin.
2. Peers and peerage shall not be recognized.
3. No privilege shall accompany any award of honor, decoration or any distinction, nor shall any such award be valid beyond the lifetime of the individual who now holds or hereafter may receive it.

Article 15. (Right to elect public officials; essence of public office; preservation of a secret ballot)

1. The people have the inalienable right to choose their public officials and to dismiss them.
2. All public officials are servants of the whole community and not of any group thereof.
3. Universal adult suffrage is guaranteed with regard to the election of public officials.
4. In all elections, secrecy of the ballot shall not be violated. A voter shall not be answerable, publicly or privately, for the choice he has made.

Article 16. (Right of petition)

Every person shall have the right of peaceful petition for the redress of damage, for the removal of public officials, for the enactment, repeal or amendment of laws, ordinances or regulations and for other matters; nor shall any person be in any way discriminated against for sponsoring such a petition.

Article 17. (State and public entity duty to compensate)

Every person may sue for redress as provided by law from the State or a public entity, in case he has suffered damage through illegal act of any public official.

Article 18. (Freedom from bondage and involuntary servitude)

No person shall be held in bondage of any kind. Involuntary servitude, except as punishment for crime, is prohibited.

Article 19. (Freedom of thought and conscience)

Freedom of thought and conscience shall not be violated.

Article 20. (Freedom of religion)

1. Freedom of religion is guaranteed to all. No religious organization shall receive any privileges from the State, nor exercise any political authority.
2. No person shall be compelled to take part in any religious act, celebration, rite or practice.
3. The State and its organs shall refrain from religious education or any other religious activity.

Article 21. (Freedom of assembly, speech, expression)

1. Freedom of assembly and association as well as speech, press and all other forms of expression are guaranteed.
2. No censorship shall be maintained, nor shall the secrecy of any means of communication be violated.

Article 22. (Freedom to choose occupation and residence and to live abroad)

1. Every person shall have freedom to choose and change his residence and to choose his occupation to the extent that it does not interfere with the public welfare.
2. Freedom of all persons to move to a foreign country and to divest themselves of their nationality shall be inviolate.

Article 23. (Academic freedom)

Academic freedom is guaranteed.

Article 24. (Individual dignity in marriage; equality of the sexes)

1. Marriage shall be based only on the mutual consent of both sexes and it shall be maintained through mutual cooperation with the equal rights of husband and wife as a basis.

2. With regard to choice of spouse, property rights, inheritance, choice of domicile, divorce and other matters pertaining to marriage and the family, laws shall be enacted from the standpoint of individual dignity and the essential equality of the sexes.

Article 25. (Right to life; promotion of society's welfare)

1. All people shall have the right to maintain the minimum standards of wholesome and cultured living.
2. In all spheres of life, the State shall use its endeavors for the promotion and extension of social welfare and security, and of public health.

Article 26. (Right to receive education; duty to educate)

1. All people shall have the right to receive an equal education correspondent to their ability, as provided by law.
2. All people shall be obligated to have all boys and girls under their protection receive ordinary education as provided for by law. Such compulsory education shall be free.

Article 27. (Right and duty to work)

1. All people shall have the right and the obligation to work.
2. Standards for wages, hours, rest and other working conditions shall be fixed by law.
3. Children shall not be exploited.

Article 28. (Right of workers to organize)

The right of workers to organize and to bargain and act collectively is guaranteed.

Article 29. (Right to property)

1. The right to own or to hold property is inviolable.
2. Property rights shall be defined by law, in conformity with the public welfare.
3. Private property may be taken for public use upon just compensation therefor.

Article 30. (Duty to pay taxes)

The people shall be liable to taxation as provided by law.

Article 31. (Guarantee to legal procedure)

No person shall be deprived of life or liberty, nor shall any other criminal penalty be imposed, except according to procedure established by law.

Article 32. (Right of access to courts)

No person shall be denied the right of access to the courts.

Article 33. (Guarantees concerning arrest)

No person shall be apprehended except upon warrant issued by a competent judicial officer which specifies the offense with which the person is charged, unless he is apprehended, the offense being committed.

Article 34. (Guarantees upon arrest; showing of adequate cause)

No person shall be arrested or detained without being at once informed of the charges against him or without the immediate privilege of counsel; nor shall he be detained without adequate cause; and upon demand of any person such cause must be immediately shown in open court in his presence and the presence of his counsel.

Article 35. (Guarantees concerning search, seizure, and entry into the home)

1. The right of all persons to be secure in their homes, papers and effects against entries, searches and seizures shall not be impaired except upon warrant issued for adequate cause and particularly describing the place to be searched and things to be seized, or except as provided by Article 33.
2. Each search or seizure shall be made upon separate warrant issued by a competent judicial officer.

Article 36. (Ban on cruel punishments)

The infliction of torture by any public officer and cruel punishment are absolutely forbidden.

Article 37. (Rights concerning trial)

1. In all criminal cases the accused shall enjoy the right to a speedy and public trial by an impartial tribunal.
2. He shall be permitted full opportunity to examine all witnesses and he shall have the right of compulsory process for obtaining witnesses on his behalf at public expense.
3. At all times the accused shall have the assistance of competent counsel who shall, if the accused is unable to secure the same by his own efforts, be assigned to his use by the State.

Article 38. (Guarantees against self-incrimination and confessions made under duress)

1. No person shall be compelled to testify against himself.
2. Confession made under compulsion, torture or threat, or after prolonged arrest or detention, shall not be admitted in evidence.
3. No person shall be convicted or punished in cases where the only proof against him is his own confession.

Article 39. (Ban on retroactive punishments and double jeopardy)

No person shall be held criminally liable for an act which was lawful at the time it was committed, or of which he has been acquitted, nor shall he be placed in double jeopardy.

Article 40. (Redress for false arrest)

Any person, in case he is acquitted after he has been arrested or detained, may sue the State for redress as provided by law.

CHAPTER IV
The Diet

Article 41. (Status of the Diet; lawmaking authority)

The Diet shall be the highest organ of state power, and shall be the sole law-making organ of the State.

Article 42. (Bicameral Diet)

The Diet shall consist of two Houses, namely the House of Representatives and the House of Councillors.

Article 43. (Organization of each House)

1. Both Houses shall consist of elected members, representative of all the people.
2. The number of the members of each House shall be fixed by law.

Article 44. (Qualifications of Diet members and their electors)

The qualifications of members of both Houses and their electors shall be fixed by law. However, there shall be no discrimination because of race, creed, sex, social status, family origin, education, property or income.

Article 45. (House of Representatives' term of office)

The term of office of members of the House of Representatives shall be four years. However, the term shall be terminated before the full term is up in case the House of Representatives is dissolved.

Article 46. (House of Councillors' term of office)

The term of office of members of the House of Councillors shall be six years, and election for half the members shall take place every three years.

Article 47. (Legal matters on elections)

Electoral districts, method of voting and other matters pertaining to the method of election of members of both Houses shall be fixed by law.

Article 48. (Ban on dual membership in both Houses)

No person shall be permitted to be a member of both Houses simultaneously.

Article 49. (Diet members' annual allowance)
Members of both Houses shall receive appropriate annual payment from the national treasury in accordance with law.

Article 50. (Special freedom from arrest)
Except in cases provided by law, members of both Houses shall be exempt from apprehension while the Diet is in session, and any members apprehended before the opening of the session shall be freed during the term of the session upon demand of the House.

Article 51. (Nonliability for in-house activities)
Members of both Houses shall not be held liable outside the House for speeches, debates or votes cast inside the House.

Article 52. (Ordinary session)
An ordinary session of the Diet shall be convoked once per year.

Article 53. (Extraordinary sessions)
The Cabinet may determine to convoke extraordinary sessions of the Diet. When a quarter or more of the total members of either House makes the demand, the Cabinet must determine on such convocation.

Article 54. (Dissolution and election of the House of Representatives; emergency session of the House of Councillors)
1. When the House of Representatives is dissolved, there must be a general election of members of the House of Representatives within forty (40) days from the date of dissolution, and the Diet must be convoked within thirty (30) days from the date of the election.
2. When the House of Representatives is dissolved, the House of Councillors is closed at the same time. However, the Cabinet may in time of national emergency convoke the House of Councillors in emergency session.
3. Measures taken at such session as mentioned in the proviso of the preceding paragraph shall be provisional and shall become null and void unless agreed to by the House of Representatives within a period of ten (10) days after the opening of the next session of the Diet.

Article 55. (Disputes concerning qualifications of Diet members)
Each House shall judge disputes related to qualifications of its members. However, in order to deny a seat to any member, it is necessary to pass a resolution by a majority of two-thirds or more of the members present.

Article 56. (Quorum; decision-making method)
1. Business cannot be transacted in either House unless one-third or more of total membership is present.
2. All matters shall be decided, in each House, by a majority of those present, except as elsewhere provided in the Constitution, and in case of a tie, the presiding officer shall decide the issue.

Article 57. (Public and secret meetings; Diet records)
1. Deliberation in each House shall be public. However, a secret meeting may be held where a majority of two-thirds or more of those members present passes a resolution therefor.
2. Each House shall keep a record of proceedings. This record shall be published and given general circulation, excepting such parts of proceedings of secret session as may be deemed to require secrecy.
3. Upon demand of one-fifth or more of the members present, votes of the members on any matter shall be recorded in the minutes.

Article 58. (Election of officials; Diet rules and discipline)
1. Each House shall select its own president and other officials.
2. Each House shall establish its rules pertaining to meetings, proceedings and internal dis-

cipline, and may punish members for disorderly conduct. However, in order to expel a member, a majority of two-thirds or more of those members present must pass a resolution thereon.

Article 59. (Lawmaking, superiority of the House of Representatives)

1. A bill becomes a law on passage by both Houses, except as otherwise provided by the Constitution.
2. A bill which is passed by the House of Representatives, and upon which the House of Councillors makes a decision different from that of the House of Representatives, becomes a law when passed a second time by the House of Representatives by a majority of two-thirds or more of the members present.
3. The provision of the preceding paragraph does not preclude the House of Representatives from calling for the meeting of a joint committee of both Houses, provided for by law.
4. Failure by the House of Councillors to take final action within sixty (60) days after receipt of a bill passed by the House of Representatives, time in recess excepted, may be determined by the House of Representatives to constitute a rejection of the said bill by the House of Councillors.

Article 60. (Budget determination, superiority of the House of Representatives)

1. The budget must first be submitted to the House of Representatives.
2. Upon consideration of the budget, when the House of Councillors makes a decision different from that of the House of Representatives, and when no agreement can be reached even through a joint committee of both Houses, provided for by law, or in the case of failure by the House of Councillors to take final action within thirty (30) days, the period of recess excluded, after the receipt of the budget passed by the House of Representatives, the decision of the House of Representatives shall be the decision of the Diet.

Article 61. (Diet approval of treaties, superiority of the House of Representatives)

The second paragraph of the preceding article applies also to the Diet approval required for the conclusion of treaties.

Article 62. (House investigations)

Each House may conduct investigations in relation to government and may demand the presence and testimony of witnesses, and the production of records.

Article 63. (Rights and duties of Ministers of State to appear in the Diet)

The Prime Minister and other Ministers of State may, at any time, appear in either House for the purpose of speaking on bills, regardless of whether they are members of the House or not. They must appear when their presence is required in order to give answers or explanations.

Article 64. (Impeachment court)

1. The Diet shall set up an impeachment court from among the members of both Houses for the purpose of trying those judges against whom removal proceedings have been instituted.
2. Matters relating to impeachment shall be provided by law.

Chapter V
The Cabinet

Article 65. (Executive power and the Cabinet)

Executive power shall be vested in the Cabinet.

Article 66. (Cabinet organization; qualifications of Ministers of State; responsibility to the Diet)

1. The Cabinet shall consist of the Prime Minister, who shall be its head, and other Ministers of State, as provided for by law.

2. The Prime Minister and other Ministers of State must be civilians.
3. The Cabinet, in the exercise of executive power, shall be collectively responsible to the Diet.

Article 67. (Nomination of the Prime Minister, superiority of the House of Representatives)

1. The Prime Minister shall be designated from among the members of the Diet by a resolution of the Diet. This designation shall precede all other business.
2. If the House of Representatives and the House of Councillors disagree and if no agreement can be reached even through a joint committee of both Houses, provided for by law, or the House of Councillors fails to make designation within ten (10) days, exclusive of the period of recess, after the House of Representatives has made designation, the decision of the House of Representatives shall be the decision of the Diet.

Article 68. (Appointment and dismissal of Ministers of State)

1. The Prime Minister shall appoint the Ministers of State. However, a majority of their number must be chosen from among the members of the Diet.
2. The Prime Minister may remove the Ministers of State as he chooses.

Article 69. (Nonconfidence resolution of the House of Representatives; Cabinet resignation)

If the House of Representatives passes a nonconfidence resolution, or rejects a confidence resolution, the Cabinet shall resign en masse, unless the House of Representatives is dissolved within ten (10) days.

Article 70. (Resignation of Cabinet)

When there is a vacancy in the post of Prime Minister, or upon the first convocation of the Diet after a general election of members of the House of Representatives, the Cabinet shall resign en masse.

Article 71. (Function of the Cabinet after resignation)

In the cases mentioned in the two preceding articles, the Cabinet shall continue its functions until the time when a new Prime Minister is appointed.

Article 72. (Functions of the Prime Minister)

The Prime Minister, representing the Cabinet, submits bills, reports on general national affairs and foreign relations to the Diet and exercises control and supervision over various administrative branches.

Article 73. (Functions of the Cabinet)

The Cabinet, in addition to other general administrative functions, shall perform the following functions:

1. Administer the law faithfully; conduct affairs of state.
2. Manage foreign affairs.
3. Conclude treaties. However, it shall obtain prior or, depending on circumstances, subsequent approval of the Diet.
4. Administer the civil service, in accordance with standards established by law.
5. Prepare the budget, and present it to the Diet.
6. Enact cabinet orders in order to execute the provisions of this Constitution and of the law. However, it cannot include penal provisions in such cabinet orders unless authorized by such law.
7. Decide on general amnesty, special amnesty, commutation of punishment, reprieve, and restoration of rights.

Article 74. (Signing of laws and cabinet orders)

All laws and cabinet orders shall be signed by the competent Minister of State and countersigned by the Prime Minister.

Article 75. (Legal action against Ministers of State)

The Minsters of State, during their tenure of office, shall not be subject to legal action without the consent of the Prime Minister. However, the right to take that action is not impaired hereby.

Chapter VI
Judiciary

Article 76. (Authority of the Judiciary; ban on extraordinary tribunals; final judgments by the Executive)

1. The whole judicial power is vested in a Supreme Court and in such inferior courts as are established by law.
2. No extraordinary tribunal shall be established, nor shall any organ or agency of the Executive be given final judicial power.
3. All judges shall be independent in the exercise of their conscience and shall be bound only by this Constitution and the laws.

Article 77. (Rule-making power of the Supreme Court)

1. The Supreme Court is vested with the rule-making power under which it determines the rules of procedure and practice, and of matters relating to attorneys, the internal discipline of the courts and the administration of judicial affairs.
2. Public procurators shall be subject to the rule-making power of the Supreme Court.
3. The Supreme Court may delegate the power to make rules for inferior courts to such courts.

Article 78. (Judgeship guarantee)

Judges shall not be removed except by public impeachment unless judicially declared mentally or physically incompetent to perform official duties. No disciplinary action against judges shall be administered by any executive organ or agency.

Article 79. (Organization, review and term of office and remuneration for the Supreme Court)

1. The Supreme Court shall consist of a Chief Judge and such number of judges as may be determined by law; all such judges excepting the Chief Judge shall be appointed by the Cabinet.
2. The appointment of the judges of the Supreme Court shall be reviewed by the people at the first general election of members of the House of Representatives following their appointment, and shall be reviewed again at the first general election of members of the House of Representatives after a lapse of ten (10) years, and in the same manner thereafter.
3. In cases mentioned in the foregoing paragraph, when the majority of the voters favors the dismissal of a judge, he shall be dismissed.
4. Matters pertaining to review shall be prescribed by law.
5. The judges of the Supreme Court shall be retired upon the attainment of the age as fixed by law.
6. All such judges shall receive, at regular stated intervals, adequate compensation which shall not be decreased during their terms of office.

Article 80. (Appointment, term of office and remuneration for inferior courts)

1. The judges of the inferior courts shall be appointed by the Cabinet from a list of persons nominated by the Supreme Court. All such judges shall hold office for a term of ten (10) years with privilege of reappointment, provided that they shall be retired upon the attainment of the age as fixed by law.
2. The judges of the inferior courts shall receive, at regular stated intervals, adequate compensation which shall not be decreased during their terms of office.

Article 81. (Supreme Court power to determine the constitutionality of laws)

The Supreme Court is the court of last resort with power to determine the constitutionality of any law, order, regulation or official act.

Article 82. (Courts open to the public)

1. Trials shall be conducted and judgment declared publicly.
2. Where a court unanimously determines publicity to be dangerous to public order or morals, a trial may be conducted privately, but trials of political offenses, offenses involving the press or cases wherein the rights of people as guaranteed in Chapter III of this Constitution are in question shall always be conducted publicly.

Chapter VII
Finance

Article 83. (Power to administer national finances)

The power to administer national finances shall be exercised as the Diet shall determine.

Article 84. (Regulation of taxes)

No new taxes shall be imposed or existing ones modified except by law or under such conditions as law may prescribe.

Article 85. (Diet authorization for expenditures)

No money shall be expended, nor shall the State obligate itself, except as authorized by the Diet.

Article 86. (Budget, consideration by the Diet)

The Cabinet shall prepare and submit to the Diet for its consideration and decision a budget for each fiscal year.

Article 87. (Reserve fund)

1. In order to provide for unforeseen deficiencies in the budget, a reserve fund may be authorized by the Diet to be expended upon the responsibility of the Cabinet.
2. The Cabinet must get subsequent approval of the Diet for all payments from the reserve fund.

Article 88. (Property and expenses of the Imperial Household)

All property of the Imperial Household shall belong to the State. All expenses of the Imperial Household shall be appropriated by the Diet in the budget.

Article 89. (Restriction on the use of public funds)

No public money or other property shall be expended or appropriated for the use, benefit or maintenance of any religious institution or association, or for any charitable, educational or benevolent enterprises not under the control of public authority.

Article 90. (State audit; Board of Audit)

1. Final accounts of the expenditures and revenues of the State shall be audited annually by a Board of Audit and submitted by the Cabinet to the Diet, together with the statement of audit, during the fiscal year immediately following the period covered.
2. The organization and competency of the Board of Audit shall be determined by law.

Article 91. (Report by Cabinet on finances)

At regular intervals and at least annually the Cabinet shall report to the Diet and the people on the state of national finances.

Chapter VIII
Local Self-Government

Article 92. (Regulation of local self-government)
Regulations concerning organization and operations of local public entities shall be fixed by law in accordance with the principle of local autonomy.

Article 93. (Local assemblies; election of members and officers)
1. The local public entities shall establish assemblies as their deliberative organs, in accordance with law.
2. The chief executive officers of all local public entities, the members of their assemblies, and such other local officials as may be determined by law shall be elected by direct popular vote within their several communities.

Article 94. (Powers of local government)
Local public entities shall have the right to manage their property, affairs and administration and to enact their own regulations within law.

Article 95. (Local consent for special laws)
A special law, applicable only to one local public entity, cannot be enacted by the Diet without the consent of the majority of the voters of the local public entity concerned, obtained in accordance with law.

Chapter IX
Amendments

Article 96. (Procedure to amend the Constitution)
1. Amendments to this Constitution shall be initiated by the Diet, through a concurring vote of two-thirds or more of all the members of each House and shall thereupon be submitted to the people for ratification, which shall require the affirmative vote of a majority of all votes cast thereon, at a special referendum or at such election as the Diet shall specify.
2. Amendments when so ratified shall immediately be promulgated by the Emperor in the name of the people, as an integral part of this Constitution.

Chapter X
Supreme Law

Article 97. (Fundamental human rights)
The fundamental human rights by this Constitution guaranteed to the people of Japan are fruits of the age-old struggle of man to be free; they have survived the many exacting tests for durability and are conferred upon this and future generations in trust, to be held for all time inviolate.

Article 98. (Supremacy of the Constitution; observance of treaties and laws of nations)
1. This Constitution shall be the supreme law of the nation and no law, ordinance, imperial rescript or other act of government, or part thereof, contrary to the provisions hereof, shall have legal force or validity.
2. The treaties concluded by Japan and established laws of nations shall be faithfully observed.

Article 99. (Duty to uphold the Constitution)
The Emperor or the Regent as well as Ministers of State, members of the Diet, judges, and all other public officials have the obligation to respect and uphold this Constitution.

Chapter XI
Supplementary Provisions

[Omitted.]

2. THE CIVIL CODE

Law No. 89, April 27, 1896, as amended

[Selected Provisions]

Source: Reprinted with permission from Appendix 4A of *Doing Business in Japan,* Zentaro Kitagawa, general ed.

BOOK I

General Provisions

Section 1. (Exercise of private rights)

1. All private rights shall conform to the principle of maintaining the public welfare.
2. The exercise of rights and performance of duties shall be carried out in accordance with the principles of good faith and trust.
3. No abuse of rights shall be permitted.

Section 1-2. (Construction)

This Code shall be construed in a manner consistent with respect for the dignity of individuals and the essential equality of the sexes.

Chapter I
Persons

Part 1. Enjoyment of Private Rights

Section 1-3. (Commencement of capacity)

The enjoyment of private rights shall commence at birth.

Section 2. (Legal capacity of aliens)

Aliens shall enjoy private rights, except where prohibited by law, ordinance, or treaty.

Chapter II
Juridical Persons

Part 1. Formation of Juridical Persons

Section 33. (Basis for formation of juridical persons)

Juridical persons may be formed only in accordance with the provisions of this Code and/or other laws.

Section 44. (Legal capacity of juridical person for unlawful act)

1. A juridical person is liable for compensation for damage done to other parties by its directors or other representatives in the performance of their duties.
2. If damage has been done to another party by an act which is not within the scope of the purposes of the juridical person, those members and directors who supported a resolution for such matter and the directors and other representatives who carried it out shall be jointly and severally liable for compensation for such damage.

Part 2. Management of Juridical Persons

Section 52. (Directors and voting)

1. A juridical person must have one or more directors.
2. Where there are two or more directors, the affairs of the juridical person shall be governed by a majority vote of the directors, unless the articles of association or the act of endowment provides otherwise.

Section 54. (Director's apparent power of representation)
No restriction placed on the power of representation of any director may be set up against a third person acting in good faith.

Chapter III
Things (*Mono*)

Section 85. (Definition)
A "thing" in this Code is a corporeal thing.

Section 86. (Immovables and movables)
1. Land and things firmly affixed thereto are immovables.
2. All other things are movables.
3. Obligation-rights payable to bearer shall be deemed to be movables.

Chapter IV
Juristic Acts (*Hōritsu Kōi*)

Part 1. General Provisions (Sōsoku)

Section 90. (The public order and good morals)
A juristic act whose object is contrary to the public order or good morals is null and void.

Section 91. (Discretionary provisions and declaration of intention)
If the parties to a juristic act have declared an intention which deviates from any provision of a law or ordinance not relating to the public order, such intention shall prevail.

Section 92. (Effect of customs)
If there is a custom deviating from any provisions of a law or ordinance not relating to the public order, such custom shall prevail if the parties to a juristic act are deemed to have intended to be bound by such custom.

Part 3. Agency

Section 99. (Effect of representation)
1. A declaration of intention made by an agent within the scope of that agent's authority who discloses the fact that he or she is acting for a principal shall be effective directly against such principal.
2. The provisions of the preceding subsection shall apply *mutatis mutandis* to a declaration of intention made by a third party to an agent.

Section 100. (Act without disclosing representation)
A declaration of intention made by an agent without disclosing that he or she is acting for a principal shall be deemed to have been made on his or her own behalf. Provided, That the provisions of Subsection 1 of the preceding section shall apply *mutatis mutandis* if the other party was aware, or should have been aware, that the declaration of intention was made on behalf of the principal.

Section 108. (Agent of other party or both parties)
In a single juristic act, no party may be an agent of the other party nor may any person be an agent of both parties. Provided, That this shall not apply with regard to the performance of obligation duties.

Section 109. (Apparent agency)
A party who has represented to a third party that he or she has conferred certain powers of agency on another party shall be responsible toward the third party for acts done by such other party within the scope of such powers.

Section 110. (Apparent agency — in excess of authority)

When an agent has done an act with a third party in excess of his or her authority, the provisions of the preceding section shall apply *mutatis mutandis* if the third party had justifiable cause to believe that the agent had authority to do such act.

Chapter VI
Prescription

Part 3. Extinctive Prescription (Shōmetsu Jikō)

Section 166. (Beginning of running of extinctive prescription)

1. Extinctive prescription begins to run from the moment when a right is capable of being exercised.
2. The provisions of the preceding subsection shall not prevent acquisitive prescription from running, as from the time of possession, in favor of a third party possessing the subject matter of a right subject to a time of commencement or to a suspensive condition. Provided, That the person holding title may at any time demand an acknowledgment from the possessor in order to interrupt the prescription.

Section 167. (Extinctive prescription of obligation-right, etc.)

1. An obligation-right shall lapse if it is not exercised for ten years.
2. A property right other than an obligation-right or ownership right shall lapse if it is not exercised for twenty years.

Section 173. (Short-term extinctive prescription for two years — continued)

The following obligation-rights shall lapse if not exercised for two years:

i. obligation-rights for payment for products and merchandise sold by producers or by wholesale or retail traders;
ii. obligation-rights of home-working artisans and manufacturers with regard to their work; and
iii. obligation-rights of school proprietors, keepers of boarding schools, teachers, and masters with regard to the education, clothing, food and lodging of pupils and apprentices.

BOOK II

Real Rights (*Bukken*)

Chapter III
Ownership Right (*Shoyūken*)

Part 1. Limitation of Ownership

Section 234. (Distance of building from boundary line)

1. In constructing a building, a distance of not less than fifty centimeters must be left from the boundary line.
2. If a person attempts to construct a building in contravention of the provisions of the preceding subsection, the owner of the adjoining land may demand that the construction be discontinued or modified. Provided, That if one year has elapsed since the commencement of construction, or if the construction has been completed, only damages may be demanded.

Section 235. (Putting opaque screen on overlooking window or veranda)

1. A person who constructs at a distance of less than one meter from the boundary line a window or veranda which overlooks the garden of another person must affix an opaque screen.

2. The distance referred to in the preceding subsection shall be determined by a line drawn at a right angle to the boundary line from that point of the window or veranda which is nearest to the adjoining land.

Section 236. (Ibid. — different custom)

If there is any custom different from what is provided for in the preceding two sections, such custom shall prevail.

BOOK III

Obligation-Rights (*Saiken*)

Chapter I
General Provisions

Part 1. Subjects of Obligation-Rights

Section 403. (Obligation-right in foreign currency)

If the amount of an obligation-right is designated in foreign currency, the obligor may make payment in Japanese currency at the rate of exchange current at the place of performance.

Section 404. (Statutory interest rate)

Where there exists no different agreement with regard to an obligation-right bearing interest, the rate of interest shall be five percent per annum.

Part 2. Effect of Obligation-Right

Section 415. (Nonperformance of obligation-duty)

If an obligor fails to perform in accordance with the main sense of the obligation-duty, the obligee may demand compensation for damages; the same shall apply in a case where performance becomes impossible for any reason imputable to the obligor.

Section 416. (Scope of damages)

1. A demand for damages shall be for compensation from the obligor for such damages as would ordinarily arise from the non-performance of the obligation-duty.
2. The obligee may also recover for damages which have arisen through special circumstances, if the parties have foreseen or could have foreseen such circumstances.

Section 419. (Damages for nonpayment of a debt)

1. The amount of damages for nonpayment of a debt shall be determined by the legal rate of interest. Provided, That in cases where the agreed rate of interest exceeds the legal rate, the former shall prevail.
2. With regard to the damages referred to in the preceding subsection, the obligee is not bound to prove actual damages nor may the obligor set up force majeure as a defense.

Section 420. (Liquidated damages and penalty)

1. The parties may determine in advance the amount of compensation for damages payable in the event of the nonperformance of an obligation-duty; in such case the court may not increase or reduce the amount.
2. The determination in advance of the amount of compensation for damages shall not prejudice an obligee's right to demand performance or rescission.
3. A penalty is presumed to be a determination in advance of the amount of compensation for damages.

Section 424. (Obligee's right of voidance)

1. An obligee may apply to the court for the voidance of any juristic act effected by the obligor with the knowledge that it would prejudice the obligee. Provided, That this shall not apply where a person who has derived benefit from such act or a subsequent purchaser was, at the time of the act or of the purchase, unaware of the fact that the act would prejudice the obligee.
2. The provisions of the preceding subsection shall not apply to a juristic act which does not have a property right for its subject.

Chapter II
Contracts *(Keiyaku)*

Part 1. General Provisions (Sōsoku)

Subpart 1. Formation of Contract

Section 521. (Offer specifying period of acceptance)

1. An offer specifying a period for acceptance may not be revoked.
2. If the offeror does not receive notice of acceptance within the period specified, the offer shall lapse.

Section 522. (Delayed acceptance)

1. When notice of acceptance has arrived after the time referred to in the preceding section, but if the offeror should have known that it was dispatched at such time that in ordinary circumstances it would have arrived on time, the offeror must without delay notify the other party of the delayed arrival, unless he or she has given notice of the delay before such arrival.
2. If the offeror fails to give notice under the preceding subsection, notice of acceptance is deemed not to have been delayed.

Section 523. (Delayed acceptance regarded as a new offer)

The offeror may treat a delayed acceptance as a new offer.

Section 524. (Offer without limiting time for acceptance)

An offer which has been made to a person at a distance without a time limit for acceptance may not be revoked before the expiration of such time as is reasonably necessary for the offeror to receive notice of acceptance.

Section 526. (Time for formation of a contract between persons distant from each other)

1. A contract between persons distant from each other is formed when notice of acceptance is dispatched.
2. In cases where no notice of acceptance is necessary either by reason of a declaration of intention to that effect by the offeror or by reason of business usage, the contract is formed when any event takes place which can be taken as a declaration of intention to accept.

Section 527. (Delayed notice of revocation arriving after notice of acceptance)

1. Even in a case where notice of the revocation of an offer has arrived after notice of acceptance has been dispatched, if the offeree should have known that the notice of revocation was dispatched at such a time that it would under normal circumstances have arrived before the dispatch of notice of acceptance, the offeree must dispatch without delay notice of the delayed arrival to the offeror.
2. If the offeree has neglected to give the notice referred to in the preceding subsection, the contract shall be deemed not to have been formed.

Section 528. (Modified acceptance)

If the offeree has accepted an offer conditionally or with any other modification, the offeree shall be deemed to have rejected the original offer and made a new offer.

Subpart 3. Rescission of Contract

Section 540. (Exercise of right of rescission)

1. If one of the parties has a right of rescission either by contract or by provisions of law, the rescission shall be effected by a declaration of intention made to the other party.
2. The declaration of intention referred to in the preceding subsection may not be revoked.

Section 541. (Rescission due to delay in performance)

If one of the parties does not perform an obligation-duty, the other party may fix a reasonable period and demand its performance, and may rescind the contract if no performance is effected within such period.

Section 543. (Rescission due to impossibility)

If performance has become impossible in whole or in part due to any cause imputable to the obligor, the obligee may rescind the contract.

Section 545. (Effect of rescission)

1. If one of the parties has exercised the right of rescission, the other party is obligated to restore the former to the original position. Provided, That the rights of third persons shall not be prejudiced thereby.
2. Interest shall be paid upon any money to be repaid in cases referred to in the preceding subsection from the time when such money was first received.
3. The exercise of a right of rescission shall not preclude a demand for compensation for damages.

Part 3. Sale (Baibai)

Section 555. (Sale)

A sale (a sales contract) becomes effective when one of the parties agrees to transfer a property right to the other party and the other party agrees to pay the purchase price to the former.

Section 557. (Earnest money)

1. Where the buyer has paid earnest money to the seller, the buyer may rescind the contract by giving up the earnest money or the seller may rescind by refunding double its amount, so long as neither of the parties has commenced performance of the contract.
2. The provisions of Section 545, Subsection 3 shall not apply in a case referred to in the preceding subsection.

Part 10. Mandate (Inin)

Section 643. (Mandate)

A mandate takes effect when one party commissions another party to perform a juristic act and the other party accepts the commission.

Section 644. (Duty of mandatary — care of good manager)

A mandatary is obligated to manage the entrusted affairs with the care of a good manager in accordance with the tenor of the mandate.

Section 645. (Ibid. — report)

A mandatary must, at any time upon demand by the mandator, report on the condition of the management of the entrusted affairs, and upon the termination of the mandate the mandatary must make a full report thereon without delay.

Section 651. (Rescission)

1. A mandate may be rescinded by either party at any time.
2. If one of the parties rescinds a mandate at a time when it would be unfavorable to the other party, such party shall compensate for any damages incurred thereby. Provided, That this shall not apply when unavoidable reasons exist for such rescission.

Part 12. Partnership (Kumiai)

Section 667. (Partnership)

1. A contract of partnership becomes effective when each of the parties agrees to carry on a joint undertaking by making a contribution thereto.
2. Contributions may consist of services.

Section 668. (Co-ownership of property)

The contribution made by each partner and the other property of the partnership shall belong to all the partners jointly.

Section 669. (Failure to make contribution of money)

Where money is to be contributed, if a partner neglects to make the contribution, such partner must, besides paying interest thereon, compensate for any damages resulting from such neglect.

Section 670. (Conduct of affairs)

1. The conduct of the affairs of the partnership shall be decided by a majority of the partners.
2. If the conduct of the affairs of the partnership has been entrusted to certain persons by the partnership contract, it shall be decided by a majority of such persons.
3. Notwithstanding the provisions of the preceding two subsections, the ordinary affairs of the partnership may be conducted solely by any partner or manager acting alone. Provided, That this shall not apply if any other partner or manager raises objection before the relevant matter is completed.

Part 14. Compromise (Wakai)

Section 695. (Compromise)

A compromise becomes effective when the parties agree to terminate a dispute between them by making mutual concessions.

Section 696. (Effect)

In cases where it has been admitted through compromise that one of the parties possesses the right constituting the subject of a dispute or that the other party does not possess such right, if it has afterwards been established that the former party did not possess the right or that the other party did possess the same, such right shall be treated by virtue of the compromise as transferred to the former party or extinguished.

Chapter V
Torts (*Fuhō Kōi*)

Section 709. (Tort — compensation for damage)

A person who intentionally or negligently violates the rights of another is obligated to compensate for damages arising therefrom.

Section 710. (Nonpecuniary damage)

A person who is liable for damages in accordance with the provisions of the preceding section must compensate therefor even with regard to nonpecuniary damage, irrespective of whether such injury was to the person, liberty or reputation of another or to such person's property rights.

Section 715. (Liability of an employer)

1. A person who employs another person for a certain undertaking is liable for damage caused by such employee to third persons in the execution of such undertaking. Provided, That this shall not apply if the employer has exercised due care in the selection of the employee and in supervision of the undertaking, or if the damages would have arisen even if due care had been exercised.

2. A person who supervises the undertaking on behalf of the employer is also subject to the responsibility under the preceding subsection.
3. The provisions of the preceding two subsections shall not prevent an employer or supervisor from exercising the right to reimbursement from employees.

Section 719. (Joint torts)

1. If two or more persons have by their joint tort caused damage to another, they are jointly and severally liable to compensate for such damage; the same shall apply if it is impossible to ascertain which of the joint participants has caused the damage.
2. Instigators and accomplices are deemed to be joint participants.

Section 722. (Manner of compensation, fault in common)

1. The provisions of Section 417 [compensation for damages to be paid in money absent contrary agreement] shall apply *mutatis mutandis* to the compensation to be made for damages arising from a tort.
2. If there is fault on the part of the injured party, the court may take such fault into account in assessing the amount of the damages.

3. THE COMMERCIAL CODE

Law No. 48, March 9, 1899, as amended

[Selected Provisions]

BOOK I

General Provisions

Chapter I
Rules Concerning the Application of Laws

Section 1. (Laws applicable to commercial matters)
As to commercial matters, in cases where there are no applicable provisions in this Code, commercial customary law shall apply, and where there is no applicable commercial customary law, the Civil Code shall apply.

Section 2. (Commercial acts by public juridical persons)
Except as otherwise provided by law or ordinance, this Code shall apply to commercial acts engaged in by public juridical persons.

Section 3. (Commercial acts with respect to only one party)
1. If an act is a commercial act with respect to one of the parties, this Code shall apply to both parties.
2. In cases where several persons make up one of the parties and an act is a commercial act with respect to one of such persons, this Code shall apply to all of them.

Chapter II
Merchants

Section 4. (Definition of merchant; constructive merchant)
1. The term merchant (*shōnin*) as used in this Code shall mean a person who, as a business, engages in commercial acts on his or her own behalf.
2. A person who engages in the sale of goods at a shop or similar establishment or a person who carries on a mining enterprise shall be deemed to be a merchant even if he or she does not engage in commercial acts as a business. The same shall apply to a company of the nature referred to in Section 52, Subsection 2.

Section 8. (Exceptional provisions for petty merchants)
The provisions in this Code relating to commercial registrations, trade names and trade books shall not apply to petty merchants.

Chapter III
Commercial Registration

Section 9. (General provision)
Matters required to be registered under this Code shall be entered upon application by the party concerned in the Commercial Register kept by the Registry with jurisdiction over the location of such party's place of business.

Section 12. (Effect of registration and public notice)
Matters required to be registered may not be set up against a bona fide third person until the registration and public notice thereof have been duly effected; even after the registration and

public notice of such matters have been effected, they may not be set up against a third person who for a justifiable reason was unaware of them.

Section 14. (Inaccurate registration)

A person who either intentionally or negligently registers inaccurate matters may not set up such inaccuracies against a bona fide third person.

Chapter IV
Trade Names

Section 16. (Selection of trade names)

A merchant may use his or her surname, his or her full name, or any other denomination as a trade name.

Section 19. (Effect of registration of trade name)

No trade name which has been registered by another person in a city, town, or village shall be registered in the same city, town, or village with regard to the same type of business.

Section 20. (Use of same trade name for purpose of unfair competition)

1. A person who has registered a trade name may demand that any other person using the same or a similar trade name for purposes of unfair competition discontinue such use. Provided, That this shall not preclude a claim for damages.
2. A person who uses a trade name of another in the same city, town, or village with regard to the same type of business shall be presumed to do so for purposes of unfair competition.

Section 25. (Transfer of business and prohibition of competition)

1. Unless the parties have expressed a different intention, where a person has transferred a business, he or she shall not engage in the same type of business in the same city, town,or village, nor in any adjacent city, town, or village, for a period of twenty years.
2. If the transferor has made a special agreement not to engage in the same type of business, such agreement shall be valid only in prefectures in which the transferred business is located and in adjacent prefectures and only for a period not exceeding thirty years.
3. Notwithstanding the provisions of the preceding two subsections, the transferor shall not engage in the same type of business for purposes of unfair competition.

Section 30. (Discontinuation of trade name)

If a person who has registered a trade name has failed to use it for a period of two years without any justifiable reason, he or she shall be deemed to have discontinued the use of such trade name.

Chapter V
Accounting Books

Section 32. (Comprehensive provisions)

1. Every merchant shall prepare accounting books and balance sheets for the purpose of making clear the conditions of the business's properties and its profits and losses.
2. In interpreting the provisions concerning the preparation of the account books, reasonable accounting practices shall be taken into consideration.

Section 33. (Accounting books and balance sheets)

* * *

2. A balance sheet shall be prepared based on the accounting books at the time of commencement of the business and thereafter once each year at a fixed time; as for a company, it shall prepare a balance sheet based on the accounting books at the time of incorporation and at the end of each accounting period.

3. Balance sheets shall be compiled and bound together, or shall be entered in a book specially kept for such purposes.
4. A balance sheet shall be signed by the person who prepared it.

Chapter VI
Business Employees

[Sections 37 to 45 concerning agency rules applicable to managers and employees omitted.]

Chapter VII
Commercial Agents

Section 46. (Definition)

A commercial agent is a person who, without being an employee, habitually acts on behalf of a particular merchant as an agent or intermediary in transactions falling within the type of business engaged in by such merchant.

Section 50. (Termination of commercial agency contract)

1. Where the parties have not fixed a term for the duration of a contract, either of them may terminate it upon giving two months' notice.
2. In cases where an unavoidable reason exists, either party may terminate a contract at any time irrespective of whether a term for the duration of the contract has been fixed or not.

BOOK II

Companies *(Kaisha)*

Chapter I
General Provisions

Section 52. (Definitions)

1. The term company as used in this Code shall mean an association formed for the purpose of engaging in commercial acts as a business.
2. An association which has for its object the acquisition of profit and is formed in accordance with the provisions of this Chapter shall be deemed to be a company even if it does not engage in commercial acts as a business.

Section 53. (Types of companies)

There shall be three types of companies, namely partnership companies *(gōmei gaisha)*, limited partnership companies (*gōshi gaisha*) and stock companies (*kabushiki kaisha*).

Section 54. (Legal status and domicile of a company)

1. A company is a juridical person.
2. The domicile of a company is the place of its principal office.

Section 57. (Existence of company)

A company comes into existence when it is registered at the place where its principal office is located.

Section 58. (Order of dissolution of a company)

1. Acting in the public interest, a court, when it determines that the continued existence of a company should not be permitted, may order the dissolution of a company upon the application of the Minister of Justice, a shareholder, an obligee, or any other interested party in the following cases:

i. where the company was established with illegal intent;
ii. where, without justifiable reason, the company has failed to commence business within one year after it has come into existence or has discontinued its business for a period of at least one year; or
iii. where, even though the Minister of Justice has delivered to such person a written demand to discontinue such act, a member or director administering the affairs of a company has continued or repeated any act exceeding or abusing the authority conferred upon the company by law or by the articles of incorporation or violating the criminal laws or ordinances.

2. In the case where an application for dissolution of a company has been made in accordance with this section, a court may, upon the application of the Minister of Justice, a shareholder, an obligee, or any other interested party, or upon its own motion, even before issuing an order of dissolution, appoint an administrator or take any other measures necessary for the preservation of the property of the company.

Chapter II
Partnership Companies (*Gōmei Gaisha*)

Part 1. Establishment

Section 62. (Execution of articles of incorporation)
In order to establish a partnership company, articles of incorporation shall be executed.

Section 63. (Mandatory information to be included in articles of incorporation)
The articles of incorporation of a partnership company must contain the following particulars and must be signed by each member:
i. the purpose;
ii. the trade name;
iii. the name and address of each member;
iv. the location of the principal office and each branch office; and
v. the nature of the contribution made by each member and the value of such contribution, including the standard of valuation used for such contribution.

Section 64. (Registration of the establishment of a partnership company)
1. The registration of the establishment of a partnership company must contain the following particulars:
i. the matters referred to in Items 1 through 3 of the preceding section;
ii. the principal office and each branch office;
iii. the period of duration or the causes for dissolution, provided that such period or causes have been determined;
iv. [deleted]
v. if there is any member who is not to represent the partnership company, the names of the members who are to represent the partnership company; and
vi. if it is provided that two or more members are jointly to represent the partnership company, the provisions as to representation.

* * *

Part 2. Internal Relations of a Partnership Company

*Section 68. (*Mutatis mutandis *application)*
Unless otherwise provided for by the articles of incorporation or by this Code, the provisions of the Civil Code concerning partnership shall apply *mutatis mutandis* to the internal relations of the partnership company.

Section 70. (Rights and duties pertaining to administration of affairs)
Unless otherwise provided for by the articles of incorporation, each member has the right and duty to administer the affairs of the partnership company.

Section 72. (Change of articles of incorporation and acts beyond the scope of the objects of a partnership corporation)

The consent of all the members is necessary in order to effect any change in the articles of incorporation or to perform any act not within the scope of the purpose of the partnership company.

Section 73. (Transfer of a member's share)

No member shall, without the consent of the other members, transfer his or her share in the partnership company, in whole or in part, to any other person.

Section 74. (Prohibition of competition; intervention by the company)

1. No member shall, without the consent of the other members, effect on his or her own behalf or on behalf of a third person any transaction which falls within the class of business carried on by the partnership company or become a member with unlimited liability or a director of any other company having for its object the same kind of business.
2. If any member has, in contravention of the provisions of the preceding subsection, effected a transaction on his or her own behalf, the other members may by a majority of their votes treat such transaction as having been effected on behalf of the partnership company.

* * *

Section 75. (Member's transaction on his or her own behalf)

1. A member may effect a transaction with the partnership company on his or her own behalf or on behalf of a third person only with the approval of a majority of the other members. * * *
2. The partnership company may guarantee the obligation-duties of a member, or effect with a third party a transaction in which the interests of the company contradict those of a member, only with the approval of a majority of the other members.

Part 3. External Relations of the Partnership Company

Section 76. (Right to represent the company)

Each of the members who administer the affairs of the partnership company shall represent the partnership company. Provided, That the partnership company may, either by the articles of incorporation or with the unanimous consent of all the members, specially designate from among such members a particular member [or, by Section 77, members] to represent the company.

Section 78. (The authority of a representative member)

1. A member who represents the partnership company is authorized to do all judicial and extra-judicial acts relating to the business of the company.
2. The provisions of Section 44, Subsection 1 and Section 54 of the Civil Code shall apply to partnership companies *mutatis mutandis.*

Section 80. (Liability of a member)

1. If the assets of a partnership company are insufficient to fully satisfy its obligation-duties, all the members are jointly and severally liable for the performance of such obligation-duties.
2. The preceding subsection shall also apply if a compulsory execution on the assets of the partnership company has proved ineffective.
3. The provision of the preceding subsection shall not apply if any member proves that the company is capable of discharging its obligation-duties and that the execution can easily be enforced.

Section 82. (Liability of a new member)

A member admitted to a partnership company after it has been established shall be liable for all the company's obligation-duties even though such obligation-duties were incurred prior to his or her admission.

Part 4. Withdrawal of a Member

Section 84. (Voluntary withdrawal of a member)

1. If the articles of incorporation of a partnership company do not specify the duration of the company or if the articles provide that the company shall exist during the life of one or more particular members, any member may withdraw from such company at the end of any business year, provided such member gives six months' prior notice.
2. If unavoidable reasons exist, a member may withdraw from the partnership company at any time, regardless of whether the duration of the company has been specified in the articles of incorporation.

Section 85. (Mandatory withdrawal of a member)

In addition to the cases referred to in the preceding section and [other specified section], a member shall withdraw for any of the following reasons:

i. the occurrence of an event specified in the articles of incorporation;
ii. consent of all the members;
iii. death of that member;
iv. bankruptcy of that member;
v. adjudication of incompetency; or
vi. expulsion.

Section 86. (Expulsion of a member and forfeiture of the power to administer or represent)

1. Where any one of the following reasons exists with regard to a member, a partnership company may, by a majority vote of the other members, demand of a court the expulsion of such member or a declaration of forfeiture of his or her power to administer the affairs of the company or to represent it:
   i. failure to perform a duty to contribute;
   ii. contravention of the provisions of Section 74, Subsection 1;
   iii. commission of a dishonest act in the administration of the affairs of the partnership company or intervention in the administration of the affairs of the partnership company without authority;
   iv. commission of a dishonest act in his or her conduct in representing the company, or representing the partnership company without authority; or
   v. failure to perform any other important duty.
2. If a member is markedly unfit to administer the affairs of a partnership company or to represent it, the partnership company may, in accordance with the provisions of the preceding subsection, demand of a court a declaration of forfeiture of such partner's power to administer the affairs of the partnership company or to represent it.
3. When a judgment expelling a member or declaring forfeiture of his or her power to administer the affairs of the company or to represent it has become final and binding, such expulsion or forfeiture shall be registered at the location of the principal office and at the location of each branch office.

Section 89. (Repayment of share)

A withdrawing member is entitled to repayment of his or her share in the partnership company even if his or her sole contribution was in the form of personal services or credit, unless the articles of incorporation provide otherwise.

Part 5. Dissolution of a Partnership Company

Section 94. (Reasons for dissolution)

A partnership company shall be dissolved for any of the following reasons:

i. expiration of the period of duration or any other reason specified in the articles of incorporation;
ii. consent of all the members;
iii. merger;

iv. withdrawal of all but one member;
v. bankruptcy of the partnership company; or
vi. a court decision ordering dissolution.

[Sections 95 to 111 mainly concerning merger of partnership companies omitted.]

Section 112. (Dissolution for unavoidable reasons)

1. If an unavoidable reason exists, any member may apply to the court for dissolution of the company.

* * *

Part 6. Liquidation

Section 116. (Status of a company in the process of liquidation)

For and within the purposes of liquidation, a company shall be deemed to still exist even after its dissolution.

Section 117. (Voluntary liquidation)

1. The method of disposal of a partnership company's assets in case of dissolution may be determined by the articles of incorporation or by agreement of all the members. * * *

* * *

[Sections 118 to 139 concerning methods of, and rights and duties connected to, liquidation omitted.]

Section 140. (Action for voiding establishment)

The establishment of a partnership company may be voided only by an action.

Section 141. (Action for voidance brought by an obligee)

If a member has established a partnership company knowing that he or she would thereby prejudice his or her obligee(s), the obligee(s) may demand a voidance of the establishment of the company by means of an action against that member and the partnership company.

Chapter III
Limited Partnership Company (*Gōshi Gaisha*)

Section 146. (Definition)

A limited partnership company is composed of members with limited liability and with unlimited liability.

Section 147. (Mutatis mutandis *application of provisions governing partnership companies)*

Unless otherwise provided for in this Chapter, the provisions governing partnership companies shall apply *mutatis mutandis* to limited partnership companies.

Section 151. (Right and duty of administering affairs)

1. Except as otherwise provided in the articles of incorporation, every member with unlimited liability shall have the right and duty to administer the affairs of the company.
2. Where there are two or more members with unlimited liability, administration of the affairs of the company shall be decided by a majority vote of such members.

Section 154. (Transfer of shares by a member with limited liability)

With the consent of all the members with unlimited liability, a member with limited liability may transfer to another person all or a part of his or her shares in the company. The above shall also apply in cases where such transfer is to be accompanied by an amendment of the articles of incorporation.

Section 155. (Limited liability member's freedom of competition)

Without the consent of the other members, a member with limited liability may effect on his or her own behalf or on that of a third person any transaction which falls within the kind of business carried on by the company, or become a member with unlimited liability or a director of any other company having for its purpose the same kind of business.

Section 156. (Ineligibility of member with limited liability to administer or represent)

A member with limited liability shall not administer the affairs of the company or represent it.

Section 157. (Liability of a member with limited liability)

1. A member with limited liability shall be bound to perform the obligation-duties of the company to the extent of the amount of his or her contribution. Provided, That if such member has already made a partial payment of his or her contribution, he or she is liable only for the balance of the contribution due.

* * *

Section 159. (Liability of self-styled member with unlimited liability)

1. Where a member with limited liability acts in such a way as to lead others to believe that he or she is a member with unlimited liability, such member shall be liable as if he or she were a member with unlimited liability to any person who effects a transaction with the company on the basis of such belief.

* * *

Chapter IV
Stock Company (*Kabushiki Kaisha*)

Part 1. Incorporation

Section 165. (Number of promoters)

In order to incorporate a stock company, one or more promoters shall prepare articles of incorporation.

Section 166. (Particulars in articles of incorporation)

1. The promoter(s) shall prepare and sign articles of incorporation which shall state the following particulars:
   i. the business purpose;
   ii. the trade name;
   iii. the total number of shares authorized to be issued by the stock company;
   iv. if shares having par value are to be issued, the par value of each share;
   v. [deleted]
   vi. the total number of shares authorized to be issued at the time of incorporation and a statement as to whether they are shares having par value or shares without par value, and the number of each;
   vii. [deleted]
   viii. the location of the principal office;
   ix. the manner by which the stock company will give public notice; and
   x. the name and address of each promoter.
2. The amount of each par value share to be issued at the time of incorporation of the company shall not be less than fifty thousand yen.
3. The total number of shares to be issued at the time of incorporation shall not be less than one-fourth of the total number of shares authorized to be issued by the stock company.
4. Public notices by a stock company shall be given by inserting such notices in the Official Gazette or in a daily newspaper in which matters relating to current events are published.

[Apart from Section 168-4, which follows, we have omitted Sections 167 to 198, concerning incorporation procedures and related rights and duties.]

Section 168-4. (Minimum capital)

The amount of capital shall not be less than ten million yen.

Part 2. Shares

Section 199. (Par value and no par value shares)

The stock company may issue either par value or no par shares, or both.

Section 200. (Liability of shareholder)

1. The liability of a shareholder shall be limited to the subscription price for the shares which he or she holds.
2. A shareholder who has a claim against the stock company may not set off that claim against the company in respect of payments for shares.

Section 202. (Face value of par value shares)

1. The face value of all par value shares shall be the same.
2. The issue price of par value shares shall not be less than the face value thereof.

Section 204. (Transferability of shares)

1. Shares may be transferred to another person. Provided, That the articles of incorporation may stipulate that such transfer requires the approval of the board of directors.
2. The transfer of shares made before the issuance of the share certificates shall not be effective against the stock company.

Section 204-2. (Ibid.)

1. If the transfer of shares requires the approval of the board of directors, the shareholder wishing to transfer shares may request approval of the transfer by way of a written document. Such written document shall state the name of the party to whom the shares will be transferred as well as the class and number of the shares to be transferred. The shareholder may also request the company to designate an alternative transferee to whom the shares may be transferred if the transfer is disapproved.
2. Where a request under the preceding subsection has been made and the transfer has been disapproved, the company shall give a written notice to that effect to the shareholder requesting transfer within two weeks from the date of the request.
3. Where a request under Subsection 1 has been made and the transfer has been disapproved, the board of directors shall designate an alternative transferee for the transfer and give written notice to that effect to the shareholder requesting transfer within two weeks from the date of the request.
4. If the notice required under Subsection 2 is not made within the designated period of time, the approval of the board of directors to the transfer request made pursuant to Subsection1 shall be deemed to have been given. The same deemed approval shall apply when notice is not given within the designated period under Subsection 3.

Section 204-3. (Preemptive right of alternative transferee)

1. The alternative transferee designated pursuant to Subsection 3 of the preceding section may, within ten days from the date of notice under said subsection, request in writing the shareholder under Subsection 1 of the preceding section to sell the shares to him or her.
2. [Upon making the request under the preceding paragraph, the alternative transferee must deposit with the company an amount equal to the net assets of the company per share (based on the most recent balance sheet) times the number of shares to be transferred.]
3. The provisions of Subsection 4 of the preceding section shall apply *mutatis mutandis* in the event a request under Subsection 1 has not been made within the period set forth in said subsection.
4. [When a request under Subsection 1 is made, the shareholder must within one week deposit the share certificates with the company and notify the alternative transferee of this.]
5. If the deposit under the preceding subsection is not made within the designated period, the alternative transferee who made a request under Subsection 1 may rescind the purchase.

Section 204-4. (Ibid.)

1. If a request under Subsection 1 of the preceding section has been made and no agreement has been reached as to the selling price, the parties concerned may, within twenty days from the date of the request made under said subsection, apply to the court for a determination of the selling price.
2. In making the determination under the preceding subsection, the court shall consider the condition of the assets of the stock company at the time of the request made under Subsection 1 of the preceding section and all other circumstances.
3. If the request for a determination under Subsection 1 is not made within twenty days, the amount deposited in accordance with the provisions of Subsection 2 of the preceding section shall be deemed to be the selling price.
4. The transfer of shares shall become effective as of the time of the payment.
5. If the selling price of the shares does not exceed the amount deposited in accordance with the provisions of Subsection 2 of the preceding section, it shall be deemed that the payment was made at the time the selling price became definite. The same shall apply with respect to the partial payment equivalent to the amount deposited, where the selling price exceeds the amount that was deposited.
6. The provisions of Section 204-2, Subsection 3 shall apply *mutatis mutandis* in the case where the shareholder has rescinded the sale because the difference between the selling price and the amount deposited was not paid.

Section 204-5. (Ibid.)

If the approval of the board of directors is required for the transfer of shares, a person who has acquired shares by auction or public sale may, by a written document stating the class and number of the shares, request the stock company to designate a person who will buy the shares if the stock company does not approve the acquisition. In this case, the provisions of Section 204-2, Subsection 3 or 4 and the preceding two sections shall apply *mutatis mutandis*.

Section 205. (Ibid.)

1. For a transfer of shares, the share certificates must be delivered.
2. The person who possesses the share certificates is presumed to be the legitimate bearer thereof.

Section 206. (Transfer of inscribed shares; transfer agents; registrars)

1. The transfer of a share cannot be set up against the stock company unless the name and address of the transferee have been entered in the register of shareholders.

* * *

Section 207. (Pledging of shares)

1. In order to effect a pledge of a share, the share certificate shall be delivered to the pledgee.
2. Unless a pledgee continues to be in possession of the share certificate, he or she cannot set up the pledge against third persons.

Section 210. (Acquisition or pledge of shares by stock company)

A stock company shall not acquire or take in pledge its own shares in excess of one-twentieth of the total issued shares except in the following cases:

i. where the shares are to be redeemed;
ii. where the acquisition results from a merger or the acquisition by transfer of the entire business of another company;
iii. where, in the course of the stock company's exercise of rights, it is necessary to acquire shares in order to achieve the stock company's business purpose; or
iv. where the shares are to be purchased in accordance with the provisions of Section 230-8-2, Subsection 2; Section 245-2; Section 349, Subsection 1; or Section 408-3 of this Code; or Section 64-2, Subsection 1 of the Limited Liability Company Act.

Section 211. (Ibid.)

In the case referred to in Item 1 of the preceding section, the stock company shall, without delay, take the procedure necessary for the voiding of the shares, and in the cases referred to in Items 2 through 4, it shall dispose of the shares or the pledge within a reasonable time.

Section 211-2. (Prohibition against holding of shares of parent company by subsidiaries)

1. Shares of a company (hereinafter referred to as "parent company") which holds a majority of the total number of the issued shares of another stock company or a majority of the capital of another limited liability company (both hereinafter referred to as "subsidiary") may not be held by the subsidiary, except:
   i. where the acquisition results from a merger or the transfer of the entire business of another company; or
   ii. where, in the course of the stock company's exercise of rights, it is necessary to acquire shares in order to achieve the stock company's business purpose.
2. In either of the two cases referred to in the preceding subsection, the subsidiary shall dispose of the shares of the parent company within a reasonable period. The same shall apply in cases where a stock company or limited liability company learns that it has become a subsidiary and at that time holds shares of the parent company.
3. When a parent company and one or more subsidiaries, or one or more subsidiaries themselves, hold a majority of the total number of issued shares of another stock company, such other stock company shall also be deemed a subsidiary of the parent company insofar as application of this Code is concerned. The same shall apply when a parent company and a subsidiary, or one or more subsidiaries themselves, hold units of contribution equal to a majority of the capital of another limited liability company.

Section 212. (Redemption of shares)

1. Shares can only be redeemed in accordance with the provisions relating to the reduction of capital. Provided, That these provisions shall not apply where such redemption is to be effected out of profits which otherwise might have been distributed to shareholders in accordance with the articles of incorporation.
2. The provisions of Section 215, Subsections 1 and 2, and Section 377, Subsection 2 shall apply *mutatis mutandis* in cases where shares are redeemed.

Section 222. (Classes of shares)

1. A stock company may issue two or more classes of shares which differ with respect to their particulars concerning the distribution of profits, interest or surplus assets, or the redemption of shares from profits.
2. In cases under the preceding subsection, the rights and the number of each class of shares shall be set forth in the articles of incorporation. Provided, That with respect to classes of shares entitled to a preference in the distribution of profits, it shall suffice with respect to the amount of the preference if the articles of incorporation stipulate only a maximum amount.
3. In a case under Subsection 1, special stipulations may be made with respect to each class of shares concerning the taking of new shares; the reverse split, stock split, or redemption of shares; the allotment of shares in a merger; or the taking of convertible debentures or debentures with warrants attached, even where no provisions have been made in the articles of incorporation.

[Sections 222-2 to 230-9 concerning convertible shares, the register of shareholders, share certificates and fractional shares omitted.]

Part 3. Internal Organization of Stock Company

Subpart 1. Shareholders' General Meeting *(Kabunushi Sōkai)*

Section 230-10. (Authority of general meeting)

The general meeting of shareholders may adopt resolutions only with respect to matters contained in this Code or specified in the articles of incorporation.

Section 231. (Decision to convene)

The convening of a general meeting of shareholders shall be determined by the board of directors, except as otherwise provided for in this Code.

Section 232. (Notice to convene)

1. In convening a general meeting, notice shall be sent to each shareholder at least two weeks prior to the day set for such meeting.
2. The notice referred to in the preceding subsection shall state the agenda of the meeting.
3. The provisions of the preceding two subsections shall not apply with respect to shareholders not entitled to vote.

Section 232-2. (Shareholders' proposal right)

1. Shareholders who have held continuously for the preceding six months either shares representing not less than one percent of the total number of issued shares or not less than three hundred shares may demand the inclusion of specific matters in the agenda of a general meeting by filing with the directors a written application six weeks before the general meeting. Provided, That this shall not apply if the matter is not a matter to be decided by the general meeting.
2. Shareholders under the preceding subsection may demand that a summary of the proposal which they are presenting for the agenda of the meeting be entered in the meeting notice referred to in the preceding section by filing with a director a written application six weeks before the general meeting. Provided, That this shall not apply if the proposal is contrary to any law or ordinance or to the articles of incorporation or if three years have not yet passed from the date of a general meeting in which the same proposal received less than ten percent of the votes.

Section 234. (Convening of ordinary shareholders' general meeting)

1. An ordinary shareholders' general meeting shall be convened at a fixed time at least once a year. * * *

* * *

Section 235. (Convening of special general meeting)

A special general meeting of shareholders may be convened whenever necessary.

Section 237. (Demand for shareholders' general meeting by minority shareholders)

1. Shareholders who have held continuously for the preceding six months shares representing not less than three percent of the total number of shares issued may demand that a special general meeting of shareholders be convened. Such demand shall be made by filing with the directors a written application which shall state the agenda of such meeting and the reasons why it is to be convened.
2. After the demand referred to in the preceding subsection has been made, if notice for convening the meeting is not promptly given, the shareholders who made the demand may themselves convene the meeting with permission of a court. The same shall apply if a notice setting a date for the meeting within six weeks from the date of the demand is not issued.
3. At a general meeting held in accordance with the provisions of the preceding two subsections, inspectors may be specially appointed to investigate the affairs of the stock company and the state of its property.

Section 237-2. (Inspector of general meeting)

1. Shareholders who have held continuously for the preceding six months shares representing not less than one percent of the total number of the issued shares may, prior to a general meeting, file with the court an application for the appointment of an inspector to investigate the procedures for the convening of a general meeting or the manner of adopting resolutions at a general meeting.
2. The inspector shall report the results of the investigation to the court.
3. If, upon receiving the report, the court deems it necessary, it may order the directors to convene a general meeting of shareholders. * * *

Section 237-3. (Directors' and auditors' duty to explain)

1. Directors and auditors shall explain matters requested by shareholders at the general meeting of shareholders. Provided, That this shall not apply if the matter is not related to a matter on the agenda of the general meeting, if the explanation would cause serious damage to the common interests of the shareholders, if the explanation would require investigation, or if there is another justifiable reason.
2. Where a shareholder has, within a reasonable period prior to the date of a general meeting, given written notice of matters concerning which he or she will request explanation at the general meeting, directors or auditors may not refuse to provide such explanation on the grounds that it would require investigation.

Section 237-4. (Chair of general meeting)

1. The chair of the general meeting shall be elected by the general meeting, unless otherwise provided in the articles of incorporation.
2. The chair shall maintain order in the general meeting and regulate the proceedings.
3. The chair may order a person who disobeys his or her instructions or who disturbs the order of the general meeting to leave.

Section 239. (Resolutions and voting)

1. Except as otherwise provided for by this Code or by the articles of incorporation, all resolutions of a shareholders' general meeting shall be adopted by a majority of votes of the shareholders present who hold shares representing more than one-half of the total number of the issued shares.
2. A shareholder may vote by proxy. Provided, That such proxy shall submit a document establishing his or her power of representation to the stock company.

* * *

Section 241. (Number of votes)

1. Each shareholder shall have one vote for each share.
2. The stock company may not vote its own shares.
3. If a company, a parent company and one or more subsidiaries, or one or more subsidiaries themselves, hold shares representing not less than one-fourth of the total number of issued shares of another stock company or hold units of contribution of not less than one-fourth of the capital of another limited liability company, such other stock company or limited liability company shall not be entitled to vote any shares it holds in the company or the parent company.

Section 242. (Nonvoting shares)

1. If a stock company issues two or more classes of shares, the articles of incorporation may provide that shareholders of a preferred class regarding the distribution of profits shall not be entitled to vote. Provided, That the holder of such shares shall be entitled to vote from the time beginning with an ordinary general shareholders meeting at which no resolution authorizing preferential distribution is submitted, or with the conclusion of an ordinary general shareholders meeting at which such a resolution is rejected, and ending with the adoption of a resolution authorizing preferential distribution.

* * *

3. The total number of shares of the type referred to in Subsection 1 shall not exceed one-third of the total number of shares issued.

Section 243. (Resolution for postponement or adjournment)

A resolution for postponement or adjournment may be adopted at a shareholders' general meeting. In such case, the provisions of Section 232 shall not apply.

Section 244. (Minutes)

1. Minutes shall be made of the proceedings of a shareholders' general meeting.

[2.-4. The minutes shall record the substance of the meeting, be signed by the directors present and meeting chair, be kept at the principal office for ten years, with copies to be kept at branch offices for five years, and be available for shareholder inspection.]

Section 245. (Requirement of resolution for special acts)

1. A resolution as provided for in Section 343 is required for a stock company to effect the following acts:
   i. the transfer of all or of an important part of the business;
   ii. the making, alteration or rescission of a contract for leasing the whole of the business, for giving a mandate to manage such business, or for sharing with another person the entire profits and losses in relation to the business, or of a similar contract; or
   iii. the taking over of the whole of the business of any other stock company.
2. The substance of the acts referred to in the preceding subsection shall be stated in the notice provided for in Section 232.

Section 245-2. (Dissenting shareholder's appraisal remedy)

Any shareholder who has notified the stock company in writing prior to the general meeting of shareholders at which a resolution referred to in Subsection 1 of the preceding section is to be made of his or her intention to oppose any of the acts referred to in said subsection, and who has opposed such resolution at the general meeting, may demand from the company the payment of the fair value of his or her shares at a price at which the shares would have been valued but for such resolution. Provided, That the same shall not apply in cases where a resolution for dissolution has been adopted simultaneously with the resolution as to the acts referred to in Item 1 of Subsection 1 of said section.

Section 245-3. (Ibid. — Procedure for repurchase)

* * *

3. If within sixty days from the date on which the resolution was adopted, the shareholder and the stock company do not reach agreement, the shareholder may, within thirty days after the expiration of the sixty-day period, file a petition with the court for a determination of the value of the shares.

* * *

Section 245-4. (Ineffective cases)

The dissenting shareholder's demand provided for in Section 245-2 shall become unavailable if the stock company abandons the act referred to in Section 245, Subsection 1.

Section 247. (Action to void resolution)

1. Shareholders, directors or auditors may institute an action for voidance of a resolution adopted at a general meeting of shareholders in the following cases:
   i. if the procedure for convening the general meeting or the manner of adopting resolutions is contrary to law or ordinance or the articles of incorporation, or is grossly unfair;
   ii. if the contents of the resolution are contrary to the articles of incorporation; or
   iii. if a grossly unfair resolution has been adopted as a result of the exercise of voting rights by a shareholder who has a special personal interest in the resolution.

* * *

Section 248. (Time limitation for actions to void a resolution)

1. An action to void a resolution shall be brought within three months from the date of such resolution.
2. Oral argument for such action shall not be commenced until after the expiration of the period referred to in the preceding subsection.

Section 249. (Security in actions to void a resolution)

1. When a shareholder has instituted an action to void a resolution, the court may, at the request of the stock company, order such shareholder to furnish adequate security. Provided, That this shall not apply if such shareholder is a director or an auditor.

* * *

Section 251. (Dismissal at discretion)

In cases where an action to void a resolution has been instituted, the court may dismiss the action, even if the procedure for convening a shareholders' meeting or the manner in which a resolution was adopted is contrary to law or ordinance or the articles of incorporation, if the court determines that the contravention was not important and did not affect the resolution.

Subpart 2. Directors and Board of Directors

Section 254. (Appointment, competency and relationship with the company)

1. Directors shall be appointed at a general meeting of shareholders.
2. The stock company shall not, even by the articles of incorporation, require that the directors be shareholders.
3. The relationship between the company and the directors shall be governed by the provisions relating to mandates.

Section 254-2. (Disqualification)

The following persons may not become directors:

i. an incompetent or quasi-incompetent;
ii. an adjudicated bankrupt who has not yet been rehabilitated;
iii. a person who has been sentenced and punished for a crime under the Commercial Code, the Stock Company Special Audit Act or the Limited Liability Company Act, and for whom two years have not yet passed since the sentence was served or was excused; or
iv. a person who has been sentenced to imprisonment or to a graver punishment for a crime other than those prescribed in the preceding subsection, and the sentence has not yet been served or excused. Provided, That this shall not apply to a person who has been granted suspension of execution of the sentence.

Section 254-3. (Fiduciary duty of directors)

The directors shall comply with laws, ordinances, and the provisions of the articles of incorporation, as well as resolutions adopted at a general meeting, and shall perform their duties faithfully on behalf of the company.

Section 255. (Number of directors)

The minimum number of directors shall be three.

Section 256. (Term of office)

1. The term of office of directors shall not exceed two years.

* * *

Section 256-2. (Quorum for a resolution appointing directors)

The number of shares owned by shareholders present at a general meeting required for a resolution appointing directors may be governed by the articles of incorporation, but shall not be less than one-third of the total number of issued shares.

Section 256-3. (Cumulative voting)

1. If a general meeting is convened to elect two or more directors, any shareholder may, unless the articles of incorporation stipulate otherwise, demand that the directors be elected by the method of cumulative voting.
2. A demand under the preceding subsection shall be made in writing at least five days before the time set for the general meeting.
3. If a demand under Subsection 1 has been made, each shareholder, in voting for a resolution electing directors, shall have the same number of votes, per share owned, as the number of directors to be elected.
4. In the case [of cumulative voting] under the preceding subsection, those candidates receiving the largest number of votes shall be deemed to have been elected as directors.
5. In a case under Subsection 1, the chair of the general meeting shall, prior to the resolution, announce that the demand referred to in said subsection has been made.
6. The written demand referred to in Subsection 2 shall be kept at the principal office for inspection by shareholders until the termination of the general meeting.

Section 257. (Removal of a director)

1. A director may be removed from office at any time by a resolution of a general meeting of shareholders. Provided, That if the term of office has been fixed, and if the director is so removed without justifiable reason before the expiration of such term, he or she may claim damages from the stock company for any damage caused by such removal.
2. The resolution referred to in the preceding subsection may not be adopted unless in accordance with the provisions of Section 343.
3. If the general meeting of shareholders has rejected the removal of a director, notwithstanding that there has been a dishonest act or grave fact contravening law, ordinance, or the articles of incorporation in connection with the performance of duties, shareholders who have held continuously for the preceding six months shares representing at least three percent of the total number of the issued shares may institute an action for the director's removal in a court within thirty days.

* * *

Section 259. (Meetings of the board of directors)

1. A meeting of the board of directors may be convened by a director. Provided, That this shall not apply if the board of directors has appointed a particular director who is to convene such a meeting.
2. In cases referred to in the proviso to the preceding subsection, another director may demand the convening of a meeting by filing a written demand containing the proposed meeting's agenda.
3. In the case of a demand under the preceding subsection, if a notice convening a meeting within two weeks from the date of the demand is not issued within five days from the date of the demand, the director making the demand may convene the meeting himself or herself.

Section 259-2. (Notice of a directors' meeting)

In convening a meeting of the board of directors, notice shall be given to each director and each auditor at least a week before the time set for such meeting. Provided, That the articles of incorporation may stipulate a shorter period.

Section 259-3. (Waiver of notice)

If the consent of all the directors and the auditors has been obtained, a meeting of the board of directors may be held without conforming to the procedure for convening meetings.

Section 260. (Authority of the board of directors)

1. The board of directors shall administer the affairs of the stock company and supervise performance of duties by the directors.

2. The board of directors shall not permit the individual directors to decide the following matters or other important matters of performance of duties:
   i. disposition or purchase of important property;
   ii. borrowing of large sums;
   iii. appointment and dismissal of managers and other important employees;
   iv. establishment, change or abolition of a branch office or other important organization.
3. A director shall report to the board of directors regarding the state of performance of duties at least once every three months.

Section 260-2. (Resolutions of the board of directors)

1. A resolution of the board of directors shall be adopted by a majority vote of the directors present, who shall constitute in number a majority of all the directors. Provided, That the articles of incorporation may stipulate more stringent requirements.
2. A director who has a special interest in the subject matter of a resolution shall not be entitled to participate in it.
3. The number of directors not entitled to participate in a resolution pursuant to the preceding subsection shall not be included when computing the number of directors under Subsection 1.

Section 260-3. (Presence of auditors)

1. Auditors may attend the meeting of the board of directors and state their opinions.
2. In cases where a director performs or is likely to perform an act which is beyond the business purpose of the company, or which is contrary to any law or ordinance or the articles of incorporation, an auditor shall report it to the board of directors.
3. In the cases referred to in the preceding subsection, an auditor may, if necessary, demand a convening of the board of directors.
4. The provisions of Section 259, Subsection 3 shall apply *mutatis mutandis* in cases where the demand referred to in the preceding subsection is made.

Section 260-4. (Minutes)

1. Minutes shall be taken of the proceedings of the meeting of the board of directors.

[2.-4. The minutes shall record the substance of the meeting, be signed by the directors and auditors present and, "with the permission of the court," be available for inspection by shareholders, if "necessary for the exercise of their rights," and by obligees of the company "in order to enforce the liability of a director or auditor."]

5. The court may not give permission if the perusal or the copying would cause serious damage to the company, its parent company or a subsidiary.

Section 261. (Representative directors)

1. The stock company shall, by a resolution of the board of directors, appoint one or more directors to represent the stock company.
2. In a case under the preceding subsection, it may be provided that two or more directors shall jointly represent the company.
3. The provisions of Section 39, Subsection 2 [any one representative director can bind the company] and Section 78 and Section 258 [concerning filling vacancies] shall apply *mutatis mutandis* to the representative director or directors.

Section 262. (Liability for director with apparent authority)

A stock company shall be liable to a bona fide third person for any act done by a director invested with any title such as president, vice-president, chief director or managing director from which it may be assumed that he or she has authority to represent the stock company, even if such person has no power of representation.

Section 263. (Keeping of documents and inspection thereof)

1. The directors shall keep the articles of incorporation at the principal office and at each branch office, and shall keep the register of shareholders, the register of fractional shares, and the register of debentures at the principal office. * * *

2. Any shareholder or obligee of the company may, at any time during business hours, inspect or copy from the documents referred to in the preceding subsection.

* * *

Section 264. (Duty to avoid competition, intervention by the company)

1. A director who intends to undertake, on his or her own behalf or on behalf of a third person, a transaction that falls within the class of business carried on by the company, shall reveal all the material facts in connection with the transaction to the board of directors and obtain its approval.
2. A director who has effected a transaction referred to in the preceding subsection shall without delay report all the material facts in connection with it to the board of directors.
3. If a director has, in contravention of the provisions of Subsection 1, made a transaction on his or her own behalf, the board of directors may treat such transaction as made on behalf of the company.
4. The right referred to in the preceding subsection shall lapse one year from the time of the transaction.

Section 265. (Transaction on one's own behalf)

1. When a director intends to acquire the stock company's products or other properties by transfer, or to transfer his or her own products or other properties to the stock company, or to receive loans from the stock company, or to make any transaction with the stock company on his or her own behalf or on behalf of a third person, he or she shall obtain the approval of the board of directors. The same shall apply when the stock company guarantees the obligation-duty of a director, or enters into with a third person other than a director a transaction in which the interests of the company conflict with those of the director.

* * *

3. The provisions of Subsection 2 of the preceding section shall apply to a director who has effected a transaction referred to in Subsection 1 of this section.

Section 266. (Liability to the stock company)

1. Directors who have done any of the following acts shall be jointly and severally liable in effecting performance or in paying damages to the stock company; in the case of Item i, directors shall be liable for the amount which has been distributed or apportioned illegally; in the case of Item ii, for the amount of property interest offered; in the case of Item iii, for the amount of loans not yet repaid; and in the cases of Items iv and v, for the amount of damage caused to the stock company:
   i. the submission to a general meeting of a proposal for the distribution of profits in contravention of the provisions of Section 290, Subsection 1, or the distribution of money in contravention of the provisions of Section 293-5, Subsection 3;
   ii. the offering of a property interest in contravention of the provisions of Section 294-2;
   iii. the loan of money to another director;
   iv. the making of a transaction referred to in Subsection 1 of the preceding section; or
   v. the doing of any act which violates any law, ordinance, or the articles of incorporation.
2. In cases where any act referred to in the preceding subsection has been done in accordance with a resolution of the board of directors, the directors who assented to such resolution shall be deemed to have committed such act.
3. Directors who participated in the resolution referred to in the preceding subsection and who did not express their dissent in the minutes shall be presumed to have assented to such resolution.
4. When a director effects a transaction in contravention of the provisions of Section 264, Subsection 1, the amount of benefit obtained by the director or a third party shall be presumed to be the amount of damage caused to the company. Provided, That this shall not apply when the right referred to in Subsection 3 of the same section is exercised.
5. The liability of directors referred to in Subsection 1 cannot be released except by a unanimous consent of all the shareholders.

6. Notwithstanding the provisions of the preceding subsection, the liability of directors in respect of a transaction referred to in Item iv of Subsection 1 may be released by a majority vote of at least two-thirds of the total number of issued shares. In this case, the directors shall disclose all material facts regarding such transaction at a general meeting of shareholders.

Section 266-2. (Right to obtain reimbursement from non-bona fide shareholders)
Directors who are liable under the provisions of the preceding section, Subsection 1, Item i, and who have satisfied such liability, shall not be prevented from seeking reimbursement from shareholders who are not bona fide.

Section 266-3. (Liability to third persons)
1. If directors have been guilty of bad faith or gross negligence in their duties, they shall be jointly and severally liable for damages to third persons.
2. The rule in the preceding subsection shall also apply in cases where a director makes a false entry, registration or notice by publication with regard to any material particulars in any application form for shares or preemptive documents, an application form for debentures, a prospectus, or documents prescribed in Section 281, Subsection 1. Provided, That a director will be excused from liability if he or she proves that he or she has not neglected to employ due care in such entry, registration or notice by publication.
3. The provisions of Section 266, Subsections 2 and 3 shall apply *mutatis mutandis* to the cases referred to in the preceding two subsections.

Section 267. (Derivative action to enforce the liability of directors)
1. Any shareholder who has held one or more shares continuously for the last six months may demand, in writing, that the stock company institute an action to enforce the liability of directors.
2. If the stock company has failed to institute an action within thirty days from the date on which the demand referred to in the preceding subsection was made, the shareholder referred to in the preceding subsection may institute such action on behalf of the company.
3. Notwithstanding the provisions of the preceding two subsections, if irreparable damage may be caused to the stock company due to the thirty day period provided for in the preceding subsection, the shareholder referred to in Subsection 1 may immediately institute the action referred to in the preceding subsection.
4. For purposes of determining the amount in dispute, the action referred to in the preceding subsection shall be deemed to involve a non-property claim. [This provision, added in 1993, operates by implicit reference to the Civil Procedure Expenses Act *(Minji Soshō Hiyō Hō)* (§§ 4(2) and 3(1)) to limit the filing fee for a derivative action to ¥8,200.]
5. When a shareholder has instituted an action pursuant to Subsection 2 or 3, the court may, at the request of the defendant, order such shareholder to furnish adequate security.
6. The provisions of Section 106, Subsection 2 shall apply *mutatis mutandis* to a request under the preceding subsection. [This means that, to make the request for security, the defendant must "make a preliminary showing that the action was brought with wrongful intent."]

Section 268. (Ibid. —jurisdiction, intervention and notification)
1. An action to enforce liability of directors shall be under the exclusive jurisdiction of the district court where the principal office is located.
2. Shareholders or the stock company may intervene in the action referred to in the preceding subsection. Provided, That this shall not apply in cases where such intervention would unduly delay the case or constitute an undue burden on the court facilities.
3. The shareholder instituting an action referred to in Subsection 2 of the preceding section shall, after bringing the action, notify the stock company of the action without delay.

Section 268-2. (Litigation expenses and attorney's fees; liability of shareholders)

1. If a shareholder who has brought an action referred to in Section 267, Subsection 2 has succeeded in the action and has incurred litigation expenses and attorney's fees, the shareholder may demand the stock company to pay such litigation expenses and attorney's fees in a reasonable amount not to exceed the scope of such expenses and fees.
2. If a shareholder loses the case, such shareholder shall not be liable in damages to the stock company, unless the shareholder has acted with wrongful intent.

* * *

Section 268-3. (Ibid. — petition for renewal of procedure)

1. If an action referred to in Section 268, Subsection 1 has been brought, and if the plaintiff and defendant have caused judgment to be rendered by their collusion for the purpose of prejudicing the rights of the stock company which are the subject matter of the case, the stock company or the shareholders may reopen the final judgment by means of an action for renewal of procedure.
2. The provisions of the preceding section shall apply *mutatis mutandis* to the action referred to in the preceding subsection.

Section 269. (Directors' remuneration)

If the amount of remuneration to be received by the directors has not been fixed by the articles of incorporation, it shall be fixed by a resolution of a general meeting of shareholders.

Subpart 3. Auditors *(Kansayaku)*

Section 273. (Term of office)

1. The term of office of an auditor shall extend until the end of the ordinary general shareholders' meeting dealing with the last settlement of accounts within three years after he or she entered office.

* * *

Section 274. (Powers of auditors)

1. An auditor shall audit the directors' performance of their duties.
2. An auditor may at any time call on the directors, managers and other business employees for a report on the business of a company, or investigate the conditions of the affairs of the company and its property.

Section 274-2. (Duty of director to report to auditor)

If a director discovers facts which give rise to an apprehension that significant damage may be incurred by the stock company, he or she shall immediately report this to an auditor.

Section 274-3. (Power of auditor of parent company to request report from a subsidiary)

1. The auditor of a parent company may, if necessary for performing his or her duties, request a subsidiary to report on its business.
2. If the * * * subsidiary has failed to report without delay, or if it is necessary to verify the report, the auditor may investigate the conditions of the business and property of the subsidiary with regard to the matters on which the report was requested.
3. If there is a justifiable reason, the subsidiary may refuse to make the report under the provisions of Subsection 1 or may refuse to permit the investigation under Subsection 2.

Section 275. (Duty to examine and to report to general meeting of shareholders)

The auditors shall examine the proposals and documents which the directors propose to submit to a general meeting of shareholders, and if the auditors recognize therein matters which are in violation of laws, ordinances or the articles of incorporation, or which are grossly improper, they shall report their opinion thereon to such general meeting.

Section 275-2. (Demand to cease unlawful act of director)

1. In cases where a director is performing an act which is not within the scope of the business purpose of the stock company or any other act in violation of laws, ordinances or the

articles of incorporation, and there is a likelihood that serious damage might be done to the stock company, an auditor may demand the director to cease such act.

2. If, in a provisional disposition, the court orders the director to cease such act, the court need not require the posting of security.

Section 275-3. (Auditor's opinion regarding appointment or removal of an auditor)

At a general meeting of shareholders, an auditor may state an opinion regarding the appointment or removal of an auditor.

Section 275-4. (Representation of action between director and company)

In cases where a stock company institutes an action against a director or where a director institutes an action against a stock company, an auditor shall represent the stock company in such action. The same shall apply in a case where a stock company receives the demand referred to in Section 267, Subsection 1.

Section 276. (Conflict of interest)

An auditor shall not at the same time be a director, manager or any other employee of a stock company or a subsidiary thereof.

Section 277. (Liability to the stock company)

If auditors have neglected any of their duties, such auditors shall be jointly and severally liable in damages to the stock company.

Section 278. (Joint and several liability with directors)

If any auditors are liable in damages either to the stock company or to a third person, and if the directors are also liable, the auditors and the directors shall be jointly and severally liable.

Section 279. (Remuneration of auditors)

1. Remuneration of auditors shall be determined by a resolution of a general meeting of shareholders unless the amount thereof is provided for in the articles of incorporation.

* * *

Section 280. (Application mutatis mutandis *of the provisions on directors)*

1. The provisions of Section 254; Section 254-2; Section 256-2; Section 257; Section 258; Section 266, Subsection 5; Section 266-3, Subsection 1; and Sections 267 to 268-3 inclusive shall apply *mutatis mutandis* to auditors.
2. The provisions of Section 266-3, Subsection 2 shall apply *mutatis mutandis* to an auditor who has made a false entry with regard to any material particulars in the auditing report.

Part 3. Issuance of New Shares (Shinkabu no hakkō)

Section 280-2. (Issuance of new shares after incorporation)

1. If shares are issued after the incorporation of the stock company, and if any of the following matters are not provided for in the articles of incorporation, they shall be determined by the board of directors. Provided, That this shall not apply to those matters otherwise provided for in this Code, or to those matters which the articles of incorporation stipulate shall be determined by a general meeting of shareholders:
   i. whether new shares are par value or no par shares, and the class and the number of shares to be issued;
   ii. the issue price of new shares and the date set for payment;
   iii. the names of the persons whose contributions are in the form of property other than money, the property forming the subject matter of such contributions, the value of such property, a statement as to whether the shares to be given therefor are par value or no par shares, and the class and the number thereof;
   iv. the amount not credited to the stated capital out of the issue price for the new shares;
   v. whether preemptive rights to new shares are to be given to shareholders, as well as a statement as to whether the shares subject to the preemptive rights are par value or no par shares, the class, the number, and the issue price thereof;

vi. whether preemptive rights under the preceding item may be transferred;
vii. whether preemptive right certificates are to be issued only by request of the shareholder, and, if so, the period for making the request;
viii. persons other than shareholders to whom new shares are to be issued at a specially reduced issue price, as well as a statement as to whether the shares issued to them are par value or no par shares, the class and the number thereof; and
ix. whether full payment of the issue price for new shares is partially reduced in accordance with the provisions of Section 280-9-2, Subsection 1, and, if so, the portion of the issue price to be paid.

2. Even if the articles of incorporation so authorize, if new shares are to be issued to persons other than shareholders at a specially reduced issue price, a resolution as provided for in Section 343 shall be adopted as to whether the shares to be issued to such persons are par value or no par shares, the number, and the minimum issue price therefor. If such new shares are to be issued, the directors shall, at a general meeting of shareholders, disclose the reason why it is necessary to offer the new shares to persons other than shareholders at a special price.

* * *

[Sections 280-3 to 280-9-2 concerning, *inter alia*, preemptive rights omitted.]

Section 280-10. (Suspension of issuance)
If the stock company issues shares either in contravention of any law or ordinance or of the articles of incorporation or in a grossly unfair manner and if there is a likelihood that shareholders will suffer disadvantage thereby, such shareholders may demand that the stock company suspend such issuance.

Section 280-11. (Liability of subscriber at unfair price)

1. Any person who, in collusion with any director, has subscribed for shares at a grossly unfair price, shall be liable to pay to the stock company an amount equivalent to the difference between a fair issue price and such unfair issue price.
2. The provisions of Sections 267 to 268-3 inclusive shall apply *mutatis mutandis* to the action for payment referred to in the preceding subsection.

Section 280-15. (Action to confirm nullity of issuance of new shares)

1. The nullity of the issuance of new shares may be asserted only by means of an action within six months of the day of the issuance of the new shares.
2. The action referred to in the preceding subsection may be brought only by shareholders, directors or auditors.

Part 4. Accounts of the Stock Company

Section 281. (Preparation of accounting documents)

1. The directors shall prepare and obtain the approval of the board of directors for the following documents and supporting schedules for every period of settlement of accounts:
   i. a balance sheet;
   ii. a profit-and-loss account;
   iii. a business report; and
   iv. proposals relating to the disposition of profits or the settlement of losses.
2. The documents referred to in the preceding subsection shall be audited by the auditors.

Section 281-2. (Submission of accounting documents)

1. The directors shall submit the documents referred to in the respective items of Subsection 1 of the preceding section to the auditors seven weeks before the scheduled date of an ordinary general meeting.
2. The directors shall submit the supporting schedules referred to in Subsection 1 of the preceding section to the auditors within three weeks from the date of submission of the documents referred to in the preceding subsection.

Section 281-3. (Auditing report on accounting documents)

1. The auditors shall submit the auditing report to the directors within four weeks after receipt of the documents under Subsection 1 of the preceding section.
2. The following matters shall be stated in the auditing report referred to in the preceding subsection:
   i. a summary of the method of auditing;
   [ii.-ix. a statement to that effect if there are misstatements, omissions, etc., or items not conforming to the law, articles of incorporation or accounting rules, etc., with regard to the accounting books, balance sheet, business report, proposals for disposition of profits, etc.];
   x. where there exists in the directors' performance of their duties any unjust conduct or serious fact in violation of laws, ordinances, or the articles of incorporation, such fact; and
   xi. where investigations necessary for auditing could not be performed, a statement to that effect and the reasons therefor.

Section 282. (Public disclosure of accounting documents)

1. The directors must keep the documents referred to in Section 281, Subsection 1 and the auditing report at the principal office of the stock company for five years, and copies thereof at branch offices for three years, commencing from two weeks prior to the date of the ordinary general meeting.
2. Any shareholder or obligee of the stock company may, at any time during business hours, demand inspection of the documents referred to in the preceding subsection and may demand delivery of a copy or an abstract of such documents, paying such fees as are fixed by the stock company.

[Sections 283 to 289 concerning, *inter alia*, accounting rules omitted.]

Section 290. (Distribution of profits)

1. Profits may be distributed to the extent of the amount of the net assets on the balance sheet minus therefrom the following amounts:
   i. the amount of stated capital;
   ii. the total sum of the capital surplus reserve and the earned surplus reserve;
   iii. the amount of the earned surplus reserve necessary to be accumulated in the period for the settlement of accounts; and
   iv. the amount, if any, by which the total sum of the amounts entered on the assets side of the balance sheet in accordance with the provisions of Section 286-2 and Section 286-3 exceeds the total sum of the surplus reserve under the preceding two items.
2. If profits have been distributed in contravention of the provisions of the preceding subsection, any obligee of the stock company may demand that such profits be refunded.

Section 293. (Distribution of profits or interest)

The distribution of profits or interest shall be made in proportion to the number of shares owned by each shareholder. Provided, That this shall not prohibit the application of the provisions of Section 222, Subsection 1.

Section 293-2. (Crediting profits to the stated capital)

The stock company may, through a resolution of a general meeting of shareholders concerning the disposition of profits, credit to the stated capital all or a part of the profits available for distribution.

Section 293-3. (Crediting the reserve fund to the stated capital)

The stock company may, by a resolution of the board of directors, credit all or a part of the reserve fund to the stated capital.

Section 293-5. (Interim dividend)

1. A stock company whose business year is one year may stipulate in the articles of incorporation that a specified date may be fixed once in a business year and by resolution of the board of directors a cash dividend may be paid to those who were shareholders as of said specified date.
2. The resolution under the preceding subsection shall be made within three months before the specified date referred to in said subsection.
3. The cash dividend under Subsection 1 shall be limited to an amount determined by deducting the following amounts from the amount of net assets shown on the last balance sheet:
   i. the total sum of the stated capital and the reserves in the last period for settlement of accounts;
   ii. the total sum of the earned surplus reserve to have been accumulated at the ordinary general meeting concerning the last period for settlement of accounts, and the earned surplus reserve required to be accumulated at the time of the cash distribution;
   iii. the amount, if any, by which the total sum of money entered as assets on the balance sheet in the last period for settlement of accounts in accordance with the provisions of Section 286-2 and Section 286-3 exceeds the total sum of the reserves under the preceding two items; and
   iv. the amount determined by a resolution of the ordinary general meeting concerning the last period for settlement of accounts to be distributed or paid from profit.
4. The directors may not distribute money under Subsection 1 if there exists any fear that at the end of the business year the net assets amount in the balance sheet will become less than the total sum of the amounts under the respective items of Section 290, Subsection 1.

* * *

Section 293-6. (Right of shareholder to peruse documents)

1. Any shareholders who hold not less than three percent of the total number of issued shares may demand to peruse or make extracts from the accounting books, records and documents.
2. The demand referred to in the preceding subsection shall be made in writing, with reasons stated.

Section 293-7. (Refusal of demand to peruse)

If a demand under the provisions of the preceding section is made, the directors shall not refuse such demand unless there exist justifiable reasons to believe the demand falls under any of the following cases:

i. where the shareholder makes a demand for a reason other than to obtain information in connection with the protection or exercise of statutory rights, or in order to hinder the management of the business of the stock company or injure the common interests of the shareholders;
ii. where the shareholder is a business competitor; or is a member, shareholder, or director of a business competitor; or holds shares in the stock company for or on behalf of a business competitor;
iii. where the shareholder makes a demand in order to inform others for profit of any fact to be obtained through the perusal or extraction of the books, records and other documents of the company; or where he or she has for profit informed others of any fact obtained through the perusal or extraction of documents of the company or of any other company within two years prior to the date of the demand; or
iv. where the shareholder has demanded perusal or extraction at an unreasonable time.

Section 294. (Inspection of company affairs and property)

1. If there is any reason to suspect that there exists any dishonest act or a serious fact constituting the contravention of any law or ordinance or the articles of incorporation in connection with the administration of the stock company's affairs, any shareholder who owns shares representing not less than one-tenth of the total number of issued shares may apply to the court for the appointment of an inspector to investigate the affairs of the stock company and the state of its property.
2. The provisions of Section 237-2, Subsections 2 and 3 shall apply *mutatis mutandis* to cases where an inspector is appointed pursuant to the preceding subsection.

Section 294-2. (Prohibition against offering property interests with regard to the exercise of shareholders' rights)

1. A stock company shall not offer any property interest to any person with respect to the exercise of rights of shareholders.
2. When a stock company has gratuitously offered a property interest to a specific shareholder, it shall be presumed that the interest has been offered with respect to the exercise of rights of shareholders. The same shall apply when a stock company has offered a property interest to a specific shareholder and the interest obtained by the stock company is markedly smaller than the interest obtained by the shareholder.
3. When a stock company has offered a property interest in contravention of Subsection 1, the person who has obtained the interest shall return it to the company. In such cases, he or she is entitled to recover whatever he or she gave to the company therefor.
4. The provisions of Sections 267 to 268-3 inclusive shall apply *mutatis mutandis* to an action for the recovery of the interest referred to in the preceding subsection.

Section 295. (Preferred claim of employees)

1. A person who has an obligation-right for the return of security money or any other obligation-right arising out of an employment relationship between a company and its employees shall have a preferred claim over the entire property of the company.
2. The preference referred to in the preceding subsection shall rank after the preference referred to in Section 306, Item 1 of the Civil Code [covering "expenses for the common benefit"].

Part 5. Debentures (Shasai)

[Omitted.]

Part 6. Amendment of the articles of incorporation (Teikan no Henkō)

Section 342. (Method to amend the articles of incorporation)

1. A resolution of the general meeting of shareholders is required to amend the articles of incorporation.
2. The substance of any proposal to amend the articles of incorporation shall be set forth in the notice provided for in Section 232.

Section 343. (Special resolution by general meeting)

The resolution provided for in Subsection 1 of the preceding section shall be adopted by a vote of two-thirds or more of the shareholders who are present, with shareholders who are present holding shares representing more than one-half of the total number of issued shares.

Section 345. (General meeting of a class of shareholders in cases of amending the articles of incorporation)

1. If a stock company has issued two or more classes of shares and if any amendment to the articles of incorporation is considered prejudicial to a certain class of shareholders, a resolution of a general meeting of that class of shareholders, in addition to that of a general meeting of shareholders, shall be required for such amendment.

2. Any resolution of a general meeting of the holders of a certain class of shares shall be adopted by a vote of two-thirds or more of the shareholders who are present, with shareholders who are present holding shares representing more than one-half of the total number of the issued shares in the class represented by such shareholders.
3. The provisions relating to a general meeting of shareholders shall apply *mutatis mutandis* to the general meeting referred to in Subsection 1, except those relating to shares not vested with the right to vote.

Section 346. (Ibid. — in cases of issuing classes of shares or merger)

The provisions of the preceding section shall apply *mutatis mutandis* in cases where special provisions are to be made in respect of specific classes of shares in accordance with the provisions of Section 222, Subsection 3, and in cases where the holders of a certain class of shares are likely to be prejudiced by the merger of the stock company.

Section 347. (Increase of total number of shares authorized to be issued)

The total number of shares authorized to be issued by the stock company cannot be increased to more than four times the total number of issued shares.

Section 348. (Voting requirements for special resolutions)

1. If the articles of incorporation are to be amended to require the approval of the board of directors to transfer shares, such resolution shall require, regardless of the provisions of Section 343, a majority vote of shareholders who hold shares, representing at least two-thirds of the total number of issued shares.
2. With respect to the resolution under the preceding subsection, the shareholders referred to in Section 242, Subsection 1 shall also have the right to vote.
3. A stock company which has issued convertible debentures may not adopt the resolution under Subsection 1 until after the period in which the demand for conversion may be made has elapsed, and a stock company which has issued debentures with preemptive rights to new shares may not adopt the resolution under Subsection 1 until after the period in which the preemptive rights to new shares may be exercised has elapsed.

Section 349. (Demand for appraisal right of dissenting shareholders)

1. Any shareholder who has notified the stock company in writing prior to the general meeting of shareholders at which the resolution referred to in Subsection 1 of the preceding section is to be adopted, of the intention to oppose the adoption of such amendment, and who has opposed it at the general meeting, may demand that the stock company purchase the shares in his or her possession at the fair market value at which the shares would have been valued but for such resolution.
2. The provisions of Sections 245-3 and 254-4 shall apply *mutatis mutandis* in the case of the preceding subsection.

[Sections 350 and 351 concerning presentation of share certificates in the event of a Section 348(1) resolution and amendment prohibiting issuance of certificates for fractions omitted. Sections 352 to 374 deleted from the Commercial Code.]

Part 6-2. Reduction of Stated Capital

Section 375. (Resolution to reduce stated capital)

1. The reduction of stated capital shall be made by a resolution as provided for in Section 343.
2. The substance of the proposal relating to the reduction of stated capital shall be stated in the notice provided for in Section 232.

[Sections 376 to 380 concerning rights in connection with capital reduction proposals omitted.]

Part 7. Reorganization of a Stock Company

Section 381. (Instituting a reorganization)

1. If, from the existing condition of a stock company and other circumstances, it is deemed that there is a fear of its becoming insolvent or of its liabilities exceeding its assets, the court may order the stock company to institute a reorganization, on the application of a director, an auditor, shareholders who have held continuously for the prior six months not less than three percent of the total number of issued shares, or of obligees having obligation-rights equivalent to at least one-tenth of the amount of the capital. The same shall apply in cases where it is deemed that there are grounds for suspecting that the stock company is insolvent or that its liabilities are in excess of its assets.
2. When it is deemed that the grounds referred to in the preceding subsection exist regarding any company, the administrative agencies supervising the affairs of stock companies may give notice thereof to the court; in such a case, the court may on its own motion order the institution of a reorganization.

[Sections 382 to 403 concerning reorganization and bankruptcy omitted.]

Part 8. Dissolution (Kaisan)

Section 404. (Reasons for dissolution)

A stock company shall be dissolved for any of the following reasons:

i. the reasons referred to in Section 94, Items i, iii, v, and vi; or
ii. a resolution of a general meeting of shareholders.

Section 405. (Procedures for resolution of dissolution)

No resolution for dissolution may be made except in compliance with the provisions of Section 343.

Section 406-2. (Judgment for dissolution)

1. In the cases referred to below, if there exist unavoidable reasons, shareholders who own not less than one-tenth of the total number of issued shares may demand that the court dissolve the stock company:
   i. when the stock company is suffering or is threatened with irreparable injury due to a crisis in the management of the stock company's affairs;
   ii. when the stock company's existence is endangered by grossly improper management or disposition of the stock company's property.
2. The provisions of Section 112, Subsection 2 shall apply *mutatis mutandis* to the cases referred to in the preceding subsection.

Section 408. (Approval of written merger agreement)

1. To effect the merger of stock companies, a written merger agreement shall be prepared and shall be approved by a general meeting of shareholders.
2. The substance of the written merger agreement shall be stated in the notice provided for in Section 232.
3. The resolution referred to in Subsection 1 may be adopted only in accordance with the provisions of Section 343.
4. In cases where the articles of incorporation of the stock company which will continue to exist after the merger contain a stipulation to the effect that the transfer of shares requires the approval of the board of directors and the articles of incorporation of the stock company which will cease to exist following the merger do not contain such a stipulation, the resolution referred to in Subsection 1 may not be adopted by the shareholders of the stock company which will cease to exist unless done in accordance with the provisions of Section 348, Subsection 1. In cases where a stipulation to that effect is placed in the articles of incorporation of a stock company which will be incorporated following a merger, if the articles of incorporation of the stock companies which will be merged do not contain stipulations to such effect, the same provisions shall apply with respect to said stock companies.

5. With respect to the general meeting which is to adopt the resolution referred to in the first sentence of the preceding subsection, the fact that the articles of incorporation of the stock company which will continue to exist will contain the stipulation referred to in said subsection shall be stated in the notice referred to in Subsection 2.

Section 408-3. (Demand for appraisal rights)

1. Any shareholder of a stock company which is to be merged who has notified the stock company in writing prior to the general meeting of shareholders referred to in Section 408, Subsection 1, of the intention to oppose the merger agreement, and who has voted against approval of such agreement at the general meeting, may demand that such stock company purchase his or her shares at the fair value which such shares would have had but for such resolution.
2. The provisions of Sections 245-3 and 245-4 shall apply *mutatis mutandis* to the case referred to in the preceding subsection.

Section 409. (Written merger agreement)

In cases where one of the merging stock companies is to continue to exist after the merger, the following particulars shall be included in the written merger agreement: * * *

Section 410. (Written consolidation agreement)

In the case of a new stock company to be incorporated as a result of a consolidation, the written consolidation agreement shall contain the following particulars: * * *

[Sections 411 to 416 concerning merger and consolidation omitted.]

Part 9. Liquidation

Subpart 1. General Provisions

Section 417. (Appointment of liquidator)

1. Except in cases of dissolution by merger or bankruptcy, upon the dissolution of the stock company, the directors shall become its liquidators, unless the articles of incorporation provide otherwise or unless other persons have been appointed by a general meeting of shareholders.
2. If, under the provisions of the preceding subsection, there is no person who is to be the liquidator, the court shall appoint a liquidator on the application of any interested person.

[Sections 419 to 456 concerning liquidation, obligees' rights, and court-ordered liquidation omitted. Sections 457-478 deleted from Commercial Code.]

Chapter VI
Foreign Companies (*Gaikoku Kaisha*)

Section 479. (Representative and business office)

1. If a foreign company intends to engage in transactions on a continuous basis in Japan, it shall appoint a representative in Japan and establish a business office at the residence of such representative or at some other place.
2. In the case referred to in the preceding subsection, such foreign company shall register such office and give notice by publication of its business office. Such registration and notice by publication shall be governed by the same provisions as those which regulate the registration and notice by publication of a branch office of a company established in Japan of the same type as the foreign company or of the type which the foreign company most closely resembles.
3. Simultaneously with the registration referred to in the preceding subsection, a foreign company also shall register the law under which it was established, as well as the name and address of its representative in Japan.
4. The provisions of Section 78 shall apply *mutatis mutandis* to the representative of a foreign company.

Section 481. (Prohibition of continuous transactions before registration)

1. A foreign company shall not engage in transactions on a continuous basis in Japan until it has registered in accordance with Section 479.
2. Any person who has engaged in transactions in contravention of the provisions of the preceding subsection shall be liable jointly and severally with the company for such transactions.

Section 482. (Compliance with the same provisions as Japanese companies)

A company which establishes its principal office in Japan or a company whose chief purpose is to carry on business in Japan shall comply with the same provisions as a company established in Japan, even though the company was established in a foreign country.

Section 485-2. (Status of foreign companies)

With regard to the application of other laws, a foreign company shall be deemed to be a company established in Japan of the same type as the foreign company or of the type which the foreign company most closely resembles. Provided, That this shall not apply in cases where laws provide otherwise.

Chapter VII
Penal Provisions

Section 486. (Special embezzlement by directors, etc.)

1. If a promoter, director, auditor, acting director or auditor (under Section 188, Subsection 3; Section 258, Subsection 2; or Section 280, Subsection 1), manager, or any other employee entrusted to undertake certain kinds of matters or specified matters relating to business, inflicts damage of a pecuniary nature on the company in breach of that person's duty, for the purpose of benefiting himself or any third person, or of damaging the stock company, such person shall be liable to either penal servitude for a term not exceeding seven years, or to a fine not exceeding three million yen.
2. [The same prohibitions and penalties apply to members of a reorganizing committee, supervisors, and receivers under Section 398, Subsection 1, and to liquidators and acting liquidators under Section 430.]

[Section 487 concerning embezzlement by representative of debenture holders omitted.]

Section 488. (Attempted special embezzlement)

An attempt to commit any of the acts referred to in the preceding two sections shall be subject to punishment.

Section 489. (Crimes of endangering property of the company)

A person referred to in Section 486, Subsection 1, or an inspector shall be liable to penal servitude for a term not exceeding five years or to a fine not exceeding two million yen in any of the following cases:

i. if such person makes an untrue statement to or conceals from a court or a general meeting of shareholders facts relating to a subscription of or payment for shares to be issued at the time of the incorporation of a stock company, or relating to the delivery of property constituting a contribution of property other than money at such time, or relating to any of the particulars referred to in Section 168, Subsection 1 or Section 280-2, Subsection 1, Item iii;

ii. if such person intentionally acquires or receives in pledge the shares of the stock company through the use of the stock company's funds, irrespective of the name he or she uses in so acting;

iii. if such person distributes profits or interest or distributes money under Section 293-5, Subsection 1 in contravention of the provisions of any law or ordinance or of the articles of incorporation; or

iv. if such person disposes of the stock company's property in speculative transactions outside the scope of the stock company's business.

Section 490. (Crime of using documents containing untrue statements)

1. A person referred to in Section 486, Subsection 1, a representative of a foreign company in Japan or a person who has been commissioned to invite subscriptions for shares or debentures shall be liable to penal servitude for a term not exceeding five years or to a fine not exceeding two million yen, if, in the course of an invitation of subscriptions for shares or debentures, such person executes application forms for shares or debentures, a prospectus, advertisements relating to an invitation or subscriptions for shares or debentures, or any other document containing untrue material statements relating to subscriptions for shares or debentures.
2. The provisions of the preceding subsection shall also apply to a person who offers shares or debentures for sale, if such person executes documents relating to such sale which contain untrue material statements.

Section 491. (Crime of borrow-and-deposit)

A person referred to in Section 486, Subsection 1 shall be liable to penal servitude for a term not exceeding five years or to a fine not exceeding two million yen, if such person engages in borrow-and-deposit for the purpose of disguising a payment; the same shall apply to a person who agrees to receive such payment.

Section 492. (Concurrent imposition of penal servitude and fine)

According to the circumstances, both penal servitude and a fine may be imposed concurrently on those persons who have committed any of the offenses referred to in the preceding six sections.

Section 492-2. (Crime of excessive issuance of shares)

Where a promoter, director, or acting director of a stock company (as referred to in Section 188, Subsection 3 or Section 258, Subsection 2) issues shares in excess of the total number of authorized shares, such person shall be liable to penal servitude for a term not exceeding five years or to a fine not exceeding two million yen.

Section 493. (Bribery by directors, inspectors, etc.)

1. If a person referred to in Section 486 or 487, an inspector or a member of an inspecting committee, in response to unlawful solicitations, has received, demanded or entered into an agreement to receive any benefit of a pecuniary nature in connection with such person's duties, such person shall be liable to penal servitude for a term not exceeding three years or to a fine not exceeding one million yen.
2. The provisions of the preceding subsection shall also apply to a person who provides the benefit referred to in the preceding subsection, makes an offer thereof, or enters into an agreement to provide such benefit.

Section 494. (Crime of bribery in connection with voting or bringing an action)

1. A person who, in response to an unlawful solicitation, has received, demanded, or entered into an agreement to receive or give any benefit of a pecuniary nature in connection with the matters referred to below shall be liable to penal servitude for a term not exceeding one year or to a fine not exceeding five hundred thousand yen:
   i. making a statement to or exercising a right to vote at an organizational general meeting, a general meeting of shareholders, a meeting of debenture holders, or a meeting of obligees;
   ii. bringing an action as prescribed in Chapter IV; intervening in an action referred to in Section 268, Subsection 2 or Section 280-11, Subsection 2; or otherwise exercising the rights of shareholders that require holdings of not less than one percent, three percent or ten percent of the total number of shares, or holdings of not less than three hundred shares; or otherwise exercising the rights of debenture holders that require holdings of not less than one-tenth of the total value of the debentures; or

iii. exercising any of the rights prescribed in Section 272; Section 280-10; Section 381, Subsection 1; Section 431, Subsection 1; Section 439, Subsections 2 and 3; and Section 452, Subsection 1.

2. The provisions of the preceding subsection shall also apply to a person who provides the benefit referred to in the preceding subsection, makes an offer thereof, or enters into an agreement to provide such benefit.

Section 495. (Confiscation or exaction of bribery)

In the cases referred to in Section 493, Subsection 1, and in Subsection 1 of the preceding section, the benefit received by the offender shall be confiscated. If it is impossible to confiscate such benefit wholly or in part, the value thereof shall be exacted from the offender.

Section 496. (Crime of evading liability for payment for shares)

A person who takes shares by using another person's name, or a fictitious name, for the purpose of evading liability for payment therefor shall be liable to penal servitude for a term not exceeding one year or to a fine not exceeding five hundred thousand yen.

Section 497. (Offer of property interest with respect to exercise of shareholders' rights)

1. If a director, auditor, acting director or auditor (under Section 188, Subsection 3; Section 258, Subsection 2; or Section 280, Subsection 1), manager, or any other employee offers a property interest to another on the company's account with respect to the exercise of shareholders' rights, he or she shall be liable to penal servitude not exceeding six months or a fine not exceeding three hundred thousand yen.
2. The same shall apply to a person who, with knowledge, obtains the interest referred to in the preceding subsection or causes another to obtain such interest.

[Section 498, which details 32 types of acts for which noncriminal fines may be imposed, and Sections 498-2 and 498-3, concerning transactions made before company registration, omitted.]

Section 499. (Application of penal provisions to juridical persons)

If any person referred to in Sections 486, 487, 489 to 491 inclusive, or Section 493, Subsection 1 is a juridical person, the penal provisions of this chapter shall apply to the directors and any other officers or managers administering the affairs of the company who have committed the acts.

BOOK III

Commercial Acts

Chapter 1
General Provisions

Section 501. (Absolute commercial acts)

The acts described below are commercial acts:

i. acts which aim to acquire movables, immovables or valuable instruments for value with the intention of disposing of them at a profit, or the disposal of objects so acquired;
ii. contracts for the supply of movables or valuable instruments which are to be acquired from others, and transactions the object of which is to acquire such movables or valuable instruments for value in order to carry out such contracts;
iii. acts on stock or commodity exchanges; and
iv. acts relating to bills of exchange and other commercial papers.

Section 502. (Commercial acts, if effected as a business)

The acts described below, when effected as a business, are commercial acts, except when such acts are effected by persons who manufacture articles or render services solely for the purpose of earning wages:

i. acts which aim to acquire for value or lease movables or immovables with the intention of leasing them, or the leasing of objects so acquired or hired;
ii. acts relating to the manufacture or processing of articles for other persons;
iii. acts relating to the supply of electricity or gas;
iv. acts relating to carriage;
v. contracts for the execution of work or for the supply of labor;
vi. acts relating to publishing, printing, or the taking of photographs;
vii. acts relating to the operation of establishments the object of which is to receive customers;
viii. money changing and other banking transactions;
ix. insurance;
x. acceptance of deposits;
xi. acts relating to brokerage or commission agency; or
xii. acceptance of an agency for commercial transactions.

Section 503. (Incidental commercial acts)

1. Acts effected by a merchant for the purpose of his or her business are commercial transactions.
2. The acts of a merchant shall be presumed to be effected for the purpose of his or her business.

Section 504. (Agency)

An act by an agent conducting commercial acts shall be valid as against his or her principal even though the agent has not disclosed the fact that he or she is acting on behalf of a principal. Provided, That this shall not prevent the other party from demanding performance from the agent if he or she did not know that the act was effected on behalf of the principal.

Section 505. (Mandate)

A mandatary conducting commercial acts may effect acts for which he or she has not received any specific mandate insofar as such acts are not contrary to the main purpose of the mandate.

Section 507. (Offer of contract made during conversation)

An offer to enter into a contract, made during a conversation, shall lapse if not immediately accepted by the offeree.

Section 508. (Offer of contract made inter absentes*)*

1. An offer to enter into a contract with regard to which no period of acceptance has been fixed, when made to a party at a distance, shall lapse if notice of its acceptance is not dispatched by the offeree within a reasonable period.
2. The provisions of Section 523 of the Civil Code shall apply *mutatis mutandis* to the situation described in the preceding subsection.

Section 509. (Duty to notify of acceptance or rejection)

When a merchant has received an offer to enter into a contract which falls within any area of the business he or she carries on from a person with whom he or she has regular business relations, said merchant shall without delay dispatch notice of acceptance or rejection. When said merchant has neglected to dispatch such notice, he or she shall be deemed to have accepted the offer.

Section 510. (Duty to hold goods in custody)

When a merchant has received goods together with an offer to enter into a contract which falls within any area of the business he or she carries on, said merchant shall, even though he or she has refused the offer, hold such goods in custody at the expense of the offeror. This shall not, however, apply in cases where the value of the goods is insufficient to cover the custody expenses or where the merchant might sustain damage through such custody.

Section 511. (Joint and several liability of obligors and sureties)

1. When two or more persons have assumed an obligation-duty with regard to one or all of them through an act which is a commercial act, the obligation-duty shall be borne jointly and severally by all such persons.
2. In cases where there is a surety, when the principal obligation-duty has arisen out of a commercial act of the principal obligor, or when the suretyship itself is a commercial act, the principal obligor and the surety shall be liable jointly and severally on the obligation-duty even though they have assumed it through separate transactions.

Section 512. (Right to demand remuneration)

A merchant who has acted for another person within the scope of his or her own business may demand reasonable remuneration.

Section 513. (Right to demand interest)

1. If a loan of money has been effected between merchants, the lender may demand legal interest thereon.
2. If a merchant, within the scope of his or her own business, has advanced money on behalf of another person, he or she may demand legal interest thereon from the date on which such advance was made.

Section 522. (Limitation period for commercial obligation-rights)

Except as otherwise provided for in this Code, an obligation-right which has arisen out of a commercial act shall be extinguished by prescription if it is not exercised within five years. Provided, That if a shorter period for prescription is provided for by other laws or ordinances, such provisions shall apply.

Chapter II
Sales (*Baibai*)

Section 524. (Deposit and auction of subject matter)

1. In the case of a sale between merchants, if the buyer refuses or is unable to take delivery of the subject matter of such a sale, the seller may deposit the subject matter with the competent authority or may sell it by public auction after giving the buyer a demand to accept it within a reasonable period specified by the seller. In such case, the seller shall dispatch notice of the fact of the public auction to the buyer without delay.
2. Perishable goods may be sold by public auction without giving the demand referred to in the preceding subsection.
3. In cases where the seller has sold the subject matter of the sale by public auction in accordance with the provisions of the preceding two subsections, he or she shall deposit the proceeds thereof with the competent authority. Provided, That this shall not affect the seller's right to appropriate the whole or a part of such proceeds to the purchase price.

Section 526. (Buyer's duty of examination and notification)

1. In the case of a sale between merchants, the buyer shall, upon taking delivery of the subject matter, examine it without delay, and if he or she discovers any defects therein or any deficiency in quantity, he or she shall immediately dispatch notice thereof to the seller; otherwise the buyer has no right to cancel the contract, to demand a reduction in the price or to claim damages. The same shall apply where within six months the buyer discovers in the subject matter of the sale a defect which was not immediately discoverable.
2. The provisions of the preceding subsection shall not apply where there has been bad faith on the part of the seller.

Section 527. (Buyer's duty regarding custody or deposit)

1. In the case described in the preceding section, the buyer shall, even though he or she has cancelled the contract, hold the subject matter of the sale in custody or deposit it with the competent authority at the seller's expense. Provided, That if the subject matter is subject

to loss or deterioration, the buyer shall with the permission of the court sell it by public auction, and shall hold the proceeds thereof in custody or deposit them with the competent authority.

2. When the buyer has effected a sale by public auction in accordance with the provisions of the preceding subsection, he or she shall dispatch notice of the fact to the seller without delay.
3. The provisions of the preceding two subsections shall not apply when the places of business of the seller and the buyer, or when they have no places of business their domiciles, are in the same city, town, or village.

Section 528. (Ibid.)

The provisions of the preceding section shall apply *mutatis mutandis* where the goods delivered by the seller to the buyer are different from those ordered; the same shall apply as regards the quantity in excess in cases where the goods delivered exceed the quantity ordered.

Chapter III
Accounts Current

[Omitted].

Chapter IV
Anonymous Partnership (*Tokumei Kumiai*)

Section 535. (Definition of anonymous partnership)

A contract of anonymous partnership is created when the parties agree that one of them shall make a contribution toward the business of the other and that they shall divide any profits arising from such business.

Section 536. (Contribution and relation to other parties)

1. The contribution made by the anonymous partner becomes the property of the proprietor of the business.
2. The anonymous partner neither acquires rights nor incurs duties with regard to third persons through the acts of the proprietor.

Section 537. (Responsibility for the use of a name)

Where the anonymous partner has consented to the use of his or her surname or full name in the proprietor's trade name or to the use of his or her own trade name as that of the proprietor, he or she shall be liable jointly and severally with the latter for any obligation-duties arising from such use.

Section 538. (Right to demand distribution of profits)

Where the contribution of the anonymous partner has been reduced by losses, he or she may not demand any share of the profits until after such losses have been made good.

Section 539. (Termination by either party)

1. When the duration of the anonymous partnership has not been fixed by the contract of partnership, or when it has been provided for therein that the partnership shall continue to exist for the life of one of the parties, either party may terminate the contract at the end of any business year, subject to the giving of six months' notice.
2. Where unavoidable reasons exist, either party may terminate the contract at any time irrespective of whether the duration of the partnership has been fixed or not.

Section 540. (Other causes for termination)

In addition to the cases referred to in the preceding section, a contract of anonymous partnership shall be ended by any of the following reasons:

i. completion of the undertaking which is the purpose of the partnership or the impossibility of such completion;
ii. death of or adjudication of incompetency of the proprietor of the business; or
iii. bankruptcy of the proprietor of the business or of the anonymous partner.

Section 541. (Effect of termination)

Upon the termination of a contract of anonymous partnership, the proprietor of the business shall return to the anonymous partner the value of his or her contribution. Provided, That in cases where the contribution has been diminished by losses, only the balance need be returned.

Section 542. (Provisions applied mutatis mutandis*)*

The provisions of Sections 150, 153, and 156 shall apply *mutatis mutandis* to an anonymous partner.

[Chapter V — Brokerage (Sections 543 to 550); Chapter VI — Commission Agency (Sections 551 to 558); Chapter VII — Freight Forwarding Business (Sections 559-568); Chapter VIII — Transportation Business (Sections 569-592); Chapter IX — Deposit (Sections 593-628); Chapter X — Insurance (Sections 629-683); and Book IV — Maritime Commerce (Sections 684 to 851) omitted].

4. ACT REGARDING EXCEPTIONAL RULES OF THE COMMERCIAL CODE CONCERNING AUDITING, ETC., OF STOCK CORPORATIONS

Law No. 22, April 2, 1974, as amended
[Selected Provisions]
Source: 2 *The Japan Business Law Journal* 443 (translation by H. Nakatsu) (Sangyō Hōrei Center Inc., 1981). Reprinted by permission.
[Updated by Edward Stokes Johnson, Jr., and Daniel H. Foote to incorporate amendments through 1993.]

Chapter I
General Provisions

Section 1. *(Purport)*

This Act shall prescribe exceptional rules of the Commercial Code (Law No. 48 of 1899) concerning auditing, etc., of stock corporations having stated capital of not less than 500,000,000 yen or total liability of not less than 20,000,000,000 yen, and of stock corporations having stated capital of not more than 100,000,000 yen.

Chapter II
Exceptional Rules For Stock Corporations Whose Stated Capital Is Not Less Than 500,000,000 Yen or Whose Total Liability Is Not Less Than 20,000,000,000 Yen

Section 2. *(Audit by accounting auditor)*

A stock corporation falling under either of the following items (hereinafter referred to as the "corporation" in this Chapter) shall have the documents referred to in Section 281, Subsection 1 of the Commercial Code (with respect to the document referred to in Item 3 of the same subsection and the accompanying schedule, only such part as relates to the accounts) audited by an accounting auditor, in addition to having them audited by the auditors:

(1) The amount of its stated capital is not less than 500,000,000 yen;

(2) The sum total of the amounts stated in the liability section of its latest balance sheet is not less than 20,000,000,000 yen.

Section 3. *(Appointment of accounting auditor)*

1. An accounting auditor shall be appointed at the general meeting of shareholders.
2. The directors shall obtain the consent of the board of auditors in presenting a proposal for appointment of an accounting auditor to the general meeting of shareholders.
3. The board of auditors may, by resolution, request the directors to place the appointment of an accounting auditor on the agenda of the general meeting of shareholders. The same shall also apply in the case of submitting any proposal relative to the election of an accounting auditor.

* * *

Section 4. *(Qualification for accounting auditor)*

1. An accounting auditor shall be either a certified public accountant (including a foreign certified public accountant) or an audit corporation.
2. Persons mentioned in the following items shall not qualify as accounting auditor:

* * *

(2) A person who is remunerated continuously for services other than those of a certified public accountant or an auditing corporation by a subsidiary (meaning a subsidiary as defined under Section 211(2) of the Commercial Code; hereinafter the same shall apply) of the corporation or a director or an auditor thereof, or the spouse of such person;

* * *

(4) An auditing corporation * * * one-half or more of whose members fall under Item 2.

Section 6. (Dismissal of accounting auditor)

1. The accounting auditor may, at any time, be dismissed by resolution of the general meeting of shareholders.
2. An accounting auditor dismissed pursuant to the provisions of the preceding subsection may request the corporation to compensate for damage arising therefrom, except where the dismissal is effected for justifiable reasons.
3. The provisions of Section 3, Subsection 2 and the former part of Subsection 3 shall apply *mutatis mutandis* in the case where a proposal to dismiss the accounting auditor is placed on the agenda of the general meeting of shareholders.

Section 6-2. (Ibid.)

1. If the accounting auditor falls under any of the following items, the board of auditors may, by resolution, dismiss such accounting auditor:
   (1) One who has violated the duties of an accounting auditor or has neglected performance of functions of accounting auditor;
   (2) One who has committed misconduct unbecoming to an accounting auditor; or
   (3) Where the pursuit of duties is obstructed or proves unbearable due to mental or physical disorder.
2. In the event that the accounting auditor has been dismissed under the provisions of the preceding subsection, an auditor designated by the board of auditors shall report such dismissal and the reasons therefor to the first general meeting of shareholders convened after the dismissal.
3. An accounting auditor dismissed pursuant to the provisions of Subsection 1 may attend the said general meeting of shareholders and state an opinion thereat.

Section 6-3. (Stating opinion on appointment, etc., of accounting auditor)

An accounting auditor may attend the general meeting of shareholders and state an opinion thereat on the appointment, refusal of reappointment or dismissal of an accounting auditor.

Section 7. (Powers, etc., of accounting auditor)

1. The accounting auditor may at any time peruse or take copies of the accounting books and documents of the corporation, or request a director, manager, or other employee to make reports concerning accounting matters.
2. The accounting auditor may, if necessary for the execution of the office, investigate the status of the business and assets of the corporation.
3. The accounting auditor may, if necessary for execution of the office, request a subsidiary to make reports concerning accounting matters.
4. The provisions of Section 274-3, Subsections 2 and 3 of the Commercial Code shall apply *mutatis mutandis* in the case of the preceding subsection.
5. The accounting auditor, in executing the office, shall not employ a certified public accountant falling under Section 4, Subsection 2, Items 1 through 3, a director, auditor, or employee of the corporation or of its subsidiary, or a person who is remunerated continuously for services other than those of certified public accountant or accounting corporation by the corporation or a subsidiary thereof.

Section 8. (Report to auditors by accounting auditor)

1. If the accounting auditor has, in executing the office, found any dishonest act or any grave fact in contravention of laws, ordinances, or the articles of incorporation relative to the execution of the office by any director, the accounting auditor shall report such information to the board of auditors.
2. The auditor may, if necessary for execution of the office, request the accounting auditor to make a report concerning an audit he or she has conducted.

Section 9. (Accounting auditor's liability to compensate for damages)

If the accounting auditors have caused damage to the corporation by neglecting their duties, such accounting auditors shall be jointly and severally liable to the corporation to compensate for such damage.

Section 10. (Liability of accounting auditor to third persons)

If an accounting auditor has caused damages to a third person by having entered a false statement in the audit report under Section 13, Subsection 1, such accounting auditor shall be jointly and severally liable to compensate for damages to the said third person. Provided, That this shall not apply to an accounting auditor who has proved that he or she did not fail to exercise due care in executing the office.

Section 11. (Joint and several liability of accounting auditor, director and auditor)

In the event that the accounting auditor is to be held liable to the corporation or a third person, if a director or an auditor is also to be held so liable, such accounting auditor, director, and/or auditor shall be deemed to bear joint and several liability.

Section 17. (Statement of opinion by accounting auditor at ordinary general meeting)

1. If the opinion of the accounting auditor differs from that of the board of auditors or an auditor regarding whether or not the documents under Section 2 conform to laws, ordinances, or the articles of incorporation, the accounting auditor (if the accounting auditor is an auditing corporation, the member in charge of execution of office; the same shall apply in the next subsection) may attend the ordinary general meeting and state an opinion thereat.
2. If the resolution is adopted at an ordinary general meeting requesting the presence of the accounting auditor, the accounting auditor shall attend ordinary general meetings and state opinions thereat.

Section 18. (Number, etc., of auditors)

1. The corporation shall have at least three auditors, at least one of whom has not been a director, manager, or other employee of the corporation or a subsidiary thereof for at least five years prior to taking office.
2. The corporation shall nominate as full-time auditors such auditors as are mutually elected by the auditors.

Section 18-2. (Formation of board of auditors)

1. Each corporation shall have a board of auditors consisting of all its auditors.
2. In addition to the powers set forth in this Act, a corporation's board of auditors shall have the power to determine, by resolution, the audit policy, the methods for investigating the corporation's business and assets, and other matters concerning the execution of the duties of the board of auditors. Provided, That the foregoing shall not prevent an individual auditor from exercising his or her powers as provided herein.
3. An individual auditor shall report the status of the execution of his or her duties as an auditor to the board of auditors at any time upon its request.

Section 18-3. (Resolutions of the board of auditors)

1. A resolution of the board of auditors shall be made by a majority vote of the corporation's auditors. Provided, That a resolution under Section 6-2, Subsection 1, shall require unanimous consent of all auditors.
2. [Commercial Code Section 259, Subsection 1; Section 259-2; Section 259-3; and Section 260-4, concerning meetings of the board of directors, made applicable to the board of auditors.]

Section 18-4. (Auditor's liability to the corporation and third persons)

1. In the event of application of Section 277; Section 280, Subsection 1; or Section 266-3, Subsection 1 of the Commercial Code to auditors, Section 266, Subsections 2 and 3, of the Commercial Code shall also apply with respect to auditor assent to board of auditors resolutions.

* * *

Chapter III
Exceptional Rules For Stock Corporations Whose Stated Capital Is Not More Than 100,000,000 Yen

Section 22. (Duties and powers of auditors)

1. The auditors of a stock corporation whose stated capital amount is not more than 100,000,000 yen (excluding a stock corporation which falls under Section 2, Item 2; hereinafter in this Chapter referred to as the "corporation") shall investigate the documents concerning accounting to be submitted to the general meeting of shareholders by the directors and report their opinion thereon to the general meeting of shareholders.
2. The auditors may at any time peruse or take copies of the accounting books and documents of the corporation, or request the director, manager, and other employees to make reports concerning accounting matters.
3. The auditors may, if necessary for execution of their offices, investigate the status of the business and assets of the corporation.
4. The provisions of the preceding three subsections shall apply *mutatis mutandis* in the case of the liquidation of the corporation.

Section 24. (Representation of corporation in action between corporation and director)

1. In the event that the corporation brings an action against a director, or a director brings an action against the corporation, a person designated by the board of directors shall represent the corporation with respect to such action.
2. Notwithstanding the provisions of the preceding subsection, the general meeting of shareholders may designate the person to represent the corporation.
3. The provisions of the preceding two subsections shall apply *mutatis mutandis* to the liquidator of the corporation.

Section 25. (Exemptions from application of Commercial Code)

The corporation shall be exempt from the application of the provisions concerning auditors as contained in the provisions of [numerous references to Commercial Code provisions omitted].

Chapter IV
Penal Provisions

Section 28. (Crime of bribery involving accounting auditor)

1. If an accounting auditor has, upon having received an unjust solicitation in connection with the office, accepted, demanded, or promised to accept a bribe, he or she shall be subject to penal servitude for not more than three years or a penal fine of not more than 1,000,000 yen.
2. In the event that an accounting auditor is an audit corporation, if a member of such audit corporation in charge of executing the office of the accounting auditor has, upon having received an unjust solicitation in connection with the office, accepted, demanded, or promised to accept a bribe, he or she shall be subject to penal servitude for not more than three years or a penal fine of not more than 1,000,000 yen. The same shall apply in the case where an accounting auditor is an audit corporation and a member of the said audit corporation has, upon having received an unjust solicitation in connection with the office of the accounting auditor, had the said accounting auditor accept, or demanded the giving to it of, or promised to accept for it, a bribe.
3. In cases under the preceding two subsections, a bribe which has been accepted shall be confiscated. If the whole or a part of the bribe cannot be confiscated, the monetary value equivalent thereto shall be redemptorily collected.

Section 29. (Crime of giving bribe)

Any person who has given, offered to give, or promised to give a bribe as referred to in Subsection 1 or Subsection 2 of the preceding section shall be subject to penal servitude for not more than three years or a penal fine of not more than 1,000,000 yen.

Section 30. (Acts subject to administrative fine)

If a person referred to in Section 498, Subsection 1 of the Commercial Code, or the accounting auditor, or a member to execute the office thereof has fallen under any of the cases set forth in the following respective items, such person shall be subject to an administrative fine of not more than 1,000,000 yen. Provided, That this shall not apply in a case where the act in question of such person shall be subject to penal sanction. [Omitted are twelve items referencing duties of directors and auditors concerning auditing that are specified in this Act and in the Commercial Code. The items refer to such duties as appointing auditors, making specified documents available to auditors and shareholders, avoiding misstatements, etc.].

5. [LIMITED LIABILITY COMPANY ACT] (LAW RELATING TO *YŪGEN KAISHA)*

Law No. 74, April 5, 1938, as amended

[Selected Provisions]

Source: 2 *EHS* No. 2230 (Eibun-Horei-Sha, 1988). Reprinted by permission.

[Updated by Daniel H. Foote to incorporate amendments through 1993.]

Chapter I
General Provisions

Section 1. (Definition)

1. A *yūgen kaisha* (hereinafter, except in Section 3, referred to as a "[close corporation]") within the meaning of this Act is an association incorporated hereunder for the purpose of engaging as a business in commercial or any other business transaction with a view to acquisition of gain.
2. A [close corporation] is a juristic person.

Section 2. (Status)

A [close corporation] shall be deemed to be a [merchant] even if it does not engage in commercial transactions as a business.

Section 3. (Trade name)

1. The trade name of a [close corporation] shall contain the word *yūgen kaisha.*
2. No person other than a [close corporation] shall use in the trade name any word which is suggestive of a *yūgen kaisha.* The same shall apply even in cases where the business of a [close corporation] has been acquired by transfer.

* * *

Chapter II
Incorporation

Section 5. (Articles of incorporation, attestation thereof)

1. In order to establish a [close corporation], articles of incorporation shall be executed.
2. The provisions of Section 167 of the Commercial Code shall apply *mutatis mutandis* to a [close corporation].

Section 6. (Particulars necessarily contained in articles of incorporation)

The articles of incorporation shall contain the following particulars and be signed by each member:

(1) The business purpose;
(2) The trade name;
(3) The total amount of the capital;
(4) The amount of one unit of contribution;
(5) The name and address of each member;
(6) The number of units of contribution to be made by each member;
(7) The location of the principal office.

Section 8. (Total number of members)

1. The total number of members shall not exceed fifty. Provided, That this shall not apply where the approval of the court has been obtained in special circumstances.
2. The provisions of the preceding subsection shall not apply in cases where any change takes place in the number of the members due either to succession or bequest.

Section 9. (Total amount of capital)

The total amount of the capital shall not be less than three million yen.

Chapter III
Rights and Duties of the Members

Section 17. (Limitation of member's liability)

The liability of a member, except as otherwise provided for in this Act, shall be limited to the amount of his or her contribution.

Section 19. (Transfer of shares)

1. Any member may transfer his or her shares wholly or in part to another member.
2. If any member intends to transfer his or her shares wholly or in part to any person who is not a member, he or she shall obtain the approval of the general meeting of members.
3. In the case of the preceding subsection, the member may, by document stating therein the intended transferee and the number of units of contribution intended to be transferred, request the company to approve said transfer or to designate another transferee if the company does not approve said transfer.
4. The provisions of Section 204-2, Subsection 2 of the Commercial Code shall apply *mutatis mutandis* in the case of a request for approval under the preceding subsection.
5. If the general meeting of members does not approve the transfer in the case of a request under Subsection 3, it shall designate another transferee. In this case, the provisions of Section 204-2, the latter clause of Subsection 3 and the latter clause of Subsection 4; Section 204-3, Subsections 1 through 3; and Section 204-4 of the Commercial Code shall apply *mutatis mutandis.*
6. If any member who is not a member has acquired units of contribution, said person may, by document stating therein the number of units of contribution, request the company, if it does not approve said acquisition, to designate a person to purchase said units of contribution. In this case, the provisions of the preceding subsection shall apply *mutatis mutandis.*
7. If, on account of a transfer, the total number of members has come to exceed the limitation prescribed in Section 8, Subsection 1, such transfer shall, except in the case of bequest, be null and void.

Chapter IV
Management of the Company

Section 25. (Director)

A [close corporation] shall have one or more directors.

Section 25-2. (Cumulative voting)

1. It may be provided for by the articles of incorporation that the election of two or more directors shall be made in accordance with cumulative voting.
2. The provisions of Section 256-3 of the Commercial Code shall apply *mutatis mutandis* to the case mentioned in the preceding subsection.

Section 26. (Decision for administration of company affairs)

In cases where there are two or more directors, the administration of the affairs of the company shall, unless otherwise provided for by the articles of incorporation, be decided by a majority of the votes of the directors. The same shall also apply in respect of the establishment, removal and abolition of a branch as well as the appointment and dismissal of a manager.

Section 27. (Representation)

1. The directors shall represent the company.
2. If there are two or more directors, each of the directors shall represent the company.
3. Notwithstanding the provisions of the preceding subsection, it may be determined by the articles of incorporation or by a resolution of a general meeting of members that a particular director shall represent the company, or that two or more directors shall jointly represent the company, or that one or more directors who shall represent the company may be elected by mutual vote of the directors based on the provisions of the articles of incorporation.

Section 29. (Duty to avoid competition)

1. A director who intends to effect on his or her own behalf or for a third person a transaction that comes under the class of business carried on by the company shall disclose all the material facts in connection with the said transaction at a general meeting of members and obtain its approval.
2. The approval mentioned in the preceding subsection shall be made by a resolution as provided for in Section 48.
3. If a director, in contravention of the provisions of Subsection 1, has effected a transaction on his or her own behalf, a general meeting of members may treat such transaction as effected on behalf of the company.
4. The right mentioned in the preceding subsection shall lapse where one year has elapsed from the time of the transaction.

Section 30. (Transaction between company and director)

1. The provisions of Subsections 1 and 2 of the preceding section shall apply *mutatis mutandis* in cases where a director seeks to acquire the company's products or other properties by transfer or to transfer his or her own products or other properties to the company or to receive loans from the company or to effect any transaction with the company on his or her own behalf or on that of a third person. The same shall also apply in the case where the company guarantees the liability of a director or otherwise effects with a person other than a director a transaction in which interests are contrary between the company and the director.
2. In the case provided for in the former part of the preceding subsection, the provisions of Section 108 of the Civil Code shall not apply.

Section 30-2. (Liability to company)

1. In the following cases, directors who have done any of the following acts shall be jointly and severally liable for reimbursing or compensating for damages to the company, in the case of Item 1 for the amount which has been distributed illegally, or in the cases of Items 2 and 3 for the amount of any damage caused to the company:
   (1) Where a proposal for the distribution of profits in contravention of the provisions of Section 290, Subsection 1 of the Commercial Code, as made applicable *mutatis mutandis* under Section 46, Subsection 1 of this Act, has been submitted to a general meeting;
   (2) Where any transaction in contravention of Section 29, Subsection 1, or Subsection 1 of the preceding section has been effected;
   (3) Where any act which violates any law or ordinance or the articles of incorporation has been done.
2. The directors who have consented to doing any act mentioned in the preceding subsection shall be deemed to have done such act.
3. The directors shall not be released from their liabilities under Subsection 1 except by the unanimous consent of all the members.
4. The provisions of Section 266, Subsection 4 of the Commercial Code shall apply *mutatis mutandis* in case of effectuation by directors of a transaction in contravention of the provisions of Section 29, Subsection 1.

Section 30-3. (Liability to third persons)

1. If directors have been guilty of wrongful intent or of gross negligence in respect of the performance of their duties, they shall be jointly and severally liable in damages to third persons also.
2. The provisions of the preceding subsection shall also apply in cases where the directors have made a false entry as to important matters to be stated in the documents referred to in Section 43, Subsection 1, or have made a false registration or public notice. Provided, That this shall not apply in a case where directors prove that they did not neglect due care in making the entry, registration, or public notice.

3. The provisions of Subsection 2 of the preceding section shall apply *mutatis mutandis* to cases under the preceding two subsections.

Section 31. (Derivative action)

1. Any member may demand, in writing, that the company bring an action to enforce the liability of directors.
2. The provisions of Section 267, Subsections 2 to 5 inclusive; and Sections 268 to 268-3 inclusive of the Commercial Code shall apply *mutatis mutandis* to an action for enforcing the liability of the directors.

Section 31-2. (Demand for stopping director's act)

In case a director performs an act which is not within the scope of the business purpose of the company, or any act against any law or ordinance or the articles of incorporation, and thereby there arises a fear of irreparable damage to the company, any member may, on behalf of the company, demand that the director stop such act.

Section 38-2. (Resolution in general meeting)

Unless otherwise provided for by this Act or by the articles of incorporation, all resolutions of a general meeting shall be adopted by a majority in number of the votes of the members present, who shall hold more than one-half of the votes of all the members.

Section 39. (Number of votes)

Each member shall have one vote for each unit of contribution. Provided, That the number of votes may be otherwise provided for by the articles of incorporation.

Section 42. (Resolution in writing)

1. In cases where a resolution of a general meeting is required, if all the members unanimously agree thereto, a resolution may be adopted in writing.
2. If all the members have expressed their consent in writing in respect of any of the matters forming the subject matter of a resolution, it shall be deemed that a resolution in writing has been adopted thereon.
3. A resolution in writing shall have the same effect as a resolution of a general meeting.
4. The provisions concerning the general meeting shall apply *mutatis mutandis* to a resolution in writing.

Chapter V
Alteration of Articles of Incorporation

Section 47. (Method to alter articles of incorporation)

To effect any alteration of the articles of incorporation, a resolution of the general meeting of members is required.

Section 48. (Special resolution by general meeting)

1. The resolution provided for in the preceding section shall be adopted with the consent of such members as shall constitute in number not less than one half of all the members and who shall hold not less than three-quarters of the votes of all the members.
2. With regard to the application of the provisions of the preceding subsection, members who are not entitled to vote shall not be computed in the total number of members, and votes which cannot be exercised shall not be computed in the number of the votes.

Section 51. (Member's right to take units of contribution)

A member shall have in proportion to his or her share a right to take units of contribution in respect of an increase in capital, unless otherwise determined by resolution as referred to in the preceding two sections.

Chapter IX
Penal Provisions

Section 89. *(Deeming to be a company under the Commercial Code)*

A [close corporation] shall be deemed to be a company within the meaning of the Commercial Code, insofar as the application of other laws excepting the Commercial Code are concerned. [Note, however, that many provisions of the Limited Liability Company Act have been omitted].

6. CODE OF CIVIL PROCEDURE

Law No. 29, April 21, 1890, as amended

[Selected Provisions]

Source: Reprinted with permission from Appendix 6A of *Doing Business in Japan*, Zentaro Kitagawa, generated.

BOOK I

General Provisions

Chapter I
Courts

Part 1. Jurisdiction

Section 1. (General forum)

A suit shall be subject to the jurisdiction of the court located at the place of the defendant's general forum.

Section 2. (General forum of a person)

1. The general forum of a person shall be determined by such person's domicile.
2. In cases where a person is not domiciled in Japan, or if the domicile is unknown, such person's general forum shall be determined according to his or her place of residence, or, if there is no place of residence, or the place of residence is unknown, it shall be determined by such person's last domicile.

Section 4. (General forum of a juridical person and of the state)

1. The general forum of a juridical person or any other association or foundation shall be determined by the location of its principal office or principal place of business, or in the event that there is no office or place of business, by the domicile of the principal person in charge of its affairs.
2. The general forum of the state shall be determined by the location of the government office that shall represent the state in the particular suit.
3. With regard to the general forum of a foreign association or foundation, the provisions of Subsection 1 shall apply to the office, place of business or person in charge of the affairs of such concerns in Japan.

Section 25. (Forum by agreement)

1. The parties may decide by agreement upon the court that will have jurisdiction, but only insofar as concerns the court of first instance.
2. The agreement referred to in the preceding subsection shall not be valid unless it is made in writing and is made with regard to a suit based on a specific legal relation.

Chapter II
Parties

Part 4. Advocates and Assistants

Section 79. (Qualifications of advocate)

1. With the exception of representatives who may effect acts of litigation in court according to the provisions of laws and orders, no person other than a lawyer *(bengoshi)* may act as an advocate. Provided, That in a summary court a person who is not a lawyer may be appointed as an advocate with the permission of the court.

* * *

Chapter III
Court Costs

Part 1. Incidence of Court Costs

Section 89. (Basic principle)
The losing party shall bear the court costs.

Section 90. (Exception-1)
Depending on the circumstances, a court may charge the winning party court costs incurred by acts which were unnecessary for the assertion or defense of such party's rights or all or a part of court costs incurred by acts which were necessary for the assertion or defense of the adversary's rights at the particular stage of the litigation.

Section 91. (Exception-2)
In cases where a party has delayed the litigation by failing to advance offensive or defensive means at the appropriate time, by failing to observe fixed dates or time periods or by any other means ascribable to such party, the court may charge such party with all or a part of the court costs arising from such delay even when such party is the winning party.

Chapter IV
Litigation Procedures

Part 4. Trial

Section 22. (Effect of foreign judgments)
A final judgment of a foreign court shall have effect only in cases satisfying the following conditions:

1. The jurisdiction of the foreign court is not denied by either statute or treaty;
2. In a case in which the losing defendant is a citizen of Japan, service of the summons or order necessary for commencement of the litigation has been received, without relying on service by public notice, or the defendant has voluntarily participated in the litigation without receiving service;
3. The judgment of the foreign court is not contrary to the public order or good morals in Japan; and
4. Guarantees of reciprocity exist.

BOOK II
First Instance Litigation Procedures

Chapter I
Complaint

Section 231. (Prohibition of duplicative lawsuits)
A party shall not institute another lawsuit with respect to a matter that is already pending in court.

BOOK III
Appeal

Chapter I
Kōso-Appeal

Section 360. (Decision from which kōso*-appeal may be made; consent to* jōkoku*-appeal)*
1. A *kōso*-appeal may be filed against a final judgment rendered by a district court in the

first instance or against a final judgment rendered by a summary court. Provided, That this shall not apply to cases where both parties have agreed not to file a *kōso*-appeal following the entry of final judgment but have reserved the right to file a *jōkoku*-appeal.

2. The provisions of Section 25, Subsection 2 shall apply *mutatis mutandis* to the agreement referred to in the preceding subsection.

Chapter II
Jōkoku-appeal

Section 393. (Court of last resort)

1. A *jōkoku*-appeal may be filed with the Supreme Court against the final judgment of a high court acting in the second instance or the first instance; and with a high court against the final judgment of a district court acting in the second instance.
2. In cases of the proviso to Section 360, Subsection 1, a *jōkoku*-appeal may be made directly to the Supreme Court against the judgment of a district court and to the high court against the judgment of a summary court.
3. A *jōkoku*-appeal may not be filed against a judgment rendered in connection with provisional attachment or provisional disposition.

Section 394. (Grounds for jōkoku*-appeal)*

A *jōkoku*-appeal may be filed only when there is an alleged misinterpretation or contravention of the Constitution in the judgment, or when a contravention of laws or orders has clearly influenced the judgment.

Section 403. (Finding of facts is binding)

Facts found in the judgment below, in accordance with legal procedures, shall be binding upon the court hearing the *jōkoku*-appeal.

[BOOK VI]
[Provisional Attachment and Provisional Disposition]

[Note: Effective January 1, 1991, Books VI and VII (Sections 737-763) of the Code of Civil Procedure were deleted; the new Civil Preservation Act (*Minji Hozen Hō,* Law No. 91 of December 22, 1989) took effect in their place. The Civil Preservation Act was intended, among other things, to simplify the procedures and, in some cases, to ease the standards for obtaining provisional relief. Since several of the cases in this book refer to now-deleted sections on provisional attachment and disposition in the Code of Civil Procedure, we have reproduced four selected provisions from Books VI and VII below. Following Section 760, we have also included the two provisions from the Civil Preservation Act that incorporate the four prior sections excerpted below.]

[Section 737. (Purpose of provisional attachment)] [See note above]

[1. Provisional attachment may be effected for the purpose of securing execution against movables or immovables with respect to a monetary obligation-right or a claim convertible into a monetary obligation-right.

2. Provisional attachment may be effected with respect to a claim not yet due.]

[Section 738. (Necessity to secure)] [See note preceding Section 737 above]

[Provisional attachment may be effected in cases where if not effected, the execution of the decision cannot be carried out or there is a fear of considerable difficulty in carrying it out or, especially, if it is to be carried out in a foreign country.]

[Section 755. (Provisional disposition relating to things at issue)]
[See note preceding Section 737 above]

[A provisional disposition relating to a thing at issue shall be permitted in cases where the realization of the right of one party will be impossible or there is fear of considerable difficulty in undertaking such right.]

[Section 760. (Provisional disposition setting provisional state of affairs)]
[See note preceding Section 737 above]
[Provisional disposition may also be made to establish a provisional state of affairs regarding the right at issue. Provided, That the said disposition shall be made only in such cases in which it is necessary to avert considerable damage to the continuing relationship involving a right or to prevent imminent violence thereto or for other reasons.]

[Civil Preservation Act, Section 20 (Necessity of order of provisional attachment)]
[See note preceding Section 737 above]
[1. An order for provisional attachment may be issued with respect to an obligation-right the object of which is payment of money, if there is a fear that it would be impossible to carry out a compulsory execution or that there would be great difficulty in doing so.
2. An order for provisional attachment may be issued even if the obligation-right referred to in the preceding subsection has a condition or term.]

[Civil Preservation Act, Section 23 (Necessity of order of provisional disposition)]
[See note preceding Section 737 above]
[1. An order for provisional disposition relating to a thing at issue may be issued, if, through a change in conditions, the realization of the rights of one party would become impossible or there is a fear that great difficulty in realizing such rights would arise.
2. An order establishing a provisional state of affairs may be issued if necessary to avert great damage or imminent danger to the rights-holder with respect to the rights at issue.]

BOOK VIII
Arbitration Procedure

Section 786. (Arbitration agreement)
An agreement to submit a dispute to one or more arbitrators shall be valid insofar as the parties are entitled to effect a compromise regarding the subject matter in dispute.

Section 787. (Arbitration agreement for future dispute)
An arbitration agreement with regard to future disputes has no effect, unless it relates to specified relations of right and the disputes arising therefrom.

Section 788. (Nomination of arbitrators)
If no provision as to the nomination of arbitrators is included in an arbitration agreement, each party shall nominate one arbitrator.

Section 789. (Method of nomination)
1. If both parties are entitled to nominate arbitrators, the first party shall notify the adversary party, in writing, of the arbitrator(s) nominated by the first party and request the adversary party to do the same within a period of seven days.
2. Upon expiration of the foregoing period, the court with jurisdiction shall, upon motion of the first party, nominate arbitrator(s).

Section 790. (Binding effect of nomination notice)
After a party has given notification to the adversary party of the nomination of arbitrators, said party shall be bound as to said nomination with regard to said adversary party.

Section 792. (Challenge of arbitrator)
1. The parties may challenge an arbitrator on the same grounds and conditions as they may challenge a judge.
2. In cases where an arbitrator nominated other than by an arbitration agreement unduly delays in the performance of his or her duty, such arbitrator may also be challenged.
3. Incapacitated persons, persons who are unable to hear or speak, and persons who are deprived of or suspended from the enjoyment of public rights may be challenged.

Section 794. (Procedure for making award)

1. The arbitrators shall, prior to making an award, question the parties and, to the extent the arbitrators deem necessary, investigate the matters which are the cause of dispute.
2. In the absence of an agreement of the parties as to arbitration procedure, the procedure shall be determined by the arbitrators according to their discretion.

Section 795. (Examination of witnesses, experts)

1. The arbitrators may examine witnesses and experts who voluntarily appear.
2. The arbitrators shall not be empowered to administer an oath to a witness or expert.

Section 796. (Cooperation of the jurisdictional court)

1. An act necessary to determine an award which the arbitrators deem necessary, but which they cannot perform, shall, upon motion of a party, be performed by the court with jurisdiction. Provided, That this shall be the case only when said motion is deemed to be appropriate.
2. A court which has ordered a witness or an expert to testify shall have the power to render a necessary decision in cases where such person refuses to testify or to give evidence.

Section 797. (Plea of illegality of arbitration procedure and power of arbitrators to continue)

The arbitrators may continue the arbitration procedure and make an award, even when the parties plead that the arbitration procedure should not be permitted, or particularly assert that no legally valid arbitration agreement has been concluded, the arbitration agreement has no concern with the dispute to be decided, or the arbitrators are not empowered to act.

Section 798. (Consultation of several arbitrators)

In the event that several arbitrators are to make an award, such award shall be decided by a majority. Provided, That this shall not apply to such cases as otherwise provided for in the arbitration agreement.

Section 800. (Effect of award)

As between the parties, an arbitration award has the same effect as a final and binding judgment.

Section 801. (A suit for cancellation of award)

1. A motion for cancellation of an award may be made in the following cases:
   i. in cases where an arbitration procedure should not be permitted;
   ii. in cases where an award requires a party to perform an act which is prohibited by law;
   iii. in cases where the parties were not represented in accordance with the provisions of law;
   iv. in cases where the parties were not examined in the arbitration procedure;
   v. in cases where the award is not accompanied by reasons; and
   vi. where the case comes under the purview of Section 420, Items 4 to 8 inclusive and conditions exist for which an action for retrial is permissible.
2. The award may not be set aside on the grounds specified in Items 4 and 5 of this section if the parties have otherwise agreed.

Section 802. (Execution based on award)

1. Execution to be undertaken by virtue of an arbitration award shall be made only when an execution judgment has announced its enforceability.
2. An execution judgment may not be rendered if a ground exists upon which application can be made for the cancellation of the award.

Section 803. (Suit for cancellation of award after the rendering of execution judgment)

After an execution judgment has been rendered, a motion for cancellation of the award may be made only when it is based on the reasons referred to in Section 801, Item 6. Provided, That this shall apply only in cases where a preliminary showing is made to the effect that, not through negligence on the part of the moving party, the reason for cancellation could not be asserted in the former procedure.

7. ACT CONCERNING THE APPLICATION OF LAWS (*HŌREI*)

Law No. 10, June 21, 1898

[Selected Provisions]

Source: Reprinted with permission from Appendix 3B of *Doing Business in Japan*, Zentaro Kitagawa, general ed.

Section 2. (Custom)

Customs which are not contrary to public order or good morals shall have the same force as law insofar as they are recognized by the provisions of a law or ordinance or relate to matters which are not provided for by laws or ordinances.

Section 7. (Formation and effect of juristic act)

1. With regard to the formation and effect of a juristic act, the question as to which country's law is to govern shall be determined by the intention of the parties.
2. In cases where the intention of the parties is unclear, the law of the place where the juristic act is done shall govern.

Section 9. (Juristic acts involving a person resident in a place governed by different law)

1. For a declaration of intention made to a person residing in a place governed by a different law, the place from which notice of the same is dispatched shall be regarded as the place of the act.
2. For the formation and effect of a contract, the place from which the offer is dispatched shall be regarded as the place of the act. In cases where the offeree is unaware, at the time of acceptance, of the place from which the offer has been dispatched, the place of the offeror's domicile shall be regarded as the place of the act.

Section 11. (Formation and effect of obligation-rights arising by operation of law)

1. The formation and effect of obligation-rights arising from the voluntary management of affairs, unjust enrichment or torts shall be governed by the law of the place where the events giving rise to such obligation-rights have occurred.
2. The provisions of the preceding subsection shall not apply to torts in cases where the events occurring in a foreign country are not unlawful according to Japanese law.
3. Even when events occurring in a foreign country are unlawful according to Japanese law, the injured person may claim compensation only for damages or other remedies recognized by Japanese law.

Section 33. (Public order and good morals)

In a case where the law of a foreign country is to govern and application of the provisions in such law would be contrary to public order and good morals, such provisions shall not apply.

8. PRACTICING ATTORNEYS ACT

Law No. 205, June 10, 1949, as amended

[Selected Provisions]

Source: Richard Wohl, Stuart Chemtob and Glen Fukushima, eds., *Practice by Foreign Lawyers in Japan* (© American Bar Association 1989), at Appendix 2. Reprinted by permission.

Chapter I.
The Mission and Duties of a Practicing Attorney

Section 1. (The mission of a practicing attorney)

1. A practicing attorney is entrusted with a mission to protect fundamental human rights and to realize social justice.
2. A practicing attorney shall, in keeping with the mission specified in the preceding subsection, sincerely perform his or her duties and endeavor to maintain social order and to improve legal systems.

Section 2. (The basic responsibility of a practicing attorney in the performance of professional duties)

A practicing attorney shall strive to remain highly cultured, to build a fine character and be well acquainted with laws, ordinances and legal practices.

Section 3. (The functions of a practicing attorney)

1. A practicing attorney may, upon the application of a party and other interested persons, or shall, upon the request of the government or public offices, perform duties relating to lawsuits, non-contentious matters, and appeals against dispositions made by administrative offices by such means as a request for investigation, raising of objection and request for review, and other general legal work.
2. A practicing attorney may, without any further qualification, engage in the business of a patent attorney and a tax agent.

Chapter II
Qualifications Necessary to be a Practicing Attorney

Section 4. (Qualifications of a practicing attorney)

A person who has completed the course for a legal apprentice shall be qualified to be a practicing attorney.

Section 5. (Special exceptions to qualifications of a practicing attorney)

Any of the following persons may be qualified to be a practicing attorney, notwithstanding the provision of the preceding section:

1. A person who has been a justice of the Supreme Court;
2. A person who has, after obtaining the qualifications to be a legal apprentice, been a judge of the Summary Court; a public prosecutor; a judicial research official; a court secretary; a secretary of the Ministry of Justice; a teacher of the Legal Research and Training Institute, the Research and Training Institute for Court Clerks or the Research and Training Institute of the Ministry of Justice; a secretary (*Sanji*) of the Legislative Bureau of the House of Representatives or the House of Councillors or a counsellor (*Sanji-kan*) of the Legislative Bureau of the Cabinet for not less than five years;
3. A person who has served in the position of professor or assistant professor of law for not less than five years at a faculty, majors program, or graduate program of a university as specified by law;
4. Any person who has served in two or more of the posts specified in the preceding two items for a total of not less than five years. Provided, That as to the posts specified in Item 2, only the years of service after he or she obtained the qualifications to be a legal apprentice shall be counted.

Section 6. *(Disqualifying reasons)*

No person specified below shall be qualified to be a practicing attorney irrespective of the provisions of the preceding two sections:

1. A person who has been sentenced to imprisonment or a heavier punishment;
2. A person in respect of whom the Impeachment Court has made a decision of dismissal;
3. A person who has been disbarred from attorneyship or prohibited from practicing as a patent attorney or has had registration as a certified public accountant struck off or has been prohibited from working as a tax agent or has been discharged from office as a public servant through disciplinary action until the lapse of three years after such disciplinary action was imposed;
4. An incompetent or quasi-incompetent person;
5. A person who has been declared bankrupt, and has not yet been reinstated.

Chapter III
Roll of Practicing Attorneys

Section 8. *(Registration as a practicing attorney)*

Any person who is to become a practicing attorney shall have his or her name registered in the roll kept in the Japan Federation of Bar Associations.

Chapter IV
The Rights and Duties of a Practicing Attorney

Section 20. *(A law office)*

1. The office of a practicing attorney shall be called a law office.
2. A law office shall be established within the district of the bar association to which the practicing attorney belongs.
3. No practicing attorney may establish two or more law offices under any name whatever. Provided, That he or she may practice at the law office of another practicing attorney.

Section 23. *(Right and duty to maintain secrecy)*

A practicing attorney or a person who was previously a practicing attorney shall have the right and duty to maintain the secrecy of any facts which he or she came to know in the performance of the profession. Provided, That this shall not apply when otherwise provided for by any law.

Section 23-2. *(Request to provide information)*

1. A practicing attorney may, with regard to the cases with which he or she is entrusted, apply to the bar association to which he or she belongs to make inquiries to public offices or public or private organizations to provide necessary information. * * *

Section 24. *(Duty to perform entrusted matters, etc.)*

A practicing attorney shall not refuse, without due reason, to undertake matters at the request of the government or public offices in accordance with the provisions of law and ordinances, or to undertake the matters designated by the bar association to which he or she belongs or by the Japan Federation of Bar Associations in accordance with the provisions of their articles of association.

Section 25. *(Cases which a practicing attorney may not undertake)*

A practicing attorney shall not undertake the cases specified below. Provided, That so far as a case specified in Item 3 is concerned, a practicing attorney may do so if the client whose case is already in his or her charge has consented thereto:

1. Cases in which he or she supported the adverse party in the consultation requested, or accepted the adverse party as client;
2. Cases in which he or she was consulted by the adverse party and the extent and form of the consultation was such that it could be considered as being based on the lawyer-client relationship;

3. Any other case he or she is requested to undertake by an adverse party to a case he or she has already undertaken;
4. Cases which he or she handled in the course of duties as a public servant;
5. Cases which he or she handled as an arbitrator in arbitration procedures.

Section 28. (Prohibition against obtaining of any right in dispute)
A practicing attorney shall not obtain any right in dispute.

Section 30. (Restrictions on concurrent assumption of a public post and engaging in business activities)
1. [Attorneys shall not concurrently practice law and hold non-elected full-time government positions other than certain specified high-level offices.]

* * *

3. A practicing attorney shall not, unless he or she obtains permission from the bar association to which he or she belongs, run any profit-making business, or become an employee of the operator of such business, or an executive member of any profit-making juristic person, or a director or an employee thereof.

Chapter V
Bar Associations

Section 31. (Object and legal personality)
1. It shall be the object of a bar association, in view of the mission and duties of practicing attorneys, to manage matters relating to the guidance, liaison and supervision of members in order to maintain their dignity and improve and advance the work of practicing attorneys.
2. A bar association shall be a juristic person.

Section 33. (Articles of association)
1. A bar association shall formulate its articles of association with the approval of the Japan Federation of Bar Associations.
2. The following matters shall be stipulated in the articles of association of a bar association:

    * * *

    3. Rules pertaining to admission of membership in or withdrawal from the association;

    * * *

    7. Rules pertaining to the practicing attorneys' ethics and maintenance of discipline of its members;
    8. Rules pertaining to standard fees to be paid to practicing attorneys;
    9. Rules pertaining to legal aid to be provided to indigent persons;

    * * *

Section 41. (Mediation of disputes)
A bar association may, upon the request of a practicing attorney, the party in question, or any other interested person, mediate any dispute regarding the professional affairs of a practicing attorney.

Chapter VI
The Japan Federation of Bar Associations

Section 45. (Establishment, object and legal personality)
1. All bar associations in the country together shall constitute the Japan Federation of Bar Associations.
2. The object of the Japan Federation of Bar Associations shall be, in view of the mission and duties of practicing attorneys, to manage matters relating to the guidance, liaison and

supervision of practicing attorneys and bar associations in order to maintain their dignity and improve and advance the work of practicing attorneys.

3. The Japan Federation of Bar Associations shall be a juristic person.

Section 47. (Membership)

Practicing attorneys and bar associations shall automatically become members of the Japan Federation of Bar Associations.

Chapter VII
The Qualifications Screening Board

[Omitted.]

Chapter VIII
Disciplinary Action

Section 56. (Grounds for disciplinary action and disciplinary authority)

1. Disciplinary action shall be taken against a practicing attorney when he or she violates this Act, or the articles of association of the bar association to which he or she belongs or of the Japan Federation of Bar Associations, or acts in a manner which is prejudicial to the good order of or the trust reposed in the said bar association or is guilty of misconduct of disgraceful nature whether in the course of or outside his or her professional duties.
2. Disciplinary action shall be imposed upon a practicing attorney by the bar association to which he or she belongs in accordance with the resolution of its Disciplinary Actions Committee.

Section 57. (Kinds of disciplinary action)

Disciplinary action shall consist of the following four kinds:

1. Reprimand;
2. Suspension from the practice of law for not more than two years;
3. Order to withdraw from the bar association to which the practicing attorney belongs;
4. Disbarment.

[Sections 58-62 establish procedures for disciplinary matters and make the Tokyo High Court the forum for appeals of disciplinary rulings by complainants or attorneys. Section 64 establishes a three-year statute of limitations for disciplinary actions.]

Chapter IX.
The Disciplinary Actions Committee and the Discipline Maintenance Committee

[Omitted.]

Chapter X
Control of the Practice of Law

Section 72. (Prohibition of the practice of law by non-lawyers)

A person other than a practicing attorney shall not, for payment, and as an occupation, engage in the practice of law by giving legal advice, providing legal representation, arbitrating, settling disputes amicably or performing any like acts in respect of lawsuits, non-contentious matters, or appeals filed with administrative agencies such as requests for investigation, the raising of objections, requests for the review of dispositions or similar matters, or act as an intermediary in such matters as are specified in this section as constituting the practice of law. Provided,That this shall not apply in such cases as otherwise specified in this Act.

Section 73. (Prohibition against the enforcement of assigned rights)

No person shall engage in the business of obtaining the transfer to himself of the rights of any other person and enforcing such rights through a lawsuit, mediation, conciliation or any other method.

Section 74. (Prohibition against false indications by non-lawyers)

1. No person who is not a practicing attorney shall use the name of a practicing attorney or call his or her office a law office.
2. No person who is not a practicing attorney shall, for gain, indicate that he or she gives legal advice or handles other legal matters.

Chapter XI
Penalties

[Omitted.]

Supplementary Provisions

[Omitted.]

9. SPECIAL MEASURES ACT CONCERNING THE HANDLING OF LEGAL BUSINESS BY FOREIGN LAWYERS

Law No. 66, May 23, 1986

[Selected Provisions]

Source: Richard Wohl, Stuart Chemtob and Glen Fukushima, eds., *Practice by Foreign Lawyers in Japan* (© American Bar Association 1989), at Appendix 1. Reprinted by permission.

CHAPTER I
General Provisions

Section 1. (Purpose)

The purposes of this Act are to ensure the stability in relation to international business law affairs and to contribute to the improvement of the handling of legal business concerning Japanese law in foreign countries, by taking, on the basis of mutual assurances, such special measures as opening the way whereby a person who is qualified to become a foreign lawyer can handle legal business concerning foreign law in Japan and regulating the handling of such legal business as in the case of a *bengoshi.*

Section 2. (Definitions)

In this Act, the meaning of the terms listed in the following items shall be as set forth in the items concerned:

(1) *bengoshi*: this shall mean a *bengoshi* [practicing attorney] provided for in the *Bengoshi* [Practicing Attorneys] Act (Law No. 205 of 1949);

(2) foreign lawyer: this shall mean a person who handles legal business as a profession in a foreign country (in the case of a federal country specified by Ministry of Justice Ordinance, the term "foreign country" shall mean its constituent unit such as a state, territory and others specified by Ministry of Justice Ordinance; hereinafter the same) and who corresponds to a *bengoshi* as defined above;

(3) *gaikokuhō jimu-bengoshi* [GJB]: this shall mean a person who has obtained the approval provided for in Section 7 and has obtained the registration in the Register provided for in Section 24;

(4) country of primary qualification: this shall mean the foreign country where a person who has been given the approval provided for in Section 7 acquired the qualification to become a foreign lawyer which served as the basis for such approval;

(5) law of the country of primary qualification: this shall mean the law which is or was effective in the country of primary qualification;

(6) legal business concerning the law of the country of primary qualification: this shall mean the legal business dealing with a legal case the whole or a major portion of which is subject or is to be subject to the application of the law of the country of primary qualification;

(7) specified foreign country: this shall mean a specified foreign country other than the country of primary qualification;

(8) law of a specified foreign country: this shall mean the law which is or was effective in a specified foreign country;

(9) designated law: this shall mean the law of a specified foreign country which is designated under the provisions of Subsection 1 of Section 16 for a person who obtained the approval under the provisions of Section 7;

(10) legal business concerning the designated law: this shall mean the legal business dealing with a legal case the whole or a major portion of which is subject or is to be subject to the application of the designated law;

(11) Japan Federation of *Bengoshi* Associations: this shall mean the Japan Federation of *Bengoshi* Associations provided for in the Practicing Attorneys Act;

(12) in Japan: this shall mean the place where this Act is enforced.

Chapter II
Functions of a *Gaikokuhō Jimu-Bengoshi*

Section 3. (Functions)

1. It shall be the functions of a [GJB] to perform the legal business concerning the law of the country of primary qualification at the request of the parties concerned or other interested persons, or, upon being entrusted by a public agency. Provided, That the performance of the following legal business shall be excluded:
   (1) representation in regard to procedures before a court, public prosecutor's office or other public agency in Japan, or the preparation of documents to be submitted to any such agency in regard to such procedures;
   (2) activities in the capacity of a counsel in a criminal case, activities in the capacity of an attendant in a juvenile protection case before a family court, or legal assistance to a fugitive criminal in an extradition case in connection with a request for the examination of extraditability made with the court;
   (3) expression of an expert opinion or other legal opinion as regards the interpretation or applicability of other laws than the law of the country of primary qualification;
   (4) service of documents in regard to the procedures taken for a foreign court or administrative agency;
   (5) representation in regard to the entrustment of preparation of notarial deeds under Item (5) of Section 22 of the Civil Execution Act (Law No. 4 of 1979);
   (6) representation or the preparation of documents (excluding written expert opinions; hereinafter the same in this section) in regard to a legal case whose primary objective is the acquisition or loss or change of rights concerning real property situated in Japan or of industrial property rights, mining rights or other rights arising upon registration thereof with an administrative agency in Japan or rights related to such rights (hereinafter referred to as "industrial property rights, etc.").
2. Even when it is a legal business that a [GJB] may perform within the scope of functions under the provisions of the preceding subsection, he or she shall be required to perform it jointly with a *bengoshi* or after receiving written advice from a bengoshi in regard to the following matters:
   (1) representation or the preparation of documents in regard to a legal case other than a legal case mentioned in Item (6) of the preceding subsection, the purpose of which is the acquisition or loss or change of rights concerning real property situated in Japan or industrial property rights, etc.;
   (2) representation or the preparation of documents in regard to a legal case concerning family relations in which a Japanese national is involved as a party;
   (3) representation or the preparation of documents in regard to a legal case concerning a will or contract of gift to become effective at death which involves property situated in Japan and owned by a person residing in Japan or a legal case concerning the division or administration of estate or other matters of inheritance which involves property situated in Japan and owned by a person who resided in Japan at the time of death and in which a Japanese national is involved as a party.

Section 4. (Prohibition against handling legal business outside of scope of functions)

A [GJB] shall not perform any legal business outside the scope of the functions prescribed in Subsection 1 of the preceding section.

Section 5. (Legal business concerning designated law)

1. A [GJB] may, despite the provisions of the preceding section, perform legal business concerning designated laws if he or she has had such laws designated in accordance with the provisions of Subsection 1 of Section 16 and had the supplementary registration of such laws made in accordance with the provisions of Subsection 1 of Section 34. However, the legal business listed in Items (1), (2) and (4) to (6) of Subsection 1 of Section 3 and the expression of an expert opinion or other legal opinion regarding the interpretation or applicability of any law other than designated laws shall be excluded.

2. The provisions of Subsection 2 of Section 3 shall apply *mutatis mutandis* in cases where a [GJB] performs the legal business concerning designated laws in accordance with the provisions of the preceding subsection.

Section 6. (Application mutatis mutandis *of Practicing Attorneys Act, etc.)*

1. The provisions of Sections 1 and 2 of the Practicing Attorneys Act shall apply *mutatis mutandis* to a [GJB].
2. The provisions of Section 72 of the Practicing Attorneys Act shall not apply to a [GJB].

Chapter III
Qualification to Become a [GJB]

Part 1. Approval by the Minister of Justice

Section 7. (Qualification to become a [GJB])

A person who is qualified to become a foreign lawyer may be qualified to become a [GJB] only when he or she has obtained the approval of the Minister of Justice.

Section 10. (Standards for approval)

1. The Minister of Justice shall not give approval to one who makes the application [to be a GJB] (hereinafter referred to as "applicant for approval") unless he or she conforms with the standards listed below:
   (1) the applicant is qualified to become a foreign lawyer and has the experience of having engaged in practice as a foreign lawyer in the foreign country where he or she acquired such qualification for five years or more after acquiring it;
   (2) the applicant does not come under any one of the following categories: [past convictions, recent disciplinary punishment, bankruptcy, etc.];
   (3) the applicant has the will to perform his or her functions faithfully and has a plan, residence and financial basis for performing such functions properly and steadily and also has the ability to compensate for damages which he or she may cause to clients.
2. Even in cases where an applicant for approval meets the standards set forth in all the items of the preceding subsection, the Minister of Justice shall not be in a position to give approval unless substantially equivalent treatment as accorded by this Act is given in the foreign country mentioned in Item (1) of the same subsection to a person who is qualified to become a *bengoshi.*
3. The Minister of Justice shall ask the opinion of the Japan Federation of *Bengoshi* Associations before giving approval.

Section 16. (Designation)

1. In cases where a person who has obtained the approval comes under one of the following items, the Minister of Justice may designate the law of a specified foreign country for such person:
   (1) when such person is qualified to become a foreign lawyer of the specified foreign country;
   (2) when such person has the same level of learning concerning the law of a specified foreign country as a person who is qualified to become a foreign lawyer of that country has and has five or more years of practice experience in regard to the handling of legal business concerning such law.

2. The provisions of Subsection 3 of Section 10 and Section 11 [concerning public notice of the approval] shall apply *mutatis mutandis* to the designation provided for in the preceding subsection.

Chapter IV
Registration, Practice and Supervision of a [GJB]

Part 1. General Provisions

[By Section 21, [GJB] are for purposes of discipline and regulation members of the Japan Federation of Bar Associations.]

Part 2. Registration of a [GJB]

[Omitted.]

Part 3. Rights and Obligations of a [GJB]

Section 44. (Indication of status as a [GJB])

A GJB shall use the title of *gaikokuhō jimu-bengoshi* when he or she performs business and shall append to such title the name of the country of primary qualification.

Section 45. ([GJB]'s office)

1. The office of a [GJB] shall be named *gaikokuhō jimu-bengoshi jimusho.*
2. The name of the office of a [GJB] shall include the names of all or one or more of the [GJB] who compose the office and shall not use the name of any other individual or organization.
3. Notwithstanding the provisions of the preceding two subsections, a [GJB] may use the name of the office of a *bengoshi* when he or she is employed by the *bengoshi.*

* * *

5. A [GJB] shall not establish more than one office, under any name, in Japan.

Section 47. (Use of the title of a foreign lawyer, etc.)

1. A [GJB] may, in performing business, use the title of a foreign lawyer in his or her country of primary qualification, only when he or she appends it to the title of *gaikokuhō jimu-bengoshi* and the name of the country of primary qualification.
2. A [GJB] may, in performing business, use the name of a juristic person, partnership or other business entity of the country of primary qualification which has as its object the conduct of legal business and to which he or she belongs, only when he or she appends it to his or her name and the name of his or her office in the following cases:
   (1) when there is no other [GJB] who uses the name of the business entity concerned;
   (2) when the [GJB] has an office in common with another [GJB] in cases where the latter is already using the name of the business entity concerned.

Section 48. (Obligation of residence)

1. A [GJB] shall be required to stay in Japan for not less than one hundred and eighty days per year.

* * *

Section 49. (Prohibition of employment of a bengoshi*, etc.)*

1. A [GJB] shall not employ a *bengoshi.*
2. A [GJB] shall not, under a partnership or other kind of agreement, run a joint enterprise with a specific *bengoshi* which has as its object the conduct of legal business, or receive a share of the fees or other profits which a specific *bengoshi* gains for the performance of legal business.

Part 4. Discipline of a [GJB]

[Omitted.]

Chapter V
Miscellaneous Provisions

[Omitted.]

Chapter VI
Penal Provisions

[Omitted.]

Supplementary Provisions

[Omitted.]

10. ACT CONCERNING PROHIBITION OF PRIVATE MONOPOLY AND MAINTENANCE OF FAIR TRADE

Law No. 54 of April 14, 1947, as amended
Major Amendments: Law No. 214 of June 18, 1949
Law No. 259 of September 1, 1953
Law No. 63 of June 3, 1977
Source: *Antimonopoly Legislation of Japan*, M. Nakagawa, ed. (Kōsei Torihiki Kyōkai, 1984). Reprinted by permission.
[Updated by Daniel H. Foote to incorporate amendments through 1992.]

Chapter I
General Provisions

Section 1. (Purpose)

This Act, by prohibiting private monopolization, unreasonable restraint of trade and unfair trade practices, by preventing excessive concentration of economic power and by eliminating unreasonable restraint of production, sales, price, technology and the like, and all other unjust restriction of business activities through combinations, agreements and otherwise, aims to promote free and fair competition, to stimulate the creative initiative of entrepreneurs, to encourage business activities of enterprises, to heighten the level of employment and people's real income, and thereby to promote the democratic and wholesome development of the national economy as well as to assure the interests of consumers in general.

Section 2. (Definitions)

1. The term "entrepreneur" as used in this Act shall mean a person who carries on a commercial, industrial, financial or any other business. Any officer, employee, agent or any other person who acts for the benefit of any entrepreneur shall be deemed to be an entrepreneur in regard to the application of the provisions of the following subsection and of Chapter III of this Act.
2. The term "trade association" as used in this Act shall mean any combination or federation of combinations of two or more entrepreneurs having as its principal purpose the furtherance of their common business interest as entrepreneurs and includes one taking any of the following forms. Provided, That a combination or federation of combinations of two or more entrepreneurs, and whose principal purpose is to operate and which is actually operating a commercial, industrial, financial or any other business for profit, shall not be included:
   (i) Any association incorporated or not incorporated of which two or more entrepreneurs are members (including any position similar thereto);
   (ii) Any foundation with or without juridical personality of which two or more entrepreneurs control the appointment or dismissal of directors or managers, the execution or existence of business;
   (iii) Any partnership of which two or more entrepreneurs are members, or any contractual combination of two or more entrepreneurs.
3. The term "officer" as used in this Act shall mean a director, a partner with unlimited liabilities and executive power, an auditor, or any person with a similar position, a manager, or other employee in charge of business of the main or branch office.
4. The term "competition" as used in this Act shall mean a situation in which two or more entrepreneurs do or may, within the normal scope of their business activities and without undertaking any important change in their business facilities or kinds of business activities, engage in any act prescribed in any one of the following items. Provided, That Item (ii) below shall not apply to such competition as provided for in

Chapter IV:

(i) Supplying the same or similar goods or services to the same consumers or users;

(ii) Getting supplies of the same or similar goods or services from the same supplier.

5. The term "private monopolization" as used in this Act shall mean that any entrepreneur, individually or by combination or conspiracy with other entrepreneurs, or in any other manner, excludes or controls the business activities of other entrepreneurs, thereby restraining substantially, contrary to the public interest, competition in any particular field of trade.

6. The term "unreasonable restraint of trade" as used in this Act shall mean that any entrepreneur, by contract, agreement or any other concerted action, irrespective of what it is called, with other entrepreneurs, mutually restrict or conduct their business activities in such a manner as to fix, maintain, or increase prices, or to limit production, technology, products, facilities, or customers or suppliers, thereby restraining substantially, contrary to the public interest, competition in any particular field of trade.

7. The term "monopolistic situation" as used in this Act shall mean that any of the following market structures and undesirable market performances exists in any particular field of business where the aggregate total amount of prices (this term refers to the prices of the goods concerned less a sum equivalent to the amount of taxes levied directly on such goods) of goods of the same type (including goods capable of being supplied without making any significant change to their business facilities or kind of business activities; hereinafter in this subsection referred to as "particular goods") and those of any other goods having a strikingly similar function and utility thereto, which are supplied in Japan (excluding those exported) or the total amount of prices (this term refers to the prices of the services concerned less a sum equivalent to the amount of taxes levied on the recipient of such services with respect thereto) of services of the same type which are supplied in Japan, during the latest one-year period as designated by a Cabinet Ordinance, is in excess of fifty billion yen:

(i) Where the market share (this refers to the ratio accounted for by the aggregate volume [in case it is not appropriate to be calculated by the quantity, the quantity shall be represented in terms of the amount of their prices; the same shall apply hereinafter in this paragraph] of the particular goods and any other goods having a strikingly similar function and utility thereto or by the volume of the services, which are supplied by the entrepreneur or entrepreneurs concerned, to total volume of those supplied in Japan [excluding those exported]) of an entrepreneur exceeds one-half or where the combined market share of two entrepreneurs exceeds three-fourths during a given one-year period;

(ii) Where there exist conditions which make it extremely difficult for any other entrepreneur to be newly engaged in the said particular field of business;

(iii) Where the increase in the price of the particular goods or services supplied by the entrepreneur concerned has been remarkable or the decrease therein has been slight for a considerable period of time in the light of changes that have occurred in the supply and demand, or in the cost of supplying such certain goods or services during such period, and where, in addition thereto, the said entrepreneur has fallen under any one of the following requirements during the said period:

(a) That the entrepreneur has earned a profit rate far exceeding that which is established by a Cabinet Ordinance as the norm for the class of business designated by such Cabinet Ordinance to which the said entrepreneur belongs; or

(b) That the entrepreneur has expended a level of selling costs and general administrative expenses far exceeding one which is considered as the norm for the field of business to which the entrepreneur belongs.

8. In the event any change has occurred in the economic conditions resulting in a drastic change in domestic industrial shipments and wholesale prices, the amount of prices as prescribed in the preceding subsection may be revised by virtue of a Cabinet Ordinance to reflect such change.
9. The term "unfair trade practices" as used in this Act shall mean any act coming under any one of the following items, which tends to impede fair competition and which is designated by the Fair Trade Commission as such:
   (i) Unjustly discriminating against other entrepreneurs;
   (ii) Dealing at unjust prices;
   (iii) Unjustly inducing or coercing customers of a competitor to deal with oneself;
   (iv) Dealing with another party on such terms as will restrict unjustly the business activities of the said party;
   (v) Dealing with another party by unjust use of one's bargaining position;
   (vi) Unjustly interfering with a transaction between an entrepreneur who competes in Japan with oneself or the company of which oneself is a stockholder or an officer and another transacting party; or, in case such entrepreneur is a company, unjustly inducing, instigating, or coercing a stockholder or an officer of such company to act against the interest of such company.

Chapter II
Private Monopolization and Unreasonable Restraint of Trade

Section 3. *(Prohibition of private monopolization or unreasonable restraint of trade)*
No entrepreneur shall effect private monopolization or any unreasonable restraint of trade.

Section 6. *(Prohibition of particular international agreements or contracts, filing requirement)*
1. No entrepreneur shall enter into an international agreement or an international contract which contains such matters as constitute unreasonable restraint of trade or unfair trade practices.
2. An entrepreneur who has entered into an international agreement or an international contract (limited to only such an agreement or a contract that belongs to the types which are prescribed by the Rules of the Fair Trade Commission as tending to contain such matters as constitute unreasonable restraint of trade or unfair trade practices) shall, in accordance with the Rules of the Fair Trade Commission, file a notification thereof with the Commission, accompanied by a copy of the said agreement or contract (in the case of an oral agreement or contract, a document describing the contents thereof), within thirty days as from the conclusion of such agreement or contract.

Section 7. *(Measures to eliminate private monopolization, unreasonable restraint of trade or particular international agreements or contracts)*
1. In case there exists any act in violation of the provisions of Section 3 or Subsection 1 or 2 of the preceding section, the Fair Trade Commission may, in accordance with the procedures as provided for in Division II, Chapter VIII, order the entrepreneur concerned to file notifications, or to cease and desist from such act, to transfer a part of his or her business, or to take any other measures necessary to eliminate such act in violation of the said provisions.
2. The Fair Trade Commission may, when it finds it particularly necessary, even when an act in violation of the provisions of Section 3 has already ceased to exist, order the entrepreneur concerned * * * to take measures to publicize that the said act has been discontinued and order any other measures necessary to ensure elimination of the said act. Provided, That the foregoing shall not apply to cases where one year has elapsed since the date of ceasing of the said act without recommendation being given to the entrepreneur concerned or without the hearing procedures being initiated with respect to the said act.

Section 7-2. (Surcharges)

1. In case any entrepreneur effects an unreasonable restraint of trade or enters into an international agreement or an international contract containing such matters as constitute an unreasonable restraint of trade, which pertains to the price of goods or services or substantially restricts the supply of such goods or services and thereby affects the price thereof, the Fair Trade Commission shall order the entrepreneur concerned * * * to pay to the Treasury a surcharge of an amount equivalent to one-half of an amount arrived at by multiplying the sales amount of such goods or services, computed in accordance with the method prescribed by a Cabinet Ordinance, for the period from the date on which the entrepreneur engaged in business activities as an implementation of such conduct to the date on which the entrepreneur ceased to engage in business activities as an implementation of such conduct (hereinafter referred to as "period of such implementation") by six percent (or by two percent for retail business or by one percent for wholesale business). Provided, That in case the amount thus computed falls below five hundred thousand yen, the Commission shall not order the payment of such a surcharge.

* * *

3. Any person who has received an order under the provisions of Subsection 1 above shall pay the surcharge as provided for in the said subsection.

* * *

6. When a period of three years has elapsed from the date of expiration of the period of such implementation (or when a period of one year has elapsed from the date on which the hearing procedures ended in case such hearing procedures had been initiated with respect to such a violation [in case the expiration of such one-year period occurs earlier than the date of the expiration of the three-year period following the expiration of the period of such implementation, then the date on which the three-year period expired]), the Fair Trade Commission shall not order such entrepreneur to pay a surcharge for such violation. Provided, That the foregoing shall not apply to cases after the Fair Trade Commission has ordered payment of the surcharge for the said violation to the Treasury under the provisions of Section 48-2 (1).

Chapter III
Trade Associations

Section 8. (Prohibited acts of a trade association, filing requirement)

1. No trade association shall engage in any act which comes under any one of the following items:
   - (i) Substantially restraining competition in any particular field of trade;
   - (ii) Entering into an international agreement or an international contract as provided for in Section 6(1);
   - (iii) Limiting the present or future number of entrepreneurs in any particular field of business;
   - (iv) Unjustly restricting the functions or activities of the constituent entrepreneurs (meaning an entrepreneur who is a member of the trade association; hereinafter the same);
   - (v) Causing entrepreneurs to employ such acts as constitute unfair trade practices.
2. Every trade association shall, when formed, in accordance with the Rules of the Fair Trade Commission, file a notification thereof with the Commission within thirty days as from the date of its formation.

* * *

Section 8-2. (Measures to eliminate prohibited acts by trade associations)

1. When there exists any act in violation of the provisions of the preceding section, the Fair Trade Commission may * * * order the trade association concerned to file a notification, or to cease and desist from such act, to dissolve the said association, or to take any other measures necessary to eliminate the said act.
2. The provisions of Section 7(2) shall apply *mutatis mutandis* to any act in violation of the provisions of Subsection 1(i), (iv) or (v) of the preceding section.
3. The Fair Trade Commission may * * * when it finds it particularly necessary, at the same time order an officer, manager or constituent * * * of the said association to take measures necessary to ensure the measures provided for in Subsection 1 above or Section 7(2) as applicable *mutatis mutandis* under the provisions of the preceding subsection.

Section 8-3. (Surcharges imposed on constituent entrepreneurs)

The provisions of Section 7-2 shall apply *mutatis mutandis* to cases where an act is committed in violation of the provisions of Section 8(1)(i) or (ii) (applying only to such an entrepreneur who is a party to an international agreement or an international contract which contains such matters which constitute an unreasonable restraint of trade). In this case, the term "any entrepreneur" appearing in Subsection 1 of Section 7-2 shall read "any trade association" and the phrase "the entrepreneur concerned" appearing therein shall read "the constituent entrepreneur (when a constituent entrepreneur is acting for the benefit of another entrepreneur, said other entrepreneur) of the trade association concerned."

Chapter III-II
Monopolistic Situations

Section 8-4. (Measures against monopolistic situations)

1. When there exists a monopolistic situation, the Fair Trade Commission may order the entrepreneur concerned * * * to transfer a part of his or her business or to take any other measures necessary to restore competition with respect to such goods or services. Provided, That the foregoing shall not apply to cases where the Commission finds that such measures may reduce the scale of business of the said entrepreneur to such an extent that the costs required for the supply of goods or services which such entrepreneur supplies will rise sharply, undermine its financial position and make it difficult for the entrepreneur to maintain its international competitiveness, or where other alternative measures may be taken which the Commission finds sufficient to restore competition with respect to such goods or services.
2. In issuing an order prescribed in the preceding subsection, the Fair Trade Commission shall give consideration, based on the items prescribed in each of the following items, to the smooth conduct of business activities by the entrepreneurs concerned and those associated with them and the stabilization of livelihood for those employed by such entrepreneurs:
   (i) Assets, income and expenditures and other aspects of accounting;
   (ii) Officers and employees;
   (iii) Location of factories, workyards and offices and other locational conditions;
   (iv) Aspects of business facilities and equipment;
   (v) The substance and technological features of patent rights, trademark rights and other intangible property rights;
   (vi) Capacity for and circumstances of production and sales, etc.;
   (vii) Capacity for and circumstances of obtaining funds and materials, etc.;
   (viii) Circumstances of supply and distribution of goods or services.

Chapter IV
Stockholding, Interlocking Directorates, Mergers and Acquisitions of Business

Section 9. (Prohibition of holding companies)

1. No holding company shall be established.
2. No company (including a foreign company; hereinafter the same) shall operate as a holding company in Japan.
3. The term "holding company" as used in the preceding two subsections shall mean a company whose principal business is to control the business activities of a company or companies in Japan by means of holding of stock (including partnership shares; hereinafter the same).

Section 9-2. (Restriction on total amount of stockholding by a large scale non-financial company)

1. For any stock company whose business is other than financial * * * and whose capital is larger than ten billion yen or whose net assets * * * are larger than thirty billion yen, in the event that the total amount of the acquisition price (or such other price as may appear in the latest balance sheet; the same meaning shall apply hereinafter) for stock of companies in Japan which it acquires or holds would exceed its capital or its net assets, whichever is larger (hereinafter referred to as "the base amount"), said company shall not acquire or hold stock in companies in Japan which exceeds said base amount. Provided, That the foregoing shall not apply to the acquisition or holding of such stock in the cases provided for in any one of the following items:
   [Nine omitted exceptions include government owned or guaranteed companies, companies granted exceptions for public policy reasons, companies that wholly acquire new companies that were formerly divisions of the acquiror, and stock acquired in enforcing a debt.]

[2.-9. Further exceptions and qualifications to Subsection 1 omitted.]

Section 10. (Prohibition of particular stockholding by a company, filing requirement)

1. No company shall acquire or hold stock of a company or companies in Japan where the effect of such acquisition or holding of stock may be substantially to restrain competition in any particular field of trade, or shall acquire or hold stock of a company or companies in Japan through unfair trade practices.
2. Every company in Japan whose business is other than financial and whose total assets exceed two billion yen and every foreign company whose business is other than financial, shall, in case it holds stock of another company or companies in Japan * * * submit, in accordance with the Rules of the Fair Trade Commission, a report on such stock held in its name or in the name of a trustee as of the end of every business year to the Commission within three months therefrom.

Section 11. (Restriction on stockholding by a financial company)

1. No company engaged in financial business shall acquire or hold stock of another company in Japan if by doing so it holds in excess of five percent (ten percent in the case of an insurance company) of the total outstanding stock thereof. Provided, That the foregoing shall not apply to such cases where authorization of the Fair Trade Commission is obtained in advance in accordance with the Rules of the Fair Trade Commission, or to such cases falling under any one of the following items:
   (i) Acquisition or holding of stock as the result of the enforcement of lien, pledge, or mortgage, or of payment in kind;
   (ii) Acquisition or holding of stock by a company engaging in securities dealing in the course of its business;
   (iii) Acquisition or holding of stock in the form of trust property of a pecuniary or securities trust. Provided, That this shall apply only to cases where the trustor or the beneficiary of such trust property can exercise his or her voting rights or where such trustor or beneficiary can issue instructions regarding the exercise of such voting rights.

* * *

Section 13. (Prohibition of particular interlocking directorates, filing requirement)

1. Neither an officer nor an employee (meaning in this section a person other than officers in the regular employment of a company) of a company shall hold at the same time a position as an officer in another company or companies in Japan wherever such an interlocking directorate may be substantially to restrain competition in any particular field of trade.
2. No company shall coerce another company or companies in Japan in competition with it in Japan, through unfair trade practices, to admit one of its officers concurrently to the position of an officer or an employee of the latter company or companies, or to admit its employee concurrently to the position of an officer of such company or companies.
3. Every officer or employee of a company who holds concurrently the position of an officer in another company or companies in Japan in competition with it in Japan, shall, in case the total assets of either company exceed two billion yen, file, in accordance with the Rules of the Fair Trade Commission, a notification thereof with the Commission within thirty days as from the date of assuming the position as such an officer.

Section 14. (Prohibition of particular stockholding by a person other than a company, filing requirement)

1. No person other than a company shall acquire or hold stock of another company or companies in Japan whenever such acquisition or holding of stock may be substantially to restrain competition in any particular field of trade, or shall acquire or hold stock of another company or companies in Japan through unfair trade practices.
2. [Reporting requirement omitted.]

Section 15. (Prohibition of particular mergers, filing requirement)

1. No company in Japan shall effect a merger falling under any one of the following items:
   (i) Where the effect of a merger would be substantially to restrain competition in any particular field of trade;
   (ii) Where the merger results from unfair trade practices.
2. A company in Japan which seeks to engage in a merger shall, in accordance with the provisions of the Rules of the Fair Trade Commission, file a notification in advance with the Commission.
3. In a case coming under the preceding subsection, no company in Japan shall effect a merger until thirty days have elapsed from the date of receipt of the notification. Provided, That the Fair Trade Commission may, when it finds it necessary, shorten the said period, or extend it by an additional period of time not exceeding sixty days with the consent of the companies concerned.
4. The Fair Trade Commission shall, where it decides to initiate hearing proceedings or makes a recommendation, with a view to ordering necessary measures relating to the merger in question pursuant to the provisions of Section 17-2, do so before the expiration of the thirty-day period as provided for in the preceding subsection, or of any shortened or extended period under the proviso thereto. Provided, That the foregoing provisions shall not apply in cases where there has been a false statement with respect to important matters in the report specified in Subsection 2 above.

Section 16. (Prohibition of particular business acquisitions, filing requirement)

The provisions of the preceding section shall apply *mutatis mutandis* to an act of a company falling under any one of the following items:

(i) Acquiring the whole or a substantial part of the business in Japan of another company;
(ii) Acquiring the whole or a substantial part of the fixed assets used for the business in Japan of another company;
(iii) Taking on a lease of the whole or a substantial part of the business in Japan of another company;

(iv) Undertaking the management of the whole or a substantial part of the business in Japan of another company;
(v) Entering into a contract which provides for a joint profit and loss accounting for business in Japan with another company.

Section 17. (Prohibition of evasion)
No acts in whatever form or manner shall be committed to evade the prohibitions or restrictions provided for in Section 9 through the preceding section inclusive.

Section 17-2. (Measures to eliminate unlawful acts relating to a company, etc.)
1. Where there exists any act in violation of the provisions of Sections 9-2(1), 10, 11(1), 15(1), or the preceding section, the Fair Trade Commission may * * * order the entrepreneur concerned to submit a report, or to dispose of the whole or a part of his or her stock holdings, to transfer a part of his or her business, or to take any other measures necessary to eliminate such act in violation of the said provisions.
2. Where there exists any act in violation of the provisions of Sections 9(1) or (2), 13, 14, or the preceding section, the Fair Trade Commission may * * * order the person violating such provisions to submit a report or file a notification, or to dispose of the whole or a part of his or her stock holdings, to resign from his or her position as an officer in a company, or to take any other measures necessary to eliminate such violation.

Section 18. (Measures against the establishment of a holding company or an illegal merger)
The Fair Trade Commission may, in a case where any company has been established in violation of the provisions of Section 9(1) or where companies have merged in violation of the provisions of Section 15(2) and (3), bring a suit to have the said establishment or merger declared null and void.

Chapter IV-II
Parallel Price Increases

Section 18-2. (Reporting requirement on parallel price increases)
[Provision requiring explanatory report to the FTC in the event of parallel price increases on similar products by companies dominant in a market omitted.]

Chapter V
Unfair Trade Practices

Section 19. (Prohibition of unfair trade practices)
No entrepreneur shall employ unfair trade practices.

Section 20. (Measures against unfair trade practices)
1. When there exists any act in violation of the preceding section, the Fair Trade Commission may * * * order the entrepreneur concerned to cease and desist from the said act, to delete the clauses concerned from the contract and to take any other measures necessary to eliminate the said act.
2. The provisions of Section 7(2) shall apply *mutatis mutandis* to an act in violation of the preceding section.

Chapter VI
Exemptions

Section 21. (Natural monopoly)
The provisions of this Act shall not apply to such acts relating to the production, sale, or supply as are done in the proper course of business by a person engaging in railway, electricity, gas, or any other business constituting a monopoly by the inherent nature of the said business.

Section 22. (Legitimate acts under special acts and orders)

1. Where there exists a special law concerning a specific industry, the provisions of this Act shall not apply to legitimate acts of an entrepreneur or a trade association conducted in accordance with such a special law or an order based upon such a law.
2. The special laws referred to in the preceding subsection shall be specified by a separate law.

Section 23. (Exercise of intangible property rights)

The provisions of this Act shall not apply to such acts recognizable as the exercise of rights under the Copyright Act, the Patent Act, the Utility Model Act, the Design Act or the Trademark Act.

Section 24. (Acts of cooperatives)

The provisions of this Act shall not apply to acts of a cooperative (including a federation of cooperatives) which conforms to the requirements stipulated in each of the following items and which has been formed in accordance with the provisions of a separate law. Provided, That the foregoing shall not apply to cases where unfair trade practices are employed, or where competition in any particular field of trade is substantially restrained resulting in an unjust rise in prices:

(i) Its purpose shall be mutual aid among small scale entrepreneurs or consumers;
(ii) It shall be voluntarily formed; and participation in and withdrawal from the cooperative shall be voluntary;
(iii) Each member shall possess equal voting rights; and
(iv) When a distribution of profits among members is made, the limits thereto shall be stipulated in a law or an order, or in the articles of association.

Section 24-2. (Resale price maintenance contracts)

1. The provisions of this Act shall not apply to legitimate acts performed by an entrepreneur who produces or sells a commodity, the uniform quality of which is easily identifiable and which is designated by the Fair Trade Commission, with another entrepreneur who buys such commodity, in order to fix and maintain the resale price thereof (this term means hereinafter the price at which the latter entrepreneur or a third entrepreneur who purchases from him or her sells such commodity). Provided, That the foregoing shall not apply if the said act would unjustly injure the interest of consumers in general or if it is done against the will of the entrepreneur who produces the said commodity, by an entrepreneur whose business is to sell the said commodity.
2. The Fair Trade Commission shall not designate a commodity under the provisions of the preceding subsection unless it comes under each of the following items:
   (i) The commodity shall be for the daily use by the consumers in general; and
   (ii) Free competition shall exist with respect to the commodity.
3. The designation of a commodity under the provisions of Subsection 1 above shall be made by notification.
4. Legitimate acts performed by an entrepreneur whose business is to publish copyrighted works or by an entrepreneur whose business is to sell such published works, in order to fix and maintain, with another entrepreneur who buys such works, the resale price thereof, shall be treated as under Subsection 1.
5. [Omitted.]
6. When an entrepreneur as stipulated in Subsection 1 above has fixed the resale price under the said subsection and has entered into a contract for the purpose of maintaining it, he or she shall, in accordance with provisions of the Rules of the Fair Trade Commission, file a notification thereof with the Commission within thirty days from the date of the conclusion of the said contract. Provided, That the foregoing shall not apply if the Fair Trade Commission stipulates otherwise in its Rules.

Section 24-3. (Depression cartels)

1. Where there exists an extreme disequilibrium of supply and demand for a particular commodity, resulting in circumstances falling under each of the following items, the provisions of this Act shall not apply to concerted activities of entrepreneurs (including an act of a trade association which causes its constituent entrepreneurs to undertake concerted activities; hereinafter the same) who produce the said commodity or a trade association consisting of such entrepreneurs (hereinafter referred to as "producers, etc."), for which authorization has been obtained under either of the following two subsections. Provided, That the foregoing shall not apply when they employ unfair trade practices or when they cause any entrepreneur to employ such acts as would constitute unfair trade practices:
   (i) The price of the said commodity is below the average cost of production, and the fear exists that it may reach the point that it would be difficult for a considerable portion of the entrepreneurs in the trade concerned to continue in business;
   (ii) It would be difficult to overcome the circumstances stipulated in the preceding item through rationalization by individual enterprises.
2. When the circumstances stipulated in the preceding subsection exist, those producers, etc., who desire to effect concerted activities relating to restrictions on output or sales, or on facilities or equipment (excluding such as will impede the renovation or improvement of facilities) may, in order to overcome such circumstances, obtain from the Fair Trade Commission authorization of the said activities in advance.
3. When the circumstances stipulated in Subsection 1 above exist and if restriction on output of the commodity in a particular trade would be extremely difficult for technical reasons, those producers, etc., who desire to effect concerted activities involving price-fixing may, in accordance with the Rules of the Fair Trade Commission, obtain from the Fair Trade Commission authorization of the said activities in advance. If, after an authorization under the preceding subsection has been obtained and concerted activities have been undertaken, it would still be extremely difficult to overcome the circumstances stipulated in Subsection 1 solely through the concerted activities stipulated in the preceding subsection, the provisions of this subsection shall apply when producers, etc., desire to effect concerted activities involving price-fixing concurrently with concerted activities stipulated in the preceding subsection.
4. The Fair Trade Commission shall not grant authorization as provided for in the preceding two subsections unless the concerted activities applied for meet the conditions provided for in the preceding two subsections and conform with each of the following items:
   (i) That they do not exceed the necessary extent to overcome the circumstances provided for in Subsection 1 above;
   (ii) That there is no likelihood of unjustly injuring the interests of the consumers in general, or of related entrepreneurs;
   (iii) That they are not unjustly discriminatory;
   (iv) That they do not restrict unjustly participation in or withdrawal from such activities.

5., 6. [Omitted.]

7. The Fair Trade Commission shall, where an objection to authorization under Subsection 2 or 3 above has been filed, conduct an open summary hearing in accordance with the Rules of the Fair Trade Commission.
8. The Fair Trade Commission shall, prior to granting authorization under Subsection 2 or 3 above, or to dismissing an application therefor, consult with the competent minister with responsibility for the business concerned. The same shall apply when the Fair Trade Commission intends to take an action provided for in Section 66(1) [cancellation or modification of authorization] with respect to such authorization under Subsection 2 or 3 above.

Section 24-4. (Rationalization cartels)

1. The provisions of this Act shall not apply to concerted activities of producers, etc., for which authorization has been obtained under the following subsection, where such activities are particularly necessary for effecting an advancement of technology, an improvement in the quality of goods, a reduction in costs, an increase in efficiency or any other rationalization of enterprises.
2. Producers, etc., desirous of undertaking concerted activities regarding restrictions on technology or kinds of product, utilization of facilities for storage of raw materials or products or for transportation thereof, or utilization or purchase of by-products, waste, or scrap, in a case as stipulated in the preceding subsection may, in accordance with the provisions of the Rules of the Fair Trade Commission, obtain authorization from the Fair Trade Commission in advance.
3. The Fair Trade Commission shall not grant authorization under the preceding subsection unless concerted activities applied for meet the conditions provided for in the preceding subsection and conform with each of the following items:
   (i) That there is no likelihood of injuring the interests of users;
   (ii) That there is no likelihood of unjustly injuring the interests of consumers in general and of related entrepreneurs (excluding customers);
   (iii) That they are not unjustly discriminatory;
   (iv) That they do not restrict unjustly the participation in or withdrawal from such activities;
   (v) That where restrictions on line of product are imposed differently on participants in the concerted activities, such differentiation is not designed unjustly to concentrate production of a particular product in the hands of any specific entrepreneurs.
4. The provisions of the proviso to Subsection 1 and of Subsections 5 to 8 inclusive of the preceding section shall apply *mutatis mutandis* to the concerted activities as provided for in Subsection 2 of this section.

Chapter VII
Damages

Section 25. (Absolute liability)

1. Any entrepreneur who has effected private monopolization or unreasonable restraint of trade or who has employed unfair trade practices shall be liable to indemnify the person injured.
2. No entrepreneur may avoid the liability as prescribed in the preceding subsection by proving the non-existence of willfulness or negligence on his or her part.

Section 26. (Restriction on exercise of the right to claim damages in court, prescription)

1. The right to claim damages as provided for in the preceding section may not be exercised in court until a decision pursuant to the provisions of Section 48(4), Section 53-3, or Section 54 has become final and conclusive or, in the event no decision has been made pursuant to said sections, until a decision pursuant to the provisions of Section 54-2(1) has become final and conclusive.
2. The right under the preceding subsection shall, upon expiration of three years from the date on which a decision referred to in said subsection has become final and conclusive, become extinct by prescription.

CHAPTER VII
Fair Trade Commission

Part 1. Organization and Authority

Section 27. (Duty and position)

1. The Fair Trade Commission shall be established in order to attain the purposes of this Act.
2. The Fair Trade Commission shall be administratively attached to the Prime Minister.

[Sections 27-2 and 28 concerning jurisdiction of the FTC and its independence omitted.]

Section 29. (Organization, appointment of chairman and commissioners and their status)

1. The Fair Trade Commission shall be composed of a chairman and four commissioners.
2. The chairman and the commissioners shall be appointed by the Prime Minister with the consent of both Houses of the Diet from among persons of learning and experience in law or economics whose age is thirty-five or more.
3. The appointment or dismissal of the chairman shall be attested by the Emperor.
4. The chairman and the commissioners shall be public service officials.

Section 30. (Term of office for chairman and commissioners)

1. The term of office for the chairman and the commissioners shall be five years * * *.
2. The chairman and the commissioners may be reappointed.

3., 4. [Omitted.]

[Sections 31, 32 and 33 concerning, inter alia, protection of FTC chairman and commissioners from dismissal for political reasons and status of FTC commissioners omitted.]

Section 34. (Quorum and voting)

1. Meetings of the Fair Trade Commission shall not be opened and the decision shall not be made unless the chairman and two or more commissioners are present.
2. All decisions of the Fair Trade Commission shall be made by majority votes of the attending commissioners. In case the votes are evenly divided the chairman shall have the power to decide.

3., 4. [Omitted.]

[Sections 35 to 39 concerning, inter alia, structure of Executive Bureau, appointment of administrative judges, other administrative matters and limitations on political participation and expression by FTC members omitted.]

Section 40. (Compulsory powers of inquiry)

The Fair Trade Commission may, when necessary for the performance of its functions, order government agencies, legal entities established by a special law or an order, entrepreneurs or organizations of entrepreneurs, or their personnel to appear before the Commission, or may require them to submit necessary reports, information or data.

[Sections 41 to 44 concerning surveys, public hearings, publications and reports to the Diet omitted.]

Part 2. Procedures

Section 45. (Report and detection of violation)

1. Any person may, when he or she considers that a matter in violation of this Act exists, report the said matter to the Fair Trade Commission and ask for appropriate measures to be taken.

2., 3. [Omitted.]

4. The Fair Trade Commission may, when it considers that a violation of this Act or a monopolistic situation exists, take appropriate measures upon its own authority.

Section 45-2. (Procedures for measures against a monopolistic situation)

1. The Fair Trade Commission, if it considers that there exists a matter that constitutes a monopolistic situation, and if it has decided to take measures under Subsection 4 of the preceding section, shall make a noticc to such effect to the competent Minister having jurisdiction over the business in which the entrepreneur concerned is engaged.
2. In case a notice under the preceding subsection has been made, the Minister may present to the Commission his or her views regarding the existence or the absence of such a monopolistic situation and his or her views regarding other alternative measures which he or she feels would be sufficient to restore competition as provided for in the proviso to Section 8-4(1).

Section 46. (Compulsory measures for investigation)

1. The Fair Trade Commission may, in order to conduct the necessary investigation with regard to a case, take any one of the following measures:
   (i) Ordering persons connected with a case or witnesses to appear for questioning, hearing their views or obtaining reports from them;
   (ii) Ordering experts to appear to have them give expert testimony;
   (iii) Ordering persons holding accounting books, documents and other matters to submit the same, or to retain such submitted matters; or
   (iv) Entering any place of business of a person connected with a case, or other necessary place, and inspecting conditions of business operations and property, accounting books, documents and other matters.
2. The Fair Trade Commission may, when it finds it proper, designate, in accordance with provisions of an order, investigators from among the personnel of the Fair Trade Commission, and cause them to take the measures as provided for in the preceding subsection.
3. [Omitted.]
4. The authority to take actions pursuant to the provisions of Subsection 1 above shall not be construed as authority for a criminal investigation.

Section 47. (Records)

The Fair Trade Commission shall, when it has conducted the necessary investigation of a case, keep an investigation record of the main points thereof, and, particularly when it has taken any measures as provided for in the preceding section, it shall set out the results thereof.

Section 48. (Recommendation to violator to take corrective measures, recommendation decision)

1. The Fair Trade Commission may, when it finds that there exists any act in violation of the provisions of Sections 3, 6(1) or (2), 8, 9(1) or (2), 9-2(1), 10, 11(1), 13, 14, 15(1) (including *mutatis mutandis* application thereof pursuant to Section 16), 17, or 19, recommend the persons who have committed such violation (including the directors and managers of a trade association and its constituent entrepreneurs when the violating act relates to the provisions of Section 8) to take appropriate measures.
2. The Fair Trade Commission may, if it finds that any act in violation of the provisions of Sections 3, 8(1)(i), (iv), or (v), or 19 has already ceased to exist, and if it finds it particularly necessary, recommend to the person who committed such violation (including the officers and managers of such trade association and the constituent entrepreneurs when the violating act relates to the provisions of Section 8(1)(i), (iv) or (v)) to take appropriate measures.
3. Any person who has received a recommendation under the provisions of the preceding subsection shall notify the Fair Trade Commission without delay whether or not he or she accepts the recommendation.
4. The Fair Trade Commission may, when the person who has received a recommendation under the provisions of the Subsection 1 or 2 has accepted it, render a decision on the lines of the said recommendation without resorting to hearing procedures.

Section 48-2. (Procedures for surcharges)

[Procedures for ordering surcharges for violations of Section 7 or 8-3 omitted.]

Section 49. (Initiation of hearing procedures)

1. The Fair Trade Commission may, in a case as stipulated in Section 48(1) or (2) or in a case where a monopolistic situation is deemed to exist (excluding cases provided for in the proviso to Section 8-4(1); the same applies in Section 54(1)), if it finds that it would be in the public interest to initiate hearing procedures on the case, initiate hearing procedures on the said case.

2., 3. [Omitted.]

4. The Fair Trade Commission shall, when it contemplates initiating procedures on a case relating to Section 8-4(1), consult with the competent Minister having jurisdiction over the business in which such entrepreneur is engaged.

Section 50. (Complaint, initiation of hearing procedures)

1. The decision to initiate hearing procedures shall be made in writing, in which the outline of the case shall be stated, and the chairman and the commissioners participating in the voting on the decision shall sign it and affix their seals thereto.
2. The hearing procedures shall be initiated by serving a certified copy of the decision to initiate hearing procedures upon a person to be ordered to take measures * * *.
3. [Omitted.]
4. The date of hearing shall be fixed on a day later than thirty days from the date of service of the certified copy of the decision. Provided, That the foregoing shall not apply when the consent of the respondent is obtained.

Section 51. (Answers)

A respondent shall, upon receipt of the certified copy of complaint, submit an answer without delay to the Fair Trade Commission.

[Sections 51-2 and 51-3 concerning hearing procedures omitted.]

Section 52. (Respondent's right of defense)

1. A respondent or his or her representative may, at a hearing proceeding, state the reason why an order of the Fair Trade Commission to take elimination, etc., measures or to pay a surcharge under the provisions of Section 7-2(1) (including cases when the said provisions are applied *mutatis mutandis* by Section 8-3) in regard to the said case should not be made, submit supporting evidence therefor, request the Fair Trade Commission to question necessary witnesses, to order expert witnesses to testify, to order holders of accounting books, documents and other matters to submit them, or to enter necessary places and inspect the conditions of business and property, accounting books and other matters; and may interrogate witnesses or expert witnesses who are required to attend hearing proceedings by order of the Fair Trade Commission.
2. A respondent may be represented by an attorney or any other appropriate person approved by the Fair Trade Commission.

Section 52-2. (Disclosure of reasons for non-adoption of evidence)

In case the Fair Trade Commission has not adopted any evidence introduced by the investigator, the respondent or his or her representative, the Commission shall state the reason for not having adopted such evidence.

Section 52-3. (Non-appearance of respondents)

The Fair Trade Commission may conduct the hearing proceedings even if the respondent or his or her representative fails to appear on the date of the said hearing proceedings without a justifiable cause.

Section 53. (Hearing proceedings, stenographic record)

1. All hearing proceedings shall be public. Provided, That when it is found necessary to protect the trade secrets of an entrepreneur, or necessary to the public interest, a hearing proceeding need not be made public.
2. [Omitted.]

[Sections 53-2 and 53-2-2 concerning evidentiary rules, including rights against self-incrimination, omitted.]

Section 53-3. (Consent decision)

The Fair Trade Commission may, after deciding to initiate hearing procedures, when the respondent, admitting the findings of fact and the application of law stated in the decision to initiate hearing procedures, submits to the Fair Trade Commission a written statement setting forth that he or she will accept the decision without resorting to subsequent hearing proceedings, and files a plan setting forth concrete measures which he or she proposes voluntarily to take in order to eliminate such violation, or to ensure the continued elimination of such violation, or to restore competition with respect to the goods or services involved in the monopolistic situation, if the Commission finds it appropriate, render a decision on the lines of the concrete measures as stated in such plan without subsequent hearing proceedings.

Section 54. (Hearing decision)

1. The Fair Trade Commission shall, when it finds after hearing proceedings that violation of the provisions of Sections 3, 6(1) or (2), 8, 9(1) or (2), 9-2(1), 10, 11(1), 13, 14, 15(1) (including cases of *mutatis mutandis* application under Section 16), 17, or 19 exists or that a monopolistic situation exists, order the respondent by a decision to take such measures as provided for in Sections 7(1), 8-2(1) or (3), 17-2, 20(1) or 8-4(1).
2. The Fair Trade Commission shall, when it finds after hearing proceedings that an act in violation of the provisions of Section 3, 8(1), (i), (iv) or (v) or 19 no longer exists and if it finds it particularly necessary, order, by a decision, the respondent to take the measures provided for in Sections 7(2) (including cases to which the said subsection is applied *mutatis mutandis* in Sections 8-2(2) and 20(2)).
3. The Fair Trade Commission shall, when it finds after hearing proceedings that such acts or monopolistic situation as provided for in Subsection 1 did not exist prior to the time when it issued the decision initiating hearing procedures, that such acts as provided for in the said subsection or a monopolistic situation existed prior to the time of the issuance of said decision but the said acts or monopolistic situation have already ceased to exist (excluding cases involving decisions under the preceding subsection), or that a monopolistic situation exists which falls under the proviso to Section 8-4(1), make clear the said fact by a decision.

Section 54-2. (Surcharge payment order)

1. The Fair Trade Commission shall, when it finds after hearing proceedings a fact as provided for in Section 7-2(1) (including cases where this provision is applicable *mutatis mutandis* by Section 8-3), order, by a decision, the respondent to pay to the Treasury a surcharge levied on such violation.
2. [Omitted.]

[Sections 54-3 to 76 concerning, *inter alia*, the FTC's making and issuing decisions, third-party interventions by private parties or government bodies, FTC applications to the courts for injunctions, and FTC rule-making powers omitted.]

Chapter IX
Suits

Section 77. (Filing suit to quash an FTC decision)

1. A suit to quash a decision of the Fair Trade Commission shall be filed within thirty days (three months in case of a decision under the provisions of Section 8-4(1)) from the date on which the decision became effective.
2. [Omitted.]

[Sections 78 to 81 concerning records and evidence from FTC hearings omitted.]

Section 82. (Quashing decisions)

The court may quash a decision of the Fair Trade Commission if the decision falls under any one of the following items:

(i) If the facts on which the decision is based are not established by substantial evidence; or
(ii) If the decision violates the Constitution or other laws or orders.

Section 83. (Remand of a decision)

The court may, when it finds it necessary that further hearing proceedings be conducted in a case where it has determined that a decision of the Fair Trade Commission should be quashed, remand the case to the Fair Trade Commission, giving the reasons for the remand.

Section 84. (Request for FTC's opinion on amount of damages)

1. When a suit for indemnification of damages under the provisions of Section 25 [absolute liability] has been filed, the court shall, without delay, request the opinion of the Fair Trade Commission with respect to the amount of damages caused by the violation as provided for in the said section.
2. If a counter claim for indemnification of damages under the provisions of Section 25 is made in court proceedings for the purpose of offsetting another claim, the provisions of the preceding subsection shall apply *mutatis mutandis.*

[Note: With regard to "offsetting" under Subsection 2, see §§505-512 of the Civil Code, and §199(2) of the Code of Civil Procedures]

[Sections 85 to 88-3 concerning, *inter alia,* Tokyo High Court's original and, in some cases, exclusive jurisdiction to hear FTC-related matters omitted.]

Chapter X
Penal Provisions

Section 89. (Penalties for private monopolization or unreasonable restraints of trade)

1. Any person committing one of the following offenses shall be punished by penal servitude for not more than three years or by a fine of not more than five million yen:
   (i) Any person who, in violation of the provisions of Section 3, effected private monopolization or unreasonable restraint of trade; or
   (ii) Any person who, in violation of the provisions of Section 8(1)(i), effected substantial restraint of competition in any particular field of trade.
2. An attempt to commit an offense falling under the preceding subsection shall be punished.

Section 90. (Penalties for prohibited international agreements or contracts, prohibited acts of trade associations, or non-observance of final and conclusive decisions)

Any person committing one of the following offenses shall be punished by penal servitude for not more than two years or by a fine of not more than three million yen:

(i) Any person who, in violation of the provisions of Section 6(1) or Section 8(1)(ii) entered into an international agreement or an international contract which contains such matters as constitute unreasonable restraint of trade;

(ii) Any person who violated the provisions of Section 8(1)(iii) or (iv); or
(iii) Any person who failed to comply with a decision under Section 48(4), Section 53-3 or Section 54(1) or (2), after it had become final and conclusive.

Section 91. (Penalties for holding company, unlawful stockholding or interlocking directorates, etc.)
Any person committing one of the following offenses shall be punished by penal servitude for not more than one year or by a fine of not more than two million yen:
(i) Any person who, in violation of the provisions of Section 9(1), established a holding company, or violated the provisions of Subsection 2 of the said section;
(ii) Any person who, in violation of the provisions of Section 9-2(1), acquired or held stock;
(iii) Any person who, in violation of the provisions of the first part of Section 10(1), acquired or held stock;
(iv) Any person who, in violation of the provisions of Section 11(1), acquired or held stock; or who, in violation of the provisions of Subsection 2 of the said section, held stock;
(v) Any person who, in violation of the provisions of Section 13(1), held concurrently positions as an officer of a company;
(vi) Any person who, in violation of the provisions of the first part of Section 14(1), acquired or held stock; or
(vii) Any person who, in connection with a prohibition or restriction contained in any of the preceding items, committed a violation of the provisions of Section 17.

Section 91-2. (Penalties for failure to file notifications, etc.)
Any person committing one of the following offenses shall be punished by a fine of not more than two million yen:
(i) Any person who, in violation of the provisions of Section 6(2), failed to file a notification, or filed a false notification;
[Subsections (ii) to (x) concerning failing to make reports, notifications, etc., required under the Act, or making false reports, notifications, etc., omitted.]

Section 92. (Concurrent punishment)
Any person committing any one of the offenses stipulated in Section 89 to 91 inclusive may, depending on the circumstances, be punished by both penal servitude and a fine.

[Sections 92-2 to 94 concerning penalties for perjury, revealing trade secrets, interfering with inspections and non-compliance with compulsory measures omitted. Sections 95 to 95-3 imposing liabilities on companies, representatives of companies and representatives of trade associations for violations by their managers, employees, agents, etc., also omitted.]

Section 95-4. (Dissolution of trade associations)
1. The court may, when it considers that sufficient grounds exist, declare a trade association to be dissolved simultaneously with the imposition of a penalty as provided for in Section 89(1)(ii) or Section 90.
2. [Omitted.]

Section 96. (Exclusive accusation by the Fair Trade Commission)
1. Any offense under Sections 89 to 91 inclusive shall be considered only after an accusation of the Fair Trade Commission has been filed.
2. – 4. [Omitted.]

[Sections 97 to 100 concerning administrative fines, revocation of patent rights and exclusion from government contracts omitted.]

11. GENERAL DESIGNATION ON UNFAIR TRADE PRACTICES

Fair Trade Commission Notification No. 15, June 18, 1982

Source: *Antimonopoly Legislation of Japan*, M. Nakagawa, ed. (Kōsei Torihiki Kyōkai, 1984). Reprinted by permission.

In accordance with the provisions of Section 2(9) of [the Antimonopoly Act], Fair Trade Commission Notification No. 11 of 1953 on Unfair Trade Practices shall be totally amended as follows * * *:

1. *(Concerted refusal to deal)*
Without proper justification, taking an act specified in one of the following items concertedly with another entrepreneur who is in a competitive relationship with oneself (hereinafter, referred to as a "competitor"):
(i) Refusing to deal with a certain entrepreneur or restricting the quantity or substance of a commodity or service involved in trade with a certain entrepreneur; or
(ii) Causing another entrepreneur to take an act which comes under the preceding item.

2. *(Other refusal to deal)*
Unjustly refusing to deal, or restricting the quantity or substance of a commodity or service involved in trade with a certain entrepreneur, or causing another entrepreneur to take any act which comes under one of these categories.

3. *(Discriminatory pricing)*
Unjustly supplying or accepting a commodity or service at prices which discriminate between regions or between trading parties.

4. *(Discriminatory treatment on transaction terms, etc.)*
Unjustly affording favorable or unfavorable treatment to a certain entrepreneur in regard to the terms or execution of a transaction.

5. *(Discriminatory treatment in a trade association, etc.)*
Unjustly excluding a specific entrepreneur from a trade association or from a concerted activity, or unjustly discriminating against a specific entrepreneur in a trade association or a concerted activity, thereby causing difficulties in the business activities of the said entrepreneur.

6. *(Unjust low price sales)*
Without proper justification, supplying a commodity or service continuously at a price which is excessively below cost incurred in the said supply, or otherwise unjustly supplying a commodity or service at a low price, thereby tending to cause difficulties to the business activities of other entrepreneurs.

7. *(Unjust high price purchasing)*
Unjustly purchasing a commodity or service at a high price, thereby tending to cause difficulties to the business activities of other entrepreneurs.

8. *(Deceptive customer inducement)*
Unjustly inducing customers of a competitor to deal with oneself by causing them to misunderstand that the substance of a commodity or service supplied by oneself, or terms of the transaction, or other matters relating to such transaction are much better or much more favorable than the actual ones or than those relating to the competitor.

9. *(Customer inducement by unjust benefits)*
Inducing customers of a competitor to deal with oneself through benefits that are unjust in the light of normal business practices.

10. *(Tie-in sales, etc.)*
Unjustly causing a trading party to purchase a commodity or service from oneself or from an entrepreneur designated by oneself by tying it to the supply of another commodity or service, or otherwise coercing the said party to deal with oneself or with an entrepreneur designated by oneself.

11. *(Dealing on exclusive terms)*
Unjustly dealing with a trading party on the condition that the said party shall not deal with a competitor, thereby tending to reduce transaction opportunities for the said competitor.

12. *(Resale price restriction)*
Supplying a commodity to a trading party who purchases the said commodity from oneself while imposing, without proper justification, one of the restrictive terms specified below:
(i) Causing the said party to maintain the sales price of the commodity that one has determined, or otherwise restricting the said party's free decision on sales price of the commodity; or
(ii) Having the said party cause an entrepreneur who purchases the commodity from the said party to maintain the sales price of the commodity that one has determined, or otherwise causing the said party to restrict the said entrepreneur's free decision on sales price of the commodity.

13. *(Dealing on restrictive terms)*
Other than any act coming under the preceding two paragraphs, dealing with a trading party on conditions which unjustly restrict any transaction between the said party and other parties with which it trades or other business activities of the said party.

14. *(Abuse of dominant bargaining position)*
Taking any act specified in one of the following items, unjustly in the light of normal business practices, by making use of one's dominant bargaining position over a trading party:
(i) Causing a trading party in an ongoing transaction to purchase a commodity or service other than the one involved in the said transaction;
(ii) Causing a trading party in an ongoing transaction to provide for oneself money, service or other economic benefits;
(iii) Setting or changing transaction terms in a way disadvantageous to a trading party;
(iv) In addition to any act coming under the preceding three items, imposing a disadvantage on a trading party regarding terms or execution of a transaction; or
(v) Causing a company which is one's trading party to follow one's directions in advance, or to get one's approval, regarding the appointment of officers of the said company (meaning those as defined by Subsection 3 of Section 2 of the Act Concerning Prohibition of Private Monopoly and Maintenance of Fair Trade).

15. *(Interference with a competitor's transaction)*
Unjustly interfering with a transaction between another entrepreneur who is in a domestic competitive relationship with oneself or with the company of which one is a stockholder or an officer and the other trading party to such transaction, by preventing the formation of a contract, or by inducing the breach of a contract, or by any other means whatsoever.

16. *(Interference with internal operation of a competing company)*
Unjustly inducing, abetting, or coercing a stockholder or an officer of a company which is in a domestic competitive relationship with oneself or with a company of which one is a stockholder or an officer, to take an act disadvantageous to such company by the exercise of voting rights, transfer of stock, divulgence of secrets, or any other means whatsoever.

12. GUIDELINES FOR THE REGULATION OF UNFAIR TRADE PRACTICES WITH RESPECT TO PATENT AND KNOW-HOW LICENSING AGREEMENTS

February 15, 1989 — Executive Bureau, Fair Trade Commission * * *
Source: Translation adapted by Yanagida Nomura & Akai from translation announced by the Fair Trade Commission.

Preamble

1. The Fair Trade Commission, on May 24, 1968, announced Guidelines for International Technology Induction Agreements and relied on [such] Guidelines when it reviewed international contracts or agreements filed under Section 6(2) of the Antimonopoly Act.

* * *

3. The legal framework for protecting intellectual property rights such as patents has a procompetitive effect by stimulating research and development by entrepreneurs, and can serve to promote the development of new markets and new technology.

Moreover, technology transactions can have a procompetitive effect when, as a result thereof, new business entities can enter a market, when the number of competing entities increases, or when technology can be utilized more efficiently.

Therefore, transfer of technology should be promoted, and guidelines that clarify the standards for examination may help to promote such transfer of technology.

On the other hand, if certain types of restrictive conditions are imposed in technology licensing agreements, they may cause an anticompetitive effect.

* * *

Taking our enforcement experience into consideration, these guidelines seek to identify as fully as possible the following three types of restrictions contained in patent and know-how licensing agreements, which constitute a substantial portion of all technology licensing agreements:

(a) Restrictions which are considered, in principle, not to constitute unfair trade practices.
(b) Restrictions which may constitute unfair trade practices.
(c) Restrictions which are highly likely to constitute unfair trade practices.

* * *

As to restrictions [in category (b)], the determination [of whether a given restriction constitutes an unfair trade practice] will be made after examining as a whole the position of licensor and licensee in the relevant market, the conditions of the relevant market, the duration of the restrictions imposed, etc., in addition to the matters set forth [in these guidelines].

[As to restrictions in category (c)], such restrictions are considered to constitute unfair trade practices unless specific justifying reasons can be presented.

* * *

Part 1. Patent Licensing Agreements

1. *Restrictions that are considered, in principle, not to constitute unfair trade practices*
Among restrictions contained in licensing agreements on patent or utility model rights * * * that are considered, in principle, not to constitute unfair trade practices * * *, since they are thought to be within a proper exercise of patent rights or utility model rights, or to have only a negligible effect on competition, the following are noteworthy * * *:
(1) Separately granting a license to manufacture, use, sell, etc.
(2) Granting a license for a limited period within the life of patent rights.
(3) Granting a license for a limited area within the whole area covered by patent rights.

(4) Restricting exploitation of patent rights to a specified field of technology.
(5) Requiring minimum production or minimum sales volume of patented goods, or minimum use of patented processes. * * *

2. *Restrictions that may constitute unfair trade practices*
Among restrictions that may constitute unfair trade practices in patent licensing agreements, the following are noteworthy. The determination whether restrictions constitute unfair trade practices will be made after considering the positions of the licensor and the licensee in the relevant market, the conditions of the relevant market, the duration of restrictions imposed, etc. * * *
(1) Making it obligatory for the licensee not to handle substitutable goods * * *, or not to employ substitutable technology * * * during the term of the licensing agreement. * * *
(2) Making it obligatory for the licensee to sell patented goods through the licensor or a person designated by the licensor, or not to sell to a person designated by the licensor. * * *
(3) Making it obligatory for the licensee to inform the licensor of knowledge or experience newly obtained by the licensee regarding the licensed patent, or to grant the licensor a non-exclusive license with respect to an improved or applied invention, etc., developed by the licensee. However, excluded are cases where the licensor bears similar obligations and the obligations of each party with respect to informing the other party or granting a non-exclusive license are roughly balanced in substance. * * *
(4) Making it obligatory for the licensee to use a trademark, etc., designated by the licensor for the patented goods. * * *
(5) Restricting the quality of the patented goods, raw materials, components, etc. However, an obligation for the licensee to maintain certain standards of quality for patented goods, raw materials, components, etc., is excluded where such obligation is confined to the extent necessary for guaranteeing the effectiveness of the licensed patent, or for maintaining the goodwill of a trademark, etc. * * *
(6) Making it obligatory for the licensee to procure raw materials, components, etc., from the licensor or a person designated by the licensor. However, excluded are cases where restrictions on the quality of raw materials, components, etc., * * * are essential to maintaining the effectiveness of the licensed patent or for maintaining the goodwill of trademark, etc., and such obligation is confined to the extent necessary for guaranteeing the effectiveness of the licensed patent or for maintaining the goodwill of a trademark, etc. * * *
(7) Restricting the ability of the licensee to export patented goods. However, excluded are cases where the restricted area falls within one of the following:
(a) The licensor has registered his or her patent rights on patented goods in the area.
(b) The licensor has been continuously marketing the patented goods in the area.
(c) The licensor has assigned the area as an exclusive sales territory to a third party. * * *

* * *

(10) Making it obligatory for the licensee to accept licensing of more than two patents as a package. However, excluded are cases where such restriction is confined to the extent necessary for guaranteeing the effectiveness of the licensed patent. * * *
(11) Imposing unilaterally disadvantageous conditions on the licensee regarding the termination of the licensing agreement, such as the right of the licensor to terminate the licensing agreement unilaterally or without giving appropriate notice. * * *

3. *Restrictions that are highly likely to constitute unfair trade practices*
Among restrictions in patent licensing agreements that are considered to constitute unfair trade practices unless specific justifiable reasons can be presented, the following are noteworthy.

(1) Restricting resale prices of the patented goods in Japan. * * *
(2) Restricting the sales prices of the patented goods by the licensee in Japan.

The latter restriction, by restricting the licensee's freedom of pricing, will lead to a significant limitation of the competitive ability of the licensee and could result in the reduction of price competition in the market for the patented goods. * * *

(3) Making it obligatory for the licensee not to handle competing goods or not to employ competing technology after the expiration or termination of the licensing agreement. * * *

(4) Restricting use of the licensed technology in spite of the expiration of the patent rights or making it obligatory for the licensee to pay royalties for use after the expiration of the patent rights. * * *

(5) Restricting the licensee, either acting by itself or jointly with a third party, in its conducting of research and development activities regarding the licensed patent or competing technology.

Under this restriction, the licensor restricts the licensee's freedom to conduct research and development activities, which are an important means of competition; this restriction also limits the future business activities of the licensee in a product or technology market, and thus could have an important and long term impact on these markets. * * *

(6) Making it obligatory for the licensee to assign the licensor the right to improved or applied inventions, etc., developed by the licensee, or to grant the licensor an exclusive license * * * with respect to improved or applied inventions, etc., developed by the licensee.

This restriction could result in underenhancement of competition or maintenance of the licensor's dominant position in a relevant market. It could further impede the licensee's incentives for research and development, and thus could impede the development of new technology by restricting the licensee's freedom to use knowledge, experience and improvements or to grant a license to a third party. * * *

When the licensor does not bear similar obligations or the obligations of both parties are not well balanced in substance, this restriction could result in setting transaction terms in a manner unduly disadvantageous to the licensee.

Part 2. Know-How Licensing Agreements

[Generally similar rules apply, including the following:]

2. *Restrictions that may constitute unfair trade practices*

Among restrictions that may constitute unfair trade practices in know-how licensing agreements, the following are noteworthy. * * *

(1) Making it obligatory for the licensee not to handle competing goods or not to employ competing technology during the term of the licensing agreement. * * *

* * *

(3) Making it obligatory for the licensee to inform the licensor of knowledge or experience newly obtained by the licensee regarding the licensed know-how or to grant the licensor a non-exclusive license with respect to an improved or applied invention, etc. * * *. However, excluded are cases where the licensor bears similar obligations and the obligations of each party with respect to informing the other party or granting a non-exclusive license are roughly balanced in substance. * * *

* * *

3. *Restrictions that are highly likely to constitute unfair trade practices*
Among restrictions in know-how licensing agreements that are considered to constitute unfair trade practice unless specific justifiable reasons can be presented, the following are noteworthy. * * *

* * *

(3) Making it obligatory for the licensee not to handle competing goods or not to employ competing technology after the expiration or termination of the licensing agreement. * * *

(4) Restricting the use of the licensed know-how even though it has become publicly known due to reasons for which the licensee is not responsible, or making it obligatory for the licensee to pay royalties for use after the licensed know-how has become publicly known.

* * *

13. FOREIGN EXCHANGE AND FOREIGN TRADE CONTROL ACT

Law No. 228, December 1, 1949, as amended

Source: *Japan Laws, Ordinances and other Regulations concerning Foreign Exchange and Foreign Trade* (Chūo Shuppan Kikaku, 1990). Reprinted by permission.
[Updated by Daniel H. Foote to incorporate amendments through 1992.]

Chapter I
General Provisions

Section 1. (Objective)

The objective of this Act shall be, on the basis of the freedom of foreign exchange, foreign trade, and other external transactions, with necessary but minimum control or adjustment, to enable proper expansion of Japan's external transactions, and thereby to facilitate the equilibrium of Japan's balance of international payments and the stability of the Japanese currency, as well as to contribute towards the sound development of Japan's national economy.

Sections 2 to 4. Deleted.

Section 5. (Scope of application)

This Act shall also be applicable to any act performed outside Japan by any representative, agent, employee, or other operator of any juridical person having its main office in Japan in regard to the property or business of such a juridical person. It shall similarly be applicable to any act performed outside Japan by any natural person having his or her place of domicile in Japan, or his or her agent, employee, or other operator in regard to the property or business of such a natural person.

Section 6. (Definitions)

1. For the uniformity of the application of this Act or any Order promulgated thereunder, each of the following terms shall have the definition given to it below:
   (i)-(iv) [Definitions omitted for: Japan, foreign countries, the Japanese currency, foreign currencies.]
   (v) A "resident" shall mean any natural person having his or her place of domicile or residence in Japan, or any juridical person having its main office in Japan. Any branch, agency, or other office in Japan of a non-resident, irrespective of whether it is legally authorized to represent its principal or not, shall be deemed to be a resident, even when its main office is in a foreign country;
   (vi) A "non-resident" shall mean any natural or juridical person other than a resident;
   (vii)-(xvi) [Definitions omitted for: means of payment, foreign means of payment, precious metals, securities, foreign securities, claimable rights, futures contract on financial indicators, etc., goods, properties.]

* * *

Section 9. (Suspension of transactions in case of emergency)

1. When a drastic change emerges in the international economic situation, and the competent Minister deems it urgently necessary, he or she may suspend any transaction governed by this Act, as provided for by Cabinet Order, within a period designated by the Cabinet Order.
2. A suspension under the provisions of the preceding subsection shall make no payments impossible which are authorized up till such suspension, and the delay of payment caused by such suspension shall be limited to the period designated by the Cabinet Order.

Chapter II
Authorized Foreign Exchange Banks and Money Exchangers

[This Chapter requires any bank that intends to engage in foreign exchange business to obtain a license from the Ministry of Finance [MOF] to be an Authorized Foreign Exchange Bank ("AFEB") (§10(1)). If the MOF deems it necessary for the prevention of drastic exchange rate fluctuation of the Japanese currency, or for the maintenance of Japan's AFEBs' international credence, it may impose restrictions on foreign exchange transactions (§11-2). AFEBs have the duty to insure that customers transacting business through them are doing so in accordance with the Act (§12). AFEBs that attempt to or actually violate the Act may have their AFEB licenses suspended for one year (§13). Sections 14 and 15 concern money exchange businesses.]

Chapter III
Payments and Receipt of Payments

Section 16. (Payments and receipt of payments)

1. When the competent Minister deems it specifically necessary for the maintenance of the equilibrium of Japan's balance of international payments, or when he or she deems it necessary for the effective enforcement of the provisions of this Act or any Order promulgated thereunder, he or she may obligate * * * any resident or non-resident who is to make a payment from Japan to abroad, or any resident who is to make a payment to, or receive a payment from, a non-resident (referred to as "payment, etc." in the present and subsequent sections), to obtain a license therefor * * * .

* * *

Section 17. (Methods of payments for external transactions)

Any resident who is to make a payment, etc., for the settlement of any claim or debt in regard to any transaction or act between a resident and non-resident through any one of those special ways designated by a Cabinet Order, such as credit or debit to an account and others, shall obtain a license therefor from the competent Minister as provided for by Cabinet Order.

Section 18. (Export and import of means of payment, etc.)

1. When the Minister of Finance deems it necessary for the effective enforcement of the provisions of this Act or any Order promulgated hereunder, he or she may obligate, as provided for by Cabinet Order, any resident or non-resident who is to export or import any means of payment or securities, to obtain a license therefor.
2. [Setting forth similar authority for MOF to require licenses for import or export of precious metals.]

Section 19. (Waiver, etc. of claimable rights)

When the competent Minister deems it specifically necessary for the maintenance of the equilibrium of Japan's balance of international payments, he or she may obligate, as provided for by Cabinet Order, any resident obligee to a non-resident obligor to obtain a license for the waiver or abandonment of his or her right in whole or part.

Chapter IV
Capital Transactions, etc.

Section 20. (Capital transactions)

A "capital transaction" shall mean any one of the below-mentioned transactions or acts (except for the acts corresponding to direct domestic investments, etc., as defined by Section 26(2) performed by any one of those mentioned in each item of Section 26(1)):

(i) A transaction concerned with the creation, alteration or extinction of a claimable right based on a deposit contract or a trust contract concluded between a resident and a non-resident * * * (hereinafter referred to as "a transaction concerned with creation, etc., of a claimable right" in this section, Section 22 and Section 23);
(ii) A transaction concerned with creation, etc., of a claimable right under a money lending or borrowing contract or a guarantee contract for an obligation, concluded [in either case] between a resident and a non-resident;
(iii) A transaction concerned with creation, etc., of a claimable right under a sales and purchase contract between a resident and non-resident of a foreign means of payment or a claimable right;
(iv) A transaction concerned with creation, etc., of a claimable right payable in a foreign currency, under a deposit contract, trust contract, money lending and borrowing contract, guarantee contract for an obligation, or sales and purchase contract of a foreign means of payment, claimable right, and others, between a resident and another resident;
(v) Acquisition of foreign securities by a resident from a non-resident * * * or acquisition of securities by a non-resident from a resident * * *;
(vi) Issuance or offer for subscription abroad of securities, or issuance or offer for subscription in Japan of foreign securities by a resident, or issuance or offer for subscription of securities in Japan by a non-resident;
(vii) Issuance or offer for subscription in a foreign country of securities denominated or payable in the Japanese currency by a non-resident;
(viii) A transaction concerned with creation, etc., of a claimable right under a futures contract on financial indicators, etc., between a resident and a non-resident;
(ix) A transaction concerned with creation, etc., of a claimable right, payment for which can be received in a foreign currency under a futures contract on financial indicators, etc., between a resident and another resident, or a transaction concerned with creation, etc. of a claimable right, payment for which can be received in the Japanese currency under a futures contract on financial indicators, etc. [certain limitations omitted];
(x) Acquisition of immovables or rights related thereto existing in a foreign country by a resident, or acquisition of the same existing in Japan by a non-resident;
(xi) Besides those mentioned in Items (i) and (ii), transfer of funds between offices in Japan and in a foreign country of one and the same juridical person (except for those designated by a Cabinet Order as being the transfer of funds for the current expenses necessary for the operations of such offices and for the current transactions thereof); or
(xii) Any other transaction or act designated by a Cabinet Order as being similar to any one of those mentioned in each of the preceding items.

Section 21. (Capital transactions requiring license from the Minister of Finance)

1. Unless a Cabinet Order otherwise provides, when any resident or non-resident is to become a party to a capital transaction referred to in either item below, the resident or the non-resident, as specified in the respective item, shall obtain a license therefor from the Minister of Finance, as provided for by Cabinet Order:
   (i) Any capital transaction falling within the purview of Items (i), (iii), (iv), (viii) or (ix) of the preceding section * * *, other than those performed by an authorized foreign exchange bank in the course of its business operations and those in which an authorized foreign exchange bank in Japan acts, in the course of its business, as an intermediary, broker or agent * * * — by the resident.
   (ii) Any capital transaction falling within the purview of Item (vii) of the preceding section — by the non-resident.

2. In cases limited to those in which the Minister of Finance deems that if any capital transaction, other than those for which a license is required under the provisions of the preceding subsection * * *, were allowed without any restriction it might result in any one of the below-mentioned consequences and render it difficult to achieve the objectives of this Act, he or she may obligate any resident or non-resident who is to carry out such a capital transaction to obtain a license therefor:
   (i) It might make the maintenance of the equilibrium of Japan's balance of international payments difficult;
   (ii) It might result in a drastic fluctuation of the Japanese currency's foreign exchange rates; or
   (iii) It might result in transfers of funds between Japan and foreign countries in a large volume, and thereby adversely affect Japanese money or capital markets.

* * *

Section 22. (Notice, etc., of capital transactions)

1. Unless a Cabinet Order otherwise provides, when any resident or non-resident is to become a party to a capital transaction referred to in any item below ([certain exclusions omitted]), the resident or non-resident, as specified in the respective item, shall give prior notice, as provided for by Cabinet Order, to the Minister of Finance [exceptions whereby notice is effectively accomplished by other means omitted]:
   (i) Among the capital transactions mentioned in Section 20, Item (ii), those transactions concerned with creation, etc., of a claimable right under a money lending and borrowing contract (except those falling under Item (iv)), or those transactions concerned with creation, etc., of a claimable right under a guarantee contract covering liabilities of those juridical persons established under foreign legislation as designated by a Cabinet Order (referred to as "foreign corporation" in this item) arising out of that foreign corporation's issuance or offer for subscription of securities in a foreign country — by the resident;
   (ii) Among the capital transactions mentioned in Section 20, Item (v), acquisition of any foreign securities by a resident from a non-resident (except those falling under Item (iv)) — by the resident;
   (iii) Among the capital transactions mentioned in Section 20, Item (v), acquisition of any securities by a non-resident from a resident — by the non-resident;
   (iv) Among the capital transactions mentioned in Section 20, Items (ii), (v), and (xi), those concerning a direct foreign investment by a resident — by the resident;
   (v) Among the capital transactions mentioned in Section 20, Item (vi), issuance or offer for subscription of any securities in a foreign country, or issuance or offer for subscription of any foreign securities in Japan, by a resident — by the resident;
   (vi) Among the capital transactions mentioned in Section 20, Item (vi), issuance or offer for subscription of any securities in Japan by a non-resident — by the non-resident;
   (vii) The capital transactions mentioned in Section 20, Item (viii) (but excluding those relating to a futures contract on financial indicators, etc., relating to currency-related financial indicators) — by the resident;
   (viii) Among the capital transactions mentioned in Section 20, Item (x), acquisition of any immovables or rights related thereto existing in Japan by a non-resident — by the non-resident.

* * *

Section 23. (Screening of the conditions for capital transactions, and recommendation for alteration thereof, etc.)

1. Any resident or non-resident who has given a notice under the provisions of Subsection 1 of the preceding section, concerning the capital transactions mentioned in[, with exceptions omitted, Items (i), (iv)-(vi), and (viii),] shall not execute the said capital transaction until a period of twenty days has elapsed, counting from the day of receipt of the notice by

the Minister of Finance. Provided, That the Minister of Finance may shorten this period when he or she deems that there is no particular harm, judging from the particulars, etc., of the capital transaction under notice.

2. In cases limited to those in which the Minister of Finance deems that if any capital transaction covered by the notice referred to in the preceding subsection were executed it might result in any one of the below-mentioned consequences and render it difficult to achieve the objectives of this Act, he or she may recommend, as provided for by Cabinet Order, the person who gave the notice either to alter the particulars of that capital transaction or to suspend the execution thereof, provided that such recommendation is given within a period of twenty days, counting from the day of his or her receipt of the notice:
   (i) It might adversely affect the international money market or derogate from the international reputation of Japan;
   (ii) It might adversely affect Japanese money or capital markets;
   (iii) It might adversely affect the business activities of a certain sector of Japanese industry or the smooth performance of the Japanese national economy; or
   (iv) It might disturb the faithful performance of treaties or other international agreements concluded by Japan, or imperil the international peace and security, or disturb the maintenance of public order.
3. The person who is given a recommendation under the provisions of the preceding subsection shall not, irrespective of the provisions of Subsection 1, execute the capital transaction covered by the notice referred to in the same subsection until a period of twenty days has elapsed, counting from the day of his or her receipt of the recommendation.
4. The person who is given a recommendation under the provisions of Subsection 2 shall inform the Minister of Finance whether he or she accedes to it or not within a period of ten days, counting from the day of his or her receipt of the recommendation.

* * *

7. When the person who has been given a recommendation under the provisions of Subsection 2 either fails to inform or informs of his or her non-accession thereto, under the provisions of Subsection 4, the Minister of Finance may direct him or her to alter the conditions of the relevant capital transaction or to suspend the execution thereof, provided that such a directive is served within a period of twenty days, counting from the day of his or her giving the recommendation under the provisions of Subsection 2.

* * *

Section 24. (Capital transactions, etc., requiring license from the Minister of International Trade and Industry)

1. In cases limited to those in which the Minister of International Trade and Industry deems that, among the capital transactions referred to in Section 20, Item (ii), * * * if any transaction or act of an exporter or importer of goods which is designated by a Cabinet Order as being directly related to export or import, or any transaction or act designated by a Cabinet Order as being that for transfer of a mining right, industrial property right, or other similar right, or for creation of a right to use such rights, were allowed without any restriction it might result in one of the consequences referred to in any item of Section 21(2) and render it difficult to achieve the objectives of this Act, he or she may obligate, as provided for by Cabinet Order, any resident who is to carry out such a capital transaction to obtain a license therefor.

2.-6. [Further details concerning MITI licenses omitted.]

Section 25. (Service transactions, etc.)

1. Any resident who is to make any transaction falling under the following items with a nonresident shall obtain a license therefor from the Minister of International Trade and Industry, as provided for by Cabinet Order:

(i) Transactions of which the objective is to offer technology concerned with design, manufacture, or utilization of specific kinds of goods designated by Cabinet Order as those considered to be obstructive to the maintenance of international peace and security (hereinafter referred to as "specific technology") in a specified area;

(ii) Transactions concerning sales and purchase of goods involving movement of goods between foreign countries designated by Cabinet Order as those considered to be obstructive to the maintenance of international peace and security.

2. [Omitted.]

3. Any resident who is to make any transaction designated by a Cabinet Order as falling under any one of the following items * * * with a non-resident shall obtain a license therefor from the competent Minister, as provided for by Cabinet Order:

(i) Service transactions (meaning transactions of which the objective is to render labor or service; the same shall apply to the next item) for processing of mineral products, transfer of mining rights, or similar matters; or

(ii) Service transactions, or transactions concerning sales and purchase involving movement of goods between foreign countries, which are considered to be obstructive to the faithful performance of treaties or other international agreements concluded by Japan.

Section 25-2. (Sanctions)

[MITI may prohibit violators of Section 25 from carrying out related transactions with non-residents for one to three years, depending on the provision violated.]

Chapter V
Direct Domestic Investments, etc.

Section 26. (Notice, etc., of direct domestic investments, etc.)

1. A "foreign investor" shall mean any one of those mentioned below, which performs any one of the direct domestic investments, etc., mentioned in each item of the next subsection:

(i) A natural person who is a non-resident;

(ii) A juridical person or other organization established under foreign legislation, or a juridical person or other organization having its main office in a foreign country;

(iii) A company of which the number of stock or the amount of capital subscription directly owned by one or more of those mentioned in Item (i) and/or the preceding item, and/or the number of stock or the amount of capital subscription designated by a Cabinet Order as being indirectly owned by the above-mentioned through another company or other companies, equal(s) or exceed(s) in the aggregate one-half of that company's total stock issue or total subscribed capital; or

(iv) Other than those mentioned in the preceding two items, a juridical person or other organization of which a majority of the board members (which means directors and other similar posts; the same shall apply below in this item) or board members having representative authority is occupied by persons mentioned in Item (i).

2. A "direct domestic investment, etc." shall mean an act which falls under any item below:

(i) Acquisition of any company's stock or share(s) ([exceptions omitted]);

(ii) Transfer of stock or share(s) of any company other than listed companies, etc., which was/were acquired by the transferor prior to his or her acquisition of non-resident status and has/have been continuously held by him or her up till the time of the transfer (limited to such transfer as made by a non-resident natural person to any one referred to in an item of the preceding subsection);

(iii) Acquisition of stock of any listed company, etc. ([where such acquisition, itself or combined with previous acquisitions, leads the acquiror to have a shareholding ratio that] equals or exceeds a ratio provided by Cabinet Order, which shall not be less than 10 percent);

(iv) Consent given to a substantial alteration of the objective of a company's business (limited to such consent as given by one or more stockholder(s) or shareholder(s) who own(s) in total one-third or more of that company's total stock issue or total subscribed capital);

(v) Establishment of a branch, etc., in Japan, or substantial alteration of the type or the business objective of a branch, etc., existing in Japan (limited to such establishment and alteration, as designated by a Cabinet Order, which is to be made by any one of those mentioned in Item (i) or (ii) of the preceding subsection);

(vi) Money lending to a juridical person having its main office in Japan, in excess of an amount determined by a Cabinet Order [exceptions omitted], for which the term exceeds one year; or

(vii) Any other act designated by a Cabinet Order as being similar to any one of those mentioned in any of the preceding items.

3. A foreign investor who has made a direct domestic investment, etc., referred to in an item in the preceding subsection [exceptions omitted] shall, as provided for by Cabinet Order, make a report to the Minister of Finance and to the Minister(s) in charge of the industry involved. Provided, That this shall not apply to a direct domestic investment, etc., for which notice must be given pursuant to the provisions of Subsection 1 of the next section.

Section 27. (Screening of the conditions of direct domestic investments, etc., and recommendation for alteration thereof, etc.)

1. A foreign investor who is to make a direct domestic investment, etc., as referred to in an item of Subsection 2 of the preceding section, which might constitute a direct domestic investment, etc., as designated by Cabinet Order, as to which the necessity exists for review under Subsection 3 below, shall provide notice in advance to the Minister of Finance and the Minister(s) in charge of the industry involved of the business purpose, amount, date of performance, and other particulars as specified by Cabinet Order for the direct domestic investment, etc.

2. A foreign investor who has given notice of a direct domestic investment, etc., under the provisions of the preceding subsection, shall not make the direct domestic investment, etc., in question until thirty days have elapsed, counting from the day on which the Minister of Finance and the Minister(s) in charge of the industry involved received said notice. Provided, That when the Minister of Finance and the Minister(s) in charge of the industry involved deem that there is no need for review under the provisions of the next subsection, judging from the business purpose and other particulars of the direct domestic investment, etc., in question, they may shorten said period.

3. When there has been notice under the provisions of Subsection 1, the Minister of Finance and the Minister(s) in charge of the industry involved may, when they deem that the need exists for a review to determine whether or not the direct domestic investment, etc., in question falls under any of the items below (referred to in this subsection, Subsection 5, and Subsection 11, as "a direct domestic investment, etc., related to national security, etc."), they may extend the period during which the execution of that direct domestic investment, etc., is prohibited to up to four months, counting from the day of their receipt of the notice:

(i) Direct domestic investment, etc., which might lead to the consequences in either (a) or (b) * * *:

(a) It might imperil the national security, disturb the maintenance of public order, or hamper the protection of the safety of the general public;

(b) It might adversely and seriously affect the smooth performance of Japan's national economy;

(ii) Because the direct domestic investment, etc., in question is made by a foreign investor with whose country no treaties or other international agreements are concluded by Japan in regard to direct domestic investment, etc., its particulars are required to be altered, or its execution is required to be suspended, so as to make conditions substantially equal to those allowed to Japan's direct investment activities (which mean those tantamount to direct domestic investment, etc., referred to in the items of Subsection 2 of the preceding section) in that country;

(iii) Judging from the use of funds and other particulars, the direct domestic investment, etc., in question constitutes, in whole or in part, a capital transaction as to which an obligation to obtain a license is imposed under the provisions of Section 21(2), and therefore its particulars are required to be altered, or its execution is required to be suspended.

4. When the Minister of Finance and the Minister(s) in charge of the industry involved have extended the period in which the direct domestic investment, etc., is not to be made pursuant to the provisions of the preceding subsection, and, as a result of the review conducted under the provisions of that subsection, deem that the said direct domestic investment, etc., is not related to national security, etc., they may shorten the extended period.
5. When the Minister of Finance and the Minister(s) in charge of the industry involved have extended the period in which the direct domestic investment, etc., is not to be made pursuant to the provisions of Subsection 3, and, as a result of the review conducted under the provisions of that subsection, deem that the said direct domestic investment, etc., is related to national security, etc., they may obtain the views of the * * * advisory council and may recommend the party * * *, either to alter the particulars of that direct domestic investment, etc., or to suspend the execution thereof. Provided, That the period within which said recommendation is to be given is that set forth in Subsection 3 or as extended under the next subsection * * *
6. [Omitted.]
7. The party who is given a recommendation under the provisions of Subsection 5 shall inform the Minister of Finance and the Minister(s) in charge of the industry involved whether it accedes to the recommendation or not within a period of ten days, counting from the day of its receipt of the recommendation.
8. A party which has informed of its accession to the recommendation under the provisions of the preceding subsection shall execute the said direct domestic investment, etc., in accordance with the recommendation.
9. A party which has informed of its accession to the recommendation under the provisions of Subsection 7 may make the direct domestic investment, etc., in question even if four months have not elapsed from the date of notice of said investment * * *, without regard to the provisions of Subsections 3 and 6.
10. When the party which has been given a recommendation under the provisions of Subsection 5 either fails to inform or informs of its non-accession thereto under the provisions of Subsection 7, the Minister of Finance and the Minister(s) in charge of the industry involved may direct it to alter the particulars of the relevant direct domestic investment, etc., or to suspend the execution thereof. Provided, That the period within which such a directive is to be served is that provided in Subsection 3 or the extended period provided in Subsection 6 * * *.
11. When, based on changed economic circumstances or other reasons, the Minister of Finance and the Minister(s) in charge of the industry involved deem that a direct domestic investment, etc., * * * has ceased to be related to national security, etc., they may cancel in whole or in part a recommendation as to alteration of the particulars of the investment that has been acceded to under Subsection 7 or an order for an alteration of the particulars of the investment under the preceding subsection.

* * *

Section 27-2. (Deemed foreign investor)

For an investment which is equivalent to a direct domestic investment, etc., undertaken by a person other than a foreign investor (including juridical persons and other associations) on behalf of a foreign investor without using the name of said foreign investor, said person other than a foreign investor shall be deemed to be a foreign investor, and the provisions of the preceding two sections shall apply.

Section 28. (Transfer of preemptive rights)

1. Any one of those mentioned in Section 26(1)(i) or (ii) which is a stockholder of a company and acquired a preemptive right accruing from its stockholding may transfer such a right to another party.
2. Unless option warrants are issued, one cannot contest the transfer referred to in the preceding subsection against the company or other third party without the company's written consent thereto.

Section 29. (Report on conclusion, etc., of technology induction agreements)

When an agreement between a resident and a non-resident (including a branch, etc., within Japan of a non-resident; the same applies hereinafter in this and the next section) for the transfer of said non-resident's industrial property rights or other rights concerning technology, or for establishment of a right to the use of the same, or for rendering technical guidance in managerial know-how, has been executed or renewed or the terms thereof have been amended (hereinafter referred to as "conclusion, etc., of technology induction agreement"), a report on said agreement shall be made to the Minister of Finance and the Minister(s) in charge of the industry involved, as provided for by Cabinet Order. Provided, That this shall not apply to the conclusion, etc., of technology induction agreements as to which [prior] notice must be made under the provisions of subsection 1 of the next section.

Section 30. (Notice and recommendation of alteration, etc., of conclusion, etc., of technology induction agreements)

1. When a resident is to conclude, etc., a technology induction agreement with a non-resident which might constitute the conclusion, etc., of a technology induction agreement, as designated by Cabinet Order, as to which the necessity exists for review under Subsection 3 below, said resident shall as provided for by Cabinet Order, provide notice in advance to the Minister of Finance and the Minister(s) in charge of the industry involved of the terms of said agreement and other particulars as specified by Cabinet Order.
2. A resident who has given notice of the conclusion, etc., of a technology induction agreement under the provisions of the preceding subsection shall not conclude, etc., the technology induction agreement in question until thirty days have elapsed, counting from the day on which the Minister of Finance and the Minister(s) in charge of the industry involved received said notice. Provided, That when the Minister of Finance and the Minister(s) in charge of the industry involved deem that there is no need for review under the provisions of the next subsection, judging from the type of technology and other particulars of the conclusion, etc., of technology induction agreement in question, they may shorten said period.
3. When there has been notice under the provisions of Subsection 1, the Minister of Finance and the Minister(s) in charge of the industry involved may, when they deem that the need exists for a review to determine whether or not the conclusion, etc., of technology induction agreement in question might lead to the consequences in either item below (* * *; hereafter in this subsection and in Subsection 5 referred to as "conclusion, etc., of technology induction agreement related to national security, etc."), they may extend the period during which the execution of that conclusion, etc., of technology induction agreement is prohibited to up to four months, counting from the day of their receipt of the notice:
   (i) It might imperil the national security, disturb the maintenance of public order, or hamper the protection of the safety of the general public;
   (ii) It might adversely and seriously affect the smooth performance of Japan's national economy.

4. When the Minister of Finance and the Minister(s) in charge of the industry involved have extended the period in which the conclusion, etc., of technology induction agreement is not to be made pursuant to the provisions of the preceding subsection, and, as a result of the review conducted under the provisions of that subsection, deem that the said conclusion, etc., of technology induction agreement is not related to national security, etc., they may shorten the extended period.
5. When the Minister of Finance and the Minister(s) in charge of the industry involved have extended the period in which the direct domestic investment, etc., is not to be made pursuant to the provisions of the Subsection 3, and, as a result of the review conducted under the provisions of that subsection, deem that the said conclusion, etc., of technology induction agreement is related to national security, etc., they may obtain the views of the * * * advisory council and may recommend the party who has filed notice * * * either to alter the terms of that conclusion, etc., of technology induction agreement in whole or in part or to suspend the execution thereof. Provided, That the period within which said recommendation is to be given is that set forth in Subsection 3 or as extended under the next subsection * * *.
6. [Omitted.]
7. The provisions of Subsections 7 through 12 of Section 27 shall apply *mutatis mutandis* to recommendations under Subsection 5 of this section. * * *

Section 31. (Exclusions from application)

The provisions of the preceding two sections shall not apply to the conclusion, etc., of technology induction agreement for technology developed independently by a branch, etc., within Japan of a non-resident and for such other conclusions, etc., of technology induction agreement as specified by Cabinet Order.

[Sections 32 through 46 deleted.]

Chapter VI
Foreign Trade

Section 47. (Principle for exports)

Export of goods shall be permitted with a minimum of restrictions, insofar as is consistent with the objectives of this Act.

Section 48. (License for export, etc.)

1. A person who is to export specified kinds of goods to specified destinations designated by Cabinet Order as those considered to be obstructive to the maintenance of international peace and security shall obtain a license from the Minister of International Trade and Industry, as provided for by Cabinet Order.
2. When the Minister of International Trade and Industry deems it necessary for the effective enforcement of the provisions of the preceding subsection, he or she may obligate, as provided for by Cabinet Order, any person who is to export specified kinds of goods as referred to in the same subsection to a destination other than the specified destinations referred to in the same subsection to obtain a license therefor.
3. In addition to those cases provided for in the preceding two subsections, the Minister of International Trade and Industry may obligate, as provided for by Cabinet Order, any person who is to export specified kinds of goods or goods to a specified destination, or who is to export goods under specified ways of transaction or settlements, to obtain approval, within the limits necessary for the maintenance of the balanced balance of payments and for the sound development of foreign trade and the national economy.

Section 51. (Embargo in case of emergency)

When the Minister of International Trade and Industry deems it urgently necessary, he or she may, as provided for by Order, place an embargo on the shipment of goods, for a period not exceeding one (1) month, specifying the type or the destination of the goods.

Section 52. (Approval for import)

For the purpose of sound development of foreign trade and the national economy, a person who is to import goods may be obligated, as provided for by Cabinet Order, to obtain approval therefor.

Section 53. (Sanctions)

1. The Minister of International Trade and Industry may prohibit any person who has exported goods as referred to in Section 48(1) without obtaining a license under the provisions of the same subsection from conducting exports or carrying out transactions with a non-resident for the provision of specified technology, for a period not exceeding three years.
2. The Minister of International Trade and Industry may prohibit any person (excluding those provided for in the preceding subsection) who has contravened this Act, any Order promulgated hereunder, or any disposition made hereunder in regard to exporting or importing goods, from carrying out export or import transactions for a period not exceeding one year.

Chapter VI-II
Advisory Council on Foreign Exchange and Other Transactions

[Omitted.]

Chapter VII
Demurral

Section 56. (Public hearing on demurral)

1. When a demurral is filed against or a request for reinvestigation is submitted to a competent Minister in regard to his or her disposition made under the provisions of this Act or any Order promulgated hereunder, the Minister shall grant such person the opportunity for a public hearing, by serving him or her with a notice a reasonable time in advance.

* * *

Section 57. (Precedence of demurral procedures over lawsuit)

No legal action may be commenced seeking the reversal of the disposition referred to in Subsection 1 of the preceding section, until a ruling on the demurral or a decision on the request for reinvestigation concerning that disposition has been made.

[Sections 58 through 64 deleted.]

Chapter VIII
Miscellaneous Provisions

Section 65. (Authority of Fair Trade Commission)

Nothing in the provisions of this Act shall be construed to repeal, modify or affect in any way the application of the "Act Concerning Prohibition of Private Monopoly and Maintenance of Fair Trade" (Law No. 54 of 1947), or the power exercised by the Fair Trade Commission under the said Act in whatever circumstances.

Section 68. (On-the-spot inspection)

1. The competent Minister can, within the limits necessary for the enforcement of this Act, have a competent government official enter the places of business, offices, or factories of any authorized foreign exchange bank, money exchanger, or other party which performs any of the transactions governed by this Act as a business, within their business hours, for inspection of books, records, or other matters, or for interrogation of the persons concerned.

2. [Omitted.]
3. The authority for an on-the-spot inspection or interrogation under the provisions of Subsection 1 shall not be construed as being conferred for the purpose of investigation of a criminal offense.

Section 69. (Partial delegation of administrative procedures)

1. The competent Minister may, as provided for by Cabinet Order, entrust the Bank of Japan and/or authorized foreign exchange banks with a part of the administrative procedures concerning the enforcement of this Act.

* * *

Chapter IX
Penal Provisions

Section 69-6

1. Any person who comes under any one of the following items shall be liable to penal servitude not exceeding five years, or a fine not exceeding two million yen, or both. Provided, That when five times the amount of the subject matter of contravention exceeds two million yen, a fine up to that five times amount shall be applicable:
   (i) A person who carried out any transaction designated by an order provided for by Section 25(1), without obtaining a license as required by the same subsection;
   (ii) A person who carried out any exportation of goods designated by an order provided for by Section 48(1), without obtaining a license as required by the same subsection.
2. An attempted crime of Item (ii) of the preceding subsection shall be liable to punishment.

Section 70.

Any person who comes under any one of the following items shall be liable to penal servitude not exceeding three years, or a fine not exceeding one million yen, or both. Provided, That when three times the amount of the subject matter of contravention exceeds one million yen, a fine up to that three times amount shall be applicable:
[List of thirty-seven items specifying requirements under Sections 7(4); 8; 9(1); 10(1); 13; 14(1); 16-19; 21(1) and (2); 22(1), 23(1), (3), (5) and (7); 24(1)-(4); 25(2) and (3); 25-2(1)-(3); 27(1)-(4), (6), (8) and (10); 27-2; 30(1)-(4), (6), and (7); 48(2) and (3); 51; 52; and 53(1) and (2) omitted.]

Section 71.

[Provision providing for penal servitude of up to one year and/or fine of up to five hundred thousand yen for operating a foreign exchange business without the license required under Section 10(3) omitted.]

Section 72.

Any person who comes under any one of the following items shall be liable to penal servitude not exceeding six months or a fine not exceeding two hundred thousand yen:
[List of twelve items specifying requirements under sections 10(4), 11, 12, 14(2), 15, 22(1), 24(2), 26(3), 27(2), 29, 49, 67 and 68(1) omitted.]

Section 73.

1. When a representative of a juridical person (including any organization so defined under Section 26(1)(ii) or (iv) or Section 27-2; the same shall apply hereinunder in this subsection), or an agent, employee, or other operator engaged by a juridical or natural person has committed any offense mentioned in Section 69-6 through the preceding section in regard to the business or property of such juridical or natural principal, the juridical or natural principal shall be liable to the fine specified in each section, in addition to the punishment of the offender himself.

2. In the case of punishment of any organization as defined by Section 26(1)(ii) or (iv) or Section 27-2, its representative or administrator shall represent such an organization for the purpose of legal proceedings, and the provisions of the laws respecting criminal procedure in cases where a juridical person is the defendant shall apply *mutatis mutandis.*

14. THE PATENT ACT

Law No. 121, April 13, 1959
Source: Translation by Yanagida Nomura & Akai.

CHAPTER I
General Provisions

Section 1. (Purpose)

This Act aims to encourage inventions by promoting the protection and utilization of inventions, and thereby to contribute to the development of industry.

Section 2. (Definitions)

1. The word "invention" as used in this Act shall mean a highly advanced creation of technical ideas utilizing a law of nature.
2. The word "patented invention" as used in this Act shall mean an invention for which a patent has been granted.
3. The word "working" of an invention as used in this Act shall mean any of the following acts:
   (i) In the case of an invention of a thing, acts of manufacturing, using, assigning, leasing, displaying for the purpose of assignment or lease, or importing the thing;
   (ii) In the case of an invention of a process, acts of utilizing the process;
   (iii) In the case of an invention of a process of manufacturing a thing, acts of using, assigning, leasing, displaying for the purpose of assignment or lease, or importing the thing manufactured by the process, in addition to the acts mentioned in the preceding paragraph.

Section 27. (Registration in patent register)

1. The following matters shall be registered in the Patent Register at the Patent Office:
   (i) The establishment, transfer, extinction or restriction on disposal or alteration of a patent right under Section 75(1);
   (ii) The establishment, maintenance, transfer, modification or restriction on disposal of an exclusive or non-exclusive license; and
   (iii) The establishment, transfer, modification, extinction or restriction on disposal of rights in a pledge on a patent right, an exclusive or a non-exclusive license.

* * *

CHAPTER II
Patents and Applications

Section 29. (Patentability requirements)

1. Any person who has made an invention that has industrial application may obtain a patent therefor, except in the case of the following inventions:
   (i) Inventions that were publicly known in Japan prior to the filing of the patent application;
   (ii) Inventions that were publicly worked in Japan prior to the filing of the patent application; or
   (iii) Inventions that were described in a publication distributed in Japan or any foreign country prior to the filing of the patent application.
2. If, prior to the filing of the patent application, an invention could easily have been made by a person with ordinary skill in the art to which the invention pertains on the basis of an invention referred to in any of the items of the preceding subsection, a patent shall not be granted for such invention, notwithstanding the preceding subsection.

Section 32. (Unpatentable inventions)

Notwithstanding Section 29, a patent shall not be granted for the following types of inventions:

(i) Inventions of substances to be manufactured by the process of transformation of the atom; or

(ii) Inventions that threaten the public order, good morals or public health.

Section 33. (Right to obtain a patent)

1. The right to obtain a patent may be transferred.
2. The right to obtain a patent may not be made the subject of a pledge.
3. In case the right to obtain a patent is jointly owned, no joint owner may transfer his or her share without having obtained the consent of the other joint owner(s).

Section 35. (Inventions of employees)

1. An employer, a juridical person or a national or local public entity ("employer") shall have a non-exclusive license on the subject patent where an employee, an executive officer of a legal entity or a national or local public official ("employee") has obtained a patent for an invention that by its nature falls within the scope of the business of the employer and acts resulting in the invention were part of the past or present duties of the employee performed on behalf of the employer ("employee's invention") or where a successor in title to the right to obtain a patent for an employee's invention has obtained a patent therefor.
2. In the case of an invention made by an employee that is not an employee's invention, any contractual provision, service regulation, or other stipulation that provides in advance that the right to obtain a patent or the patent itself shall pass to the employer or that the employee shall have an exclusive license on such invention shall be null and void.
3. The employee shall have the right to reasonable remuneration where he or she has enabled the right to obtain a patent or the patent for an employee's invention to pass to the employer or where he or she has given the employer an exclusive right to such invention in accordance with a contract, service regulations, or other stipulations.
4. The amount of remuneration to the employee shall be decided by reference to the profits that the employer will make from the invention and to the amount of contribution of the employer to the making of the invention.

Section 36. (Patent applications)

1. Any person desiring a patent shall submit a request to the Director General of the Patent Office stating the following: [name and address of applicant and inventor, date, and title of invention.]
2. The request shall be accompanied by the specifications and any necessary drawings and shall include the following:
   (i) The title of the invention;
   (ii) A brief explanation of the drawings;
   (iii) A detailed explanation of the invention; and
   (iv) The patent claim(s).
3. The detailed explanation of the invention under Item (iii) of the preceding subsection shall state the purpose, nature, and effect of the invention in such a manner that it may easily be carried out by a person having ordinary skill in the art to which the invention pertains.

* * *

Section 39. (First-to-file rule)

1. Where two or more patent applications relating to the same invention are filed on different dates, only the first applicant may obtain a patent for the invention.
2. Where two or more patent applications relating to the same invention are filed on the same date, only one such applicant, determined by agreement after mutual consultation among all the applicants, may obtain a patent for the invention. If no agreement is reached or no consultation is possible, none of the applicants may obtain a patent for the invention.

3. Where an invention claimed in a patent application is the same as a device claimed in a utility model application and the applications are filed on different dates, the patent applicant may obtain a patent only if the corresponding application was filed before the application for the utility model.
4. Where an invention claimed in a patent application is the same as a device claimed in a utility model application and the applications are filed on the same date, only one applicant, determined by agreement after mutual consultation between the applicants, may obtain the patent or the utility model registration. If no agreement is reached or no consultation is possible, the patent applicant shall not obtain a patent for the invention.
5. Where a patent application or a utility model application is withdrawn or invalidated, such application shall, for the purpose of the four preceding subsections, be deemed never to have been made.
6. A patent application or a utility model application filed by a person who is neither the inventor nor the creator nor the successor in title to the right to obtain a patent or utility model registration shall, for the purposes of Subsections 1 to 4, be deemed not to be a patent application or a utility model application.

* * *

Section 43. (Priority claim under the Paris Convention)

1. A person desiring to declare a priority claim for a patent application under D(1) of Section 4 of the Paris Convention shall, simultaneously with the patent application, submit to the Director General of the Patent Office a document setting forth a statement to that effect and specifying the country party to the Paris Convention in which the application was first filed, or considered under C(4) of said section to have been first filed, or recognized under A(2) of said section to have been first filed, as well as the filing date of such application.

* * *

Chapter III
Examination

Section 48-2. (Examination of applications)

The examination of a patent application shall be carried out when a request for examination of the application is made.

Section 51. (Publication of applications)

1. Where the examiner finds no reason for refusing a patent application, the examiner shall render a ruling that the application is to be published.
2. When a ruling that a patent application is to be published has been rendered, the Director General of the Patent Office shall publish the application after transmitting the ruling to the applicant.
3. The publication of the application shall be effected by publishing the following particulars in the Patent Gazette: [details omitted.]
4. During the two months following the publication of the application, the Director General of the Patent Office shall make the application files and their attachments available for public inspection in the Patent Office.

Section 52. (Effect of publication)

1. After the publication of the application, the applicant for a patent shall have an exclusive right commercially to work the invention claimed in the patent application.
2. Sections 100 to 106 shall apply *mutatis mutandis* to the right under the preceding subsection.
3. If a patent application has been abandoned, withdrawn, or invalidated after the publication of the application; if the examiner's decision or a trial hearing decision that the patent application is to be refused has become final and conclusive; if the patent right has been

deemed never to have existed pursuant to Section 112(6); or if, with the exception of cases coming within the proviso to Section 125, a court judgment that the patent is to be invalidated has become final and conclusive, the right under Subsection 1 shall be deemed never to have arisen.

4. If a person having the right under Subsection 1 has exercised that right and if the patent application has been abandoned, withdrawn, or invalidated or if the examiner's decision or a court judgment that the patent application is to be refused has become final and conclusive, such person shall be liable for indemnifying any damage caused to another party by the exercise of that right. The same shall apply where the right is exercised with respect to an invention that as a result of amendment or the declining of an amendment of the specifications or drawings attached to the patent application no longer falls within the scope of the patent claim(s) at the time of the registration of the establishment of the patent.

Section 55. (Opposition to granting of a patent)

1. Within three months from the publication of a patent application, any person may file with the Director General of the Patent Office an opposition to the granting of a patent * * *.
2. The opponent shall file a written opposition stating the grounds therefor, together with an indication of the supporting evidence.

Section 58. (Rulings on opposition)

1. After the expiration of the time limit for amending the written opposition * * *, the examiner shall render a ruling on the opposition.
2. The ruling shall be in writing and shall state the reasons therefor.

* * *

4. No appeal shall lie from a ruling under Subsection 1.

Section 65. (Relationship to litigation)

1. The examination procedure may, if necessary, be suspended until a court judgment has become final and conclusive or litigation proceedings have been concluded.
2. The court may, if necessary, suspend its proceedings until the examiner's decision has become final and conclusive.

Chapter III-II
Laying Open of Applications

Section 65-2. (Laying open of applications)

1. Eighteen months after the filing of an application for a patent, the Director General of the Patent Office shall lay the application open for public inspection, unless the application has already been published.
2. [Details concerning information to be published in Patent Gazette omitted.]

Section 65-3. (Effect of laying open)

1. After the laying open of the patent application, if the applicant has previously sent a written warning describing the contents of the invention claimed in the application, the applicant may demand of a person who has commercially worked the invention after receiving the warning but before publication of the application the payment of compensation in a sum equivalent to what the applicant would normally be entitled to receive for the working of the invention if it were patented. Even in the absence of the warning, the same shall apply to a person who has commercially worked the invention before the publication of the application, knowing that the invention was the one claimed in the patent application.

* * *

4. Sections 52(3) and (4), * * * [and] 101 * * * of this Act and Sections 719 and 724 [torts] of the Civil Code shall apply *mutatis mutandis* to the exercise of the right to demand compensation under Subsection 1. * * *

Chapter IV
Patent Right

Part 1. Patent Right

Section 66. (Registration of establishment of patent)
1. A patent right shall come into force upon registration of its establishment.

* * *

Section 67. (Term of patent)
1. The term of a patent right shall be 15 years from the date of publication of the patent application. Provided, That such term shall not exceed 20 years from the filing date of the patent application.
2. Where a patent application is deemed to have been filed at the time of submission of an amendment in accordance with Section 40, the 20 years in the preceding subsection shall be counted from the day following the filing of the original patent application.

Section 68. (Exclusive right)
The patentee shall have an exclusive right commercially to work the patented invention, except that where the patent is the subject of an exclusive license, the foregoing shall not apply to the extent that the licensee exclusively possesses the right to work the patented invention.

Section 70. (Scope of a patented invention)
1. The technical scope of a patented invention shall be determined on the basis of the statements of the patent claim(s) in the specifications attached to the request.

* * *

Section 72. (Relationship to another's patented invention)
Where a patented invention would utilize another person's patented invention, registered utility model, or registered design or design similar thereto under an application filed prior to the filing of the patent application concerned, or where the patent right conflicts with another person's design right under an application for registration of a design filed prior to the filing of the patent application concerned, none of the patentee or any exclusive or non-exclusive licensee shall commercially work the patented invention.

Section 77. (Exclusive licenses)
1. A patentee may grant an exclusive license on the patent right.
2. An exclusive licensee shall have the exclusive right commercially to work the patented invention, to the extent stipulated in the [license agreement].
3. An exclusive license may be transferred only together with the business in which it is worked, or only with the consent of the patentee, or in the case of inheritance or other general succession.
4. An exclusive licensee may establish a pledge or grant a non-exclusive license on the exclusive license only upon the consent of the patentee.

* * *

Section 78. (Non-exclusive licenses)
1. A patentee may grant non-exclusive license(s) on his or her patent right.
2. A non-exclusive licensee shall have the right commercially to work the patented invention in accordance with this Act or the [license agreement].

Section 79. (Non-exclusive license by virtue of prior use)
If, at the time of filing of a patent application, * * * a person who has made an invention by himself or herself without knowledge of the contents of an invention claimed in the patent application, or who has learned how to make the invention from such a person, has been commercially working the invention in Japan or has been making preparations for the same, such person shall have a non-exclusive license on the patent right under the patent

application, within the scope for which the invention is being worked or for which preparations for working were being made and within the business purpose of such working or preparations.

Section 83. (Decision on grant of non-exclusive license in case of non-working)

1. Where a patented invention has not been sufficiently and continuously worked during a period of three years or more in Japan, a person who intends to work the patented invention may request the patentee or the exclusive licensee to hold consultations on the grant of a non-exclusive license thereon. * *
2. If no agreement is reached or no consultation is possible under the preceding subsection, a person who intends to work the patented invention may demand the Director General of the Patent Office to make a decision.

Section 86. (Formalities of Director General's decision)

* * *

2. If the Director General's decision is that a non-exclusive license should be established, the following matters shall be designated:
   (i) The scope of the non-exclusive license that should be established; and
   (ii) The amount of consideration, including method and time of payment, therefor.

Section 93. (Non-exclusive license in the public interest)

1. If the working of a patented invention is especially necessary given the public interest, any person intending to work such invention may demand of the patentee or exclusive licensee an agreement concerning grant of a non-exclusive license.
2. If no agreement is made or it is impossible to make such an agreement, any person desiring to work such a patented invention may demand a decision of the Minister of International Trade and Industry.

* * *

Part 2. Infringement

Section 100. (Demand to cease and desist)

1. A patentee or exclusive licensee may demand a person who is infringing or is likely to infringe the patent right or exclusive license to cease and desist such infringement.
2. A patentee or an exclusive licensee may, at the time of making the demand under the preceding subsection, demand any act necessary for the prevention of infringement such as the destruction of the things constituting infringement, including, in the case of a patented process, destruction of things made by the process.

Section 101. (Acts deemed to be infringement)

The following acts shall be deemed to be an infringement of a patent right or exclusive license:

(i) In the case of a patent for an invention of a thing, acts of manufacturing, assigning, leasing, displaying for the purpose of assignment or lease, or importing, in the course of trade, things to be used exclusively for the manufacture of the thing; and

(ii) In the case of a patent for an invention of a process, acts of manufacturing, assigning, leasing, displaying for the purpose of assignment or lease, or importing, in the course of trade, things to be used exclusively for the working of such invention.

Section 102. (Presumption, etc., of amount of damage)

1. Where a patentee or exclusive licensee demands from a person who has intentionally or negligently infringed the patent right or exclusive license compensation for damage caused by the infringement, the profits gained by the infringer shall be presumed to be the amount of damage sustained by the patentee or exclusive licensee.
2. A patentee or exclusive licensee may demand from a person who has intentionally or negligently infringed the patent right or exclusive license the amount of money which the

patentee or exclusive licensee would normally be entitled to receive for the working of the patented invention, as the amount of damage sustained by said patentee or exclusive licensee.

3. The preceding subsection shall not preclude a claim to damages exceeding the amount referred to therein. In such a case, if there has been neither willfulness nor gross negligence on the part of the person who has infringed the patent right or the exclusive license, the court may take this into consideration when determining the amount of damages.

Section 103. (Presumption of negligence)

A person who has infringed a patent right or exclusive license of another person shall be presumed to have been negligent with respect to the act of infringement.

Section 104. (Presumption regarding manufacturing process)

Where a patent has been granted for an invention of a process of manufacturing a thing, if such thing was not publicly known in Japan prior to the patent application, any thing identical to that thing shall be presumed to have been manufactured by such patented process.

Chapter VI
Trial Hearing

Section 121. (Trial hearing for determination of refusal)

1. A person who has received a determination that his or her application is to be refused may, if dissatisfied with the determination, demand a trial hearing thereon within 30 days of being served with the determination.

* * *

Section 123. (Trial hearing for invalidation of patent)

1. In the following cases, a trial hearing may be demanded for the invalidation of the patent * * *:
   (i) Where the patent has been granted in violation of Section 25, 29, 29-1, 32, 38, or 39(1) to (4);
   (ii) Where the patent has been granted contrary to the provisions of a treaty;
   (iii) Where the patent has been granted on a patent application that does not comply with the requirements of Section 36(3) or (4) * * *;
   (iv) Where the patent has been granted on a patent application filed by a person who is not the inventor and has not succeeded to the right to obtain a patent for the invention concerned;

   * * *
2. Even after the extinguishment of a patent right, a trial hearing under the preceding subsection may be demanded.

* * *

Section 125. (Trial hearing for invalidation of a patent)

When a decision that a patent should be invalidated has become final and conclusive, the patent right shall be deemed not to have ever existed; * * *.

Section 168. (Relationship to litigation)

1. If necessary during a trial hearing, the proceedings may be suspended until the decision of another trial hearing becomes final and conclusive or a litigation proceeding is completed.
2. If necessary during a litigation proceeding, the court may suspend proceedings until a trial hearing decision becomes final and conclusive.

Chapter VII
Retrial Hearing

Section 171. (Demand for retrial hearing)

1. A party may demand a retrial hearing after a decision is issued in a trial hearing.

* * *

Section 172. (Demand by third party)

1. If the claimant and respondent in a trial hearing have conspired to have a trial hearing decision rendered for the purpose of injuring the right or interest of a third party, such third party may demand a retrial hearing.

* * *

Chapter VIII
Litigation

Section 178. (Actions against trial hearing decisions)

1. A suit against * * * a ruling of dismissal of a demand for a trial or retrial hearing shall come under the exclusive jurisdiction of the Tokyo High Court.
2. An action under the preceding subsection may be instituted only by a party or intervenor or a person whose demand to intervene in the trial or retrial has been refused.

* * *

4. A suit with regard to the matters on which a trial hearing may be demanded may be instituted only against a trial decision.

* * *

Chapter XI
Penal Provisions

Section 196. (Offense of infringement)

1. Any person who has infringed a patent right or an exclusive license shall be punishable by penal servitude not exceeding five years or by a fine not exceeding ¥5,000,000.
2. Any person who has infringed the right under Section 52(1) shall, if the establishment of the patent right comes to be registered, be punishable by penal servitude not exceeding five years or by a fine not exceeding ¥5,000,000.
3. The prosecution of the offenses under the two preceding subsections shall be initiated upon complaint.

Section 197. (Offense of fraudulent act)

A person who has obtained a patent right or decision by means of a fraudulent act shall be punishable by penal servitude of not more than three years or by a fine of not more than ¥3,000,000.

15. THE TRADEMARK ACT

Law No. 127, April 13, 1959, as amended

Source: Adapted from Teruo Doi, *Intellectual Property Protection and Management: Law and Practice in Japan* (Institute of Comparative Law, Waseda University, 1992), Appendix 4. Reprinted by permission.

Chapter I
General Provisions

Section 1. (Purpose)

This Act aims, through protection of trademarks, to maintain the business goodwill of those who use trademarks and thereby to contribute to the development of industry as well as to protect the interests of consumers.

Section 2. (Definitions, etc.)

1. The word "trademark" as used in this Act shall mean letters, figures, or signs, or any combination of these and colors (hereinafter referred to as "mark") which falls under the following items:
   (i) One which a person who, as a business, produces, processes, certifies, or assigns goods, uses on such goods; or
   (ii) One which a person who, as a business, renders or certifies services, uses for such services.

* * *

3. The word "use" as used in this Act shall mean the following acts:
   (i) Acts of attaching a mark to goods or packages of goods;
   (ii) Acts of assigning, delivering, displaying for the purpose of assignment or delivery, or importing goods to which, or to the packages of which, a mark is attached;
   (iii) Acts of attaching, in the course of rendering service, a mark on things that are offered for use by persons who receive such service (including those to be assigned or rented; the same applies in subsequent provisions);
   (iv) Acts of using, in the course of rendering service, things bearing a mark that are offered for use by persons who receive such service;
   (v) Acts of displaying, in the course of rendering service, things bearing a mark that are to be used in rendering such service (including those to be offered for use by persons who receive such service; the same applies in subsequent provisions);
   (vi) Acts of attaching, in the course of rendering service, a mark to a thing which belongs to a person who receives such service and is subjected to such service; and
   (vii) Acts of displaying or distributing advertisements, price lists, or business papers relating to goods or service to which a mark is attached.
4. In the application of this Act, the scope of matters that are similar to particular goods may include services, and the scope of matters that are similar to particular services may include goods.

Chapter II
Trademark Registration and Application

Section 3. (Requirements for trademark registration)

1. Trademark registration may be obtained for any trademark which is to be used for goods or services relating to one's own business, with the exception of the following trademarks:
   (i) A trademark which consists only of a mark indicating a generic name of such goods or services in a manner commonly used;
   (ii) A trademark which is customarily used for such goods or services;

(iii) A trademark which consists only of a mark indicating in a manner commonly used the place of origin, place of sale, quality, raw materials, efficacy, use, quantity, shape, price or the manner or time of production or use of such goods, or the place of rendering, quality, things to be used in the rendering, efficacy, use, quantity, mode, price or the method or time of the rendering of such services;

(iv) A trademark which consists only of a mark indicating a common surname or application in a manner commonly used;

(v) A trademark which consists only of an extremely simple and common mark; and

(vi) In addition to those listed in the preceding items, a trademark by which consumers are unable to identify to whose business such goods or services are related.

* * *

Section 4. (Trademarks not entitled to registration)

1. Notwithstanding the provisions of the preceding section, the following trademarks are not entitled to trademark registration:

(i) A trademark which is identical with or similar to the national flag or the national emblem of any other country;

* * *

(viii) A trademark which consists of the portrait, name, well-known pseudonym or pen name of another person;

* * *

(x) A trademark which is well-known among consumers as indicating the goods or services related to the business of another person or a trademark similar to it and which is to be used for such goods or services or goods or services similar to them;

(xi) A registered trademark of another person based on an application for trademark registration filed before the filing of the application for trademark registration in question or a trademark similar to it which is to be used for the designated goods or the designated services (meaning the goods or services designated in accordance with the provisions of Section 6(1) (including an instance where it is applicable *mutatis mutandis* under Section 68(1)); the same applies in subsequent provisions) or goods or services similar to them;

(xii) A trademark which is identical with a registered defensive mark of another person (meaning a mark which has obtained defensive mark registration; the same applies in subsequent provisions) and is to be used for the designated goods or designated services pertaining to such defensive mark registration;

(xiii) A trademark of another person for which one year has not yet elapsed from the day on which such person's trademark right extinguished (when a trial decision to invalidate such person's trademark registration was rendered, the day it became conclusive; the same applies in subsequent provisions) (other than one which has not been used by such other person for more than one year before the day on which the trademark right extinguished) or a trademark similar to it which is to be used for the designated goods or designated services pertaining to such trademark right or goods or services similar to them;

* * *

(xv) A trademark which is likely to cause confusion with the goods or services pertaining to the business of another person (other than one falling under any of Items (10) to (14)); and

(xvi) A trademark which is likely to cause confusion as to the quality of goods or services.

* * *

Section 5. (Application for trademark registration)

1. A person who wants a trademark registration shall file with the Director General of the Patent Office an application which contains the following matters, together with a document showing the trademark for which he or she intends to obtain trademark registration and a document containing necessary explanations:

(i) [Name and domicile of applicant];
(ii) The date of submission; and
(iii) Designated goods or designated services, and the classification of the goods or services as prescribed by cabinet order referred to in Section 6(1).

* * *

Section 6. *(One application for one trademark)*

1. An application for trademark registration shall be filed for each trademark designating one or more goods or services for which it is to be used and which fall under one of the classes of goods or services prescribed by cabinet order.
2. The classification of goods and services referred to in the preceding subsection is not intended to provide the scope of similarity among goods or services.

Section 7. *(Associated trademarks)*

1. The owner of a trademark right shall not obtain trademark registration for a trademark which is similar to his or her registered trademark and to be used for the designated goods or designated services pertaining to such registered trademark or his or her registered trademark or a trademark similar to it which is to be used for goods or services similar to the designated goods or designated services pertaining to such registered trademark, unless said owner of a trademark right files an application for trademark registration of an associated trademark.

* * *

Section 8. *(Priority based on filing)*

1. Where two or more applications for trademark registration have been filed for identical or similar trademarks to be used for identical or similar goods or services on different days, only the first applicant for trademark registration shall obtain trademark registration for such trademark.
2. [Trademark registration right for same day filings to be resolved by negotiation by the filers.]

* * *

[Sections 9 and 9-2 incorporate the Paris Convention priority filing system.]

Chapter III
Examination

Section 14. *(Examination)*

The Director General of the Patent Office shall cause an examiner to examine each trademark registration application and motion of objection to registration.

Section 15. (Examiner's decision of refusal)

The examiner shall render a decision of refusal on an application for trademark registration when the application falls under any one of the following items:

(i) [When there should be no registration in accordance with Sections 3, 4(1), 7(1) or 3, 8(2) or (5), 51(2), 53(2) of this Act or Section 25 of the Patent Act, as applied *mutatis mutandis.*]

* * *

(iii) When the application for trademark registration does not meet the requirements set forth in Section 6(1); or
(iv) [When registration falls within the one year grace period applicable under the Paris Convention for similar filings in Paris Convention countries.]

Section 16. *(Publication of an application)*

1. The examiner shall, if no reason is found for refusing the trademark registration application, render a ruling to the effect that public notice of the application should be made.

* * *

3. Publication of an application shall be made by inserting in the Official Trademark Gazette the following particulars: [details omitted].

* * *

Chapter IV
Trademark Right

Part 1. Trademark Right

Section 18. (Registration)

1. A trademark right shall come into existence upon registration of its establishment.

* * *

Section 19. (Duration)

1. A trademark right shall expire ten years after the date of registration of its establishment.
2. The duration of a trademark right is renewable upon application for renewal registration. Provided, That the following instances are excepted:
   (i) When the trademark comes to fall under Section 4(1)(i) * * * or (xvi); and
   (ii) When neither the owner of the trademark right, the holder of an exclusive use right, nor the holder of an ordinary use right has been using the registered trademark * * * for any designated goods or designated services in Japan within three years before the filing of an application for renewal registration. * * *
3. [Item 2 of the preceding subsection is inapplicable "if there is a justifiable reason for not using the registered trademark."]

Section 20. (Renewal registration)

[Procedure designated for application for renewal of duration of trademark right, including requirement that application be made within six months before the expiration of the trademark right.]

Section 25. (Effect of a trademark right)

The owner of a trademark right shall exclusively have the right to use the registered trademark with respect to the designated goods or the designated services. Provided, That this shall not apply, when an exclusive use right has been established with respect to such trademark right, within the scope that the holder of an exclusive use right exclusively possesses the right to use the registered trademark.

Section 26. (Limitation on scope of right)

1. The effect of a trademark right shall not extend to the following trademarks:.
   * * *
   (ii) A trademark which consists of the generic name of the designated goods or goods similar thereto, the place of origin, the place of sale, quality, raw materials, efficacy, use, quantity, shape, price or the method or time of production or use of such goods, or of the generic name of services which is similar to the designated goods, the place of rendition, quality, things to be used in the rendition, efficacy, use, quantity, manner, price or the method or time of rendition, of such services and is indicated in a commonly used way;
   (iii) A trademark which consists of the generic name of the designated service or services similar thereto, the place of rendition, quality, things to be used in the rendition, efficacy, use, quantity, manner, price or the method or time of rendition of such services, or the generic name of goods similar to the designated service, the place of origin, the place of sale, quality, raw materials, efficacy, use, quantity, shape, price or the method or time of use of such goods and is indicated in a commonly used way; and
   (iv) A trademark which is commonly used for the designated goods or the designated service or goods or services similar thereto.
   * * *

Section 27. (Scope of a registered trademark, etc.)

1. The scope of a registered trademark shall be determined in accordance with the description in the application.
2. The scope of the designated goods or the designated service shall be determined in accordance with the descriptions in the application.

Section 28. (Adjudication of scope)

1. With regard to the effect of a trademark right, adjudication of the issue may be demanded of the Patent Office.

* * *

Section 29. (Relationship with design rights, etc.)

When the use of a registered trademark for the designated goods or the designated service in a given manner conflicts with a design right of another person pertaining to an application for design registration filed before the filing date of the registered trademark or with copyright of another person accrued before the filing date of the registered trademark, the owner of the trademark right, the holder of an exclusive use right, or the holder of an ordinary use right shall not use the registered trademark in such manner for the conflicting part of the designated goods or the designated service.

Section 30. (Exclusive use right)

[Trademark right holder may grant exclusive use right, the scope of which is as stipulated by the act of its establishment.]

Section 31. (Ordinary use right)

[Trademark right holder may grant an "ordinary use right" (*i.e.*, non-exclusive), the scope of which is as stipulated by the act of its establishment.]

Section 32. (Right to use a trademark by virtue of prior use)

1. When a person who, without an intention of unfair competition, has used in Japan a trademark identical with or similar to a registered trademark of another person for the designated goods or goods similar thereto before the filing of an application for trademark registration by such other person and the said trademark has become well-known among consumers as indicating the goods or service pertaining to the user's business as the result of such use at the time of the filing of the said application for trademark registration * * * and such person continuously uses the trademark for such goods or service, such person shall have the right to use such trademark for such goods or service. The same shall apply to a person who has succeeded to the said business.
2. The owner of the trademark right or the holder of an exclusive use right may demand the person who has the right to use the trademark in accordance with the provisions of the preceding subsection to attach an indication suitable for preventing confusion between the goods or service pertaining to the business of such person and the goods or service pertaining to the business of the owner of the trademark right or holder of the exclusive use right.

Section 33. (Prior use before invalidation trial)

When a person who falls under any one of the following items has used in Japan a trademark identical with or similar to a registered trademark for the designated goods or the designated service or goods or service similar thereto before the registration of a demand under Section 46(1) without knowing that the said trademark registration falls under any one of the items of the said subsection and the said trademark has become well-known among consumers as indicating the goods or service pertaining to such person's business, and such person continuously uses the trademark for such goods or service, such person shall have the right to use the trademark for such goods or service. The same shall apply to a person who has succeeded to the said business:

(i) The original owner of the trademark right, in a case where one of two or more trademark registrations granted for identical or similar trademarks to be used for identical or similar designated goods or designated service has been invalidated;
(ii) The original owner of the trademark right, in a case where such person's trademark registration has been invalidated and a trademark registration has been granted to a person who has the title to an identical or similar trademark to be used for identical or similar designated goods or designated services;

* * *

Part 2. Infringement

Section 36. (Demand to cease infringement)

* * *

2. A trademark right or exclusive use right owner may, at the time of making the demand under the previous subsection [to cease and desist infringement], demand the destruction of things constituting the act of infringement * * * or any other act necessary for prevention of infringement.

Section 37. (Acts deemed infringing)

The following acts shall be deemed to infringe upon a trademark right or an exclusive use right:

(i) Use of a trademark similar to the registered trademark for the designated goods or designated services, or use of the trademark or a trademark similar thereto for goods or services similar to the designated goods or designated services;
(ii) An act of possessing for the purpose of assignment or delivery of the designated goods or goods similar to the designated goods or designated services to which or to the package of which the registered trademark or a trademark similar thereto is attached;
(iii) An act of possessing or importing, in the course of rendering the designated services or services similar to the designated services or designated goods, things bearing the registered trademark or a trademark similar thereto which are to be offered for use by persons who receive such services, for the purpose of rendering such services using such things;
(iv) [Same as above but covering "an act of assigning, delivering or possessing or importing for the purpose of assignment or delivery"];
(v) An act of possessing things on which the registered trademark or a trademark similar thereto is indicated for the purpose of using the registered trademark or a trademark similar thereto for the designated goods or designated services or goods or services similar thereto;
(vi) An act of assigning, delivering, or possessing for the purpose of assignment or delivery things on which the registered trademark or a trademark similar thereto is indicated in order to have the registered trademark or a trademark similar thereto be used for the designated goods or designated services similar thereto;
(vii) An act of manufacturing or importing things on which the registered trademark or a trademark similar thereto is indicated in order to use the registered trademark or a trademark similar thereto or to cause it to be used for the designated goods or designated services or for goods or services similar thereto; and
(viii) An act of manufacturing, assigning, delivering or importing as a business things which are used solely for the purpose of manufacturing things on which the registered trademark or a trademark similar thereto is to be indicated.

Section 38. (Presumption of amount of damages)

1. [Amount of damages to trademark or exclusive right holder for willful or negligent infringement presumed to be profits earned by infringer.]
2. [Trademark or exclusive right holder may demand as damages an amount equivalent to what would normally be received for a license to the infringer.]

3. [In determining damages, court may take it into account if the infringement is not done maliciously or with gross negligence.]

Chapter V
Trial Hearing

Section 44. (Trial hearing on refusal)

1. [A person objecting to a determination of refusal may, within 30 days of being served with the transcript of the determination, demand a trial hearing.]

* * *

Section 46. (Trial hearing for invalidation of a trademark registration)

1. When a trademark registration falls under any one of the following items [which concern the trademark not having met or having come not to meet the requirements for registration], a trial hearing may be demanded for invalidating the said trademark registration. In such event, if there exist two or more designated goods or designated services for the registered trademark, a trial hearing may be demanded for each such designated good or service.

* * *

Section 48. (Trial hearing for invalidation of renewal)

[Trial hearings may be demanded for challenging renewal registrations that should not have been or should not continue to be granted.]

Section 50. (Trial hearing for cancellation of a trademark registration)

1. When the owner of a trademark right, the holder of an exclusive use right, and the holders of ordinary use rights have not been using the registered trademark for each designated good or designated service in Japan continuously for more than three years, a trial hearing may be demanded for cancelling the said trademark registration for such designated good or designated service.
2. [If the trademark right has not been used in the previous three years, the registration must be canceled unless a "justifiable reason" is demonstrated for not having used the trademark.]

Section 53-2. (Trial hearing for cancellation of a trademark registration)

[Right to demand trial hearing for cancellation by right holder in a Paris Convention country.]

Section 56. (Application mutatis mutandis *of the Patent Act)*

[Patent Act provisions concerning trial hearings, effects of trial decisions, and relationship to litigation made applicable *mutatis mutandis.*]

Chapter VI
Retrial Hearing and Litigation

Section 57. (Demand for retrial hearing)

[Parties concerned may demand retrial hearings.]

Section 58. (Third party demands)

[If claimant and respondent in hearing have conspired to have a decision rendered for the purpose of injuring a third party, such third party may demand a retrial hearing.]

Chapter VII
Defensive Marks

Section 64. (Requirements for defensive mark registration)

1. The owner of a trademark right may, when such person's registered trademark for goods has become well-known among consumers as indicating the designated goods pertaining to his or her business, and when another person uses the registered trademark for goods other than the designated goods of such registered trademark and goods similar thereto or for services other than services similar to the designated goods and thereby creates a likelihood of confusion between such goods or services and the designated goods pertaining to the trademark right owner's business, obtain a defensive mark registration for a mark identical with his or her registered trademark for goods or service susceptible of such confusion.
2. The owner of a trademark right may, when such person's registered trademark for services has become well-known among consumers as indicating the designated service pertaining to his business, and when another person uses the registered trademark for services other than the designated service of such registered trademark and services similar thereto or for goods other than goods similar to the designated service and thereby creates a likelihood of confusion between such services or goods and the designated service pertaining to the trademark right owner's business, obtain a defensive mark registration for a mark identical with his or her registered trademark for services or goods susceptible of such confusion.

Section 65. (Change of application)

1. An applicant for a trademark registration may change the registration application to a defensive mark registration application.

* * *

Section 67. (Acts deemed infringing)

The following acts shall be deemed to infringe upon a trademark right or an exclusive use right:

(i) Use of the registered defensive mark for the designated goods or designated service;

[Items (ii)-(vii) parallel Section 37(ii)-(vii), but apply to defensive marks.]

Chapter VIII
Miscellaneous Provisions

Section 73. (Indication of trademark registration)

[Trademark right owner and licensee(s), when using the mark, must endeavor to affix to the goods or things used in connection with a service a trademark registration notice as prescribed by MITI ordinance.]

Chapter IX
Penal Provisions

Section 78. (Offense of infringement)

A person who has infringed a trademark or exclusive use right shall be punishable with penal servitude of not more than five years or with a fine of not more than five million yen.

16. UNFAIR COMPETITION PREVENTION ACT

Law No. 47, May 19, 1993

Source: Institute of Intellectual Property, Tokyo, Japan. Reprinted by permission.

Section 1. (Purpose)

The purpose of this Act is to contribute to the sound development of the national economy by providing measures for the prevention of, and compensation for damages from, unfair competition in order to ensure fair competition among business entities and the full implementation of international agreements related thereto.

Section 2. (Definitions)

1. As used in this Act, the term "unfair competition" means any one of the following:
   (i) The act of using an indication which is identical or similar to a goods or other indication (as used herein a "goods or other indication" means the name, trade name, trademark, mark, container or packaging of goods in relation to a person's business, or any other indication of goods or business) of another person, which is widely known among consumers, or the act of assigning, delivering, displaying for the purpose of assignment or delivery, exporting, or importing goods that use such a goods or other indication, and thereby causing confusion with another person's goods or business;
   (ii) The act of using as one's own a goods or other indication which is identical or similar to another person's well-known goods or other indication, or the act of assigning, delivering, displaying for the purpose of assignment or delivery, exporting, or importing goods that use such a goods or other indication;
   (iii) The act of assigning, leasing, displaying for the purpose of assignment or lease, exporting or importing goods that imitate the configuration (excluding a configuration which is commonly used for goods of the same kind as those of another person [or, in the case of goods that are not of the same kind, goods which have an identical or similar function and utility to those of another person]) of another person's goods (excluding goods for which three years have elapsed from the date on which sales thereof first commenced);
   (iv) The act of acquiring a trade secret by means of theft, fraud, coercion or other improper means (hereinafter referred to as an "improper acquisition") or using or disclosing a trade secret acquired through an improper acquisition (including showing to a specific person or group of persons while maintaining secrecy; hereinafter the same applies);
   (v) The act of acquiring a trade secret while aware that such trade secret has been acquired through improper acquisition or, through gross negligence, not being aware of such circumstance; or the act of using or disclosing a trade secret so acquired;
   (vi) The act of using or disclosing a trade secret after becoming aware, subsequent to its acquisition, that such trade secret has been acquired through improper acquisition or, through gross negligence, not becoming aware of such circumstance;
   (vii) The act of using or disclosing a trade secret which has been disclosed by the business entity holding it (hereinafter referred to as the "holder"), for the purpose of unfair business competition or of otherwise acquiring an unfair benefit, or for the purpose of inflicting injury on such holder;
   (viii) The act of acquiring a trade secret while being aware or, through gross negligence, not being aware that there has been an improper disclosure of such trade secret (meaning an act of disclosing a trade secret for a purpose stipulated in the preceding item, or an act of disclosing a trade secret in breach of a legal duty to maintain secrecy, in a case as stipulated in the preceding item; hereinafter the same applies) or that such trade secret has been acquired through improper disclosure; or the act of using or disclosing a trade secret so acquired;

(ix) The act of using or disclosing an acquired trade secret after becoming aware, subsequent to its acquisition, that there has been improper disclosure of such trade secret or that such trade secret has been acquired through improper disclosure, or, through gross negligence, not being aware of such circumstance;

(x) The act of indicating on goods or for services, or in an advertisement therefor or in a document or correspondence used for a transaction, which is likely to mislead with respect to the place of origin, quality, contents, manufacturing method, use or quantity of such goods or the quality, contents, use or quantity of such services, or the act of assigning, delivering, displaying for the purpose of assignment or delivery, exporting or importing goods with such an indication or offering a service with such an indication;

(xi) The act of announcing or circulating a falsehood which injures the business reputation of a third person in a competitive relationship;

(xii) The act of an agent or representative, or a person who, within one year of the date of such act, was an agent or representative of an owner of a right relating to a trademark (such right shall be limited herein to a right equivalent to a trademark right and hereinafter referred to simply as a "right") in a state party to the Paris Convention (used herein as defined in Section 4, Subsection 1, Item (ii) of the Trademark Act (Law No. 127 of 1959)), without justifiable reason and without the consent of the owner of such right, using a trademark which is identical or similar to the trademark relating to which the right relates, in respect of goods or service identical or similar to those to which such right relates, or the act of assigning, delivering, displaying for the purpose of assignment or delivery, exporting or importing goods using such trademark which is identical or similar to the goods to which the right relates, or offering a service, using such trademark, which is identical or similar to the service to which such right relates.

* * *

4. As used in this Act, the term "trade secret" means manufacturing method, sales method or any other technical or business information useful in a commercial activity, which is maintained as a secret and not known to the general public.

Section 3. *(Right to request an injunction)*

1. A person whose business interests are infringed or are likely to be infringed by unfair competition is entitled to request an injunction preventing or suspending such infringement against the person who is infringing such business interests or is likely to do so.
2. A person whose business interests are infringed or are likely to be infringed by unfair competition is entitled, at the time of the request referred to in the preceding subsection, to request the destruction of the objects which constitute the act of infringement (including objects created by the act of infringement), the removal of the facilities used for the act of infringement, or any other acts necessary to prevent or suspend the infringement.

Section 4. *(Claim for damages)*

A person who intentionally or negligently infringes the business interests of another person through unfair competition shall be liable to compensate for damages which result therefrom. Provided, That this shall not apply to damages which arise from use of a trade secret after the rights described in Section 8 below are extinguished in accordance with that section.

Section 5. *(Presumption of amount of damages, etc.)*

[Omitted.]

Section 6. *(Submission of documents)*

In an action related to infringement of business interests through unfair competition, the court, pursuant to an application by a party to the action, may order the other party to submit documents necessary to calculate the amount of damages caused by the said infringement. Provided, That this does not apply in the case where the person who holds such a document has a justifiable reason for refusing to submit it.

Section 7. (Measures to restore business reputation)

The court may order a person who intentionally or negligently has committed unfair competition and thereby has injured the business reputation of another person to take those measures necessary to restore the business reputation of such person in lieu of compensation for damages or in addition to such damages, upon the request of the person whose business reputation was so injured.

Section 8. (Extinction by prescription)

The right to request an injunction pursuant to the provisions of Section 3(1) to suspend or prevent, from among those acts set forth in Items (iv) through (ix) of Section 2(1), acts involving the use of a trade secret, shall be extinguished by prescription in the case where the person who commits such act continues it and the holder whose business interests have been infringed or are likely to be infringed by such act does not exercise such right within three years from the time that such holder becomes aware of such facts and of the person committing such act. The right shall be extinguished by prescription, in any event, when ten years have elapsed from the time of commencement of such act.

[Sections 9 and 10, containing prohibitions on the commercial use of emblems of foreign states and marks of international organizations, omitted.]

Section 11. (Exemptions)

1. The provisions of Sections 3 to 8, 13 (excluding those portions concerning Item (iii) thereof) and 14 do not apply to those acts which are stipulated in the items below which fall within the type of unfair competition set forth for such item:
   (i) unfair competition as described in Section 2(1), Item (i), (ii), (x) or (xii):
   the act of using or indicating in a normally-used manner a common name of goods or business (excluding the name of a place of origin of goods which is made from grapes or uses grapes as an ingredient, and has become a common name) or a goods or other indication that is commonly used for identical or similar goods or business (hereinafter such a common name or commonly-used indication, together referred to as a "common name"), or the act of assigning, delivering, displaying for the purpose of assignment or delivery, exporting or importing goods using or indicating a common name in a normally-used manner (including, in the case of unfair competition as described in Items (x) or (xii) of the same subsection, an act of offering a service using or indicating, in a normally-used manner, a common name);
   (ii) unfair competition as described in Section 2(1), Item (i), (ii) or (xii):
   the act of using one's own personal name, for no unfair purpose ("unfair purpose" hereby defined and hereinafter used as a purpose to obtain an unfair profit, a purpose to cause injury to another person or any other unfair purpose), or the act of assigning, delivering, displaying for the purpose of assignment or delivery, exporting or importing goods using, for no unfair purpose, one's own personal name (including, in the case of unfair competition as described in any of the above items, an act of offering a service using, for no unfair purpose, one's own personal name);
   (iii) unfair competition as described in Section 2(1), Item (i):
   the act of a person's using, for no unfair purpose, a goods or other indication identical or similar to a widely known goods or other indication of another person, if such person had used such indication before it became widely known or had succeeded to a business related to such indication, or the act of assigning, delivering, displaying for the purpose of assignment or delivery, exporting or importing goods which use, for no unfair purpose, such indication;
   (iv) unfair competition as described in Section 2(1), Item (ii):
   the act of a person's using, for no unfair purpose, a goods or other indication identical or similar to a well-known goods or other indication of another person, if such person had used such indication before it became well-known or had succeeded to a

business related to such indication, or the act of assigning, delivering, displaying for the purpose of assignment or delivery, exporting or importing goods which use, for no unfair purpose, such indication;

(v) unfair competition as described in Section 2(1), Item (iii):
the act of assigning, leasing, displaying for the purpose of assignment or lease, exporting or importing goods, done by a person, who has obtained by assignment such goods that, as described in the item, imitate the configuration of another person's goods (provided that such person, at the time of obtaining such goods by assignment, was unaware that such goods imitated the configuration of another person's goods and was not unaware of such circumstance through gross negligence);

(vi) unfair competition as described in Section 2(1), Items (iv) through (ix):
the act of using or disclosing a trade secret within the scope of the legal title acquired through a transaction done by a person, who has acquired the trade secret through such transaction (provided that such person, at the time of such acquisition, was not aware that there had been an improper disclosure of such trade secret or that such trade secret had been acquired through an improper disclosure or improper acquisition and was not unaware of such circumstance through gross negligence).

2. A person who suffers or is likely to suffer an infringement to its business interests through one of the acts set forth in Item (ii) or (iii) of the preceding subsection is entitled to request, in accordance with the type of unfair competition set forth in the following items, against any person who falls under such item, that an appropriate indication be used to prevent confusion with the former's own goods or business:

(i) an act set forth in Item (ii) of the preceding subsection:
a person using his or her own personal name (including a person who assigns, delivers, displays for the purpose of assignment or delivery, exports or imports, by himself, goods which use his or her own personal name);

(ii) an act set forth in Item (iii) of the preceding subsection:
a person using a goods or other indication identical or similar to that of another person and a person who succeeds to a business related to such an indication (including a person who assigns, delivers, displays for the purpose of assignment or delivery, exports or imports, by himself, goods using such an indication).

Section 13. (Penal provisions)

Any person who falls under any of the following items shall be sentenced to imprisonment for a term not exceeding three years or fined an amount not exceeding ¥3,000,000:

(i) a person who commits, for an unfair purpose, any act of unfair competition set forth in Section 2(1), Item (i) or (x);

(ii) a person (excluding a person coming under the preceding item) who indicates a falsehood on goods or for services, or in an advertisement or in a document or correspondence used for a transaction, which is likely to mislead, with respect to the place of origin, quality, contents, manufacturing method, use or quantity of such goods or the quality, contents, use or quantity of such services;

(iii) a person who violates any provision of Section 9 or Section 10.

Section 14. (Juridical persons)

In the case where a representative of a juridical person or an agent, servant or other employee of a juridical person or a natural person has committed, in connection with the business of such juridical or natural person, any of the violations set forth in the preceding section, in addition to the violator being penalized, such a juridical person shall be fined an amount not exceeding ¥100,000,000 and such a natural person shall be liable to the same fine as set forth in the preceding section.

Table of Cases

[Note: The principal cases are in italic type. The cited cases are in roman type. References are to pages on which the cases appear or are cited.]

Table of Statutes
(including regulations and rules)

[Note: Roman type designates pages on which the statutes are cited. Italic type designates the page numbers for the text of statutes reproduced in the Appendices.]

Index

P